BIBLIOGRAPHY
OF RELIGION
IN THE SOUTH

BIBLIOGRAPHY
OF RELIGION
IN THE SOUTH

BY

CHARLES H. LIPPY

MERCER
MUP

ISBN 0-86554-161-2

Bibliography of Religion in the South
Copyright © 1985
Mercer University Press, Macon GA 31207
All rights reserved
Printed in the United States of America

Library of Congress Cataloging in Publication Data

Lippy, Charles H.
    Bibliography of religion in the South.

    1. Christian sects—Southern States—Bibliography.
2. Southern States—Church history—Bibliography.
3. Southern States—Religion—Bibliography.   I. Title.
Z7778.S59L56   1985   [BR535]   016.28'00975   85-13575
ISBN 0-86554-161-2 (alk. paper)

CONTENTS

For the Armstrongs
Virginia, Patrick,
David, Laura, and Rebecca

PREFACE

ANALYSTS OF AMERICAN CULTURE have long directed attention to the South as a region with a distinctive consciousness, identity, and style. The interpenetration of religion and society in the South has spawned hundreds of studies that explore topics ranging from the history of religious groups in the region to the influence of religion on the literature and architecture of the region. This bibliography is designed to identify and describe the secondary literature about religion in the South from many different perspectives. As a rule, it does not identify primary materials, whether papers and records of individuals or groups or published articles, books, and monographs. It includes discussion of the reference materials that point students to other works, synoptic studies of the region's religious culture, works looking at the religions of the native American groups from the area and the impact of Christianity on them, and the growing literature on black religion. As well, it looks at studies of the various religious groups—Protestant denominations, Roman Catholicism, Judaism, sectarian bodies, and numerically smaller movements—that have found a place for themselves in Dixie. In addition, it looks at the relation between religion and other aspects of human life, such as education, art and architecture, music, and literature. The bibliography also appraises work on the relationship of religion and the social order and on the religious thought and theology advanced by Southerners. It includes, too, discussion of studies that focus on movements such as revivalism and the Pentecostal-Holiness thrust that cut across established denominational boundaries. And it identifies work that scrutinizes the religious life of Appalachia and the rural South.

This work is thus organized in part topically and in part institutionally. Some may think it more convenient to find all materials relating to a particular tradition under a single heading; for example, to have all titles dealing with the Presbyterians, regardless of their focus, in one chapter. But so much of Southern experience has affected all religious groups—all had to respond to the presence of Black Americans and the Indians, all Protestant groups at least had to deal with the issues raised in the furor over fundamentalism—that it seemed prudent to place such materials in topically focused chapters while retaining chapters on individual denominations and the like to identify works that treated their own internal institutional developments. Otherwise, the same events and movements would be discussed over and over in different chapters. Consequently, users of this volume will no doubt find it necessary to look at several chapters in order to get a comprehensive perspective on any topic or group.

A good bibliography, of course, should be comprehensive. But as every bibliographer knows, efforts at comprehensiveness always fall short of the mark. An article or a monograph will somehow escape notice. Reviewers will be quick to note omissions. Nonetheless, I believe this work offers the most complete examination of the literature on religion in the South to date. Perhaps future editions will allow the inclusion of important works that I have failed to uncover this time. But even in a quest for comprehensiveness, principles of selection determine choice of materials to include. In this study, one such principle was to concentrate on scholarly works rather than popular works, though some of these have indeed been included. As well, I have by and large omitted inclusion of articles and essays which have appeared in mass circulation publications—denominational periodicals, popular journals, and the like. I have also consciously omitted many books that have an occasional chapter or make a passing reference to topics or individuals important to the religious culture of the South, choosing instead to emphasize coverage of articles, monographs, dissertations, and theses whose major focus is religion. Chapters on the various traditions that are vital components of Southern religion do include some local studies and biographical or autobiographical materials. In these two areas, additional principles of selection helped determine choice of titles to include. Thousands of local congregations have printed histories as part of anniversary celebrations. It would be virtually impossible to locate all of them, for many are not copyrighted. In addition, the majority are not readily accessible. Hence I have included only those local studies for which I could verify publication data. As well, countless individuals from both the ranks of the clergy and the laity are the subjects of biographies. To include, for example, every biography ever published of every person who happened to be a Methodist or a Baptist from the South would be as impossible as including every local church history. The biographical materials that I have included tend to concentrate on clergy or religious professionals as well as on a few lay persons who, in my subjective scholarly estimate, played vital roles in helping shape the course of their denominations or groups. I am aware that other scholars might well make different choices. Indeed, another writer of a volume such as this would no doubt decide to comment on different works than those I have highlighted.

Each chapter is organized in two major sections. The first section is commentary on the secondary literature, noting the major work in an area, offering critical appraisal of its value, and suggesting areas for further inquiry. The second is a topically organized bibliography that provides standard bibliographical information not only for the many titles noted in the narrative, but also for hundreds of additional works. As I have mentioned, the material surveyed concentrates almost exclusively on secondary sources. Some preference has been given to journal articles and essays published in the past twenty-five years, although older materials are also included. I have made a conscious effort to identify works about concerns often minimized or neglected in much of the literature. Roman Catholicism in the South, black religion, and native American Indian religions are only three examples. Finally, the bibliographical listings seek to provide examples of the range of materials that treat individual topics.

Within the narrative, numbers appearing in parentheses following the mention of a work identify where in the listing one may find complete bibliographical information about that particular study. For example, (37) means that the item mentioned is entry 37 in the bibliography at the conclusion of that chapter. If bibliographical information for a work mentioned is included in the listing for another chapter, the number of the chapter, followed by a colon, precedes the item number. For example, (2:29) means that full information on the work noted may be found in entry 29 in the listing for chapter 2.

My interest in developing a critical bibliography of religion in the South stems from my participation in a National Endowment for the Humanities Summer Seminar for College Teachers conducted by John Shelton Reed, professor of sociology at the University of North Carolina in Chapel Hill, in the summer of 1983. Professor Reed has offered continued support and judicious advice as the project grew from a seminar paper to a book. I am grateful to Professor Adrienne Bond for bringing my earlier efforts to the attention of Mercer University Press. Much of the initial work on this manuscript was done while on sabbatical leave from Clemson University in the spring of 1984. It goes without saying that I could not have completed my work without that leave. While on sabbatical, I had the privilege of being designated a Visiting Scholar in the department of history at the University of North Carolina in Chapel Hill. I appreciate the effort of Professor Donald G. Mathews for arranging that appointment as well as his continuing counsel.

Many scholars offered advice and criticism of various parts of the bibliography. They include Professors Peter W. Williams of Miami University,

F. Maurice Ethridge of Tennessee Technological University, Samuel S. Hill of the University of Florida, Charles Reagan Wilson of the University of Mississippi, Grant Wacker of the University of North Carolina in Chapel Hill, Randall M. Miller of Saint Joseph's University, Will B. Gravely of the University of Denver, and Denis Paz, Theda Perdue, and H. Lewis Suggs of Clemson University.

The bulk of the work in tracking down bibliographical references was done at the Davis Library (University of North Carolina in Chapel Hill), the Perkins Library (Duke University), the Hill Library (North Carolina State University), and the Duke Divinity School Library. I appreciate the courtesies extended to me by the staffs of each. Much of the final checking of titles and bibliographical information was done, of course, at the Cooper Library of Clemson University. My debt to its staff, especially to Ms. Marian Withington, is immense. The final manuscript has benefited greatly from the suggestions made by the many persons to whom Mercer University Press sent various chapters for preliminary reading.

Finally, I could not have completed the manuscript without having entered the technological age and learning my way amid the world of computers and word processors. Hence my greatest debt is to Joseph E. Carter, who graciously shared his expertise in computer science, patiently answered my questions, and frequently used his skills to get me out of technological dilemmas generated by my embryonic computer literacy.

Charles H. Lippy
Clemson University
31 December 1984

1 RESOURCES FOR THE STUDY OF RELIGION IN THE SOUTH

WITH THE INCREASE over the past two and a half decades of scholarly interest in the role played by regionalism in American life, new resource materials for students of religion in the South have become available. Among the foremost of these is the *Encyclopedia of Religion in the South* (112), an indispensable tool for initial study of any aspect of Southern religion. Edited by Samuel S. Hill, perhaps the preeminent scholar of the region's religious culture, the *Encyclopedia* offers treatment of topics, groups, institutions, and ideas that cover the gamut of Southern religion. In addition, this valuable work contains capsule histories of developments by state (which have been published separately; see 2:34), notes those sites that have peculiar religious significance within the region, and appraises dimensions of the popular or folk religious culture of the South. As well it provides biographical sketches of individuals whose work has shaped Southern religion, augmenting the more general biographical dictionary edited by Henry Warner Bowden (105). The *Encyclopedia* also includes numerous essays of a background nature that place religious developments in the South in context both within American culture and within the larger western religious tradition. Main entries are followed by suggestions for further reading, most of which are also noted in this volume.

Those seeking information of an encyclopedic nature concerning the American religious scene in general on matters which provide the setting for distinctively Southern phenomena will find Charles H. Lippy and Peter W. Williams, eds., *Encyclopedia of Religion in America* (113) useful. One area the *Encyclopedia of Religion in the South* neglects to include, however, is the complex of Asian religions that have gained a following in recent years in the South both because of the growing numbers of Americans in the South who have espoused Asian teachings and because of the increased Asian immigrant population of the region, who have transplanted the religious traditions of their homelands to the South.

Many of the standard bibliographical guides dealing with American history and/or religion retain value for the contemporary student, particularly in pointing out older studies. The massive *Bibliography of Bibliographies in Religion* project (2) is helpful in identifying some of the earlier research tools. The various editions of Henry P. Beers, *Bibliographies in American History* (3-4), are also worthy of perusal. Among the bibliographical works that focus on American religion, two are especially important for students of Southern religion. An *Alphabetical Subject Index and Index Encyclopedia to Periodical Articles in Religion, 1890-1899,* compiled by Ernest C. Richardson (294), while by no means restricted to topics dealing with religion in the South or even in the United States, is nevertheless virtually indispensable, for it identifies more than 55,000 articles written in the closing decade of the nineteenth century. Also still a basic beginning point is Nelson R. Burr, *A Critical Bibliography of Religion in America* (6). Although now nearly one quarter of a century old and therefore not including the most recent work in any field, Burr's bibliography remains the most comprehensive in terms of coverage and the most judicious in terms of comment.

Since many advances in scholarship receive their initial statement in dissertations and periodical articles, those works that abstract or index such materials are essential to serious research. University Microfilms International's *Dissertation Abstracts* (11) continues to be the major guide to dissertation studies, but two others are also pertinent to those seeking titles treating Southern religion. *Doctoral Dissertations in the Field of Religion, 1940-1952,* prepared by the Council on Graduate Studies in Religion (10), is still helpful, although current researchers should be aware that many dissertations that focus on Southern religion come from other disciplines, especially literature, history, sociology, and, more recently, interdisciplinary programs in areas such as black studies and women's studies. *Dissertations in American Church History, 1889-1932,* published under the auspices of the Catholic University of America (9), provides numerous titles of older work dealing with the early days of Roman Catholicism in the South although, like the others, it is not by any means limited to Southern topics.

A particularly useful guide to recent periodical literature, which includes brief abstracts, some analytical in nature, of numerous items dealing with religion in the South, is Robert deV. Brunkow, *Religion and Society in America: An Annotated Bibliography* (5). The major limitation of this work lies in its restriction of coverage to work appearing in those journals indexed in

America: History and Life. The most comprehensive reference work for periodical literature in religion is *Religion Index One: Periodicals,* formerly known as the *Index to Religious Periodical Literature.* Again, although its focus is broader than Southern religion, it notes many titles that pertain to the religious life of the region. Its use should be augmented by consulting the *Catholic Periodical Index* for works centering on Southern Catholicism and the *Index to Jewish Periodicals* for occasional titles on Judaism in the South.

As well, one should consult the journals published by state historical societies, denominational agencies, and other scholarly groups that have a special concern for Southern culture. Many of the serials sponsored by state historical societies include annual or occasional bibliographies of periodical literature centering on their own states; some list monographs and dissertations as well. None restricts coverage to religion, but all include topics pertaining to religion. Two journals that publish bibliographies of exceptional value for students of Southern religion are the *Journal of Southern History* and *Mississippi Quarterly.* The former publishes an annual bibliography of articles on all aspects of Southern culture arranged topically. Those interested in religion should consult not only that section of the listing, but also those dealing with black studies and with social and intellectual history especially. The annual bibliographies in *Mississippi Quarterly* focus on Southern literature and highlight secondary works of all sorts that discuss Southern writers. Both are indispensable aids to researchers on religion in the South.

There are as well numerous topical bibliographies that help persons pursuing the study of Southern religion. Those with special interest in Southern Catholicism, for example, should consult John Tracy Ellis and Robert Trisco, *A Guide to American Catholic History* (37), as well as Edward R. Vollmar, *The Catholic Church in America: an Historical Bibliography* (81). While the former is annotated and the latter is not, except for an occasional phrase or two, the Vollmar work is more extensive and particularly useful in identifying older materials (the revised edition appeared more than twenty years ago) and studies that have appeared in relatively unknown journals and monographs. More recent materials are surveyed by James J. Hennesey in *American Catholic Bibliography, 1970-1982* (42). The standard bibliographies focusing on American Judaism (28, 31, 63, 65), however, are less useful in pointing out works that study that tradition's story in the South since they tend to highlight analyses that are more synoptic than regional in orientation.

Numerous bibliographies identify materials pertaining to the various Protestant denominations, though most are in need of updating and none has an exclusively Southern orientation. For the Presbyterians, see Martha B. Aycock, ''A Checklist of Doctoral Dissertations on American Presbyterian and Reformed Subjects, 1965-1972'' (20); Harold B. Prince, comp., *A Presbyterian Bibliography* (60); Leonard J. Trinterud, *A Bibliography of Ameri-*

can Presbyterianism during the Colonial Period (79); T. H. Spence's older "Brief Bibliography of Presbyterian History" (72); and the more narrowly focused essay by Haskell Monroe, "Presbyterians in Texas—A Bibliographical Essay" (54). Several focus on the Baptists: Leo T. Crismon, "Literature of the Baptists" (29); Edward C. Starr's invaluable *A Baptist Bibliography* (73); and Charles W. Deweese, "State Baptist Historical Journals" (34). The most helpful work for the Methodists is still in process of completion: Kenneth E. Rowe, comp., *Methodist Union Catalog: Pre-1976 Imprints* (67). A greater range of titles surveys studies treating various aspects of the Episcopal story. Among the more recent is Frank E. Sugeno, ed., "Episcopal and Anglican History, 1973-1975: An Annotated Bibliography" (74); Sandra Hughes Boyd, comp., "The History of Women in the Episcopal Church: A Selected Annotated Bibliography" (27); and Denis G. Paz, "The Episcopal Church in Local History since 1950: An Annotated Bibliography" (58). Older but still helpful works include Robert S. Bosher, comp., "The Episcopal Church and American Christianity: A Bibliography (26); W. Robert Insko, "A Short Bibliography of the History of the Episcopal Church in Kentucky" (46); John M. Kinney, comp., "Bibliography of Diocesan Histories" (50); Patricia Farrell Sharber's doctoral dissertation, "Social History of Tennessee Episcopalians, 1865-1935, with a Guide to Research in Local Religious History" (69); and Niels H. Sonne, "Bibliographical Materials on the Episcopal Church" (71). Richard T. Hughes, "Twenty-Five Years of Restoration Scholarship" (44), is a judicious discussion of materials pertinent to the story of the Disciples of Christ and the Churches of Christ. On the Church of the Brethren, see Donald F. Durnbaugh and Lawrence W. Schultz, "A Brethren Bibliography, 1713-1963" (36).

Scholars of Southern religion have long recognized the prevalence of countless sectarian groups in the region, many of which have links with the Holiness and/or Pentecostal movements. But few detailed studies of Southern sectarianism have appeared in print. Research in this area, though, is now facilitated by the publication in the last decade of two ambitious bibliographies written by Charles Edwin Jones, *A Guide to the Study of the Holiness Movement* (47) and *A Guide to the Study of the Pentecostal Movement* (48). Jones provides a brief history of each group included and lists a dazzling array of primary and secondary materials carefully arranged by topic or genre, but does not offer extensive comment on any of the titles. Nonetheless, his work highlights how fertile Southern culture has been in giving birth to and sustaining a variety of sectarian movements and is the basic beginning point for identifying the major sources available for future research. Also helpful is Donald W. Dayton, *The American Holiness Movement: A Bibliographical Introduction* (32). For titles dealing with Black Pentecostalism, see James Tinney, *Black Pentecostalism: An Annotated Bibliography* (78). Yet to appear is a comprehensive bibliographical study of those sectarian movements that lie outside the Pentecostal-Holiness orbit.

The surge of scholarly interest in ethnic studies over the past two decades has yielded several bibliographical guides that introduce materials on the various tribal cultures of the native Americans whose societies once flourished in the South. The most valuable is the *Newberry Library Center for the History of the American Indian Bibliography Series,* prepared under the general editorship of Francis Jennings. Individual volumes that have appeared to date provide an entrée into materials on the Cherokee, Choctaw, Creek, and other Southeastern cultures (39, 40, 49, 57, 59). There is also a volume on Christian missions to the Indians (64) that should be supplemented by chapter 11 of Francis P. Prucha, *A Bibliographical Guide to the History of Indian-White Relations in the United States* (61) and its supplement (62). The Newberry Library Series, like the present work, divides material into two sections: a connected critical commentary on work done in an area and a more extensive bibliographical listing containing many titles that are not discussed in the narrative. The volumes, though, are very selective in scope, and coverage is far from exhaustive in any area. Research on the religions of the Southern tribes and the interaction of those traditions with Christianity and the other religions of the European conquerors would be enriched by a guide to literature in state historical journals appraising tribal cultures similar to that prepared by Arlene B. Hirschfelder (43) for journals in the New England and Middle Atlantic states.

Academic and popular interest in the mountain and rural cultures of the South, particularly in the Appalachian region, has also risen over the past two decades, largely as a result of programs associated with the Kennedy and Johnson administrations and designed to combat rural poverty. In this area, the most useful and also most comprehensive aid to research on Appalachian religion is the *Appalachian Bibliography* (19), published under the auspices of West Virginia University and updated periodically. Other works that seek to identify resources in this area include those of Lynn Dickerson and Barbara Vann (35), Charlotte T. Ross (66), and Marie G. Noss (56).

Indispensable for the study of Black religion in the United States in general are two works prepared by Ethel L. Williams and Clifton E. Brown: *The Howard University Bibliography of African and Afro-American Religious Studies* (83), which notes library locations of materials included, and *Afro-American Religious Studies* (82). Walter Schatz, ed., *Directory of Afro-American Resources* (155), is helpful in locating unpublished primary materials.

The religious dimension of Southern life has permeated much of the writing of the region's authors, as literary critics have long noted. Studies of both major and minor figures are catalogued in Louis D. Rubin, ed., *A Biblio-*

graphical Guide to the Study of Southern Literature (68) and its sequel, *Southern Literature, 1968-1975: A Checklist of Scholarship,* edited by Jerry T. Williams (84). One hopes that this ambitious project will receive another update covering the criticism and analyses of the last decade. Occasionally one will find additional titles in more general reference guides such as Duke University Press's continuing *American Literary Scholarship: An Annual* (18) and its *Articles in American Literature* volumes (51-53). Also see the continuing series, *Bibliography of American Literature* (24). More extensive checklists of criticism on individual authors have also been published in many cases. They are noted in the bibliographical listing at the end of chapter 16.

Numerous libraries contain important manuscript holdings and archival materials, including diaries, letters, and unpublished papers of the region's religious leaders and authors. Perhaps the most extensive resources of this sort are those found in the Southern Historical Collection at the University of North Carolina in Chapel Hill, which have been described in several published guides (122, 133, 158). But such materials are to be found scattered throughout the South in the collections of most of the region's historical societies and university libraries, particularly those which have established centers for research on the South such as the Center for the Study of Southern Culture at the University of Mississippi. Many of these, including college and university libraries that are repositories for denominational materials, are noted in the bibliography at the close of this chapter. Among the special collections that contain items of interest to students of Southern religion are those of the various denominations. The Protestant Episcopal Church, for example, has extensive holdings that have been described more fully than those of other denominations in in the *Historical Magazine of the Protestant Episcopal Church* (120). One should not neglect the materials to be found in the collections of local and subregional historical societies. The Guilford County (North Carolina) Historical Society, for example, has a splendid collection of materials relating to the early Moravian settlements in the area around Winston-Salem, North Carolina. Several general guides to archival and manuscript collections are fortunately available, though many are dated. One should note Edmund L. Binsfield, "Church Archives in the United States and Canada" (121); Nelson R. Burr, "Sources for the Study of American Church History in the Library of Congress" (123); Robert B. Downs, *Resources of Southern Libraries* (127); the old but reliable *Guide to Archives and Manuscripts in the United States* compiled by Philip M. Hamer (134); the *National Union Catalog of Manuscript Collections* (150), a continuing project of the Library of Congress; and the *Directory of Archives and Manuscript Repositories in the United States* (149), published by the National Archives and Records Service.

Several archival collections are valuable for the study of Judaism in the South. They include the American Jewish Archives (166) and the American Jewish Historical Society Archives at Brandeis University (167). Various Presbyterian groups have important collections (202, 203). The United Methodist Church recently opened an important archival center housed on the campus of Drew University (266). Some denominational groups have extensive holdings in state archival collections. Two examples are the Georgia Baptist Historical Society collection at Mercer University (196) and the Florida Baptist Historical Collection at Stetson University (191). For the latter there is an older, but still useful index of materials compiled by Harry Garwood (132). On a state basis, the most complete holdings of Catholic materials are at the Catholic Archives of Texas (176); parts of that collection were described in an older study by Claude Lane, *Catholic Archives of Texas: History and Preliminary Inventory* (143). Some of the more helpful Catholic diocesan archives are noted in the bibliography at the end of this chapter.

The bibliography of resource and reference materials in this chapter provides a selected listing of general guides to published materials, including those that treat the larger social and religious context within which Southern religion has charted its course. It then identifies bibliographies of topical materials of special interest to students of Southern religion. There is also a brief listing of periodicals that prepare bibliographies on an annual or occasional basis, as well as a section that cites those periodical indexes of greatest value in locating articles on Southern religion and its role in Southern life. Another section highlights encyclopedias, dictionaries, and atlases that would be of use in initial exploration of topics concerning religion in the South, while separate sections detail published guides to archival, manuscript, and special research collections likely to contain materials germane to the study of Southern religion and the major collections themselves.

BIBLIOGRAPHY

I. BIBLIOGRAPHICAL GUIDES: GENERAL

(1) American Theological Library Association. *A Bibliography of Postgraduate Masters' Theses in Religion Accepted by American Theological Seminaries*. Niels H. Sonne, ed. Chicago: ATLA, 1951.

(2) Barrow, John G. *A Bibliography of Bibliographies in Religion*. Austin: n.p., 1955.

(3) Beers, Henry P. *Bibliographies in American History: Guide to Materials for Research*. Rev. ed. New York: H. W. Wilson, 1942.

(4) _____. *Bibliographies in American History, 1942-1978*. Woodbridge CT: Research Publications, 1982.

(5) Brunkow, Robert deV., ed. *Religion and Society in America: An Annotated Bibliography*. Santa Barbara: ABC-Clio, 1983.

(6) Burr, Nelson R., ed. *A Critical Bibliography of Religion in America.* 2 vols. *Religion in American Life,* 4:1-2. James Ward Smith and A. Leland Jamison, eds. Princeton: Princeton University Press, 1961.

(7) _____. *Religion in American Life.* Goldentree Bibliographies in American History. New York: Appleton-Century-Crofts, 1971.

(8) Case, Shirley J., et al. *A Bibliographical Guide to the History of Christianity.* Rev. ed. New York: Peter Smith, 1951.

(9) Catholic University of America. *Dissertations in American Church History, 1889-1932.* Washington: Privately printed, 1933.

(10) Council on Graduate Studies in Religion. *Doctoral Dissertations in the Field of Religion, 1940-1952.* New York: Columbia University Press, 1954.

(11) *Dissertation Abstracts: Abstracts of Dissertations and Monographs in Microfilm.* Ann Arbor: University Microfilms International, 1938– . Title varies.

(12) Downs, Robert B. *American Library Resources: A Bibliographical Guide.* Chicago: American Library Association, 1951; *Supplement, 1950-61.* Chicago: American Library Association, 1961; *Supplement, 1961-70.* Chicago: American Library Association, 1972; *Supplement, 1971-80.* Chicago: American Library Association, 1981.

(13) Gaustad, Edwin S. *American Religious History.* American Historical Association Service Center for Teachers of History Publication 65. Washington: Service Center for Teachers of History, 1966.

(14) Jackson, Samuel M. "A Bibliography of American Church History, 1820-1893." *The American Church History Series* 12. Philip Schaff, ed. New York: Christian Literature Publishing, 1894.

(15) *Religious Books, 1876-1982.* 4 vols. New York: R.R. Bowker, 1983.

(16) Sandeen Ernest R., and Frederick Hall. *American Religion and Philosophy: A Guide to Information Sources.* Detroit: Gale Research, 1978.

(17) U.S. Library of Congress, General Reference and Bibliography Division. *A Guide to the Study of the United States of America.* Donald H. Mugridge and Blanche McCrum, eds., 752-84. Washington: Library of Congress, 1960.

II. BIBLIOGRAPHICAL GUIDES: TOPICAL

(18) *American Literary Scholarship: An Annual.* Durham: Duke University Press, 1966– .

(19) *Appalachian Bibliography, 1980.* Morgantown WV: West Virginia University Library, 1980.

(20) Aycock, Martha B. "A Checklist of Doctoral Dissertations on American Presbyterian and Reformed Subjects, 1965-1972." *Journal of Presbyterian History* 53 (1975): 168-83.

(21) Bell, Barbara L. *Black Bibliographical Sources: An Annotated Bibliography.* New Haven: Yale University Press, 1970.

(22) Berkowitz, Morris I., and J. Edmund Johnson, eds. *Social Scientific Studies of Religion: A Bibliography*. Pittsburgh: University of Pittsburgh Press, 1967.

(23) Bieder, Robert E. "Anthropology and History of the American Indian." Bibliography Issue. *American Quarterly* 33 (1981): 309-26.

(24) Blanck, Jacob N. *Bibliography of American Literature*. Comp. for the Bibliographical Society of America. New Haven: Yale University Press, 1955- . 7 vols. to date.

(25) Boles, John B. "Religion in the South: Recent Historiography." Paper presented to the Southern Historical Association, 6 November 1982.

(26) Bosher, Robert S., comp. "The Episcopal Church and American Christianity: A Bibliography." *Historical Magazine of the Protestant Episcopal Church* 19 (1950): 369-84.

(27) Boyd, Sandra Hughes, comp. "The History of Women in the Episcopal Church: A Selected Annotated Bibliography." *Historical Magazine of the Protestant Episcopal Church* 50 (1981): 423-33.

(28) Brickman, William W. *The Jewish Community in America*. New York: Burt Franklin, 1977.

(29) Crismon, Leo T. "Literature of the Baptists." *Religion in Life* 25 (1955-56): 117-31.

(30) Cunningham, Horace H. "The Southern Mind Since the Civil War." In *Writing Southern History*. Arthur S. Link and Rembert W. Patrick, eds., 383-409. Baton Rouge: Louisiana State University Press, 1965.

(31) Cutter, Charles, and Micha Falk Oppenheim. *Jewish Reference Sources: A Selective, Annotated Bibliographic Guide*. New York and London: Garland Publishers, 1982.

(32) Dayton, Donald W. *The American Holiness Movement: A Bibliographical Introduction*. Wilmore KY: B. L. Fisher Library, Asbury Theological Seminary, 1971.

(33) DeGroot, A. T. *Churches and the North American Indians: A Chronology and Sample Denominational Bibliographies*. Peoria AZ: Privately printed, 1979.

(34) Deweese, Charles W. "State Baptist Historical Journals." *Baptist History and Heritage* 14 (1978): 34, 36.

(35) Dickerson, Lynn, and Barbara Vann. "Regional Studies: Appalachia, 1905-1972." *Appalachian Heritage* 5 (Winter 1977): 41-57.

(36) Durnbaugh, Donald F., and Lawrence W. Schultz. "A Brethren Bibliography, 1713-1963: Two Hundred Fifty Years of Brethren Literature." *Brethren Life and Thought* 9 (1964): 3-177.

(37) Ellis, John Tracy, and Robert Trisco. *A Guide to American Catholic History*. Santa Barbara: ABC-Clio, 1982.

(38) Field, Thomas W. *An Essay Towards an Indian Bibliography*. New York: Scribner, Armstrong, 1873. Reprinted, Detroit: Gale Research, 1967.

(39) Fogelson, Raymond D. *The Cherokees: A Critical Bibliography*. Newberry Library Center for the History of the American Indian Bibliography Series. Francis Jennings, ed. Bloomington: Indiana University Press for the Newberry Library, 1978.

(40) Green, Michael D. *The Creeks: A Critical Bibliography*. Newberry Library Center for the History of the American Indiana Bibliography Series. Francis Jennings, ed. Bloomington: Indiana University Press for the Newberry Library, 1980.

(41) Haywood, Charles. *A Bibliography of North American Folklore and Folksong*. New York: Greenberg, 1951; New York: Dover Publishing, 1961.

(42) Hennesey, James, S.J. *American Catholic Bibliography, 1970-1982*. Working Papers Series 12, No. 1. Notre Dame: Cushwa Center for the Study of American Catholicism, 1982.

(43) Hirschfelder, Arlene B. *Annotated Bibliography of the Literature on American Indians Published in State Historical Society Publications: New England and Middle Atlantic States*. Millwood NY: Kraus Intern Publications, 1982.

(44) Hughes, Richard T. "Twenty-Five Years of Restoration Scholarship." *Restoration Quarterly* 25 (1982): 233-56; 26 (1983): 39-62.

(45) Hultkrantz, Ake. "North American Indian Religion in the History of Research: A General Survey." *History of Religions* 6 (1966): 91-107, 183-207; 7 (1967): 13-34, 112-48.

(46) Insko, W. Robert. "A Short Bibliography of the History of the Episcopal Church in Kentucky." *Register of the Kentucky Historical Society* 53 (1955): 263-68.

(47) Jones, Charles E. *A Guide to the Study of the Holiness Movement*. Metuchen: Scarecrow Press, 1974.

(48) _____. *A Guide to the Study of the Pentecostal Movement*. 2 vols. Metuchen: Scarecrow Press, 1983.

(49) Kidwell, Clara S., and Charles Roberts. *The Choctaws: A Critical Bibliography*. Newberry Library Center for the History of the American Indian Bibliography Series. Francis Jennings, ed. Bloomington: Indiana University Press for the Newberry Library, 1980.

(50) Kinney, John M., comp. "Bibliography of Diocesan Histories." *Historical Magazine of the Protestant Episcopal Church* 43 (1974): 69-100.

(51) Leary, Lewis G., ed. *Articles on American Literature, 1900-1950*. Durham: Duke University Press, 1954.

(52) _____, with Carolyn Bartholet and Catharine Roth. *Articles on American Literature, 1950-1967*. Durham: Duke University Press, 1970.

(53) _____, with John Auchard. *Articles on American Literature, 1968-1975*. Durham: Duke University Press, 1979.

(54) Monroe, Haskell. "Presbyterians in Texas—A Bibliographical Essay." *Journal of Presbyterian History* 50 (1972): 326-51.

(55) Murdock, George P. *Ethnographic Bibliography of North America*. New Haven: Human Relations Area Files, 1975.

(56) Noss, Marie G. *Books on the Southern Mountain Area That Contain Religion or Sections on Religion, 1947-55*. Berea KY: Berea College, n.d.

(57) O'Donnell, James H. III. *Southeastern Frontiers—Europeans, Africans, and American Indians, 1513-1840: A Critical Bibliography*. Newberry Library Center for the History of the American Indian Bibliography Series. Francis Jennings, ed. Bloomington: Indiana University Press for the Newberry Library, 1982.

(58) Paz, Denis G. "The Episcopal Church in Local History Since 1950: An Annotated Bibliography." *Historical Magazine of the Protestant Episcopal Church* 49 (1980): 389-409.

(59) Porter, Frank W. III. *Indians in Maryland and Delaware: A Critical Bibliography*. Newberry Library Center for the History of the American Indian Bibliography Series. Francis Jennings, ed. Bloomington: Indiana University Press for the Newberry Library, 1980.

(60) Prince, Harold B., comp. and ed. *A Presbyterian Bibliography: The Published Writings of Ministers Who Served the Presbyterian Church in the United States During Its First Hundred Years, 1861-1961, and Their Locations in Eight Significant Small Colleges in the U.S.* Metuchen: Scarecrow Press, 1983; Philadelphia: ATLA, 1983.

(61) Prucha, Francis P. *A Bibliographical Guide to the History of Indian-White Relations in the United States*, chap. 11. Chicago: University of Chicago Press, 1977.

(62) _____. *Indian-White Relations in the United States: A Bibliography of Works Published 1975-1980*, chap. 9. Lincoln: University of Nebraska Press, 1982.

(63) Rischin, Moses. *An Inventory of American Jewish History*. Cambridge: Harvard University Press, 1954.

(64) Ronda, James P., and James Axtell. *Indian Missions: A Critical Bibliography*. Newberry Library Center for the History of the American Indian Bibliography Series. Francis Jennings, ed. Bloomington: Indiana University Press for the Newberry Library, 1978.

(65) Rosenbach, A. S. W. *An American Jewish Bibliography*. New York: American Jewish Publication Society, 1926.

(66) Ross, Charlotte T., ed. *Bibliography of Southern Appalachia*. Boone NC: Appalachian Consortium, 1976.

(67) Rowe, Kenneth E., comp. *Methodist Union Catalog: Pre-1976 Imprints*. Metuchen: Scarecrow Press, 1975– . 5 vols. to date.

(68) Rubin, Louis D. *A Bibliographical Guide to the Study of Southern Literature*. Baton Rouge: Louisiana State University Press, 1969.

(69) Sharber, Patricia Farrell. "Social History of Tennessee Episcopalians, 1865-1935, with a Guide to Research in Local Religious History." D.A. dissertation, Middle Tennessee State University, 1973.

(70) Smith, Mary Lorraine. *Historic Churches of the South: A Collection of Articles Published in Holland's "The Magazine of the South."* Atlanta: Tupper and Love, 1952.

(71) Sonne, Niels H. "Bibliographical Materials on the Episcopal Church." *Religion in Life* 25 (1956): 442-51.

(72) Spence, T. H. "Brief Bibliography of Presbyterian History." *Religion in Life* 25 (1956): 603-612.

(73) Starr, Edward C. *A Baptist Bibliography: Being a Register of Printed Material by and about Baptists*. Philadelphia: Judson Press for the Samuel Colgate Baptist Historical Collection, Colgate Univesity, 1947-76.

(74) Sugeno, Frank E., ed. "Episcopal and Anglican History, 1973-75: An Annotated Bibliography." *Historical Magazine of the Protestant Episcopal Church* 46 (1977): 115-48.

(75) Swanton, John R. *Source Material for the Social and Ceremonial Life of the Choctaw Indians*. United States Bureau of American Ethnology Bulletin 103. Washington: Government Printing Office, 1931.

(76) Thomas, Sr. Ursula. "Sources for the Study of Oklahoma Catholic Missions: A Critical Bibliography." *Chronicles of Oklahoma* 16 (1938): 346-77.

(77) Thompson, Edgar T., and A. M. Thompson. *Race and Religion: A Descriptive Bibliography Compiled with Special Reference to the Relations between Whites and Blacks in the United States*. Chapel Hill: University of North Carolina Press, 1949.

(78) Tinney, James. *Black Pentecostalism: An Annotated Bibliography*. Washington: By the author, 1979.

(79) Trinterud, Leonard J. *A Bibliography of American Presbyterianism during the Colonial Period*. Presbyterian Historical Society Publications 8. Philadelphia: Presbyterian Historical Society, 1968.

(80) Turner, Harold W. *Bibliography of New Religious Movements in Primal Societies, 2: North America*. Boston: G. K. Hall, 1978.

(81) Vollmar, Edward R. *The Catholic Church in America: An Historical Bibliography*. 2d ed. New York: Scarecrow Press, 1963.

(82) Williams, Ethel L., and Clifton F. Brown, *Afro-American Religious Studies*. Metuchen: Scarecrow Press, 1972.

(83) ———, and Clifton F. Brown. *The Howard University Bibliography of African and Afro-American Religious Studies with Locations in American Libraries*. Wilmington: Scholarly Resources, 1977.

(84) Williams, Jerry T., ed. *Southern Literature, 1968-1975: A Checklist of Scholarship*. Boston: G. K. Hall, 1978.

(85) Woodress, James. *American Fiction, 1900-1950: A Guide to Information Sources*. Detroit: Gale Research, 1974.

In addition, many journals and newsletters publish occasional or annual bibliographies of books, articles, and dissertations pertinent to the focus of the periodical that may treat religious topics. Included in this category are:

(86) *American Catholic Studies Newsletter*. Cushwa Center for the Study of American Catholicism, University of Notre Dame.

(87) *Baptist History and Heritage.*

(88) *Civil War History.*

(89) *Florida Historical Quarterly.*

(90) *Georgia Historical Quarterly.*

(91) *Historical Magazine of the Protestant Episcopal Church.*

(92) *Journal of Mississippi History.*

(93) *Journal of Presbyterian History.*

(94) *Journal of Southern History.*

(95) *Maryland Historical Magazine.*

(96) *Methodist History.*

(97) *Newsletter of the Afro-American Religious History Group of the American Academy of Religion.* Office of Special Studies, College of the Holy Cross, Worcester MA.

(98) *Mississippi Quarterly.*

(99) *North Carolina Historical Review.*

(100) *Quaker History.*

(101) *Southwestern Historical Quarterly.*

(102) *Virginia Magazine of History and Biography.*

III. ENCYCLOPEDIAS, DICTIONARIES, ATLASES, AND SIMILAR WORKS

(103) Allen, Clifton Judson, et al., eds. *Encyclopedia of Southern Baptists.* 2 vols. Nashville: Broadman Press, 1958.

(104) Baker, Robert A., ed. *A Baptist Source Book with Particular Reference to Southern Baptists.* Nashville: Broadman Press, 1966.

(105) Bowden, Henry W. *Dictionary of American Religious Biography.* Westport: Greenwood Press, 1977.

(106) Code, Joseph B. *Dictionary of the American Hierarchy, 1789-1964.* New York: Joseph F. Wagner, 1964.

(107) Crismon, Leo, and George R. Jewell. *Kentucky Baptist Atlas.* Middletown KY: Kentucky Historical Society, 1964.

(108) Gaustad, Edwin S. *An Historical Atlas of Religion in America.* Rev. ed. New York: Harper and Row, 1976.

(109) Greene, Glen Lee. *Louisiana Baptist Historical Atlas.* Alexandria LA: Executive Board of the Louisiana Baptist Convention, 1973.

(110) Harmon, Nolan B. *Encyclopedia of World Methodism.* 2 vols. Nashville: United Methodist Publishing House, 1974.

(111) Hastings, James, and John A. Selbie, et al., eds. *Encyclopaedia of Religion and Ethics.* 13 vols. Reprinted, New York: Charles Scribner's Sons, 1955.

(112) Hill, Samuel S., ed. *Encyclopedia of Religion in the South.* Macon: Mercer University Press, 1984.

(113) Lippy, Charles H., and Peter W. Williams, eds. *Encyclopedia of Religion in America*. 3 vols. New York: Charles Scribner's Sons, in press.

(114) Melton, J. Gordon. *Encyclopedia of American Religions*. Wilmington NC: McGrath Publishing House, 1978.

(115) Schaff, Philip, ed. *New Schaff-Herzog Encyclopedia of Religious Knowledge*. Rev. ed. 13 vols. Grand Rapids: Baker Book House, 1960.

(116) Weis, Frederick L. *The Colonial Churches and the Colonial Clergy of the Middle and Southern Colonies, 1607-1776*. Publications of the Society of Descendants of the Colonial Clergy, vol. 3. Lancaster MA: n.p., 1938.

(117) _____. *The Colonial Clergy and the Colonial Churches of Maryland, Delaware, and Georgia*. Publications of the Society of Descendants of the Colonial Clergy, vol. 5. Lancaster MA: n.p., 1950.

(118) _____. *The Colonial Clergy of Virginia, North Carolina, and South Carolina*. Publications of the Society of Descendants of the Colonial Clergy, vol. 7. Boston: n.p., 1955.

IV. GUIDES TO ARCHIVAL, MANUSCRIPT, AND RESEARCH COLLECTIONS

(119) Ash, Lee. *Subject Collections*. 5th ed. New York: Bowker, 1978.

(120) Bellamy, V. Nelle. "The Library and Archives of the Church Historical Society." *Historical Magazine of the Protestant Episcopal Church* 36 (1967): 387-96.

(121) Binsfield, Edmund L. "Church Archives in the United States and Canada: A Bibliography." *American Archivist* 21 (1958): 311-32.

(122) Blosser, Susan Sokol, and Clyde N. Wilson. *The Southern Historical Collection: A Guide to Manuscripts*. Chapel Hill: University of North Carolina Library, 1970.

(123) Burr, Nelson R. "Sources for the Study of American Church History in the Library of Congress." *Church History* 22 (1953): 227-38.

(124) Chapman, Berlin B. "Valuable Manuscripts on Oklahoma Indian History in the Bureau of Catholic Indian Missions, Washington, D.C." *Chronicles of Oklahoma* 26 (1948): 247.

(125) D'Antoni, Blaise C. "The Church Records of North Louisiana." *Louisiana History* 15 (1974): 59-67.

(126) Day, James M. *Handbook of Texas Archival and Manuscript Depositories*. Austin: Texas Library and Historical Commission, 1960.

(127) Downs, Robert B. *Resources of Southern Libraries*. Chicago: American Library Association, 1938.

(128) _____. "A Survey of Research Materials in North Carolina Libraries." Mimeographed, 1936.

(129) _____, ed. *Resources of North Carolina Libraries*. Raleigh: Governor's Commission on Library Resources, 1965.

(130) Drewry, Elizabeth B. "Material in the National Archives Relating to Florida, 1789-1870." *Florida Historical Quarterly* 22 (1944): 97-115.

(131) Edwards, Morgan, comp., assisted by Oliver Hart. "Materials toward a History of the Baptists in the Provinces of Maryland, Virginia, North Carolina, South Carolina, Georgia." Unpublished manuscript, 1772. Furman Manuscripts, Furman University Library.

(132) Garwood, Harry. *The Florida Baptist Historical Collection Index*. Deland: Florida Baptist Historical Society, 1960.

(133) *Guide to the Manuscripts in the Southern Historical Collection*. Chapel Hill: University of North Carolina Library, 1947.

(134) Hamer, Philip M., ed. *A Guide to Archives and Manuscripts in the United States*. New Haven: Yale University Press, 1961.

(135) Historical Records Survey of Virginia. *Inventory of Church Archives of Virginia*. Richmond: Historical Records Survey of Virginia, 1940- .

(136) Holweck, Frederick G. "The Historical Archives of St. Louis." *Catholic Historical Review* 1 (1918): 24-39.

(137) Hough, Brenda. "The Archives of the Society for the Propagation of the Gospel." *Historical Magazine of the Protestant Episcopal Church* 46 (1977): 309-22.

(138) Jacobsen, Phebe R. *Quaker Records in Maryland*. Annapolis: Hall of Records Commission, State of Maryland, 1966.

(139) Keller, Clara D. *American Library Resources Cumulative Index, 1870-1970*. Chicago: American Library Association, 1981.

(140) Kentucky Historical Society. *Kentucky Historical Society Microfilm Catalog*. N.p.p.: Kentucky Historical Society, 1975.

(141) Kirkham, E. Kay. *A Survey of American Church Records for the Period Before the Civil War East of the Mississippi River*. 2 vols. Salt Lake City: Deseret Book, 1959-1960.

(142) Kramer, William A. "Why Concordia Historical Institute?" *Concordia Historical Institute Quarterly* 51 (1978): 70-75.

(143) Lane, Claude. *Catholic Archives of Texas: History and Preliminary Inventory*. Houston: Sacred Heart Dominican College, 1961.

(144) McAvoy, Thomas T. "Catholic Archives and Manuscript Collections." *American Archivist* 24 (1961): 409-14.

(145) Manucy, Albert C. "Florida in North Carolina Spanish Records." *Florida Historical Quarterly* 25 (1947): 85-87.

(146) "Manuscript Collections of the South Carolina Historical Society," *South Carolina Historical Magazine* 78 (1977): 253-63.

(147) Mode, Peter G. *Source Book and Bibliographical Guide for American Church History*. Menasha WI: George Banta Publishing, 1921.

(148) Moore, John Hammond. *Research Materials in South Carolina: A Guide*. Columbia: University of South Carolina Press, 1967.

(149) National Historical Publications and Records Commission. *Directory of Archives and Manuscript Repositories in the United States*. Washington: National Archives and Records Service, General Services Administration, 1978.

(150) *National Union Catalog of Manuscript Collections, 1959- .* Washington: Library of Congress, 1962–. 20 vols. to date.

(151) Nolan, Charles E. *A Southern Catholic Heritage.* New Orleans: Archdiocese of New Orleans, 1976- . One volume to date.

(152) Rairdon, Jack T. "A Descriptive Guide to the Resource Materials of the International Headquarters, Church of the Nazarene, 1908-1948." M.A. thesis, University of Oklahoma, 1950.

(153) Riordan, Michael J. *Cathedral Records from the Beginning of Catholicism in Baltimore to the Present Time.* Baltimore: Catholic Mirror Press, 1914.

(154) Robbins, John A., et al., comps. *American Literary Manuscripts: A Checklist of Holdings in Academic, Historical and Public Libraries in the United States.* 2d ed. Athens: University of Georgia Press, 1977.

(155) Schatz, Walter, ed. *Directory of Afro-American Resources.* New York: R. R. Bowker, 1970.

(156) Schell, Edwin. "Methodist Records and History at the Grassroots in Northern Virginia." *American Archivist* 27 (1964): 381-85.

(157) Scherer, Lester B. "Black Baptists in the United States: Research Needs and Resources." *American Baptist Quarterly* 1 (1982): 69-73.

(158) Smith, Everard H. III. *The Southern Historical Collection: Supplementary Guide to Manuscripts, 1970-75.* Chapel Hill: University of North Carolina Library, 1976.

(159) Stewart, John, and Kenny A. Franks. *State Records, Manuscripts and Newspapers at the Oklahoma State Archives and Oklahoma Historical Society.* Oklahoma City: Oklahoma Department of Libraries and Oklahoma Historical Society, 1975.

(160) Sweet, William Warren. "Church Archives in the United States." *Church History* 8 (1939): 43-48.

(161) Tilley, Nannie M., and Noma Lee Goodwin. *Guide to Manuscript Collections in the Duke University Library.* Historical Papers of the Trinity College Historical Society, Nos. 27-28. Durham: Duke University Press, 1947.

(162) *User's Guide to the American Indian Correspondence: The Presbyterian Historical Society Collection of Missionaries' Letters, 1833-1893.* Westport CT: Greenwood Press, n.d.

(163) Walker, Charles O. "The Committee on Baptist History, 1948-1978." *Viewpoints: Georgia Baptist History* 6 (1978): 83-96.

(164) Wilson, Louis R., and Robert B. Downs. "Special Collections for the Study of History and Literature in the Southeast." *Publications of the Bibliographical Society of America* 28 (1934): 97-131.

V. SELECTED ARCHIVAL, MANUSCRIPT, AND RESEARCH COLLECTIONS

(165) Academy of American Franciscan History Library, Potomac MD.

(166) American Jewish Archives, Cincinnati OH.

(167) American Jewish Historical Society Library, Waltham MA.

(168) Archivum Romanum Societatis Jesu, Rome, Italy.

(169) Asbury Theological Seminary, Wilmore KY.

(170) Austin Presbyterian Theological Seminary, Austin TX.

(171) Baltimore Yearly Meeting of Friends (Hicksite), Baltimore MD.

(172) Baltimore Yearly Meeting of Friends (Homewood), Baltimore MD.

(173) Baylor University, Waco TX.

(174) Carolina Discipliana Library, Wilson NC.

(175) Cathedral House Archives, Protestant Episcopal Church in the Diocese of West Texas, San Antonio TX.

(176) Catholic Archives of Texas, Austin TX.

(177) Catholic University of America, Washington DC.

(178) Center for Restoration Studies, Brown Library, Abilene Christian University, Abilene TX.

(179) Christian Church History Collection, Elon College Library, Elon College NC

(180) Church Historical Society, Episcopal Church Archives, Austin TX.

(181) Concordia Historical Institute, St. Louis MO.

(182) Dalcho Historical Society of the Protestant Episcopal Church in South Carolina, Charleston SC.

(183) Dargan-Carver Library, Baptist Sunday School Board, Nashville TN.

(184) Disciples of Christ Historical Society, Nashville TN.

(185) Duke University, Durham NC.

(186) Eden Archives, Evangelical and Reformed Church and United Church of Christ, St. Louis MO.

(187) Emory University, Atlanta GA.

(188) Episcopal Diocese of Kentucky Archives, Louisville, KY.

(189) Episcopal Diocese of Missouri Archives, St. Louis MO.

(190) Filson Club Manuscript Department, Louisville KY.

(191) Florida Baptist Historical Society, Stetson University, Deland FL.

(192) Florida Historical Society Library, University of South Florida, Tampa FL.

(193) Free Will Baptist Historical Collection, Free Will Baptist Bible College, Nashville, TN.

(194) Free Will Baptist Historical Collection, Mt. Olive College, Mt. Olive NC.

(195) Furman University, Special Collections, Greenville SC.

(196) Georgia Baptist Historical Collection, Mercer University, Macon GA.

(197) Georgia Historical Society, Savannah GA.

(198) Georgetown University Archives, Washington DC.

(199) Guilford College Library, Greensboro NC.

(200) Harding Graduate School of Religion, Memphis TN.

(201) Hendrix College Library, Conway AR.

(202) Historical Foundation of the Cumberland Presbyterian Church, Memphis TN.

(203) Historical Foundations of the Presbyterian and Reformed Churches, Montreat NC.

(204) Huguenot Society of South Carolina, Charleston SC.

(205) Institute for the Study of Texan Culture, San Antonio TX.

(206) Interdenominational Theological Center, Atlanta GA.

(207) Jewish Historical Society of Maryland, Baltimore MD.

(208) Kentucky Conference of the United Methodist Church, Commission on Archives and History, Lexington KY.

(209) Kentucky Historical Society, Frankfort KY.

(210) Lexington Theological Seminary, Lexington KY.

(211) Library of the United Methodist Publishing House, Nashville TN.

(212) Livingstone College, Salisbury NC.

(213) Louisiana Historical Association, Tulane University, New Orleans LA.

(214) Louisiana State University Archives, Baton Rouge LA.

(215) Louisville Presbyterian Theological Seminary, Louisville KY.

(216) Lovely Lane Museum of the United Methodist Historical Society, Baltimore MD.

(217) Lutheran Church—Missouri Synod, Southeastern District Archives, Washington DC.

(218) Lutheran Church in America, Florida Synod Archives, Tampa FL.

(219) Lutheran Church in America, Indiana-Kentucky Synod Archives, Indianapolis IN.

(220) Lutheran Church in America, Maryland Synod Archives, Baltimore MD.

(221) Lutheran Church in America, North Carolina Synod Archives, Salisbury NC.

(222) Lutheran Theological Southern Seminary, Columbia SC.

(223) Maryland [Episcopal] Diocesan Library, Peabody Institute Library, Baltimore MD.

(224) Maryland Historical Society, Baltimore MD.

(225) Maryville College Library, Maryville TN.

(226) Methodist Collection, Central Methodist College, Fayette MO.

(227) Mississippi Baptist Historical Society, Mississippi College, Clinton MS.

(228) Mississippi Methodist Archives, Millsaps College, Jackson MS.

(229) Missouri Baptist Historical Society, William Jewell College Library, Liberty MO.

(230) Missouri Historical Society Archives, St. Louis MO.

(231) Moravian Archives, Winston-Salem NC.

(232) New Orleans Baptist Theological Seminary, New Orleans LA.

(233) North Carolina Baptist Historical Collection, Wake Forest University, Winston-Salem NC.

(234) North Carolina Collection, University of North Carolina, Chapel Hill NC.

(235) Northwest Texas Annual Conference Archives, United Methodist Church, McMurry College, Abilene TX.

(236) Oklahoma Annual Conference Archives, United Methodist Church, Oklahoma City University Library, Oklahoma City OK.

(237) Oklahoma Historical Society Library, Oklahoma City OK.

(238) Order of Preachers, Province of St. Joseph Archives, Dominican House of Studies, Washington DC.

(239) Primitive Baptist Library and Archives, Elon College NC.

(240) Protestant Episcopal Church Diocese of Maryland Archives, Baltimore MD.

(241) Roman Catholic Archdiocese of Baltimore Archives, Baltimore MD.

(242) Roman Catholic Archdiocese of New Orleans Chancery Archives, New Orleans LA.

(243) Roman Catholic Archdiocese of San Antonio Archives, San Antonio, TX.

(244) Roman Catholic Diocese of Amarillo Archives, Amarillo TX.

(245) Roman Catholic Diocese of Charleston Archives, Charleston SC.

(246) Roman Catholic Diocese of Covington Archives, Covington KY.

(247) Roman Catholic Diocese of Galveston-Houston Archives, Houston TX.

(248) Roman Catholic Diocese of Lafayette Archives, Lafayette LA.

(249) Roman Catholic Diocese of Natchez-Jackson Archives, Jackson MS.

(250) Roman Catholic Diocese of Savannah Archives, Savannah GA.

(251) St. Louis University, St. Louis MO.

(252) St. Mary's Seminary and University, Baltimore MD.

(253) St. Paul's Church, Augusta GA.

(254) South Carolina Historical Society, Charleston SC.

(255) South Caroliniana Library, University of South Carolina, Columbia SC.

(256) Southern Baptist Theological Seminary, Louisville KY.

(257) Southern Historical Collection, University of North Carolina, Chapel Hill NC.

(258) Southern Jewish Historical Society, Richmond VA.

(259) Southern Methodist University, Dallas TX.

(260) Southwestern Baptist Theological Seminary, Fort Worth TX.

(261) Texas Catholic Historical Society, Austin TX.

(262)   Texas Christian University, Fort Worth TX.

(263)   Texas State Historical Association, Austin TX.

(264)   Tulane University, New Orleans LA.

(265)   Union Theological Seminary, Richmond VA.

(266)   United Methodist Archives, Drew University, Madison NJ.

(267)   University of Alabama, University AL.

(268)   University of Georgia, Athens GA.

(269)   University of Mississippi, Oxford MS.

(270)   University of Notre Dame, Notre Dame IN.

(271)   University of Oklahoma, Norman OK.

(272)   University of Richmond, Richmond VA.

(273)   University of Texas, Austin TX.

(274)   Virginia Baptist Historical Society, University of Richmond, Richmond VA.

(275)   Virginia [Episcopal] Diocesan Library, Richmond VA.

(276)   Virginia Historical Society, Richmond VA.

(277)   Wofford College, Spartanburg SC.

VI. INDEXES TO PERIODICAL LITERATURE

(278)   *America: History and Life.*

(279)   *American Literature Abstracts.*

(280)   *Arts and Humanities Citation Index.*

(281)   *Catholic Periodical Index: A Cumulative Author and Subject Index to a Selected List of Catholic Periodicals.* Formerly *Catholic Periodical and Literature Review.*

(282)   *Christian Periodical Index: A Subject Index to Selected Periodical Literature.*

(283)   *Current Contents.*

(284)   *Guide to Religion and Social Science in Periodical Literature.*

(285)   *Historical Abstracts.*

(286)   *Humanities Index.*

(287)   *Index to Jewish Periodicals.*

(288)   *Poole's Index to Periodical Literature.*

(289)   *Reader's Guide to Periodical Literature.*

(290)   Ragazzi, John I., and Theodore C. Hines. *A Guide to Indexed Periodicals in Religion.* Metuchen: Scarecrow Press, 1975.

(291)   *Religion Index One: Periodicals.* Formerly *Index to Religious Periodical Literature.*

(292)   *Religious and Theological Abstracts.*

(293) *Religious Press Directory.*

(294) Richardson, Ernest Cushing, comp. and ed. *An Alphabetical Subject Index and Index Encyclopedia to Periodical Articles on Religion, 1890-1899.* New York: Charles Scribner's Sons for the Hartford Seminary Press, 1907-11.

(295) *Southern Baptist Periodical Index.*

(296) *United Methodist Periodical Index.* Formerly *Methodist Periodical Index.*

(297) Walsh, Michael J. *Religious Bibliographies in Serial Literature: A Guide.* Westport: Greenwood Press, 1981.

(298) *Writings in American History.*

2 RELIGION IN THE SOUTH: AN OVERVIEW

"THE BIBLE BELT" may well be the first image that comes to mind when the casual observer initially ponders religion in the South. Historically, the term is a relatively recent one, coined by H. L. Mencken in 1925. Whether a source of pride to fundamentalists or other biblical literalists to denote the centrality of one approach to Scripture in much of Southern Protestantism or a label of derision indicating the narrow range of vision that outsiders especially have claimed characterizes the region's religious life, "the Bible Belt" at least points to the prominence of religion in Southern culture.

Mencken, of course, is usually regarded as a critic of Southern culture in general who, according to Charles Anghoff (101), dismissed the South as the "bunghole of the United States, a cesspool of Baptists, a miasma of Methodism, snake-charmers, phony real-estate operators, and syphilitic evangelists." While contemporary students of Menckeniana suggest that Mencken was not attempting to degrade the South (116)—since he was, after all, a Baltimore Episcopalian—he nevertheless did recognize the impact of a particular form of Protestant evangelicalism as the dominant style of religious affirmation within Dixie.

But Mencken was far from alone in sensing the centrality to Southern culture of evangelical Protestantism as institutionalized in the Baptist and Methodist traditions. Mencken wrote in the 1920s, a time when other sorts of analysts were likewise arguing that despite the promotion of claims that a "New South" had emerged in the wake of nascent industrialization following Reconstruction and the ways in which the Great War had brought the South into a national orbit, the region still sustained a distinctive cultural ethos. Many

of these students of Southern life of a half century ago grounded their thinking in the discipline of sociology, particularly the sociology of regionalism
associated with Howard Odum and his circle at the University of North Carolina in Chapel Hill. Until the 1960s this school of thought dominated academic discussion of Southern religion, and its impact lives on in the work of
many contemporary students of Southern life.

Much of this older appraisal took published form in essays rather than in
monographs. Edwin M. Poteat, for example, in an essay published in 1934
(53), noted that religious makeup of the South was more homogeneous than
that of any other section of the United States, rooted in an evangelical orthodoxy that shunned sophisticated theological reflection and things modern. It
also served, he claimed, to buttress white supremacy and to delineate a proper
sphere for religion that removed the possibility of religion's being an active
force promoting social change. Consequently, Poteat neglected to include
discussion of black religious life in his overview, although, as will be noted
later, one could argue that the conscious or unconscious efforts of the white
majority to perpetuate distinct white and black societies, with the latter kept
clearly subordinate to the former, may themselves have been central to the
dominance of a Protestantism that stressed personal conversion and saw ethical issues almost exclusively through individualistic lenses. But even within
the cozy evangelicalism of white Baptists and Methodists, formal religious
ties were recognized as related to socioeconomic status. John Dollard's classic study, *Class and Caste in a Southern Town* (114), revealed the extent to
which denominations were pegged to a popular perception of social status.
Many of the same insights permeated W. J. Cash's comments on the role of
religion in *The Mind of the South* (13). Indeed, one of the earliest discussions
to suggest that those who would understand the dynamics of Southern religion needed to pay heed to the subtleties of black-white interaction was that
of Clyde L. Manschreck in his lecture ''Religion in the South: Problem and
Promise'' (45), published in 1959 as the civil rights movement was gaining
momentum. Fundamentalism and racial segregation taken together, argued
Manschreck, and not fundamentalism alone, provided the key to the South's
religious life. Fred J. Hood, *Reformed America* (38), is very helpful in providing a careful appraisal of many of the historical forces that generated the
ethos within which Southern religion developed.

Perhaps the most perceptive overview of Southern religion in essay form,
though now obviously outdated in some respects, is Joseph H. Fichter and
George L. Maddox, ''Religion in the South: Old and New,'' which appeared
in 1965 (24). While Fichter and Maddox followed earlier interpreters in
stressing the theological fundamentalism, individualistic ethic, and resistance to change inherent in Southern white Protestantism, they, too, identified the problem of race as central to the overall story. As well, they

highlighted two other dimensions of Southern religious history that most previous commentators had omitted: Roman Catholicism and Judaism. Both traditions have deep roots in the Southern heritage, but have easily been eclipsed
by the magnitude of evangelical Protestantism. Each will receive independent treatment in this work. But the importance of Fichter's and Maddox's
insight lay in its suggestion that the pluralism that has marked the nation's
religious history has also been present in the South, even if that presence has
been muted.

More sustained analysis of Southern religious life traces its roots to Kenneth K. Bailey's study, *Southern White Protestantism in the Twentieth Century* (6), the backdrop of which was set in his earlier essay, "Southern White
Protestantism at the Turn of the Century" (7). While much work prior to Bailey's had told the story by denomination, naturally emphasizing Baptist and
Methodist developments, his studies recognized that the religious thrust of
the South did not respect denominational divisions. In other words, the evangelical dimension cut across institutional lines, creating more similarities than
differences in the everyday beliefs and practices of white Southerners regardless of their denominational affiliations. That same realization has also
occasionally led to somewhat humorous attempts to delineate precisely what
distinguishes Southern denominations, as in George Harmon's popular essay, "How to Tell a Baptist from a Methodist in the South" (29). But Bailey
arrived at some of the same conclusions as had his predecessors: Southern
white religion and Southern culture were so delicately intertwined that it was
difficult, if not impossible, in many circumstances to label a phenomenon as
"religious" or as "cultural." He did not push the point, though, to probe
precisely why such deep-seated interconnections have developed. He did
suggest that the major dilemma confronting Southern religion at mid-century
was the matter of racial discrimination and racial separation. While this conviction may have simply mirrored the mounting societal concern at the time
of his writing for civil rights and an end to blatant discrimination, he may
have been closer than he thought to identifying the reason for the close links
between the dominant white culture and evangelical Protestantism in the
South, for both were forged in an environment that sought to maintain white
supremacy and perpetuate first black slavery and then black inferiority. As
with virtually all other students of the Southern religious experience before
him, Bailey also minimized the influence of those who were not evangelicals
from "mainstream" denominations in painting his portrait of Southern white
Protestantism.

Since the appearance of *Southern Churches in Crisis* in 1967 (36), no one
has been more of a catalyst for promoting the serious study of Southern religion than Samuel S. Hill. In this study, Hill followed the lead of previous
analysts in arguing for the centrality of individual religious experience (con-

version) in Southern religion. But Hill was at the same time critical of this emphasis, claiming it had generated a crisis not only because it had fostered an individualistic ethic, but also because it had transformed Baptist and Methodist groups into symbols of an "established" majority. Sensitive to the history of Christianity, Hill reminded readers that both groups owed their origins to impulses for reform and change and that both had gained adherents in their early years because they represented the concerns of a minority outside the mainstream of society. Consequently both traditions historically had potent prophetic impact on their parent cultures because they operated as "sectarian" bodies, not dominant denominations. The result, he claimed, was that Southern evangelical Protestantism was a "culture-religion" different from the forces that had given it birth. If Hill offered a challenge to earlier interpretations in his implicit claim that Southern evangelical Protestant bodies had lost touch with the forces that had given them birth, he nevertheless echoed much earlier work in ignoring the black religious experience and in failing to probe the ways in which a stance of avoiding interaction across racial lines had made the individualistic ethic plausible and propelled from the fringes to the mainstream that style of Protestantism which valued private over collective religious experience.

Hill's more recent work, such as *The South and the North in American Religion* (35), does attempt to counter such criticism. This study, a revision of a series of lectures, compares religious developments regionally in three different time periods ("epochs"): 1795-1810, 1835-1850, and 1885-1900. Arguing that the South has maintained a religious "ethos without a social ethic," Hill here does take account of black religious developments, especially in the 1885-1900 period, and claims that the South gradually made religion a private concern (individual conversion) in order to maintain public order. While this appraisal is more sophisticated than that advanced in *Southern Churches in Crisis,* it nevertheless is predicated on the assumption that a stress on conversion necessarily means the lack of social concern or, more simply put, that personal religious experience automatically leads to a personal rather than social ethic. That such need not be the case and has not always been the case has been argued by other scholars whose work is examined in chapter 20.

Hill's overall "culture-religion" thesis has also been the subject of two studies: Gene M. Adams, "An Analytical Study of Southern Religion of the 1970's as Based on Samuel S. Hill's Southern Culture-Religion Thesis" (5), which looks at the ministry of Dallas's First Baptist Church, and Hart M. Nelsen and others, "Image of God and Religious Ideology and Involvement: A Partial Test of Hill's Southern Culture-Religion" (50). Both have found support for Hill's basic contention that Southern religion is concerned with saving souls to the exclusion of saving society. C. C. Goen's "Cultural Captivity of the American Churches'' (27) is a more general application of Hill's ''central theme'' to American religion as a whole.

Hill has also edited three valuable collections of essays. *Religion and the Solid South* (33) contains trenchant articles on the fundamentalist world view, religion and the plantation system, and the role of women in Southern religion. *On Jordan's Stormy Banks* (32), a reprint of material first appearing in 1976 in *Southern Exposure* with some new essays, through narrative and illustration suggests the multifaceted nature of Southern Protestantism, its important economic dimension, and its primacy as a total world view more than a compartmentalized feature of individual life. *Religion in the Southern States: A Historical Study* (34), which concludes with a brilliant essay by Hill surveying Southern religious history as a whole, contains the essays on each state that also appear in the *Encyclopedia of Religion in the South* (1:112). Most of the essays, however, trace state religious history by denomination; only the essay on Kentucky by Fred J. Hood moves beyond this narrow approach to explore the more subtle ways in which religion became so vital to the social fabric of the South.

Numerous synoptic studies of Southern religious culture are more popular in style and impressionistic in content. Of these, the most insightful is by the renowned Southern writer Erskine Caldwell. The son of a minister of the Associate Reformed Presbyterian Church, Caldwell drafted the essays in *Deep South: Memory and Observation* (11) as reflections on his childhood and adolescent perceptions of the meaning of his father's work and the problems he encountered. While the work has been little noticed, it is an indictment of the kind of ''culture-religion'' Hill has analyzed in that Caldwell repeatedly condemns the hypocrisy that he noticed in a social order in which many claimed to be Christian but regarded other human beings, particularly blacks, as inferior. Also from a personal perspective is *Haunted by God: The Cultural and Religious Experience of the South* by James M. Dabbs (16). Its thesis, stated more implicitly than explicitly, is that the evangelical imprint has operated more as a means to evade personal and collective social responsibility, resulting in a malaise when the disjunction between religious affirmation and empirical reality is recognized. C. Dwight Dorough, *Bible Belt Mystique* (20), an attempt to describe the role of revivalism in the rural South, tends to the simplistic, and Frye Gaillard, *Race, Rock, & Religion: Profiles from a Southern Journalist* (26), while occasionally insightful, offers little by way of fresh interpretation.

Several important essays describe and appraise the impact of Southern evangelical Protestantism and, in some cases, offer correctives to several assumptions that lie behind the synoptic studies mentioned thus far. Ernest Kurtz, for example, focused on the 1930s in ''The Tragedy of Southern Religion'' (41), claiming that the evangelical ethos had produced a society that emphasized "doing" over "being" and was consequently a "shame culture" rather than a "guilt culture." Four studies offer modest corrections to the perspective that concentrates on the uniformity of the evangelical style or, in some cases, its actual dominance in some locales. The volume of essays entitled *Varieties of Southern Evangelicalism,* edited by David Edwin Harrell, Jr., (28), demonstrates conclusively that Southern evangelicals are not fashioned from a single mold, particularly as it highlights the prevalence of white sectarianism in the South (especially in rural areas) and the very different evangelical style that has permeated much of Southern black religion. W. Frank Ainsley and John W. Florin, "The North Carolina Piedmont: An Island of Religious Diversity" (100), while not widely known, offers evidence that religious pluralism has a distinguished heritage and has long played an important role in at least one Southern state, while Charles O. Walker, "Georgia's Religion in the Colonial Era, 1733-1790" (150), suggests that such pluralism may be traced back to the early days of settlement in that state when Anglicans, Lutherans, Presbyterians, Congregationalists, Quakers, Baptists, and Jews all flourished there. Timothy F. Reilly, "Heterodox New Orleans and the Protestant South, 1800-1861" (144), while noting the obvious differences that mark the Louisiana situation because of the strong Catholic presence stretching back to the days of Spanish and French possession of the region and the emergence of a vibrant antebellum Unitarianism, shows how both require qualification of a facile assumption of evangelical Protestant hegemony.

Donald W. Shriver, Jr., now president of Union Theological Seminary in New York City, concludes that forces such as the civil rights movement, changing demographics, and new industrial patterns have left a mark on Southern religion in "Southern Churches in Transition" (57), while Richard Machalek and Michael Martin, " 'Invisible' Religions: Some Preliminary Evidence" (42), found an increase in the number of persons in metropolitan areas of the Deep South who claim no religious affiliation, though they are quick to point out that the absence of formal religious affiliation does not necessarily mean the absence of a religious world view influenced by the evangelical stance. A more simplistic popular tendency to attribute final causality of natural phenomena to the Divine without necessarily incorporating that sense into the presumably mainstream evangelical perspective remains a substratum of the religious scene, as evidenced by comparing the study of William M. Clements on popular reaction to the tornado that struck Jonesboro, Arkansas, in 1973 (107), with that of Wayne Viitanen on reaction to the earthquakes that ravaged New Madrid, Missouri, in 1811-1812 (149). The prevalence of a more strident fundamentalism than that found in the Baptist and Methodist groups emerges from Jeffrey K. Hadden and Charles E. Swann, *Prime-Time Preachers* (115), the best study of the "televangelism" of the "electronic church," and from Samuel S. Hill and Dennis E. Owen, *The New Religious Political Right* (31), which explores the rise of the Moral Majority and its relative strength in the South. Nonetheless, despite this growing recognition of pluralism and diversity, others have found that the established patterns of Southern white Protestant hegemony, an unofficially "established" evangelical world view and a "popular" fundamentalism, have not lost their strength or influence. Sociological evidence supporting this contention may be found in the " 'The Bible Belt': Southern Religion," chapter six of John Shelton Reed's *The Enduring South: Subcultural Persistence in Mass Society* (54).

But how did an evangelical style of Protestantism become so thoroughly entrenched in the South? The most penetrating response to that question in a study that seeks to look at the region as a whole rather than one area or state is Donald G. Mathews, *Religion in the Old South* (47). Drawing on an interdisciplinary methodological scheme, the value of which he argued in an earlier essay (48), Mathews here amplifies a thesis developed initially in "The Second Great Awakening as an Organizing Process, 1780-1830: An Hypothesis" (130)—namely, that evangelicalism brought a sense of order to society that functioned so effectively as to gain dominance. It is important to note that Mathews speaks of the evangelical "style" rather than focusing on denominations, for he is convinced that the same basic style supports the Baptists, Methodists, and others who in time came to dominate Southern religion. More important is the challenge Mathews raises to those interpretations of Southern white Protestantism that make a causal connection between the evangelical call for conversion and the lack of a social ethic. It is Mathews's contention, although the argument is strained at times, that the need to maintain an ideology of white supremacy over blacks and male supremacy over women was primarily responsible for the rise of an individualistic morality in the South and the corresponding failure of a social ethic to gain a strong foothold. In developing his position, Mathews provides provocative chapters on both black religion and the role of women in antebellum Southern religion. The need to maintain a focus extending beyond white culture is also an idea advanced in a different vein by William G. McLoughlin in "Red, White, and Black in the Antebellum South" (44). Also see McLoughlin's *The Cherokee Ghost Dance* (43).

Mathews's work, however, concentrates on an epoch when evangelical religion of some stripe had already captured the loyalty of most white Southerners. Such was not always the case. While some antebellum Southerners as well conceded the prevalence of some kind of Christianity in the region (see, for example, Kenneth R. Wesson, "Traveler's Accounts of the Southern Character: Antebellum and Early Postbellum Period" [64]), in the colonial period some bemoaned the poor state of religion. David W. Jordan's study of Anglican Joseph Presbury (39), among others, notes this sense that religious life reached a low ebb in the early colonial South. Even the one Southern colony popularly thought to have been settled for religious purposes, Maryland, was most likely not originally conceived as (nor did it long remain) a haven for Roman Catholics, as demonstrated in R. J. Lahey, "The Role of Religion in Lord Baltimore's Colonial Enterprise" (124). Nor did the evangelical hegemony arrive everywhere in the South at the same time. Presbyterian John Miller, for instance, recorded a mix of religious conditions in a journal kept while traveling in the South and midwest in the early nineteenth century (109).

Many commentators argue, however, that what gave the impetus to the evangelical surge was the Great Awakening of the eighteenth century, a movement that swept the English colonies from Maine to Georgia and everywhere brought dramatic transition to the prevalent religious, social, and economic patterns, of the day. An overview of the Great Awakening throughout the South still awaits writing, but numerous important studies on its impact in particular areas suggest the direction such a study might take. To date the most significant work has centered on Virginia, perhaps because the rise of evangelicalism there brought a multifaceted upheaval to a social order revolving around a landed gentry and a religious establishment focused on the Church of England. A good beginning point is the old, but classic study by Wesley M. Gewehr, *The Great Awakening in Virginia, 1740-1790* (77), but the questions and research methods for all future studies are those advanced in the work of Rhys Isaac. Drawing on interpretive constructs developed by cultural anthropologists and with a keen sensitivity to how language and symbols shape human understanding and behavior by generating cognitive structures and paradigms of reality, Isaac has forcefully argued that the key to the "evangelical South" lies with the rise of the Separate Baptist movement of the eighteenth century, rather than with the Regular Baptists or the Methodists who ultimately reaped the fruit of that movement. Isaac echoes Donald Mathews in regarding evangelicalism as a phenomenon that is "community-building." But Isaac goes well beyond all others in probing the subtle and delicate ways in which the Separate Baptists and their evangelical style created a world view to challenge the dominance of the gentry and established Anglicanism and to provide an alternative that was more plausible in interpreting empirical reality for increasing numbers of people. Isaac developed his essential argument in several articles (80-83), but they receive full and impressive articulation in *The Transformation of Virginia, 1740-1790* (84), destined to become a classic.

Other studies amplify some of the areas of concern advanced by Isaac. For example, William L. Lumpkin, *Baptist Foundations in the South: Tracing through the Separates the Influence of the Great Awakening, 1754-1787*

(89), covers much of the same ground, but without the refinement of Isaac's work. Maury Klein's several articles on the Scots-Irish (87) provide limited but valuable insight into life in the Shenandoah region that was the crucible for much of early evangelicalism in the era of the Awakening. One local study, "Social Change and Cultural Conflict in Virginia: Lunenburg County, 1746 to 1774" by Richard R. Beeman (69), arrives at essentially the same conclusions as did Isaac and offers a narrower range of evidence supporting the contention. Further support for Isaac's contentions comes in J. Stephen Kroll-Smith, "Transmitting a Revival Culture: The Organizational Dynamic of the Baptist Movement in Colonial Virginia, 1760-1777" (88). Treating some of the same matters in South Carolina, but devoid of the interdisciplinary methodology and sensitivity to subtle detail that marks Isaac's work, is John W. Brinsfield, *Religion and Politics in Colonial South Carolina* (105), which is really more of a study of the mechanics of the establishment and disestablishment of the Church of England in the colony than a careful appraisal of the evangelical forces behind the moves to end establishment. More substantive on the dynamics operating within Anglican circles is Frederick V. Mills, *Bishops by Ballots* (90).

Much more traditional in approach, but important in the overall picture, are those studies that treat Samuel Davies, a New Light Presbyterian whose work was regarded as central to the Awakening in Virginia, but which must be reevaluated in the light of Isaac's analysis. The now dated essays on Davies by George H. Bost are still a good starting point: "Samuel Davies, Preacher of the Great Awakening" (73) and "Samuel Davies, the South's Great Awakener" (74). The two most comprehensive studies of Davies are Robert S. Alley, "The Reverend Mr. Samuel Davies: A Study in Religion and Politics, 1747-1759" (68), and George W. Pilcher, *Samuel Davies: Apostle of Dissent in Colonial Virginia* (97).

Ultimately, though, all students of the era of the Awakening must come to grips with the figure of George Whitefield, whose itinerant preaching throughout the colonies helped make the Awakening a common phenomenon among the people who formed the United States. Literature on Whitefield is voluminous, although there remains a need for more sustained scholarly appraisal of his work throughout the colonies. The best general study is Stuart C. Henry, *George Whitefield: Wayfaring Witness* (79). Richard J. Cox has looked at Whitefield and the Awakening in Maryland (75); William Howland Kenney III, at Whitefield's labors in South Carolina (85) and elsewhere (86); while David T. Morgan, Jr., has attempted to probe the significance of Whitefield's preaching in the Carolinas and Georgia in two essays (91, 92); and Theda Perdue has focused on Whitefield in Georgia in two thoughtful pieces (95, 96). An attempt to appraise the import of Whitefield from a vantage point two centuries later is Jennings B. Sanders, "George Whitefield Two

Hundred and Twenty-five Years After His First American Visit: An Interpretation'' (98).

Not all are agreed, however, that the Great Awakening of the eighteenth century nurtured the seeds that grew into the later evangelicalism of the South. Others have looked to the wave of revivals that broke out in the frontier regions of Kentucky and gave birth to the campmeeting, in modern dress still a staple of much Southern religion, as the catalyst which paved the way for the evangelical ascendancy in the South. John B. Boles, *The Great Revival, 1787-1805: The Origins of the Southern Evangelical Mind* (71), provides the most powerful statement of this position. Many other works attempt to assess the impact of the frontier campmeeting and its brand of revivalism on Southern life. They will be noted in chapter 15, which deals with the phenomenon of revivalism.

It may be futile to try to determine a single matrix of events, movements, or figures that nurtured the evangelical style in the South as it assumed prominence. A host of forces, some more significant in one part of the region than in others, most likely contributed to cultivating and reshaping evangelicalism until it became intertwined with other phenomena to issue in the complex we know as Southern culture or, more properly, the culture of Southern white Protestantism. What is more clear, however, is that evangelicalism has never been the only religious style espoused by white Protestants nor is it a monolith everywhere the same in the South. Niels H. Sonne, for example, in *Liberal Kentucky, 1780-1828* (147), examines the same time period as Boles, but focuses on the prevalence of religious liberalism in some circles, which derived from an appreciation of the Enlightenment approach to religious belief and experience as well as from the religious philosophy associated with Thomas Jefferson of Virginia.

But a rational Protestantism did not carry the day. Elmer G. Million, in ''Protestantism in the Kentucky Blue Grass, 1865-1940'' (132), traces the breakdown of that early liberalism in a study that complements Sonne's work. In a classic older study, *Freedom of Thought in the Old South* (22), Clement Eaton noted how the South became much more conservative in matters political and religious after 1820. There was a need to find workable props to justify an agrarian social system grounded in slavery, once pressures began to build elsewhere in the nation to abolish slavery and move in the direction of an industralized economy. R. M. Weaver argued the same point in ''The Older Religiousness in the South'' (62), when he claimed that the South rejected a world view rooted in rationalism because of its potential to question the social *modus operandi;* a more conservative religious style was a safer bulwark to avoid the currents of unwanted change. Two narrower studies also suggest that the desire to maintain the social status quo, particularly with regard to slavery, may have contributed as much to the evangelical sweep of the white Protestant South as the plausibility of evangelicalism itself. Dumas Malone in an old but well-done biography, carefully demonstrated how Thomas Cooper, the first president of what is now the University of South Carolina, and his Enlightenment religious liberalism became increasingly unpopular as the South became more self-consciously proslavery (128). Clarence E. Hix, Jr.'s dissertation, "The Conflict Between Presbyterianism and Free Thought in the South, 1776-1838" (14:40), likewise noted how the South ceased to be open to rationalism in religious matters as it became more defensive of its "peculiar institution" and cultural mores. More recently, historian John Hope Franklin (25) has argued that the convergence of religious evangelicalism and social conservatism in the antebellum era left a legacy of resistance to change in the South that endured long after the matter of slavery was resolved. But in a study restricted to one religious group, "Virginia Baptists and the Myth of the Southern Mind, 1865-1900" (110), W. Harrison Daniel sought to show that what is often taken as Southern conservatism in religion and politics is not distinctively Southern at all, but a reflection of the prejudices of mainstream American society. Regardless of the presence of alternatives to white evangelical Protestantism and of similar social and intellectual developments in other sections of the nation, the South did marry its dominant culture to evangelicalism to the extent that its dominating presence is the first characteristic of the region's religion identified by contemporary analysts.

The following bibliographical listing includes notation of some classic studies of American religion that place Southern developments in a broader context. It then lists those works that seek to give an overview of religion in the South or of Protestantism in the South. The titles also include materials that treat the Great Awakening and the genesis of Southern evangelicalism. Finally the bibliography identifies pertinent synoptic studies that treat development within a particular state or subregion of the South.

BIBLIOGRAPHY

I. OVERVIEWS OF AMERICAN RELIGION

Several titles in the bibliography to chapter 1 are relevant here, especially those in Section III.

(1) Ahlstrom, Sydney E. *A Religious History of the American People*. New Haven: Yale University Press, 1972.

(2) Albanese, Catherine L. *America: Religions and Religion*. Belmont, CA: Wadsworth, 1981.

(3) Handy, Robert T. *A History of the Churches in the United States and Canada*. New York: Oxford University Press, 1977.

(4) Hudson, Winthrop S. *Religion in America.* 3d ed. New York: Charles Scribner's Sons, 1981.

II. OVERVIEWS OF RELIGION IN THE SOUTH

(5) Adams, Gene M. "An Analytical Study of Southern Religion of the 1970's as Based on Samuel S. Hill's Southern Culture-Religion Thesis." Ph.D. dissertation, Florida State University, 1980.

(6) Bailey, Kenneth K. *Southern White Protestantism in the Twentieth Century.* New York: Harper and Row, 1964.

(7) _____. "Southern White Protestantism at the Turn of the Century." *American Historical Review* 68 (1963): 618-35.

(8) Baker, Tod A., and Robert B. Steed, eds. *Religion and Politics in the South: Mass and Elite Perspectives.* New York: Praeger, 1983.

(9) Boles, John B. "Religion in the South: A Tradition Recovered." *Maryland Historical Magazine* 77 (1982): 388-401.

(10) Bruce, Dickson D., Jr. "Religion, Society and Culture in the Old South: A Comparative View." *American Quarterly* 26 (1974): 399-416.

(11) Caldwell, Erskine. *Deep South: Memory and Observation.* Athens: University of Georgia Press, 1980. Part I published 1966 as "In the Shadow of the Steeple."

(12) Carleton, Stephen. "Continuity and Change in Southern Religion, 1820-1845: The Baptists, the Presbyterians, and the Methodists." Ph.D. dissertation, University of Chicago, 1968.

(13) Cash, W. J. *The Mind of the South.* New York: Alfred A. Knopf, 1941.

(14) Clark, Thomas D. *The Emerging South,* 248-70. New York: Oxford University Press, 1961.

(15) Clausen, Christopher. "Mencken and the Bible Belt." *Menckeniana* no. 70 (Fall 1979): 7-11.

(16) Dabbs, James M. *Haunted by God: The Cultural and Religious Experience of the South.* Richmond: John Knox Press, 1972.

(17) Daniel, W. Harrison. "The Effects of the Civil War on Southern Protestantism." *Maryland Historical Magazine* 69 (1974): 44-63.

(18) Dawson, Joseph M. *The Spiritual Conquest of the Southwest.* Nashville: Sunday School Board of the Southern Baptist Convention, 1927.

(19) Dollar, George W. *A History of Fundamentalism in America.* Greenville SC: Bob Jones University Press, 1973.

(20) Dorough, C. Dwight. *Bible Belt Mystique.* Philadelphia: Westminster Press, 1974.

(21) _____. "Religion in the Old South: A Pattern of Behavior and Thought." Ph.D. dissertation, University of Texas, 1947.

(22) Eaton, Clement. *Freedom of Thought in the Old South.* Durham: Duke University Press, 1940.

(23) Ezell, John. *The South Since 1865.* 2d ed. New York: Macmillan, 1975.

(24) Fichter, Joseph H., and George L. Maddox. "Religion in the South, Old and New." *The South in Continuity and Change*. John C. McKinney and Edgar T. Thompson, eds., 359-83. Durham: Duke University Press, 1965.

(25) Franklin, John Hope. "The Great Confrontation: The South and the Problem of Change." *Journal of Southern History* 38 (1972): 3-20.

(26) Gaillard, Frye. *Race, Rock and Religion: Profiles from a Southern Journalist*. Charlotte: East Woods Press, 1982.

(27) Goen, C. C. "Cultural Captivity of the American Churches." *Foundations* 12 (1969): 197-207.

(28) Harrell, David Edwin Jr., ed. *Varieties of Southern Evangelicalism*. Macon GA: Mercer University Press, 1981.

(29) Harmon, George. "How to Tell a Baptist from a Methodist in the South." *Harper's Magazine* 226 (Feb. 1963): 58-63.

(30) Herzog, Frederick. "Liberal Theology or Culture Religion?" *Union Seminary Quarterly Review* 29 (1974): 233-34.

(31) Hill, Samuel S., and Dennis E. Owen. *The New Religious Political Right*. Nashville: Abingdon Press, 1982.

(32) ———, ed. *On Jordan's Stormy Banks*. Macon GA: Mercer University Press, 1983.

(33) ———, ed. *Religion and the Solid South*. Nashville: Abingdon Press, 1972.

(34) ———, ed. *Religion in the Southern States: A Historical Study*. Macon GA: Mercer University Press, 1983.

(35) ———. *The South and the North in American Religion*. Athens GA: University of Georgia Press, 1980.

(36) ———. *Southern Churches in Crisis*. New York: Holt, Rinehart and Winston, 1967.

(37) Holifield, E. Brooks. "Three Strands of Jimmy Carter's Religion." *New Republic* 174 (5 June 1976): 15-17.

(38) Hood, Fred J. *Reformed America*. Tuscaloosa: University of Alabama Press, 1980.

(39) Jordan, David W. "A Search for Salvation in the Corrupt New World." *Historical Magazine of the Protestant Episcopal Church* 43 (1974): 45-55.

(40) Kalman, Harold, and John DeVisser. *Pioneer Churches*. New York: W.W. Norton, 1976.

(41) Kurtz, Ernest. "The Tragedy of Southern Religion." *Georgia Historical Quarterly* 66 (1982): 217-47.

(42) Machalek, Richard, and Michael Martin. " 'Invisible' Religions: Some Preliminary Evidence." *Journal for the Scientific Study of Religion* 15 (1976): 311-22.

(43) McLoughlin, William G. *The Cherokee Ghost Dance*. Macon GA: Mercer University Press, 1984.

(44) _____. "Red, White, and Black in the Antebellum South." *Baptist History and Heritage* 7 (1972): 69-75.

(45) Manschreck, Clyde L. "Religion in the South: Problem and Promise." *The South in Perspective*. Francis B. Sims, ed., 77-91. Farmville VA: Longwood College, 1959.

(46) Marty, Martin E. "Ethnicity: the Skeleton of Religion in America." *Church History* 41 (1972): 5-21.

(47) Mathews, Donald G. *Religion in the Old South*. Chicago: University of Chicago Press, 1977.

(48) _____. "Religion in the Old South: Speculation on Methodology." *South Atlantic Quarterly* 73 (1974): 34-52.

(49) Mencken, Henry L. "The Sahara of the Bozart." In *Prejudices*. 2d series, 136-54. New York: Alfred A. Knopf, 1920.

(50) Nelsen, Hart M., et al. "Image of God and Religious Ideology and Involvement: A Partial Test of Hill's Southern Culture-Religion." *Review of Religious Research* 15 (February 1973): 37-44.

(51) Posey, Walter B. *Frontier Mission: A History of Religion West of the Southern Appalachians to 1861*. Lexington: University of Kentucky Press, 1966.

(52) _____. *Religious Strife on the Southern Frontier*. Baton Rouge: Louisiana State University Press, 1965.

(53) Poteat, Edwin M., Jr. "Religion in the South." In *Culture in the South*. W. T. Crouch, ed., 248-69. Chapel Hill: University of North Carolina Press, 1934.

(54) Reed, John Shelton. " 'The Bible Belt': Southern Religion." In *The Enduring South: Subcultural Persistence in Mass Society*. Chap. 6. Chapel Hill: University of North Carolina Press, 1972.

(55) Robertson, Archibald T. *That Old-Time Religion*. Boston: Houghton, Mifflin, 1950.

(56) Shinn, Roger L. "A Good Word for Some Southern Ways." *Christianity and Crisis* 19 (19 October 1959): 148-51.

(57) Shriver, Donald W., Jr. "Southern Churches in Transition." *New South* 25 (Winter 1970): 40-47.

(58) Slotkin, Richard. *Regeneration through Violence: The Mythology of the American Frontier, 1660-1860*. Middletown CT: Wesleyan University Press, 1973.

(59) Stroupe, Henry S. "The Beginnings of Religious Journalism in North Carolina, 1823-1865." *North Carolina Historical Review* 30 (1953): 1-22.

(60) Tate, Allen. "Remarks on Southern Religion." In *I'll Take My Stand: The South and the Agrarian Tradition*, 155-75. New York: Harper and Brothers, 1930.

(61) Tweedie, Stephen W. "Viewing the Bible Belt." *Journal of Popular Culture* 11 (1978): 865-76.

(62) Weaver, R. M. "The Older Religiousness in the South." *Sewanee Review* 51 (1943): 237-49.

(63) Wentz, Richard E. "Region and Religion in America." *Foundations* 24 (1981): 148-56.

(64) Wesson, Kenneth R. "Travelers' Accounts of the Southern Character: Antebellum and Early Postbellum Period." *Southern Studies* 17 (1978): 305-18.

(65) Woodward, C. Vann. "The Southern Ethic in a Puritan World." *William and Mary Quarterly* 3d series 25 (1968): 343-70.

III. THE GREAT AWAKENING
AND THE BEGINNING OF SOUTHERN EVANGELICALISM

(66) Aldridge, Alfred O. "George Whitefield's Georgia Controversies." *Journal of Southern History* 9 (1943): 357-80.

(67) Allen, Carlos R., Jr. "The Great Revival in Virginia, 1783-1812." M.A. thesis, University of Virginia, 1948.

(68) Alley, Robert S. "The Reverend Mr. Samuel Davies: A Study in Religion and Politics." Ph.D. dissertation, Princeton University, 1963.

(69) Beeman, Richard R. "Social Change and Cultural Conflict in Virginia: Lunenburg County, 1746-1774." *William and Mary Quarterly* 3d series 35 (1978): 455-76.

(70) Benson, Louis F. "President Davies as Hymn Writer." *Presbyterian Historical Society Journal* [now *Journal of Presbyterian History*] 2 (1904): 277-86, 343-73.

(71) Boles, John B. *The Great Revival, 1787-1805: The Origins of the Southern Evangelical Mind.* Lexington: University of Kentucky Press, 1972.

(72) Bost, George A. "Samuel Davies as President of Princeton." *Journal of Presbyterian History* 26 (1948): 165-81.

(73) _____. "Samuel Davies, Preacher of the Great Awakening." *Journal of Presbyterian History* 26 (1948): 65-86.

(74) _____. "Samuel Davies, the South's Awakener." *Journal of Presbyterian History* 33 (1955): 135-55.

(75) Cox, Richard J. "Stephen Bordley, George Whitefield, and the Great Awakening in Maryland." *Historical Magazine of the Protestant Episcopal Church* 46 (1977): 297-307.

(76) Dolmeister, Carl R. "The Apostle As Southerner." *Southern Literature Journal* 4 (1971): 74-82.

(77) Gewehr, Wesley M. *The Great Awakening in Virginia, 1740-1790.* Durham: Duke University Press, 1930.

(78) Gilborn, Craig. "Samuel Davies' Sacred Muse." *Journal of Presbyterian History* 41 (1963): 63-79.

(79) Henry, Stuart C. *George Whitefield: Wayfaring Witness.* New York: Abingdon Press, 1957.

(80) Isaac, Rhys. ''Dramatizing the Ideology of Revolution: Popular Mobilization in Virginia, 1774 to 1776.'' *William and Mary Quarterly* 3d series 33 (1976): 357-85.

(81) _____. ''Evangelical Revolt: The Nature of the Baptists' Challenge to the Traditional Order of Virginia, 1765 to 1775.'' *William and Mary Quarterly* 3d series 31 (1974): 345-68.

(82) _____. ''Preachers and Patriots: Popular Culture and the Revolution in Virginia.'' In *The American Revolution*. Alfred F. Young, ed., 127-56. Dekalb IL: Northern Illinois University Press, 1976.

(83) _____. ''Religion and Authority: Problems of the Anglican Establishment in Virginia in the Era of the Great Awakening and the Parson's Cause.'' *William and Mary Quarterly* 3d series 30 (1973): 3-36.

(84) _____. *The Transformation of Virginia, 1740-1790*. Chapel Hill: University of North Carolina Press for the Institute of Early American History and Culture, 1981.

(85) Kenney, William H. III. ''Alexander Garden and George Whitefield: The Significance of Revivalism in South Carolina, 1738-1741.'' *South Carolina Historical Magazine* 71 (1970): 1-16.

(86) _____. ''George Whitefield, Dissenter Priest of the Great Awakening, 1739-1741.'' *William and Mary Quarterly* 3d series 26 (1969): 75-93.

(87) Klein, Maury. ''The Scotch Irish.'' *American History Illustrated* 13:9 (1979): 30-38, 13:10 (1979): 32-39, 14:1 (1979): 8-12, 15-17.

(88) Kroll-Smith, J. Stephen, ''Transmitting a Revival Culture: The Organizational Dynamic of the Baptist Movement in Colonial Virginia, 1760-1777.'' *Journal of Southern History* 50 (1984): 551-68.

(89) Lumpkin, William L. *Baptist Foundations in the South: Tracing through the Separates the Influence of the Great Awakening, 1754-1787*. Nashville: Broadman Press, 1961.

(90) Mills, Frederick V., Sr. *Bishops by Ballot: An Eighteenth Century Ecclesiastical Revolution*. New York: Oxford University Press, 1978.

(91) Morgan, David T., Jr. ''The Consequences of George Whitefield's Ministry in the Carolinas and Georgia, 1739-1740.'' *Georgia Historical Quarterly* 55 (1971): 62-82.

(92) _____. ''George Whitefield and the Great Awakening in the Carolinas and Georgia, 1739-1740.'' *Georgia Historical Quarterly* 54 (1970): 517-39.

(93) _____. ''The Great Awakening in North Carolina, 1740-1775: The Baptist Phase.'' *North Carolina Historical Review* 45 (1968): 264-83.

(94) Nelson, Andrew T. '' 'Enthusiasm' in Carolina, 1740.'' *South Atlantic Quarterly* 44 (1945): 397-405.

(95) Perdue, Theda. ''George Whitefield in Georgia: Evangelism.'' *Atlanta Historical Journal* 22 (Spring 1978): 43-51.

(96) _____. ''George Whitefield in Georgia: Philanthropy.'' *Atlanta Historical Journal* 22 (Fall/Winter 1978): 53-62.

(97) Pilcher, George W. *Samuel Davies: Apostle of Dissent in Colonial Virginia*. Knoxville: University of Tennessee Press, 1972.

(98) Sanders, Jennings B. "George Whitefield Two Hundred and Twenty-five Years After His First American Visit: An Interpretation." *Georgia Historical Quarterly* 48 (1964): 64-73.

(99) Stokes, Durward T. "North Carolina and the Great Revival of 1800." *North Carolina Historical Review* 43 (1966): 401-12.

IV. STATE, LOCAL, AND TOPICAL STUDIES

(100) Ainsley, W. Frank, and John W. Florin. "The North Carolina Piedmont: An Island of Religious Diversity." *West Georgia College Studies in the Social Sciences* 12 (1973): 30-34.

(101) Anghoff, Charles. *H. L. Mencken: A Portrait from Memory*. New York: Thomas Yoseloff, 1956.

(102) Boles, John B. *Religion in Antebellum Kentucky*. Lexington: University Press of Kentucky, 1976.

(103) Bonomi, Patricia U., and Peter R. Eisenstadt. "Church Adherence in the Eighteenth-Century British American Colonies. *William and Mary Quarterly* 3d series 39 (1982): 245-86.

(104) Bradley, Michael R. "The Puritans of Virginia: Their Influence on the Religious Life of the Old Dominion." Ph.D. dissertation, Vanderbilt University, 1972.

(105) Brinsfield, John W. *Religion and Politics in Colonial South Carolina*. Easley SC: Southern Historical Press, 1983.

(106) Carty, James W. *Nashville as a World Religious Center*. Nashville: Cullom and Ghertner, 1958.

(107) Clements, William M. "The Jonesboro Tornado: A Case Study in Folklore, Popular Religion, and Grass Roots History." *Red River Valley Historical Review* 2 (1975): 273-86.

(108) Coker, William S. "Religious Censuses of Pensacola, 1796-1801." *Florida Historical Quarterly* 31 (1982): 54-63.

(109) Cross, Jasper W., ed. "John Miller's Missionary Journal—1816-1817: Religious Conditions in the South and Midwest." *Journal of Presbyterian History* 47 (1969): 226-61.

(110) Daniel, W. Harrison. "Virginia Baptists and the Myth of the Southern Mind, 1865-1900." *South Atlantic Quarterly* 73 (1974): 85-98.

(111) Dawson, Jan C. "The Puritan and the Cavalier: The South's Perception of Contrasting Traditions." *Journal of Southern History* 44 (1978): 597-614.

(112) DesChamps, Margaret Burr. "Union or Division? South Atlantic Presbyterians and Southern Nationalism, 1820-1861." *Journal of Southern History* 20 (1954): 484-98.

(113) Dickinson, George E. "Religious Practices of Adolescents in a Southern Community, 1964-1974." *Journal for the Scientific Study of Religion* 15 (1976): 361-64.

(114) Dollard, John. *Class and Caste in a Southern Town*. New Haven: Yale University Press, 1937.

(115) Hadden, Jeffrey K., and Charles E. Swann. *Prime-Time Preachers*. Reading MA: Addison-Wesley, 1981.

(116) Jerome, W. P. "A Baltimore Episcopalian." *Menckeniana* no. 51 (Fall 1974): 7-9.

(117) Jervey, Edward D. "Henry L. Mencken and American Methodism." *Journal of Popular Culture* 12 (1978): 75-87.

(118) Johnson, Guion. "Religious Denominations." *Antebellum North Carolina: A Social History*. Chapel Hill: University of North Carolina Press, 1937.

(119) Johnson, Gwen Mills. "Churches and Evangelism in Jackson, Mississippi, 1920-1929." *Journal of Mississippi History* 34 (1972): 307-329.

(120) Jones, John G. *A Concise History of the Introduction of Protestantism into Mississippi and the Southwest, 1772-1862*. St. Louis: P. M. Pinckard, 1866.

(121) Kanigel, Robert. "Did H. L. Mencken Hate the Jews?" *Menckeniana* no. 73 (Spring 1980): 1-7.

(122) Kaufman, Harold F. *Mississippi Churches: A Half Century of Change*. Mississippi State University Social Science Research Center Bulletin 12 (Starkville: Mississippi State University, 1959).

(123) _____. "Religious Organization in Kentucky." Kentucky Agricultural Experiment Station *Bulletin* 524 (1948).

(124) Lahey, R. J. "The Role of Religion in Lord Baltimore's Colonial Enterprise." *Maryland Historical Magazine* 72 (1977): 492-511.

(125) LeMay, Joseph. *Men of Letters in Colonial Maryland*. Knoxville: University of Tennessee Press, 1972.

(126) Ledbetter, R. E. "The Planting and Growth of Protestant Denominations in Texas Prior to 1850." Ph.D. dissertation, University of Chicago, 1950.

(127) McGrain, J. W., Jr. "Ayd and Criminal Aid." *Menckeniana* no. 45 (Spring 1973): 11-12.

(128) Malone, Dumas. *The Public Life of Thomas Cooper, 1783-1839*. New Haven: Yale University Press, 1926.

(129) Mariner, Kirk. *Revival's Children: A Religious History of Virginia's Eastern Shore*. Salisbury MD: Peninsular Press, 1979.

(130) Mathews, Donald G. "The Second Great Awakening as an Organizing Process, 1780-1830: An Hypothesis." *American Quarterly* 21 (1969): 23-43.

(131) Middleton, Arthur F. "The Colonial Virginia Parish." *Historical Magazine of the Protestant Episcopal Church* 40 (1971): 431-46.

(132) Million, Elmer G. "Protestantism in the Kentucky Blue Grass, 1865-1900." Ph.D. dissertation, University of Chicago, 1950.

(133) Monk, Robert C. "Unity and Diversity Among Eighteenth Century Colonial Anglicans and Methodists." *Historical Magazine of the Protestant Episcopal Church* 38 (1969): 51-69.

(134) Moore, George V. *Interchurch Cooperation in Kentucky, 1865-1965*. Private ed. Lexington: Keystone Printery, 1965.

(135) Moore, Margaret DesChamps. "Protestantism in the Mississippi Territory." *Journal of Mississippi History* 29 (1967): 358-70.

(136) _____. "Religion in Mississippi in 1860." *Journal of Mississippi History* 22 (1960): 233-38.

(137) Morrison, Alfred J. "The Virginia Literary and Evangelical Magazine, 1818-1828." *William and Mary Quarterly* first series 19 (1911): 266-72.

(138) Norton, Herman A. *Religion in Tennessee, 1777-1945*. Knoxville: University of Tennessee Press, 1981.

(139) Norton, Wesley. "Religious Newspapers in Antebellum Texas." *Southwestern Historical Quarterly* 79 (1975): 145-65.

(140) Owens, Gwinn. "Mencken and the Jews, Revisited." *Menckeniana* no. 74 (Summer 1980): 6-10.

(141) Pieper, Mary G. "Church Organization in Bradley County, Tennessee in 1950." Thesis, University of Tennessee, 1952.

(142) Red, William S. *The Texas Colonists and Religion, 1821-1836*. Austin: E. L. Shettles, 1924.

(143) Richardson, Paul D. "Some Social Influences in the Development of Major Religious Denominations in Kentucky." Ph.D. dissertation, University of Kentucky, 1956.

(144) Reilly, Timothy F. "Heterodox New Orleans and the Protestant South, 1800-1861." *Louisiana Studies* 12 (1973): 533-51.

(145) Smith, Cortland V. "Church Organization as an Agency of Social Control: Church Discipline in North Carolina, 1800-1860." Ph.D. dissertation, University of North Carolina in Chapel Hill, 1967.

(146) Smith, Jesse G. *Heroes of the Saddle Bag: A History of Christian Denominations in the Republic of Texas*. San Antonio: Naylor, 1951.

(147) Sonne, Niels H. *Liberal Kentucky, 1780-1828*. New York: Columbia University Press, 1939.

(148) Stroupe, Henry S. *The Religious Press in the South Atlantic States, 1802-1865*. Durham: Duke University Press, 1956.

(149) Viitanen, Wayne. "The Winter the Mississipi Ran Backwards: Early Kentuckians Report the New Madrid, Missouri Earthquake of 1811-1812." *Register of the Kentucky Historical Society* 71 (1973): 51-68.

(150) Walker, Charles O. "Georgia's Religion in the Colonial Era, 1733-1790." *Viewpoints: Georgia Baptist History* 5 (1976): 17-44.

(151) Weeks, Stephen B. *The Religious Development in the Province of North Carolina*. First published 1892. Reprint, New York: Johnson Reprint, 1973.

3 Native American Religions and Indian Missions

LONG BEFORE evangelical styles of Protestantism came to dominate Southern culture, indeed long before the European invaders began their conquest of the land, numerous aboriginal groups had fashioned their own civilizations in the area. Their presence is rarely noted in studies of Southern religion, apart from consideration of Christian missionary efforts among them, yet their story is part of the overall drama of Southern religion, for these societies had to respond to the challenge of missionary Christianity and experienced severe dislocation with the forced removal to the Indian territory (now part of Oklahoma) in the 1830s. It has been easy to ignore the Indian religions that once flourished in the South because they baffled the first Europeans. Convinced of the superiority of their own brands of Christianity, the European colonists—and their descendants—simply did not take the time to explore the intricacies of these religions and the delicate ways in which fundamental religious beliefs and practices were integral to the whole of Indian societal life. It was easier to regard native Americans as heathen to be converted than to understand the religious cosmos that endowed Indian life with rich meaning.

Recent scholarly interest in native Americans has at last begun to correct this deficiency, but centuries of forced acculturation and the lack of written sources predating European conquest mean that students of Indian life today will probably never have a complete understanding of the religious world of the ''five civilized tribes'' and the other indigenous clusters who once regarded the South as their own. Robert F. Berkhofer, Jr., in *The White Man's Indian: Images of the American Indian from Columbus to the Present* (1), forcefully demonstrates the ways in which preconceptions and unfounded assumptions determined how Europeans and Americans alike perceived the Indian cultures of the New World. The doctoral dissertation of Maxwell Ford Taylor, Jr., "The Influence of Religion on White Attitudes towards Indians in the Early Settlement of Virginia" (338), explores the both the subtle and obvious ways that the affirmation of Christianity affected dealings with the various Indian societies.

The best overall introduction to Southern Indian life is Charles M. Hudson, *The Southeastern Indians* (10). Hudson devotes two chapters to what might be called the explicitly religious dimensions of tribal culture, one treating belief systems and one dealing with ceremonialism. Focusing more specifically on ceremonialism is James H. Howard, *The Southeastern Ceremonial Complex and Its Interpretation* (45), but Howard explores primarily the persistence of ancient ceremonialism on the Oklahoma reservations following removal. An older, but still valuable overview of the mythic ideology that undergirded group life is John R. Swanton, *Myths and Tales of the Southeastern Indians* (16). The earlier lack of concern for tribal religious life is obvious in R.S. Cotterill, *The Southern Indians: The Story of the Civilized Tribes before Removal* (4), which makes only two passing references to religion, although it is otherwise a useful survey.

In studying the religion of particular native aboriginal groups, contemporary scholars remain indebted to the early ethnographic work of James Mooney, whose interest in Indian culture continues to be a starting point in the study of many Native American societies. His "Myths of the Cherokees" (62) is still a basic collection of materials. Building on the field notes of Frans Olbrechts, Jack F. Kilpatrick and Anna G. Kilpatrick have attempted to reconstruct the mythology of the Eastern Band of Cherokees (49). The Kilpatricks, individually or together, have as well provided the basic collection of Oklahoma Cherokee mythology in *Friends of Thunder* (50) and appraised the conjunction of religion and medicine in *The Sacred Formulas of the Western Cherokees* (53) and changes in healing rituals that followed on sustained contact with Christianity (48). Other synoptic accounts include Ruth Elgin Suddeth, "The Myths of the Cherokees" (71) and Howard L. Meredith and Virginia E. Milam, "A Cherokee Vision of Eloh" (59), which gives a cursory description of the most fundamental Cherokee beliefs. Specific components of Cherokee religious beliefs have guided the work of numerous other scholars. For example, David H. Corkran has analyzed "The Nature of the Cherokee Supreme Being" (26); Charles M. Hudson has focused on the "Cherokee Concept of Natural Balance" (46), a characteristic theme in the Cherokee world view; the venerable James Mooney directed attention to "The Cherokee River Cult" (61); while Raymond D. Fogelson has provided a careful "Analysis of Cherokee Sorcery and Witchcraft" (32).

Central to Cherokee religious and cultural life—if the two can be distinguished—is the Green Corn festival, a mythico-ceremonial complex that includes dimensions of fertility, healing, and renewal rites and more. Two essays by John Witthoft, "Green Corn Ceremonialism in the Eastern Woodlands" (74) and "The Green Corn Medicine and the Green Corn Festival" (75), are basic to an appreciation of this vital aspect of Cherokee life. Also integral to the Cherokee religious world view is the "sacred fire" and its attendant stomp dance. David H. Corkran has offered two brief contextual studies of this phenomenon and its import in tribal life, "The Sacred Fire of the Cherokee" (27) and "Cherokee Sun and Fire Observances" (25). The preservation of Cherokee ceremonialism and its revival in Oklahoma has been noted in three important studies: George McCoy and H. F. Fulling, *History of the Stomp Dance or "Sacred Fire" of the Cherokee Indian Nation* (57); Janet Campbell and Archie Sam, "The Primal Fire Lingers" (22); and James H. Howard, "Bringing Back the Fire: The Revival of a Natchez-Cherokee Ceremonial Ground" (44).

While scholars have tended to devote more attention to the Cherokees than to other tribal clusters of the South and Southeast, some have attempted to describe and analyze the religious life of the other "civilized" tribes. Curiously, W. David Baird's *The Choctaw People* (80) and Donald E. Green's *The Creek People* (94)—both of which are part of the Indian Tribal Series, virtually ignore the religious cultures of these peoples. Among those studies of the Choctaws that do treat religion seriously, Angie Debo's classic *The Rise and Fall of the Choctaw Republic* (83) demonstrates how religion was interwoven with virtually every aspect of group life. Three other students provide an entree into the Choctaw world view: T. N. Campbell, "The Choctaw Afterworld" (82); Henry S. Halbert, "Funeral Customs of the Mississippi Choctaws" (87); and David Bushnell, "Myths of the Louisiana Choctaw" (81). The last two, however, are dated in approach, and Halbert's is occasionally marred by his own Roman Catholic convictions. Halbert was a teacher at a Catholic Mission School for the Choctaws who did attempt to understand the world of the people with whom he worked in this and other studies. Little work of substance has been directed to religion among the Chickasaws.

Half a century ago, John R. Swanton sought to describe the Creek version of the Green Corn festival, basing his work in "The Green Corn Dance" (104) on an early nineteenth-century account by John Howard Payne. The inseparability of religion and medicine in Creek daily life provides the focus for another study by Swanton, "Religious Beliefs and Medical Practices of the Creek Indians" (105). James O. Buswell focused on the Seminoles in his doctoral dissertation, "Florida Seminole Religious Ritual: Resistance and Change" (90). Also see William C. Sturtevant, "The Medicine Bundles and Busks of the Florida Seminoles" (103). James N. Howard has recently called attention to religion among the Seminoles removed to Indian territory in *Oklahoma Seminoles: Medicines, Magic, and Religion* (96).

The literature on the interaction of tribal cultures with the Christianity of the European conquerors and later Americans far exceeds work to date that presumes the integrity of tribal religion. The most recent and perhaps most careful study of the interaction that came when Christians began a missionary movement among tribal groups is Henry Warner Bowden, *American Indians and Christian Missions: Studies in Cultural Conflict* (113). Its telling subtitle reveals the basic thesis of this important work. Two additional studies are essential in filling out the overall story of Protestant missionary efforts among tribal peoples. Robert F. Berkhofer, Jr., *Salvation and the Savage: An Analysis of Protestant Missions and American Indian Response, 1787-1862* (112), is particularly sensitive to the undercurrent of religious and cultural superiority that marked much early missionary effort, while R. Pierce Beaver, *Church, State, and the American Indians: Two and a Half Centuries of Partnership in Missions between Protestant Churches and Government* (111), is more taken by the ways in which missionary work consciously or unconsciously buttressed governmental policies of acculturation and assimilation—a matter that will be discussed in greater detail—and the complementary ways in which government agents and agencies offered indirect support to those missionary efforts that did not aggressively encourage tribal societies to preserve their integrity. In addition see also John U. Terrell, *The Arrow and the Cross: A History of the American Indian and the Missionaries* (130). Catholic missionary efforts, particularly in Spanish Florida and Texas, antedate all Protestant efforts at conversion of the Indians. There is not, however, a contemporary scholarly monograph which looks at the overall story of Catholic Indian missions in what became the United States. The only synoptic study remains John Gilmary Shea, *History of the Catholic Missions among the Indian Tribes of the United States, 1529-1854,* which first appeared in 1855 (219).

The chronologically earlier efforts of Roman Catholics to ''Christianize'' the Indians—often eclipsed by Protestant missions because of the tendency of scholars to restrict their view to the English colonies that formed the nucleus of the United States at the time of independence—lie at the core of Andrew A. Lambing's old apologia, ''Who Was the Apostle to the Indians?'' (205). Although preceded by more than half a century by ''Beginnings of the Capuchin Mission in Texas'' (154), Catholic work there first received sustained general treatment in Thomas P. O'Rourke, C.S.B., *The Franciscan Missions in Texas, 1690-1793* (174), a study now superseded by the work of Carlos Castaneda (5:73-75). Walter F. McCaleb, *The Spanish Missions of Texas* (171), although not rigorously academic, also provides an important overview. Many shorter studies of Catholic missions in Texas have been offered by Marion A. Habig (162-165), but Habig writes too simply and superficially for these essays and monographs to provide a complete picture. When Catholicism came to the English colonies, much energy was devoted to seeking Indian conversions by the Jesuit Andrew White, who was an early figure of prominence in Lord Baltimore's Maryland enterprise (185, 192). Catholic labors among the Southern tribes in Oklahoma are discussed in Mary Urban Kehoe, "The Educational Activities of Distinguished Catholic Missionaries among the Five Civilized Tribes" (204). Also helpful in piecing together the Catholic story, though not easy to locate, are various published reports of the Bureau of Catholic Indian Missions (197-198).

A matter of debate in reflecting on the role of Spanish missions concerns the degree to which the Spanish colonial regimes regarded the work of the priests as a legitimate religious enterprise and the degree to which it was viewed as a "frontier institution," part of a colonial defense program. That is, were Spanish motives based on desire to promote conversion or on a desire to have religious missions serve as a buffer to protect the main colonial settlements and an aid in controlling the Indians? Spanish missions in Florida have been the subject of much of this discussion as reflected in Herbert F. Bolton, "The Mission as a Frontier Institution in the Spanish-American Colonies" (136), and Robert A. Matter's refutation of the notion that the missions were central to Spanish colonial defense, "Missions in the Defense of Spanish Florida, 1566-1710" (144).

There were as well early Spanish Catholic endeavors in the areas that later became Virginia and Georgia. Catholic missions in Virginia, the northernmost area penetrated, were little more than a disappointment and failure. Their story is ably told in both documents and narrative in Clifford M. Lewis and Albert J. Loomie, eds., *The Spanish Jesuit Mission in Virginia, 1570-1572* (152). Franciscan efforts, especially among the Guale Indians of Georgia, never fully recovered from the Guale revolt against Spanish encroachment in the 1590s. On this matter, see Lewis H. Larson, "Historic Guale Indians of the Georgia Coast and the Impact of the Spanish Mission Effort" (151), which deals with the period leading up to the revolt, and Mary Ross, "The Restoration of the Spanish Missions in Georgia, 1598-1606" (153), which treats the not very successful efforts to resume missionary work a few years later. Other Spanish missions in the South during the colonial epoch had greater prosperity until the eighteenth century when colonists from South Carolina and certain of the Creeks destroyed the work. The rise and demise of this effort is recounted in Mark Boyd, Hale G. Smith, and John W. Griffin, *Here Once They Stood: The Tragic End of the Apalachee Mission* (139).

Within the English colonies that became the United States, missions to the Indians prior to independence were erratic at best. Much of the formal interest revolved around missionaries sent by the Church of England's Society for the Propagation of the Gospel. But these missionaries were also often charged with the religious instruction of slaves brought from Africa and frequently found that the shortage of clergy and low density of the population meant that much of their ministry was directed to white settlers. What work did exist betrayed a mixture of motives and attitudes as it had with the Spanish. This complex is evident in the title of the best brief introduction to such endeavors: "Christianity, Civilization and the Savage: The Anglican Mission to the American Indians" by Gerald J. Goodwin (321). Later attempts at Indian missions by other Protestant groups revealed the same phenomenon as demonstrated in Michael C. Coleman's doctoral dissertation, "Presbyterian Missionaries and Their Attitudes to the American Indians, 1837-1893" (387). The combination of a sense of duty to convert with a conviction that conversion would improve the lot of the Indians or "civilize" them according to prevailing white standards especially motivated Gideon Blackburn, Presbyterian missionary to the Cherokees before removal. His intentions are appraised by Dorothy C. Bass in "Gideon Blackburn's Mission to the Cherokees: Christianization and Civilization" (225). Such ambivalence has a long history, as Frederick A. Norwood recounted for another Protestant body in "The Invisible American—Methodism and the Indian" (378). At least one early Anglican missionary, however, learned some Indian folk wisdom, for after he returned to England following an unhappy tour as a missionary to the Indians in Georgia, John Wesley, later founder of the Methodist movement, published a volume of recipes for home medications, some of which were based on his observation of Indian healing practices (369).

The most complete story of Protestant missions among the Cherokees up the time of removal is William G. McLoughlin, *Cherokees and Missionaries, 1789-1839* (242). A classic example of ethnohistory, McLoughlin's study brilliantly demonstrates how missionaries were important agents of change in virtually every aspect of tribal life. They not only sought conversions, but they also tried, with a good deal of success, to introduce education, agricultural techniques, economic ideas, and political organizational patterns that reflected the surrounding Anglo-American modus operandi. But the tale McLoughlin tells has other dimensions. On the one hand, as McLoughlin also noted in an earlier essay ("Cherokee Anti-Mission Sentiment, 1824-1828" [239; also 14]), the Cherokees did resent the speed of acculturation that the missionaries urged on them and had periods when they resisted the mission work.

But as well, in time, some of the missionaries came to identify with the aspirations of the Cherokees as they sought to resist pressure to abandon their ancestral land; consequently they were at odds with government policy, particularly during the era of removal. Those, such as the Baptists and Methodists, who were willing to allow converted Cherokees to assume some religious leadership in the enterprise, were the ones ultimately with the most to lose in conflict with official United States policy and the most to gain in terms of status within the tribe if they stood with the Indians in their struggles with the government. When institutional Methodism waffled in support of missionaries who espoused the Indian cause, the Baptists became the favored denomination of those Indians who chose to align themselves with Christianity. Attempts on the part of the state of Georgia to pressure the Cherokees by coercing missionaries to promote governmental policy are exposed in "Georgia's Attack on the Missionaries" (235), a story reprinted from the *New York Spectator*, 23 August 1831. The conflict is captured in more general terms in "The Protestant Missionary and the Government Indian Policy, 1775-1850," a doctoral dissertation written by Harold C. Howard (115). Even after removal was accomplished, missionaries frequently challenged government policy as reservation life destroyed tribal integrity and consigned to poverty those who refused to acculturate according to white society's standards. For the story after removal, see Francis P. Prucha, *American Indian Policy in Crisis: Christian Reformers and the Indians, 1865-1900* (119), which also touches on a topic of growing controversy as the nineteenth century ended that will be discussed more fully—namely, the use of government funds to support Indian schools sponsored by religious bodies. On earlier connections between government policy and missions, see the relevant chapters in Berkhofer's *Salvation and the Savage*, previously noted; Bernard W. Sheehan, *Seeds of Extinction: Jeffersonian Philanthropy and the American Indian* (125); and Prucha's earlier study, *American Indian Policy in the Formative Years* (120), which covers the period between 1790 and removal.

But neither the Baptists nor the Methodists were the first to establish Cherokee missions. The initial efforts were those of the Moravians, who had made even earlier inroads with tribal groups in Maryland before directing attention to the Cherokees and the Creeks. Early enthusiasm for Indian missions in Moravian circles is revealed in George H. Loskiel, *History of the Mission of the United Brethren among the Indians in North America,* published in 1794 (413). Moravian work among Indians in the Southeast is told in the now dated study by Edmund Schwarze, *History of the Moravian Missions among Southern Indian Tribes of the United States* (414). Two important articles detail the beginnings of Moravian endeavors among the Cherokees and among the Creeks: Clemens DeBaillou, "The Diaries of the Moravian Brotherhood at the Cherokee Mission in Spring Place, Georgia, for the Years 1800-1804" (228), and Carl Mauelshagen and Gerald N. Davis, "The Moravians' Plan for a Mission among the Creek Indians, 1803-1804" (309). Work among the Cherokees was more promising, for as Carolyn Thomas Foreman, who has written extensively on specific missions in Indian Territory after removal, has shown (302), the Creeks especially manifested little interest in Christianity until removal destroyed what stability their culture had retained.

Southern Baptists have told the story of that denomination's mission work among Native Americans in two semipopular works, both of which warrant updating in view of changes in scholarly understanding of the dynamics of mission work: Robert Hamilton, *The Gospel among the Red Man: The History of the Southern Baptist Indian Missions* (353) and Carl C. Rister, *Baptist Missions among the American Indians* (359). Fortunately, some of that updating is provided in Lexie Wiggins's doctoral dissertation, ''A Cultural History of the Southern Baptist Indian Mission Movement'' (363). While Baptists in time became the favored Protestant group among the Cherokees and other Southeastern clusters, they did not undertake serious mission work prior to the conclusion of the War of 1812. The most academic study of the beginning of Baptist missions is ''A History of Early Baptist Missions among the Five Civilized Tribes'' (357), a doctoral dissertation by James W. Moffitt, a portion of which appeared as ''Early Baptist Missionary Work among the Cherokee'' (245). The premier figure among the Baptist missionaries to the Indians was Isaac McCoy, whose work was not limited to Southern tribes. McCoy is a man worthy of more intensive study, for during his labors he came to espouse the notion of a separate Indian state as a means both to preserve tribal heritage as well as to facilitate missionary work. The best brief overview of McCoy is ''Reverend Isaac McCoy'' by Franklin G. Adams (349), though it is somewhat uncritical in its appreciation of McCoy. One monograph and two dissertations provide a more balanced perspective. The first is George A. Schultz, *An Indian Canaan: Isaac McCoy and the Vision of an Indian State* (361). The others are Randolph O. Yeager, ''Indian Enterprises of Isaac McCoy, 1817-1846'' (365), and Edward Roustio, ''A History of the Life of Isaac McCoy in Relation to Early Indian Migrations and Missions as Revealed in His Unpublished Manuscripts'' (360).

The work of Methodists, the second most popular Protestant denomination among Southern tribes before and after removal, has been recounted in several essays. In addition to the material in his *Cherokees and Missionaries,* noted above, William G. McLoughlin has written ''Cherokees and Methodists, 1824-1834'' (241; also 14). Also focusing on early Methodist work is Mary T. Peacock, ''Methodist Missionary Work among the Cherokees before the Removal'' (247). The Methodist efforts in Indian Territory have been ably recounted by Walter N. Vernon: ''Beginnings of Indian Methodism in Oklahoma'' (381), ''Methodist Beginnings among Southwest Oklahoma Indians'' (383), and ''Early Echoes from Bloomfield Academy'' (382). His monograph, *One in the Lord: A History of Ethnic Minorities in the South Central Jurisdiction, the United Methodist Church* (384), is broader in scope, but does include discussion of Indian missions in Oklahoma and elsewhere.

Development of Presbyterian missions among the Choctaw and Chickasaw Indians prior to and after removal has been the subject of a series of articles by William L. Hiemstra: "Early Presbyterian Missions among the Choctaw and Chickasaw Indians in Mississippi" (277), "Presbyterian Missionaries and Mission Churches among the Choctaw and Chickasaw Indians, 1832-1865" (279), "Presbyterian Missions among the Choctaw and Chickasaw Indians, 1860-61" (280), and "Presbyterian Mission Schools among the Choctaws and Chickasaws, 1845-1861" (278). His work should be supplemented for the early period by A. Mark Conard, "The Cherokee Mission of Virginia Presbyterians" (227), and Samuel C. Williams, "An Account of the Presbyterian Mission to the Cherokees, 1757-1759" (258). Complementing Hiemstra's study for the period after removal is Natalie M. Denison, "Missions and Missionaries of the Presbyterian Church, U.S., among the Choctaws—1866-1907" (270). The most thorough treatment of one aspect of Protestant work with the Choctaws in Oklahoma is Carolyn Thomas Foreman's three-article series on "The Choctaw Academy" (274). Pioneer Presbyterian missionaries among the Choctaws were Cyrus Byington and Cyrus Kingsbury. There have been numerous studies in article form of the work of each. A good beginning is provided in Edward B. Austin, "Cyrus Byington" (261), and Arthur H. DeRosier, Jr., "Cyrus Kingsbury—Missionary to the Choctaws" (271).

Theda Perdue, "Letters from Brainerd" (248), provides an illuminating glimpse into the missionary efforts among the Cherokees sponsored by the American Board of Commissioners for Foreign Missions, work which began in 1817 and ended with the removal to Oklahoma and which was not marked by great success, largely because of the Board's insistence on an educated clergy and teachers and a concomitant reluctance to use the Cherokees themselves in any leadership roles. ABCFM Indian missions are put in the broader context of the Board's work by Clifton J. Phillips in his *Protestant America and the Pagan World: The First Half Century of the American Board of Commissioners for Foreign Missions, 1810-1860* (407). In addition, several brief studies of individual missions and missionaries sponsored by the Board are noted in Section XXII of the bibliography at the close of this chapter.

Numerous other Protestant bodies have also recounted their work among Indian groups. Rayner W. Kelsey, *Friends and the Indians, 1655-1917* (342), is the most comprehensive treatment of missions sponsored by the Quakers, who evidenced perhaps the greatest openness to the integrity of Indian cultures. Kelsey's study includes, but is not restricted to, materials concerning Southern and Southeastern tribes. The very limited work of the Lutherans is the subject of Jens Christian Kjaer, "The Lutheran Mission at Oaks, Oklahoma" (428). Richard H. Harper discussed Dutch Reformed missions in Indian Territory in a two-part series, "The Missionary Work of the Reformed

(Dutch) Church in America in Oklahoma'' (426), while Mormon labors are the focus of Grant Foreman, ed., ''Missionaries of the Latter-Day Saints Church in Indian Territory'' (425). One should not neglect consideration of Mennonite missions, which differ from the others because they were the outgrowth of the establishment of a Mennonite colony in Oklahoma rather than part of a program engineered by a denominational or cooperative missionary agency. Two older essays tell the story from the inside: Herbert M. Dalke, ''Seventy-five Years of Missions in Oklahoma'' (416), and Edmund G. Kaufman, ''Mennonite Missions among the Oklahoma Indians'' (418).

As traumatic as removal was for both tribal groups and missionary efforts, others dilemmas soon appeared. Among these, perhaps the most awkward centered around the presence of black slavery in the Indian nations. Adopting the practice from the dominant white culture around them, many of the Southern tribes took black slaves with them in the removal to Indian territory. As abolitionist sentiment increased in the United States, missionaries were confronted with the problem of seeking to educate and convert Indians who engaged in a practice which was seen to be in conflict with the ethical standards they proclaimed. The most perceptive analyst of this situation is again William G. McLoughlin, who explored the many nuances of the problem in ''Red Indians, Black Slavery, and White Racism: America's Slaveholding Indians'' (431; also 14) and also provided a ''case study'' in ''Indian Slaveholders and Presbyterian Missionaries, 1837-1861'' (430; also 14). But also see Theda Perdue, *Slavery and the Evolution of Cherokee Society, 1540-1866* (67). Three earlier studies also deserve scrutiny when attempting to unravel the many complicated strands of Indian missions and black slavery. Two focus on the Choctaws: Arthur H. DeRosier, Jr., ''Pioneers with Conflicting Ideals: Christianity and Slavery in the Choctaw Nation'' (272), and James D. Morrison, ''Note on Abolitionism in the Choctaw Nation'' (432). The third, which concentrates on the paradoxes inherent in the situation, is Robert T. Lewitt, ''Indian Missions and Antislavery Sentiment: A Conflict of Evangelical and Humanitarian Ideals'' (429).

In the 1890s, another controversy erupted, one that raised thorny issues of separation of church and state and also questioned the intent of missions. It dealt with the use of public funds to support schools which originated as vehicles for missions. As public education came to the reservations, the state was ill-equipped to launch a full-scale educational enterprise, but in many instances entered into cooperative arrangements with religious bodies whereby mission schools received subsidy from the government. The arrangement relieved the state from the necessity of constructing a school system from scratch, while the contractual agreements allowed for a continuing missionary presence, albeit in a supposedly secular arena. Much of the public debate was tinged with anti-Catholic sentiments then prevalent, for many of the schools operating under Catholic auspices were staffed by nuns who continued to wear their habits even though they were, in some sense, employees of the state. Hence opponents of the program claimed that the practice violated principles of the separation of church and state and demonstrated favoritism to particular religious bodies. The literature of controversy on this topic is voluminous, filling the pages of popular religious journals of the late nineteenth and early twentieth centuries. One complete section of the bibliography that follows lists representative articles and other works that treat the ''Indian school'' or ''nun's garb'' question, and those titles will not be detailed here. The best contemporary study is Francis P. Prucha, *Churches and the Indian Schools* (457). The controversy was not limited to arrangements with the Roman Catholics. Howard Meredith, ''Whirlwind: A Study of Church-State Relations'' (332), explores the conflict that emerged with the Protestant Episcopal Church when Indian agents felt the Episcopalian-run Whirlwind Day School was not promoting the kind of acculturation process that the state advocated. The general controversy was never formally resolved, but faded gradually as the state assumed more direct control over education and the missionaries turned to other arenas of activity.

A final dimension of the interaction of Indian religion(s) with Christianity deserves note. In several instances, syncretistic religious styles emerged that blended features of tribal religion with aspects of Christianity. The most conspicuous developments came after settlement in Indian Territory and may well reflect efforts of some of the tribal clusters to revitalize their cultural life through creating new religious forms that tapped ancient resources while at the same time adjusting to a new religious and political context. Not all of these movements affected every Southeastern group forced to the reservations, though there has been spill-over from other native American groups through social contact. One syncretistic approach that emerged in the Oklahoma context is the subject of R. Martin House, '' 'The Only Way' Church and the Sac and Fox Indians'' (467). More well known is the movement centering around the ritual use of peyote, institutionalized in the Native American Church. Here the work of Carol K. Rachlin and Alice Marriott (469-470) and of Weston LeBarre (468) provides a foundation for the future scholarly inquiry.

The bibliography that follows is organized topically. It includes general studies of Indian religion as well as sections listing studies of religious beliefs and practices of specific Southern tribes. These are titles that survey the literature on Roman Catholic missions in Florida, Texas, and elsewhere. Also included are works that appraise Protestant missions in general as well as the missionary efforts of individual Protestant bodies to particular tribal groups. The bibliography catalogues in addition many titles dealing with the controversies over slaveholding Indians and the contract schools. It concludes with a brief listing of studies which focus on the more recent syncretistic religious styles.

BIBLIOGRAPHY

Also relevant to this chapter are several of the bibliographical guides and resources listed in the bibliography to chapter 1.

I. GENERAL STUDIES

(1) Berkhofer, Robert F., Jr. *The White Man's Indian: Images of the American Indian from Columbus to the Present.* New York: Knopf, 1978.

(2) Brant, Charles S. "Indian-White Cultural Relations in Southwestern Oklahoma." *Chronicles of Oklahoma* 37 (1959): 433-39.

(3) Capps, Walter H., ed. *Seeing with a Native Eye.* New York: Harper and Row, 1976.

(4) Cotterill, R. S. *The Southern Indians: The Story of the Civilized Tribes before Removal.* Norman: University of Oklahoma Press, 1954.

(5) Eastman, Elaine Goodale. "The American Indian and His Religion." *Missionary Review of the World* 60 (1937): 128-30.

(6) Gill, Sam D. "Native American Religions." *Council on the Study of Religion Bulletin* 9 (1978): 125-28.

(7) _____. "Native American Religions: A Review Essay." *Religious Studies Review* 5 (1979): 251-58.

(8) _____. *Native American Religions: An Introduction.* Belmont CA: Wadsworth Publishing, 1982.

(9) Hultkrantz, Ake. *The Religions of the American Indians.* Berkeley: University of California Press, 1979.

(10) Hudson, Charles M. *The Southeastern Indians.* Knoxville: University of Tennessee Press, 1976.

(11) _____. "Vomiting for Purity: Ritual Emesis in the Aboriginal Southeastern United States." *Symbols and Society.* Carole E. Hill, ed., 93-102. Southern Anthropological Society Proceedings 9 (Athens: University of Georgia Press, 1975).

(12) Kleber, Louis C. "Religion among the American Indians." *History Today* 28 (1978): 81-87.

(13) Lindquist, G. E. E. *The Red Man in the United States: An Intimate Study of the Social, Economic, and Religious Life of the American Indian.* New York: George H. Doran, 1923.

(14) McLoughlin, William G. *The Cherokee Ghost Dance: Essays on the Southeastern Indians, 1789-1861.* Macon GA: Mercer University Press, 1984.

(15) Schermerhorn, John F. "Report Respecting the Indians, Inhabiting the Western Parts of the United States." *Massachusetts Historical Society Collections,* 2d series 2 (1814): 1-45.

(16) Swanton, John R. *Myths and Tales of the Southeastern Indians*. United States *Bureau of Ethnology Bulletin* 88. Washington: Government Printing Office, 1929. Reprint, New York: AMS Press, 1976.

(17) Underhill, Ruth. *Red Man's Religion: Beliefs and Practices of the Indians North of Mexico*. Chicago: University of Chicago Press, 1972. First published, 1965.

(18) Wax, Murray L., and Rosalie H. Wax. "Religion among American Indians." *Annals of the American Academy of Political and Social Science* 436 (1978): 27-39.

II. THE CHEROKEES

(19) Albanese, Catherine L. "Exploring Regional Religion: A Case Study of the Eastern Cherokee." *History of Religions* 23 (1984): 344-71.

(20) Bartram, William. *Travels through North and South Carolina, Georgia, East and West Florida, the Cherokee Country, the Extensive Territories of the Muscogulges or Creek Confederacy, and the Country of the Choctaws*. First published, 1791. New ed. Francis Harper, ed. New Haven: Yale University Press, 1958.

(21) Brown, Dewi. "Address of Dewi Brown, a Cherokee Indian." *Massachusetts Historical Society Proceedings* first series 12 (1871-1873): 30-31.

(22) Campbell, Janet, and Archie Sam. "The Primal Fire Lingers." *Chronicles of Oklahoma* 53 (1975): 463-75.

(23) Corkran, David H. "A Cherokee Migration Fragment." *Southern Indian Studies* 4 (1952): 27-28.

(24) _____. "Alexander Longe's 'A Small Postscript on the Ways and Manners of the Indians Called Cherokees, the Contents of the Whole So That You May Find Everything by Pages.'" *Southern Indian Studies* 21 (1969): 1-49.

(25) _____. "Cherokee Sun and Fire Observances." *Southern Indian Studies* 7 (1955): 33-38.

(26) _____. "The Nature of the Cherokee Supreme Being." *Southern Indian Studies* 8 (1956): 27-35.

(27) _____. "The Sacred Fire of the Cherokee." *Southern Indian Studies* 5 (1953): 21-26.

(28) Davis, John B. "Some Cherokee Stories." *Annals of Archaeology and Anthropology of the University of Liverpool* 3 (1910): 26-49.

(29) DeBaillou, Clemens. "A Contribution to the Mythology and Conceptual World of the Cherokee Indians." *Ethnohistory* 8 (1961): 92-102.

(30) Evans, E. Raymond. "Notable Persons in Cherokee History: Stephen Foreman." *Journal of Cherokee Studies* 2 (1977): 230-39.

(31) Finger, John R. *The Eastern Band of Cherokees, 1819-1900*. Knoxville: University of Tennessee Press, 1984.

(32) Fogelson, Raymond D. "An Analysis of Cherokee Sorcery and Witchcraft." In *Four Centuries of Southern Indians*. Charles M. Hudson, ed., 113-31. Athens: University of Georgia Press, 1975.

(33) _____. "Change, Persistence, and Accommodation in Cherokee Medico-Magical Beliefs." *Symposium on Cherokee and Iroquois Culture*. William N. Fenton and John Gulick, eds. *Bureau of American Ethnology Bulletin* 180:213-25. Washington: U.S. Government Printing Office, 1961.

(34) _____. "The Cherokee Ballgame Cycle: An Ethnologist's View." *Ethnomusicology* 15 (1971): 327-38.

(35) Gearing, Frederick O. "Priests and Warriors: Social Structures for Cherokee Politics in the 18th Century." In *American Anthropological Association Memoir* 93. Menasha WI: American Anthropological Association, 1962.

(36) Gilbert, William H., Jr. "The Eastern Cherokees." In Smithsonian Institution. *Bureau of American Ethnology Bulletin* 133, Paper 23: 169-413. Washington: U.S. Government Printing Office, 1943.

(37) Gillespie, John D. "Some Eastern Cherokee Dances Today." *Southern Indian Studies* 13 (1961): 29-43.

(38) Gregory, Jack, and Rennard Strickland. *Cherokee Spirit Tales: Tribal Myths, Legends, and Folklore*. Fayetteville AR: Indian Heritage Association, 1969.

(39) Gulick, John. *Cherokees at the Crossroads*. Chapel Hill: Institute for Research in Social Science, 1960.

(40) Hagar, Stansbury. "Cherokee Star-lore." In *Boas Anniversary Volume: Anthropological Papers Written in Honor of Franz Boas*. Berthold Laufer, ed., 354-66. New York: Stechert, 1906.

(41) Hedges, James S. "Attributive Mutation in Cherokee Nation Historical Myth." *North Carolina Folklore Journal* 21 (1973): 147-54.

(42) Herndon, Marcia. "The Cherokee Ballgame Cycle: An Ethnomusicologist's View." *Ethnomusicology* 15 (1971): 339-52.

(43) Holman, Harriet R. "Cherokee Dancing Remembered: Why the Eastern Band Abjured the Old Eagle Dance." *North Carolina Folklore Journal* 26 (1976): 101-106.

(44) Howard, James H. "Bringing Back the Fire: The Revival of A Natchez-Cherokee Ceremonial Ground." *American Indian Crafts and Culture* 4 (1970): 9-12.

(45) _____. *The Southeastern Ceremonial Complex and Its Interpretation*. Missouri Archaeology Society Memoir 6. Columbia MO: Missouri Archaeological Society, 1968.

(46) Hudson, Charles. "Cherokee Concept of Natural Balance." *The Indian Historian* 3:4 (1970): 51-54.

(47) Kilpatrick, Jack F., and Anna G. Kilpatrick. "Cherokee Rituals Pertaining to Medicinal Roots." *Southern Indian Studies* 16 (1964): 24-28.

(48) _____. "Christian Motifs in Cherokee Healing Rituals." *Perkins School of Theology Journal* 18:2 (1965): 32-36.

(49) _____, and Anna G. Kilpatrick. "Eastern Cherokee Folktales: Reconstruction from the Field Notes of Frans M. Olbrechts." In Smithsonian Institution. *Bureau of American Ethnology Bulletin* 196, Paper 80:379-447. Washington: U.S. Government Printing Office, 1966.

(50) _____, and Anna G. Kilpatrick. *Friends of Thunder: Folktales of Oklahoma Cherokee*. Dallas: Southern Methodist University Press, 1964.

(51) _____, and Anna G. Kilpatrick. "Notebook of a Cherokee Shaman." In Smithsonian Institution. *Contributions to Anthropology* 2:83-125. Washington: Smithsonian Institution Press, 1970.

(52) _____, and Anna G. Kilpatrick. *Run Toward the Nightland: Magic of the Oklahoma Cherokees*. Dallas: Southern Methodist University Press, 1967.

(53) _____. "The Siquanid Dil 'tidegi Collection." In *Sacred Formulas of the Western Cherokees*. Series 1, 1. Dallas: Bridwell Library, Southern Methodist University, 1962.

(54) _____, and Anna G. Kilpatrick. *Walk in Your Soul: Love Incantations of the Oklahoma Cherokees*. Dallas: Southern Methodist University Press, 1965.

(55) Kupferer, Harriet J. "The 'Principal People,' 1960: A Study of Cultural and Social Groups of the Eastern Cherokee." In Smithsonian Institution. *Bureau of American Ethnology Bulletin* 196, Paper 78:215-325. Washington: U.S. Government Printing Office, 1966.

(56) Kurath, Gertrude P. "Effects of Environment on Cherokee-Iroquois Ceremonialism, Music, and Dance." In *Symposium on Cherokee and Iroquois Culture*. William N. Fenton and John Gulick, eds. Smithsonian Institution. *Bureau of American Ethnology Bulletin* 180:173-95. Washington: U.S. Government Printing Office, 1961.

(57) McCoy, George, and H. F. Fulling. *History of the Stomp Dance or "Sacred Fire" of the Cherokee Indian Nation*. Marshall Walker, ed. Blackgum OK: Marshall Walker, 1961.

(58) Malone, Henry T. *Cherokees of the Old South: A People in Transition*. Athens: University of Georgia Press, 1956.

(59) Meredith, Howard L., and Virginia E. Milam. "A Cherokee Vision of Eloh." *The Indian Historian* 8,4 (1975): 19-23.

(60) Mooney, James. "The Cherokee Ball Play." *American Anthropologist* old series 3 (1890): 105-32.

(61) _____. "The Cherokee River Cult." *Journal of American Folklore* 13 (1900): 1-10.

(62) _____. "Myths of the Cherokees." In Smithsonian Institution. *Bureau of American Ethnology Nineteenth Annual Report, 1897-98*, Part I:3-576. Washington: U.S. Government Printing Office, 1900. Reprint, New York: Johnson Reprint, 1970; reprinted with "Sacred Formulas of the Cherokees," Nashville: Charles and Randy Elder, Booksellers, 1982.

(63) _____. "The Sacred Formulas of the Cherokees. In Smithsonian Institution. *Bureau of Ethnology Seventh Annual Report, 1885-1886*. Washington: U.S. Government Printing Office, 1891. 301-97. Reprinted with "Myths of the Cherokees," Nashville: Charles and Randy Elder, Booksellers, 1982.

(64) _____, and Frans M. Olbrechts. "The Swimmer Manuscript: Cherokee Sacred Formulas and Medicinal Prescriptions." In Smithsonian Institution. *Bureau of American Ethnology Bulletin* 99. Washington: U.S. Government Printing Office, 1932.

(65) Olbrechts, Frans M. "Cherokee Belief and Practice with Regard to Childbirth." *Anthropos* 26 (1931): 17-33.

(66) _____. "Some Cherokee Methods of Divination." *International Congress of Americanists Proceedings* 23:547-52. New York: The Science Press Printing, 1928.

(67) Perdue, Theda. *Slavery and the Evolution of Cherokee Society, 1540-1866.* Knoxville: University of Tennessee Press, 1979.

(68) Spade, Watt, and Willard Walker. *Cherokee Stories.* Middletown CT: Wesleyan University Anthropology Lab, 1966.

(69) Speck, Frank G., and Leonard Broom. *Cherokee Dance and Drama.* Berkeley: University of California Press, 1951.

(70) _____. "Concerning Iconology and the Masking Complex in Eastern North America." *University* [of Pennsylvania] *Museum Bulletin* 15 (1950): 6-57.

(71) Suddeth, Ruth Elgin. "The Myths of the Cherokees." *Georgia Review* 10 (1956): 84-91.

(72) Thomas, Robert K. "The Redbird Smith Movement." In *Symposium on Cherokee and Iroquois Culture.* William N. Fenton and John Gulick, eds. Smithsonian Institution. *Bureau of American Ethnology Bulletin* 180:159-66. Washington: U.S. Government Printing Office, 1961.

(73) Witthoft, John, and Wendell S. Hadlock. "Cherokee-Iroquois Little People." *Journal of American Folklore* 59 (1946): 413-22.

(74) _____. "Green Corn Ceremonialism in the Eastern Woodlands." *Occasional Contributions from the Museum of Anthropology of the University of Mississippi* 13 (1949).

(75) _____. "The Green Corn Medicine and the Green Corn Festival." *Journal of the Washington Academy of Sciences* 36 (1946): 213-19.

(76) _____. "Notes on a Cherokee Migration Story." *Journal of the Washington Academy of Sciences* 37 (1947): 304-305.

(77) _____. "Some Eastern Cherokee Bird Stories." *Journal of the Washington Academy of Sciences* 36 (1946): 177-80.

(78) _____. "Stone Pipes of the Historic Cherokees." *Southern Indian Studies* 1 (1949): 43-62.

(79) Woodward, Grace. *The Cherokees.* Norman: University of Oklahoma Press, 1970.

III. THE CHOCTAWS AND CHICKASAWS

(80) Baird, W. David. *The Choctaw People.* Phoenix: Indian Tribal Series, 1973.

(81) Bushnell, David I., Jr. "Myths of the Louisiana Choctaw." *American Anthropologist* new series 12 (1910): 526-35.

(82) Campbell, T. N. "The Choctaw Afterworld." *Journal of American Folklore* 72 (1959): 146-54.

(83) Debo, Angie. *The Rise and Fall of the Choctaw Republic*. Norman: University of Oklahoma Press, 1934.

(84) Dunkle, W. F. "A Choctaw Indian's Diary." *Chronicles of Oklahoma* 4 (1926): 61-69.

(85) Eggan, Fred. "Historical Changes in the Choctaw Kinship System." *American Anthropologist*, new series 39 (1937): 34-52.

(86) Halbert, Henry S. "A Choctaw Migration Legend." *American Antiquarian and Oriental Journal* 16 (1894): 215-16.

(87) _____. "Funeral Customs of the Mississippi Choctaws." *Publications of the Mississippi Historical Society* 3 (1900): 353-66.

(88) _____. "Nanih Waiya, the Sacred Mound of the Choctaws." *Publications of the Mississippi Historical Society* 2 (1899): 223-34.

(89) Wright, Alfred. "Choctaws." *Missionary Herald* 25 (1828): 187-88.

IV. THE CREEKS AND SEMINOLES

(90) Buswell, James O. "Florida Seminole Religious Ritual: Resistance and Change." Ph.D. dissertation, St. Louis University, 1972.

(91) Coe, Charles H. *Red Patriots: The Story of the Seminoles*. Gainesville: University of Florida Press, 1974. First published, 1898.

(92) Debo, Angie. *The Road to Disappearance: A History of the Creek Indians*. Norman: University of Oklahoma Press, 1941.

(93) Driver, Harold E. "Religion, Magic, Medicine." *Indians of America*. 2d rev. ed., 393-430. Chicago: University of Chicago Press, 1969.

(94) Green, Donald E. *The Creek People*. Phoenix: Indian Tribal Series, 1973.

(95) Green, Michael D. *The Politics of Indian Removal: Creek Government and Society in Crisis*. Lincoln: University of Nebraska Press, 1982.

(96) Howard, James N. *Oklahoma Seminoles: Medicines, Magic, and Religion*. Norman: University of Oklahoma Press, 1984.

(97) Kersey, Harry A., Jr. "Private Societies and the Maintenance of Seminole Tribal Integrity, 1899-1957." *Florida Historical Quarterly* 56 (1978): 297-316.

(98) _____. "The Seminole Indians of Florida." *Southeastern Indians Since the Removal Era*. Walter L. Williams, ed. Athens: University of Georgia Press, 1979.

(99) MacCauley, Clay. "The Seminole Indians of Florida." *Fifth Annual Report of the Bureau of American Ethnology, 1883-84*. Washington: Government Printing Office, 1887.

(100) McReynolds, Edwin C. *The Seminoles*. Norman: University of Oklahoma Press, 1957.

(101) Speck, Frank G. "Ceremonial Songs of the Creek and Yuchi Indians." *University of Pennsylvania Museum Anthropological Publications* 1:2 (1911): 157-245.

(102) Sturtevant, William C. "Creek into Seminole." *North American Indians in Historical Perspective.* E. B. Leacock and N. O. Lurie, eds. New York: Random House, 1971.

(103) _____. "The Medicine Bundles and Busks of the Florida Seminoles." *Florida Anthropologist* 7 (1954): 31-70.

(104) Swanton, John R., ed. "The Green Corn Dance." *Chronicles of Oklahoma* 10 (1932): 170-95.

(105) _____. "Religious Beliefs and Medical Practices of the Creek Indians." *Forty-second Annual Report of the United States Bureau of American Ethnology (1924-1925),* 473-672. Washington: Government Printing Office, 1928.

V. OTHER TRIBAL GROUPS

(106) Brown, Donald N. "The Ghost Dance Religion among the Oklahoma Cheyenne." *Chronicles of Oklahoma* 30 (1952): 408-16.

(107) Heckewelder, John G. E. *History, Manners and Customs of the Indian Nations Who Once Inhabited Pennsylvania and the Neighboring States. Memoirs of the Historical Society of Pennsylvania* 12 (1876). Reprint, New York: Arno Press, 1971.

(108) "Witchcraft along the Rio Grande." *Palacio* 80 (1974): 21-37.

VI. INDIAN MISSIONS: SCHOLARLY GENERAL STUDIES

(109) Axtell, James. "The European Failure to Convert the Indians: An Autopsy." In *Papers of the Sixth Algonquin Conference, 1974.* William Cowan, ed., 272-90. Ottawa: National Museum of Canada, 1975.

(110) Beaver, R. Pierce. *The Native American Christian Community: A Directory of Indian, Aleut, and Eskimo Churches.* Monrovia CA: Missions Advanced Research and Communications Center, 1979.

(111) _____. *Church, State, and the American Indians: Two and a Half Centuries of Partnership in Missions Between Protestant Churches and Government.* St. Louis: Concordia Publishing House, 1966.

(112) Berkhofer, Robert F., Jr. *Salvation and the Savage: An Analysis of Protestant Missions and American Indian Reponse, 1787-1862.* New York: Atheneum, 1976.

(113) Bowden, Henry Warner. *American Indians and Christian Missions: Studies in Cultural Conflict.* Chicago: University of Chicago Press, 1981.

(114) Hinman, George W. *The American Indian and Christian Missions.* New York: Fleming H. Revell, 1933.

(115) Howard, Harold C. "The Protestant Missionary and the Government Indian Policy, 1775-1850." Ph.D. dissertation, Loyola University, 1965.

(116) Jennings, James C. "The American Indian Ethos: A Key for Christian Missions?" *Missiology* 5 (1977): 487-98.

(117) Lindquist, G. E. E. *Indians in Transition: A Study of Protestant Missions to Indians in the United States.* New York: Division of Home Missions, National Council of Churches, 1951.

(118) Nash, Gary B. "Notes on the History of Seventeenth-Century Missionization in Colonial America." *American Indian Culture and Research Journal* 2:2 (1978): 3-8.

(119) Prucha, Francis P. *American Indian Policy in Crisis: Christian Reformers and the Indians, 1865-1900*. Norman: University of Oklahoma Press, 1976.

(120) _____. *American Indian Policy in the Formative Years: The Indian Trade and Intercourse Acts, 1790-1834*. Cambridge: Harvard University Press, 1962.

(121) Rainwater, Percy L. "Conquistadors, Missionaries, and Missions." *Journal of Mississippi History* 27 (1965): 123-47.

(122) Ronda, James P. " 'We Are Well As We Are': An Indian Critique of Seventeenth-Century Christian Missions." *William and Mary Quarterly* 3d series 34 (1977): 166-83.

(123) Rushdoony, Rousas J. "Christian Missions and Indian Culture." *Westminster Theological Journal* 12 (November 1949): 1-12.

(124) Schusky, Ernest L. "American Indians on Their Own." *Christian Century* 94 (1977): 303-306.

(125) Sheehan, Bernard W. *Seeds of Extinction: Jeffersonian Philanthropy and the American Indian*. Chapel Hill: University of North Carolina Press, 1973.

(126) Starkloff, Carl F. "Church between Cultures: Missions on Indian Reservations." *Christian Century* 93 (1976): 955-59.

(127) _____. "Cultural Problems in Mission Catechesis among Native Americans." *Occasional Bulletin of Missionary Research* 3 (1979): 138-40.

(128) _____. "Mission Method and the American Indian." *Theological Studies* 38 (1977): 621-53.

(129) Stevens, Michael E. "The Ideas and Attitudes of Protestant Missionaries to the North American Indians, 1643-1776." Ph.D. dissertation, University of Wisconsin at Madison, 1978.

(130) Terrell, John U. *The Arrow and the Cross: A History of the American Indian and the Missionaries*. Santa Barbara CA: Capra Press, 1979.

(131) Waller, Eugene C. "A Survey of the Church and Indian Schools and Colleges of the Southern Appalachians." Thesis, University of Tennessee, 1931.

VII. INDIAN MISSIONS: PERSONAL REMINISCENCES

(132) Methvin, J. J. "Reminiscences of Life Among the Indians." *Chronicles of Oklahoma* 5 (1927): 166-79.

(133) Pelter, Rodolphe C. *Reminiscences of Past Years in Mission Service among the Cheyenne*. Newton KS: Herald Publishing, 1936.

(134) Rainwater, Percy L. "Indian Missions and Missionaries." *Journal of Mississippi History* 28 (1966): 15-39.

VIII. SPANISH MISSIONS IN FLORIDA

(135) Bannon, John Francis. "The Mission as a Frontier Institution: Sixty Years of Interest and Research." *Western Historical Quarterly* 9 (1979): 303-22.

(136) Bolton, Herbert E. "The Mission as a Frontier Institution in the Spanish-American Colonies." *American Historical Review* 23 (1917): 42-61.

(137) Boyd, Mark F. "Enumeration of Florida Spanish Missions in 1675." *Florida Historical Quarterly* 26 (1948): 181-85.

(138) _____, ed. "Further Consideration of the Apalachee Missions." *Americas* 9 (1953): 459-79.

(139) _____, Hale G. Smith, and John W. Griffin. *Here Once They Stood: The Tragic End of the Apalachee Mission*. Gainesville: University of Florida Press, 1951.

(140) _____. "Mission Sites in Florida." *Florida Historical Quarterly* 17 (1939): 255.

(141) Geiger, Maynard J. *The Franciscan Conquest of Florida (1573-1618)*. Washington: Catholic University of America Press, 1937.

(142) Kenny, Michael. "The First Jesuit Mission in Florida." *U.S. Catholic Historical Society Historical Records and Studies* 33 (1941): 42.

(143) Matter, Robert A. "Mission Life in Seventeenth Century Florida." *Catholic Historical Review* 66 (1981): 401-20.

(144) _____. "Missions in the Defense of Spanish Florida 1566-1710." *Florida Historical Quarterly* 54 (1975): 18-38.

(145) Spellman, Charles W. "The 'Golden Age' of the Florida Missions, 1632-1674." *Catholic Historical Review* 51 (1965): 354-72.

(146) Vargas Ugarte, Ruben, "The First Jesuit Mission in Florida." U.S. Catholic Historical Society *Historical Records and Studies* 25 (1935): 59-148.

(147) Zubillaga, Felix. *La Florida, la Mision Jesuitica (1566-1572) y la colonizacion espanola*. Rome: Biblioteca Instituti Historica, S.J., 1941.

(148) _____, ed. *Monumenta Antiquae Floridae (1566-1572)*. Roma: Monumenta Historica Soc. Jesu, 1946.

IX. SPANISH MISSIONS IN GEORGIA AND VIRGINIA

(149) Johnson, J. G. "The Yamassee Revolt of 1597 and the Destruction of the Georgia Missions." *Georgia Historical Quarterly* 7 (1923): 44-53.

(150) Lanning, John T. *The Spanish Missions of Georgia*. Chapel Hill: University of North Carolina Press, 1935.

(151) Larson, Lewis H. "Historic Guale Indians of the Georgia Coast and the Impact of the Spanish Mission Effort." In *Tacachale: Essays on the Indians of Florida and Southeastern Georgia during the Historic Period*. Jerald T. Milanich and Samuel Proctor, eds., 120-49. Gainesville: University Presses of Florida, 1978.

(152) Lewis, Clifford M., and Albert J. Loomie, eds. *The Spanish Jesuit Mission in Virginia, 1570-1572*. Chapel Hill: University of North Carolina Press for the Virginia Historical Society, 1953.

(153) Ross, Mary. "The Restoration of the Spanish Missions in Georgia, 1598-1606." *Georgia Historical Quarterly* 10 (1926): 171-99.

X. ROMAN CATHOLIC MISSIONS IN TEXAS AND LOUISIANA

(154) "Beginnings of the Capuchin Mission in Texas." *U.S. Catholic Historical Magazine* 2 (1888): 259-300.

(155) Bolton, Herbert E. "Founding of the Mission Rosario." *Texas State Historical Association Quarterly* 10 (1906): 113-39.

(156) ———. "Founding of the Missions on the San Gabriel River, 1745-1749." *Southwestern Historical Quarterly* 17 (1914): 323-78.

(157) ———. "Native Tribes about the East Texas Missions." *Texas State Historical Association Quarterly* 11 (1908): 249-76.

(158) Domenech, Emmanuel H. D. *Journal d'un Missionaire au Texas et au Mexique, 1846-1852.* Paris: Gaume frères, 1857.

(159) Donohue, William H. "Mary of Agreda and the Southwest United States." *Americas* 9 (1953): 291-314.

(160) Dunn, William E. "Apache Mission on the San Saba River." *Southwestern Historical Quarterly* 17 (1914): 379-414.

(161) ———. "Missionary Activities among the Eastern Apaches Previous to the Founding of San Saba Mission." *Texas State Historical Association Quarterly* 15 (1912): 186-200.

(162) Habig, Marion A., O.F.M. *The Alamo Chain of Missions: A History of San Antonio's Five Old Missions.* Chicago: Franciscan Herald Press, 1968.

(163) ———, et al., eds. and trans. "Benito Fernandez: Memorial of Father Benito Fernandez Concerning the Canary Islanders, 1741." *Southwestern Historical Quarterly* 82 (1979): 265-96.

(164) ———. "Mission San Jose y San Miguel de Aguayo, 1720-1824." *Southwestern Historical Quarterly* 65 (1968): 498-516.

(165) ———. *San Antonio's Mission San Jose: State and National Historic Site, 1720-1968.* San Antonio: Naylor, 1968.

(166) Heusinger, Edward. *Early Explorations and Mission Establishments in Texas.* San Antonio: Naylor, 1936.

(167) Lambing, Andrew A. "Scenes from the Texas Mission of Half a Century Ago." *American Catholic Historical Researches* 3 (1887): 2-11.

(168) Leone, Allesandro. "Da una Lettera del P. Allesandro." *Lettere Edificanti Provincia Napolitana* 8,1 (1899): 64-68.

(169) Leutenegger, Benedict, and Marion A. Habig, eds. "Report on the San Antonio Missions in 1792." *Southwestern Historical Quarterly* 77 (1974): 487-98.

(170) ———. "Two Franciscan Documents on Early San Antonio, Texas: I. San Antonio and Father Antonio de Olivares, O.F. M., 1716; II. San Antonio and Father Benito Fernandez [1740]." *Americas* 26 (1969): 191-206.

(171) McCaleb, Walter F. *The Spanish Missions of Texas.* San Antonio: Naylor, 1954.

(172) Madlem, W. *San Jose Mission.* San Antonio: Naylor, 1934.

(173) O'Hagen, Thomas. "In the Footsteps of Texas Missionaries." *Catholic World* 71 (1900): 340-51.

(174) O'Rourke, Thomas P., C.S.B. *The Franciscan Missions in Texas, 1690-1793*. Washington: Catholic University of America Press, 1927. Reprint, New York: AMS Press, 1974.

(175) Persons, Billie. "Secular Life in the San Antonio Missions." *Southwestern Historical Quarterly* 62 (1958): 45-62.

(176) Santos, Richard G. "Proposed View of Mission San Antonio de Valero, circa 1790." *Texana* 3 (1965): 197-202.

(177) Santos Hernandez, Angel. "Presencia Misionera en la Antigua Luisiana." *Missionalia Hispanica* 32 (1975): 77-101.

(178) Simpson, Lesley Byrd, ed. *The San Saba Papers: A Documentary Account of the Founding and Destruction of San Saba Mission*. Paul D. Nathan, trans. San Francisco: John Howell, 1959.

(179) "A Texas Missionary Trip." *Annals of the Propagation of the Faith, Baltimore* 67 (1904): 131-38.

(180) "Texas Missions in 1785." *Mid-America* 11 (1945): 38-58.

(181) Webb, Mure L. "Religious and Educational Efforts among Texas Indians in the 1850's." *Southwestern Historical Quarterly* 69 (1965): 22-37.

(182) Weddle, Robert S. *San Juan Bautista: Gateway to Spanish Texas*. Austin: University of Texas Press, 1968.

(183) _____. *The San Saba Mission: Spanish Pivot in Texas*. Austin: University of Texas Press, 1964.

XI. CATHOLIC MISSIONS IN MARYLAND AND MISSOURI

(184) Campbell, B. U. "Early Missions among the Indians in Maryland." *Maryland Historical Magazine* 1 (1906): 293-316.

(185) Dalrymple, E. A., ed. *Relatio Itineris in Marylandium Declaratio Coloniae Domini Baronis de Baltimoro ad Annum 1638. . . . Narrative of a Voyage to Maryland, by Father Andrew White, S.J. An Account of the Colony of the Lord Baron of Baltimore. Extracts from Different Letters of Missionaries, from the Year 1635 to the Year 1677*. Fund Publication 7. Baltimore: Maryland Historical Society, 1874.

(186) Garraghan, Gilbert J., ed. "An Early Missouri River Journal." *Mid-America* 13 (1931): 236-54.

(187) _____. "The Kickapoo Mission." *St. Louis Catholic Historical Review* 4 (1922): 25-50.

(188) Porter, Frank W. III. "A Century of Accommodation: The Nanticokes in Colonial Maryland." *Maryland Historical Magazine* 74 (1979): 175-92.

(189) Rahill, Peter. "Catholics Penetrated Missouri's Indian Border." *Social Justice Review* 68 (1975): 87-92, 120-23.

(190) Rothensteiner, John E. "Early Missionary Efforts among the Indians in the Diocese of St. Louis." *St. Louis Catholic Historical Review* 2 (1920): 57-96.

(191) _____. "The Flathead and Nez Perce Delegation to St. Louis, 1831-1839." *St. Louis Catholic Historical Review* 2 (1920): 183-97.

(192) Tierney, Richard H. "Father Andrew White, S.J., and the Indians." United States Catholic Historical Society *Historical Records and Studies* 15 (1921): 89-103.

XII. OTHER ROMAN CATHOLIC INDIAN MISSIONS

(193) Aguirre, H. Jeronimo. "Mission de Tejas: Carta del H. Jeronimo Aguirre al Superior de Poyanne, Lovaino, 19 de Marzo de 1875." *Cartas de Poyanne* 3 (1879): 101-107.

(194) Bekkers, B. J. "The Catholic Church in Mississippi during Colonial Times." *Mississippi Historical Society Publications* 6 (1902): 351-57.

(195) Brouillet, J. B. A. *The Bureau of Catholic Indian Missions—the Work of the Decade Ending December 31, 1883*. Washington: n.p., 1883.

(196) _____. *Work of the Catholic Indian Missions of the United States of America*. Washington: n.p., 1879.

(197) Bureau of Catholic Indian Missions. *The Bureau of Catholic Indian Missions, 1874 to 1895*. Washington: Church News Publishing, 1895.

(198) _____. *Status of the Catholic Indian Missions in the United States, 1876*. Baltimore: n.p., 1876.

(199) Curtis, Ralph E., Jr. "Relations between the Quapaw National Council and the Roman Catholic Church, 1876-1927." *Chronicles of Oklahoma* 55 (1977): 211-21.

(200) Fightmaster, Maxine. "Sacred Heart Mission Among the Potawatomi Indians." *Chronicles of Oklahoma* 50 (1972): 156-76.

(201) Fittipaldi, Silvio E. "The Catholic Church and the American Indians." *Horizons* 5 (1978): 73-75.

(202) Foreman, Carolyn Thomas. "St. Agnes Academy for the Choctaws." *Chronicles of Oklahoma* 48 (1970): 323-30.

(203) Healy, George R. "The French Jesuits and the Idea of the Noble Savage." *William and Mary Quarterly* 3d series 15 (1958): 143-67.

(204) Kehoe, Mary Urban. "The Educational Activities of Distinguished Catholic Missionaries among the Five Civilized Tribes." *Chronicles of Oklahoma* 24 (1936): 166-82.

(205) Lambing, Andrew A. "Who Was the Apostle to the Indians?" *American Catholic Historical Researches* 4 (1888): 124-32.

(206) Laracy, John. "Sacred Heart Mission and Abbey." *Chronicles of Oklahoma* 5 (1927): 234-50.

(207) Manley, D. "The Catholic Church and the Indians." *Catholic World* 55 (1872): 473-81.

(208) Michalicka, John. "First Catholic Church in Indian Territory—1872: St. Patrick's Church at Atoka." *Chronicles of Oklahoma* 50 (1972): 479-85.

(209) Nieberding, Velma. "Catholic Education among the Osage." *Chronicles of Oklahoma* 32 (1954): 290-307.

(210) _____. "Chief Splitlog and the Cayuga Mission Church." *Chronicles of Oklahoma* 52 (1974): 18-28.

(211) _____. "St. Agnes School of the Choctaws." *Chronicles of Oklahoma* 23 (1955): 183-92.

(212) _____. "St. Mary's of the Quapaws." *Chronicles of Oklahoma* 31 (1953): 2-14.

(213) _____, ed. "A Trip to Quapaw in 1903." *Chronicles of Oklahoma* 31 (1953): 142-67.

(214) _____. "The Very Reverend Urban DeHasque, S.T.D., L.L.D., Pioneer Priest of Indian Territory." *Chronicles of Oklahoma* 38 (1960): 35-42.

(215) Nolan, Charles E. "Recollections of Tulsa, Indian Territory, from Sister Mary Agnes New Church, O. Carm.." *Chronicles of Oklahoma* 49 (1971): 92-99.

(216) Rahill, Peter J. *The Catholic Indian Missions and Grant's Peace Policy, 1870-1884*. Washington: Catholic University of America Press, 1954.

(217) Robertson, Dario F. "The Catholic Mission and Indian Reservations." *Social Thought* 3 (1977): 15-29.

(218) Ryan, Patrick J. "Indians and Martyrs Reconsidered." *America* 133 (18 October 1975): 226-28.

(219) Shea, John Gilmary. *History of the Catholic Missions among the Indian Tribes of the United States, 1529-1854*. First published, 1855. Reprint, New York: Arno Press, 1969.

(220) Starkloff, Carl F. "A Reflection on 'The Catholic Church and the American Indians.'" *Horizons* 5 (1978): 255-58.

(221) Stephan, J. A. *The Bureau of Catholic Indian Missions, 1874 to 1895*. Washington: Church News Publishing, 1895.

(222) Wintz, Jack. "Respect Our Indian Values." *St. Anthony Messenger* 83 (1975): 34-40.

XIII. PROTESTANT MISSIONS TO THE CHEROKEES

(223) Ballenger, T. L. "Joseph Franklin Thompson: An Early Cherokee Leader." *Chronicles of Oklahoma* 30 (1952): 285-91.

(224) Bass, Althea. *Cherokee Messenger*. Norman: University of Oklahoma Press, 1936.

(225) Bass, Dorothy C. "Gideon Blackburn's Mission to the Cherokees: Christianization and Civilization." *Journal of Presbyterian History* 52 (1974): 203-226.

(226) Collins, Linton M. "Activities of the Missionaries among the Cherokees." *Georgia Historical Quarterly* 6 (1922): 285-322.

(227) Conard, A. Mark. "The Cherokee Mission of Virginia Presbyterians." *Journal of Presbyterian History* 58 (1980): 35-48.

(228) DeBaillou, Clemens. "The Diaries of the Moravian Brotherhood at the Cherokee Mission in Spring Place, Georgia, for the Years 1800-1804." *Georgia Historical Quarterly* 54 (1970): 571-76.

(229) Everts, Jeremiah. *Cherokee Removal: The "William Penn" Essays and Other Writings.* Knoxville: University of Tennessee Press, 1981.

(230) Foreman, Carolyn Thomas. "The Cherokee Gospel Teachings of Dwight Mission." *Chronicles of Oklahoma* 12 (1934): 454-69.

(231) Foreman, Grant, ed. "Dwight Mission." *Chronicles of Oklahoma* 12 (1934): 42-51.

(232) Foreman, Minta Ross. "Reverend Stephen Foreman, Cherokee Missionary." *Chronicles of Oklahoma* 18 (1940): 229-42.

(233) Gardner, Robert G. "Landmark Banner and Cherokee Baptist." *Viewpoints: Georgia Baptist History* 4 (1974): 27-38.

(234) Garrett, Kathleen. "Worcester, the Pride of the West." *Chronicles of Oklahoma* 30 (1952): 386-96.

(235) "Georgia's Attack on the Missionaries." *Journal of Cherokee Studies* 4 (1979): 82-92. Reprinted from the *New York Spectator,* 23 August 1831.

(236) Higginbotham, Mary Alves. "The Creek Path Mission." *Journal of Cherokee Studies* 1 (1976): 72-86.

(237) Hutchins, John. "The Trial of Reverend Samuel A. Worcester." *Journal of Cherokee Studies* 2 (1977): 356-74.

(238) Lackey, Vinson. "New Springplace." *Chronicles of Oklahoma* 17 (1939): 178-83.

(239) McLoughlin, William G. "Cherokee Anti-Mission Sentiment, 1824-1828." *Ethnohistory* 21 (1974): 361-70 [see 14].

(240) _____. "The Cherokee Baptist Preacher and the Great Schism of 1844-45." *Foundations* 24 (1981): 137-47 [see 14].

(241) _____. "Cherokees and Methodists, 1824-1834." *Church History* 50 (1981): 44-63 [see 14].

(242) _____. *Cherokees and Missionaries, 1789-1839.* New Haven: Yale University Press, 1984.

(243) _____. "Civil Disobedience and Evangelism among the Missionaries to the Cherokees, 1829-1839." *Journal of Presbyterian History* 51 (1973): 116-39 [see 14].

(244) _____. "Parson Blackburn's Whiskey and the Cherokee Indian Schools, 1809-1810." *Journal of Presbyterian History* 57 (1979): 427-45 [see 14].

(245) Moffitt, James W. "Early Baptist Missionary Work among the Cherokee." *East Tennessee Historical Society Publications* 12 (1940): 16-27.

(246) Malone, Henry T. "The Early Nineteenth Century Missionaries in the Cherokee Country." *Tennessee Historical Quarterly* 10 (1951): 127-39.

(247) Peacock, Mary T. "Methodist Missionary Work among the Cherokee Indians before the Removal." *Methodist History* 3 (1965): 20-39.

(248) Perdue, Theda. "Letters from Brainerd." *Journal of Cherokee Studies* 4 (1979): 6-9.

(249) _____, ed. *Cherokee Editor: The Writings of Elias Boudinot.* Knoxville: University of Tennessee Press, 1983.

(250) Queener, V. M. "Gideon Blackburn." *East Tennessee Historical Society Publications* 6 (1934): 12-28.

(251) Routh, E. C. "Early Missionaries to the Cherokees." *Chronicles of Oklahoma* 15 (1937): 449-65.

(252) Thoburn, Joseph B., ed. "Letters of Cassandra Sawyer Lockwood: Dwight Mission, 1834." *Chronicles of Oklahoma* 33 (1955): 202-237.

(253) Torrey, Charles C. "Notes of a Missionary among the Cherokees." Grant Foreman, ed. *Chronicles of Oklahoma* 16 (1938): 171-89.

(254) Tuttle, Sarah. *Conversations on the Mission to the Arkansas Cherokee.* Boston: Massachusetts Sabbath School Society, 1833.

(255) _____. *Conversations on the Cherokee Mission.* Boston: Massachusetts Sabbath School Union, 1830.

(256) West, Sam. "Brief Statement of Facts Concerning Old Baptist Mission Church, Cherokee Nation." *Chronicles of Oklahoma* 24 (1946): 106-107.

(257) White, Pliny H. "A Memorial of Rev. Samuel Austin Worcester." *Congregational Quarterly* 3 (1861): 279-85.

(258) Williams, Samuel C. "An Account of the Presbyterian Mission to the Cherokees, 1757-1759." *Tennessee Historical Magazine* 2d series 1 (1931): 125-38.

(259) _____. "Christian Missions to the Overhill Cherokees." *Chronicles of Oklahoma* 12 (1934): 66-73.

(260) Wright, Muriel H. *Springplace: Moravian Mission and the Ward Family of the Cherokee Nation.* Guthrie OK: Co-operative Publishing, 1940.

XIV. PROTESTANT MISSIONS TO THE CHOCTAWS AND CHICKASAWS

(261) Austin, Edward B. "Cyrus Byington." *Arkansas Historical Quarterly* 7 (1948): 81-86.

(262) Baird, W. David. "Spencer Academy, Choctaw Nation, 1842-1900." *Chronicles of Oklahoma* 45 (1967): 25-43.

(263) Benson, Henry C. *Life among the Choctaw Indians and Sketches of the South-West.* Cincinnati: Swormstedt and Poe, 1860. Reprint, New York: Johnson Reprint, 1970.

(264) Brewer, Phil D. "Rev. Willis F. Folsom." *Chronicles of Oklahoma* 4 (1926): 55-60.

(265) Bryant, Keith L., Jr. "The Choctaw Nation in 1843: A Missionary's View." *Chronicles of Oklahoma* 44 (1966): 319-21.

(266) Bryce, J. Y., ed. "About Some of Our First Schools in Choctaw Nation." *Chronicles of Oklahoma* 6 (1928): 354-94.

(267) Cassal, Hilary. "Missionary Tour in the Chickasaw Nation and Western Indian Territory." *Chronicles of Oklahoma* 34 (1956): 397-416.

(268) Copeland, Charles C. "Letter Mailed from Eagle Town, Choctaw Nation, 1842." *Chronicles of Oklahoma* 35 (1957): 229-33.

(269) Debo, Angie. "Education in the Choctaw Country after the Civil War." *Chronicles of Oklahoma* 10 (1932): 383-91.

(270) Denison, Natalie Morison. "Missions and Missionaries of the Presbyterian Church., U.S., among the Choctaws—1866-1907." *Chronicles of Oklahoma* 24 (1946): 426-28.

(271) De Rosier, Arthur H., Jr. "Cyrus Kingsbury—Missionary to the Choctaws." *Journal of Presbyterian History* 50 (1972): 267-87.

(272) _____. "Pioneers with Conflicting Ideals: Christianity and Slavery in the Choctaw Nation." *Journal of Mississippi History* 21 (1959): 174-89.

(273) Farr, Eugene I. "Religious Assimilation: A Case Study of the Adoption of Christianity by the Choctaw Indians of Mississippi." Th.D. dissertation, New Orleans Baptist Theological Seminary, 1948.

(274) Foreman, Carolyn Thomas. "The Choctaw Academy." *Chronicles of Oklahoma* 6 (1928): 453-80; 9 (1931): 382-411; 10 (1932): 77-114.

(275) Goode, William H. *Outposts of Zion, with Limnings of Mission Life*. Cincinnati: Poe and Hitchcock, 1863.

(276) Graham, William. "Lost Among the Choctaws During a Tour in the Indian Territory, 1845." *Chronicles of Oklahoma* 50 (1972): 226-33.

(277) Hiemstra, William L. "Early Presbyterian Missions among the Choctaw and Chickasaw Indians in Mississippi." *Journal of Mississippi History* 10 (1948): 8-16.

(278) _____. "Presbyterian Mission Schools among the Choctaws and Chickasaws, 1845-1861." *Chronicles of Oklahoma* 27 (1949): 33-40.

(279) _____. "Presbyterian Missionaries and Mission Churches among the Choctaw and Chickasaw Indians, 1832-1865." *Chronicles of Oklahoma* 26 (1948): 459-67.

(280) _____. "Presbyterian Missions among the Choctaw and Chickasaw Indians, 1860-1861." *Presbyterian Historical Society Journal* (now *Journal of Presbyterian History*) 37 (1959): 51-59.

(281) Hunt, Elizabeth H. "Two Letters from Pine Ridge Mission." *Chronicles of Oklahoma* 50 (1972): 219-25.

(282) Isern, Thomas D. "Chickasaw Academy." *Methodist History* 19 (1981): 131-45.

(283) "Letter of Cyrus Kingsbury to Mission Headquarters." *Presbyterian Historical Society Journal* (now *Journal of Presbyterian History*) 37 (1959): 50.

(284) Lewis, Anna, ed. "Diary of a Missionary to the Choctaws, 1860-1861." *Chronicles of Oklahoma* 17 (1939): 428-47.

(285) _____, ed. "The Diary of Sue McBeth, a Missionary to the Choctaws, 1860-1861." *Chronicles of Oklahoma* 21 (1943): 186-95.

(286) _____. ''Letters Regarding Choctaw Missions and Missionaries.''
       Chronicles of Oklahoma 17 (1939): 287-95.

(287) *Life and Letters of Miss Mary C. Greenleaf, Missionary to the Chickasaw
       Tribe.* Boston: Massachusetts Sabbath School Society, 1858.

(288) Love, William A. ''The Mayhew Mission to the Choctaws.'' *Mississippi
       Historical Society Publications* 11 (1910): 363-402.

(289) McLoughlin, William G. ''The Choctaw Slave Burning: A Crisis in Mis-
       sion Work Among the Indians.'' *Journal of the West* 13 (1974): 113-27 [see
       also 14].

(290) Morrison, William B. ''The Choctaw Mission of the American Board of
       Commissioners for Foreign Missions.'' *Chronicles of Oklahoma* 4 (1926):
       166-83.

(291) Phelps, Dawson A. ''The Chickasaw Mission.'' *Journal of Mississippi His-
       tory* 13 (1951): 226-35.

(292) _____. ''The Choctaw Mission: An Experiment in Civilization.'' *Jour-
       nal of Mississippi History* 14 (1952): 35-62.

(293) Spalding, Arminta Scott. ''Cyrus Kingsbury: Missionary to the Choc-
       taws.'' Ph.D. dissertation, University of Oklahoma, 1975.

(294) _____. ''From the Natchez Trace to Oklahoma: Development of Chris-
       tian Civilization among the Choctaws, 1800-1860.'' *Chronicles of Okla-
       homa* 45 (1967): 2-24.

(295) Spear, Eloise G. ''Choctaw Indian Education with Special Reference to
       Choctaw County, Oklahoma: An Historical Appraisal.'' Ph.D. disserta-
       tion, University of Oklahoma, 1977.

(296) Tuttle, Sarah. *Conversations on the Choctaw Missions.* Boston: Massachu-
       setts Sabbath School Union, 1830.

(297) _____. *Letters on the Chickasaw and Osage Missions.* Boston: Massa-
       chusetts Sabbath School Union, 1831.

(298) Vaughn, Courtney Ann. ''Job's Legacy: Cyrus Byington, Missionary to the
       Choctaws in Indian Territory.'' *Red River Valley Historical Review* 3 (1978):
       5-18.

XV. PROTESTANT MISSIONS TO THE CREEKS AND SEMINOLES

(299) Derrick, W. Edwin. ''Coweta Mission: Struggle for the Mind and Soul of
       the Creek Indians.'' *Red River Valley Historical Review* 4 (1979): 4-13.

(300) Fife, Sharon A. ''Baptist Indian Church: Thlewarle Mekko Sapkv Coko.''
       Chronicles of Oklahoma 48 (1970): 451-66.

(301) Foreman, Carolyn Thomas. ''Lee Compere and the Creek Indians.''
       Chronicles of Oklahoma 42 (1964): 291-99.

(302) _____. ''Report of the Reverend R. M. Loughridge to the Board of For-
       eign Missions Regarding the Creek Mission.'' *Chronicles of Oklahoma* 26
       (1948): 278-84.

(303) Hazard, Ebenezer. "Remarks on Mr. Schermerhorn's Report Concerning the Western Indians." Massachusetts Historical Society *Collections* 2d series 4 (1816): 65-69.

(304) Hinds, Roland. "Early Creek Missions." *Chronicles of Oklahoma* 17 (1939): 48-61.

(305) Jackson, Joe C. "Church School Education in the Creek Nation, 1898 to 1907." *Chronicles of Oklahoma* 46 (1968): 312-30.

(306) Kersey, Harry A., Jr., and Donald E. Pullease. "Bishop William Crane Gray's Mission to the Seminole Indians in Florida, 1893-1914." *Historical Magazine of the Protestant Episcopal Church* 42 (1973): 257-73.

(307) _____. "Educating the Seminole Indians of Florida, 1879-1970." *Florida Historical Quarterly* 49 (1970): 19-21.

(308) Lauderdale, Virginia E. "Tullahassee Mission." *Chronicles of Oklahoma* 26 (1948): 285-300.

(309) Mauelshagen, Carl, and Gerald H. Davis. "The Moravians' Plan for a Mission among the Creek Indians, 1803-1804." *Georgia Historical Quarterly* 51 (1967): 358-64.

(310) Parkhill, Harriet Randolph. *Mission to the Seminoles*. Orlando FL: By the Author, 1909.

(311) Smoot, Joseph G., ed. "An Account of Alabama Indian Missions and Presbyterian Churches in 1828 from the Travel Diary of William S. Potts." *Alabama Review* 18 (1965): 134-52.

(312) Sturtevant, William C. "R. H. Pratt's Report on the Seminole in 1879." *Florida Anthropologist* 9 (March 1956): 1-5.

XVI. PROTESTANT MISSIONS
TO THE COMANCHES, KIOWAS, AND OSAGES

(313) Corwin, Hugh D. "Protestant Mission Work among the Comanches and Kiowas." *Chronicles of Oklahoma* 46 (1968): 41-57.

(314) Graves, Mrs. W. W. "In the Land of the Osages—Harmony Mission." *Missouri Historical Review* 19 (1965): 409-18.

(315) Mondello, Salvatore. "Isabel Crawford and the Kiowas." *Foundations* 21 (1978): 322-39; 22 (1979): 28-42, 99-115.

(316) Wardell, Morris L. "Protestant Missions among the Osages, 1820 to 1838." *Chronicles of Oklahoma* 2 (1924): 285-97.

XVII. MISCELLANEOUS INDIAN MISSIONS
OF THE CHURCH OF ENGLAND
AND THE PROTESTANT EPISCOPAL CHURCH

(317) Botkin, Sam L. "Indian Missions of the Episcopal Church in Oklahoma." *Chronicles of Oklahoma* 36 (1958): 40-47.

(318) [Bray, Thomas]. *Missionalia: or, a Collection of Missionary Pieces relating to the Conversion of the Heathen: both the African Negroes and American Indians*. London: W. Roberts, 1727.

(319) Foreman, Carolyn Thomas. "Journal of a Tour in the Indian Territory." *Chronicles of Oklahoma* 10 (1932): 219-56.

(320) Franks, Kenny A. "Missionaries in the West: An Expedition of the Protestant Episcopal Church in 1844." *Historical Magazine of the Protestant Episcopal Church* 44 (1975): 318-33.

(321) Goodwin, Gerald J. "Christianity, Civilization and the Savage: The Anglican Mission to the American Indian." *Historical Magazine of the Protestant Episcopal Church* 42 (1973): 93-110.

(322) Hawkins, Ernest. *Historical Notices of the Missions of the Church of England in the North American Colonies, previous to the Independence of the United States: Chiefly from the MS. Documents of the Society for the Propagation of the Gospel in Foreign Parts.* London: B. Fellowes, 1845.

(323) "Historical Sketch of the Society for Propagating the Gospel among the Indians and Others in North America." Massachusetts Historical Society *Collections* 2d series 2 (1814): 45-48.

(324) Hock, Alvin S. "The Church in Indian Territory," *Protestant Episcopal Church Historical Magazine* (now *Historical Magazine of the Protestant Church*) 8 (1939): 372-87.

(325) Hunnewell, James F., et al. *The Society for Propagating the Gospel among the Indians and Others in North America, 1787-1887.* [Cambridge]: Printed for the Society by University Press, 1887.

(326) Jones, Jerome W. "The Established Virginia Church and the Conversion of Negroes and Indians, 1620-1760." *Journal of Negro History* 46 (1961): 12-23.

(327) Kersey, Harry A., and Donald E. Pullease. "Bishop William Crane Gray's Mission to the Seminole Indians in Florida, 1893-1914." *Historical Magazine of the Protestant Episcopal Church* 42 (1973): 257-74.

(328) Klingberg, Frank J. "Early Attempts at Indian Education in South Carolina: A Documentary." *South Carolina Historical Magazine* 61 (1960): 1-10.

(329) _____. "The Indian Frontier in South Carolina as Seen by the S.P.G. Missionary." *Journal of Southern History* 5 (1939): 479-500.

(330) Knox, William. *Three Tracts respecting the Conversion and Instruction of the Free Indians, and Negroe Slaves in the Colonies. Addresses to the venerable Society for Propagation of the Gospel in Foreign Parts.* London: n.p., [1770].

(331) Lewis, Norman. "English Missionary Interest in the Indians of North America, 1578-1700." Ph.D. dissertation, University of Washington, 1968.

(332) Meredith, Howard. "Whirlwind: A Study of Church-State Relations." *Historical Magazine of the Protestant Episcopal Church* 43 (1974): 297-304.

(333) Pennington, Edgar L. "The Reverend Francis LeJau's Work Among Indians and Negro Slaves." *Journal of Southern History* 1 (1935): 442-58.

(334) Rainwater, Percy L. "Indian Missions and Missionaries." *Journal of Mississippi History* 28 (1966): 15-39.

(335) Robinson, W. Stitt, Jr. "Indian Education and Missions in Colonial Virginia." *Journal of Southern History* 18 (1952): 152-68.

(336) Smith, Franklin C. "Pioneer Beginnings at Emmanuel, Shawnee." *Chronicles of Oklahoma* 24 (1946): 2-14.

(337) Stinson, Richard L. "The Development of Indian Mission Policy and Practice in the National Period." *Historical Magazine of the Protestant Episcopal Church* 37 (1968): 51-65.

(338) Taylor, Maxwell F., Jr. "The Influence of Religion on White Attitudes towards Indians in the Early Settlement of Virginia." Ph.D. dissertation, Emory University, 1970.

XVIII. MISCELLANEOUS QUAKER INDIAN MISSIONS

(339) Brainerd, Ezra. "Jeremiah Hubbard, Hoosier Schoolmaster and Friends Missionary among the Indians." *Chronicles of Oklahoma* 29 (1951): 23-31.

(340) Gibson, Arrell M. "Wyandotte Mission: The Early Years, 1871-1900." *Chronicles of Oklahoma* 36 (1958): 137-54.

(341) Hopkins, Gerald T. "A Quaker Pilgrimage: Being a Mission to the Indians from the Indian Committee of the Baltimore Yearly Meeting, to Fort Wayne, 1804." William H. Love, ed. *Maryland Historical Magazine* 4 (1909): 1-24.

(342) Kelsey, Rayner W. *Friends and the Indians, 1655-1917*. Philadelphia: Associate Executive Committee of Friends on Indian Affairs, 1917.

(343) Knowles, David E. "Some Account of a Journey to the Cherokees, 1839-1840." *Bulletin of Friends' Historical Society of Philadelphia* [now *Quaker History*] 6 (November 1915): 70-78.

(344) LeVan, Sandra W. "The Quaker Agents at Darlington." *Chronicles of Oklahoma* 51 (1973): 92-99.

(345) Neely, Sharlotte. "The Quaker Era of Cherokee Indian Education, 1880-1892." *Appalachian Journal* 2 (1975): 314-22.

(346) Ragland, Hobert D. "Missions of the Society of Friends among the Indian Tribes of the Sac and Fox Agency." *Chronicles of Oklahoma* 33 (1955): 169-82.

(347) Thomson, S. Carrie. "The Shawnee Friends Mission." *Chronicles of Oklahoma* 2 (1924): 392-94.

(348) Tolles, Frederick B. "Nonviolent Contact: The Quakers and the Indians." *Proceedings of the American Philosophical Association* 107 (15 April 1963): 93-101.

XIX. MISCELLANEOUS BAPTIST INDIAN MISSIONS

(349) Adams, Franklin G. "Reverend Isaac McCoy." Kentucky Historical Society *Collections* 2 (1881): 271-75.

(350) Belt, Loren J. "Baptist Missions to the Indians of the Five Civilized Tribes of Oklahoma." Th.D. dissertation, Central Baptist Theological Seminary, 1955.

(351) Dane, John P. "A History of Baptist Missions among the Plains Indians of Oklahoma." Th.D. dissertation, Central Baptist Theological Seminary, 1955.

(352) Fauth, Albert H. "A History of the American Indian Mission Association and Its Contribution to Baptist Indian Missions." Th.D. dissertation, Central Baptist Theological Seminary, 1953.

(353) Hamilton, Robert. *The Gospel among the Red Man: The History of the Southern Baptist Indian Missions*. Nashville: Baptist Sunday School Board, 1930.

(354) Hutcherson, Curtis A. "The Contributions of Dr. Johnson Lykins and Robert Simerwell to the Preservation, Advancement, and Evangelization of the American Indians." Th.D. dissertation, Central Baptist Theological Seminary, 1952.

(355) McCoy, Isaac. *History of Baptist Indian Missions: Embracing Remarks on the Former and Present Conditions of the Aboriginal Tribes, Their Settlement within Indian Territory, and Their Future Prospects*. Reprint, New York: Johnson Reprint, 1970. First published 1840.

(356) McDonald, Joseph R. "A History of the Western Oklahoma Indian Baptist Association." Th.D. dissertation, Central Baptist Theological Seminary, 1957.

(357) Moffitt, James W. "A History of Early Baptist Missions among the Five Civilized Tribes." Ph.D. dissertation, University of Oklahoma, 1946.

(358) _____. "Some Results of Early Baptist Indian Missions, 1801-1861." *Review and Expositor* 45 (1948): 209-216.

(359) Rister, Carl C. *Baptist Missions among the American Indians*. Atlanta: Home Missions Board, Southern Baptist Convention, 1944.

(360) Roustio, Edward. "A History of the Life of Isaac McCoy in Relation to Early Indian Migrations and Missions as Revealed in His Unpublished Manuscripts." Th.D. dissertation, Central Baptist Theological Seminary, 1954.

(361) Schultz, George A. *An Indian Canaan: Isaac McCoy and the Vision of an Indian State*. Norman: University of Oklahoma Press, 1972.

(362) Smith, Timothy S. *Missionary Abominations Unmasked; or, A View of Carey Mission . . . . under the Superintendence of the Rev. Isaac McCoy*. South Bend: The Beacon Office, 1833. Reprint, South Bend: Windle Printing, 1946.

(363) Wiggins, Lexie O., Jr. "A Critical History of the Southern Baptist Indian Mission Movement." Ph.D. dissertation, University of Oklahoma, 1980.

(364) Wyeth, Walter N. *Isaac McCoy: A Memorial*. Philadelphia: W. N. Wyeth, 1895.

(365) Yeager, Randolph O. "Indian Enterprises of Isaac McCoy, 1817-1846." Ph.D. dissertation, University of Oklahoma, 1954.

XX. MISCELLANEOUS METHODIST INDIAN MISSIONS

(366) Babcock, Sidney H. "John Jasper Methvin, 1846-1941." *Chronicles of Oklahoma* 19 (1941): 113-18.

(367) _____, and John Y. Bryce. *History of Methodism in Oklahoma: Story of the Indian Mission Annual Conference of the Methodist Episcopal Church. South*. Oklahoma City: Times Journal Publishing, 1937.

(368) Barclay, Wade C. *History of Methodist Missions*. 3 vols. New York: Board of Missions and Church Extension of the Methodist Church, 1949-1957.

(369) Bardell, Eunice Bonow. "Primitive Physick: John Wesley's Receipts." *Pharmacy in History* 21 (1979): 111-21.

(370) Brockway, Allan R., ed. "The American Indian Today." *Engage/Social Action* 5 (1977): 17-47.

(371) Bryce, John Y. "Beginning of Methodism in Indian Territory." *Chronicles of Oklahoma* 7 (1929): 475-86.

(372) Chisholm, Johnnie B. "Harley Institute." *Chronicles of Oklahoma* 4 (1926): 116-28.

(373) Corwin, Hugh D. "The Folsom Training School." *Chronicles of Oklahoma* 42 (1964): 46-52.

(374) Eichenberger, Flora Paine. "A Reminiscence of a Methodist Minister's Daughter." *Chronicles of Oklahoma* 7 (1929): 260-65.

(375) Green, Frank L. "H. K. W. Perkins, Missionary to the Dalles." *Methodist History* 9 (April 1971): 34-44.

(376) Harper, Robert H. *In the Land of New Acadia*. Nashville: Board of Missions, Methodist Episcopal Church, South, 1930.

(377) Moore, F. M. *A Brief History of the Missionary Work in the Indian Territory, of the Indian Mission Conference, Methodist Episcopal Church, South, and an Appendix Containing Personal Sketches of Many of the Workers in This Field*. Muskogee OK: Phoenix Printing, 1899.

(378) Norwood, Frederick A. "The Invisible American—Methodism and the Indian." *Methodist History* 8 (January 1970): 3-24.

(379) Patton, William. "Journal of a Visit to Indian Missions, Missouri Conference." *Bulletin of the Missouri Historical Society* 10 (1954): 167-80.

(380) Stewart, Martha. "The Indian Mission Conference of Oklahoma." *Chronicles of Oklahoma* 40 (1962): 330-36.

(381) Vernon, Walter N. "Beginnings of Indian Methodism in Oklahoma." *Methodist History* 17 (April 1979): 127-54.

(382) _____. "Early Echoes from Bloomfield Academy." *Chronicles of Oklahoma* 52 (1974): 237-43.

(383) _____. "Methodist Beginnings among Southwest Oklahoma Indians." *Chronicles of Oklahoma* 59 (1981): 392-411.

(384) _____, ed. *One in the Lord: A History of Ethnic Minorities in the South Central Jurisdiction, the United Methodist Church*. Oklahoma City: Commission on Archives and History, South Central Jurisdiction, United Methodist Church, 1977.

XXI. MISCELLANEOUS PRESBYTERIAN INDIAN MISSIONS

(385) Beaver, R. Pierce. "Methods in American Missions to the Indians in the Seventeenth and Eighteenth Centuries: Calvinist Models for Protestant Foreign Missions." *Journal of Presbyterian History* 47 (1969): 124-48.

(386) Coleman, Michael C. "Not Race, but Grace: Presbyterian Missionaries and American Indians, 1837-1893." *Journal of American History* 67 (1980): 41-60.

(387) ———. "Presbyterian Missionaries and Their Attitudes to the American Indians, 1837-1893." Ph.D. dissertation, University of Pennsylvania, 1977.

(388) Morrison, William B. *The Red Man's Trail.* Richmond: Presbyterian Committee of Publication, 1932.

(389) Waltmann, Henry G. "John C. Lourie and Presbyterian Indian Administration, 1870-1882." *Journal of Presbyterian History* 54 (1976): 259-76.

(390) Washburn, Cephas. *Reminiscences of the Indians.* Richmond: Presbyterian Committee of Publication, 1869.

XXII. MISCELLANEOUS INDIAN MISSIONS SPONSORED BY THE AMERICAN BOARD OF COMMISSIONERS FOR FOREIGN MISSIONS

(391) Anderson, Rufus. *Memorial Volume of the First Fifty Years of the American Board of Commissioners for Foreign Missions.* Boston: The Board, 1861.

(392) Andrew, John A. III. *Rebuilding the Christian Commonwealth: New England Congregationalists and Foreign Missions, 1800-1830.* Lexington: University of Kentucky Press, 1976.

(393) Bartlett, Samuel C. *Sketches of the Missions of the American Board.* Boston: The Board, 1872.

(394) Bass, Althea. "William Schenck Robertson." *Chronicles of Oklahoma* 37 (1959): 28-34.

(395) Bullen, Robert W. "Joseph Bullen, Some Biographical Notes." *Journal of Mississippi History* 27 (1965): 265-67.

(396) Edwards, John. "An Account of My Escape from the South in 1861." Muriel H. Wright, ed. *Chronicles of Oklahoma* 43 (1965): 58-89.

(397) Foreman, Carolyn Thomas. "Augusta Robertson Moore." *Chronicles of Oklahoma* 13 (1935): 399-420.

(398) ———. "Fairfield Mission." *Chronicles of Oklahoma* 37 (1959): 373-88.

(399) ———. "Hopefield Mission in Osage Nation, 1823-1837." *Chronicles of Oklahoma* 28 (1959): 193-205.

(400) Holway, Hope. "Ann Eliza Worcester Robinson as a Linguist." *Chronicles of Oklahoma* 37 (1959): 35-44.

(401) Jones, Dorsey D. "Cephas Washburn and His Work in Arkansas." *Arkansas Historical Quarterly* 3 (1944): 125-36.

(402) Lindsey, Lilah Denton. "Memoirs of the Indian Territory Mission Field." *Chronicles of Oklahoma* 36 (1958): 181-98.

(403) Loomis, Augustus W. "Scenes in the Indian Territory: Kowetah Mission." *Chronicles of Oklahoma* 46 (1968): 64-72.

(404) Miller, Floyd E. "Hillside Mission." *Chronicles of Oklahoma* 4 (1926): 223-28.

(405) Miller, Lona Eaton. "Wheelock Mission." *Chronicles of Oklahoma* 29 (1951): 314-23.

(406) Oliphant, J. Orin. *Through the South and the West with Jeremiah Evarts in 1826.* Lewisburg PA: Bucknell University Press, 1956.

(407) Phillips, Clifton J. *Protestant America and the Pagan World: The First Half Century of the American Board of Commissioners for Foreign Missions, 1810-1860.* Cambridge: Harvard University Press, 1969.

(408) Reed, Ora Eddleman. "The Robe Family—Missionaries." *Chronicles of Oklahoma* 26 (1948): 301-12.

(409) Strong, William E. *The Story of the American Board: An Account of the First Hundred Years of the American Board of Commissioners for Foreign Missions.* Boston: Pilgrim Press, 1910.

(410) Thomson, Louise. "A Cross Section in the Life of a Missionary Teacher among the Indians." *Chronicles of Oklahoma* 17 (1939): 323-32.

(411) Tracy, E. C. *Memoir of the Life of Jeremiah Evarts, Esq.* Boston: Crocker and Brewster, 1845.

(412) Wright, Muriel H. "Notes on the Life of Mrs. Hannah Worcester Hicks Hitchcock and the Park Hill Press." *Chronicles of Oklahoma* 19 (1941): 348-55.

XXIII. MISCELLANEOUS MORAVIAN INDIAN MISSIONS

(413) Loskiel, George J. *History of the Mission of the United Brethren among the Indians in North America.* London: Brethren's Society for the Furtherance of the Gospel, 1794.

(414) Schwarze, Edmund. *History of the Moravian Missions among Southern Indian Tribes of the United States.* Bethlehem PA: Times Publishing, 1923.

XXIV. MISCELLANEOUS MENNONITE INDIAN MISSIONS

(415) Board of Missions, General Conference, Mennonite Church. *Among the Cheyenne and Arapaho Indians in Oklahoma: Seventy-Five Years of General Conference Mission Work.* Newton KS: Board of Missions, General Conference, Mennonite Church, 1955.

(416) Dalke, Herbert M. "Seventy-five Years of Missions in Oklahoma." *Mennonite Life* 10 (July 1955): 100-107.

(417) Juhnke, James C. "General Conference Mennonite Missions to the American Indians in the Late Nineteenth Century." *Mennonite Quarterly Review* 54 (1980): 117-34.

(418) Kaufman, Edmund G. "Mennonite Missions among the Oklahoma Indians." *Chronicles of Oklahoma* 40 (1962): 41-54.

(419) Krehbiel, Christian. "The Beginnings of Missions in Oklahoma." Elva Krehbiel Leisy, trans. *Mennonite Life* 10 (July 1955): 108-13.

(420) Linscheid, Ruth C. *Red Moon.* Newton KS: United Printing, 1973.

XXV. MISCELLANEOUS INDIAN MISSIONS

(421) Balyeat, Frank A. "Joseph Samuel Morrow, Apostle to the Indians." *Chronicles of Oklahoma* 36 (1957): 297-313.

(422) Corwin, Hugh D. "Saddle Mission and Church." *Chronicles of Oklahoma* 36 (1958): 118-30.

(423) Foreman, Carolyn Thomas. "New Hope Seminary, 1844-1897." *Chronicles of Oklahoma* 22 (1944): 271-99.

(424) _____. "North Fork Town." *Chronicles of Oklahoma* 29 (1951): 79-111.

(425) Foreman, Grant, ed. "Missionaries of the Latter Day Saints Church in Indian Territory." *Chronicles of Oklahoma* 13 (1935): 196-213.

(426) Harper, Richard H. "The Missionary Work of the Reformed (Dutch) Church in America in Oklahoma." *Chronicles of Oklahoma* 18 (1940): 252-65, 328-47; 19 (1941): 170-79.

(427) Holway, Hope. "Union Mission, 1826-1837." *Chronicles of Oklahoma* 40 (1962): 355-78.

(428) Kjaer, Jens Christian. "The Lutheran Mission at Oaks, Oklahoma." *Chronicles of Oklahoma* 28 (1950): 42-51.

XXVI. INDIAN MISSIONS AND THE SLAVERY CONTROVERSY

(429) Lewitt, Robert T. "Indian Missions and Antislavery Sentiment: A Conflict of Evangelical and Humanitarian Ideals." *Mississippi Valley Historical Review* (now *Journal of American History*) 50 (1963): 39-55.

(430) McLoughlin, William G. "Indian Slaveholders and Presbyterian Missionaries, 1837-1861." *Church History* 42 (1973): 535-51 [see also 14].

(431) _____. "Red Indians, Black Slavery, and White Racism: America's Slaveholding Indians." *American Quarterly* 26 (1974): 367-85 [see also 14].

(432) Morrison, James D. "Note on Abolitionism in the Choctaw Nation." *Chronicles of Oklahoma* 38 (1960): 78-84.

(433) Speck, F. G. "The Negroes and the Creek Nation." *Southern Workman* 38 (1908): 106-110.

XXVII. THE CONTROVERSY OVER GOVERNMENT FUNDS FOR MISSION SCHOOLS

(434) Casey, M. P. "Indian Contract Schools." *Catholic World* 71 (1902): 629-37.

(435) "Catholics and Indian Schools." *Outlook* 102 (1912): 234-35.

(436) "Critics of Religious Garb in Indian Schools." *Literary Digest* 44 (2 March 1912): 428.

(437) Dorchester, Daniel. "Government Schools and Contract Schools." *Lend a Hand* 10 (1893): 118-26.

(438) Edwards, Martha L. "A Problem of Church and State in the 1870's." *Mississippi Valley Historical Review* (now *Journal of American History*) 11 (1924): 37-53.

(439) Elliott, Richard B. "Government Secularization of the Education of Catholic Indian Youth." *American Catholic Quarterly Review* 25 (1900): 148-68.

(440) "Indian Appropriations for Sectarian Schools." *Outlook* 79 (28 January 1905): 221-22.

(441) "Indian Church Schools: The Way Out." *Outlook* 82 (3 February 1906): 247-48.

(442) "Indian Funds for Sectarian Schools." *Independent* 63 (19 December 1907): 1507-1508.

(443) "Indian Government Schools." *Outlook* 100 (30 March 1912): 718-19.

(444) Indian Rights Association. *Indian Trust Funds for Sectarian Schools*. Philadelphia: Indian Rights Association, 1905.

(445) _____. *Shall Public Funds Be Expended for the Support of Sectarian Schools?* Philadelphia: Indian Rights Association, 1914.

(446) "The Indian Schools." *Independent* 60 (12 April 1906): 883-84.

(447) *Indian Tribal Funds: The Case for the Catholic Indians Stated*. New York: Marquette League, n.d.

(448) Leupp, Francis E. "Indian Funds and Mission Schools." *Outlook* 83 (9 June 1906): 315-19.

(449) Marty, Martin. "The Indian Problem and the Catholic Church." *Catholic World* 48 (1889): 577-84.

(450) *Memorandum Relative to Commissioner Morgan's Indian School Policy, and to the Mission School for the Education of the Indians*. N.p.p.: n.p., n.d.

(451) Mitchell, Fredric. "Church-State Conflict: A Little-Known Part of the Continuing Church-State Conflict Found in Early Indian Education." *Journal of American Indian Education* 2 (May 1963): 7-14.

(452) _____, and James W. Skelton. "The Church-State Conflict in Early Indian Education." *History of Education Quarterly* 6 (1966): 41-51.

(453) Morgan, Thomas J. *Roman Catholics and Indian Education: An Address by Hon. T. J. Morgan, Ex-Commissioner of Indian Affairs, Del'v'd in Music Hall, Boston, Mass., Sunday, April 16, 1893*. Boston: American Citizen, 1893.

(454) National League for the Protection of American Institutions. *A Petition Concerning Sectarian Appropriations for Indian Education*. New York: n.p., 1892.

(455) "The Nuns'-Garb Question." *Literary Digest* 45 (12 October 1912): 626.

(456) Palladino, L. B. *Education for the Indian: Fancy and Reason on the Subject: Contract Schools and Non-Sectarianism in Indian Education*. New York: Benziger Brothers, 1892.

(457) Prucha, Francis P. *Churches and the Indian Schools*. Lincoln: University of Nebraska Press, 1979.

(458) "Public Money Diverted for Catholic Schools." *Christian Century* 62 (1945): 101, 243, 338.

(459) "Religious Garb in Indian Schools." *Independent* 72 (15 February 1912): 374-75.

(460) "Religious Garb in Indian Schools." *Literary Digest* 44 (24 February 1912): 379-80.

(461) Rothensteiner, John E. "The Champion of the Catholic Indian Schools." *Central Blatt and Social Justice* (now *Social Justice Review*) 17 (1924): 161-63.

(462) Sievers, Harry J. "The Catholic Indian School Issue and the Presidential Election of 1892." *Catholic Historical Review* 38 (1952): 129-55.

(463) "The State, the Church, and the Indian." *Outlook* 79 (11 February 1905): 370-72.

(464) "Trust Funds for Catholic Schools." *Nation* 80 (9 February 1905): 106.

(465) *The Two Sides of the School Question, as Set Forth in the Annual Meeting of the National Education Association, Held at Nashville, Tennessee, July, 1889, by Cardinal Gibbons and Bishop Keane on the One Hand, and Edwin D. Mead and Hon. John Jay on the Other.* Boston: Committee of One Hundred, 1890.

(466) "Unfair Indian Fighting." *Outlook* 79 (4 February 1905): 263-65.

XXVIII. INDIAN SECTARIANISM

(467) House, R. Morton. " 'The Only Way' Church and the Sac and Fox Indians." *Chronicles of Oklahoma* 43 (1965): 443-66.

(468) LaBarre, Weston. *The Peyote Cult.* New York: Schocken Books, 1969.

(469) Marriott, Alice, and Carol K. Rachlin. *Peyote.* New York: New American Library, 1971.

(470) Rachlin, Carol K. "Native American Church in Oklahoma." *Chronicles of Oklahoma* 42 (1964): 262-72.

4 THE RELIGIOUS EXPERIENCE OF SOUTHERN BLACKS: BLACK-WHITE INTERACTION IN SOUTHERN RELIGION

BLACK AMERICANS have been part of Southern life since the arrival in Virginia of the first slave in 1619. But not until recently, as a consequence of the civil rights movement of the 1950s and 1960s, has the story of Black religious life come to be regarded as integral to the overall heritage of Southern religion. The omission of Black religion from serious consideration is no doubt the result of the same complex of forces that produced the history of oppression in slavery and repression in discrimination. Just as white domination in slavery required professing superiority to blacks and consciously ignoring the dynamics of black culture, so the domination of white evangelical Protestantism required ignoring the dynamics of black religion or at least seeing it as inferior to and on the periphery of the mainstream of Christianity. What attention religiously whites gave to blacks emerged from a troubled conscience. Mindful of their Christian duty to convert the heathen, white slaveowners had in one side of their souls an urge to instruct the slaves in the basic precepts of Christianity. In the other side they recognized that to teach slaves could be tantamount to acknowledging the humanity if not the equality of those slaves who received the freedom that Christianity promised with baptism. Too often forgotten is the conviction among black Christians even in the days of slavery that in Christianity they found a God beyond racial distinction and a way to view the world that transcended racial differences.

As white interpreters analyzed "religion in the South," they fell into the same dilemma. One side of their scholarly consciences no doubt prodded them to include analysis of the black experience and its contributions to the religious life of the region, while the other recognized that to do so would be to expose the lingering weaknesses in the dominant white evangelical style, with its emphasis on personal rather than social ethics that allowed it to sidestep the links between religion and racism. When scholars did treat the black experience in religion, they tended to put it into categories of its own, a phenomenon—and a curious one at that—that existed alongside of the "real" religion of the white evangelical Protestants, but which had few interconnections with it and certainly little impact on its development. As a result white scholars especially have tended to forget that the story of Southern religion and of the development of the various denominations in the South is a biracial phenomenon, one marked from the beginning by black-white interaction. Some of the problems were brought to the attention of scholars nearly half a century ago in an essay by Haven P. Perkins, "Religion for Slaves: Difficulties and Methods" (53). Also see Charles H. Long, "Perspectives for a Study of Afro-American Religion in the United States" (18).

Yet when interpreters, whether black or white, have focused their attention on religion in the life of Southern blacks, they have almost uniformly come to one conclusion: religion has been the single most important force operating within American black culture from the days of slavery to the present. The first synoptic views of the black religious experience, not restricted in scope to the religious life of blacks in the South, came from the hands of black scholars, and while they are dated and need revision in light of more recent knowledge, particularly of the antebellum period, they remain basic starting points that reveal the appreciation the authors had for the cohesive and unifying power of black religious institutions. They were convinced that to understand the character of black history in the United States and the dynamics of black culture one had to look first at the black church. First among these older studies is W. E. B. DuBois, *The Souls of Black Folk* (8). This collection of poignant essays stresses the ways in which religion provided not only comfort in the present, but hope for the future to a people comfortless and hopeless by the standards of the society around them because of slavery and discrimination. Without religion, argued DuBois in a theme that undergirds his dramatic portrayal of the pulse of black culture at the turn of the twentieth century, black society would have lacked the strength to withstand the dehumanizing power of white oppression. Many of these themes were developed more fully by DuBois in his *The Negro Church* (7). Intended as a more academic study is Carter G. Woodson, *The History of the Negro Church* (33). In the first full treatment of black religion in the United States from slavery to the twentieth century, Woodson echoed DuBois in claiming for the church the central role in black culture. The two other older classic studies are Benjamin E. Mays and Joseph W. Nicholson, *The Negro's Church* (21), and E.

Franklin Frazier, *The Negro Church in America* (10). All these writers noted the systematic attempts of slave traders to snuff out remnants of tribal religions that might have survived the calamities of transatlantic passage. All assumed that the contours of black Christianity were taken over from the style of Protestantism preached to the slaves prior to emancipation. All noted the development of independent black denominations in the nineteenth century—some in the North prior to the Civil War, but most in the South coming after—and all commented on the central role played by the church within the black community in the South once freedom was attained. They also analyzed the leadership role accruing to black clergy as representatives of the people. Of these older studies, the one by Frazier is perhaps the most comprehensive in terms of treating the sweep of American black religious history, urban and rural variants, and the inner dynamics of black religion. But it should be consulted along with C. Eric Lincoln, *The Black Church since Frazier* (17), which contains not only the text of Frazier's work, but also additional materials by Lincoln that not only update the story but also point to new avenues of interpretation that emerged after the civil rights movement and a deeper sensitivity to the penetration of racism in scholarship had made an impact. Among other pioneering studies are Ruby F. Johnston's *The Development of Negro Religion* (14) and her *The Religion of Negro Protestants* (15).

The first major dissenting voice, which suggested there was another side to the story, was that of Joseph R. Washington, Jr. In his *Black Religion* (27), Washington did not deny the major themes suggested by his predecessors, but insisted that the Christianity that flourished among black Americans was not the same as normative orthodox Christianity that could trace roots back to the first century A.D. Rather, Washington asserted, the Christianity espoused by black Americans was a folk religion, a watered-down version of mainstream Christianity that owed its distortion to the white slaveowners who foisted on Afro-Americans a gospel that stressed only selected features of the New Testament and the Christian tradition, those designed to foster subservience and obedience with the hope of future rewards for faithfulness now. Washington's book had a tone of resentment. It was clear, perhaps because of the impact of neoorthodox theology on his thinking, that he regarded white Protestantism as genuine and black Christianity as a poor stepchild. That opinion was dramatically reversed in Washington's second book, *The Politics of God* (29). In this work, Washington advanced the thesis that white Christianity itself was a folk religion that had diluted its own integrity because it had perpetuated an insidious racism that had no place in the authentic proclamation of the gospel. No longer did he bemoan the ways in which black Christianity differed from white Christianity nor did he any longer demand that blacks experience the Christian tradition as did whites. Rather he suggested that the only way white Christianity could become faithful to the gospel was to experience the redemption that could come only from the hands of a suffering community, the black church, for the suffering inflicted by slavery and discrimination had rendered the black church the only means of redemption for the folk religion of white Protestantism. In *Black Sects and Cults* (28), Washington directed attention to the numerous smaller Christian movements that have attracted the allegiance of blacks, but rather than viewing them as aberrations on the fringe or as mere urban adaptations of a Southern rural religious style, Washington claimed that the sectarian movements were a clear demonstration of the ways in which an ethic of justice combined with a striving for power had penetrated black Christianity throughout its history in the United States.

Many of the ideas advanced by Washington, particularly his views of the complicated dynamics of the relationship between black Christianity and white Protestantism, formed the core for what has become known as "black theology." This essay will not treat black theology in detail. While it represents a serious effort to examine the black religious experience systematically and with the same intellectual sophistication that has marked the theological enterprise historically in the Western religious traditions, black theology has found its most vocal proponents in persons who have labored in universities and seminaries outside the South, though as individuals many of them—Preston Williams and George Kelsey, for examples—have Southern roots. One reason, of course, why so much of black theology has emerged in Northern seminaries and universities is the systematic exclusion of blacks from Southern graduate schools until the past two to three decades. In addition, as with much of religious thought in any tradition, it is still not at all clear that the theological reflections of academics have a significant impact on the rank and file. Rather, such work tends to be addressed more to the circle of theologians and the educated elite within a tradition and consequently to have a limited influence on the religious experience of ordinary folk. The best survey of black theology, linking contemporary developments to the more historically oriented work of Washington, is James Cone, "Black Religious Thought," in *Encyclopedia of Religion in America* (1:113).

That the multifaceted functions of religion within the black community had a direct connection to the protest movements of the civil rights era is the thrust of Gayraud S. Wilmore's important work, *Black Religion and Black Radicalism* (32). Wilmore forcefully demonstrates how the pressures of discrimination and the striving for stable identity fashioned black religious institutions into well-organized cadres of individuals committed to implementing within the cultural order the social principles of justice and equality that had emerged from religious conviction. Unwittingly, then, white religion's attempt to push black religion to the periphery following emancipation had a catalytic effect in promoting racial and ethnic pride that ultimately demanded an end to oppression and repression. One of the few Southern voices recognizing the implications of the white response to black religion, from the efforts to control Black religious experience during slavery to the post-Civil war social and religious separatism fostered by discrimination, was that of Willis D. Weatherford. Weatherford, whose insistence that religion had social as well as individual ethical nuances will be noted in another chapter, was a minority voice in the South, but his *American Churches and the Negro: An Historical Study from Early Slave Days to the Present* (31) serves as a reminder that some white Southerners were sensitive to the complexity of black religion and understood the consequences of white discrimination and oppression.

But all commentators are agreed that one cannot understand the American black religious experience without taking a close look at the religion of slaves. The standard study that synthesizes much of the earlier scholarship on slave religion is Albert J. Raboteau, *Slave Religion: The "Invisible Institution" in the Antebellum South* (55). One advantage of Raboteau's work is its comparison and contrast of the black religious experience that developed in North America with the rather different, somewhat more syncretistic religious style that was emerging at the same time in Latin America and the Caribbean. Similar in focus to Raboteau's study, but drawing more heavily on local church records to make its case, is Mechal Sobel, *Trabelin' On: The Slave Journey to an Afro-Baptist Faith* (60). Lawrence Levine, in the opening chapter of *Black Culture and Black Consciousness,* entitled "The Sacred World of Black Slaves" (48), adds to the picture by drawing on anthropological methods and interpretive constructs. The later antebellum period is the subject of Olli Alho, *The Religion of the Slaves: A Study of the Religious Tradition and Behavior of Plantation Slaves in the United States, 1830-1865* (35). Alho overemphasizes folkloric dimensions of slave religion, but otherwise his study is quite conventional. John W. Blassingame, in *The Slave Community: Plantation Life in the Antebellum South* (37), and Michael R. Bradley, "The Role of the Black Church in the Colonial Slave Society" (38), both highlight the function of religion in creating a sense of community within slave society, in offering opportunities for leadership abilities to come to the fore, in granting some relief from the oppression of the system, and in providing psychological and religious support for individual identity. But the best short treatment of slave religion is found in Eugene D. Genovese, *Roll, Jordan, Roll: The World the Slaves Made* (44). While Genovese tends to examine slave society from a Marxist perspective and might therefore be expected to minimize the importance of religion to the slaves, he cogently argues that the religion of the slaves was the most important single component in slave culture and the major factor in providing support mechanisms that allowed slaves to endure a system of systematic oppression. Donald Blake Touchstone's doctoral dissertation,

"Planters and Slave Religion in the Deep South" (62), argued persuasively that there was a greater willingness on the part of plantation owners to acknowledge and accept a black religious life that was not the same as white religious experience once the major Protestant denominations in the country had split into Northern and Southern branches over the slavery issue. They simply recognized then that no longer would those whites who sought to minister to slaves be advocating abolition of slavery, but offering a message that made loyalty, obedience, and diligent labor religious virtues.

Not all Afro-Americans in the South were plantation slaves. The story of the free blacks is summarized in Ira Berlin, *Slaves without Masters: The Free Negro in the Antebellum South* (36). Berlin, however, gives brief attention to religion, but his work is the best to date and he does at least note that there were some Roman Catholic inroads among the free black population. John T. O'Brien, "Factory, Church, and Community: Blacks in Antebellum Richmond" (52), focuses more narrowly on urban slaves and a smaller number of free blacks in one locale. His conclusion stresses the importance of the well-organized churches, offspring of and generally controlled by white denominations, that had developed to meet the religious needs of urban slaves. There were, of course, some who sought to combine ministry to urban slaves and free blacks. One such person was Charles Colcock Jones, about whom more will be said. But the mission enterprises he supported among urban blacks, slave and free, in Charleston, South Carolina, as well as among plantation slaves in Georgia, is deftly chronicled by T. Erskine Clarke in *Wrestlin' Jacob: A Portrait of Religion in the Old South* (41).

As previously indicated, however, there was considerable ambivalence among Southern whites concerning precisely what moral duty they had to provide for the conversion and religious nurture of the slaves, an ambivalence that marks as well the story of denominational efforts to promote ministry among the slaves. From an institutional standpoint, the picture was clouded because the denominations in most cases had constituencies in both the North and South until shortly before the Civil War erupted and therefore had to balance antislavery and proslavery sentiment, calls for aggressive missions to the slaves and calls for minimal ministry, support for allowing blacks themselves to assume leadership roles in religious work and a reluctance to let control over black religious life slip from white hands. One attempt to tell the overall story of plantation missions is Milton C. Sernett, *Black Religion and American Evangelicalism: White Protestants, Plantation Missions, and the Flowering of Negro Christianity, 1787-1865* (57). But the story stretches back further, and it begins with the work of agents sponsored by the Church of England's Society for the Propagation of the Gospel in the seventeenth and eighteenth centuries. The work of these missionaries was not always well received by white colonists, who feared that educating and evangelizing the slaves would work against the perpetuation of the slave labor system. That story is appraised by John C. Van Horne in "Impediments to the Christianization and Education of Blacks in Colonial America: The Case of the Associates of Dr. Bray" (159). An older, but complementary overview is given by Mary F. Goodwin, "Christianizing and Educating the Negro in Colonial Virginia" (97). A classic first-hand account of the antipathy of white slaveowners, ambivalence among slaves, and occasional hostility among Indians (who were likewise objects of these missionary endeavors) is given in Frank Klingberg, ed., *The Carolina Chronicle of Dr. Francis LeJau, 1706-1717* (113). LeJau, a one-time Huguenot, was a prominent S.P.G. missionary. The ways in which early Anglicans sought to reconcile slavery with their own religious ethics is one subject of Denzil T. Clifton, "Anglicanism and Negro Slavery in Colonial America" (84). As I have suggested previously, part of the ambivalence was the concern that conversion and subsequent baptism placed slaves on an equal basis with masters and was tantamount to recognizing their freedom. The colonial legislative assemblies gradually solved this dilemma by adding to slave codes or similar enactments a provision stating that baptism and conversion did not effect a change in one's status if one were a slave. An interesting twist, though, is found in Warren M. Billings, "The Cases of Fernando and Elizabeth Key: A Note on the Status of Blacks in Seventeenth-Century Virginia" (74). This slave couple sued for their freedom because they were baptized Christians; Elizabeth Key's case was successful, but that of her husband was not. The episode, however, did prompt much of the interest in achieving a legislative response that would deal with such situations permanently.

Perhaps because the Church of England and its post-American Revolution child, the Protestant Episcopal Church, had been established in those areas where slavery early took the firmest hold or perhaps because at least until the late eighteenth or early nineteenth century, the most well-known slaveholders had some sort of connection with the denomination, later Anglican and Episcopalian missionary efforts among Afro-Americans never received the depth of response that those of the more evangelically and emotionally inclined Baptists and Methodists did. It may also have been a question of style, insofar as numerous scholars have noted that the Baptist and Methodist appeal to inner experience was more resonant with the rhythm of Black understanding than the rationalistic ethos of the Anglicans. On this point in particular, see R. E. Hood, "From a Headstart to a Deadstart: The Historical Basis for Black Indifference toward the Episcopal Church, 1800-1860" (105). However, Episcopalians continued modest missionary efforts until the outbreak of hostilities between North and South. This work and the mixed motivation that sustained it can be seen in Stiles B. Lines, "Slaves and Churchmen: The Work of the Episcopal Church among Southern Negroes,

1830-1860'' (116) and J. Carleton Hayden, ''Conversion and Control: Dilemma of Episcopalians in Providing for the Religious Instruction of Slaves, Charleston, South Carolina, 1845-1860'' (103).

Some impetus to missions to slaves came from the Great Awakening, the import of which has already been noted in chapter 2. The same recognition of the equality of all before God that gave rise to the evangelical challenge to Anglican, coastal, and planter-class hegemony also sparked an interest in the conversion of slaves. In Virginia, some of this interest may be traced to Samuel Davies, one of the preachers of the evangelical Awakening; see George W. Pilcher, ''Samuel Davies and the Instruction of Negroes in Virginia'' (136). Denominationally, the Baptists and the Methodists reaped most of the results of the Awakening, and at first at least, the two likewise were among the most active in ministry to slaves. Both, however, as national bodies ultimately divided into regional bodies over the question of slavery.

The overall Baptist story, in terms of attitudes for and against slavery and missions to the slaves, is recounted in an old study that lacks critical judgment in some areas: Mary P. Putnam, *The Baptists and Slavery* (140). More insightful are scholarly articles that treat only aspects of the story. For example, one of the group's first encounters with slavery in the South has been analyzed in a brilliant essay by William G. McLoughlin and Winthrop D. Jordan, ''Baptists Face the Barbarities of Slavery in 1710'' (119). W. Harrison Daniel has ably appraised Baptist attitudes toward and ministries to slaves in Virginia in the period between the American Revolution and the Civil War in two articles, ''Virginia Baptists and the Negro in the Early Republic'' (88), and ''Virginia Baptists and the Negro in the Antebellum Era'' (87). Antebellum Baptist work with slaves in South Carolina is the subject of an unpublished thesis, ''Religious Work of South Carolina Baptists among the Slaves from 1781 to 1830'' by Annie H. Mallard (121). The results of Baptist work with slaves in Georgia prior to the end of the Civil War is the focus of Julia Floyd Smith, ''Marching to Zion: The Religion of Black Baptists in Coastal Georgia Prior to 1865'' (58). As the cotton culture prospered and the population grew, expansion westward from Georgia through Alabama and Mississippi to Louisiana, Arkansas, and Texas saw the extension of slavery through the so-called ''deep South.'' The evangelical denominations likewise moved westward, accepting if not supporting slavery, while feebly attempting to bring Christianity to the slaves. The combination of support for slavery as a labor system and missions to the slaves in one of the areas settled in the first decades of the nineteenth century has been studied by Orville W. Taylor in ''Baptists and Slavery in Arkansas: Relations and Attitudes'' (154). On this point, also see the more general study of David T. Bailey, ''Slavery and the Churches: The Old Southwest'' (70), and Walter B. Posey, ''The Baptists and Slavery in the Lower Mississippi Valley'' (137). The Baptists and Methodists found themselves competitors in slave missions as the South expanded, as Timothy F. Reilly pointed out in "Slavery and the Southwestern Evangelist in New Orleans (1800-1861)" (142). New Orleans may hardly be the typical case, however, for its complex history made it one of the few centers of genuine religious pluralism in the old South. Even after the Baptists split into regional denominations in 1845, Southern Baptists were not necessarily of a single mind with regard to slavery, although there were strident efforts to support and defend the system. On this issue see Glen Jeansonne, "Southern Baptists Attitudes toward Slavery, 1845-1861" (111).

"The Methodist Mission to the Slaves" is chronicled in Thomas L. Williams's doctoral dissertation of that title (163), while two essays tell the story in more synoptic fashion. Important for its attempt to probe the psychology behind Methodist attitudes and their implications for later developments is William B. Gravely, "Early Methodism and Slavery: The Roots of a Tradition" (98). The other cursory overview is Durward Long, "The Methodist Church and Negro Slavery in America, 1784-1844" (117). Methodists had to contend with the strident antislavery attitudes of their founder, John Wesley, but those views could to a certain extent be ignored after the United States became independent since Wesley was also a strident Tory and opponent of the American Revolution. The classic study of Methodism and slavery, however, remains Donald G. Mathews, *Slavery and Methodism: A Chapter in American Morality, 1780-1845* (125). Part of Mathews's work is capsuled in his "The Methodist Mission to the Slaves, 1829-1844" (123). Mathews shows how the presence of slavery affected Methodism's own self-understanding, for as Methodist work in slave areas reaped such harvests, the denomination's General Conference increasingly muted its once firm condemnation of the institution of slavery. But Methodism, following John Wesley, emphasized striving towards perfection, a stance that also led more and more individuals to regard slavery and slaveholding as sins that thwarted the attainment of perfection and, in subtle ways, thwarted the transformation of American society into the epitome of holiness. Complementary to Mathews's study for the early period is Walter B. Posey, "Influence of Slavery upon the Methodist Church in the Early South and Southwest" (138). The hardening of the Southern Methodist defense of slavery as the final showdown between North and South neared can be examined in Lewis M. Purifoy, Jr.'s competently researched and written doctoral dissertation, "The Methodist Episcopal Church, South, and Slavery, 1844-1865" (139), while the perpetuation of racism within Methodist circles and the willingness of the church's leadership to assist former slaves in forming their own Wesleyan denomination—thereby maintaining a separation of the races—is the focus of Eugene Southall, "The Attitude of the Methodist Episcopal Church, South, Toward the Negro from 1844 to 1870" (150).

Presbyterians had some more difficult theological issues with which to wrestle in dealing with their slaves, for the Calvinist notion of predestination contained the implication that one's estate in this life was ordained by God and therefore not subject to manipulation by human beings. Yet who could say that Afro-Americans might not be among God's elect? As W. Harrison Daniel has shown in "Southern Presbyterians and the Negro in the Early National Period" (86), many Presbyterians came to acknowledge that blacks had souls but accepted slavery as the best social arrangement. The same held true as the South and slavery followed cotton westward, as George C. Whatley III has demonstrated in "The Alabama Presbyterian and His Slave, 1830-1864" (161). As others, Presbyterians could trace the paradox in their views to the turmoil of the Revolutionary era when they also had to reconcile maintenance of a slave labor system with an ideology of freedom and equality. On this latter point, see J. Earl Thompson, Jr., "Slavery and Presbyterianism in the Revolutionary Era" (156). In the nineteenth century, as Andrew Murray demonstrated in "Bright Delusion: Presbyterians and African Colonization" (130), some Presbyterians looked to resettlement of black Americans in Africa as the only way out of the racial impasse.

But no Presbyterian confronted the ambiguities of slavery more than Charles Colcock Jones. From a prominent Southern slaveholding family, Jones studied at Princeton Theological Seminary and there imbibed some of the antislavery sentiment that was increasing in the North. Returning to the South, he determined to commit his life first, somewhat idealistically, to ending the slave system, and then, more in keeping with accommodation to harsh social reality, to ministry to the slaves. His work is surveyed and appraised in several essays. Wayne C. Tyner, "Charles Colcock Jones: Missionary to Slaves" (158), notes that Jones's approach was ultimately ameliorative, but Donald G. Mathews, "Charles Colcock Jones and the Southern Evangelical Crusade to Form a Biracial Community" (122), as the title suggests, claims that an ideal of a racially inclusive society never left Jones. Barbara Anne Byrnes, "Charles C. Jones and the Intellectual Crisis of the Antebellum South" (79), stresses the sense of guilt among slaveholders who found it increasingly difficult to accept the justification of slavery on religious grounds, particularly when the work of persons like Jones gave clear evidence of its falsity. Jones's leadership in Presbyterian urban ministry with both slaves and free blacks is the subject of T. Erskine Clarke, "An Experiment in Paternalism: Presbyterians and Slaves in Charleston, South Carolina" (83) as well as of his monograph, *Wrestlin' Jacob,* previously noted.

Roman Catholic missions to the slaves are too frequently neglected because they were not very successful in obtaining converts or in challenging the slave system itself. An old, but useful summary is Stephen L. Theobald, "Catholic Missionary Work among the Colored People of the United States

(1776-1866)'' (155), while the now dated study by John C. Murphy, *An Analysis of the Attitudes of American Catholics toward the Immigrant and the Negro* (128), attempts to probe ideology and its relation to intention and action. An important recent study whose range is not restricted to the South is Maria Genovino Caravaglios, *The American Catholic Church and the Negro Problem in the XVIII-XIX Centuries* (81). The need to look more closely at Roman Catholic work with African slaves has been forcefully brought to the attention of scholars by Randall M. Miller, "Black Catholics in the Slave South: Some Needs and Opportunities for Study" (126). Miller's "The Failed Mission: The Catholic Church and Black Catholics in the Old South" (127) is perhaps the best brief scholarly analysis to date of the faltering Roman Catholic labors with black Americans, slave and free. As with other religious bodies, so, too, with American Catholics: the attempt to minister to slaves was distorted because Catholics themselves were slaveholders. Much of the early Catholic mission work in the United States oriented to whites as well as blacks was spearheaded by the Jesuits, whose dilemmas as slaveholders have been recounted in Peter C. Finn, "The Slaves of the Jesuits in Maryland" (95). Some blacks not only became devout Catholics, but they also took up the religious life. On this matter, see Michael J. McNally, "A Minority of a Minority: The Witness of Black Religious Women in the Antebellum South" (120).

Other religious bodies also found themselves involved with slavery either as sponsors of mission work or groups whose adherents were caught in the morass of slaveholding and its attendant problems, though perhaps not to the extent of those already discussed. Southern Jews, for example, another minority present from the early days of European settlement and one in the twentieth century identified in the popular mind with a procivil rights position, were in many cases slave owners and traders and confronted the same ambiguities as others in sorting through the morality of their actions. The best study, and a solid one, of Southern Jews' attitudes and actions is Bertram W. Korn, *Jews and Negro Slavery in the Old South, 1789-1865* (114). Rarely, but occasionally, Afro-Americans would identify themselves as Jews. For one instance, see Ralph Melnick, "Billy Simons: The Black Jew of Charleston" (50). Lutherans in the South were also slaveowners and defended slavery on economic grounds: while Lutheran efforts to convert Afro-Americans were not extensive, by the mid-nineteenth century, there were some slaves who had identified with this tradition less from choice than from having owners who happened to be Lutherans. Two articles tell the story: Thomas R. Noon, "Early Black Lutherans in the South (to 1865)" (132), and Douglas C. Stange, " 'A Compassionate Mother to Her Poor Negro Slaves': The Lutheran Church and Negro Slavery in Early America" (151). The American Home Missionary Society, essentially a Congregationalist agency, also supported a limited mission ministry to Afro-American slaves in the South. The work and its scant results are the subject of a doctoral dissertation by Charles T. Thrift, Jr., "The Operations of the American Home Missionary Society in the South, 1826-1861" (157). The Mormon migration westward brought Joseph Smith's followers for a time into the slave state of Missouri. Mormon doctrine, until the late 1970s, insisted that blacks were inferior to whites, though it was not necessarily the contact with slavery in Missouri that led to that doctrine. For a general view, see Newell G. Bringhurst, "The Mormons and Slavery—A Closer Look" (76).

What results did all these efforts to convert and minister to the slaves have? First, it is clear that the evangelical denominations that espoused an affective religious experience as the basis for conversion—the Baptist and the Methodist—became the churches with which most blacks who converted identified and which would over time give birth to the strongest and largest black denominations. Precisely how many converts there were while slavery remained the basis of the Southern labor system will no doubt be forever unknown, though some denominations did attempt to keep statistics of the number of their "colored" members. It is also becoming increasingly clear that blacks were more actively involved in biracial congregations, despite the system of slavery, than most analysts have hitherto conceded. Second, there was a connection between religion and attempts to rebel against the system on the part of the slaves. The leaders of the two most well-known revolts, one of which was quashed before it began, were Denmark Vesey and Nat Turner. Both had close ties to slave religion and religious leaders. Instructive in showing connections between rebellion and religion as well as in illustrating how white fear of slave insurrection played into the ambiguity shared by many over what should be done about religious instruction for the slaves are Vincent Harding, "Religion and Resistance among Ante-Bellum Negroes, 1800-1860" (45), and his powerful *There Is a River: The Black Struggle for Freedom in America* (46). Third, prior to the Civil War, there did exist examples of biracial local congregations. There is also evidence of black converts moving into positions of leadership not only in the slave community but occasionally in the white community. Indeed, as Kenneth K. Bailey demonstrated in "Protestantism and Afro-Americans in the Old South" (71), there were even some predominantly white congregations with black pastors. Fourth, as antislavery sentiment in the nation mounted and then as the Civil War brought a radical realignment of the Southern social structure, some biracial congregations divided along racial lines, ostensibly because blacks wanted more autonomy. A case study of a biracial congregation in Tennessee that by Reconstruction had split into two bodies is Mechal Sobel, " 'They Can Never Both Prosper Together': Black and White Baptists in Nashville, Tennessee" (149). When splits did occur, the new black congregations and denominations generally maintained the polity and doctrines of the former biracial groups. On this point, see Will B. Gravely, "The Rise of African Churches in America (1786-1822): Re-examining the Contexts" (363), which has important implications for the Southern situation even though it focuses on Northern groups. Fifth, labors among slaves also paved the way for the emergence of a distinctive black Christian identity that was to be of greater import in the decades after emancipation, according to Timothy L. Smith, "Slavery and Theology: The Emergence of Black Christian Consciousness in Nineteenth-Century America" (59). Sixth, the watered-down version of Protestantism presented to the slaves, so deplored by Joseph Washington, did mean that some Afro-Americans refused to escape when opportunity presented itself and did truly believe that loyalty and obedience to masters were hallmarks of the Christian slave. On this point, see Randall M. Miller, " 'It Is Good to be Religious': A Loyal Slave on God, Masters, and the Civil War" (51). Finally, slave ministry forced whites to make a decision whether to promote or to oppose slavery itself.

Religious dimensions of Southern proslavery arguments, as well as the ways in which antislavery advocates, primarily in the North but also in the South, linked their position to religion, have spawned a voluminous interpretive literature. H. Shelton Smith's *In His Image But . . . : Racism in Southern Religion, 1780-1910* (241), while traditionalist in approach, is a meticulous study of the direct and indirect ways in which a racist mentality penetrated the core of Southern religion, even in the thinking of those who were given to antislavery sentiment. Smith's work stands as a potent reminder that mission enterprises directed toward the slaves and qualms about the morality of maintaining a slave labor system did not mean that their advocates espoused racial equality or even the ideal of a racially pluralistic society. A solid overall study is James D. Essig, *The Bonds of Wickedness: American Evangelicals against Slavery* (186). The best appraisals of the feeble antislavery movement in the South prior to the Civil War are Gordon Finnie, "The Antislavery Movement in the Upper South before 1840" (191), which looks at the failure of the enterprise, and Donald G. Mathews, "Religion and Slavery: The Case of the American South" (228). Mathews's basic contention is that while there were committed antislavery and abolitionist elements in the major evangelical denominations (Baptist, Methodist, Presbyterian), religious and social structures rendered it impossible for them to mount a cohesive movement. Where such a movement did surface, it received the active endorsement and support of the black churches, as Carol V. P. George demonstrated in "Widening the Circle: The Black Church and the Abolitionist Crusade, 1830-1860" (192). Many religious groups with constituencies in both the North and the South had a particularly difficult time in coming to grips with competing proslavery and antislavery sentiment within their ranks, especially groups that were themselves minority movements subject to other sorts of recrimination in the larger society. The Roman Catholic Church is a case in point. The inner tensions are adeptly portrayed in the excellent revised dissertation of Madeleine H. Rice, *American Catholic Opinion in the Slavery Controversy* (237). On the Catholic situation, also see Benjamin J. Blied, "Catholicism and Abolitionism" (172). Similar tensions confronted newer religious movements, as in the case of what are now the Disciples of Christ and the Churches of Christ (a single phenomenon at the time of their origins in the frontier revivals). Founder Alexander Campbell's wrestling with these issues is summarized by Earl E. Eminhizer, "Alexander Campbell's Thoughts on Slavery and Abolition" (184). Sometimes episodes occurred that were construed by slaveowners as attacks on the South's "peculiar institution" when they were not that at all. John B. Boles, in "Tension in a Slave Society: The Trial of the Reverend Jacob Gruber" (173), recounts one such incident when this Methodist preacher conducted a campmeeting in Maryland in 1819 with a racially mixed audience. The resulting panic among slaveowners led to Gruber's arrest on charges of inciting slaves to revolt, though he was acquitted. But in the very early years of the antislavery movement, the Baptists of Virginia are typical. James D. Essig, "A Very Wintry Season: Baptists and Slavery, 1785-1797" (188), noted the range of attitudes that prevailed among these folk: some eschewed slave ownership as a sign of unChristian worldliness, some attempted to ignore its blight, while others argued that the system might be reformed from within. As Essig noted, the last position paved the way for the later assertion in proslavery religious circles that slavery was a positive good in society.

Those who had reservations about slavery, especially clergy, often kept their views to themselves lest their ministry to slaveowners lost its effectiveness. One such person is the North Carolina Presbyterian minister who is the focus of George Troxler, "Eli Caruthers: A Silent Dissenter in the Old South" (250). "Robert L. Stanton, Abolitionist of the Old South," the subject of Timothy F. Reilly's article (236), was born in New England, but was called to a pastorate in New Orleans and then to the presidency of Oakland College in Mississippi. His antislavery views ultimately led him to abandon work in the South and remove to Ohio in 1845. Some attempted to straddle the fence, hoping for gradual emancipation and perhaps recolonization in Africa, but detested abolitionism and abolitionists as fanatics who did not appreciate the delicacy of the Southern situation. Presbyterian pastor and later college president Robert J. Breckenridge fits into this category, as evidenced in Will D. Gilliam, Jr., "Robert Jefferson Breckenridge, 1800-1871" (194). Increasingly, however, Southern evangelicals felt pressures from their counterparts in the North and in Britain to acknowledge the inconsistency between their religious and social perspectives. Thomas F. Harwood, "British Evangelical

Abolitionism and American Churches in the 1830's'' (199), documents some of the external forces at work, as does W. Harrison Daniel, "English Presbyterians, Slavery, and the American Crisis of the 1860s'' (181), who noted the cool reception Southerner Moses D. Hoge received in England because of his position on slavery. James B. Stewart, "Evangelicalism and the Radical Strain in Southern Antislavery Thought During the 1820's'' (248), pinpointed one of the telling arguments: slavery was seen to be the primary cause for a presumed decline in piety in the South because it undercut evangelical moral values.

Before the Civil War erupted, the Methodists, Baptists, and Presbyterians all split along regional lines. C. Bruce Staiger's older study, "Abolitionism and the Presbyterian Schism of 1837-38'' (247), shows how slavery was a factor in that denomination's earlier division presumably over the value of revivalism, though later separations on the eve of the Civil War were more directly related to slavery. The Methodist division into the Methodist Episcopal Church and the Methodist Episcopal Church, South, came in 1844. As Donald G. Mathews has shown in "The Methodist Schism of 1844 and the Popularization of Antislavery Sentiment'' (227), the break hardened positions on both sides of the question. When the Baptist split came in 1845, Northerners feared that the new Southern Baptist Convention would ignore religious instruction of the slaves in consequence of its freedom to advocate proslavery views without the tempering presence of northern codenominationalists. Northern Baptists established an agency to continue labors among Afro-Americans, as recounted in John R. McKivigan, "The American Baptist Free Mission Society: Abolitionist Reaction to the 1845 Baptist Schism'' (221).

Attempts to justify slavery on religious and biblical grounds were not, of course, limited to the immediate antebellum period, the era of the denominational divisions over the issue. As James R. Hertzler has shown (200), the sermons preached before the trustees of the Georgia colony sought to justify slavery through biblical precept. Much of the biblical argument, as it developed among Southern religionists, centered around an interpretation of the mythic story of Ham as recounted in the Hebrew Bible, the Christian Old Testament. While it is perhaps a bit short of specific evidence and too heavy on analysis in its attempt to apply Claude Lévi-Strauss's notion of myth as a means to mediate contradictions in the social order and Clifford Geertz's understanding of religion as a model of and for reality, Thomas V. Peterson, *Ham and Japheth: The Mythic World of Whites in the Antebellum South* (233) is instructive in showing how use of biblical arguments became central to the religious justification of slavery. Also provocative, if controversial, is Jack P. Maddex, Jr., " 'The Southern Apostasy' Revisited: The Significance of Proslavery Christianity'' (226). Working from a Marxist perspective, Maddex claims that religious arguments were less reflections of a defensive position than they were of a class ideology, for those who espoused them tended to support other kinds of reform that could be construed as libertarian if not liberal.

But it is unlikely that those who argued for slavery would have accepted that analysis. Rather, many saw the perpetuation of slavery as integral to the establishment of the evangelical Eden in the New World, if not a necessary ingredient in paving the way for the millennium, when the close of history would witness the working out of human dilemmas and contradictions in God's terms. Drew Gilpin Faust, for example, in ''Evangelicalism and the Meaning of the Proslavery Argument: The Reverend Thornton Stringfellow of Virginia'' (189), shows how her Baptist subject supported all manner of reform in education, diet, and temperance advocacy, but still insisted that slavery was central to the soul of evangelical Christianity. Two studies of James Henley Thornwell, Presbyterian clergyman and theologian, are also instructive on this point: Charles C. Bishop, ''The Pro-Slavery Argument Reconsidered: James Henley Thornwell, Millennial Abolitionist'' (171), and Philip Leonard's M.A. thesis, ''The Contributions of Presbyterian Orthodoxy to the Pro-Slavery Argument as Exemplified by the Writings of James Henley Thornwell'' (215). But as Jack P. Maddex, Jr., has noted in ''Proslavery Millennialism: Social Eschatology in Antebellum Southern Calvinism'' (225), Southern visions of that culture as a precursor of the millennial kingdom received a serious blow with emancipation and defeat in the Civil War.

Among specific religious groups, a few studies highlight the impact of proslavery thinking. The curious case of Southern Catholics has already been noted, but what is striking is the way in which European immigrant clergy who came to minister in Southern Catholic missionary endeavors tended rather quickly to adopt the prevailing proslavery views of the culture around them. This point has been argued in two important works, one contemporary with the time and one more recent: Giovanni Antonio Grassi, *Notizie varie sullo stato presente della repubblica degli Stati Uniti dell' America* (195), which appeared in 1818, and Sr. Dorothea Olga McCants, *They Came to Louisiana: Letters of a Catholic Mission, 1854-1882* (218), published in 1970. Not all Catholics, however, went this route; see Maria Genovino Caravaglios, ''A Roman Critique of the Pro-Slavery Views of Bishop Martin of Natchitoches, Louisiana'' (177), a particularly interesting case since Natchitoches was the center of one of the enclaves of black Catholics in the South. Unitarians also present a curious case. In the North, Unitarians had become popularly associated not only with liberal stances in religious belief, but also with numerous social reform efforts, including the antislavery movement. But in the South, only the former characteristic tended to be true. Douglas C. Stange, in *Unitarians and Antislavery: Patterns of Antislavery Among American Unitari-*

ans, 1831-1860 (246) and several articles (243-45), has shown how Southern Unitarians generally were more favorably disposed toward slavery than their Northern counterparts. Of the many studies treating the evangelical Protestant denominations' involvement in proslavery advocacy, Lewis M. Purifoy, "The Southern Methodist Church and the Proslavery Argument" (235), is among the most academically solid.

Reconstruction brought many changes institutionally to black religion in the South. Among the most important was the withdrawal of blacks from the white denominations into new, separate black denominations, into congregations of independent black groups that had formed earlier in the North, into separate congregations within predominantly white denominations, or into churches associated with Northern white denominations (again, usually racially separate). As William B. Gravely argued in "The Social, Political, and Religious Significance of the Formation of the Colored Methodist Episcopal Church" (272), now known as the Christian Methodist Episcopal Church, the move to form new denominations such as this one, which emerged from the Methodist Episcopal Church, South, was an important exercise in religious freedom and voluntarism, but it also institutionalized racial segregation. Southern Baptists also witnessed the exodus of most black members, as David O. Moore documented in "The Withdrawal of Blacks from Southern Baptist Churches following Emancipation" (288). Two other studies are important in appraising the shifts within the Southern Baptist tradition: John L. Bell, Jr., "Baptists and the Negro in North Carolina during Reconstruction" (256), and W. Harrison Daniel, "Virginia Baptists and the Negro, 1865-1902" (264).

While the CME formed through a combined black and white initiative, establishment of racially separate congregations was spurred more often by whites than by blacks, and, as Kenneth K. Bailey demonstrated in his revisionist "The Post-Civil War Racial Separations in Southern Protestantism: Another Look" (255), stopped a trend toward biracial congregations that had been on the ascendancy. Nevertheless, the emergence of separate black churches and denominations and the growth of Northern black denominations among Southern blacks did much to provide an ideology of racial uplift—one of the points made by Clarence F. Walker in *A Rock in a Weary Land: The African Methodist Episcopal Church During the Civil War and Reconstruction* (306)—even as it may have aided the freed blacks to accommodate to white expectations, as Robert L. Hall has argued was the case in "Tallahassee's Black Churches, 1865-1885" (275). The new situation also thrust black clergy into a preeminent role within the black community and often within the political sector as well. Two studies that treat this matter are Ronald L. Lewis, "Cultural Pluralism and Black Reconstruction: The Public Career of Richard Cain" (285), a man whose life work included service as a

South Carolina State Senator, United States Congressman, college president, and AME bishop; and Mary J. Bratton, "John Jasper of Richmond: From Slave Preacher to Community Leader" (258). Jasper's ministry at the First African Baptist Church in Richmond brought him national attention. Other valuable articles that have looked at particular local areas as case studies include Thomas F. Armstrong, "The Building of a Black Church: Community in Post Civil War Liberty County, Georgia" (254), and James Smallwood, "The Black Community in Reconstruction Texas: Readjustments in Religion and the Evolution of the Negro Church" (300).

The predominantly white denominations also had to redirect the character of their work among Southern blacks. J. Carleton Hayden, amplifying material in his doctoral dissertation, which concentrated on Virginia (277), charted the new directions Episcopal work took in "After the War: The Mission and Growth of the Episcopal Church among Blacks in the South, 1865-1877" (276), calling attention as well to the muted racism that undergirded much of this ministry. Two studies by John T. Gillard, old but still valuable, discuss the work of the Roman Catholic Church: *The Catholic Church and the American Negro* (437) and *Colored Catholics in the United States* (438). Also in a now outdated but still instructive work, T. B. Moroney assessed "The Condition of Catholic Colored Mission Work in the United States" (290). Origins of new programs of Catholic ministry with former slaves are the focus of William Osborne, "Slavery's Sequel: A Freedman's Odyssey" (449), while John A. Hogan, "Church Work among the Negroes: Letter Dated Galveston, Texas, August 3, 1901" (441), looks at one local situation as a case study. In Louisiana, for example, the long Catholic presence stretching back to French occupation placed Roman Catholics in a unique position, for among the "Creoles de couleur" there was an enclave of black Catholics that antedated the slavery controversy and continued to be part of the black Catholic story after emancipation. The best overall study is Gary B. Mills, *The Forgotten People: Cane River's Creoles of Color* (447), but there are as well two studies of individual congregations that are instructive in providing a glimpse of this often neglected dimension of Black identification with Roman Catholicism: Msgr. Henry Beckers, *A History of the Immaculate Conception Catholic Church, Natchitoches, Louisiana, 1717-1973* (426), and J. J. Callahan, et al., *The History of St. Augustine's Parish: Isle Brevelle, Natchez, La.* (434). The American Baptist Convention sought an entree among the freed blacks, but as Adolph H. Grundman demonstrated in "Northern Baptists and the Founding of Virginia Union University: The Perils of Paternalism" (273), they were not immune to racism or to abetting blacks who sought personal aggrandizement through associating with paternalistic Northerners. Northern Presbyterians also tried to expand work among the former slaves. Their story is told by Steven E. Brooks in "Out of the Galleries: The Northern Presby-

terian Mission in Reconstruction North Carolina'' (260). But also see John
L. Bell, Jr., ''The Presbyterian Church and the Negro in North Carolina during Reconstruction'' (257). Studies of two individuals capture the spirit of
Methodist work. Anne C. Loveland, ''The 'Southern Work' of the Reverend
Joseph C. Hartzell, Pastor of Ames Church in New Orleans, 1870-1873'' (287)
looks at the work of one Northern Methodist ''missionary'' who attempted
to develop educational institutions for blacks and who encountered much resentment from local leaders in the Methodist Episcopal Church, South. Also
see Ralph Morrow, *Northern Methodism and Reconstruction* (291). The links
between Methodism and educational opportunities for blacks are also the focus of William B. Gravely, ed., ''A Black Methodist on Reconstruction in
Mississippi: Three Letters by James Lynch in 1868-1869'' (269), and Gravely's ''James Lynch and the Black Christian Mission During Reconstruction''
in David W. Wills and Richard Newman, eds., *Black Apostles at Home and
Abroad* (424). The Congregationalists' American Missionary Association also
engaged in a considerable work, again emphasizing education, among Southern blacks both before and immediately after the Civil War, though with only
modest success for much of the same reason that Congregationalist missions
to the Indians reaped a scant harvest: the intellectual bent of the denomination
and its insistence on an educated (white) clergy were simply not consonant
with the needs and style of the blacks with whom they worked. Several articles by Larry W. Pearce (320-22) and Joe M. Richardson (323-26) chronicle the labors of those sent by the American Missionary Association. But also
see Clara Merritt DeBoer's doctoral dissertation, ''The Role of Afro-Americans in the Origin and Work of the American Missionary Association, 1839-
1877'' (315). The modest Lutheran work following Reconstruction is highlighted in ''The Alpha Synod of Lutheran Freedmen (1889-1891)'' by Thomas
R. Noon (618). The best brief study of the religious ethos of this era among
Southern blacks is Leon Litwack's ''The Gospel and the Primer,'' a chapter
in his *Been in the Storm So Long: The Aftermath of Slavery* (286).

One result of these endeavors is the continuing identification of numbers
of Southern blacks with denominations that are predominantly white. Those
who remained or became affiliated with the Protestant Episcopal Church first
had their story told in popular, uncritical fashion in George F. Bragg, Jr., *The
History of the Afro-American Group of the Episcopal Church* (584). More
recently, John M. Burgess, *Black Gospel/White Church* (588), and Robert A.
Bennett, ''Black Episcopalians: A History from the Colonial Period to the
Present'' (580), have brought a more academic approach to the literature on
blacks within this denomination. Charles L. Hoskins, *Black Episcopalians in
Georgia* (602), gives a chronicle of developments there from the colonial
period to 1980, but he does not assess reasons why black Episcopalians retained their denominational allegiance after the Civil War when black de-

nominations became an important part of the overall story. An important, albeit sketchy, overview of the black experience within what is now the United Methodist Church is Julius E. DelPino, "Blacks in the United Methodist Church from Its Beginning to 1968" (594), while influences on Methodist worship form the focus of Maceo D. Pembroke, "Black Worship Experience in the United Methodist Church" (620). The most comprehensive study, however, is William B. McClain, *Black People in the Methodist Church: Whither Thou Goest?* (614). Relatively little work has been done on the labors of black Methodists who were associated structurally first with the Northern wing of the denomination and then with the segregated annual conferences following the 1939 merger until they were phased out in the late 1960s and early 1970s. The best study, albeit brief, is Homer M. Keever, "The Methodist Church (1866) in North Carolina" (606). But also see *Passionate Journey: History of the 1866 South Carolina Annual Conference* by John W. Curry (593) for a more full chronicle of the former predominantly black unit that had the largest membership of any of these conferences prior to being administratively united with the predominantly white conferences. The need for more intensive research on the black experience within the Methodist tradition (and, one might add, within other predominantly white religious groups) has been stressed by David M. Reimers in "Negro Leadership in the Methodist Episcopal Church, 1900-1920: A Plea for Research in Negro Church History" (626). Robert T. Maxey has chronicled the history of black involvement in the Disciples of Christ denomination in popular fashion in *One Wide River* (616). But there is, of course, much more to the story of Southern black religious life.

The history of the numerous black denominations is an important dimension of Southern religious life, as is the attractiveness of sectarian alternatives (particularly those identified with the Holiness and/or Pentecostal thrust of American Christianity). The most solid overview is William E. Montgomery's doctoral dissertation, "Negro Churches in the South, 1865-1915" (384). The best and quite readable account of the overall story of Methodism among blacks, including appraisal of the several black Methodist denominational groups, is Harry V. Richardson, *Dark Salvation: The Story of Methodism as It Developed among Blacks in America* (396). The standard history of the largest of these groups, the African Methodist Episcopal Church, is Daniel Payne and Charles S. Smith, *History of the African Methodist Episcopal Church* (388). But also see George A. Singleton, *The Romance of African Methodism* (408). A more recent interpretive study is Alain Rogers, "The African Methodist Episcopal Church—A Study in Black Nationalism" (398), while a reasonable statewide survey is Charles S. Long, *History of the African Methodist Episcopal Church in Florida* (378). Two standard studies tell the story of the sister African Methodist Episcopal Zion Church: the two-volume work of David M. Bradley (336) and William J. Walls, *The African Methodist Episcopal Zion Church* (416). For the Christian Methodist Episcopal Church's development, see Charles H. Phillips, *The History of the Colored Methodist Church in America* (391), and Othal Hawthorne Lakey, *The Rise of "Colored Methodism": A Study of the Background and the Beginnings of the Christian Methodist Episcopal Church* (374). But two older studies are also important, more for what they reveal about the social and psychological significance of separate black Methodist denominations among the former slaves than for meeting the canons of contemporary scholarship: Wesley J. Gaines, *African Methodism in the South: Or Twenty-Five Years of Freedom* (357), and Israel L. Butt, *History of African Methodism in Virginia: Or, Four Decades in the Old Dominion* (338).

A careful, insightful approach to the rise of black Baptist churches and groups is James M. Washington, "The Origins and Emergence of Black Baptist Separatism, 1863-1897" (417), a Yale doctoral dissertation now extensively revised and expanded for publication by Mercer University Press in 1986. Also see Charles H. Rankin's master's thesis, "The Rise of Negro Baptist Churches in the South through the Reconstruction Period" (393). Introductions to the Baptist story are also provided in Edward L. Wheeler's brief article, "Beyond One Man: A General Survey of Black Baptist Church History" (421), and Lewis G. Jordan's monograph (again as important for mood as for scholarship), *Negro Baptist History, U.S.A., 1750-1930* (370). In terms of denominational labels, the National Baptist Convention is the largest of the Black Baptist groups. A nonacademic, anecdotal account of interest is Owen D. Pelt and Ralph Lee Smith, *The Story of the National Baptists* (390). Four older studies, lacking in scholarly rigor, which have a somewhat narrower focus are Patrick H. Thompson, *The History of Negro Baptists in Mississippi* (415); Thomas O. Fuller, *History of the Negro Baptists of Tennessee* (355); Stevenson N. Reid, *The History of Colored Baptists in Alabama* (395); and William Hicks, *History of Louisiana Negro Baptists* (365). Not all Southern Black Baptist congregations identified with the National Baptist Convention. One group, the New Covenant Baptist Association, began with a nucleus of thirteen congregations organized with the assistance of anti-Confederate Baptists. Continuing to the present, the New Covenant Baptist Association's developments have been chronicled in Mark S. Sexton, *The Chalice and the Covenant: A History of the New Covenant Baptist Association, 1868-1975* (402). But clearly there is a crying need for scholars to plumb black Baptist developments in the period since Reconstruction.

Over the years thousands of Southern blacks have found religious homes in groups associated with the Holiness-Pentecostal strain of American Christianity. Often linked to the possession of charismatic gifts, these sects and movements draw in a powerful way on the affective dimension of religious expression central to much of the Black experience. Reasons for the attractiveness of such groups are the focus of George Eaton Simpson, "Black Pentecostalism in the United States" (407), while Arnor S. Davis, "The Pentecostal Movement in Black Christianity" (348) offers a brief overview. As with other groups in the Pentecostal-Holiness orbit, the black clusters emphasize personal holiness, the conviction that one can gain assurance of sanctification in a second-level experience, often cataclysmic in nature, that follows on the initial experience of salvation or conversion. The role played by "Sanctification in Negro Religion" is the subject of an essay by William A. Clark (343), drawing largely on sociological and functionalist approaches. Leonard Lovett has addressed "Black Holiness-Pentecostalism: Implications for Ethics and Social Transformation" in a doctoral dissertation (379), while Allen O. Battle, looking at the Church of God in Christ, a black Pentecostal-Holiness sect with headquarters in Memphis, Tennessee, has noted how the experience of sanctification or holiness works to enhance a sense of personal identity and status (331). Arthur E. Paris, studying the Mount Calvary Holy Church of America, a Northern black Holiness-Pentecostal sect with eighty local congregations, has advanced the thesis that black holiness religion represents an adaptation of the black Southern evangelical style to Northern urban life in *Black Pentecostalism: Southern Religion in an Urban World* (386). While they are far from academic in style, German R. Ross, *History and Formative Years of the Church of God in Christ* (399), and Henry Fisher, *The History of the United Holy Church of America, Inc.* (353), are two of the few monograph-length studies of individual black Pentecostal-Holiness groups. A provocative study of one congregation of the United Holy Church of America in Richmond, Virginia, is provided by James A. Forbes, "Ministry of Hope from a Double Minority" (354), who notes the peculiar dilemmas and possibilities for creative ministry that confront a group that is a minority (Pentecostal-Holiness) within a minority (black Americans).

But not all blacks who are drawn to sectarian movements give allegiance to Pentecostal-Holiness groups. In the early twentieth century, the charismatic Father Divine attracted many Southern black followers. One phase of the story is told in Fred L. Pearson and Joseph A. Tomberlin, "John Doe, Alias God: A Note on Father Divine's Georgia Career" (389). But also see C. Eric Lincoln and Lawrence H. Mamiya, "Daddy Jones and Father Divine: The Cult as Political Religion" (376), for comment on the implications of the movement around Father Divine for black identity and what a later generation would term "Black Power."

For decades, scholars assumed that the forced removal of Africans to the New World, the systematic efforts of slave traders and slave owners to extinguish African cultural patterns in order to render the slaves malleable for easier control, and the allegiance to Christianity that many black Americans developed as missionary work brought them the gospel meant that few, if any, of the African mores, religious beliefs and practices, or tribal customs survived in the American context. In recent years, however, scholars have expended considerable effort to disprove this theory and identify those dimensions of the Black experience in which Africanisms reverberate even today. A splendid, careful appraisal of the ways in which African religious elements continue to permeate the Black experience in the United States is Leonard E. Barrett, *Soul-Force: African Heritage in Afro-American Religion* (3). A far briefer and consequently less satisfactory treatment is Romeo B. Garrett, "African Survivals in American Culture" (476). William C. Suttles, Jr., advanced the hypothesis that the continuing presence of tribal belief and practice was among the complex of forces that lay behind attempts at slave insurrections prior to the Civil War (508).

While there is consensus in the academy that there are African survivals, it is also clear that few exist in pure form. Rather, in many instances the prolonged contact with American Christianity as well as the heritage under slavery has made them part of a potpourri that has generated a black folk culture and attendant religious forms. An older general study is Newbell N. Puckett, *Folk Beliefs of the Southern Negro* (498). A more recent, solid general study of this phenomenon, with a comparative orientation, is Henry H. Mitchell, *Black Belief: Folk Beliefs in America and West Africa* (488). This cross-cultural interplay is also integral to black preaching and popular images of the role of the preacher. On this point, see Nancy B. McGhee, "The Folk Sermon: A Facet of the Black Literary Heritage" (485), and the more narrowly focused *The Word on the Brazos: Negro Preacher Tales from the Brazos Bottoms of Texas* by J. Mason Brewer (464). Bruce A. Rosenberg, *The Art of the American Folk Preacher* (500), while predominantly black in focus, neglects to consider African connections. African dimensions may also be seen in retrospect in many of the ceremonies and rituals that were part of slave life. For example, Sudie Duncan Sides has studied marriage practices before emancipation in "Slave Weddings: Plantation Life in the Southern States Before the Civil War" (502), David R. Roediger has examined funeral practices in "And Die in Dixie: Funerals, Death, and Heaven in the Slave Community, 1700-1865" (56), while in a related essay, " 'The Roses So Red and the Lilies So Fair': Southern Folk Cemeteries in Texas," (482), Terry G. Jordan has directed attention to burial practice. Both before and after emancipation, freedom celebrations also frequently assumed a religious cast. See, for example, William B. Gravely, "The Dialectic of Double-Consciousness in Black American Freedom Celebrations" (477), and William H. Wiggins, Jr.'s dissertation, " 'Free at Last!': A Study of Afro-American Emancipation Day Celebrations" (518). Of course, of much interest in the realm of African connections is the black spiritual. Titles that reflect studies of the spiritual and its connections to gospel music are identified in the chapter on art, architecture, and music.

Much of the effort at assimilation after the Civil War came in the area of education. While several of these programs have been noted in the discussion of literature concerning mission work in the Reconstruction era, there are several studies that deal exclusively with attempts to provide educational opportunities for Southern Blacks. Horace M. Bond's old but classic study, *The Education of the Negro in the American Social Order* (526), while more expansive in scope, does note some of the educational work in the South. More recent important studies include Ronald E. Butchart, *Northern Schools, Southern Blacks and Reconstruction: Freedmen's Education, 1862-1875* (529); Robert C. Morris, *Reading 'Riting, and Reconstruction: The Education of Freedmen in the South, 1861-1870* (559); and the more narrowly focused *Soldiers of Light and Love: Northern Teachers and Georgia Blacks, 1865-1873* by Jacqueline Jones (548).

An extensive literature deals with Roman Catholic educational labors. Here the standard study remains Mother M. Agatha (Mary Cecelia Ryan), *Catholic Education and the Negro* (521), which, like Bond's monograph, does not limit coverage to the South, but includes Catholic work there both before and after the Civil War. One older study worth noting because of its focus on a more limited region is Michael F. Rouse, *A Study of the Development of Negro Education under Catholic Auspices in Maryland and the District of Columbia* (564), which should be complemented by Bettye Gardner, "Ante-Bellum Black Education in Baltimore" (537); Gardner also notes the schools sponsored by Methodists, Presbyterians, Quakers, and the African Methodist Church. As Theresa A. Rector, "Black Nuns as Educators" (562), has shown, Catholics in some instances—and perhaps more than their Protestant counterparts—sought to use blacks as teachers. Other monographs devoted to treating educational endeavors among blacks are the older *Methodist Adventures in Negro Education* (570) by Jay S. Stowell and and James Brawley's more recent *Two Centuries of Methodist Concern: Bondage, Freedom and Education of Black People* (527). There is also a study that concentrates on the thirteen schools founded in Virginia by Baptists prior to 1906: Lester F. Russell, *Black Baptist Secondary Schools in Virginia, 1887-1957: A Study in Black History* (567).

Many of the Protestant educational endeavors centered on providing training for clergy, for the clergy quickly assumed the primary leadership role within the black community following the Civil War. Indeed, perhaps until the civil rights movement of the mid-twentieth century reached its zenith and a number of secular leaders emerged among black Americans, the clergy retained its position of preeminence. John F. Marszalek, "The Black Leader in 1919—South Carolina as a Case Study" (657), noted that the spokesman for the black community was most likely to be a Baptist minister who had received his education at a church-related college. But the clergy's role extended well beyond the sphere of religion. Randolph M. Walker, "The Role of the Black Clergy in Memphis during the Crump Era" (668), appraised the political leadership of black ministers from 1927-1948, arguing that although they may have acquiesced to paternalism and accommodationism, they nevertheless exerted tremendous influence over their people.

Perhaps the most conspicuous example of the broader role of the black preacher is provided by Martin Luther King, Jr., and his work in the civil rights movement. An intimate view of King, written before his tragic assassination, is Lerone Bennett, Jr., *What Manner of Man: A Biography of Martin Luther King, Jr.* (673). Jim Bishop, *The Days of Martin Luther King, Jr.* (674), offers a journalistic portrait of King's life. The best critical studies are David L. Lewis, *King: A Critical Biography* (698), and C. Eric Lincoln, ed., *Martin Luther King, Jr.: A Profile* (699). But also see the more popular *Martin Luther King, Jr.*, by Don McKee (701). Important for understanding the varied religious and theological underpinnings of King's civil rights activities are T. Edmund, "Martin Luther King and the Black Protest Movement" (684), which emphasizes King's blending of Christian doctrine with Gandhian nonviolence, and Warren E. Steinkraus, "Martin Luther King's Personalism and Non-Violence" (720), which examines the impact of the Boston Personalist theological school and King's intellectual experiences as a theological student. The most comprehensive study of the ideology that supported King's ministry is Kenneth L. Smith and Ira Zepp, *Search for the Beloved Community* (718).

But by the later twentieth century, analysts were commenting on the decline of the black church and the demise of the leadership role of the black clergy. E. Wilbur Bock addressed the latter issue in "The Decline of the Negro Clergy: Changes in Formal Religious Leadership in the United States in the Twentieth Century" (639). Arnold Vedlitz, and others, "Politics and the Black Church in a Southern Community" (667), noted that the black church remains an important influence within the black community, but has lost ground to political activists who may have no formal religious affiliation or at least do not operate out of a religious framework. A case study of the changing role of the black church in the wake of secular Black Power and related movements is James A. Moss, "The Negro Church and Black Power" (659).

Biographical materials about the hundreds of men and women who have shaped the Southern black religious experience are legion. Still valuable is William J. Simmons, *Men of Mark: Eminent, Progressive and Rising* (716), first published in 1887. Another older (1888) but important collection about Georgia black Baptist leaders is E. R. Carter, *Biographical Sketches of Our*

Pulpit (678). Several Southern denominational leaders are included in R. R. Wright, Jr., *The Bishops of the African Methodist Episcopal Church* (727). A good introduction to the work of South Carolina's Henry McNeal Turner in the nineteenth century is Edwin S. Redkey, *Respect Black: The Writings and Speeches of Henry McNeal Turner* (713). Numerous Southern blacks are also included in the two volumes by Henry Young, *Major Black Religious Leaders* (729). The vital contribution of black women to religious life may be discerned in several sketches found in Bert James Loewenberg and Ruth Bogin, eds., *Black Women in Nineteenth Century American Life* (700), which is not restricted to the South in its coverage.

But in many parts of the South, particularly in rural areas, black religious traditions that stretch back beyond the Civil War to the days of slavery, if not to life in Africa, live on, richly blending dimensions of evangelical Christianity with a folk culture shaped by a history of slavery and continuing oppression and rooted in a distant African past. The vitality of this ongoing heritage is evidenced in narrative form in Charles Wilson, "The Conversion Ritual in a Rural Black Baptist Church" (671), and conveyed more dramatically in pictorial form in Eldon J. Weisheit, "The Black Belt Revisited" (670).

The bibliography that follows begins with a listing of the most important general surveys of the American and Southern black religious experience, and then focuses on those works that deal with the religion of the slaves and antebellum free blacks. It then turns to works that analyze the relations of the white religious groups with slavery, looking first at missionary efforts among the slaves and then to the links between white religion and proslavery and antislavery arguments, including the numerous denominational divisions over slavery. The next sections highlight white religious work among freed blacks during Reconstruction and the early postbellum epoch and the story of the black Protestant denominational and sectarian movements. Roman Catholic enterprises among black Southerners are then documented. African and folk elements in black religion are listed next, followed by studies of the many educational enterprises sponsored by white religious groups but directed toward a black constituency. Works dealing with blacks who have remained within predominantly white religious bodies are noted next. Finally, there are listings of studies concerned with twentieth-century issues and trends and selected black religious leaders. Other relevant titles may be found scattered throughout the volume, but especially in the chapters on literature, on the social order, on the various denominations, and on art, architecture, and music.

BIBLIOGRAPHY

Many titles in chapter 3, "Native American Religions and Indian Missions," are relevant to this chapter, particularly those treating the early missions directed both to Indians and to slaves and those dealing with the slaveholding Indians. Also relevant are scattered titles in chapter 2, "Religion in the South: An Overview," and some of the bibliographical resources found in chapter 1. Titles dealing with racism and links between religion and the civil rights movement are found in chapter 20, while studies of spirituals are identified in chapter 17.

I. OVERVIEWS OF BLACK RELIGION

(1) Bailey, Leroy. "A Comparative Analysis of *The Negro Church in America,* by E. Franklin Frazier and *Black Religion,* by Joseph R. Washington, Jr." M.A. thesis, Howard University, 1971.

(2) Banks, William L. *The Black Church in the U.S.: Its Origin, Growth, Contributions, and Outlook.* Chicago: Moody Press, 1972.

(3) Barrett, Leonard E. *Soul-Force: African Heritage in Afro-American Religion.* Garden City: Anchor Press/Doubleday, 1974.

(4) Becker, William H. "The Black Church: Manhood and Mission." *Journal of the American Academy of Religion* 40 (1972): 316-33.

(5) Bragg, George F. "Beginning of Negro Church Work in the South." *Living Church* 65 (20 August 1921): 505.

(6) Butcher, Margaret Just. *The Negro in American Culture: Based on Materials Left by Alain Locke,* chaps. 2, 3, 5. New York: Knopf, 1956.

(7) DuBois, W. E. B. *The Negro Church.* Atlanta: Atlanta University Press, 1903.

(8) _____. *The Souls of Black Folk.* Chicago: A. C. McClurg, 1903.

(9) Earnest, Joseph B., Jr., *The Religious Development of the Negro in Virginia.* Charlottesville: Michie, 1914.

(10) Frazier, E. Franklin. *The Negro Church in America.* New York: Schocken Books, 1964.

(11) Haygood, Atticus G. "The Negro in the South." *Quarterly Review of the Methodist Episcopal Church, South* 19 (1891): 300-315.

(12) Hilger, Rothe. "The Religious Experience of the Negro." M.A. thesis, Vanderbilt University, 1931.

(13) James, Samuel H. "The Religious Experience of the Negro in America." Master's thesis, Andover Newton Theological School, 1943.

(14) Johnston, Ruby F. *The Development of Negro Religion.* New York: Philosophical Library, 1954.

(15) _____. *The Religion of Negro Protestants.* New York: Philosophical Library, 1956.

(16) Krueger, E. T. "Negro Religious Expression." *American Journal of Sociology* 38 (1932): 22-31.

(17) Lincoln, C. Eric. *The Black Church Since Frazier.* New York: Schocken Books, 1973. Includes text of Frazier, *The Negro Church in America.*

(18) Long, Charles H. "Perspectives for a Study of Afro-American Religion in the United States." *History of Religions* 11 (1971): 54-66.

(19) McBeth, Leon. "Images of the Black Church in America." *Baptist History and Heritage* 16 (1981): 19-28, 40.

(20) McCall, Emmanuel L. *The Black Christian Experience*. New York: Broadman Press, 1972.

(21) Mays, Benjamin E., and Joseph W. Nicholson, *The Negro's Church*. New York: Institute of Social and Religious Research, 1933.

(22) _____. *The Negro's God as Reflected in His Literature*. Boston: Chapman and Grimes, 1938.

(23) Reed, Richard C. "A Sketch of the Religious History of the Negroes in the South." *Papers of the American Society of Church History* 2d series 4 (1914): 177-204.

(24) Smith, Allen H. "The Negro Church: A Critical Examination of the Christian Church among Negroes in the United States." Typescript, Yale Divinity School, 1961.

(25) Wallace, W. J. L. "The Black Church: Past and Present." *A.M.E. Zion Quarterly Review* 82 (Summer 1970): 63-72.

(26) Washington, Booker T., and W. E. B. DuBois. "Religion in the South." In *The Negro in the South*. Philadelphia: George W. Jacobs, 1907.

(27) Washington, Joseph R. *Black Religion: The Negro and Christianity in the United States*. Boston: Beacon Press, 1964.

(28) _____. *Black Sects and Cults: The Power Axis in an Ethnic Ethic*. Garden City: Anchor Press/Doubleday, 1972.

(29) _____. *The Politics of God: The Future of the Black Churches*. Boston: Beacon Press, 1967.

(30) Watson, James J. "The Religion of the Negro." Ph.D. dissertation, University of Pennsylvania, 1912.

(31) Weatherford, Willis D. *American Churches and the Negro: An Historical Study from Early Slave Days to the Present*. Boston: Christopher Publishing House, 1957.

(32) Wilmore, Gayraud S. *Black Religion and Black Radicalism: An Examination of the Black Experience in Religion*. Garden City: Anchor Press/Doubleday, 1973.

(33) Woodson, Carter G. *The History of the Negro Church*. Washington: Associated Publishers, 1921.

II. THE RELIGION OF SLAVES AND ANTEBELLUM FREE BLACKS

(34) Adefila, Johnson Ajibade. "Slave Religion in the Antebellum South: A Study of the Role of Africanisms in the Black Response to Christianity." Ph.D. dissertation, Brandeis University, 1975.

(35) Alho, Olli. *The Religion of the Slaves: A Study of the Religious Tradition and Behavior of Plantation Slaves in the United States, 1830-1865*. Helsinki: Academia Scientarium Fennica, 1976.

(36) Berlin, Ira. *Slaves Without Masters: The Free Negro in the Antebellum South.* New York: Pantheon Press, 1975.

(37) Blassingame, John W. *The Slave Community: Plantation Life in the Antebellum South,* 60-75. New York: Oxford University Press, 1972.

(38) Bradley, Michael R. "The Role of the Black Church in the Colonial Slave Society." *Louisiana Studies* 14 (1975): 413-21.

(39) Bruce, Dickson D., Jr. "Play, Work, and Ethics in the Old South." *Southern Folklore Quarterly* 41 (1977): 33-51.

(40) Cade, John B. "Out of the Mouths of Ex-Slaves: Religion and Recreation of Activities." *Journal of Negro History* 20 (1934): 327-34.

(41) Clarke, T. Erskine. *Wrestlin' Jacob: A Portrait of Religion in the Old South.* Richmond: John Knox Press, 1979.

(42) Franklin, John Hope. *Negro Episcopalians in Ante-Bellum North Carolina.* New Brunswick NJ: n.p., 1944. Reprinted from *Historical Magazine of the Protestant Episcopal Church* 13 (1944).

(43) Genovese, Eugene D. "Black Plantation Preachers in the Slave South." *Louisiana Studies* 11 (1972): 188-214.

(44) _____. *Roll, Jordan, Roll: The World the Slaves Made,* 161-284. New York: Random House, 1974.

(45) Harding, Vincent. "Religion and Resistance among Antebellum Negroes, 1800-1860." In *The Making of Black America.* August Meier and Elliott Rudwick, eds., 1:179-97. New York: Atheneum, 1969.

(46) _____. *There Is a River: The Black Struggle for Freedom in America.* New York: Harcourt, Brace, Jovanovich, 1981.

(47) Johnson, Clifton H., et al. *God Struck Me Dead: Religious Conversion Experiences and Autobiographies of Ex-Slaves.* Philadelphia: Pilgrim Press, 1969.

(48) Levine, Lawrence W. *Black Culture and Black Consciousness,* chap. 1. New York: Oxford University Press, 1977.

(49) Mallard, Robert. *Plantation Life before Emancipation.* Richmond: Whittet and Shepperson, 1892.

(50) Melnick, Ralph. "Billy Simons: The Black Jew of Charleston." *American Jewish Archives* 32 (1980): 3-8.

(51) Miller, Randall M. " 'It is Good to be Religious': A Loyal Slave on God, Masters, and the Civil War." *North Carolina Historical Review* 54 (1977): 66-71.

(52) O'Brien, John T. "Factory, Church, and Community: Blacks in Antebellum Richmond." *Journal of Southern History* 44 (1978): 509-36.

(53) Perkins, Haven P. "Religion for Slaves: Difficulties and Methods." *Church History* 10 (1941): 228-45.

(54) Pierson, William D. "White Cannibals, Black Martyrs: Fear, Depression, and Religious Faith as Causes of Suicide among New Slaves." *Journal of Negro History* 62 (1977): 147-59.

(55) Raboteau, Albert J. *Slave Religion: The "Invisible Institution" in the Antebellum South.* New York: Oxford University Press, 1978.

(56) Roediger, David R. "And Die in Dixie: Funerals, Death, and Heaven in the Slave Community, 1700-1865." *Mississippi Review* 22 (1981): 163-83.

(57) Sernett, Milton C. *Black Religion and American Evangelicalism: White Protestants, Plantation Missions, and the Flowering of Negro Christianity, 1787-1865.* Metuchen: Scarecrow Press, 1975.

(58) Smith, Julia Floyd. "Marching to Zion: The Religion of Black Baptists in Coastal Georgia Prior to 1865." *Viewpoints: Georgia Baptist History* 6 (1978): 47-54.

(59) Smith, Timothy L. "Slavery and Theology: The Emergence of Black Christian Consciousness in Nineteenth-Century America." *Church History* 41 (1972): 497-512.

(60) Sobel, Mechal. *Trabelin' On: The Slave Journey to an Afro-Baptist Faith.* Westport: Greenwood Press, 1979.

(61) Stowe, Charles E. "The Religion of Slavery." *The Crisis* 5 (1912): 36-38.

(62) Touchstone, Donald Blake. "Planters and Slave Religion in the Deep South." Ph.D. dissertation, Tulane University, 1973.

(63) Wiley, Bell I. *Southern Negroes, 1861-1865,* chap. 6. New Haven: Yale University Press, 1965.

(64) Williams, Michael P. "The Black Evangelical Ministry in the Antebellum Border States: Profiles of Elders John Berry Meachum and Noah Davis." *Foundations* 21 (1978): 225-41.

(65) Wilson, Gold Refined. "The Religion of the American Slave: His Attitude Towards Life and Death." *Journal of Negro History* 8 (1923): 41-71.

(66) Wood, Peter H. " 'Jesus Christ Has Got Thee at Last': Afro-American Conversion as a Forgotten Chapter in Eighteenth-Century Southern Intellectual History." *Bulletin of the Center for the Study of Southern Culture and Religion* 3 (November 1979): 1-7.

(67) Woolridge, Nancy Bullock. "The Slave Preacher: Portrait of a Leader." *Journal of Negro Education* 14 (1945): 28-37.

(68) Yonker, Thomas W. "The Negro Church in North Carolina, 1700-1900." Master's thesis, Duke University, 1955.

III. WHITE RELIGION(S) AND SLAVERY: MINISTRY TO THE SLAVES

(69) Agonito, Joseph. "St. Ingoes Manor: A Nineteenth Century Jesuit Plantation." *Maryland Historical Magazine* 72 (1977): 83-98.

(70) Bailey, David T. "Slavery and the Churches: The Old Southwest." Ph.D. dissertation, University of California at Berkeley, 1978.

(71) Bailey, Kenneth K. "Protestantism and Afro-Americans in the Old South: Another Look." *Journal of Southern History* 41 (1975): 451-72.

(72) Barber, Jesse B. *Climbing Jacob's Ladder: Story of the Work of the Presbyterian Church U.S.A. among the Negroes.* New York: Board of National Missions, Presbyterian Church in the U.S.A., 1930.

(73) Bassett, John S. "North Carolina Methodism and Slavery." *Historical Papers of the Trinity College Historical Society* 4th series (1900): 1-11.

(74) Billings, Warren M. "The Cases of Fernando and Elizabeth Key: A Note on the Status of Blacks in Seventeenth Century Virginia." *William and Mary Quarterly* 3d series 30 (1973): 467-74.

(75) Bragg, George F. "The Church's Early Work for the Colored Race." *Living Church* 65 (1921): 351-54.

(76) Bringhurst, Newell G. "The Mormons and Slavery—A Closer Look." *Pacific Historical Review* 50 (1981): 329-38.

(77) Brown, Larry. "Historic Roles of Christianity during Slavery." *Transition* 1 (1973): 182-92.

(78) Bruner, Clarence. "The Religious Instruction of the Slaves in the Antebellum South." Doctoral dissertation, George Peabody College, 1933.

(79) Byrne, Barbara Anne. "Charles C. Jones and the Intellectual Crisis of the Antebellum South." *Southern Studies* 19 (1980): 274-85.

(80) Callaway, T. F. "The Old South and the Negro Slaves." *Christian Index* 118 (1928): 3.

(81) Caravaglios, Maria Genovino. *The American Catholic Church and the Negro Problem in the XVIII-XIX Centuries*. Ernest L. Unterkoefler, ed. Charleston SC: Caravaglios, 1974.

(82) Cass, Michael M. "Charles C. Jones, Jr., and the 'Lost Cause'." *Georgia Historical Quarterly* 55 (1971): 222-33.

(83) Clarke, T. Erskine. "An Experiment in Paternalism: Presbyterians and Slaves in Charleston, South Carolina." *Journal of Presbyterian History* 53 (1975): 223-38.

(84) Clifton, Denzil T. "Anglicanism and Negro Slavery in Colonial America." *Historical Magazine of the Protestant Episcopal Church* 40 (1970): 29-70.

(85) Daniel, W. Harrison. "The Methodist Episcopal Church and the Negro in the Early National Period." *Methodist History* 11 (1973): 40-53.

(86) _____. "Southern Presbyterians and the Negro in the Early National Period." *Journal of Negro History* 58 (1973): 291-312.

(87) _____. "Virginia Baptists and the Negro in the Antebellum Era." *Journal of Negro History* 56 (1971): 1-16.

(88) _____. "Virginia Baptists and the Negro in the Early Republic." *Virginia Magazine of History and Biography* 80 (1972): 60-69.

(89) DeVinne, Daniel. *The Methodist Episcopal Church and Slavery: A Historical Survey of the Relation of the Early Methodists to Slavery*. New York: F. Hart, 1857.

(90) Drake, Thomas E. *Quakers and Slavery in America*. New Haven: Yale University Press, 1950.

(91) Ellerbee, A. W. "The Episcopal Church among the Slaves." *American Church Review* 7 (1855): 429-37.

(92) Engelder, Conrad J. "The Churches and Slavery: A Study of the Attitudes toward Slavery of the Major Protestant Denominations." Ph.D. dissertation, University of Michigan, 1964.

(93) "The Established Virginia Church and the Conversion of Negroes and Indians, 1620-1760." *Journal of Negro History* 46 (1961): 12-23.

(94) Fickling, Susan Maria Markey. *Slave-Conversion in South Carolina, 1830-1860*. Columbia: University of South Carolina Press, 1924.

(95) Finn, Peter C. "The Slaves of the Jesuits in Maryland." M.A. thesis, Georgetown University, 1974.

(96) Fortenbaugh, Robert. "American Lutheran Synods and Slavery, 1830-1860." *Journal of Religion* 13 (1933): 72-92.

(97) Goodwin, Mary F. "Christianizing and Educating the Negro in Colonial Virginia." *Historical Magazine of the Protestant Episcopal Church* 1 (1932): 143-52.

(98) Gravely, William B. "Early Methodism and Slavery: The Roots of a Tradition." *Wesleyan Quarterly Review* 2 (1965): 84-100.

(99) Green, Fletcher M. "Northern Missionary Activities in the South, 1846-1861." *Journal of Southern History* 21 (1925): 147-72.

(100) Greenburg, Michael. "Slavery and the Protestant Ethic." *Louisiana Studies* 15 (1976): 209-39.

(101) Guice, John A. "American Methodism and Slavery to 1844." B.D. paper, Duke University, 1930.

(102) Harrison, William P., ed. *The Gospel among the Slaves: A Short Account of Missionary Operations among the African Slaves of the Southern States*. Nashville: Publishing House of the Methodist Episcopal Church, South, 1893.

(103) Hayden, J. Carleton. "Conversion and Control: Dilemma of Episcopalians in Providing for the Religious Instruction of the Slaves, Charleston, South Carolina, 1845-1860." *Historical Magazine of the Protestant Episcopal Church* 40 (1971): 143-71.

(104) Hildebrand, Reginald F. "Methodist Episcopal Policy on the Ordination of Black Ministers, 1784-1864." *Methodist History* 20 (1982): 124-42.

(105) Hood, R. E. "From a Headstart to a Deadstart: The Historical Basis for Black Indifference toward the Episcopal Church, 1800-1860." *Historical Magazine of the Protestant Episcopal Church* 51 (1982): 269-96.

(106) Horton, Joseph P. "Religious and Educational Contributions of the Methodists to the Slaves." B.D. thesis, Southern Methodist University, n.d.

(107) Hughes, John E. "History of the Southern Baptist Convention's Ministry to the Negro, 1845-1904." Th.D. dissertation, Southern Baptist Theological Seminary, 1971.

(108) Jackson, James C. "The Religious Education of the Negro in South Carolina Prior to 1850." *Historical Magazine of the Protestant Episcopal Church* 36 (1967): 35-61.

(109) Jackson, Luther P. "Religious Development of the Negro in Virginia from 1760-1860." *Journal of Negro History* 16 (1931): 168-239.

(110) _____. "Religious Instruction of Negroes, 1830-1860, with Special Reference to South Carolina." *Journal of Negro History* 15 (1930): 72-114.

(111) Jeansonne, Glen. "Southern Baptist Attitudes toward Slavery, 1845-1861." *Georgia Historical Quarterly* 55 (1971): 510-22.

(112) Klein, Herbert S. "Anglicanism, Catholicism and the Negro Slave." *Comparative Studies in Society and History* (1966): 295-327. Also in *Slavery in the New World*. Laura Foner and Eugene D. Genovese, eds., 138-66. Englewood Cliffs: Prentice-Hall, 1969.

(113) Klingberg, Frank, ed. *The Carolina Chronicle of Dr. Francis LeJau, 1706-1717*. University of California Publications in History 53. Berkeley: University of California Press, 1956.

(114) Korn, Bertram W. *Jews and Negro Slavery in the Old South, 1789-1865*. Elkins Park MD: Reform Congregation Keneseth Israel, 1961. Also in *Publications of the American Jewish Historical Society* 50 (1961): 151-201.

(115) Kull, Irving S. "Presbyterian Attitudes toward Slavery." *Church History* 7 (1938): 101-14.

(116) Lines, Stiles B. "Slaves and Churchmen: The Work of the Episcopal Church among Southern Negroes, 1830-1860." Ph.D. dissertation, Columbia University, 1960.

(117) Long, Durward. "The Methodist Church and Negro Slavery in America, 1784-1844." *Wesleyan Quarterly Review* 3 (1966): 3-17.

(118) Loring, Eduard N. "Charles C. Jones: Missionary to Plantation Slaves, 1831-1847." Ph.D. dissertation, Vanderbilt University, 1976.

(119) McLoughlin, William G., and Winthrop D. Jordan. "Baptists Face the Barbarities of Slavery in 1710." *Journal of Southern History* 29 (1963): 495-501.

(120) McNally, Michael J. "A Minority of a Minority: The Witness of Black Religious Women in the Antebellum South." *Review for Religious* 40 (1981): 260-69.

(121) Mallard, Annie H. "Religious Work of South Carolina Baptists among the Slaves from 1781 to 1830." M.A. thesis, University of South Carolina, 1946.

(122) Mathews, Donald G. "Charles Colcock Jones and the Southern Evangelical Crusade to Form a Biracial Community." *Journal of Southern History* 41 (1975): 299-320.

(123) _____. "The Methodist Mission to the Slaves, 1829-1844." *Journal of American History* 51 (1965): 615-31.

(124) _____. "Religion and Slavery: The Case of the American South." In *Anti-Slavery, Religion and Reform: Essays in Memory of Roger Anstey*. Christine Bolt and Seymour Drescher, eds., 207-32. Folkestone, England: Dawson, 1980.

(125) _____. *Slavery and Methodism: A Chapter in American Morality, 1780-1845*. Princeton: Princeton University Press, 1965.

(126) Miller, Randall M. "Black Catholics in the Slave South: Some Needs and Opportunities for Study." *Records of the American Catholic Historical Society* 86 (1975): 93-106.

(127) ———. "The Failed Mission: The Catholic Church and Black Catholics in the Old South." In *The Southern Common People: Studies in Nineteenth-Century Social History.* Edward Magdol and Jon L. Wakelyn, eds., 37-54. Westport CT: Greenwood Press, 1980.

(128) Murphy, John C. *An Analysis of the Attitudes of American Catholics toward the Immigrant and the Negro.* Washington: Catholic University of America Press, 1940.

(129) Murphy, Miriam T. "Catholic Missionary Work among the Colored People of the United States, 1766-1866." *American Catholic Historical Society of Philadelphia Records* 35 (1924): 101-36.

(130) Murray, Andrew E. "Bright Delusion: Presbyterians and African Colonization." *Journal of Presbyterian History* 58 (1980): 224-37.

(131) Nelson, William S. "The Christian Church and Slavery in America." *Howard University Review* 2 (1925): 41-71.

(132) Noon, Thomas R. "Early Black Lutherans in the South to 1865." *Concordia Historical Institute Quarterly* 50 (1977): 50-53.

(133) Opper, Peter K. "North Carolina Quakers: Reluctant Slaveholders." *North Carolina Historical Review* 52 (1975): 37-58.

(134) Palm, Reba W. "Protestant Churches and Slavery in Matagorda County." *East Texas Historical Journal* 14 (Spring 1976): 3-8.

(135) Pierre, C. E. "The Work of the Society for the Propagation of the Gospel in Foreign Parts among the Negroes in the Colonies." *Journal of Negro History* 1 (1916): 349-60.

(136) Pilcher, George W. "Samuel Davies and the Instruction of Negroes in Virginia." *Virginia Magazine of History and Biography* 74 (1966): 293-300.

(137) Posey, Walter B. "The Baptists and Slavery in the Lower Mississippi Valley." *Journal of Negro History* 41 (1956): 117-30.

(138) ———. "Influence on Slavery upon the Methodist Church in the Early South and Southwest." *Mississippi Valley Historical Review* (now *Journal of American History*) 17 (1930-1931): 530-42.

(139) Purifoy, Lewis M., Jr. "The Methodist Episcopal Church, South, and Slavery, 1844-1865." Ph.D. dissertation, University of North Carolina in Chapel Hill, 1965.

(140) Putnam, Mary B. *The Baptists and Slavery.* Ann Arbor: George Wahr, 1913.

(141) Quarles, Benjamin F. "Ante-Bellum Relations between the First African Baptist Church of New Orleans and White Agencies." *The Chronicle* 18 (1955): 26-36.

(142) Reilly, Timothy F. "Slavery and the Southwestern Evangelist in New Orleans (1800-1861)." *Journal of Mississippi History* 41 (1979): 301-17.

(143) Reinders, Robert C. "The Churches and the Negro in New Orleans, 1850-1860." *Phylon* 22 (1961): 241-48.

(144) Satterfield, James H. "The Baptists and the Negro Prior to 1863." Th.D. dissertation, Southern Baptist Theological Seminary, 1919.

(145) Schreyer, George M. "Methodist Work among the Plantation Negroes in the South Carolina Conference from 1829 to 1865." B.D. thesis, Duke University, 1939.

(146) Sharrow, Walter G. "John Hughes and a Catholic Response to Slavery in Antebellum America." *Journal of Negro History* 57 (1972): 254-69.

(147) Sims, Charles F. "The Religious Education of the Southern Negroes." Th.D. dissertation, Southern Baptist Theological Seminary, 1926.

(148) Singleton, George A. "Religious Instruction of the Negro in the United States before the Rebellion." M.A. thesis, University of Chicago, 1929.

(149) Sobel, Mechal. " 'They Can Never Both Prosper Together': Black and White Baptists in Nashville, Tennessee." *Tennessee Historical Quarterly* 38 (1979): 296-307.

(150) Southall, Eugene. "The Attitude of the Methodist Episcopal Church, South, Toward the Negro from 1844 to 1870." *Journal of Negro History* 16 (1931): 359-70.

(151) Stange, Douglas C. " 'A Compassionate Mother to Her Poor Negro Slaves': The Lutheran Church and Negro Slavery in Early America." *Phylon* 29 (1968): 272-81.

(152) _____. "Our Duty to Preach the Gospel to Negroes: Southern Lutherans and American Slavery." *Concordia Historical Institute Quarterly* 42 (1969): 171-82.

(153) Stein, Stephen J. "George Whitefield on Slavery: Some New Evidence." *Church History* 42 (1973): 243-56.

(154) Taylor, Orville W. "Baptists and Slavery in Arkansas: Relations and Attitudes." *Arkansas Historical Quarterly* 38 (1979): 199-226.

(155) Theobald, Stephen L. "Catholic Missionary Work among the Colored People of the United States (1776-1866)." *American Catholic Historical Society of Philadelphia Records* 35 (1924): 324-44.

(156) Thompson, J. Earl, Jr. "Slavery and Presbyterianism in the Revolutionary Era." *Journal of Presbyterian History* 54 (1976): 121-41.

(157) Thrift, Charles T., Jr. "The Operations of the American Home Missionary Society in the South, 1826-1861." Ph.D. dissertation, University of Chicago, 1936.

(158) Tyner, Wayne C. "Charles Colcock Jones: Missionary to Slaves." *Journal of Presbyterian History* 55 (1977): 363-80.

(159) Van Horne, John C. "Impediments to the Christianization and Education of Blacks in Colonial America: The Case of the Associates of Dr. Bray." *Historical Magazine of the Protestant Episcopal Church* 50 (1981): 243-69.

(160) Walker, James G. *Presbyterians and the Negro.* Greensboro NC: n.p., n.d.

(161) Whatley, George C. III. "The Alabama Presbyterian and His Slave, 1830-1864." *Alabama Review* 13 (1960): 46-51.

(162) Weeks, Stephen B. *Southern Quakers and Slavery: A Study in Institutional History*. Baltimore: Johns Hopkins University Press, 1896.

(163) Williams, Thomas L. "The Methodist Mission to the Slaves." Ph.D. dissertation, Yale University, 1943.

(164) Wilson, J. Leighton. "Religious Instruction of the Colored People." *The Southern Presbyterian Review* 16 (1863): 190 + .

IV. WHITE RELIGION(S) AND SLAVERY: ANTISLAVERY AND PROSLAVERY DIVISIONS

Several titles in Section III are also relevant to this topic.

(165) Allen, Carlos R., Jr. "David Barrow's Circular Letter of 1798." *William and Mary Quarterly* 3d series 20 (1963): 440-51.

(166) Allen, Jeffrey B. "Were Southern White Critics of Slavery Racists? Kentucky and the Upper South, 1791-1824." *Journal of Southern History* 44 (1978): 169-90.

(167) Barber, Verle L. "The Slavery Controversy and the Presbyterian Church." Ph.D. dissertation, University of Chicago, 1928.

(168) Basker, Roosevelt A. "Pro-Slavery Arguments of Southern Religious Leaders as Illustrated by the Old School Presbyterians." M.A. thesis, University of Chicago, 1935.

(169) Bell, Stephen H. "Phillip Phillips Nealy and Secession." *Alabama Historical Quarterly* 38 (1976): 45-50.

(170) Bellot, Leland J. "Evangelicals and the Defense of Slavery in Britain's Old Colonial Empire." *Journal of Southern History* 37 (1971): 19-40.

(171) Bishop, Charles C. "The Pro-Slavery Argument Reconsidered: James Henley Thornwell, Millennial Abolitionist." *South Carolina Historical Magazine* 73 (1972): 18-26.

(172) Blied, Benjamin J. "Catholicism and Abolitionism." *Salesianum* 33 (1938): 170-78.

(173) Boles, John B. "Tension in a Slave Society: The Trial of the Reverend Jacob Gruber." *Southern Studies* 18 (1979): 179-97.

(174) Bradley, L. Richard. "The Curse of Canaan and the American Negro." *Concordia Theological Monthly* 42 (1971): 100-110.

(175) Brokhage, Joseph D. *Francis Patrick Kenrick's Opinion on Slavery*. Washington: Catholic University of America Press, 1955.

(176) Burr, Nelson R. "United States Senator James Dixon, 1814-1873: Episcopal Anti-Slavery Statesman." *Historical Magazine of the Protestant Episcopal Church* 50 (1981): 29-72.

(177) Caravaglios, Maria Genovino. "A Roman Critique of the Pro-Slavery Views of Bishop Martin of Natchitoches, Louisiana." *Records of the American Catholic Historical Society* 83 (1972): 67-81. Also Philadelphia: American Catholic Historical Society, 1972.

(178) Carroll, Kenneth L. "William Southeby, Early Quaker Antislavery Writer." *Pennsylvania Magazine of History and Biography* 89 (1965): 416-27.

(179) Cobb, Jimmy G. "A Study of White Protestants' Attitudes towards Negroes in Charleston, South Carolina, 1790-1845." Ph.D. dissertation, Baylor University, 1976.

(180) Crowther, Edward R. "Mississippi Baptists, Slavery, and Secession: A Study in Religious Ideology." M.A. thesis, Mississippi College, 1981.

(181) Daniel, W. Harrison. "English Presbyterians, Slavery, and the American Crisis of the 1860s." *Journal of Presbyterian History* 58 (1980): 50-62.

(182) Davis, J. Treadwell. "Nashoba: Frances Wright's Experiment in Self-Emancipation." *Southern Quarterly* 11 (1972): 63-90.

(183) DesChamps, Margaret B. "Antislavery Presbyterians in the Carolina Piedmont." *Proceedings of the South Carolina Historical Association* 24 (1954): 6-13.

(184) Eminhizer, Earl E. "Alexander Campbell's Thoughts on Slavery and Abolition." *West Virginia History* 33 (1972): 109-23.

(185) Epps, Archie C. "The Christian Doctrine of Slavery: A Theological Analysis." *Journal of Negro History* 46 (1961): 243-49.

(186) Essig, James D. *The Bonds of Wickedness: American Evangelicals against Slavery*. Philadelphia: Temple University Press, 1982.

(187) _____. "The Lord's Free Man: Charles G. Finney and His Abolitionism." *Civil War History* 24 (1978): 25-45.

(188) _____. "A Very Wintry Season: Virginia Baptists and Slavery, 1785-1797." *Virginia Magazine of History and Biography* 88 (1980): 170-85.

(189) Faust, Drew Gilpin. "Evangelicalism and the Meaning of the Proslavery Argument: The Reverend Thornton Stringfellow of Virginia." *Virginia Magazine of History and Biography* 85 (1977): 3-17.

(190) Fife, Robert O. "Alexander Campbell and the Christian Church in the Slavery Controversy." Ph.D. dissertation, Indiana University, 1960.

(191) Finnie, Gordon. "The Antislavery Movement in the Upper South before 1840." *Journal of Southern History* 35 (1969): 319-42.

(192) George, Carol V. P. "Widening the Circle: The Black Church and the Abolitionist Crusade, 1830-1860." In *Antislavery Reconsidered: New Perspectives on the Abolitionists*. Lewis Perry and Michael Fellman, eds., 195-218. Baton Rouge: Louisiana State University Press, 1979.

(193) Gilliam, Will D. "Robert J. Breckenridge: Kentucky Unionist." *Register of the Kentucky Historical Society* 69 (1971): 362-85.

(194) _____. "Robert Jefferson Breckenridge, 1800-1871." *Register of the Kentucky Historical Society* 72 (1974): 207-233, 319-36.

(195) Grassi, Giovanni A. *Notizie varie sullo stato presente della republica degli Stati Uniti dell' America*. Rome: Presso L. P. Salvioni, 1818.

(196) Gravely, William B. "Methodist Preachers, Slavery and Caste: Types of Social Concern in Antebellum America." *Duke Divinity School Review* 34 (1969): 209-29.

(197) _____. "A Preacher's Covenant against Slavery, 1795." *South Carolina United Methodist Advocate* 135 (18 March 1971): 8-9, 11.

(198) Halbrooks, G. Thomas. "Francis Wayland: Influential Mediator in the Baptist Controversy over Slavery." *Baptist History and Heritage* 13 (1978): 21-35.

(199) Harwood, Thomas F. "British Evangelical Abolitionism and American Churches in the 1830's." *Journal of Southern History* 28 (1962): 287-306.

(200) Hertzler, James R. "Slavery in the Yearly Sermons before the Georgia Trustees." *Georgia Historical Quarterly* 59 [supplement] (1975): 118-26.

(201) Hildebrand, Reginald F. " 'An Imperious Sense of Duty': Documents Illustrating an Episode in the Methodist Reaction to the Nat Turner Revolt." *Methodist History* 19 (1981): 155-74.

(202) Howard, Victor B. "The Anti-Slavery Movement in the Presbyterian Church, 1835-1861." M.A. thesis, Ohio State University, 1961.

(203) _____. "The Kentucky Presbyterians in 1849: Slavery and the Kentucky Constitution." *Register of the Kentucky Historical Society* 75 (1975): 217-40.

(204) _____. "Presbyterians, the Kansas-Nebraska Act, and the Election of 1856." *Journal of Presbyterian History* 49 (1971): 133-56.

(205) _____. "The Slavery Controversy and a Seminary for the Northwest." *Journal of Presbyterian History* 43 (1965): 227-53.

(206) _____. "The Southern Aid Society and the Slavery Controversy." *Church History* 41 (1972): 208-224.

(207) Isaac, Ephraim. "Genesis, Judaism, and the 'Sons of Ham'." *Slavery and Abolition* 1 (1980): 3-17.

(208) Jenkins, William S. *Pro-Slavery Thought in the Old South*. Chapel Hill: University of North Carolina Press, 1935.

(209) Johnson, Clifton H. "Abolitionist Missionary Activities in North Carolina." *North Carolina Historical Review* 40 (1963): 295-320.

(210) _____. "John Gregg Fee: Kentucky Abolitionist." *The Crisis* 79 (1972): 330-32.

(211) Jordan, Marjorie Waggoner. "Mississippi Methodists and the Division of the Church over Slavery." Ph.D. dissertation, University of Southern Mississippi, 1972.

(212) Keller, Ralph A. "Methodist Newspapers and the Fugitive Slave Law: A New Perspective for the Slavery Crisis in the North." *Church History* 43 (1974): 319-39.

(213) Kostlevy, William C. "Luther Lee and Methodist Abolitionism." *Methodist History* 20 (1982): 90-103.

(214) Kraditor, Aileen S. *Means and Ends in American Abolitionism: Garrison and His Critics on Strategy and Tactics, 1834-1850*. New York: Vintage Books, 1970.

(215) Leonard, Philip. "The Contributions of Presbyterian Orthodoxy to the Pro-Slavery Argument as Exemplified by the Writings of James Henley Thornwell." M.A. thesis, University of Virginia, 1967.

(216) Loveland, Anne C. "Evangelicalism and 'Immediate Emancipation' in American Antislavery Thought." *Journal of Southern History* 32 (1966): 172-88.

(217) _____. "Richard Furman's 'Questions on Slavery'." *Baptist History and Heritage* 10 (1975): 177-81.

(218) McCants, Sr. Dorothea O. *They Came to Louisiana: Letters of a Catholic Mission, 1854-1882*. Baton Rouge: Louisiana State University Press, 1970.

(219) McKiever, Charles. *Slavery and the Emigration of North Carolina Friends*. Murfreesboro NC: Johnson Publishing, 1970.

(220) McKitrick, Eric L. *Slavery Defended: The Views of the Old South*. Englewood Cliffs: Prentice-Hall, 1963.

(221) McKivigan, John R. "The American Baptist Free Mission Society: Abolitionist Reaction to the 1845 Baptist Schism." *Foundations* 21 (1978): 340-55.

(222) _____. "The Antislavery 'Comeouter' Sects: A Neglected Dimension of the Abolitionist Movement." *Civil War History* 26 (1980): 142-60.

(223) Maclear, James F. "The Evangelical Alliance and the Abolitionist Crusade." *Huntington Library Quarterly* 42 (1979): 141-64.

(224) McNeilly, James H. *Religion and Slavery: A Vindication of the Southern Churches*. Nashville: Publishing House of the Methodist Episcopal Church, South, 1911.

(225) Maddex, Jack P., Jr. "Proslavery Millennialism: Social Eschatology in Antebellum Southern Calvinism." *American Quarterly* 31 (1979): 46-62.

(226) _____. " 'The Southern Apostasy' Revisited: The Significance of Proslavery Christianity." *Marxist Perspectives* 2 (1979): 132-41.

(227) Mathews, Donald G. "The Methodist Schism of 1844 and the Popularization of Antislavery Sentiment." *Mid-America* 51 (1969): 3-23.

(228) _____. "Religion and Slavery: The Case of the American South." In *Anti-Slavery, Religion and Reform: Essays in Memory of Roger Anstey*. Christine Bolt and Seymour Drescher, eds., 207-32. Fokestone, Eng.: Dawson, 1980.

(229) Matthews, Paul A. "Francis Wright and the Nashoba Experiment: A Transitional Period in Antislavery Attitudes." *East Tennessee Historical Society Publications* 46 (1974): 37-52.

(230) Mitchell, Joseph. "Travelling Preacher and Settled Farmer." *Methodist History* 5 (1967): 3-14.

(231) Nuermberger, Ruth Anna Ketring. *The Free Produce Movement: A Quaker Protest against Slavery*. Durham: Duke University Press, 1942.

(232) Pearson, Alden B., Jr. "The Tragic Dilemma of a Border-State Moderate: The Rev. George E. Eagleton's Views on Slavery and Secession." *Tennessee Historical Quarterly* 32 (1973): 360-73.

(233) Peterson, Thomas V. *Ham and Japheth: The Mythic World of Whites in the Antebellum South*. Metuchen: Scarecrow Press, 1978.

(234) Posey, Walter B. "The Slavery Question in the Presbyterian Church in the Old Southwest." *Journal of Southern History* 15 (1949): 31-42.

(235) Purifoy, Lewis M. "The Southern Methodist Church and the Proslavery Argument." *Journal of Southern History* 32 (1966): 325-41.

(236) Reilly, Timothy F. "Robert L. Stanton, Abolitionist of the Old South." *Journal of Presbyterian History* 53 (1975): 33-49.

(237) Rice, Madeline H. *American Catholic Opinion in the Slavery Controversy.* New York: Columbia University Press, 1944.

(238) Rogers, Tommy W. "Dr. Frederick A. Ross and the Presbyterian Defense of Slavery." *Journal of Presbyterian History* 45 (1967): 112-24.

(239) Shankman, Arnold. "Converse, the *Christian Observer,* and Civil War Censorship." *Journal of Presbyterian History* 52 (1974): 227-44.

(240) Shanks, Caroline L. "The Biblical Anti-Slavery Argument of the Decade 1830-1840." *Journal of Negro History* 16 (1931): 132-57.

(241) Smith, H. Shelton. *In His Image But . . . .: Racism in Southern Religion, 1780-1910.* Durham: Duke University Press, 1972.

(242) _____. "Moral Crisis in a Troubled South." *Journal of Religious Thought* 14 (1956): 37-42.

(243) Stange, Douglas C. "Abolitionism as Maleficence: Southern Unitarians Versus 'Puritan Fanaticism'—1831-1860." *Harvard Library Bulletin* 26 (1978): 146-71.

(244) _____. "Abolitionism as Treason: The Unitarian Elite Defends Law, Order, and the Union." Harvard *Library Bulletin* 28 (1980): 152-70.

(245) _____. "From Treason to Antislavery Patriotism: Unitarian Conservatives and the Fugitive Slave Law." *Harvard Library Bulletin* 25 (1977): 466-88.

(246) _____. *Unitarians and Antislavery: Patterns of Antislavery Among American Unitarians, 1831-1860.* Rutherford NJ: Fairleigh Dickinson University Press, 1977.

(247) Staiger, C. Bruce. "Abolitionism and the Presbyterian Schism of 1837-38." *Mississippi Valley Historical Review* (now *Journal of American History*) 36 (1949): 391-414.

(248) Stewart, James B. "Evangelicalism and the Radical Strain in Southern Antislavery Thought During the 1820's." *Journal of Southern History* 39 (1973): 379-96.

(249) Taylor, Hubert V. "Slavery and the Deliberating of the Presbyterian General Assembly, 1833-1838." Ph.D. dissertation, Northwestern University, 1964.

(250) Troxler, George. "Eli Caruthers: A Silent Dissenter in the Old South." *Journal of Presbyterian History* 46 (1967): 95-111.

(251) Weeks, Louis III. "John Holt Rice and the American Colonization Society." *Journal of Presbyterian History* 46 (1968): 26-41.

V. BLACK RELIGION IN THE SOUTH
DURING RECONSTRUCTION
AND IN THE EARLY POSTBELLUM PERIOD

(252) Anscombe, Francis C. "The Contributions of the Quakers to the Reconstruction of the Southern States." Ph.D. dissertation, University of North Carolina in Chapel Hill, 1926.

(253) _____. "The Work of the Baltimore Association: The Quakers and Reconstruction in North Carolina." M.A. thesis, University of North Carolina in Chapel Hill, 1924.

(254) Armstrong, Thomas F. "The Building of a Black Church in Post Civil War Liberty County, Georgia." *Georgia Historical Quarterly* 66 (1982): 346-67.

(255) Bailey, Kenneth K. "The Post-Civil War Racial Separations in Southern Protestantism: Another Look." *Church History* 46 (1977): 453-73.

(256) Bell, John L., Jr. "Baptists and the Negro in North Carolina during Reconstruction." *North Carolina Historical Review* 42 (1965): 391-409.

(257) _____. "The Presbyterian Church and the Negro in North Carolina during Reconstruction." *North Carolina Historical Review* 40 (1963): 15-36.

(258) Bratton, Mary J. "John Jasper of Richmond: Free Slave Preacher to Community Leader." *Virginia Cavalcade* 29 (1979): 32-39.

(259) Brewe, H. Peers. "The Protestant Episcopal Freeman's Commission, 1865-1878." *Historical Magazine of the Protestant Episcopal Church* 26 (1967): 361-81.

(260) Brooks, Stephen E. "Out of the Galleries: The Northern Presbyterian Mission in Reconstruction North Carolina." M.A. thesis, University of North Carolina in Chapel Hill, 1974.

(261) Brown, Ira V. "Lyman Abbott and Freedmen's Aid, 1865-1869." *Journal of Southern History* 15 (1949): 22-38.

(262) Clark, Thomas D., ed. *The South Since Reconstruction*, 449-53, 466-73. Indianapolis: Bobbs-Merrill, 1973.

(263) Cunningham, Effie L. Harris. *Work of Disciples of Christ with Negro Americans*. St. Louis: UCMS, [1922].

(264) Daniel, W. Harrison. "Virginia Baptists and the Negro, 1865-1902." *Virginia Magazine of History and Biography* 76 (1968): 340-63.

(265) Dykes, Charles B. "Theology versus Thrift in the Black Belt." *Popular Science Monthly* 60 (1902): 360-64.

(266) Edwards, Larry. "Religious Education by Blacks During Reconstruction." *Religious Education* 69 (1974): 412-21.

(267) Ferry, Henry J. "Racism and Reunion: A Black Protest by Francis James Grimke." *Journal of Presbyterian History* 50 (1972): 77-88.

(268) Forrest, Edna Mae. "The Religious Development of the Negro in South Carolina since 1865." Master's thesis, Howard University, 1928.

(269) Gravely, William B., ed. "A Black Methodist on Reconstruction in Mississippi: Three Letters by James Lynch in 1868-1869." *Methodist History* 11 (1973): 2-18.

(270) _____. "The Decision of A.M.E. Leader, James Lynch, to Join the Methodist Episcopal Church: New Evidence." *Methodist History* 16 (July 1977): 263-69.

(271) _____. "Hiram Revels Protests Racial Separation in the Methodist Episcopal Church (1876)." *Methodist History* 8 (1970): 13-20.

(272) _____. "The Social, Political, and Religious Significance of the Formation of the Colored Methodist Episcopal Church (1870)." *Methodist History* 18 (1979): 3-25.

(273) Grundman, Adolph H. "Northern Baptists and the Founding of Virginia Union University: The Perils of Paternalism." *Journal of Negro History* 63 (1978): 26-41.

(274) Hagood, Lewis M. "The Southern Problem." *Methodist Review* 7 (1891): 428-34.

(275) Hall, Robert L. "Tallahassee's Black Churches, 1865-1885." *Florida Historical Quarterly* 58 (1979): 185-96.

(276) Hayden, J. Carleton. "After the War: The Mission and Growth of the Episcopal Church among Blacks in the South, 1865-1877." *Historical Magazine of the Protestant Episcopal Church* 42 (1973): 403-27.

(277) _____. "Reading, Religion, and Racism: The Mission of the Episcopal Church to Blacks in Virginia, 1865-1877." Ph.D. dissertation, Howard University, 1972.

(278) Heckman, Oliver S. "Northern Church Penetration into the South, 1860-1880." Ph.D. dissertation, Duke University, 1939.

(279) Hertzberg, Steven. "Southern Jews and Their Encounter with Blacks: Atlanta, 1850-1915." *Atlanta Historical Journal* 21 (1977): 7-24.

(280) Jervey, Edward D. "Motives and Methods of the Methodist Episcopal Church in the Period of Reconstruction." *Methodist History* 4 (1965): 17-25.

(281) Jones, Terry L. "Attitudes of Alabama Baptists Toward Negroes, 1890-1914." M.A. thesis, Samford University, 1968.

(282) Kealing, Hightower T. "The Colored Ministers of the South." *AME Church Review* 1 (1884): 139-44.

(283) Kennedy, Sr. M. Mercedes. "The Struggle for Education in the Parish (Civil) of Natchitoches, Louisiana, 1847-1951." M.A. thesis, Our Lady of the Lake University, 1952.

(284) Lamar, J. S. "Religious Future of the Negroes of the South." *Christian Quarterly* 6 (1874): 211.

(285) Lewis, Ronald L. "Cultural Pluralism and Black Reconstruction: The Public Career of Richard Cain." *Crisis* 85 (1978): 57-60, 64-65.

(286) Litwack, Leon. *Been in the Storm So Long: The Aftermath of Slavery*, 450-501. New York: Random House, 1979.

(287) Loveland, Anne C. "The 'Southern Work' of the Reverend Joseph C. Hartzell, Pastor of Ames Church in New Orleans, 1870-1873." *Louisana History* 16 (1975): 391-407.

(288) Moore, David O. "The Withdrawal of Blacks from Southern Baptist Churches Following Emancipation." *Baptist History and Heritage* 16 (1981): 12-18.

(289) More, Joanne Patterson. *In Christ's Stead: On Life and Work among the Negroes of the Southern States, Autobiographical Sketches*. Chicago: Woman's Baptist Home Missionary Society, 1902.

(290) Moroney, T. B. "The Condition of Catholic Colored Mission Work in the United States." *American Ecclesiastical Review* 61 (1919): 640-48.

(291) Morrow, Ralph E. *Northern Methodism and Reconstruction*. East Lansing: Michigan State University Press, 1956.

(292) Newton, John B. *The Commission on Work among the Colored People, Its Work and Progress*. Alexandria VA: Hill Print, 1888. Reprinted from *Virginia Seminary Magazine* 1,2 (1888).

(293) Presbyterian Church in the U.S.A. Board of Missions for Freedmen. *A Sketch of the Origin and Work of the Presbyterian Board of Missions for Freedmen*. Pittsburgh: Presbyterian Board of Missions for Freedmen, 1888.

(294) Richardson, Joe M. "Jonathan C. Gibbs: Florida's Only Negro Cabinet Member." *Florida Historical Quarterly* 42 (1964): 363-68.

(295) Roth, Donald F. " 'Grace Not Race': Southern Negro Church Leaders, Black Identity, and Missions to West Africa, 1865-1919." Ph.D. dissertation, University of Texas at Austin, 1975.

(296) Russell, James S. "Past and Present among the Negroes of Southern Virginia." *Spirit of Missions* 74 (1909): 307-310.

(297) Sessions, Gene A. "Camp Meeting at Willowtree, 1881." *Journal of American Folklore* 87 (1974): 361-64.

(298) Shield, R. N. "A Southern View of the Race Question." *Quarterly Review of the Methodist Episcopal Church, South* 8 (1890): 335.

(299) Sisk, Glenn N. "Churches in the Alabama Black Belt, 1875-1917." *Church History* 23 (1954): 153-74.

(300) Smallwood, James. "The Black Community in Reconstruction Texas: Readjustments in Religion and the Evolution of the Negro Church." *East Texas Historical Journal* 16 (1978): 16-28.

(301) Story, John W. "The Negro in Southern Baptist Thought, 1854-1900." Ph.D. dissertation, University of Kentucky, 1968.

(302) Strange, Robert. *Church Work among the Negroes in the South*. Chicago: Western Theological Seminary, 1907.

(303) Tripling, Paul W. "The Negro Excision from Baptist Churches in Texas, 1861-1870." Th.D. dissertation, Southwestern Baptist Theological Seminary, 1967.

(304) Thomas, Bettye C. "Public Education and Black Protest in Baltimore, 1865-1900." *Maryland Historical Magazine* 71 (1976): 381-91.

(305) Thompson, Ernest Trice. "Black Presbyterians, Education and Evangelicalism after the Civil War." *Journal of Presbyterian History* 51 (1973): 174-98.

(306) Walker, Clarence E. *A Rock in a Weary Land: The African Methodist Episcopal Church During the Civil War and Reconstruction*. Baton Rouge: Louisiana State University Press, 1982.

(307) Wharton, Vernon L. *The Negro in Mississippi, 1865-1890,* 256-65. Chapel Hill: University of North Carolina Press, 1947.

(308) Wheeler, Edward L. "Uplifting the Race: The Black Minister in the New South, 1865-1902." Ph.D. dissertation, Emory University, 1982.

(309) Work, Monroe N. "The Negro Church and the Negro Community." *Southern Workman* 37 (1908): 428-32.

(310) _____. "The Negroes of Warsaw, Georgia." *Southern Workman* 37 (1908): 29-40.

(311) Wynes, Charles E. "Bishop Thomas V. Dudley and the Uplift of the Negro." *Register of the Kentucky Historical Society* 65 (1967): 230-38.

VI. THE WORK OF THE AMERICAN MISSIONARY ASSOCIATION

(312) American Missionary Association. *History of the American Missionary Association: Its Churches and Educational Institutions among the Freedmen, Indians, and Chinese with Illustrative Facts and Anecdotes*. New York: S. W. Green, 1874.

(313) "The American Missionary Association and the Congregationalists Have Established Educational Foundations in Southern States." *Southern Workman* 5 (1876): 50.

(314) Cady, George L. "Hampton Institute and the American Missionary Association." *Southern Workman* 63 (1934): 135-39.

(315) DeBoer, Clara Merritt. "The Role of Afro-Americans in the Origin and Work of the American Missionary Association, 1839-1877." Ph.D. dissertation, Rutgers University, 1973.

(316) Drake, Richard B. "The American Missionary Association and the Southern Negro, 1881-1888." M.A. thesis, Emory University, 1957.

(317) Haywood, Jacqueline Slaughter. "The American Missionary Association in Louisiana during Reconstruction." Ph.D. dissertation, University of California at Los Angeles, 1974.

(318) Hubbard, Henry W. *American Missionary Association: Work among the Colored People of the South*. New York: Congregational Rooms, n.d.

(319) Johnson, Clifton H. "The American Missionary Association, 1846-1861: A Study of Christian Abolitionism." Ph.D. dissertation, University of North Carolina in Chapel Hill, 1959.

(320) Pearce, Larry W. "The American Missionary Association and the Freedmen in Arkansas, 1863-1878." *Arkansas Historical Quarterly* 30 (1971): 123-44.

(321) _____. "The American Missionary Association and the Freedmen's Bureau in Arkansas, 1866-1868." *Arkansas Historical Quarterly* 30 (1971): 242-59.

(322) _____. "The American Missionary Association and the Freedmen's Bureau in Arkansas, 1868-1878." *Arkansas Historical Quarterly* 31 (1972): 246-61.

(323) Richardson, Joe M. "The American Missionary Association and Black Education in Civil War Missouri." *Missouri Historical Review* 69 (1975): 433-88.

(324) _____. "Christian Abolitionism: The American Missionary Association and the Florida Negro." *Journal of Negro Education* 40 (1971): 35-44.

(325) _____. "The Failure of the American Missionary Association to Expand Congregationalism Among Southern Blacks." *Southern Studies* 18 (1979): 51-73.

(326) _____, ed. " 'We Are Truly Doing Missionary Work': Letters from American Missionary Association Teachers in Florida, 1864-1874." *Florida Historical Quarterly* 54 (1975): 178-95.

(327) Rogers, George A., and R. Frank Saunders, Jr. "The American Missionary Association in Liberty County, Georgia: An Invasion of Light and Love." *Georgia Historical Quarterly* 62 (1978): 304-15. See also Rogers and Saunders. *Swamp Water and Wiregrass,* 109-22. Macon GA: Mercer University Press, 1984.

(328) Schweninger, Loren. "The American Missionary Association and Northern Philanthropy in Reconstruction Alabama." *Alabama Historical Quarterly* 32 (1970): 129-56.

VII. BLACK DENOMINATIONAL AND SECTARIAN MOVEMENTS AND CHURCHES

(329) Allen, Easter W. "The Negro's Religion and Its Effect upon the Recreational Activities in Bladen County, North Carolina." Master's thesis, Springfield College, 1936.

(330) Allison, Madeline G. "Bethel A.M.E. Church in Columbia, S.C." *The Crisis* 25 (1922): 75.

(331) Battle, Allen O. "Status Personality in a Negro Holiness Sect." Ph.D. dissertation, Catholic University of America, 1961.

(332) Berlack, Freeman R. "A Study of Religious Cults among Negroes in Richmond, Virginia." B.D. thesis, Virginia Union University, 1940.

(333) Berry, Lewellyn L. *A Century of the African Methodist Episcopal Church, 1840-1940.* New York: Gutenberg Printing, 1942.

(334) Boothe, Charles O. *The Cyclopedia of the Colored Baptists of Alabama, Their Leaders and Their Work.* Birmingham: Alabama Publishing, 1895.

(335) Bowling, Richard H. "Keeping an Old Church Alive." *Southern Workman* 61 (1932): 200-208.

(336) Bradley, David M. *A History of the A.M.E. Zion Church.* 2 vols. Nashville: Parthenon Press, 1956-1970.

(337) Brooks, Walter H. "The Priority of the Silver Bluff Church and Its Promoters." *Journal of Negro History* 7 (1922): 172-96.

(338) Butt, Israel L. *History of African Methodism in Virginia: or, Four Decades in the Old Dominion.* Hampton VA: Hampton Institute Press, 1908.

(339) Carey, Archibald J. "The Negro Methodist Churches in America." *A.M.E. Church Review* 78 (1961): 20-26.

(340) Carter, Edward R. *The Black Side: A Partial History of the Business, Religious, and Educational Side of the Negro in Atlanta, Ga.* Atlanta: n.p., 1894.

(341) Carter, Luther C., Jr. "Negro Churches in a Southern Community." Ph.D. dissertation, Yale University, 1955.

(342) "Churches, Early Negro, in Kingston, Jamaica, and Savannah, Georgia." *Journal of Negro History* 1 (1916): 69-92.

(343) Clark, William A. "Sanctification in Negro Religion." *Social Forces* 15 (1937): 544-51.

(344) Cobbins, Bishop Otto B., et al. *History of the Church of Christ (Holiness) U.S.A., 1895-1965.* Chicago: National Publication Board, Church of Christ (Holiness) U.S.A., 1966.

(345) Coleman, Clinton R. "A Study of a Black Ghetto Church, the Pennsylvania Avenue A.M.E. Zion Church, Baltimore, Maryland." M. Div. paper, Howard University School of Religion, 1971.

(346) Cooke, J. W. "Stoney Point, 1866-1969." *Filson Club Historical Quarterly* 50 (1976): 337-52.

(347) Crawford, D. D., comp. *Statistical Report of Negro Baptists of Georgia for the Year 1915.* Macon GA: William Pullins, Printer, 1915.

(348) Davis, Arnor S. "The Pentecostal Movement in Black Christianity." *Black Church* 2 (1972): 65-88.

(349) Dodson, Dan. "The Role of Institutional Religion in Ethnic Groups of Dallas." Master's thesis, Southern Methodist University, 1936.

(350) Durden, Robert F. "The Establishment of Calvary Protestant Episcopal Church for Negroes in Charleston." *South Carolina Historical Magazine* 65 (1964): 63-84.

(351) Evans, Zeila S., with J. T. Alexander, eds. *Dexter Avenue Baptist Church, 1877-1977.* Montgomery Al: Dexter Avenue Baptist Church, 1978.

(352) "The First African M.E. Church in the South." *A.M.E. Church Review* 75 (1959): 10-16.

(353) Fisher, Henry. *The History of the United Holy Church of America, Inc.* [Durham NC]: n.p., [194?].

(354) Forbes, James A. "Ministry of Hope from a Double Minority." *Theological Education* 9 (Summer 1973, supplement): 305-16.

(355) Fuller, Thomas O. *History of the Negro Baptists of Tennessee.* Memphis: Haskins Print, 1936.

(356) Gaines, Miriam. "The John Little Mission, Louisville, Ky." *Southern Workman* 62 (1933): 161-70.

(357) Gaines, Wesley J. *African Methodism in the South: or Twenty-Five Years of Freedom*. Atlanta: Franklin Publishing, 1890.

(358) Garvin, Philip, and Julia Welch. *Religious America*, 141-69. New York: McGraw-Hill, 1974.

(359) General Association of Colored Baptists. *Diamond Jubilee of the General Association of Colored Baptists in Kentucky*. Louisville: American Baptist, 1943.

(360) "Giving Out of Deep Poverty." *The Church at Home and Abroad* 1 (1887): 448.

(361) Graham, John H. *A Study of Revel's Methodist Church of Greenville, Mississippi*. Atlanta: Interdenominational Theological Center, 1960.

(362) _____. *A Study of Wesley Methodist Church, York, South Carolina*. Atlanta: Gammon Theological Seminary Department of Sociology, 1959.

(363) Gravely, Will B. "The Rise of African Churches in America (1786-1822): Re-examining the Contexts." *Journal of Religious Thought* 41 (1984): 58-73.

(364) Harris, Waldo P. III. "Locations Associated with Daniel Marshall and the Kiokee Church." *Viewpoints: Georgia Baptist History* 6 (1978): 25-46.

(365) Hicks, William. *History of Louisiana Negro Baptists*. Nashville: National Baptist Publishing House, 1915.

(366) "A Historic Building." *The Church at Home and Abroad* 23 (1898): 516.

(367) Holleweger, Walter J. "A Black Pentecostal Concept: A Forgotten Chapter of Black History." *Concept*, special issue 30 (June 1970).

(368) Hood, J. W. *One Hundred Years of the African Methodist Episcopal Zion Church; or the Centennial of African Methodism*. New York: A.M.E. Zion Book Concern, 1895.

(369) Jackson, R. J. *History of Walker Baptist Association of Georgia*. Augusta: Chronicle Job Print, 1909.

(370) Jordan, Lewis G. *Negro Baptist History, U.S.A., 1750-1930*. Nashville: Sunday School Publishing Board, National Baptist Convention, 1930.

(371) Kealing, H. T. *History of African Methodism in Texas*. Waco: C. F. Blanks, 1885.

(372) Kennard, Richard. *A Short History of the Gilfield Baptist Church of Petersburg, Virginia*. Petersburg VA: Owen, 1913.

(373) Koger, Azzie B. *Negro Baptists of Maryland*. Baltimore: Clarke Press, 1946.

(374) Lakey, Othal H. *The Rise of "Colored Methodism": A Study of the Background and the Beginnings of the Christian Methodist Episcopal Church*. Dallas: Crescendo Book Publications, 1972.

(375) Lewis, Thomas P. *Condensed Historical Sketch of Tabernacle Baptist Church, Augusta, Georgia, from Its Organization in 1885 to February, 1904*. Augusta: The Georgia Baptist Book Print, 1904.

(376) Lincoln, C. Eric, and Lawrence H. Mamiya. "Daddy Jones and Father Divine: The Cult as Political Religion." *Religion in Life* 49 (1980): 6-23.

(377) Lockley, Edith. "The Negro Spiritualist Churches of Nashville." Master's thesis, Fisk University, 1935.

(378) Long, Charles S. *History of the A.M.E. Church in Florida*. Philadelphia: A.M.E. Book Concern, 1939.

(379) Lovett, Leonard. "Black Holiness-Pentecostalism: Implications for Ethics and Social Transformation." Ph.D. dissertation, Emory University, 1978.

(380) McAfee, Sara Jane. *History of the Woman's Missionary Society in the Colored Methodist Episcopal Church, Comprising Its Foundations, Organizations, Pathfinders, Subsequent Developments and Present Status*. Rev. ed. Phenix City AL: Phenix City Herald, 1945.

(381) McAnich, Glen A. "We'll Pray For You: Methodist Ethnocentrism in the Origins of the African Methodist Episcopal Church in Baltimore." M.A. thesis, University of North Carolina in Chapel Hill, 1973,

(382) Manly, Basil, Jr. "Reminiscences of the First African Church, Richmond, Va." *Baptist Memorial and Monthly Chronicle* 14 (1855): 262-65, 289-92, 321-27, 353-56.

(383) Mixon, Winfield H. *History of the African Methodist Episcopal Church in Alabama, with Biographical Sketches with an Introduction by Rt. Rev. Henry McNeal Turner*. N.p.p.: n.p., n.d.

(384) Montgomery, William E. "Negro Churches in the South, 1865-1915." Ph.D. dissertation, University of Texas at Austin, 1975.

(385) Moore, John J. *History of the A.M.E. Zion Church*. York PA: Teachers Journal Office, 1884.

(386) Paris, Arthur. *Black Pentecostalism: Southern Religion in an Urban World*. Amherst: University of Massachusetts Press, 1982.

(387) Parrish, Charles H. *Golden Jubilee of the General Association of Colored Baptists in Kentucky: The Story of Fifty Years' Work from 1865-1915, Including Many Photos and Sketches*. Louisville: Mayes Printing, 1915.

(388) Payne, Daniel A., and Charles S. Smith. *History of the African Methodist Episcopal Church*. 2 vols. New York: Johnson Reprint, 1968. First published 1891, 1922.

(389) Pearson, Fred L., and Joseph A. Tomberlin. "John Doe, Alias God: A Note on Father Divine's Georgia Career." *Georgia Historical Quarterly* 60 (1976): 43-48.

(390) Pelt, Owen D., and Ralph L. Smith. *The Story of the National Baptists*. New York: Vantage Press, 1960.

(391) Phillips, Charles H. *The History of the Colored Methodist Episcopal Church in America: Comprising Its Organization, Subsequent Development, and Present Status*. Jackson TN: C.M.E. Church Publishing House, 1898. Rev. ed., 1925.

(392) "Pilgrimage to First Negro Church." *The Crisis* 79 (1972): 162-63.

(393) Rankin, Charles H. "The Rise of Negro Baptist Churches in the South through the Reconstruction Period." Master's thesis, New Orleans Baptist Theological Seminary, 1955.

(394) Redkey, Edwin S. *Black Exodus: Black Nationalist and Back-to-Africa Movements, 1890-1910*. New Haven: Yale University Press, 1969.

(395) Reid, Stevenson N. *History of Colored Baptists in Alabama*. [Gadsden AL?]: n.p., 1949.

(396) Richardson, Harry V. *Dark Salvation: The Story of Methodism as It Developed among Blacks in America*. Garden City: Doubleday Anchor, 1976.

(397) Richardson, James C. *With Water and Spirit: A History of the Black Apostolic Denominations in the United States*. Washington: Spirit Press, 1980.

(398) Rogers, Alain. ''The African Methodist Episcopal Church—A Study in Black Nationalism.'' *The Black Church* 1 (1972): 17-43.

(399) Ross, German R. *History and Formative Years of the Church of God in Christ*. Memphis: Church of God in Christ Publishing House, 1969.

(400) Rush, Christopher. *A Short Account of the Rise and Progress of the African Methodist Episcopal Church in America*. New York: By the author, 1843.

(401) ''St. John African Methodist Episcopal Church, Norfolk, Virginia.'' *A.M.E. Church Review* 72 (1955): 16-17.

(402) Sexton, Mark S. *The Chalice and the Covenant: A History of the New Covenant Baptist Association, 1868-1975*. Winston-Salem: Hunter Publishing, 1976.

(403) Shaw, J. Beverly F. *The Negro in the History of Methodism*. Nashville: Parthenon Press, 1954.

(404) Shropshire, James M. ''A Socio-Historical Characterization of the Black Pentecostal Movement in America.'' Ph.D. dissertation, Northwestern University, 1974.

(405) Sideboard, Henry Y. ''The Historical Background of the Colored Methodist Episcopal Church.'' B.D. paper, Howard University School of Religion, 1938.

(406) Simms, James M. *The First Colored Baptist Church in North America, Constituted at Savannah, Georgia, June 20, A.D. 1788*. Philadelphia: J. B. Lippincott, 1888.

(407) Simpson, George E. ''Black Pentecostalism in the United States.'' *Phylon* 35 (1974): 203-11.

(408) Singleton, George A. *The Romance of African Methodism: A Study of the African Methodist Episcopal Church*. New York: Exposition Press, 1952.

(409) Smith, Sid. ''Growth of Black Baptist Churches in the Inner City.'' *Baptist History and Heritage* 16 (1981): 49-60.

(410) Sweet, William Warren. ''Negro Churches in the South: A Phase of Reconstruction.'' *Methodist Review* 104 (1921): 405-18.

(411) Tanner, Carl M. ''Bethel A.M.E. Tabernacle.'' *A.M.E. Church Review* 78 (1963): 26-33.

(412) Tarr, H. ''Elijah in Mississippi.'' *Jewish Digest* 8 (1963): 71-80.

(413) Tate, Robert Jr. ''A Study of Negro Churches in Durham, North Carolina.'' B.D. thesis, Duke University, 1939.

(414) Thomas, Edgar G. *The First African Baptist Church of North America*. Savannah: n.p., 1925.

(415) Thompson, Patrick H. *The History of Negro Baptists in Mississippi*. Jackson: R. W. Bailey Printing, 1898.

(416) Walls, William J. *The African Methodist Episcopal Zion Church: Reality of the Black Church*. Charlotte: A.M.E. Zion Publishing House, 1974.

(417) Washington, James M. "The Origins and Emergence of Black Baptist Separatism, 1863-1897." Ph.D. dissertation, Yale University, 1979.

(418) Wayman, Alexander W. *Cyclopedia of African Methodism*. Baltimore: Methodist Episcopal Book Depository, 1882.

(419) West, C. S. "A Colored Church Self-Sustaining." *The Church at Home and Abroad* 4 (1888): 43.

(420) Weston, Abraham. "How African Methodism was Introduced in the Up Country." *A.M.E. Church Review* 80 (1964): 44-46.

(421) Wheeler, Edward L. "Beyond One Man: A General Survey of Black Baptist Church History." *Review and Expositor* 70 (1973): 309-19.

(422) Whitted, J. *A History of the Negro Baptists of North Carolina*. Raleigh: Edwards and Broughton, Printing, 1908.

(423) Wills, David W. "Aspects of Social Thought in the African Methodist Episcopal Church, 1884-1910." Ph.D. dissertation, Harvard University, 1975.

(424) _____and Richard Newman, eds. *Black Apostles at Home and Abroad: Afro-Americans and the Christian Mission from the Revolution to Reconstruction*. Boston: G. K. Hall, 1982.

(425) Wright, Richard R., Jr., ed. *The Encyclopedia of the African Methodist Episcopal Church*. 2d ed. Philadelphia: n.p., 1947.

VIII. ROMAN CATHOLICISM AND SOUTHERN BLACKS

Many titles in the previous sections of this chapter are relevant to this topic.

(426) Beckers, Msgr. Henry. *A History of the Immaculate Conception Catholic Church, Natchitoches, Louisiana, 1717-1973*. Privately printed, 1973.

(427) "Bishop Jeanmard and the Erath, La. Case." *St. Augustine's Messenger* 33 (1956): 24-27.

(428) Bowman, John W. "Mouton Switch." *St. Augustine's Messenger* 19 (1941): 219-21.

(429) _____. "Where the West Begins." *St. Augustine's Messenger* 19 (1941): 170-74.

(430) _____. "A Year and a Day." *St. Augustine's Messenger* 20 (1942): 171-74.

(431) Bryan, C. Braxton. "The Negro in Virginia." *Southern Workman* 34 (1905): 51-54, 100-108, 170-79.

(432) Butsch, Joseph. "Negro Catholics in the United States." *Catholic Historical Review* 3 (1917): 33-51.

(433) Callaghan, Brian L. "Fifty Years in Louisiana." *The Colored Harvest* 27 (1948): 8-11.

(434) Callahan, Rev. J. J., et al. *The History of St. Augustine's Parish: Isle Brevelle, Natchez, La.* Natchitoches LA: n.p., 1956.

(435) Cooley, Leo P. "Bishop England's Solution of the Negro Problem." M.A. thesis, St. John's University, 1940.

(436) Detiege, Sr. Audrey Marie. *Henriette Delille, Free Woman of Color: Foundress of the Sisters of the Holy Family.* New Orleans: Sisters of the Holy Family, 1976.

(437) Gillard, John T. *The Catholic Church and the American Negro.* Baltimore: St. Joseph's Society Press, 1929.

(438) _____. *Colored Catholics in the United States.* Baltimore: Josephite Press, 1941.

(439) Guidry, Sr. Mary Gabrilla, S.S.F. *The Southern Negro Nun: An Autobiography.* New York: Exposition Press, 1974.

(440) Hepburn, D. "Negro Catholics in New Orleans." *Our World* 5 (1950): 14-31.

(441) Hogan, John A. "Church Work among the Negroes: Letter dated Galveston, Texas, August 3, 1901." *Woodstock Letters* 30 (1901): 223-30.

(442) Howard, Clarence J. "Anniversary in Louisiana." *St. Augustine's Messenger* 21 (1943): 220-23.

(443) Kemper, Donald J. "Catholic Integration in St. Louis, 1935-1947." *Missouri Historical Review* 73 (1978): 1-22.

(444) Labbe, Dolores E. *Jim Crow Comes to Church: The Establishment of Segregated Catholic Parishes in South Louisiana.* Lafayette LA: University of Southwestern Louisiana, 1971.

(445) McKenna, Horace B. "Colored Catholics in St. Mary's County, Maryland." *Woodstock Letters* 79 (1950): 55-78.

(446) Mensing, Raymond C., Jr. "The Rise and Fall of the Pseudo Poor Clare Nuns of Skidaway Island." *Georgia Historical Quarterly* 61 (1977): 318-28.

(447) Mills, Gary B. *The Forgotten People: Cane River's Creoles of Color.* Baton Rouge: Louisiana State University Press, 1977.

(448) Murphy, Miriam T. "Catholic Missionary Work among the Colored People of the United States, 1766-1866." *American Catholic Historical Society of Philadelphia Records* 35 (1924): 101-36.

(449) Osborne, William. "Slavery's Sequel: A Freedman's Odyssey." *Jubilee* 3 (1955): 10-23.

(450) Perry, Galbraith B. *Twelve Years among the Colored People: A Record of the Work of Mt. Calvary Chapel of St. Mary the Virgin, Baltimore.* New York: James Pott, 1884.

(451) Sherwood, Grace H. *The Oblates' Hundred and One Years.* New York: Macmillan, 1931.

(452) "Southern States and Catholic Negroes." *The Crisis* 1 (1911): 10.

(453) Spalding, David. "The Negro Catholic Congresses, 1889-1894." *Catholic Historical Review* 55 (1969): 337-57. Reprinted, *Freeing the Spirit* (Summer 1972): 7-16.

(454) Tarry, Ellen. "The City of Jude." *Catholic Digest* 5 (October 1941): 73-76.

(455) Theobald, Stephen L. "Catholic Missionary Work among the Colored People of the United States (1776-1876)." *American Catholic Historical Society of Philadelphia Records* 35 (1924): 324-44.

IX. AFRICAN AND FOLK ELEMENTS IN SOUTHERN BLACK RELIGION

Titles dealing with spirituals and other musical topics are found in the listing for chapter 17.

(456) Adams, Edward C. L. *Congaree Sketches: Scenes from Negro Life in the Swamps of the Congaree and Tales by Tad and Scrip of Heaven and Hell with Other Miscellany*. Chapel Hill: University of North Carolina Press, 1927.

(457) "Alabama Folk Lore." *Southern Workman* 33 (1904): 49-52.

(458) Allen, Richard. "The Folk Sermon." In *Black American Literature*. Ruth Miller, ed., 115-35. Beverly Hills: Glencoe Press, 1971.

(459) Anderson, John Q. "The New Orleans Voodoo, Ritual Dance, and Its Twentieth Century Survivals." *Southern Folklore Quarterly* 24 (1960): 135-43.

(460) "The Baptist, Methodist, and Presbyterian Preachers from 'Negro Tales from Bolivar Country, Mississippi'." *Southern Folklore Quarterly* 19 (1955): 104-26.

(461) "Beliefs and Customs Connected with Death and Burial." *Southern Workman* 26 (1897): 18-19.

(462) Bolton, H. Carrington. "Decoration of Graves of Negroes in South Carolina." *Journal of American Folklore* 4 (1891): 214.

(463) Bradford, R. "Swing Low, Sweet Chariot: Religious Rites of the Southern Negro." *Colliers* 96 (21 September 1935): 16-17+.

(464) Brewer, J. Mason. *The Word on the Brazos: Negro Preacher Tales from the Brazos Bottoms of Texas*. Austin: University of Texas Press, 1953. Rev. ed., 1976.

(465) Brewer, John M. *Worser Days and Better Times: The Folklore of the North Carolina Negro*. Chicago: Quadrangle Books, 1965.

(466) Brownlow, Paul C. "The Pulpit and Black America: 1865-1877." *Quarterly Journal of Speech* 58 (1972): 431-40.

(467) Butler, Alfloyd. "The Blacks' Contribution of Elements of African Religion to Christianity in America: A Case Study of the Great Awakening in South Carolina." Ph.D. dissertation, Northwestern University, 1975.

(468) Bryant, M. Winifred. "Negro Services." *American Missionary Magazine* 46 (1892): 301-302.

(469) Carter, Lawrence E. "Black Preaching: Poetry and a Text." *Freeing the Spirit* 3 (1974): 33-36.

(470) Chamberlain, Alexander F. "Negro Creation Legend." *Journal of American Folklore* 3 (1890): 302.

(471) Culverhouse, Patricia. "Black Religion: Folk or Christian?" *Foundations* 13 (1970): 295-315.

(472) Cummings, Melbourne S. "The Rhetoric of Bishop Henry McNeal Turner." *Journal of Black Studies* 12 (1981-82): 457-70.

(473) "Customs and Superstitions in Louisiana." *Journal of American Folklore* 1 (1888): 136-39.

(474) Ferris, William R., Jr. "The Negro Conversion Experience." *Keystone Folklore Quarterly* 15 (1970): 35-51.

(475) "Folk-Lore from St. Helena, South Carolina." *Journal of American Folklore* 38 (1935): 217-38.

(476) Garrett, Romeo B. "African Survivals in American Culture." *Journal of Negro History* 51 (1966): 239-45.

(477) Gravely, William B. "The Dialectic of Double-Consciousness in Black American Freedom Celebrations, 1808-1863." *Journal of Negro History* 67 (1982): 302-317.

(478) Ingersoll, Ernest. "Decoration of Negro Graves." *Journal of American Folklore* 5 (1892): 68-69.

(479) Johnson, Clifton E., ed. *God Struck Me Dead: Religious Conversion Experiences and Autobiographies of Ex-Slaves.* Philadelphia: Pilgrim Press, 1969.

(480) Johnson, Guy B. *Folk Culture of St. Helena Island.* Chapel Hill: University of North Carolina Press, 1930.

(481) Jones, Alice Marie. "The Negro Sermon: A Study in the Sociology of Folk Culture." M.A. thesis, Fisk University, 1942.

(482) Jordan, Terry G. " 'The Roses So Red and the Lilies So Fair': Southern Folk Cemeteries in Texas." *Southwestern Historical Quarterly* 83 (1980): 227-58.

(483) Kennedy, William T. "The Genius of Black Preaching." *A.M.E. Zion Quarterly Review* 83 (1971): 104-108.

(484) Lett, Anna. "Some West Tennessee Superstitions about Conjurers, Witches, Ghosts, and the Devil." *Tennessee Folklore Society Bulletin* 36 (1970): 37-45.

(485) McGhee, Nancy B. "The Folk Sermon: A Facet of the Black Literary Heritage." *College Language Association Journal* 13 (September 1969): 51-61.

(486) Martin, D. S. "On Religious Excitement: The Peculiar Craze of Kentucky Negroes with the Appearance of General Fremont." *Journal of American Folklore* 4 (1891): 5-6.

(487) Mathews, Dom Basil. "Vodun and Catholicism." *Catholic World* 158 (October 1943): 65-72.

(488) Mitchell, Henry H. *Black Relief: Folk Beliefs of Blacks in America and West Africa*. New York: Harper and Row, 1975.

(489) *Negro Tales from Pine Bluff, Arkansas, and Calvin, Michigan*. Bloomington: University of Indiana Press, 1948.

(490) Newell, William W. "Reports of Voodoo Worship in Hayti [*sic*] and Louisiana." *Journal of American Folklore* 2 (1889): 41-47.

(491) Oertel, Hanns. "Notes on Six Negro Myths from the Georgia Coast." *Journal of American Folklore* 2 (1889): 309.

(492) Owen, Mary Alicia. "Voodooism in Missouri." *Journal of American Folklore* 3 (1890): 9-10.

(493) Parsons, Elsie C. *Folklore of the Sea Islands, South Carolina*. Cambridge: American Folklore Society, 1923.

(494) Pendleton, Louis. "Negro Folklore and Witchcraft in the South." *Journal of American Folklore* 3 (1890): 201-207.

(495) Pipes, William H. *Say Amen, Brother! Old-Time Negro Preaching: A Study in American Frustration*. New York: William-Frederick Press, 1951.

(496) Pitman, Frank W. "Fetishism, Witchcraft, and Christianity among the Slaves." *Journal of Negro History* 2 (1926): 650-68.

(497) Powdermaker, Hortense. *After Freedom: A Cultural Study of the Deep South*, chap. 4. New York: Viking Press, 1939.

(498) Puckett, Newbell N. *Folk Beliefs of the Southern Negro*, chap. 3. New York: Viking Press, 1968. First published 1926.

(499) Rogers, George A., and R. Frank Saunders, Jr. "The Liberty County Christ Craze of 1889." In *Swamp Water and Wiregrass*, 191-204. Macon GA: Mercer University Press, 1984.

(500) Rosenberg, Bruce A. *The Art of the American Folk Preacher*. New York: Oxford University Press, 1970.

(501) Seale, Lea, and Marianna Seale. "Easter Rock: A Louisiana Negro Ceremony." *Journal of American Folklore* 55 (1942): 212-28.

(502) Sides, Sudie Duncan. "Slave Weddings and Religion: Plantation Life in the Southern States Before the American Civil War." *History Today* 24 (1974): 77-87.

(503) Smiley, Portia. "Folk-Lore from Virginia, South-Carolina [*sic*], Georgia and Florida." *Journal of American Folklore* 32 (1919): 837-83.

(504) Spillers, Hortense J. "Martin Luther King and the Style of the Black Sermon." *Black Scholar* 3 (1971): 14-27.

(505) Steiner, Roland. "Seeking Jesus: A Religious Rite of Negroes in Georgia." *Journal of American Folklore* 14 (1901): 172.

(506) _____. "Sol Lockheart's Call." *Journal of American Folklore* 13 (1900): 67-70.

(507) _____. "Superstitions and Beliefs from Central Georgia." *Journal of American Folklore* 12 (1899): 261-71.

(508) Suttles, William C., Jr. "African Religious Survivals as Factors in American Slave Revolts." *Journal of Negro History* 56 (1971): 97-104.

(509) Tallant, Robert. *Voodoo in New Orleans.* New York: Macmillan, 1946.

(510) Terry, Richard R. *Voodooism in Music and Other Essays.* New York: Books for Libraries Press, 1968.

(511) Touchstone, Donald Blake. "Voodoo in New Orleans." *Louisiana History* 13 (1972): 371-86.

(512) "Two Negro With Stories." *Journal of American Folklore* 12 (1899): 145-56.

(513) "Voodoo and Vodun." *Journal of American Folklore* 10 (1897): 21-34.

(514) "A Voodoo Festival near New Orleans." *Journal of American Folklore* 10 (1897): 21-34.

(515) Watson, Andrew P. "Primitive Religion among Negroes in Tennessee." M.A. thesis, Fisk University, 1932.

(516) Whitney, Anna Weston. "Why the Devil Never Wears a Hat." *Journal of American Folklore* 12 (1899): 274.

(517) Whitten, Norman E., Jr. "Contemporary Patterns of Malijn Occultism among Negroes in North Carolina." *Journal of American Folklore* 75 (1962): 311-25.

(518) Wiggins, William H., Jr. "'Free at Last!': A Study of Afro-American Emancipation Day Celebrations." Ph.D. dissertation, Indiana University, 1974.

(519) Williamson, George. "Superstitions from Louisiana." *Journal of American Folklore* 18 (1905): 229-30.

(520) Work, Monroe N. "Some Geechee Folklore." *Southern Workman* 34 (1905): 633-35, 696-97.

X. RELIGION, EDUCATION, AND SOUTHERN BLACKS

(521) Agatha, Mother M. (Mary Cecelia Ryan). *Catholic Education and the Negro.* Washington: n.p., 1942.

(522) Avery, William A. "Better Education for Negro Rural Ministers." *Southern Workman* 49 (1920): 458-67.

(523) _____. "Negro Teachers and Ministers Cooperate in South Carolina." *Southern Workman* 50 (1921): 503-510.

(524) Barnette, Henlee H. "Negro Students in Southern Baptist Seminaries." *Review and Expositor* 53 (1956): 207-210.

(525) Bishop, Samuel H. "The Church and Negroes." *Spirit of Missions* 74 (1909): 207-209, 931-33.

(526) Bond, Horace M. *The Education of the Negro in the American Social Order.* New York: Prentice-Hall, 1934.

(527) Brawley, James. *Two Centuries of Methodist Concern: Bondage, Freedom and Education of Black People*. New York: Vantage Press, 1974.

(528) Brown, Frank R. "Educational Philosophy and Program for Higher Education of Hood Theological Seminary, A.M.E. Zion Church, Salisbury, N.C." *A.M.E. Zion Quarterly Review* 84 (1972): 148-50.

(529) Butchart, Ronald E. *Northern Schools, Southern Blacks and Reconstruction: Freedmen's Education, 1862-1875*. Westport CT: Greenwood Press, 1980.

(530) Caution, Tollie L. "Protestant Episcopal Church: Policies and Rationale upon Which Support of Its Negro Colleges Is Predicated." *Journal of Negro Education* 29 (1960): 274-83.

(531) Chitty, Arthur Ben. "St. Augustine's College, Raleigh, North Carolina." *Historical Magazine of the Protestant Episcopal Church* 35 (1966): 207-19.

(532) Coleman, C. D. "Christian Methodist Episcopal Church: The Rationale and Policies upon Which Support of Its Colleges Is Predicated." *Journal of Negro Education* 29 (1960): 315-18.

(533) "The Colver Theological Institute, at Richmond, Va." *Southern Workman* 1 (March 1872): 3.

(534) "Comparison of Some Ethnic and Religious Attitudes of Negro and White College Students in the Deep South." *Social Forces* 30 (1952): 426-28.

(535) Corey, Charles H. *History of the Richmond Theological Seminary with Reminiscences of Thirty Years' Work among the Colored People of the South*. Richmond: J. W. Randolph, 1895.

(536) Fisher, Miles M., ed. *Virginia Union University and Some of Her Achievements: Twenty-Fifth Anniversary, 1899-1924*. Richmond: Brown Print Shop, 1924.

(537) Gardner, Bettye. "Ante-Bellum Black Education in Baltimore." *Maryland Historical Magazine* 71 (1976): 360-66.

(538) George, Arthur H. "The History of Johnson C. Smith University, 1867 to the Present." Doctoral dissertation, New York University, 1954.

(539) Gibson, DeLois. "A Historical Study of Philander Smith College, 1877-1969." Ph.D. dissertation, University of Arkansas, 1972.

(540) Graham, John H. *The Role of Gammon Theological Seminary in Ministerial Training and Services for the Negro Churches, 1940-1954*. Atlanta: n.p., 1956.

(541) Graham, William L. "Patterns of Intergroup Relations in the Cooperative Establishment, Control, and Administration of Paine College, Georgia, by Southern Negro and White People: A Study of Intergroup Process." Doctoral dissertation, New York University, 1955.

(542) Griffin, Paul R. "Black Founders of Reconstruction Era Methodist Colleges: Daniel A. Payne, Joseph C. Price, and Isaac Lane, 1863-1890." Ph.D. dissertation, Emory University, 1983.

(543) Hargett, Andrew H. "Religious Attitudes as Expressed by Students of Savannah State College." *Journal of Negro Education* 20 (1951): 237-40.

(544) Holmes, Dwight O. W. *The Evolution of the Negro College*. New York: Teachers College, Columbia University, 1934.

(545) "Hood Seminary: A Unique Training Center." *Church School Herald-Journal* 56 (1971): 1-2.

(546) Jenkins, Clara B. "A Historical Study of Shaw University, 1865-1963." Ph.D. dissertation, University of Pittsburgh, 1965.

(547) Johnson, Alandus C. "History of Paine College, Augusta, 1903-1946." Ph.D. dissertation, University of Georgia, 1970.

(548) Jones, Jacqueline. *Soldiers of Light and Love: Northern Teachers and Georgia Blacks, 1865-1873*. Chapel Hill: University of North Carolina Press, 1980.

(549) Kersey, Harry A., Jr. "St. Augustine School: Seventy-five Years of Negro Parochial Education in Gainesville, Florida." *Florida Historical Quarterly* 51 (1972): 58-63.

(550) Little, John. "The Work of the Presbyterian Church for the Negro." *Southern Workman* 33 (1904): 439-48.

(551) Lunceford, Bill E. "An Historical Study of the Development of Theological Education for Negro Baptist Ministers in the South from 1619 until 1954." Master's thesis, Southern Baptist Theological Seminary, 1955.

(552) McKinney, Richard I. *Religion in Higher Education among Negroes*. New Haven: Yale University Press, 1945.

(553) Martin, Sandy Dwayne. "The American Baptist Home Missionary Society and Black Higher Education in the South, 1865-1920." *Foundations* 24 (1981): 310-27.

(554) Mayo, Amory D. *The Work of Certain Northern Churches in the Education of the Freedmen, 1862-1900*. Washington: Government Printing Office, 1903.

(555) Mays, Benjamin E. "A Dream Comes True." *A.M.E. Church Review* 74 (1958): 55+.

(556) _____. "Education of Negro Ministers." *Journal of Negro Education* 2 (1933): 342-51.

(557) "Missionary in Alabama: Catholic Priest Builds Schools and Churches for Negroes, Cajuns Deep in Southern Backwoods." *Ebony* 7 (1952): 65-70.

(558) Moore, Elton. "An Investigation of the Mississippi Baptist Seminary." Master's thesis, New Orleans Baptist Theological Seminary, 1950.

(559) Morris, Robert C. *Reading, 'Riting, and Reconstruction: The Education of Freedmen in the South, 1861-1870*. Chicago: University of Chicago Press, 1981.

(560) Patterson, Joseph N. "A Study of the History of the Contribution of the American Missionary Association to the Higher Education of the Negro: With Special Reference to Five Selected Colleges Founded by the Association." Ph.D. dissertation, Cornell University, 1956.

(561) Phraner, Wilson. "School Work in the South." *The Church at Home and Abroad* 5 (1889): 541-43.

(562) Rector, Theresa A. "Black Nuns as Educators." *Journal of Negro Education* 51 (1982): 238-53.

(563) Richardson, Frederick. "American Baptists' Southern Mission." *Foundations* 18 (1975): 136-45.

(564) Rouse, Michael F. *A Study of the Development of Negro Education under Catholic Auspices in Maryland and the District of Columbia.* Johns Hopkins University Studies in Education 22. Baltimore: Johns Hopkins University Press, 1935.

(565) Rowley, Margaret Nelson. "The Joseph Kaplan Human Relations Program at Morris Brown College." *A.M.E. Church Review* 78 (1962): 65-67.

(566) "Rural Preachers at Bettis Academy." *Southern Workman* 52 (1923): 422-24.

(567) Russell, Lester F. *Black Baptist Secondary Schools in Virginia, 1887-1957: A Study in Black History.* Metuchen: Scarecrow Press, 1981.

(568) "The St. Paul School." *Southern Workman* 55 (1926): 295-96.

(569) Stevenson, J. D. "Tuskegee's Religious Work." *Southern Workman* 39 (1910): 401 + .

(570) Stowell, Jay S. *Methodist Adventures in Negro Education.* New York: Methodist Book Concern, 1922.

(571) "Summer School for Colored Church Workers." *Southern Workman* 52 (1923): 473-74.

(572) Taylor, Prince A., Jr. "A History of Gammon Theological Seminary." Doctoral dissertation, New York University, 1948.

(573) Thompson, Ernest Trice. "Black Presbyterians, Education and Evangelism after the Civil War." *Journal of Presbyterian History* 51 (1973): 174-98.

(574) Wallace, J. P. Q. "The History of Payne Theological Seminary." *A.M.E. Church Review* 68 (1952): 62-63.

(575) Walls, William J. *The Romance of a College.* New York: Vantage Press, 1963.

(576) Wilson, Prince E. "Some Aspects of the Morris Brown College Academic Program." *A.M.E. Church Review* 78 (1962): 48-53.

(577) Woodcock, Eleanor J. "The Personnel Services of Morris Brown College." *A.M.E. Church Review* 78 (1962): 54-57.

XI. BLACKS IN BIRACIAL
BUT PREDOMINANTLY WHITE RELIGIOUS BODIES

Numerous titles in the preceding sections are relevant to this topic, as are selected titles in the listings for the various denominations.

(578) Allen, L. Scott. "Toward Preserving the History of the Central Jurisdiction." *Methodist History* 7 (1968): 24-30.

(579) Barber, William J. *Disciple Assemblies of Eastern North Carolina.* St. Louis: Bethany Press, 1966.

(580) Bennett, Robert A. "Black Episcopalians: A History from the Colonial Period to the Present." *Historical Magazine of the Protestant Episcopal Church* 43 (1974): 231-46, 305-21.

(581) Brackenridge, R. Douglas. "Lawrence W. Bottoms: The Church, Black Presbyterians, and Personhood." *Journal of Presbyterian History* 56 (1978): 47-60.

(582) Bragg, George F., Jr. *The Colored Harvest in the Old Virginia Diocese.* N.p.p.: n.p., n.d.

(583) _____. "The Episcopal Church and the Negro Race." *Historical Magazine of the Protestant Episcopal Church* 4 (1935): 45 + .

(584) _____. *The History of the Afro-American Group of the Episcopal Church.* Baltimore: Church Advocate Press, 1922. Reprint, New York: Johnson Reprint, 1968.

(585) _____. *The Story of Old Stephen's, Petersburg, Va. & the Origin of the Bishop Payne Divinity School.* Baltimore: n.p., 1917.

(586) Branch, Harold T. "Implications of Multiple Affiliation for Black Baptists." *Baptist History and Heritage* 16 (1981): 41-48, 60.

(587) Bryden, George M. *The Episcopal Church among the Negroes of Virginia.* Richmond: Richmond Printing, 1937.

(588) Burgess, John M. *Black Gospel/White Church.* New York: Seabury Press, 1982.

(589) Carter, Paul A. "The Negro and Methodist Union." *Church History* 21 (1952): 55-69.

(590) Cooper, John C. "The Black Man's Burden." *Metanoia* 4 (1972): 2-6.

(591) Cort, Cyrus. "Losing Caste Preaching for Darkies." *Christian Intelligencer* 83 (1912): 392.

(592) Crum, Mason. *The Negro in the Methodist Church.* New York: Editorial Department, Division of Education and Civilization, Board of Missions and Church Extension, Methodist Church, 1951.

(593) Curry, John W. *Passionate Journey: History of the 1866 South Carolina Annual Conference.* St. Mathews SC: Bill Wise Printing, 1980.

(594) DelPino, Julius E. "Blacks in the United Methodist Church from Its Beginning to 1968." *Methodist History* 19 (1980): 3-20.

(595) Demby, Edward T. *The Mission of the Episcopal Church among the Negroes of the Diocese of Arkansas.* Little Rock: n.p., [190?].

(596) Eighmy, John L. "The Baptists and Slavery: An Examination of the Origins and Benefits of Segregation." *Social Science Quarterly* 49 (1968): 666-73.

(597) Fairly, John S. *The Negro in His Relation to the Church.* Charleston SC: Walker, Evans and Cogswell, Printers, 1889.

(598) Felton, Ralph A. *The Ministry of the Central Jurisdiction of the Methodist Church.* Madison NJ: n.p., 1954.

(599) Foster, Gaines M. "Bishop Cheshire and Black Participation in the Episcopal Church: The Limits of Paternalism." *North Carolina Historical Review* 54 (1977): 49-65.

(600) Gibson, Joseph K. "The Methodist Evangelistic Movement among Negroes in America." B.D. thesis, Livingstone College, 1948.

(601) Hickman, Thomas L. "A Study of the Status of Negroes as Members of White Baptist Churches in the State of North Carolina, 1776-1863." Master's thesis, Howard University, 1947.

(602) Hoskins, Charles L. *Black Episcopalians in Georgia: Strife, Struggle, and Salvation*. Savannah: St. Matthew's Episcopal Church, 1980.

(603) Jenkins, Warren M. *Steps along the Way: The Origin and Development of the South Carolina Conference of the Central Jurisdiction of the Methodist Church*. Columbia SC: Socamead Press, 1967.

(604) Johnson, Richard H. "A Critical Study of Religious Work among Negroes of St. Mary's County, Maryland, Since 1865, with Special Reference to Catholic, Episcopal, and Methodist Churches." M.A. thesis, Howard University, 1948.

(605) Kater, John L. "The Episcopal Society for Cultural and Racial Unity and Its Role in the Episcopal Church in the United States." Ph.D. dissertation, McGill University, 1972.

(606) Keever, Homer M. "The Methodist Church (1866) in North Carolina." *Methodist History* 20 (1982): 192-208.

(607) Kershaw, J. "Rights of Negro Clergy in Protestant Episcopal Convention of South Carolina." *Church Review* 46 (1885): 466.

(608) Kirkland, H. Burnam. "The Methodist Church and the Negro." B.D. thesis, Union Theological Seminary, 1944.

(609) Krebs, Ervin E. *The Lutheran Church and the American Negro*. Columbus OH: Board of American Missions, 1950.

(610) Little, John. "Lessons from Experience: Presbyterian Colored Missions, Louisville, Ky." *Missionary Review* 59 (1926): 312-15.

(611) Lyda, Hap. "History of the Black Christian Churches (Disciples of Christ) in the United States through 1899." Ph.D. dissertation, Vanderbilt University, 1971.

(612) McCall, Emmanuel L. "Home Mission Board Ministry in the Black Community." *Baptist History and Heritage* 16 (1981): 29-40.

(613) McCarriar, Herbert G., Jr. "A History of the Missionary Jurisdiction of the South of the Reformed Episcopal Church." *Historical Magazine of the Protestant Episcopal Church* 41 (1972): 197-220.

(614) McClain, William B. *Black People in the Methodist Church: Whither Thou Goest?* Cambridge MA: Schenkman Publishing, 1984.

(615) McCloud, J. Oscar. "Perspective on Reunion." *Church and Society* 60 (May-June 1970): 29-38.

(616) Maxey, Robert T. *One Wide River*. Louisville: College of the Scriptures, 1960.

(617) Murray, Andrew E. *Presbyterians and the Negro: A History*. Philadelphia: Presbyterian Historical Society, 1966.

(618) Noon, Thomas R. "The Alpha Synod of Lutheran Freedmen (1889-1891)." *Concordia Historical Institute Quarterly* 50 (1977): 64-70.

(619) Payne, H. N. "Our Colored Synods." *The Church at Home and Abroad* 4 (1888): 165-66.

(620) Pembroke, Maceo D. "Black Worship Experience in the United Methodist Church." *Religion in Life* 44 (1975): 309-17.

(621) Pennington, Edgar L. "The Episcopal Church in the Alabama Black Belt." *Alabama Review* 4 (1951): 117-26.

(622) Phillips, A. L. *The Presbyterian Church in the United States: "The Southern Presbyterian Church" and the Colored People . . . Acts viii: 27.* Birmingham: Roberts and Son, 1890.

(623) Pool, Frank K. "The Southern Negro in the Methodist Episcopal Church." Ph.D. dissertation, Duke University, 1939.

(624) Raney, G. Wesley, "Black Congregationalism: Its Past and Future." B.D. paper, Andover Newton Theological School, 1969.

(625) Reimers, David M. "Negro Bishops and Diocesan Segregation in the Protestant Episcopal Church, 1870-1954." *Historical Magazine of the Protestant Episcopal Church* 31 (1962): 231-42.

(626) _____. "Negro Leadership in the Methodist Episcopal Church, 1900-1920: A Plea for Research in Negro Church History." *Wesleyan Quarterly Review* 3 (1966): 243-51.

(627) Rice, Joseph S. "The Challenge of the Negro to the Southern Presbyterian Church." Master's thesis, Princeton Theological Seminary, 1946.

(628) Riley, Walter H. *Forty Years in the Lap of Methodism: History of the Lexington Conference of the Methodist Episcopal Church.* Louisville: Mayes Printing, 1915.

(629) Schmalz, Annie M. "A Presbyterian Conference for Colored Women." *Southern Workman* 54 (1925): 416-18.

(630) Shaw, James B. F. *The Negro in the History of Methodism.* Nashville: Parthenon Press, 1954.

(631) Simpkins, Patrick L. "North Carolina Quakers and Blacks: Education and Membership." *Negro History Bulletin* 35 (November 1972): 160-62.

(632) Stanley, J. Taylor. *A History of Black Congregational Christian Churches of the South.* New York: United Church Press for the American Missionary Association, 1978.

(633) Walker, Claude. "Negro Disciples in Kentucky, 1840-1925." Bachelor's paper, College of the Bible, 1959.

(634) Whitefield, Charles R. D. *Brief History of the Negro Disciples of Christ in Eastern North Carolina: Past Achievements and Future Aims.* Kinston NC: Whitfield Printery, n.d.

(635) Wilson, Frank T., ed. "Living Witnesses: Black Presbyterians in Ministry." *Journal of Presbyterian History* 53 (1975): 187-222.

(636) Wilson, W. W. "The Methodist Episcopal Church in Her Relations to the Negro in the South." *Methodist Review* 75 (1941): 713-23.

(637) Woodward, Joseph H. *The Negro Bishop Movement in the Episcopal Diocese of South Carolina*. McPhersonville SC: H. Woodward, 1916.

(638) Worcester, John. "Southern Blacks and Reunion." *Presbyterian Outlook* 154 (November 1972): 6.

XII. TWENTIETH CENTURY ISSUES AND TRENDS

(639) Bock, E. Wilbur. "The Decline of the Negro Clergy: Changes in Formal Religious Leadership in the United States in the Twentieth Century." *Phylon* 29 (1968): 48-64.

(640) Brown, Agnes. "The Negro Churches of Chapel Hill." M.A. thesis, University of North Carolina in Chapel Hill, 1939.

(641) Burkett, Randall, and Richard Newman, eds. *Black Apostles: Afro-American Clergy Confront the Twentieth Century*. Boston: G. K. Hall, 1978.

(642) "The Ceremony of 'Foot Wash' in Virginia." *Southern Workman* 24 (1896): 82, 102-12.

(643) Clark, Kenneth B. *The Negro Protest: James Baldwin, Malcolm X, Martin Luther King Talk with Kenneth B. Clark*. Boston: Beacon Press, 1963.

(644) Ellison, John M. "The Negro Church in Rural Virginia." *Southern Workman* 60 (1931): 67-73, 201-210, 307-14.

(645) _____. "The Negro Preacher as a Social Prophet." *Baptist Herald* 30 (May-June 1973): 3-7.

(646) _____, and Charles H. Hamilton. *The Negro Church in Rural Virginia*. Virginia Agricultural Bulletin 27340. Blacksburg: Virginia Polytechnic University, 1930.

(647) Felton, Ralph A. *These My Brethren: A Study of 570 Negro Churches and 1542 Negro Homes in the Rural South*. Madison NJ: Drew Theological Seminary Department of the Rural Church, 1950.

(648) Friedrichs, R. W. "The Role of the Negro Minister in Politics in New Orleans." Ph.D. dissertation, Tulane University, 1967.

(649) Fuller, Thomas O. *The Story of Church Life among Negroes in Memphis, Tennessee, for Students and Workers, 1900-1938*. Memphis: n.p., 1938.

(650) Hewitt, Doris W. *The Relation of Security and Religiosity of the Low-Income Southern Negro Youth*. Tallahassee: n.p., 1965.

(651) Jackson, Benjamin F. "An Adequate Program of Religious Education for the Small Negro Baptist Church in Northwest Baltimore Which Has Inadequate Facilities." M.A. thesis, Howard University, 1942.

(652) Johnson, Charles S. "Youth and the Church." In *The Black Church in America*. Hart M. Nelsen, et al., eds., 91-99. New York: Basic Books, 1971.

(653) Kater, John L., Jr. "Experiment in Freedom: The Episcopal Church and the Black Power Movement." *Historical Magazine of the Protestant Episcopal Church* 48 (1979): 67-81.

(654) Lawton, Samuel M. *The Religious Life of South Carolina Coastal and Sea Island Negroes*. Nashville: George Peabody College for Teachers, 1939.

(655) Lincoln, C. Eric. "Extremist Attitudes in the Black Muslim Movement." *New South* 18 (1963): 3-10.

(656) McKinney, Richard I. "The Black Church: Its Development and Present Impact." *Harvard Theological Review* 64 (1971): 452-81.

(657) Marszalek, John F. "The Black Leader in 1919—South Carolina as a Case Study." *Phylon* 36 (1975): 249-59.

(658) Mitchell, Henry H. *Black Preaching.* Philadelphia: J. B. Lippincott, 1970.

(659) Moss, James A. "The Negro Church and Black Power." *Journal of Human Relations* 17 (1969): 119-28.

(660) "Muslims in Alabama." *Time* 95 (2 February 1970): 12.

(661) Nelsen, Hart M., Thomas W. Madron, and Raytha L. Yokley. "Black Religion's Promethean Motif: Orthodoxy and Militancy." *American Journal of Sociology* 81 (1975): 139-46.

(662) Proctor, Samuel D. "The Black Community and the New Religious Right." *Foundations* 25 (1982): 180-87.

(663) Richardson, Harry V. *Dark Glory: A Picture of the Church among Negroes in the Rural South.* New York: Published for Home Missions Council of North America and Phelps-Stokes Fund by Friendship Press, 1947.

(664) Schab, Fred. "Attitudinal Differences of Southern White and Negro Adolescent Males regarding the Home, School, Religion and Morality." *Journal of Negro Education* 40 (1971): 108-110.

(665) Smith, Kelly Miller. *Social Crisis Preaching. The Lyman Beecher Lectures, 1983.* Macon GA: Mercer University Press, 1984.

(666) Thomas, James S. "A Study of the Social Role of the Negro Rural Pastor in Four Selected Southern Areas." Ph.D. dissertation, Cornell University, 1952.

(667) Vedlitz, Arnold, et al. "Politics and the Black Church in a Southern Community." *Journal of Black Studies* 10 (1980): 367-75.

(668) Walker, Randolph M. "The Role of the Black Clergy in Memphis during the Crump Era." *West Tennessee Historical Society Papers* 33 (1979): 29-47.

(669) Weatherford, Allen E. "Recreation in the Negro Church in North Carolina." *Journal of Negro Education* 13 (1944): 499-508.

(670) Weisheit, Eldon J. "The Black Belt Revisited." *Concordia Historical Institute Quarterly* 48:2 (1975): 44-50.

(671) Williams, Charles. "The Conversion Ritual in a Rural Black Baptist Church." In *Holding On to the Land and the Lord: Kinship, Ritual, Land Tenure, and Social Policy in the Rural South.* Robert L. Hall and Carol B. Stack, eds., 69-79. Southern Anthropological Society Proceedings 15. Athens: University of Georgia Press, 1982.

XIII. BIOGRAPHICAL AND AUTOBIOGRAPHICAL STUDIES

(672) Alexander, Mithrapuram K. *Martin Luther King: Martyr for Freedom.* New Delhi: New Light Publishers, 1968.

(673) Bennett, Lerone, Jr. *What Manner of Man: A Biography of Martin Luther King, Jr.* Chicago: Johnson Publishing, 1964.

(674) Bishop, Jim. *The Days of Martin Luther King, Jr.* New York: G.P. Putnam's Sons, 1971.

(675) Bleiweiss, Robert M., et al. *Marching to Freedom: The Life of Martin Luther King, Jr.* Middletown CT: American Education Publications, 1968.

(676) Bosco, Teresio. *Martin Luther King.* Turin: Societa editrice internazionale, 1969.

(677) Carter, George E. "Martin Luther King: Incipient Transcendentalist." *Phylon* 40 (1979): 318-24.

(678) Carter, E. R. *Biographical Sketches of Our Pulpit.* Chicago: Afro-American Press, 1969. First published 1888.

(679) Clayton, Edward T. *Martin Luther King: The Peaceful Warrior.* Englewood Cliffs: Prentice-Hall, 1968.

(680) Davis, Lenwood G. "Frederick Douglass as a Preacher, and One of His Last Most Significant Letters." *Journal of Negro History* 66 (1981): 140-43.

(681) Dean, David M. *Defender of the Race: James Theodore Holly, Black Nationalist Bishop.* Boston: Lambeth Press, 1979.

(682) DeKay, James T. *Meet Martin Luther King, Jr.* New York: Random House, 1969.

(683) Douglas, Carlyle C. "Ralph Abernathy." *Ebony* 25 (January 1970): 40-50.

(684) Edmund, T. "Martin Luther King and the Black Protest Movement." *Gandhi Magazine* 20 (1976): 235-49.

(685) Feuerlicht, Robert S. *Martin Luther King, Jr.: A Concise Biography.* New York: American R.D.M., 1966.

(686) Garber, Paul R. "Martin Luther King, Jr.: Theologian and Precursor of Black Theology." Ph.D. dissertation, Florida State University, 1973.

(687) Gerbeau, Herbert. *Martin Luther King.* Paris: Editions Universitaires, 1968.

(688) Gullins, William R. *The Heroes of the Virginia Annual Conference of the A.M.E. Church.* Norfolk: n.p., 1899.

(689) Harrigan, James P. "Martin Luther King and the Ethic of Militant Nonviolence." Ph.D. dissertation, Duke University, 1973.

(690) Harris, William C. "James Lynch: Black Leader in Southern Reconstruction." *Historian* 34 (November 1971): 40-61.

(691) Harrison, Deloris. *We Shall Live in Peace: The Teachings of Martin Luther King, Jr.* New York: Hawthorn Books, 1968.

(692) Hartel, Klaus-Dieter. *Martin Luther King: Vorkampfer für Frieden und Menschenwurde.* Giessen: Brunnen-Verlag, 1968.

(693) "Heroism and Sacrifices of Colored Preachers in the South." *Southern Workman* 1,8 (1872): 2.

(694) Jones, Lawrence N. "Interpreters of Our Faith: Martin Luther King, Jr." *A.D. United Church Herald Edition* 2 (April 1973): 18-22.

(695) Josca, Guiseppe. *Martin Luther King.* Milan: Della Volpe, 1968.

(696) Lane, Isaac. *Autobiography: With a Short History of the A.M.E. Church in America and of Methodism.* Nashville: Publishing House of the Methodist Episcopal Church, South, 1916.

(697) *Leading Afro-Americans of Vicksburg, Mississippi: Their Enterprises, Churches, Schools.* Vicksburg: Biographa, 1908.

(698) Lewis, David L. *King: A Critical Biography.* Baltimore: Penguin Books, 1971. Also New York: Praeger, 1970.

(699) Lincoln, C. Eric, ed. *Martin Luther King, Jr.: A Profile.* New York: Hill and Wang, 1970.

(700) Loewenberg, Bert James, and Ruth Bogin, eds. *Black Women in Nineteenth Century American Life.* University Park: Pennsylvania State University Press, 1976.

(701) McKee, Don. *Martin Luther King, Jr.* New York: G. P. Putnam's Sons, 1969.

(702) Manis, Andrew M. "Silence or Shockwaves: Southern Baptist Responses to the Assassination of Martin Luther King, Jr." *Baptist History and Heritage* 15 (1980): 19-27, 35.

(703) Millender, Dharathula H. *Martin Luther King, Jr.: A Boy with a Dream.* Indianapolis: Bobbs-Merrill, 1969.

(704) Miller, Harriet Parks. *Pioneer Colored Christians.* Clarkesville TN: W. P. Titus, 1911.

(705) Miller, William R. *Martin Luther King, Jr.: His Life, Martyrdom and Meaning for the World.* New York: Weybright and Talley, 1969.

(706) Moore, N. Webster. "John Berry Meachum (1789-1854): St. Louis Pioneer, Black Abolitionist, Educator, and Preacher." *Missouri Historical Society Bulletin* 29 (1973): 96-103.

(707) Muller, Gerald T. *Martin Luther King, Jr.: A Civil Rights Leader.* Minneapolis: Denison, 1971.

(708) Newsome, Clarence G. "Mary McLeod Bethune in Religious Perspective: A Seminal Essay." Ph.D. dissertation, Duke University, 1982.

(709) Noack, Hans G. *Der Gewaltlose Aufstand: Martin Luther King und der Kampf des Amerikanischen Neger.* Baden-Baden: Signal-Verlag, 1965.

(710) Patterson, Lillie. *Martin Luther King, Jr.: Man of Peace.* Champaign IL: Garrard Publishing, 1969.

(712) Preston, Edward. *Martin Luther King: Fighter for Freedom.* New York: Doubleday, 1968.

(712) Reddick, L. D. *Crusader Without Violence: A Biography of Martin Luther King, Jr.* New York: Harper and Brothers, 1959.

(713) Redkey, Edwin S., ed. *Respect Black: The Writings and Speeches of Henry McNeal Turner.* New York: Arno Press, 1971.

(714) Roundtree, Louise M., comp. *An Index to Biographical Sketches and Publications of the Bishops of the A.M.E. Zion Church.* Salisbury NC: n.p., 1963.

(715) Sharma, Mohan L. "Martin Luther King: Modern America's Greatest The-ologian of Social Action." *Journal of Negro History* 53 (1968): 259-63.

(716) Simmons, William J. *Men of Mark: Eminent, Progressive, and Rising.* Cleveland: George M. Rewell, 1887. Reprint, New York: Arno Press, 1968.

(717) Slack, Kenneth. *Martin Luther King.* London: S.C.M. Press, 1970.

(718) Smith, Kenneth, and Ira G. Zepp, Jr. *Search for the Beloved Community: The Thinking of Martin Luther King, Jr.* Valley Forge: Judson Press, 1974.

(719) Smylie, James H. "On Jesus, Pharaohs, and the Chosen People: Martin Lu-ther King as Biblical Interpreter and Humanist." *Interpretation* 24 (1970): 74-91.

(720) Steinkraus, Warren E. "Martin Luther King's Personalism and Non-Vio-lence." *Journal of the History of Ideas* 34 (1973): 97-111.

(721) Thompson, Julius E. "Hiram Revels: A Biography." Ph.D. dissertation, Princeton University, 1973.

(722) Tucker, David M. *Black Pastors and Leaders: Memphis, 1819-1972.* Memphis: Memphis State University Press, 1975.

(723) VanDeburg, William L. "Frederick Douglass: Maryland Slave to Religious Liberal." *Maryland Historical Magazine* 69 (1974): 27-43.

(724) Wagner, Clarence M. *Profiles of Black Georgia Baptists.* Gainesville GA: privately published, 1980.

(725) Wesley, Charles H. *Richard Allen: Apostle of Freedom.* Washington: As-sociated Publishers, 1935.

(726) Williams, Ethel L., ed. *Biographical Dictionary of Negro Ministers.* 3d ed. New York: Scarecrow Press, 1976.

(727) Wright, Richard R., Jr. *Bishops of the African Methodist Episcopal Church.* Nashville: Printed by the A.M.E. Sunday School Union, 1963.

(728) Wynes, Charles. "William Henry Heard: Politician, Diplomat, A.M.E. Churchman." *Southern Studies* 20 (1981): 384-93.

(729) Young, Henry. *Major Black Religious Leaders.* 2 vols. Nashville: Abing-don Press, 1977-1979.

(731) Zepp, Ira G., Jr. "The Intellectual Sources of the Ethical Thought of Martin Luther King, Jr., as Traced in His Writings With Special Reference to the Beloved Community." Doctoral dissertation, Ecumenical Institute of The-ology of St. Mary's Seminary and University, 1971.

5 ROMAN CATHOLICISM IN THE SOUTH

ROMAN CATHOLICS had established American missions and parishes in what became the American South long before English settlers, who came to dominate the region, began to establish roots further north. Spanish Catholics were carving a place for themselves in Florida nearly a half century before the first permanent English colony was established in Virginia. In time, a Spanish style of Catholicism also made its way into what is now Texas, while French Catholicism penetrated what became Alabama and Louisiana with the founding of Mobile and New Orleans early in the eighteenth century. Yet it was an Anglo-American Catholicism that gave shape to the structure of American and, consequently, Southern Catholicism because of the founding of Maryland, a proprietary colony controlled at first by an influential English Catholic family, the Calverts. Hence the ethnic pluralism that later became characteristic of American Catholicism in general marked Southern Catholic history from the beginning. Today, while Catholics remain a minority of the Southern population in most regions, they still confront ethnic pluralism, albeit of a different sort, with the influx of Mexican-Americans in Texas, for example, or of Cuban-Americans in Florida.

When Rome first gave formal organization to American Catholicism, Baltimore became the nation's initial bishopric in 1789. Within half a century, diocesan structures were in place in Bardstown (Kentucky), Charleston, Richmond, Mobile, Natchez, and Nashville, and the diocese of New Orleans and Florida had been absorbed when those regions became American territory. Hence relatively early on, the hierarchical structure was in place to facilitate growth and expansion, although even today the South's Catholic population, with the exception of South Florida, remains heavily concentrated in Louisiana and the Gulf coast of Texas and Mississippi. Elsewhere in the South, Catholicism continues to be primarily an urban phenomenon.

In many ways, Southern Catholics have imbibed the cultural style of Dixie while remaining apart from the mainstream. Southern Catholics, for example, as noted in chapters 4 and 20, confronted matters of slavery and race in much the same fashion as other Southerners, and most aligned themselves with the Confederate cause in the Civil War, although the Roman Catholic Church in the United States did not divide over the issue. chapter 4 includes many titles dealing with Catholic missions to slaves and with black Catholics. Catholic missions among the Indians, as demonstrated in chapter 3, were similar to their Protestant analogues in yielding fewer converts than desired and in operating on a basis of disregard for the integrity of native American religious life. Parish missions and renewal movements, noted in chapter 15, have fostered dedication to Catholicism similar to, though less extensive than, the results of revivals for the Protestant majority. And, like their Protestant counterparts, Southern Catholics have also established numerous church schools and colleges, as documented in chapter 18. Southern writers who are Catholic, such as Flannery O'Connor and Walker Percy, have left an indelible mark on Southern literature and indeed on American literature as a whole. Works examining the importance of religion in their writing and religious themes in their works are included in the discussion in chapter 16.

But Southern Catholics have also remained a people apart, enduring a long struggle in many Southern states to secure political rights and marked as ''outsiders'' because of papal allegiance, a highly liturgical approach to worship, maintenance of a celibate clergy, and the like. In many areas of the South, where the Catholic population is the least dense, marriage outside the faith has also been a matter of concern since the pool of coreligionists is so small. Yet many of the situations that American Catholicism at large has faced have also confronted the church in the South. The controversies over lay control of parishes (lay trusteeism), for example, were problems American Catholicism met in the nineteenth century wherever it had adherents in the nation. And anti-Catholic prejudice or ''nativism'' has been a continuing concern for all American Catholics, but perhaps more so for Southern Catholics once nativism's violent stages had ebbed, since anti-Catholic sentiment has tended to endure beneath the surface more in the South than in other regions of the country. Works treating anti-Catholic sentiment in Southern life are included in chapter 20. Hence it is fair to conclude that Southern Catholics have maintained a dual identity. Once the one hand, they are culturally Southern, but on the other hand, they are religiously Catholic. The two have yet to become synonymous.

Numerous studies of American Catholicism provide the backdrop for Southern developments and the religious context in which they occurred. John Tracy Ellis, *American Catholicism* (3) remains a standard, complemented by Andrew M. Greeley, *The Catholic Experience: An Interpretation of the History of American Catholicism* (7). The most recent general study is James J. Hennesey, *American Catholics: A History of the Roman Catholic Community in the United States* (8). In that work and in his "Roman Catholicism: The Maryland Tradition" (9), Hennesey noted how the Anglo-American style emerging from the Maryland experience, rather than the more ultramontane tradition characteristic of much continental Catholicism, dominated American Catholicism well into the nineteenth century. On this point, also see S. R. Lee, "The Maryland Influence on American Catholicism" (14).

Brief overviews of peculiarly Southern Catholic developments are provided in Alfred O. Hero, *The Southerner and World Affairs* (10), chap. 12, and Thomas R. Mickler's now dated master's thesis, "The Catholic Church in the Southland" (22). Perhaps the best short treatment is the essay on Roman Catholicism in the South by Randall M. Miller in the *Encyclopedia of Religion in the South* (1:112). By far the finest study of antebellum Catholicism in the South is the collection of essays, uniformly provocative and well done, edited by Miller and Jon L. Wakelyn, *Catholics in the Old South: Essays on Church and Society* (23). Taken together, the essays reveal the extent to which Southern Catholics adopted the cultural attitudes of the society around them while remaining religiously distinctive. Also see Stephen C. Worsley, "Catholicism in Antebellum North Carolina" (286). James J. Pillar, "Catholicism in the Lower South" (29) is especially good in its discussion of the controversy over lay control of churches in the regions along the Gulf Coast in the first half of the nineteenth century, while Vincent J. O'Connell, "The Church in the South" (27), offers an equally reliable appraisal of trends in the first half of the twentieth century.

Much of the secondary literature about Southern Catholicism is found in an array of diocesan, state, and local studies. Many document the vital role played by numerous Catholic orders, male and female, that spearheaded Catholic expansion through countless mission and educational endeavors. Numerous works that center on the history and contributions of various orders are listed in the bibliography at the close of this chapter. Without the labors of groups such as the Jesuits, Capuchins, and Redemptorists, the Sisters of Charity of the Incarnate Word, the Sisters of Loretto, the Ursulines, and the Sisters of Charity of Nazareth (Kentucky), to mention just a few, Southern Catholicism would have a far different history. The problem, however, is that many of the diocesan, state, and local studies and many of the biographies of individuals who played critical roles in Catholic growth are found in relatively obscure and often inaccessible journals and monographs.

In addition, many are filiopietistic and hagiographic in tone, and therefore must be used with caution. The commentary that follows will treat only the more accessible resources, though the bibliographical listings at the conclusion of the chapter include coverage of this genre of materials.

R. Emmett Curran, *The Maryland Jesuits: 1634-1833* (88), notes not only the pivotal role of that order in nurturing the Catholic population of colonial Maryland and the increasing importance of Irish Jesuits in American work, but also the work of Maryland Jesuits in establishing Catholic missionary outposts elsewhere in Dixie. Part of the difficulty Maryland Catholics confronted in the early years might be termed "guilt by association," since as long as the overwhelmingly Catholic French colonial enterprise in North America was perceived as a threat to English colonial expansion, Catholics in Maryland were assumed to be disloyal to the British cause because it was believed they would identify with their French coreligionists in any final confrontation over colonial supremacy of eastern North America. On this point, see Mark J. Stegmaier, "Maryland's Fear of Insurrection at the Time of Braddock's Defeat" (266). Andrew White, prominent early Maryland Catholic, penned several accounts of his impressions of the colony and the prospects for the church there (281-285). But also see Gilbert J. Garraghan, "Catholic Beginnings in Maryland" (116). Henry S. Spalding, *Catholic Colonial Maryland* (258), is the most comprehensive account of the early story in Lord Baltimore's colony. Also see Thomas J. Stanton's more narrowly focused *A Century of Growth: Or, the History of the Church in Western Maryland* (264).

On Catholic developments in neighboring Virginia, see Peter Guilday's still valuable *The Catholic Church in Virginia* (129). Antebellum Catholic history in Virginia provides the basis for John M. Lenhart, "The Catholic Church in the State of Virginia, 1785-1843" (177). Francis J. Magri, "Catholicity in Virginia during the Episcopate of Bishop McGill" (197), covers the story for the third quarter of the nineteenth century. A survey of Catholic growth in the Carolinas and Georgia was written more than a century ago by Jeremiah J. O'Connell: *Catholicity in the Carolinas and Georgia* (218).

Roman Catholicism in Texas has received the most comprehensive and the most historiographically sound analysis of that tradition in any state in the work of Mexican-American historian Carlos E. Castaneda. The seven-volume *Our Catholic Heritage in Texas* (74) carefully traces the story from the days of Spanish missions in the sixteenth century down to the mid-twentieth century. Appreciative comment on Castaneda's work is found in two essays by Felix D. Almarez: "Carlos E. Castaneda and *Our Catholic Heritage:* The Initial Volumes" (38) and "Carlos Eduardo Castaneda, Mexican-American Historian: The Formative Years, 1896-1927" (437). Supplementing Castaneda's work on the period of reorganization when Texas first declared independence from Mexico and then was annexed to the United States is the doctoral dissertation of Sr. Mary Bernignus Sheridan, "Bishop Odin and the New Era of the Catholic Church in Texas, 1840-1860" (254). Also see the pamphlet series, *The Texians and the Texans* (152), produced under the auspices of the Institute of Texan Cultures at the University of Texas at San Antonio, which offers brief overviews of the various ethnic groups that make up much of Texas Catholicism.

Early Catholic expansion into Kentucky received attention in one nineteenth century work that is still of value: Martin J. Spalding, *Sketches of Early Catholic Missions of Kentucky* (262). But also see Mary Ramona Mattingly's now somewhat dated monograph, *The Catholic Church on the Kentucky Frontier* (202). Kentucky's Bardstown became a diocesan see in 1808 and soon thereafter witnessed the establishment of two American orders of nuns nearby: the Sisters of Loretto at the Foot of the Cross and the Sisters of Charity of Nazareth, as well as the founding of the first order of Dominican nuns in the country. While there are numerous filiopietistic and somewhat exaggerated studies of the first two, there is also one older study of the Sisters of Loretto based on credible scholarship: Thomas F. O'Connor, "A Kentucky Contribution to Religion on the Frontier" (219).

Michael V. Gannon, *The Cross in the Sand: The Early Catholic Church in Florida, 1513-1870* (114), has become the standard for that state, but one should not neglect to consult as well the scholarly exposition and evaluation provided by Gregory J. Keegan and Leandro Tormo Sanz, *Experiencia en la Florida (siglos XVI y XVII)* (159). Later developments are ably appraised by Michael McNally in a doctoral dissertation, "Cross in the Sun: The Growth and Development of Catholicism in South Florida, 1868-1968" (195). Another reliable older study, reprinted about a decade ago, is Michael J. Curley, *Church and State in the Spanish Floridas, 1783-1822* (86). Exceptionally well-documented for a study of a diocesan administration and containing much valuable information on Roman Catholic developments in northwest Florida and Alabama in the third quarter of the nineteenth century is Oscar H. Lipscomb, "The Administration of John Quinlan, Second Bishop of Mobile, 1859-1883" (180). Lipscomb has studied early Alabama developments and the situation of the church during the Civil War years in two other articles (181-182). An older cognate study, reprinted in 1970, that emphasizes the colonial period in this same region is Mary Teresa Austin Carroll, *A Catholic History of Alabama and the Floridas* (71).

Roger Baudier, *The Catholic Church in Louisiana* (50) remains the basic work for this American center of a Catholicism more French in heritage than Anglo-American, but the work suffers from serious problems of disorganization. Jean Delanglez, S.J., *The French Jesuits in Lower Louisiana* (91), although reprinted a decade ago, is so polemic in tone as to be of little real value to contemporary students. Better, but still lacking in rigorous scholarly analysis, is A. H. Biever, *Jesuits in New Orleans and the Mississippi Valley* (61). More reliable and academic in thrust is James J. Pillar, *The Catholic Church in Mississippi, 1837-1865* (236). Also see Richard O. Gerow, comp., *Catholicity in Mississippi* (121). On Tennessee, see George J. Flanigan, *Catholicity in Tennessee, 1541-1937* (107), a work that merits updating. A good study of the population movement patterns that brought Catholics into Tennessee and adjacent areas is Donald F. Forrester's older master's thesis, "A Study of the Migration of Catholics to the Tennessee Valley Region from 1769-1810" (108). James Cardinal Gibbons, *Reminiscences of Catholicity in North Carolina* (122) is valuable more for its anecdotes and the sense of ethos they provide than for rigorous analysis. Thomas E. Brown, *Bible Belt Catholicism: A History of the Roman Catholic Church in Oklahoma, 1905-1945* (68), merits attention for its sensitivity to the minority context within which Southern Catholicism has developed as well as for its awareness of the subtle but multifaceted anti-Catholic bigotry that continues to permeate Protestantism in Oklahoma and elsewhere. Catholic beginnings in Oklahoma are recounted by Urbande Hasque, *Early Catholic History of Oklahoma* (139). The University of Oklahoma Press has published a useful series of short monographs examining the stories of the various ethnic groups in the Oklahoma population. Members of these groups are in many cases overwhelmingly Roman Catholic. Titles in the series, *Newcomers to a New Land,* are listed individually in the bibliography at the close of this chapter. For the story in Arkansas, see John M. Lucey, *The Catholic Church in Arkansas* (186).

Several local studies deserve comment. Clyde F. Crews, "Hallowed Ground: The Cathedral of the Assumption in Louisville History" (310), demonstrates how this Catholic focal point has had a profound impact on community life. Also well done is George F. Flanigan, *The Centenary of Sts. Peter and Paul's Parish, Chattanooga, Tennessee* (324). More popular but less valuable to scholars is Charles L. Dufour, *1833 . . . . St. Patrick's of New Orleans . . . 1958* (318). Frederick G. Holweck, "The Beginnings of the Church in Little Rock" (340), represents solid research, as does Vincent J. Fecher, *A Study of the Movement for German National Parishes in Philadelphia and Baltimore, 1787-1802* (322), which treats a problem that faced American Catholicism everywhere—namely, how to accommodate ethnic pluralism within a single, unified church.

John E. Rothensteiner's two-volume *History of the Archdiocese of St. Louis* (394), while in need of updating, pays meticulous attention to detail. Less valuable to scholars but more readable is William B. Faherty, S.J., *Dream by the River: Two Centuries of Saint Louis Catholicism, 1766-1967* (320). A companion work, somewhat older but equally readable (although without notes) and written by one who later became Archbishop of Indianapolis, is Paul C. Schulte, *The Catholic Heritage of St. Louis: A History of the Old Cathedral Parish* (411). St. Louis was another city where Catholicism had to deal with ethnic diversity, sometimes painfully. See two articles by Frederick G. Holweck: "The Language Question in the Old Cathedral of St. Louis" (341) and "Public Worship in St. Louis before Palm Sunday, 1843" (342). Much later language issues again came to the fore in the decrees of Vatican II that mandated celebration of the Mass in English. For this story in St. Louis, see Peter J. Rahill, "New Language for St. Louis Cathedral" (383). Particularly pivotal in shaping St. Louis Catholicism was Joseph Rosati, the first bishop of the diocese from 1826 to 1843. Peter J. Rahill gives a responsible overview of Rosati's work in "St. Louis under Bishop Rosati" (385). But also see two essays by Charles L. Souvay, "Rosati's Election to the Coadjutorship of New Orleans" (536) and "Rosati's Elevation to the See of St. Louis" (537), and John E. Rothensteiner's detailed study, "The Northeastern Part of the Diocese of St. Louis under Bishop Rosati" (395). The standard biography of Rosati, a revised doctoral dissertation reprinted in 1974, is Frederick J. Easterly, *The Life of the Rt. Rev. Joseph Rosati, First Bishop of St. Louis, 1789-1843* (456). Another key figure not only in St. Louis Catholicism but also in the diocese of Louisiana and Florida was L. William Du Bourg. Two brief pieces analyze his work and impact: Peter J. Rahill, "The St. Louis Episcopacy of L. William DuBourg" (384), and William B. Faherty, "The Personality and Influence of Louis William Valentine DuBourg: Bishop of Louisiana and the Floridas" (460).

Noteworthy as well are several studies by John M. Lenhart, who has paid particular attention to ethnic factors, especially the significant German community, in Wheeling, West Virginia. The concern of Wheeling's German Catholics for social issues is the subject of "Catholic Action in the German Congregation of Wheeling, West Virginia, 1865-1955" (348), while socioeconomic class standing of the same community forms the basis of his "Economic Valuation of the German Catholic Congregation in Wheeling W. Va., 1856-1955" (349). Often overlooked even in studies of ethnicity within the Catholic tradition is the presence of ethnic subgroups. Again looking at Wheeling, Lenhart addresses this matter in "Ethnic Groups of the German Congregation of the Wheeling District, 1820-1849" (350). Ethnic identity could also mean some minor variations in both worship style and style of pastoral ministry. Lenhart treats the former in "Order of Services in the German Congregation, Wheeling, W.Va., 1858-1956" (352) and the latter in "Statistics of Pastoral Functions of the German Congregation at Wheeling, W.Va." (353).

Perhaps no other single family was more significant in providing leadership to American Catholics during the late eighteenth and early nineteenth century than the Carrolls of Maryland. Charles Carroll, signer of the Declaration of Independence, may have been the most well-known Catholic in the new United States. The most recent biography is Thomas O. Hanley, *Charles Carroll of Carrollton: The Making of a Revolutionary Gentleman* (477), which rightly argues that Carroll and his family were part of a Catholic elite and therefore somewhat separated from the bulk of the Catholic population (however small that population was). Nevertheless, Charles Carroll and his family were, according to Hanley, the patriarchs of Maryland Catholicism. More scholarly and perhaps the finest biographical study remains Ellen Hart Smith, *Charles Carroll of Carrollton* (535), recently reprinted. Two other studies merit mention: Kate Mason Rowland, *The Life of Charles Carroll of Carrollton, 1737-1832, with His Correspondence and Public Papers* (528), is a detailed exposition in two volumes, although somewhat hagiographic in tone, while James B. Bonder's master's thesis, "Life of Charles Carroll of Carrollton" (441), is a solid short biography.

A cousin to Charles Carroll, John Carroll, became the first American Roman Catholic bishop when Baltimore became a diocesan see in 1789. James Hennesey, "An Eighteenth Century Bishop: John Carroll of Baltimore" (482), provides the best brief overview. Remarkable for its attention to detail is Peter Guilday, *The Life and Times of John Carroll: Archbishop of Baltimore, 1735-1815* (473). Guilday's two-volume work, however, is superseded by Annabelle M. Melville, *John Carroll of Baltimore: Founder of the American Catholic Hierarchy* (503). The bibliography at the close of this chapter also notes several articles that deal with specific aspects of Carroll's work, especially as it relates to the growth and expansion of Catholicism elsewhere in the South.

In 1808 Bardstown, Kentucky, also became an episcopal see under the leadership of French-born Benedict Joseph Flaget. The standard biography, reprinted in 1970 but first published in the mid-nineteenth century, is Martin J. Spalding, *Sketches of the Life, Times, and Character of the Rt. Rev. Benedict Joseph Flaget, First Bishop of Louisville* (539). It is unlikely that other studies will entirely replace Spalding's even if they are more sophisticated in their analyses, since many of the primary materials Spalding used have since been lost or destroyed.

Charleston's first bishop, John England, was not only a regional leader in Catholic circles, but a national one as well. During England's episcopacy, Southern and American Catholicism confronted a massive influx of Irish immigrants who were to leave an enduring imprint on the character of American Catholicism, for quickly Irish Catholics came to dominate the hierarchy (and remain dominant today). England himself was Irish and had to contend with nativist tendencies among his own constituency as well as among the Southern population around him. Much of his career was devoted to demonstrating the "Americanness" not only of Irish Catholics but of Catholicism itself. This particular aspect of England's ministry is the focus of Patrick W. Carey, *An Immigrant Bishop: John England's Adaptation of Irish Catholicism to American Republicanism* (448). The most complete biography is still Peter Guilday, *The Life and Times of John England: First Bishop of Charleston, 1786-1842* (474). Joseph L. O'Brien, *John England, Bishop of Charleston: The Apostle to Democracy* (512), is a popular study, based almost entirely on Guilday's earlier work, while Dorothy Fremont Grant, *John England: American Christopher* (472) is excessively hagiographic and therefore of little value to serious students. For a very brief overview, see Thomas P. Phelan, "Rt. Rev. John England, First Bishop of Charleston" (524).

The tensions over slavery that rocked but did not divide American Catholicism come into sharp relief in Michael V. Gannon, *Rebel Bishop: The Life and Era of Augustin Verot* (466). Verot, who remained loyal to the Confederacy, was noted both as a defender of slavery and as a critic of the severity and excesses of the slave system. After the Civil War, he championed the freedmen's cause as Bishop of Savannah while remaining vicar apostolic of Florida.

If Flaget was the first bishop resident in Kentucky and consequently did much to bring order to Catholic work there, much of the growth of Catholicism in Kentucky and adjacent areas, particularly Missouri, resulted from the missionary labors of Charles Nerinckx, who was as well the guiding force behind the formation of the American order, the Sisters of Loretto at the Foot of the Cross. Camillus P. Maes's *The Life of Rev. Charles Nerinckx* (497) is still a good beginning point in the study of this important figure, although it has been superseded by William J. Howlett, *Life of the Rev. Charles Nerinckx: Pioneer Missionary of Kentucky and Founder of the Sisters of Loretto at the Foot of the Cross* (484). Howlett's study, however, was written with a popular audience in mind and lacks scholarly acumen. Helene Magaret, *Giant in the Wilderness: A Biography of Father Charles Nerinckx* (498), is so hagiographic as to deserve classification as a work of fiction rather than of biography. Two essays summarize Nerinckx's work further west in Missouri: John Gilmary Shea's "Pioneer of the West—Rev. Charles Nerinckx" (531), and John E. Rothensteiner, "Father Charles Nerinckx and His Relations to the Diocese of St. Louis" (527).

Martin J. Spalding, whose biography of Flaget has already been noted, was Flaget's successor as Bishop of Louisville. He later was named to what for much of the nineteenth century was the premier American see, the archbishopric of Baltimore. His nephew, John Lancaster Spalding, also a critical figure in American Catholic history, wrote an early biography *The Life of the Most Reverend M. J. Spalding* (538). Fortunately, there is a recent biography as well, one commendable for its scholarship: Thomas W. Spalding, *Martin John Spalding: American Churchman* (540).

By the reckoning of some, James Andrew Corcoran ranks as the foremost nineteenth-century American Roman Catholic theologian. Corcoran spent the bulk of his early life in Charleston, but moved to Philadelphia after the Civil War. Sr. M. M. Lowman's doctoral dissertation, "James Andrew Corcoran: Editor, Theologian, Scholar (1820-1889)" (494), is the best study to date. Another figure of national stature within Catholicism and the whole of American religion is James Cardinal Gibbons, who expended much energy interpreting the American context to Roman authorities during a time when massive Eastern and Southern European immigration, industrialization, and urbanization were reshaping the contours of American Catholicism. Gibbons's direct association with the South, however, is essentially restricted to his service as Archbishop of Baltimore. John Tracy Ellis, *Life of James Cardinal Gibbons, Archbishop of Baltimore, 1834-1921* (457) is still the standard biography and a reliable study. Finally, one relatively obscure figure deserves mention because of his involvement in an episode that remains a bone of contention between American Protestants and Catholics, Edward Fitzgerald, bishop of Little Rock at the time of the First Vatican Council in 1870. The controversial issue is the doctrine of papal infallibility, which asserts that the Pope is incapable of error when speaking *ex cathedra* on matters of faith and morals, a doctrine that attained official status when promulgated by the First Vatican Council. There were only two dissenting votes, thanks to much political maneuvering and a commitment among many to bolster papal prestige in the wake of loss of political power during the unification of Italy. Several American bishops opposed to official promulgation of the doctrine went home before the vote was taken, but Fitzgerald cast one of the two dissenting votes. An all too brief account is Svend Peterson, "The Little Rock against the Big Rock" (523). There remains a dearth of biographical studies of Southern Roman Catholic lay persons.

Southern Catholicism in the late twentieth century, while different from the Catholicism that took root in colonial Maryland, remains a part of Southern culture but apart from Southern culture. Still a regional minority, Southern Catholics are nevertheless members of a church that ranks as the largest Christian body in the nation. Hence their presence cannot be ignored and deserves more serious scrutiny by students of Southern religious life.

The bibliography that concludes this chapter follows the same format as that of other chapters. It first lists general topical studies of Southern Catholicism, then state and local studies, and finally biographical and autobiographical studies. Matters of current bibliography are frequently treated in the *American Catholic Studies Newsletter,* published by the Cushwa Center for the Study of American Catholicism at the University of Notre Dame.

BIBLIOGRAPHY

Numerous titles in the listings for chapters 1, 2, 3, 4, 15, 16, 18, 19, and 20 are also particularly relevant to the study of Roman Catholicism in the South.

I. ROMAN CATHOLICISM IN THE SOUTH: GENERAL AND TOPICAL STUDIES

(1) Agonito, Joseph. "Ecumenical Stirrings: Catholic-Protestant Relations During the Episcopacy of John Carroll." *Church History* 45 (1976): 358-73.

(2) _____, and Madeline Wellner, eds. "Reverend Charles Nerinckx's Pamphlet, 'A Look in the Present State of the Roman Catholic Religion in America' " *American Catholic Historical Society of Philadelphia Records* 83 (1972): 3-36.

(3) Ellis, John Tracy. *American Catholicism*. 2d ed. Chicago: University of Chicago Press, 1969.

(4) _____. *Catholics in Colonial America*. Baltimore: Helicon Press, 1965.

(5) Fichter, Joseph H. *Southern Parish: Dynamics of a City Church*. Chicago: University of Chicago Press, 1951.

(6) Gleason, Philip, ed. *Contemporary Catholicism in the United States*. Notre Dame: University of Notre Dame Press, 1969.

(7) Greeley, Andrew M. *The Catholic Experience: An Interpretation of the History of American Catholicism*. Garden City: Doubleday, 1967.

(8) Hennesey, James J. *American Catholics: A History of the Roman Catholic Community in the United States*. New York: Oxford University Press, 1982.

(9) _____. "Roman Catholicism: The Maryland Tradition." *Thought* 51 (1976): 282-95.

(10) Hero, Alfred O., Jr. *The Southerner and World Affairs,* chap. 12. Baton Rouge: Louisiana State University Press, 1965.

(11) Ives, John M. *The Ark and the Dove*. New York: Longmans, Green, 1936.

(12) LaFarge, John. *A Report on the American Jesuits*. New York: Farrar, Straus, and Cudahy, 1956.

(13) _____. "Some Aspects of the Jesuit-Baltimore Controversy." *Thought* 4 (1930): 638-66.

(14) Lee, S. R. "The Maryland Influence on American Catholicism." *American Catholic Historical Society of Philadelphia Records* 41 (1930): 328-52.

(15) "Letters Concerning Some Missions of the Mississippi Valley, A.D. 1815-1827." *American Catholic Historical Society of Philadelphia Records* 14 (1903): 141-216.

(16) Liu, William T. "The Marginal Catholics in the South: A Revision of Concepts." *American Journal of Sociology* 65 (1960): 383-90.

(17) _____. "A Study of the Social Integration of Catholic Migrants in a Southern Community." Ph.D. dissertation, Florida State University, 1958.

(18) McAvoy, Thomas T. "The Formation of the Catholic Minority in the United States, 1820-1860." *Review of Politics* 10 (1948): 13-34; see also *The Formation of the American Catholic Minority*. Philadelphia: Fortress Press, 1967.

(19) McKernan, Louis F. "Bishop England's Views on Church and State." M.A. thesis, Columbia University, 1962.

(20) McMurry, Vincent deP. "The Catholic Church During Reconstruction, 1865-1877." M.A. thesis, Catholic University of America, 1951.

(21) Martensen, Katherine. "Region, Religion, and Social Action: The Catholic Committee of the South, 1939-1956." *Catholic Historical Review* 68 (1982): 249-67.

(22) Mickler, Thomas R. "The Catholic Church in the Southland." M.A. thesis, Georgetown University, 1923.

(23) Miller, Randall M., and Jon L. Wakelyn, eds. *Catholics in the Old South: Essays on Church and Society*. Macon GA: Mercer University Press, 1983.

(24) Mulvey, Sr. Mary Doris. *French Catholic Missionaries in the Present United States (1604-1791)*. Catholic University of America Studies in American Church History 23. Washington: Catholic University of America Press, 1936.

(25) Murphy, Robert J. "The Catholic Church in the United States during the Civil War Period (1852-1866)." *American Catholic Historical Society of Philadelphia Records* 39 (1928): 271-346.

(26) Nast, Lenora H. "The Role of the Clergy in Jewish-Christian Relations in Baltimore from 1945 to 1975." Ph.D. dissertation, St. Mary's Seminary and University, 1978.

(27) O'Connell, Vincent J. "The Church in the South." *The American Apostolate: American Catholics in the Twentieth Century*. Leo R. Ward, ed. Westminster MD: Newman Press, 1952.

(28) Owens, M. Lilliana. "The Origins of the Sisters of Loretto at the Foot of the Cross." *Filson Club Historical Quarterly* 3 (1965): 226-45.

(29) Pillar, James J. "Catholicism in the Lower South." In *The Americanization of the Gulf Coast, 1803-1850*. Lucius F. Ellsworth, ed., 34-43. Pensacola: Historic Pensacola Preservation Board, 1972.

(30) Pohlkamp, Diomede. "Spanish Franciscans in the Southeast." *Franciscan Educational Conference Annual Report* 18 (1936): 124-50.

(31) Schmandt, Raymond H., ed. "Episcopal Support of Catholic Intellectual Activity—A Note on the Fourth Provincial Council of Baltimore." *Catholic Historical Review* 64 (1978): 51-56.

(32) Seary, John L. "The Society of Jesus in the United States, 1773-1814." M.A. thesis, Catholic University of America, 1927.

(33) Shea, John Gilmary. *History of the Catholic Church in the United States*. 4 vols. New York: J. G. Shea, 1886-92.

(34) Wakin, Edward, and Joseph F. Scheur. *The De-Romanization of the American Catholic Church*. New York: Macmillan, 1966.

II. ROMAN CATHOLICISM IN THE SOUTH: STUDIES BY STATE

(35) "Allegany Friars in Texas." *Provincial Annals* (Province of the Most Holy Name, O.F.M.) 5 (1946): 275-81.

(36) Allen, Ethan. *Maryland Toleration: or, Sketches of the Early History of Maryland, to the Year 1650.* Baltimore: J. S. Waters, 1855.

(37) Allison, Young E. "Chapter of Trappist History in Kentucky." [Louisville] *Historical Quarterly* 1 (1926): 68-81.

(38) Almarez, Felix D., Jr. "Carlos E. Castaneda and *Our Catholic Heritage: The Initial Volumes (1933-1943).*" *Social Science Journal* 13 (1976): 27-37.

(39) _____. *Crossroads of Empire: The Church and State on the Rio Grande Frontier of Coahuila and Texas, 1700-1821.* San Antonio: n.p., 1979.

(40) Aloysius, Fr. O. M. *Mission, Garrett Co., Md., 1820-1920.* Cumberland MD: Enterprise Publishing, 1921.

(41) "Applications for the Maryland Missions." *Woodstock Letters* 9 (1880): 73-94.

(42) Assenmacher, Hugh. *A Place Called Subiaco: A History of the Benedictine Monks in Arkansas.* Little Rock: Rose, 1977.

(43) Augustin, James M. *Sketch of the Catholic Church in Louisiana.* New Orleans: J. M. Augustine and T. H. Ryan, 1893.

(44) "Aus dem Grundungstagen einer Deutschen Gemeinde in Virginia." *Central Blatt and Social Justice* (now *Social Justice Review*) 16 (1923): 197-98, 271-72.

(45) Badin, Stephen T. "The Catholic Church in Kentucky." *American Catholic Historical Researches* 29 (1912): 141-74.

(46) _____. *Origine et progres de la Mission du Kentucky.* Paris: A. LeClere, 1821.

(47) Baker, T. Lindsay. *The First Polish Americans: Silesian Settlements in Texas.* College Station: Texas A & M University Press, 1979.

(48) Barnum, Francis. "Development of the Early Jesuit Missions." *American Catholic Historical Society of Philadelphia Records* 34 (1923): 362-73.

(49) _____. "Development of the Early Jesuit Missions." *Woodstock Letters* 52 (1923): 216-25.

(50) Baudier, Roger. *The Catholic Church in Louisiana.* New Orleans: A. W. Hyatt Stationery Manufacturing, 1939.

(51) _____. "Marian Devotion in Louisiana." *Ave Maria* 57 (1943): 687-89.

(52) Bayard, Ralph. *Lone-Star Vanguard: The Catholic Re-Occupation of Texas, 1838-1848.* St. Louis: Vincentian Press, 1945.

(53) Beattie, Robert F. "Beginnings of Catholicity in Virginia." M.A. thesis, St. Mary's Seminary and University, 1929.

(54) Bernard, Harry. "Le Roman Religioniste en Louisiana." *La Revue de L'Universite Laval* 2 (1948): 888-95.

(55) Bernard, Mother Mary. *The Story of the Sisters of Mercy in Mississippi, 1860-1930*. New York: Kenedy, 1931.

(56) Bernard, Richard M. *The Poles in Oklahoma*. Norman: University of Oklahoma Press, 1980.

(57) Bevins, Ann B. "Sisters of the Visitation: One Hundred Years in Scott County, Mt. Admirabilis and Cardome." *Register of the Kentucky Historical Society* 74 (1976): 30-39.

(58) Bicha, Karel D. *The Czechs in Oklahoma*. Norman: University of Oklahoma Press, 1980.

(59) Bier, Charles J. "Convalescing in Texas." *Salesianum* 68 (1953): 1-9.

(60) Bieter, A. J. "The Church in Texas." *Columbia* 16 (September 1936): 13, 20.

(61) Biever, A. H. *Jesuits in New Orleans and the Mississippi Valley*. New Orleans: Hauser, 1924.

(62) Blessing, Patrick. *The British and Irish in Oklahoma*. Norman: University of Oklahoma Press, 1980.

(63) Bolton, Herbert E. "The Spanish Abandonment and Re-occupation of Texas." *Texas State Historical Association Quarterly* 9 (1905): 85-137.

(64) _____. "Spanish Mission Records at San Antonio." *Texas State Historical Association Quarterly* 10 (1907): 297-307.

(65) Bosworth, Timothy W. "Anti-Catholicism as a Political Tool in Mid-Eighteenth-Century Maryland." *Catholic Historical Review* 61 (1975): 535-63.

(66) Bringazi, M. S. "Redemptorists in Texas." *Extension* 26 (1931): 26.

(67) Brown, Kenny L. *The Italians in Oklahoma*. Norman: University of Oklahoma Press, 1980.

(68) Brown, Thomas E. *Bible Belt Catholicism: A History of the Roman Catholic Church in Oklahoma, 1905-1945*. New York: U.S. Catholic Historical Society, 1977.

(69) Browne, Patrick W. "Salamanca and the Beginnings of the Church in Florida." *American Ecclesiastical Review* 84 (1931): 581-87.

(70) Carayon, Auguste. *Bannissement des Jesuites de la Louisiane: Relation et Lettres Inedites*. Paris: L'Ecureux, 1865.

(71) Carroll, Mary Teresa Austin. *A Catholic History of Alabama and the Floridas*. New York: Kenedy, 1908. Reprinted, Freeport NY: Books for Libraries, 1970.

(72) _____. *The Ursulines in Louisiana, 1727-1824*. New Orleans: H. Smith, 1886.

(73) Castaneda, Carlos E. "Earliest Catholic Activities in Texas." *Catholic Historical Review* 17 (1931): 278-95. Also Austin: Texas Catholic Historical Society, 1931.

(74) _____. *Our Catholic Heritage in Texas*. 7 vols. Austin: Von Boeckmann-Jones, 1936-58.

(75) _____. "The Sons of St. Francis in Texas." *Americas* 1 (1945): 289-302.

(76) Chabot, Frederick C. *Mission La Purissima Concepcion*. San Antonio: Naylor, 1935.

(77) Clark, Michael D. "Jonathan Boucher and the Toleration of Roman Catholics in Maryland." *Maryland Historical Magazine* 71 (1976): 194-203.

(78) Clarke, R. C. "Beginnings of Texas." *Texas Historical Association Quarterly* 5 (1901-02): 171-205; 6 (1902-03): 1-26.

(79) Clavreul, H. P. "Lettre de M. Clavreul, Missionnaire en Florida, a MM, les Membres des Conseils Centraux de L'Oeuvre de la Propagation de la Foi, Paris, 19 aout 1872." *Annales de la Propagation de la Foi* 44 (1872): 427-38.

(80) _____. *Notes on the Catholic Church in Florida*. St. Leo FL: Abbey Press, n.d.

(81) Connor, Jeannette T. *Colonial Records of Spanish Florida*. Deland: Florida State Historical Society, 1925.

(82) Conrad, Glenn R. "L'Immigration Alsacienne en Louisiane, 1753-1759." *Revue d'histoire de l'Amerique francaise* 32 (1978): 57-94.

(83) Cooney, J. M. "In Catholic Kentucky." *Ave Maria* 32 (1930): 737-42.

(84) Crump, Thomas F. "The History of the Bardstown Diocese, 1758-1818." M.A. thesis, Xavier University (Cincinnati), 1953.

(85) Cruzat, Heloise Hulse. "The Ursulines of Louisiana." *Louisiana Historical Quarterly* 2 (1919): 5-23.

(86) Curley, Michael J. *Church and State in the Spanish Floridas, 1783-1822*. Washington: Catholic University of America Press, 1940. Reprint, New York: AMS Press, 1974.

(87) Curran, Francis X. "The Jesuits in Kentucky, 1831-1846." *Mid-America* 35 (1953): 223-46.

(88) Curran, R. Emmett. *The Maryland Jesuits: 1634-1833*. Baltimore: Maryland Province, Society of Jesus, 1976.

(89) Deiler, J. Hanno. *The Settlement of the German Coast of Louisiana*. Philadelphia: American Germanica Press, 1909.

(90) _____. *Zur Geschichte der deutschen Kirchegemeinden in Staate Louisiana*. New York: By the author, 1894.

(91) Delanglez, Jean, S.J. *The French Jesuits in Lower Louisiana (1700-1763)*. Catholic University of America Studies in American Church History 21. Washington: Catholic University of America Press, 1935. Reprint, New York: AMS Press, 1974.

(92) Devitt, Edward I., ed. "Papers Relating to the Early History of Maryland Mission." *Woodstock Letters* 9 (1880): 157-80; 10 (1881): 3-28, 89-120, 209-24; 11 (1882): 3-24, 117-40.

(93) _____. "The Suppression and Restoration of the Society in Maryland." *Woodstock Letters* 33 (1904): 371-81.

(94) Dewey, Ralph E. S. "Letter from a Scholastic in Texas, dated San Antonio, Texas, Oct. 16th, 1873." *Woodstock Letters* 3 (1874): 64-68.

(95) _____. "Letter from a Scholastic in Texas, dated San Antonio, Jan. 28th, 1874." *Woodstock Letters* 3 (1874): 133-34.

(96) Din, Gilbert C. "The Irish Mission to West Florida." *Louisiana History* 12 (1971): 315-34.

(97) Dabbs, J. Autrey, trans. and ed. "Texas Missions in 1785, Document: Report of Father President of the Mission, 1785." *Mid-America* 11 (1940): 38-58.

(98) Dromo, John. "The Jesuit Order in Kentucky (1831-1868)." M. A. thesis, University of Louisville, 1954.

(99) Durkin, Joseph T. "Catholic Training for Maryland Catholics, 1773-1786." *U.S. Catholic Historical Society Records and Studies* 32 (1941): 70-82.

(100) East Tennessee Deanery Council of the Nashville Diocesan Council of Catholic Women. *East Tennessee Deanery Handbook*. N.p.p.: East Tennessee Deanery, 1952.

(101) "An Echo of the Old Order of Church and State in Louisiana." *American Catholic Historical Society of Philadelphia Records* 24 (1914): 288-95.

(102) Edwards, Richard B. "Pioneer Catholics in Kentucky." *Register of the Kentucky Historical Society* 68 (1970): 252-64.

(103) Emerick, A. J. "The Jesuits in Florida." *Woodstock Letters* 55 (1926): 215-25.

(104) Englehardt, Zephyrin. "Florida's First Bishop." *Catholic Historical Review* 4 (1918): 479-85.

(105) "Expulsion of the Jesuits from Louisiana in 1763." *Woodstock Letters* 4 (1875): 88-100; 5 (1876): 161-73; 6 (1877): 19-30.

(106) Fitzmorris, Sr. M. Angela. *Four Decades of Catholicism in Texas, 1820-1860*. Washington: Catholic University of America Press, 1926.

(107) Flanigan. George J. *Catholicity in Tennessee, 1541-1937*. Nashville: Ambrose Printing, 1937.

(108) Forrester, Donald F. "A Study of the Migration of Catholics to the Tennessee Valley Region from 1769-1810." M.A. thesis, Catholic University of America, 1934.

(109) Fortier, Alcee. *History of Louisiana*. 4 vols. New York: Goupiel, 1904.

(110) "Franciscan Diocese of Texas." (St. John the Baptist Province, O.F.M.) *Provincial Chronicle* 22 (1950): 29-56, 72, 90-107.

(111) "From Pensacola to St. Augustine in 1827." *Florida Historical Quarterly* 25 (1947): 135-66.

(112) Gaffey, James P. *Francis Clement Kelley and the American Catholic Dream*. 2 vols. Bensenville IL: Heritage Foundation, 1980.

(113) Gannon, Michael V. "Altar and Hearth: The Coming of Christianity, 1521-1565." *Florida Historical Quarterly* 44 (1965): 17-44.

(114) _____. *The Cross in the Sand: The Early Catholic Church in Florida, 1513-1870*. Gainesville: University of Florida Press, 1965.

(115) Garaventa, Louis T. "Bishop James Gibbons and the Growth of the Roman Catholic Church in North Carolina, 1868-1872." M.A. thesis, University of North Carolina in Chapel Hill, 1973.

(116) Garraghan, Gilbert J. "Catholic Beginnings in Maryland." *Thought* 9 (1934): 5-31, 261-85.

(117) _____. "A Jesuit Westward Movement." *Mid-America* 6 (1936): 165-81.

(118) _____. "The Mission of Central Missouri." *St. Louis Catholic Historical Review* 2 (1920): 157-82.

(119) Gately, Sr. Francis Magdalen. "Religious Conditions in Early Colonial Maryland (1634-1655)." M.A. thesis, Boston College, 1941.

(120) Geiger, Maynard. *Early Franciscans in Florida and Their Relation to Spain's Colonial Effort.* Paterson NJ: St. Anthony Guild Press, 1936.

(121) Gerow, Richard O., comp. *Catholicity in Mississippi.* Natchez: By the author, 1939.

(122) Gibbons, James [Cardinal]. *Reminiscences of Catholicity in North Carolina.* N.p.p.: n.p., 1891.

(123) Gleiss, Paul G. "German Jesuit Missionaries in 18th Century Maryland." *Woodstock Letters* 75 (1946): 199-206.

(124) Glodt, John T. "Our Florida Martyr Priests." *American Ecclesiastical Review* 69 (1923): 498-513, 614-31.

(125) Gold, Robert L. "The Departure of Spanish Catholicism from Florida, 1763-1765." *Americas* 22 (1966): 377-88.

(126) Gorrell, John J. "Earliest Franciscan Missionary Labors in Texas." *St. Francis Home Journal* 36 (1936): 76-78, 108-11.

(127) _____. "Early Franciscan Missions in Texas." *St. Francis Home Journal* 33 (1933): 333-34, 345.

(128) Greenleaf, Richard E. "The Inquisition in Spanish Louisiana, 1762-1800." *New Mexico Historical Review* 50 (1975): 45-72.

(129) Guilday, Peter. *The Catholic Church in Virginia.* New York: U.S. Catholic Historical Society, 1924.

(130) _____. "The Priesthood of Colonial Maryland (1634-1773)." *American Ecclesiastical Review* 90 (1934): 14-31.

(131) Guy, Francis J. "The Catholic Church in Arkansas (1541-1843)." M.A. thesis, Catholic University of America, 1932.

(132) H. F. "The Franciscans Seek the Maryland Mission in 1642." *American Catholic Historical Society Researches* 22 (1905): 289-91.

(133) Habig, Marion A. *The Alamo Mission: San Antonio de Valero.* Chicago: Franciscan Herald, 1977.

(134) _____. "First Marian Shrine in the United States." *American Ecclesiastical Review* 134 (1957): 81-89.

(135) _____, ed. *Nothingness Itself: Selected Writings of Venerable Father Antonio Margil, 1690-1724.* Chicago: Franciscan Herald, 1976.

(136) Haile, Herbert. *Catholic Women of Tennessee, 1937-1956*. Nashville: Marshall and Bruce, 1956.

(137) Hale, Douglas. *The Germans from Russia in Oklahoma*. Norman: University of Oklahoma Press, 1980.

(138) Hammon, Walter. "New Page in an Old Diary." [New York] *Provincial Annals* 11 (1954): 87-90.

(139) Hasque, Urbande. *Early Catholic History of Oklahoma*. Oklahoma City: Southwest Courier, 1928.

(140) Hennesey, James J. "The Vision of John Carroll." *Thought* 54 (1979): 322-23.

(141) Historical Commission, Diocese of Little Rock. *A History of Catholicity in Arkansas from the Earliest Missionaries down to the Present Time*. Little Rock: The Guardian, 1925.

(142) Hogan, John A. *On the Mission in Missouri, 1857-1868*. Kansas City: J. A. Heilmann, 1892. Reprint, Glorietta NM: Rio Grande, 1976.

(143) Holmes, Jack D. L. "Educational Opportunities in Spanish West Florida, 1781-1821." *Florida Historical Quarterly* 60 (1981): 3-19.

(144) _____. "Spanish Religious Policy in West Florida: Enlightened or Expedient?" *Journal of Church and State* 15 (1973): 259-69.

(145) Holweck, Frederick G. "The Arkansas Mission under Rosati." *St. Louis Catholic Historical Review* 1 (1918): 243-67.

(146) Holworthy, Sr. Mary Xavier. *Diamonds for the King*. Corpus Christi: Incarnate Word Academy, 1945.

(147) Holzmeister, DePaul. "The Catholic Church in the Oklahoma Panhandle." [Cincinnati] *Provincial Chronicles, O.F.M.* 28 (1956): 265-71.

(148) "How the Benedictines Came to Enter Texas." *Central Blatt and Social Justice* (now *Social Justice Review*) 24 (1931): 132.

(149) Hurley, James M. "Political Status of Roman Catholics in North Carolina." *American Catholic Historical Society of Philadelphia Researches* 38 (1927): 237-96.

(150) Hyland, F. E. "The Church in Georgia." *Extension* 48 (October 1953): 24-25.

(151) "Imposter 'Bishop' in Illinois and Kentucky in 1827." *American Catholic Historical Researches* 8 (1892): 81-83.

(152) Institute of Texan Cultures. *The Texians and the Texans*. Pamphlet series. San Antonio: University of Texas at San Antonio Institute of Texan Cultures, 1970- .

(153) "Instruction for the Government of the Parochial Clergy of the Diocese of Louisiana." *U.S. Catholic Historical Magazine* 1 (1887): 418-42.

(154) Jordan, David W. "A Plea for Maryland Catholics." *Maryland Historical Magazine* 67 (1972): 429-35.

(155) "Journal of Missions in Kentucky." *Woodstock Letters* 8 (1879): 74-80.

(156) Juarez, Jose R. "La Iglesia Catholica y el Chicano en Sud Texas, 1836-1911." *Aztlan* 4 (1973): 217-55.

(157) Jung, Margetta P. "Texas's First Catholic Mission." *Ave Maria* 43 (1936): 430-33.

(158) Keane, James P. "Status of Catholics in Maryland, 1689-1760." M.A. thesis, Catholic University of America, 1950.

(159) Keegan, Gregory J., and Leandro Tormo Sanz. *Experiencia en la Florida (siglos XVI y XVII)*. Madrid: Consigo Superior de Investigaciones Cientifica, Institutio Santo Torbio de Mongrovejo, 1957.

(160) Keller, Allan. "The Catholics in Maryland." *Early American Life* 9 (1978): 18-21, 78-79.

(161) Kenny, Michael. *Catholic Culture in Alabama*. New York: The America Press, 1931.

(162) _____. *Romance of the Floridas*. Milwaukee: Bruce, 1934.

(163) _____. "What History Says of Florida's Beginnings." *Catholic World* 162 (1945): 232-37.

(164) Kohlmann, Anthony. "Letter to Father William Strickland, Poland Street, London, dated Georgetown, Feb. 23, 1807." *Woodstock Letters* 12 (1883): 86-87.

(165) _____. "Letter to Father William Strickland, Poland Street, London, dated Georgetown, March 9, 1808." *Woodstock Letters* 12 (1883): 88.

(166) _____. "Letter to Father William Strickland, Poland Street, London, dated Philadelphia, April 23, 1807." *Woodstock Letters* 12 (1883): 89.

(167) Krugler, John D. "The Calvert Family, Catholicism, and Court Politics in Early Seventeenth-Century England." *The Historian* 63 (1981): 378-92.

(168) _____. "Lord Baltimore, Roman Catholics and Toleration: Religious Policy in Maryland during the Early Catholic Years." *Catholic Historical Review* 75 (1979): 49-75.

(169) _____. "Sir George Calvert's Resignation as Secretary of State and the Founding of Maryland." *Maryland Historical Magazine* 67 (1973): 239-54.

(170) LaFarge, John. "The Jesuit-Baltimore Controversy." *Historical Bulletin* 12 (1934): 23-24.

(171) _____. "The Missions of Old Maryland." *America* 50 (1934): 586-87.

(172) _____. "The Survival of the Catholic Faith in Southern Maryland." *Catholic Historical Review* 21 (1935): 1-20.

(173) Lahey, Raymond J. "The Role of Religion in Lord Baltimore's Colonial Enterprise." *Maryland Historical Magazine* 72 (1977): 83-98.

(174) Lammers, Herman J. "History of the St. Vincent dePaul Society: The Particular Council of Louisville, Kentucky, 1854-1932." M.A. thesis, Catholic University of America, n.d.

(175) Lemarie, Charles. *Mgr. J.-B. David, 1761-1841: Les Origines religieuses de Kentucky*. Angers: By the author, 1973.

(176) Lemieux, Donald. "Some Legal and Practical Aspects of the Office of *Commissaire Ordonnateur* of French Louisiana." *Louisiana Studies* 14 (1975): 379-93.

(177) Lenhart, John M. "The Catholic Church in the State of Virginia, 1785-1843." *Social Justice Review* 49 (1956): 274-78.

(178) _____. "The Double Jurisdiction in French Louisiana, 1722-1766." *Franciscan Studies* 28 (1947): 344-47.

(179) _____. "German Catholics in Colonial Louisiana (1721-1803)." *Central Blatt and Social Justice* (now *Social Justice Review*) 25 (1932): 17-19, 53-55, 88-91, 126-29.

(180) Lipscomb, Oscar H. "The Administration of John Quinlan, Second Bishop of Mobile, 1859-1883." *Records of the American Catholic Historical Society of Philadelphia* 78 (1967).

(181) _____. "Catholic Missions in Early Alabama." *Alabama Review* 18 (1965): 124-31.

(182) _____. "Catholics in Alabama, 1861-1865." *Alabama Review* 20 (1967): 278-88.

(183) Little, Mary Bartholomew. "The Development of the Catholic Religion in Northeast Missouri." M.A. thesis, St. Louis University, 1946.

(184) Little Rock, Arkansas, Diocesan Historical Commission. *The History of Catholicity in Arkansas*. Little Rock: n.p., 1925.

(185) Lockett, Wickliffe. "Early Catholicity in Kentucky and the See of Bardstown." M.A. thesis, University of Louisville, 1929.

(186) Lucey, John M. *The Catholic Church in Arkansas*. Little Rock: n.p., 1906.

(187) _____. "The Catholic Church in Arkansas." *Arkansas Historical Association Publications* 2 (1908): 424-61.

(188) _____. *Souvenir of a Silver Jubilee*. Little Rock: n.p., 1892.

(189) Lyon, Eugene. *The Enterprise of Florida: Pedro Menendez de Aviles and the Spanish Conquest of 1565-1568*. Gainesville: University Presses of Florida, 1976.

(190) McBeath, James J. "The Irish Empresarios in Texas." M.A. thesis, Catholic University of America, 1953.

(191) [McGee, John Forest]. "A Living Story of the Faith in the Oklahoma Panhandle." [Province of St. John the Baptist, O.F.M.] *Provincial Chronicles* 21 (1949): 127-31.

(192) _____. "The Story of the Friars Minor in the 'Franciscan Diocese of Texas'." [St. John the Baptist Province, O.F.M.] *Provincial Chronicles* 21 (1949): 29-56, 90-113.

(193) McGrain, John W., Jr. "Priest Neale, His Mission House, and His Successors." *Maryland Historical Magazine* 62 (1967): 254-84.

(194) _____. "Priest Neale and his Successors, Part II." *Maryland Historical Magazine* 63 (1968): 137-57.

(195) McNally, Michael J. T. "Cross in the Sun: The Growth and Development of Catholicism in South Florida, 1868-1968." Ph.D. dissertation, University of Notre Dame, 1982.

(196) McNutty, John P. "Diocesan Priests in Florida's Beginnings." *Catholic World* 162 (1946): 527-32.

(197) Magri, Francis J. "Catholicity in Virginia during the Episcopate of Bishop McGill (1850-1872)." *Catholic Historical Review* 2 (1917): 415-26.

(198) *Marianite Centennial in Louisiana, 1848-1948.* New Orleans: Provincial House, Holy Angels Academy, 1948.

(199) Matter, Robert A. "Economic Bases of the Seventeenth-Century Florida Missions." *Florida Historical Quarterly* 50 (1973): 18-38.

(200) _____. "Mission Life in Seventeenth-Century Florida." *Catholic Historical Review* 67 (1981): 401-20.

(201) _____. "Missions in the Defense of Spanish Florida, 1566-1710." *Florida Historical Quarterly* 54 (1975): 18-38.

(202) Mattingly, Mary Ramona. *The Catholic Church on the Kentucky Frontier (1785-1812).* Washington: Catholic University of America, 1936.

(203) Melville, Annabelle M. "John Carroll and Louisiana, 1803-1815." *Catholic Historical Review* 64 (1978): 398-440.

(204) "Memoir Concerning the Church of Louisiana, dated Nov. 21, 1728." *American Catholic Historical Researches* 22 (1905): 124-27.

(205) Menard, Russel B. "Maryland's 'Time of Troubles': Sources of Political Disorder in Early St. Mary's." *Maryland Historical Magazine* 76 (1981): 124-40.

(206) Michalicki, John. "The First Catholic Church in Indian Territory—1872." *Chronicles of Oklahoma* 50 (1972): 479-85.

(207) Milanich, Jerald T. "Tacacacuru and the San Pedro de Mocama Mission." *Florida Historical Quarterly* 51 (1972): 283-91.

(208) "Missouri—The First Mission from Maryland." *Woodstock Letters* 14 (1885): 305-16.

(209) Morris, Sr. Mary Mercedes. "The Sisters of Mercy of Oklahoma, 1884-1944." M.A. thesis, Catholic University of America, 1947.

(210) Mulherin, Sr. Mary Jeane. "The First Years of the Catholic Layman's Association of Georgia, 1916-1921." M.A. thesis, Catholic University of America, 1954.

(211) Murdoch, Richard K. "Governor Cesedes and the Religious Problem in East Florida, 1786-1787." *Florida Historical Quarterly* 26 (1948): 325-44.

(212) Murphy, Joseph F. *Tenacious Monks: The Oklahoma Benedictines, 1875-1975.* Shawnee OK: St. Gregory's Abbey, 1975.

(213) Murray, Christopher P. "The Catholic Church among the Negroes of Tennessee." M.A. thesis, St. Mary's Seminary and University, 1927.

(214) Nash, Michael. "Our Fathers in Kentucky: An Historical Note." *Woodstock Letters* 22 (1893): 25-27.

(215) Nolan, Charles E. *Bayou Carmel: The Sisters of Mount Carmel of Louisiana, 1833-1903*. Kenner LA: Nolan, 1977.

(216) O'Brien, E. J. "Jesuits in Spanish Florida." M.A. thesis, Loyola University (Chicago), 1942.

(217) O'Brien, James J. "Sketch of the Expulsion of the Society of Jesus from Louisiana." Louisiana Historical Society *Publications* 9 (1916): 9-24.

(218) O'Connell, Jeremiah J. *Catholicity in the Carolinas and Georgia*. New York: D. and J. Sadler, 1879. Reprint, Westminster MD: Ars Sacra, 1964, and Spartanburg SC: Reprint, 1972.

(219) O'Connor, Thomas. "A Kentucky Contribution to Religion on the Frontier." *Register of the Kentucky Historical Society* 34 (1936): 131-38.

(220) O'Daniel, Victor F., trans. and ed. "Bishop Flaget's Report of the Diocese of Bardstown to Pope Pius VII, April 10, 1815." *Catholic Historical Review* 1 (1915): 305-19.

(221) _____. *Dominicans in Early Florida*. U.S. Catholic Historical Society Monograph Series 12. New York: U.S. Catholic Historical Society, 1930.

(222) [Odin, J. M.]. "Missionary Life in Texas Fifty Years Ago." *U.S. Catholic Historical Magazine* 4 (1891-92): 210-19.

(223) O'Donohue, Sr. Mary Aquinas. "Sisters of Mercy in Texas, 1875-1945." M.A. thesis, Catholic University of America, 1948.

(224) Oetgen, Jerome. "The Origins of the Benedictine Order in Georgia." *Georgia Historical Quarterly* 53 (1969): 165-83.

(225) O'Neill, Charles E., ed. *Charlevoix's Louisiana: Selections from the History and the Journal*. Baton Rouge: Louisiana State University Press, 1977.

(226) "Origin and Progress of the Mission of Kentucky." *Catholic World* 21 (1875): 825-35.

(227) O'Rourke, Thomas P. "The Franciscan Missions in Texas (1690-1793)." Ph.D. dissertation, Catholic University of America, 1927.

(228) Ousley, Stanley. "The Kentucky Irish American." *Filson Club Historical Quarterly* 53 (1979): 178-95.

(229) Owens, Sr. M. Lilliana. "Growth of the Lorettines in Missouri." *American Catholic Historical Society of Philadelphia Records* 71 (1960): 93-112.

(230) _____. "Loretto Foundations in Louisiana and Arkansas." *Louisiana History* 2 (1961): 202-29.

(231) _____. "The Pioneer Days of the Lorettines in Missouri, 1823-1841." *American Catholic Historical Society of Philadelphia Records* 70 (1960): 67-87.

(232) Palmer, Bonaventure. "Bishop John William Shaw and the Diocese of San Antonio, 1910-1918." M.A. thesis, Catholic University of America, 1960.

(233) Pariseau, A. A. "History of the Society of Mary in Texas." M.A. thesis, Loyola University (Chicago), 1939.

(234) Parisot, P. F. *Reminiscences of a Texas Missionary*. San Antonio: Johnson Brothers Printing, 1899.

(235) Paul. *Paulist Fathers in Tennessee, 1900-1950*. Memphis: Wimmer Brothers, [1950?].

(236) Pillar, James J. *The Catholic Church in Mississippi*. New Orleans: Hauser Press, 1964.

(237) Plaissance, Aloysius. "Benedictine Monks in Alabama, 1876-1956." *Alabama Review* 11 (1958): 56-63.

(238) Porteus, Laura L., trans. and ed. "Marriage Contracts of the Spanish Period in Louisiana." *Louisiana Historical Quarterly* 10 (1927): 385-97.

(239) Rahill, Peter J. "Who Was the Second Bishop of Louisiana?" *Social Justice Review* 63 (1970-1971).

(240) Renggli, M. Beatrice. "From Rickenbach to Maryville: An Account of the Journey (1874)." M. Agnes Voltha, trans. *American Benedictine Review* 27 (1976): 247-69.

(241) Resch, Peter A. *Shadows Cast Before: The Early Chapters of the History of the Society of Mary in the St. Louis Country*. Kirkwood MO: Maryhurst Press, 1948.

(242) Rice, Bernadine. "The Irish in Texas." *American Irish Historical Society Journal* 30 (1932): 60-70.

(243) Ritta, M. "Catholicism in Colonial Maryland." *Records of the American Catholic Historical Society of Philadelphia* 51 (1940): 65-83.

(244) Robertson, James A. "Notes on Early Church Government in Spanish Florida." *Catholic Historical Review* 17 (1931): 151-74.

(245) Rohrs, Richard C. *The Germans in Oklahoma*. Norman: University of Oklahoma Press, 1980.

(246) Rooney, Sr. Nellie. "A History of the Catholic Church in the Pan-handle Plains Area of Texas from 1875 to 1916." M.A. thesis, Catholic University of America, 1954.

(247) Rouse, Parke J. "Conquistadors on the Chesapeake." *Americas* 32 (1980): 28-33.

(248) Russell, William T. *Maryland: The Land of Sanctuary*. Baltimore: J. H. Furst, 1907.

(249) Rybalt, John E. "Missouri in 1847: The Pastoral Visit of Archbishop Kenrick." *Bulletin of the Missouri Historical Society* 35 (1979): 202-97.

(250) Schauinger, J. Herman. "Kentucky: Cradle of Catholicism in the Old World." *Ave Maria* 94 (4 November 1961): 5-10.

(251) Scheibl, H. J. "Catholics in the History of Texas." *Americas* 48 (1933): 526-27.

(252) Schmitt, E. J. P. *Catalogue of Franciscan Missionaries in Texas (1528-1859)*. Austin: n.p., 1901.

(253) Schmitz, Jose W. "Beginning of the Society of Mary in Texas, 1852-1866." *Mid-America* 14 (1943): 3-28.

(254) Sheridan, Sr. Mary Bernignus. "Bishop Odin and the New Era of the Catholic Church in Texas." Ph.D. dissertation, St. Louis University, 1938.

(255) Smith, Michael M. *The Mexicans in Oklahoma*. Norman: University of Oklahoma Press, 1980.

(256) Solis, Jose de. "Diary of a Visit of Inspector of the Texas Missions Made by Fray Gaspar Jose de Solis, in the Year 1767-1768." Margaret K. Kress, trans. *Southwestern Historical Quarterly* 35 (1931): 28-72.

(257) Souvay, Charles L. "Episcopal Visitation to the Diocese of New Orleans, 1827-1828." *St. Louis Catholic Historical Review* 1 (1919): 215-30.

(258) Spalding, Henry S. *Catholic Colonial Maryland: A Sketch*. Milwaukee: Bruce, 1931.

(259) _____. "English-Maryland Catholics in Kentucky." *Month* 157 (1931): 128-32.

(260) _____. "The Priest's House—A Relic of Early Catholicity in Kentucky." *Illinois Catholic Historical Review* 9 (1927): 372-76.

(261) Spalding, Martin J., and Bonaventure Hammer. *Aussage aus der Geschichte der Diocese Louisville*. 2 vols. Louisville: George D. Deuser, 1852.

(262) _____. *Sketches of Early Catholic Missions of Kentucky*. Louisville: B. J. Webb and Brother, 1844.

(263) Spelman, Sr. M. Cajetan. "The Church on the Kentucky Frontier." M.A. thesis, University of Notre Dame, 1945.

(264) Stanton, Thomas J. *A Century of Growth: Or, the History of the Church in Western Maryland*. 2 vols. Baltimore: John Murphy, 1900.

(265) Steck, Francis Borgia. *Forerunners of Captain de Leon's Expedition to Texas, 1670-1675*. Austin: Texas Catholic Historical Society, 1932.

(266) Stegmaier, Mark J. "Maryland's Fear of Insurrection at the Time of Braddock's Defeat." *Maryland Historical Magazine* 71 (1976): 467-83.

(267) Thomas, Sr. Ursula. "The Catholic Church on the Oklahoma Frontier." *Mid-America* 9 (1938): 170-207.

(268) _____. "The Catholic Church on the Oklahoma Frontier." Ph.D. dissertation, St. Louis University, 1938.

(269) [Timon, John]. "The Church in Texas: Bishop Timon's Account of His Visitation in 1840-1841." *American Catholic Historical Researches* 14 (1897): 187-89.

(270) Treacy, William P. *Old Catholic Maryland and Its Early Jesuit Missions*. Swedesboro NJ: n.p., 1889.

(271) Van Miert, Louis, ed. "Some Historical Documents Concerning the Mission of Maryland, 1807-1820, with Biographical Sketches and Notes by Father Louis Van Miert, S.J." *Woodstock Letters* 30 (1901): 333-52.

(272) Veglia, Eugenie, S.J. "The Sisters of Saint Joseph in Louisiana." B.A. thesis, Loyola University (New Orleans), 1936.

(273) Vogel, Claude L. *The Capuchins in French Louisiana (1722-1766)*. Catholic University of America Studies in American Church History 7. Washington: Catholic University of America Press, 1928. Reprint, New York: Arno Press, 1974.

(274) ———. "The Capuchins in Lower Louisiana." *Franciscan Educational Conference Annual Report* 18 (1936): 198-233.

(275) Webb, B. J. "Catholicity in Kentucky: The Elder Family of Missouri and Kentucky." *American Catholic Quarterly Review* 5 (1880): 653-65.

(276) ———. "Catholicity in Kentucky: Grace Newton Simpson." *American Catholic Quarterly Review* 6 (1881): 609-16.

(277) ———. *The Centenary of Catholicity in Kentucky.* Louisville: C. A. Rogers, 1884.

(278) Weddle, Robert S. "San Juan Bautista: Mother of Texas Missions." *Southwestern Historical Quarterly* 72 (1968): 542-63.

(279) Weibel, John E. *The Catholic Missions of North-East Arkansas, 1867-1893.* Sr. M. Agnes Voth, O.S.B., trans. Lee A. Dew, ed. State University AR: Arkansas State University Press, 1967. First published 1893.

(280) West Tennessee Deanery Council of the Diocesan Council of Catholic Women. *The Catholic Church in West Tennessee.* N.p.p.: West Tennessee Deanery Council of the Diocesan Council of Catholic Women, 1951.

(281) White, Andrew. "An Account of the Colony of the Lord Baron of Baltimore, 1633." *Narratives of Early Maryland, 1633-1684.* Clayton C. Hall, ed., 1-10. New York: Charles Scribner's Sons, 1910.

(282) ———. "A Brief Account of the Voyage into Maryland." In *Narratives of Early Maryland, 1633-1684.* Clayton C. Hall, ed., 25-45. New York: Charles Scribner's Sons, 1910.

(283) ———. *Relatio Itineris in Marylandiam.* Baltimore: Maryland Historical Society, 1874.

(284) ———. *A Relation of Maryland: Together with a Map of the Contrey, the Conditions of Plantation, His Majesties Charter to Lord Baltemore.* New York: Johnson Reprint, 1976. First published 1635.

(285) ———. *A Relation of the Successful Beginnings of the Lord Baltemore's Plantation in Maryland: Being an Extract of Certaine Letters Written from Thence, by Some of the Adventurers to Their Friends in England.* Albany NY: J. Munsell, 1865. First published 1634.

(286) Worsley, Stephen C. "Catholicism in Antebellum North Carolina." *North Carolina Historical Review* 60 (1983): 399-430.

(287) Zwinge, Joseph S.J. "The Jesuit Farms in Maryland." *Woodstock Letters* 39 (1910): 374-82; 40 (1911): 65-77, 180-99; 41 (1912): 85-97, 195-222, 275-91; 42 (1913): 1-13, 137-50, 336-52; 43 (1914): 183-89, 194-200.

(288) ———. "Our Fathers and the Colonization of Maryland." *Woodstock Letters* 36 (1907): 78-92.

III. ROMAN CATHOLICISM IN THE SOUTH: LOCAL STUDIES

(289) Agonito, Joseph. "St. Inigoes Manor: A Nineteenth-Century Jesuit Plantation." *Maryland Historical Magazine* 72 (1977): 83-98.

(290) Anneken, Mary G. "A Study of the Growth of Catholicism in Covington, Kentucky, 1830-1868." M.A. thesis, University of Notre Dame, 1946.

(291) Bailey, James H. *A Century of Catholicism in Historic Petersburg: A History of St. Joseph's Parish, Petersburg*. Petersburg VA: Catholic Historical Society of the Diocese of Richmond, 1942.

(292) _____. "A History of the Diocese of Richmond from Its Establishment, 1820, to the Episcopate of Bishop Gibbons, 1872." Ph.D. dissertation, Georgetown University, 1953.

(293) _____. *A History of the Diocese of of Richmond: The Formative Years*. Richmond: Chancery Office, 1956.

(294) Baker, T. Lindsay, ed. and trans. "Four Letters from Texas to Poland in 1855." *Southwestern Historical Quarterly* 77 (1974): 381-89.

(295) Battersby, W. J. *The Christian Brothers in Memphis: A Chronicle of One Hundred Years, 1871-1971*. Memphis: Christian Brothers College, 1971.

(296) Baudier, Roger. "The First Sodality of the Blessed Virgin in New Orleans, 1730." *U.S. Catholic Historical Society Records and Studies* 30 (1939): 47-53.

(297) Beitzell, Edwin W. *The Jesuit Missions of St. Mary's County, Maryland*. 2d ed. Abell MD: By the author, 1976.

(298) Bezou, Henry C. *Metairie: A Tongue of Land to Pasture: An Account of the Development of the Faith Community in East Jefferson Deanery Commemorating the Fiftieth Anniversary of St. Francis Xavier Parish, Metairie, Louisiana*. Gretna LA: Pelican, 1973.

(299) "Bohemia, Cecil County, Maryland." *Woodstock Letters* 13 (1884): 333-44; 14 (1885): 102-11, 221-31.

(300) Bowen, John. "A History of the Baltimore Cathedral to 1876." M.A. thesis, Catholic University of America, 1963.

(301) Bramlage, Catherine. "Origin, History, and Educational Activities of the Benedictine Sisters of Covington, Kentucky." M.A. thesis, University of Notre Dame, 1938.

(302) Breunig, J. "Catholic Revival in Tennessee." *America* 88 (1953): 704-705.

(303) "A Brief Story of Louisiana." [Cincinnati] *Provincial Chronicles, O.F.M.* 23 (1951): 152-72.

(304) Britt, Sr. Gertrude Marie. "Catholic Beginnings of the Wheeling Diocese." M.A. thesis, Catholic University of America, 1939.

(305) Buetenbach, Sara Ann. "The Development of the Catholic Church in Louisville." Master's thesis, University of Louisville, 1941.

(306) Buotich, D. D. *Historical Sketch of Sacred Heart Parish and Its Mission in Northwestern Texas*. Amarillo: Rev. J. R. Allard, 1922.

(307) Catholic Youth Organization, Diocese of Galveston, Houston District. *The Story of the Development of the Kingdom of God on Earth in that Portion of the Vineyard Which for One Hundred Years has been the Diocese of Galveston*. Houston: Catholic Youth Organization and Centennial Book Committee, 1947.

(308) Colley, Van Buren. *History of the Diocesan Shrine of the Immaculate Conception*. Atlanta: Diocesan Shrine of the Immaculate Conception, 1955.

(309) Comeau, Alfonso. "A Study of the Trustee Problem in the St. Louis Cathedral Church of New Orleans, Louisiana, 1842-1844." M.A. thesis, University of Notre Dame, 1947.

(310) Crews, Clyde F. "Hallowed Ground: The Cathedral of the Assumption in Louisville History." *Filson Club Historical Quarterly* 51 (1977): 249-61.

(311) Cronin, John C. "Material for the History of Old St. Peter's Parish, Baltimore, Maryland, 1770-1841." M.A. thesis, St. Mary's Seminary and University, 1937.

(312) Cummins, Damian L. "Catholic Beginnings in Nodaway County, Missouri." M.A. thesis, St. Louis University, 1930.

(313) _____. "Pioneer Catholics of Nodaway County, Missouri, 1846-1873." *Mid-America* 2 (1931): 207-24.

(314) *Diamond Jubilee, 1847-1922, of the Diocese of Galveston and St. Mary's Cathedral.* LaPorte TX: [St. Mary's Seminary], 1922.

(315) Doyon, Bernard, O.M.I. *The Cavalry of Christ on the Rio Grande, 1849-1883.* Milwaukee: Bruce, 1956.

(316) Dressel, John J. "St. Patrick's Parish, Baltimore, Maryland, 1792-1922." M.A. thesis, St. Mary's Seminary and University, 1941.

(317) du Fief, Mary Margaret. "A History of Saint Aloysius' Parish, Washington, D.C., 1859-1909." M.A. thesis, Georgetown University, 1961.

(318) Dufour, Charles L. *1833 . . . St. Patrick's of New Orleans . . . 1958.* New Orleans: St. Patrick's Parish, 1958.

(319) Eyraud, Jean, and Donald Millet, comps. and eds. *A History of St. John the Baptist Parish with Biographical Sketches.* Marrero LA: Hope Haven Press, 1939.

(320) Faherty, William B., S.J. *Dream by the River: Two Centuries of Saint Louis Cathedral, 1766-1967.* St. Louis: Piraeus, 1973.

(321) Fay, M. Anita Rosaire. "Growth and Development of the Diocesan Organization of the Baltimore Diocese." M.A. thesis, Villanova University, 1951.

(322) Fecher, Vincent J., S.V.D. *A Study of the Movement for German National Parishes in Philadelphia and Baltimore, 1787-1802.* Rome: Apud Aedes Universitatis Gregorianne, 1955.

(323) Fitzwilliam, Mary C. "Relations of the Ursuline Community of New Orleans with Other Ursuline Communities from 1727-1803." M.A. thesis, St. Louis University, 1940.

(324) Flanigan, George J. *The Centenary of Sts. Peter and Paul's Parish, Chattanooga, Tennessee.* Chattanooga: Ss. Peter and Paul Parish, 1952.

(325) Flusche, Emil. "A Group of Colonies Founded by Three Brothers." *Central Blatt and Social Justice* (now *Social Justice Review*) 25 (1932): 276-77.

(326) Friend, A. B. "Alabama: Letter Dated Selma, Alabama, June 7th, 1877." *Woodstock Letters* 17 (1888): 52-72.

(327) Garesche, Ferdinand P. "Texas: Letter Dated Gonzalez, Texas, Jan. 31st, 1887." *Woodstock Letters* 16 (1887): 136-39.

(328) _____. "Texas: Letter Dated Gonzalez, Texas, March 12th, 1888." *Woodstock Letters* 17 (1888): 202-204.

(329) _____. "Texas: Letter Dated Seguin, Texas." *Woodstock Letters* 11 (1882): 185-90.

(330) _____. "Texas: Letter Dated Seguin, Texas, July 10, 1881." *Woodstock Letters* 10 (1881): 282-85.

(331) _____. "Texas: Letter Dated Seguin, Texas, Oct. 3, 1882." *Woodstock Letters* 11 (1882): 60-65.

(332) Garraghan, Gilbert J. *Catholic Beginnings in Kansas City, Missouri.* Chicago: Loyola University Press, 1921.

(333) _____. *Saint Ferdinand De Florissant: The Story of an Ancient Parish.* Chicago: Loyola University Press, 1923.

(334) Gerow, Richard O. *Cradle Days of St. Mary's at Natchez.* Natchez: By the author, 1941.

(335) Habig, Marion A. "Our First Church of Mary Immaculate." *American Ecclesiastical Review* 131 (1954): 313-19.

(336) _____. "Our Oldest Church of Mary Immaculate." *American Ecclesiastical Review* 133 (1956): 5-9.

(337) Haggerson, Elizabeth. "The History of the Diocese of Mobile, 1826-1859." M.A. thesis, University of Notre Dame, 1942.

(338) Heaney, Jane Frances. "A Century of Pioneering: A History of the Ursuline Nuns in New Orleans (1727-1827)." M.A. thesis, St. Louis University, 1949.

(339) Holmes, Jack D. L. "Irish Priests in Spanish Natchez." *Journal of Mississippi History* 29 (1967): 169-80.

(340) Holweck, Frederick G. "The Beginnings of the Church in Little Rock." *Catholic Historical Review* 6 (1920): 156-71.

(341) _____. "The Language Question in the Old Cathedral of St. Louis." *St. Louis Catholic Historical Review* 2 (1920): 5-17.

(342) _____. "Public Worship in St. Louis, before Palm Sunday, 1843." *St. Louis Catholic Historical Review* 4 (1922): 5-12.

(343) Hugh. "Tampa, Fla. Letter dated Tampa, Fla. Church of St. Louis, Diocese of St. Augustine, Jan. 5, 1890." *Woodstock Letters* 19 (1890): 82-85.

(344) Johnson, Richard H. "A Critical Study of Religious Work among Negroes of St. Mary's County, Maryland, since 1865, with Special Reference to the Catholic, Episcopal, and Methodist Churches." M.A. thesis, Howard University, 1948.

(345) Krier, P. A. "Missouri: Letter Dated Westphalia, Osage Co., Mo., July 15th, 1882." *Woodstock Letters* 11 (1882): 295-97.

(346) Lachowsky, M. Wilma. "Centenary History of St. Peter's Parish, St. Charles, Missouri, 1850-1950." M.A. thesis, St. Louis University, 1952.

(347) Lally, William M. "The History of St. Mark the Evangelist Parish, St. Louis, Missouri, 1893-1957." M.A. thesis, St. Louis University, 1958.

(348) Lenhart, John M. "Catholic Action in the German Congregation of Wheeling, West Virginia, 1865-1955." *Social Justice Review* 50 (1957): 96-99.

(349) _____. "Economic Valuation of the German Catholic Congregation in Wheeling, W.Va., 1856-1955." *Social Justice Review* 49 (1956): 140-43.

(350) _____. "Ethnic Groups of the German Congregation of the Wheeling District, 1820-1949." *Social Justice Review* 49 (1956): 130-33.

(351) _____. *Historical Notes on Sacred Heart Church, Charleston, West Virginia*. N.p.p.: n.p., 1941.

(352) _____. "Order of Services in the German Congregation, Wheeling, W.Va., 1858-1956." *Social Justice Review* 49 (1957): 312-14.

(353) _____. "Statistics of Pastoral Functions of the German Congregation at Wheeling, W.Va." *Social Justice Review* 50 (1957): 61-63.

(354) Lennon, Mary Isidore. "Social History of the Sisters of Mercy in St. Louis." M.A. thesis, St. Louis University, 1934.

(355) Lyons, John A. *Historical Sketches of Old St. Theresa's in Meade County, Kentucky*. Louisville: By the author, n.d.

(356) McCarthy, Sr. Mary Helen. "History of the Sisters of Mercy of Belmont, North Carolina, 1869-1933." M.A. thesis, Catholic University of America, 1934.

(357) McDermott, John F., et al. *Old Cahokia: A Narrative and Documents Illustrating the First Century of its History*. St. Louis: St. Louis Historical Documents Foundation, 1949.

(358) McGann, Sr. Agnes Geraldine. *Sisters of Charity of Nazareth in the Apostolate 1812-1976*. St. Meinrad: n.p., 1976.

(359) McGill, Anna Blanche. *The Sisters of Charity of Nazareth, Kentucky*. New York: The Encyclopedia Press, 1917.

(360) McGraw, Daniel. "Appeal of the Catholics of Natchez, Mississippi, to Archbishop Carroll for a Priest, 1816." *American Catholic Historical Researches* 19 (1902): 64.

(361) McTigue, Sr. Mary Xavier. "History of St. Leo's Parish, St. Louis, Missouri, 1888-1950." M.A. thesis, St. Louis University, 1951.

(362) Mackin, Sr. Aloysius, ed. "Wartime Scenes from Convent Windows: St. Cecilia's, 1860 through 1865." *Tennessee Historical Quarterly* 39 (1980): 401-22.

(363) Magri, F. Joseph. *The Catholic Church in the City and Diocese of Richmond*. Richmond: Whittet and Shepperson, 1906.

(364) Maguire, N. T. "The Beginnings and Progress of Catholicity in Washington, Willkes Co., Georgia." *American Catholic Historical Researches* 11 (1894): 17-28.

(365) Marrama, Conrad J. "The Sisters of St. Joseph in the Diocese of Wheeling." M.A. thesis, St. Mary's Seminary and University, 1939.

(366) Molitor, Donald F. "The History of Glennonville and Adjacent Catholic Colonization Ventures in Southeast Missouri: A Study in Changing Rural-Urban Patterns, 1905-1947." M.A. thesis, St. Louis University, 1975.

(367) Montenarelli, Giuseppi M. "Lettera LXXVII." *Lettere Edificanti Provincia napolitana* series 3 (1879-1880): 183-84.

(368) Morgan, Mary L. "The Vestry Records of St. Mary's Roman Catholic Church, Charleston, South Carolina, 1806-1823." M.A. thesis, University of South Carolina at Columbia, 1982.

(369) Mulry, George A. "Picture of Missionary Life in Chase County, Maryland." *U.S. Catholic Historical Magazine* 4 (1891-1892): 269-89.

(370) Mysliwiec, John S. "History of the Catholic Poles of St. Louis." M.A. thesis, St. Louis University, 1936.

(371) Niehaus, Earl F. *The Irish in New Orleans, 1800-1860*. Baton Rouge: Louisiana State University Press, 1965.

(372) Nolan, Charles E. *Bayou Carmel: The Sisters of Mount Carmel of Louisiana (1833-1903)*. Kenner LA: By the Author, 1977.

(373) Odin, Jean-Marie. "Extrait d'une Lettre de Mgr. Odin, Eveque de Galveston a M. Duplay, Superieur du Grand-Seminaire a Lyon. Galveston le 12 juillet, 1858." *Annales de la Propagation de la Foi* 31 (1859): 442-45.

(374) Oechsle, Placidus. *Historical Sketch of the Congregation of Our Lady of Perpetual Help at Altus, Arkansas: Golden Jubilee, 1930*. N.p.p.: n.p., [1930?].

(375) Orf, S. J. *Chronicle of St. Peter's Parish, Jefferson City, Missouri: Golden Jubilee, 1896*. N.p.p.: n.p., [1896?].

(376) Owen, Allison. "The Catholic Maritime Club of New Orleans." *Catholic Charities Review* 35 (1949): 45-47.

(377) Parisot, P. F., and C. J. Smith, comps. *History of the Catholic Church in the Diocese of San Antonio, Texas*. San Antonio: Carrico and Bowen, 1897.

(378) Pike, J. J. *History of St. Charles Church and Centenary of the Congregation, 1806-1906*. St. Mary KY: n.p., 1907.

(379) Quinlan, John B. "Florida: Letter dated Church of St. Louis, Tampa, Fla., July 6, 1890." *Woodstock Letters* 19 (1890): 316-18.

(380) _____. "Galveston, Texas: Letter." *Woodstock Letters* 16 (1887): 282-83.

(381) Quinn, Denis. *Heroes and Heroines of Memphis (1873-1879)*. Providence RI: E. L. Freeman and Sons, 1887.

(382) Quinn, Jane. "Nuns in Ybor City: The Sisters of St. Joseph and the Immigrant Community." *Tampa Bay History* 5 (1983): 28-32.

(383) Rahill, Peter J. "New Language for St. Louis Cathedral." *Missouri Historical Review* 69 (1975): 449-60.

(384) _____. "The St. Louis Episcopacy of L. William DuBourg." *Records of the American Catholic Historical Society of Philadelphia* 77 (1966): 67-98.

(385) _____. "St. Louis Under Bishop Rosati." *Missouri Historical Review* 66 (1972): 495-519.

(386) Reed, John C. "Catholic Refugee Families in St. Louis, 1948-1954." *American Catholic Sociological Review* 15 (1954): 323-31.

(387) Reily, John T. *Conewego: A Collection of Catholic Local History*. Martinsburg WV: Herald Printing, 1885.

(388) Riordan, Michael J. "The Archdiocese and Province of Baltimore." *The Catholic Church in the United States of America* 2. New York: Editing, 1912.

(389) Robertson, Thelma S. "History of the Catholic Institutions of Nelson County [KY] from 1785 to 1835." M.A. thesis, University of Kentucky, 1929.

(390) Roth, Benedict, and Francis R. Sadlier. *Brief History of the Churches of the Diocese of St. Augustine, Florida*. 10 parts. St. Leo FL: Abbey Press, n.d.

(391) Rothensteiner, John E. *Chronicles of an Old Missouri Parish*. St. Louis: Amerika Printing, 1917.

(392) _____. "First Years of Bishop Kenrick's Administration of St. Louis Diocese." *St. Louis Catholic Historical Review* 5 (1923): 205-29.

(393) _____. "Historical Antecedents of the Diocese of St. Louis." *Illinois Catholic Historical Review* 4 (1922): 243-54.

(394) _____. *History of the Archdiocese of St. Louis*. 2 vols. St. Louis: Herder, 1928.

(395) _____. "The Northeastern Part of the Diocese of St. Louis under Bishop Rosati." *Catholic Historical Review* 2 (1919-20): 175-95, 269-85, 396-416; 3 (1920-21): 61-72, 126-45, 284-302, 389-403; 4 (1921-22): 34-42, 135-53.

(396) Runge, Fenton J. "National Parishes in the City of Saint Louis." M.A. thesis, St. Louis University, 1955.

(397) Ryan, John J. *Chronicle and Sketch of the Church of St. Ignatius of Loyola, Baltimore, 1856-1906*. Baltimore: A. Hoen, 1907.

(398) Ryan, Sr. Mary Timothy. "History of Sancta Maria in Ripa, St. Louis, Missouri, 1901-1924." M.A. thesis, St. Louis University, 1941.

(399) Ryan, Paul E. *History of the Diocese of Covington, Kentucky: On the Occasion of the Centenary of the Diocese, 1853-1953*. Covington: Chancery Office, 1954.

(400) Ryan, T. J. "History of St. Mary's Home, Savannah, Georgia." M.A. thesis, Loyola University (Chicago), 1942.

(401) Ryan, Thomas R. "Orestes A. Brownson's Lectures in St. Louis, Missouri, 1852 and 1854." *Records of the American Catholic Historical Society of Philadelphia* 89 (1978): 45-59.

(402) St. Augustin de Tranchepain, Mere. *Relation du Voyage des Premieres Ursulines a la Nouvelle Orleans et leur etablissement en cette ville*. New York: Cramoisy de Jean Marie Shea, 1950.

(403) St. Augustine Cathedral. *History of Nuestra Senora de la Leche Buen Parto, and Saint Augustine*. St. Augustine: Cathedral Parish of St. Augustine, 1937.

(404) "St. John's Church and Residence, Frederick, Md." *Woodstock Letters* 5 (1876): 29-36, 99-114, 174-88.

(405) St. Leo Abbey. *Silver Jubilee of Abbey and Abbot of St. Leo, Florida, 1927.* St. Leo FL: St. Leo Abbey, [1927?].

(406) "St. Mary's Church and Residence, Alexandria, Virginia." *Woodstock Letters* 13 (1884): 344-56; 14 (1885): 97-112, 243-57.

(407) Salmon, Fr. "Father Salmon, Missionary in Kentucky, Describes to Bishop Carroll His Journey from Baltimore and the Condition of the Church and Character of the People of the State—1799." *American Catholic Historical Researches* 28 (1911): 105-107.

(408) Schafly, James J. "Birth of Kansas City's Pioneer Church." *Missouri Historical Review* 44 (1950): 364-72.

(409) Schlecter, N. L. "Missouri: A Short History of Osage County." *Woodstock Letters* 13 (1884): 357-61, 14 (1885): 22-28.

(410) Schreiber, Albert. *Mesquite Does Bloom.* San Antonio: Standard Printing, 1942.

(411) Schulte, Paul C. *The Catholic Heritage of St. Louis: A History of the Old Cathedral Parish.* St. Louis: Catholic Herald, 1934.

(412) Semple, Henry C., ed. *The Ursulines in New Orleans and Our Lady of Prompt Succor: A Record of Two Centuries, 1729-1925.* New York: P. J. Kenedy and Sons, 1925.

(413) Sisters of Charity. "Sacred Heart Chapel at the National Leprosarium, Carville, Louisiana." [Cincinnati] *Province Chronicle* 31 (1959) 305-310.

(414) Sisters of Charity of the Incarnate Word. *Brief History of the Sisters of Charity of the Incarnate Word of the Diocese of Galveston, 1866-1941.* Galveston: n.p., 1941.

(415) Sisters of Divine Providence. *Memoirs of Fifty Years.* San Antonio: Sisters of Divine Providence, 1916.

(416) "Some Correspondence Relating to the Diocese of New Orleans and St. Louis, 1818-1843, from the Archepiscopal Archives of Quebec." *American Catholic Historical Society of Philadelphia Records* 19 (1908): 185-213, 305-25.

(417) Souvay, Charles L. "Centennial of the Church in St. Louis." *Catholic Historical Review* 4 (1918): 52-75.

(418) ———. "DuBourg and the Biblical Society (New Orleans, 1813)." *St. Louis Catholic Historical Review* 2 (1920): 18-25.

(419) ———. "Rummaging Through Old Parish Records: An Historical Sketch of the Church of Lafayette, Louisiana, 1821-1921." *St. Louis Catholic Historical Review* 3 (1921): 242-94.

(420) Suellentrop, C. "A Pioneer German Catholic Settlement in Tennessee." *Central Blatt and Social Justice* (now *Social Justice Review*) 25 (1932): 204-205.

(421) Texas, Diocese of San Antonio. "Mission der Deutschen Beschuhlen Karmeliter in Texas." *Die Katholischen Missionen* 23 (1895): 114-16.

(422) Thompson, T. P. *The St. Louis Cathedral of New Orleans,* New Orleans: n.p., n.d.

(423) Thornton, Francis A., ed. *The Notable Catholic Institutions of St. Louis and Vicinity.* St. Louis: Finkenbiner-Reed Publishing, 1911.

(424) Tunnick, Wilfrid. "St. Pius X Monastery." *American Benedictine Review* 8 (1957): 55-63.

(425) Turner, Thomas W. "A Visit to Catholic New Orleans." *Chronicle* 5 (1932): 52-53.

(426) Van Antwerp, Mrs. Sydney. "Michael Portier, First Bishop of Mobile, 1795-1859." *Alabama Review* 24 (1971): 205-13.

(427) Walker, Theron J. *First Hundred Years of the Cathedral Church in Robertson County, Tennessee: Centennial of St. Michael's Church, 1942.* N.p.p.: n.p., [1942?].

(428) Walsh, Grace. *The Cathedral Church in Lynchburg, 1829-1936.* Lynchburg VA: Coleman and Bradley, 1936.

(429) Watts, Henry C. "Conewago: Our First Shrine to the Sacred Heart." *U.S. Catholic Historical Society Records and Studies* 2 (1932): 138-69.

(430) Wise, Sr. Mary Charles. "History of the Catholic Church in St. Mary's County, Maryland." M.A. thesis, Catholic University of America, 1944.

(431) Woulfe, Sr. M. Theresa. *The Ursulines in New Orleans, 1727-1925.* New York: n.p., 1925.

(432) Wright, Willard E., ed. "Letters from the Diocese of Little Rock, 1861-1865." *Arkansas Historical Quarterly* 18 (1959): 366-74.

(433) Wuest, Joseph, comp. *History of the Redemptorists at Annapolis, Md., from 1853-1903, with a Short History of the Preceding Hundred and Fifty Years of Catholicity in the Capital of Maryland.* Ilchester MD: College Press, 1904.

(434) Yealy, Francis J. *Sainte Genevieve: The Story of Missouri's Oldest Settlement.* St. Genevieve MO: Bicentennial Historical Committee, 1935.

IV. ROMAN CATHOLICISM IN THE SOUTH: BIOGRAPHICAL AND AUTOBIOGRAPHICAL STUDIES

(435) Allen, Ethan. "Rev. Thomas Bacon, 1745-1768, Incumbent of St. Peter's, Talbot Co., and All Saints, Frederick Co., Maryland." *American Quarterly Church Review* 17 (1865): 430-51.

(436) ———. "Rev. Thomas Craddock, Rector of St. Thomas' Parish, Baltimore County, Maryland, 1745." *Church History* 7 (1854-55): 302-12.

(437) Almarez, Felix D., Jr. "Carlos Eduardo Castaneda, Mexican-American Historian: The Formative Years, 1896-1927." *Pacific Historical Review* 42 (1973): 319-34.

(438) Archibald, Georgellen. "Biography of Augustine Van De Vyver (1844-1911), Sixth Bishop of Richmond, 1889-1911." M.A. thesis, Catholic University of America, 1961.

(439) Baker, T. Lindsay. "The Early Years of Rev. Wincenty Barzynski." *Polish American Studies* 32 (1975): 29-52.

(440) Baum, Charles J. "Ignatius Aloysius Reynolds, Second Bishop of Charleston." M.A. thesis, St. Mary's Seminary and University, 1932.

(441) Bonder, James B. "Life of Charles Carroll of Carrollton." M.A. thesis, Villanova University, 1939.

(442) Bowman, Charles H. Jr. "Dr. John Carr Monk: Sampson City's Latter Day 'Cornelius'." *North Carolina Historical Review* 50 (1973): 52-72.

(443) Brislen, Sr. M. Bernetta. "The Episcopacy of Leonard Neale, Second Archbishop of Baltimore." *U.S. Catholic Historical Society Records and Studies* 34 (1945): 20-111.

(444) Brown, Emmalene. "Charles Rudolph Uncles: Maryland's First Negro Josephite Priest, 1858-1933." M.A. thesis, Morgan State University, 1972.

(445) Burch, Francis. "The Apostle of Kentucky." *St. Meinrad Historical Essays* 1 (1928): 25-31.

(446) Butler, Ruth Lapham, trans. *Journal of Paul du Ru [Feb. 1-May 8, 1700], Missionary Priest to Louisiana.* Chicago: Caxton Club, 1934.

(447) Cadwalader, Mary H. "Charles Carroll of Carrollton: A Signer's Story." *Smithsonian* 6 (1975): 64-71.

(448) Carey, Patrick W. *An Immigrant Bishop: John England's Adaptation of Irish Catholicism to American Republicanism.* New York: U.S. Catholic Historical Society, 1982.

(449) _____. "John England and Irish American Catholicism, 1815-1842: A Study of Conflict." Ph.D. dissertation, Fordham University, 1975.

(450) _____. "John F. O. Fernandez: Enlightened Lay Catholic Reformer, 1815-1820." *Review of Politics* 43 (1981): 112-29.

(451) Carmel, Sr. Mary. "Problems of William Louis DuBourg, Bishop of Louisiana, 1815-1826." *Louisiana History* 4 (1963) 55-72.

(452) Clarke, Mary Whatley. "Father Michael Muldoon." *Texana* 3 (1971): 179-229.

(453) Delaney, John J. *Dictionary of American Catholic Biography.* Garden City: Doubleday, 1984.

(454) Driscoll, David R., Jr. "Stephen Theodore Badin." M.A. thesis, University of Louisville, 1953.

(455) Durkin, Joseph T., S.S., ed. *Confederate Chaplain: A War Journal of the Rev. James B. Sheeran, C.SS.R., 14th Louisiana, C.S.A.* Milwaukee: Bruce, 1960.

(456) Easterly, Frederick J., C.M. *The Life of the Rt. Rev. Joseph Rosati, First Bishop of St. Louis, 1789-1843.* Washington: Catholic University of America Press, 1942. Reprint: New York: AMS Press, 1974.

(457) Ellis, John Tracy. *The Life of James Cardinal Gibbons, Archbishop of Baltimore, 1834-1921.* Milwaukee: Bruce Publishing, 1952.

(458) Evans, John Whitney. "John LaFarge, *America,* and the Newman Movement." *Catholic Historical Review* 64 (1978): 614-43.

(459) Faherty, William B. "In the Footsteps of Bishop Joseph Rosati." *Italian Americana* 1 (1975): 281-91.

(460) _____. "The Personality and Influence of Louis William Valentine DuBourg: Bishop of Louisiana and the Floridas (1776-1833)." In *Frenchmen and French Ways in the Mississippi Valley*. John F. McDermott, ed., 43-55. Urbana: University of Illinois Press, 1969.

(461) _____. "Peter Verhaegen: Pioneer Missouri Educator and Church Administrator." *Missouri Historical Review* 60 (1966): 407-15.

(462) Fleming, M. Saint Agnes. "The Influence of Father Abram Ryan, Civil War Chaplain." M.A. thesis, Villanova University, 1945.

(463) Fogarty, Gerald P. "Archbishop Peter Kenrick's Submission to Papal Infallibility." *Archivum Historiae Pontificiae* 16 (1979): 205-22.

(464) Fox, Sr. Columba. *The Life of the Right Reverend John Baptist Mary David, 1761-1841: Bishop of Bardstown and Founder of the Sisters of Charity of Nazareth*. New York: U.S. Catholic Historical Society, 1925.

(465) Gaffey, James P. *Francis Clement Kelley and the American Catholic Dream*. 2 vols. Bensenville IL: Heritage Foundation, 1980.

(466) Gannon, Michael V. *Rebel Bishop: The Life and Era of Augustin Verot*. Milwaukee: Bruce Publishing, 1964.

(467) _____. "Sebastian Montero, Pioneer American Missionary, 1566-1572." *Catholic Historical Review* 51 (1965): 335-53.

(468) Geiger, Mary Virginia. *Daniel Carroll, A Framer of the Constitution*. Washington: Catholic University of America Press, 1943.

(469) Geiger, Maynard. *Biographical Dictionary of the Franciscans in Spanish Florida and Cuba (1528-1841)*. Paterson NJ: St. Anthony Guild Press, 1940.

(470) Germillion, Joseph B. *The Journal of a Southern Pastor*. Chicago: Fides Publishers Association, 1957.

(471) Gibson, Sr. Laurita. "Catholic Women of Colonial Maryland." M.A. thesis, Catholic University of America, 1939.

(472) Grant, Dorothy Fremont. *John England: American Christopher*. Milwaukee: Bruce, 1949.

(473) Guilday, Peter. *The Life and Times of John Carroll: Archbishop of Baltimore, 1735-1815*. 2 vols. New York: Encyclopedia Press, 1922. Reprint, Westminster MD: Newman, 1954.

(474) _____. *The Life and Times of John England: First Bishop of Charleston, 1786-1842*. 2 vols. New York: America Press, 1927. Reprint, New York: Arno Press, 1969.

(475) Gwynn, Denis. "Dr. Wiseman as a Roman Agent for Baltimore." *Homiletic and Pastoral Review* 41 (1940): 11-18.

(476) Halsey, Columba E., O.S.B. "The Life of Samuel Eccleston, Fifth Archbishop of Baltimore, 1801-1851." *Records of the American Catholic Historical Society of Philadelphia* 76 (1965): 69-156.

(477) Hanley, Thomas O. *Charles Carroll of Carrollton: The Making of a Revolutionary Gentleman*. Washington: Catholic University of America Press, 1970.

(478) _____, ed. *The John Carroll Papers*. 3 vols. Notre Dame: University of Notre Dame Press, 1976.

(479) Hartenbach, William. "Leo Deneckere, Bishop of New Orleans." M.A. thesis, Catholic University of America, 1968.

(480) Hay, Robert P. "Charles Carroll and the Passing of the Revolutionary Generation." *Maryland Historical Magazine* 66 (1972): 54-62.

(481) Hay, Thomas R. "Lucius B. Northrop, Commissary General of the Confederacy." *Civil War History* 9 (1963): 5-23.

(482) Hennesey, James. "An Eighteenth Century Bishop: John Carroll of Baltimore." *Archivum Historiae Pontificiae* 16 (1978): 171-204.

(483) Hickel, John J. "Charles Nerinckx, Founder of the Lorettines to 1824." M.A. thesis, St. Louis University, 1969.

(484) Howlett, William J. *Life of Rev. Charles Nerinckx: Pioneer Missionary of Kentucky and Founder of the Sisters of Loretto at the Foot of the Cross*. 2d ed. Techny IL: Mission Press, 1940.

(485) Ives, Levi Silliman. *The Trials of a Mind in Its Progress to Catholicism*. Boston: Donahoe, 1854.

(486) Jacks, Leo V. *Claude DuBois, Bishop of Galveston*. St. Louis: Herder, 1946.

(487) Kelley, Francis C. *The Bishop Jots It Down*. New York: Harper and Brothers, 1939.

(488) Kirkfleet, Cornelius J., O. Praem. *The Life of Patrick Augustine Feehan, Bishop of Nashville, First Archbishop of Chicago, 1829-1902*. Chicago: Matre Press, 1922.

(489) Knab, Raymond. "Father Joseph Prost, Pioneer Redemptorist in the United States." *U.S. Catholic Historical Society Records and Studies* 22 (1932): 32-84.

(490) LaFarge, John, S.J. *An American Amen: A Statement of Hope*. New York: Farrar, Straus and Cudahy, 1958.

(491) _____. *The Manner Is Ordinary*. New York: Harcourt, Brace, 1953.

(492) Lebreton, D.R. *Chala-ima: The Life of Adrien-Emmanuel Rouquette*. Baton Rouge: Louisiana State University Press, 1947.

(493) Lipscomb, Oscar H. "Alabama's First Bishop Had a Sense of Humor." *Alabama Review* 35 (1982): 3-13.

(494) Lowman, Sr. M. M. "James Andrew Corcoran: Editor, Theologian, Scholar (1820-1889)." Ph.D. dissertation, St. Louis University, 1958.

(495) McCann, James G. "Bishop John England, Pioneer Catholic Spokesman on Church-State Relations." M.A. thesis, Loyola University (Chicago), 1958.

(496) McKenna, Stephen. "Our Lady's Bishop: Archbishop William Gross—Savannah, Georgia; Oregon." *Central Blatt and Social Justice* (now *Social Justice Review*) 24 (1931): 53-55, 88-89, 129-32, 176-78, 212-14, 249-51, 286-87, 322-23.

(497) Maes, Camillus P. *The Life of Rev. Charles Nerinckx*. Cincinnati: R. Clarke, 1880.

(498) Magaret, Helene. *Giant in the Wilderness: A Biography of Father Charles Nerinckx*. Milwaukee: Bruce Publishing, 1952.

(499) Malone, Michael T. "Levi Silliman Ives: Priest, Bishop, Tractarian, Roman Catholic Convert." Ph.D. dissertation, Duke University, 1970.

(500) Marling, Joseph M. "A Pioneer Priest of Western Missouri." *American Ecclesiastical Review* 133 (1955): 361-69.

(501) Marschall, John P. "Francis Patrick Kenrick, 1851-1863: The Baltimore Years." Ph.D. dissertation, Catholic University of America, 1965.

(502) Matthies, Katherine. "Charles Carroll of Carrollton." *Daughters of the American Revolution Magazine* 110 (1976): 300-304.

(503) Melville, Annabelle M. *John Carroll of Baltimore: Founder of the American Catholic Hierarchy*. New York: Charles Scribner's Sons, 1955.

(504) Mideke, Sr. Mary Alicia. "Bishop Meerschaert, First Bishop of Oklahoma, 1847-1924." M.A. thesis, Catholic University of America, 1950.

(505) Miller, Samuel J. "Peter Richard Kenrick: Bishop and Archbishop of St. Louis, 1806-1896." American Catholic Historical Society of Philadelphia *Records* 84 (1973): 1-163.

(506) Moran, Michael. "The Writings of Francis Patrick Kenrick, Archbishop of Baltimore." American Catholic Historical Society of Philadelphia *Records* 41 (1930): 230-61.

(507) Murrett, John C. *Tar Heel Apostle*. New York: Longmans, Green, 1944.

(508) Murtha, Ronin J. "The Life of the Most Reverend Ambrose Marechal, Third Archbishop of Baltimore, 1768-1828." Ph.D. dissertation, Catholic University of America, 1965.

(509) Nott, Sharrard. "Jesuit Martyrs in Virginia." *America* 54 (1935): 131-32.

(510) O'Brien, James J. *Louisiana and Mississippi Martyrs*. New York: Paulist Press, 1928.

(511) ———. "Our Louisiana and Mississippi Martyrs." *Woodstock Letters* 58 (1929): 24-38.

(512) O'Brien, Joseph L. *John England, Bishop of Charleston: The Apostle to Democracy*. New York: Edward O'Toole, 1934.

(513) O'Daniel, Victor F. *The Father of the Church in Tennessee: Richard Pius Miles, O.P.* New York: The Dominicana, 1926.

(514) ———. *A Light of the Church in Kentucky: Samuel Thomas Wilson, O.P.* Washington: The Dominican, 1932.

(515) O'Grady, Joseph P. "Anthony M. Kieley." *Catholic Historical Review* 54 (1968-1969): 613-35.

(516) Ore, Luis Geronimo de. *The Martyrs of Florida, 1513-1616*. Maynard Geiger, trans. Franciscan Studies 18. New York: Joseph F. Wagner, 1936.

(517) O'Rourke, Timothy J. *Maryland Catholics on the Frontier: The Missouri and Texas Settlements*. Parsons KS: Brefny, 1973.

(518) Owens, Sr. M. Lilliana. *Most Reverend Anthony J. Schuler, S.J., D.D.* El Paso: Revista Catolica, 1953.

(519) Panczyk, Matthew L. "James Whitefield, Fourth Archbishop of Baltimore: The Episcopal Years, 1828-1834." *Records of the American Catholic Historical Society* 76 (1965): 21-53.

(520) Patricia Jean, Sr. S.L. *Only One Heart: The Story of a Pioneer Nun in America.* Garden City: Doubleday, 1963.

(521) Perrichon, Abbe J. *Vie de Mgr. Dubuis, L'Apotre de Texas.* Lyons: Librairie Vitte, 1900.

(522) Peterman, Thomas J. "Thomas Andrew Becker, the First Catholic Bishop of Wilmington, Delaware, and Sixth Bishop of Savannah, Georgia, 1831-1899." Ph.D. dissertation, Catholic University of America, 1982.

(523) Peterson, Svend. "The Little Rock against the Big Rock." *Arkansas Historical Quarterly* 2 (1943): 164-70.

(524) Phelan, Thomas P. "Rt. Rev. John England, First Bishop of Charleston." *American Irish Historical Society Journal* 14 (1914): 115-26.

(525) Pohlkamp, Diomede. *The First Franciscan Missionary in Kentucky.* Louisville: St. Anthony Hospital, 1944.

(526) Richardson, Eudora Ramsay. "Giles Brent, Catholic Pioneer of Virginia." *Thought* 6 (1932): 650-64.

(527) Rothensteiner, John E. "Father Charles Nerinckx and His Relations to the Diocese of St. Louis." *St. Louis Catholic Historical Review* 1 (1919): 157-75.

(528) Rowland, Kate Mason. *The Life of Charles Carroll of Carrollton, 1737-1832, with His Correspondence and Public Papers.* 2 vols. New York: G. P. Putnam's Sons, 1898.

(529) Schauinger, Joseph Herman. *Cathedrals in the Wilderness.* Milwaukee: Bruce Publishing, 1952.

(530) _____. *William Gaston, Carolinian.* Milwaukee: Bruce Publishing, 1945.

(531) Shea, John Gilmary. "Pioneer of the West—Rev. Charles Nerinckx." *American Catholic Quarterly Review* 5 (1880): 486-508.

(532) _____. "Ven. Anthony Margil of Jesus, of the Order of St. Francis, Apostle of Texas and Guatemala." *Ave Maria* 21 (1885): 105-108, 128-31.

(533) Shearer, Donald, O.M.Cap. *Ignatius Cardinal Persico, O.M.Cap.* New York: Joseph F. Wagner, 1932.

(534) Skeabeck, Andrew H. "The Early Life of William H. Gross, C.S.S.R., Fifth Bishop of Savannah, 1837-1885." M.A. thesis, Catholic University of America, 1949.

(535) Smith, Ellen Hart. *Charles Carroll of Carrollton.* Cambridge: Harvard University Press, 1942. Reprint, New York: Russell and Russell, 1971.

(536) Souvay, Charles L. "Rosati's Election to the Coadjutorship of New Orleans." *Catholic Historical Review* 3 (1917): 3-21.

(537) _____. "Rosati's Elevation to the See of St. Louis." *Catholic Historical Review* 3 (1917): 165-86.

(538) Spalding, John Lancaster. *The Life of the Most Reverend M. J. Spalding.* New York: Catholic Publication Society, 1973.

(539) Spalding, Martin J. *Sketches of the Life, Times, and Character of the Rt. Rev. Benedict Joseph Flaget, First Bishop of Louisville*. Louisville: Webb and Levering, 1852. Reprinted, New York: Arno Press, 1970.

(540) Spalding, Thomas W. *Martin John Spalding: American Churchman*. Washington: Catholic University of America Press in association with Consortium Press, 1973.

(541) _____, ed. "Some Early Letters of Martin John Spalding." *Filson Club Historical Quarterly* 47 (1973): 333-42.

(542) Stritch, Thomas J. "Three Catholic Bishops from Tennessee." *Tennessee Historical Quarterly* 37 (1978): 3-35.

(543) Sullivan, Stephen A. "Missionary Career of Father Price in North Carolina." M.A. thesis, St. Mary's Seminary and University, 1936.

(544) Voth, M. Agnes. "Mother M. Beatrice Ringgli, O.S.B., Foundress of the American Olivetan Benedictine Sisters, Jonesboro, Arkansas." *American Benedictine Review* 25 (1974): 389-409.

(545) Weibel, J. E. *Vierzig Jahre Missionar in Arkansas*. Lucerne, Switzerland: Raber, 1927.

(546) Xavier, Sr. Mary. *Father Jaillet: Saddlebag Priest of the Nueces*. Austin: Von Boeckmann-Johnes, 1949.

(547) Yzermans, Vincent A., ed. *Days of Hope and Promise: The Writings and Speeches of Paul J. Hallinan, Archbishop of Atlanta*. Collegeville MN: Liturgical Press, 1973.

6 JUDAISM IN THE SOUTH

ALTHOUGH THEY ACCOUNT for less than one percent of the total population of the South and are consequently virtually unnoticeable in most areas apart from major urban centers such as Atlanta or Miami, Jews have been part of the Southern religious picture since the seventeenth century and part of the American enterprise since the arrival of Columbus in 1492. The story of Southern Judaism has not yet been adequately probed by scholars, perhaps because outside of several cities the Jewish population is so scattered as to make careful scrutiny difficult if not impossible. The problem is compounded by the nature of Judaism itself and by the multifaceted ways in which individuals identify themselves with the Hebrew heritage. The combination of religious, ethnic, and cultural dimensions in Judaism presents such an intertwined complex that it is difficult to discern at times precisely what is religious, what is ethnic, or what is cultural for purposes of analysis.

Of course, it may as well be argued that such attempts at separation represent the imposition of external criteria on what is internally an integrated whole. In addition, those who approach Judaism sociologically quickly become perplexed because what have become standard measurements of religiosity—frequency of attendance at religious services, and the like—simply do not apply. Distinctions among Orthodox, Conservative, and Reform Jews render monolithic interpretation of the Jewish experience irresponsible academically. Then, too, one must be sensitive to the frightening presence of anti-Semitism in Southern culture, a matter that will be noted in greater detail in chapter 20. Hence, as many commentators have noted, the study of Judaism in the South (as elsewhere) is fraught with paradoxes: while Jews have been intimately involved in all facets of Southern life, they remain on the fringes; while Jews can be identified, they cannot be neatly categorized in religious terms.

Numerous works on the American Jewish experience contain information on Judaism in the South and provide insight into the broader American context that has nurtured Jewish life in the region. Two helpful introductions are Nathan Glazer, *American Judaism* (6), and Joseph L. Blau, *Judaism in America: From Curiosity to Third Faith* (2). Jacob R. Marcus, ed., *American Jewry: Documents* (15); Marcus, ed., *Memoirs of American Jews, 1775-1865* (16); and Joseph L. Blau and Salo W. Baron's three volume collection, *Jews in the United States, 1790-1840: A Documentary History* (1), also contain much material vital to understanding the emergence and development of Southern Jewry. Anita Libman Lebeson's *Recall to Life: The Jewish Woman in America* (13) provides pertinent discussion in several sections.

Several studies indicate the diversity and richness that mark Southern Judaism, as well as its complexity. Perhaps the best brief introduction, though now somewhat dated, is found in Alfred O. Hero, Jr., *The Southerner and World Affairs,* ch. 13 (10). Hero noted that Southern Jews tend to be less cosmopolitan than their coreligionists elsewhere in the country, having absorbed some of the region's attitudes with regard to racial matters and demonstrating less public support for Israel than other American Jews. He attributed some of these characteristics to the higher degree of contact Southern Jews had with non-Jews, which issued in a lower degree of participation in public Jewish activity (whether religious, philanthropic, or otherwise) and a greater tendency to convert to Christianity or to maintain silence. A lingering fear of anti-Semitism, buttressed by incidents such as the bombing of an Atlanta synagogue in 1958, has helped perpetuate this situation. Other studies have amplified some of the points Hero made. Two collections of essays of unusually high quality echo many of Hero's claims: Leonard Dinnerstein and Mary Dale Palsson, eds., *Jews in the South* (3), and Nathan M. Kaganoff and Melvin I. Urofsky, eds., *"Turn to the South": Essays on Southern Jewry* (12). Eli N. Evans, *The Provincials: A Personal History of Jews in the South* (5), emphasizes the constant struggle of Southern Jews against assimilation into a predominantly Protestant culture, whether that assimilation be coerced or the result of intermingling in daily life. Evans noted as well how the Southern situation is exacerbated because Jews in Dixie live outside the geographical mainstream of American Judaism (as well as outside the regional cultural mainstream). The efforts of Southern Jews to maintain some semblance of community life are the focus of Harry Simonoff, *Under Strange Skies* (20). *Jews of the South: Selected Essays,* edited by Samuel Proctor and Louis Schmier, with Malcolm Stern (17), provides a glimpse of the favor of Southern Jewish life. Not heavily analytical and somewhat anecdotal, the essays do offer several perceptive family histories.

The earliest enduring Jewish communities in the South were centered in Charleston and Savannah. An old but detailed and reliable study provides an initial examination of the South Carolina story down to the beginning of the twentieth century: Barnett A. Elzas, *The Jews of South Carolina from the Earliest Times to the Present Day* (29). The Charleston experience is recounted in scholarly fashion in Charles Reznikoff and Uriah Z. Engelman, *The Jews of Charleston: A History of an American Jewish Community* (78), an account that also concludes with early twentieth-century developments. Even in the early years, however, divisions between Sephardic and Ashkenazic elements in the Charleston community produced internal dissension, a story deftly told in Solomon Breibart, "Two Congregations in Charleston, S.C. Before 1791: A New Conclusion" (48). Also see Breibart's "The Synagogues of Kahal Kadosh Beth Elohim, Charleston" (47). Barnett Elzas published a series of short works on numerous Jewish cemeteries in South Carolina, including those in Charleston, Camden, Columbia, Georgetown, Orangeburg, and Sumter (53-58, 60-61). In addition, he wrote a now dated congregational study, *History of Congregation Beth Elohim, of Charleston, S.C., 1800-1810* (52). One important study of the Charleston Jewish community challenges the commonly held assertion that assimilation has been a continuing trend. Working from survey data collected in the early 1970s, Frank Petrusak and Steven Steinert, "The Jews of Charleston: Some Old Wine in New Bottles" (76), argue that Jews there retain a strong sense of self-identification as Jews, demonstrated in support for both local synagogue and Israel, and consequently form a distinctive religious and ethnic grouping within Charleston society.

Savannah's Jewish community traces its heritage to the initial English colonial settlement in the 1730s, and while it has not been subject to as detailed examination as the Charleston Jewish community, it shares many of the same features in its development (for example, early conflict between Sephardic and Ashkenazic groups). See especially Malcolm Stern, "New Light on the Jewish Settlement of Savannah" (91). However, Savannah's Jews did confront a more hostile gentile populace in the eighteenth century, and twice during the eighteenth century most Jews left Georgia. See David T. Morgan, "Judaism in Eighteenth-Century Georgia" (34). But also see B. H. Levy's recent *Savannah's Old Jewish Cemeteries* (74), which includes capsule biographies of the persons buried there. Particularly prominent in early Savannah Jewish development was the Sheftall family. Two edited works by Malcolm H. Stern help clarify their vital role: "The Sheftall Diaries" (120), and "Growing Up in Pioneer Savannah" (118), the story of Levi Sheftall.

By the time of World War I, Atlanta boasted the South's largest Jewish community, but again one that was internally divided between those inclined to the Orthodox tradition and those attracted to Reform; the two groups co-operated only in certain philanthropic areas. Growth of Atlanta's Jewish population was triggered largely by the upswing in immigration that came in the closing decades of the nineteenth century and the early twentieth century. Three studies begin to unravel the Atlanta developments: Steven Hertsberg, "The Jewish Community of Atlanta from the End of the Civil War until the End of the Frank Case" (70): Arnold Shankman, "Atlanta Jewry—1900-1930" (86); and Solomon Sutker, "The Jews of Atlanta: Their Structure and Leadership Patterns" (92). Atlanta, of course, was the locale of the most obvious rash of Southern anti-Semitism in the twentieth century. In 1913, Jewish factory superintendent Leo Frank was falsely accused of murdering a thirteen-year-old female employee. Found guilty in 1915 in a trial that received national publicity and brought the embers of Southern anti-Semitism to full fire, Frank was abducted from the jail and lynched by a mob. The standard study is Leonard Dinnerstein, *The Leo Frank Case* (4), but also see the popularly written *A Little Girl is Dead* by Harry Golden (8), and the provocative essay by Eugene Levy, "Is the Jew a White Man?: Press Reaction to the Leo Frank Case, 1913-1915" (14). Studies of Judaism elsewhere in Georgia include three by Louis Schmier on Valdosta (83-85).

Janice A. Byrd has recounted "A History of the Jews of Mississippi" in a master's thesis (22). For the story in the Lone Star State, see Henry Cohen, *The Jews in Texas* (24). Louis Ginsberg offers vignettes of developments in the Old Dominion in *Chapters on Jews of Virginia, 1658-1900* (32). For Louisiana, see Leo Shpall's now dated study, *The Jews in Louisiana* (37). As part of a series on ethnic groups in Oklahoma, Henry J. Tobias prepared his *The Jews in Oklahoma* (38); its focus extends well beyond matters religious.

There are as well several scholarly studies of Jewish communities in Southern cities other than those already mentioned. Bertram W. Korn, whose numerous books and essays on aspects of the Southern Jewish experience are models for work that remains to be done, has provided an excellent scholarly appraisal, with illustrations, of *The Early Jews of New Orleans* (72); he traces developments there down to the mid-nineteenth century. New Orleans presents a rather different case, since Jewish settlement began under French control and emerged in a different content politically and religiously than elsewhere. As Julian B. Feibelman argued in his doctoral dissertation, "A Social and Economic Study of the New Orleans Jewish Community" (66), the peculiar circumstances of New Orleans encouraged Jews to take on the trappings of their surroundings to a fuller extent than the cultural climate did in the English-controlled areas, with the result that, he claims, there is no religiously or culturally "distinctive" Jewish community in the city, a point that merits further study for verification. On New Orleans see also Leonard Reissman, "The New Orleans Jewish Community" (77). For Norfolk see Malcolm H. Stern, "Moses Myers and the Early Jewish Community of Norfolk" (119).

Korn has also written a carefully documented study of *The Jews of Mobile, Alabama, 1763-1841* (73). A Gulf port, Mobile nurtured one of the earlier enduring Jewish communities in the South. Richmond, Virginia, has also been home to another longstanding Jewish community in Dixie, one which has been the subject of many studies. The most comprehensive, however, merits updating, for it is nearly three-quarters of a century old and ends its treatment with the epoch of the First World War. Nonetheless, Herbert T. Ezekiel and Gaston Lichtenstein, *The History of the Jews of Richmond from 1769 to 1917* (63) is a carefully documented study that probes the lives of significant leaders in Richmond Jewry, astutely examines the dilemmas that confronted the community during the Civil War, offers brief histories of individual synagogues, and also looks at communal religious and philanthropic activities. Another well documented work is Fedora S. Frank, *Five Families and Eight Young Men: Nashville and Her Jewry, 1850-1861* (68). While restricted in terms of the time span covered, Frank's study is invaluable in unraveling the early development of Jewish life in Nashville. Mark H. Elovitz, *A Century of Jewish Life in Dixie: The Birmingham Experience* (51), explores and documents the numerous economic, religious, social, and philanthropic activities of this Alabama city's Jews and also pays particular attention to the internal conflict that Zionism, the establishment of Israel as an independent nation, and its subsequent history to the early 1960s brought to Jewish citizens. One statewide study deserves mention: Abraham I. Shinedling, *West Virginia Jewry: Origins and History, 1850-1938* (36). This three-volume work contains a mass of details, some bordering on trivia. But while it is short on analysis, its index alone makes it a basic reference work for probing Jewish developments in West Virginia.

One aspect of the Southern Jewish story that is often neglected is the vision some early American Jewish leaders had of the South as a potential utopia for Jews or at least as a base for the establishment of Jewish communities that would remove Jewish immigrants from the assimilating, corruptive influences of the Eastern urban centers. In the early nineteenth century, there was some effort to form a communitarian settlement in Florida that would combine adherence to biblical precept with socialistic principles. Its story is told in Jacob Toury, "M. E. Levy's Plan for a Jewish Colony in Florida: 1825" (39). Also see Samuel Proctor, "Pioneer Jewish Settlement in Florida" (35). More widely known was what has become known as the Galveston Movement, a scheme to use that Texas city as a base to relocate thousands of Jews in the interior of both the United States and Canada, removed from the congestion and corruption of cities on the east coast. Two articles recount this effort: Ronald A. Axelrod, ''Rabbi Henry Cohen and the Galveston Immigration Movement, 1907-1914'' (41), and Gary D. Best, ''Jacob H. Schiff's Galveston Movement: An Experiment in Immigration Deflection, 1907-1914'' (44).

A few studies of prominent figures in Southern Jewish history merit mention. Barnett A. Elzas more than three-quarters of a century ago published work on two individuals who played key roles in South Carolina developments: *Joseph Salvador: Jewish Merchant Prince Who Came to South Carolina* (101) and *Moses Lindo: A Sketch of the Most Prominent Jew in Charleston in Provincial Days* (102). Important in Charleston literary circles as well as in the Jewish community was *The Moise Family*, whose story has been told by Harold Moise (113). In addition to the titles on the Sheftalls already mentioned, also see David T. Morgan's ''The Sheftalls of Savannah'' (114). Two other essays that examine the life of Moses Elias Levy and his work in Florida are George R. Fairbanks, ''Moses Elias Levy Yulee'' (103), and Leon Huhner, ''Moses Elias Levy, Florida Pioneer'' (106).

Note should also be made of numerous archival collections in addition to those listed in chapter 1. Many Jewish communities and congregations in the South have now established archives. For example, such collections may be found in Atlanta, Baltimore, Charleston, Jacksonville, Memphis, Nashville, New Orleans, Richmond, and Savannah. A strong Jewish press in the region has combined materials of a religious nature with matters of more general and cultural interest. Among others, Atlanta, Baltimore, Charlotte, Dallas, Houston, Jacksonville, Kansas City, Miami, New Orleans, Richmond, St. Louis, and Tuscaloosa have all been centers (and in several cases remain such) for the publication of Jewish newspapers. Research on Judaism in the South has also been enriched by the work, conferences, and publications of the Southern Jewish Historical Society, especially the *Journal of the Southern Jewish Historical Society*, which has been in print since 1958. Other periodicals that frequently feature articles on Judaism in the South include *American Jewish Archives, Western States Jewish Historical Quarterly*, and *American Jewish Historical Quarterly*.

Judaism has been part of Southern religious life for three centuries. The complexities and the richness of its story deserve greater scholarly attention.

The bibliography that follows organizes studies of Southern Judaism into four sections: general and topical studies, statewide studies, local studies, and biographical and autobiographical studies.

BIBLIOGRAPHY

Some titles in the listing for chapters 1, 4, and 20 are also especially relevant to the study of Judaism in the South.

I. JUDAISM IN THE SOUTH:
GENERAL AND TOPICAL STUDIES

(1) Blau, Joseph L., and Salo W. Baron. *Jews of the United States, 1790-1840: A Documentary History*. 3 vols. New York: Columbia University Press, 1963.

(2) _____. *Judaism in America: From Curiosity to Third Faith*. Chicago: University of Chicago Press, 1976.

(3) Dinnerstein, Leonard, and Mary Dale Palsson, eds. *Jews in the South*. Baton Rouge: Louisiana State University Press, 1973.

(4) _____. *The Leo Frank Case*. New York: Columbia University Press, 1968.

(5) Evans, Eli N. *The Provincials: A Personal History of Jews in the South*. New York: Atheneum, 1973.

(6) Glazer, Nathan. *American Judaism*. Rev. ed. Chicago: University of Chicago Press, 1972.

(7) Golden, Harry. *Jewish Roots in the Carolinas*. Charlotte: Carolina Israelite, 1955.

(8) _____. *A Little Girl is Dead*. Cleveland: World Publishing, 1965.

(9) _____. *Our Southern Landsmen*. New York: G. P. Putnam's Sons, 1974.

(10) Hero, Alfred O., Jr. *The Southerner and World Affairs*, chap. 13. Baton Rouge: Louisiana State University Press, 1965.

(11) Huhner, Leon. *Jews in America after the American Revolution*. New York: Gertz Brothers, 1959.

(12) Kaganoff, Nathan M., and Melvin I. Urofsky, eds. *"Turn to the South": Essays on Southern Jewry*. Charlottesville: University of Virginia Press, 1979.

(13) Lebeson, Anita Libman. *Recall to Life: The Jewish Woman in America*. South Brunswick NJ: T. Yoseloff, 1970.

(14) Levy, Eugene. "Is the Jew a White Man?: Press Reaction to the Leo Frank Case, 1913-1915." *Phylon* 35 (1974): 212-22.

(15) Marcus, Jacob R., ed. *American Jewry: Documents*. Cincinnati: Hebrew Union College Press, 1959.

(16) _____, ed. *Memoirs of American Jews, 1775-1865*. Rev. ed. 3 vols. in 2. New York: KTAV Publishing House, 1974. First published 1955-1956.

(17) Proctor, Samuel, and Louis Schmier, with Malcolm Stern, eds. *Jews of the South: Selected Essays*. Macon GA: Mercer University Press, 1984.

(18) Reed, John Shelton. "Shalom, Y'All: Jewish Southerners." In *One South: An Ethnic Approach to Regional Culture*, chap. 7. Baton Rouge: Louisiana State University Press, 1982.

(19) Schmier, Louis, ed. *Reflections of Southern Jewry: Letters of Charles Wessolowsky, 1878-1879*. Macon GA: Mercer University Press, 1982.

(20) Simonoff, Harry. *Under Strange Skies*. New York: Philosophical Library, 1971.

II. JUDAISM IN THE SOUTH: STUDIES BY STATE

(21) Altfeld, E. Milton. *The Jew's Struggle for Religious Civil Liberty in Maryland*. Baltimore: Curlander, 1924.

(22) Byrd, Janice. "A History of the Jews in Mississippi." M.A. thesis, Mississippi College, 1979.

(23) Cohen, Henry, et al. *One Hundred Years of Jewry in Texas*. [Dallas?]: Jewish Advisory Committee, [1936?].

(24) _____. *The Jews in Texas*. Baltimore: Friedenwald, [1895?].

(25) Cowen, Elfrida D. "Moses Elias Levy's Agricultural Colony in Florida." *Proceedings of the American Jewish Historical Society* 25 (1917): 132-34.

(26) Elzas, Barnett A. *A Century of Judaism in South Carolina, 1800-1900*. Charleston: YMHA, [1904].

(27) _____. *Documents Relative to a Proposed Settlement of Jews in South Carolina in 1748*. Charleston: Daggett Printing, 1903.

(28) _____. *The Jews of South Carolina*. Charleston: Daggett Printing, [1903].

(29) _____. *The Jews of South Carolina from the Earliest Times to the Present Day*. Philadelphia: J. B. Lippincott, 1905.

(30) _____. *Leaves from My Historical Scrap Book*. Charleston: n.p., 1907. 2d series, Charleston: n.p., 1908.

(31) _____. *Pamphlets Relating to the History of the Jews in South Carolina*. Charleston: n.p., n.d.

(32) Ginsberg, Louis. *Chapters on Jews of Virginia, 1658-1900*. Petersburg VA: n.p., 1969.

(33) Glushkow, A. D., ed. *A Pictorial History of Maryland Jewry*. Baltimore: n.p., 1955.

(34) Morgan, David T. "Judaism in Eighteenth-Century Georgia." *Georgia Historical Quarterly* 58 (1974): 41-54.

(35) Proctor, Samuel. "Pioneer Jewish Settlement in Florida." In *Proceedings of the Conference on the Writing of Regional History in the South*, 81-115. Miami: n.p., 1956.

(36) Shinedling, Abraham I. *West Virginia Jewry: Origins and History, 1850-1938*. 3 vols. Philadelphia: Press of M. Jacobs, 1963.

(37) Shpall, Leo. *The Jews in Louisiana*. New Orleans: Steeg Printing and Publishing, 1936.

(38) Tobias, Henry J. *The Jews in Oklahoma*. Norman: University of Oklahoma Press, 1980.

(39) Toury, Jacob. "M. E. Levy's Plan for a Jewish Colony in Florida: 1825." *Michael: On the History of the Jews in the Diaspora* 3 (1975): 23-33.

(40) Watters, Gary. "The Russian Jew in Oklahoma: The May Brothers." *Chronicles of Oklahoma* 53 (1975): 479-91.

III. JUDAISM IN THE SOUTH: LOCAL STUDIES

(41) Axelrod, Ronald A. "Rabbi Henry Cohen and the Galveston Immigration

Movement, 1907-1914." *East Texas Historical Journal* 15 (1977): 24-37.

(42) Berman, Myron. "Rabbi Edward Nathan Calish and the Debate over Zionism in Richmond, Virginia." *American Jewish Historical Quarterly* 62 (1973): 295-305.

(43) _____. *Richmond's Jewry, 1769-1976: Shabbat in Shockoe.* Charlottesville: University Press of Virginia, 1979.

(44) Best, Gary D. "Jacob H. Schiff's Galveston Movement: An Experiment in Immigration Deflection, 1907-1914." *American Jewish Archives* 30 (1978): 43-79.

(45) Beton, Sol. "Sephardim—Atlanta." *Atlanta Historical Journal* 23 (1979): 119-27.

(46) Boxerman, Burton A. "The St. Louis Jewish Coordinating Council: Its Formative Years." *Missouri Historical Review* 65 (1970): 51-71.

(47) Breibart, Solomon. "The Synagogues of Kahal Kadosh Beth Elohim, Charleston." *South Carolina Historical Magazine* 80 (1979): 215-35.

(48) _____. "Two Jewish Congregations in Charleston, S.C. Before 1791: A New Conclusion." *American Jewish History* 69 (1980): 360-63.

(49) Ehrenreich, Bernard C. "Reminiscences of the First Generation." *Zeta Beta Tau Quarterly* 10 (December 1925): 21-23.

(50) Ellenson, David. "A Jewish Legal Decision by Rabbi Bernard Illowy of New Orleans and Its Discussion in Nineteenth Century Europe." *American Jewish History* 69 (1979): 174-95.

(51) Elovitz, Mark H. *A Century of Jewish Life in Dixie: The Birmingham Experience.* University AL: University of Alabama Press, 1974.

(52) Elzas, Barnett A. *History of Congregation Beth Elohim, of Charleston, S.C., 1800-1810.* Charleston: Daggett Printing, [1902].

(53) _____, comp. *The Jewish Cemeteries at Columbia, S.C.* Columbia: n.p., 1910.

(54) _____, comp. *The Jewish Cemeteries of Congregation Berith Shalome at Charleston, S.C.* Columbia: n.p., 1910.

(55) _____, comp. *The Jewish Cemetery at Camden, S.C.* Charleston: n.p., 1910.

(56) _____, comp. *The Jewish Cemetery at Georgetown, S.C.* Charleston: n.p., 1910.

(57) _____, comp. *The Jewish Cemetery at Orangeburg, S.C.* Charleston: n.p., 1910.

(58) _____, comp. *The Jewish Cemetery at Sumter, S.C.* Charleston: n.p., 1910.

(59) _____. *Jewish Marriage Notices from the Newspaper Press of Charleston, S.C. (1775-1906).* New York: Bloch Publishing, 1917.

(60) _____. comp. *The New Jewish Cemetery of K.K. Beth Elohim at Charleston, S.C.* Charleston: n.p., 1910.

(61) _____. *The Old Jewish Cemeteries at Charleston, S.C.: A Transcript of the Inscriptions of Their Tombstones, 1762-1903*. Charleston: Daggett Printing, 1903.

(62) _____. *The Reformed Society of Israelites of Charleston, S.C.* New York: Bloch Publishing, 1916.

(63) Ezekiel, Herbert T., and Gaston Lichtenstein. *The History of the Jews of Richmond from 1769 to 1917*. Richmond: The Authors, 1917.

(64) _____. *The Jews of Richmond During the Civil War*. Richmond: Press of H. T. Ezekiel, 1915.

(65) _____, and Gaston Lichtenstein. *World War Section of The Jews of Richmond*. Richmond: The Authors, 1920.

(66) Feibelman, Julian B. ''A Social and Economic Study of the New Orleans Jewish Community.'' Ph.D. dissertation, University of Pennsylvania, 1941.

(67) Fein, Isaac M. *The Making of an American Jewish Community: The History of Baltimore Jewry from 1773 to 1920*. Philadelphia: Jewish Publication Society of America, 1971.

(68) Frank, Fedora S. *Five Families and Eight Young Men: Nashville and Her Jewry, 1850-1861*. Nashville: Tennessee Book, 1962.

(69) Ginsberg, Louis. *History of the Jews of Petersburg, 1780-1950*. Petersburg VA: Williams Printing, 1954.

(70) Hertsberg, Steven. ''The Jewish Community of Atlanta from the End of the Civil War until the End of the Frank Case.'' *American Jewish Historical Quarterly* 62 (1973): 250-87.

(71) Kaplan, Benjamin. *The Eternal Stranger: A Study of Jewish Life in a Small Community*. New York: Bookman Associates, 1957.

(72) Korn, Bertram W. *The Early Jews of New Orleans*. Waltham MA: American Jewish Historical Society, 1969.

(73) _____. *The Jews of Mobile, Alabama, 1763-1841*. Cincinnati: Hebrew Union College Press, 1970.

(74) Levy, B. H. *Savannah's Old Jewish Cemeteries: Including Short Genealogies and Biographies of Persons There Interred*. Macon GA: Mercer University Press, 1983.

(75) _____. ''Savannah's Old Jewish Community Cemeteries.'' *Georgia Historical Quarterly* 66 (1982): 1-20.

(76) Petrusak, Frank, and Steven Steinert. ''The Jews of Charleston: Some Old Wine in New Bottles.'' *Jewish Social Studies* 38 (1976): 337-46.

(77) Reissman, Leonard. ''The New Orleans Jewish Community.'' *Jewish Journal of Sociology* 4 (1962): 110-23.

(78) Reznikoff, Charles, and Uriah Z. Engelman. *The Jews of Charleston: A History of an American Jewish Community*. Philadelphia: Jewish Publication Society of America, 1950.

(79) Rosenwaike, Ira. ''The Founder of Baltimore's First Jewish Congregation: Fact vs. Fiction.'' *American Jewish Archives* 28 (1976): 119-25.

(80) Rothschild, Janice O. *As But a Day: The First Hundred Years, 1867-1967*. Atlanta: Hebrew Benevolent Congregation, 1967.

(81) Sachs, Howard F. "Development of the Jewish Community of Kansas City, 1864-1908." *Missouri Historical Review* 60 (1966): 350-60.

(82) Sanders, Ira E., and Elijah E. Palnick, eds. *The Centennial History of Congregation B'nai Israel, Little Rock, Arkansas, 1866-1966*. Little Rock: n.p., [1966?].

(83) Schmier, Louis. "The First Jews of Valdosta." *Georgia Historical Quarterly* 62 (1978): 32-49.

(84) _____. "The Man from Gehau." *Atlanta Historical Quarterly* 23 (1979): 91-106.

(85) _____. " 'For Him the "Schwartzers" Couldn't Do Enough': A Jewish Peddler and His Black Customers Look at Each Other." *American Jewish History* 73 (September 1983): 39-55.

(86) Shankman, Arnold. "Atlanta Jewry—1900-1930." *American Jewish Archives* 25 (1973): 131-55.

(87) _____. "Happyville [SC], the Forgotten Colony." *American Jewish Archives* 30 (1978): 3-19.

(88) _____. "A Temple Is Bombed: Atlanta, 1958." *American Jewish Archives* 23 (1971): 125-53.

(89) Shinedling, Abraham I., and Manuel Pickus. *History of the Beckley [WV] Jewish Community and of Congregation Beth El, 1895-1955*. Beckley WV: n.p., 1955.

(90) Stein, Kenneth W. "A History of Ahavath Achim Congregation, 1887-1927." *Atlanta Historical Journal* 23 (1979): 106-18.

(91) Stern, Malcolm. "New Light on the Jewish Settlement of Savannah." *American Jewish Historical Quarterly* 52 (1963): 169-99.

(92) Sutker, Solomon. "The Jews of Atlanta: Their Structure and Leadership Patterns." Ph.D. dissertation, University of North Carolina in Chapel Hill, 1950.

(93) Tarshish, Allan. "The Organ Case." *American Jewish Historical Quarterly* 54 (1965): 401-49.

(94) "Two Views of an International Jewish Community: Brownsville, Texas, and Matamoros, Mexico." *Western States Jewish Historical Quarterly* 10 (1978): 306-310.

(95) Wax, James A. "The Jews of Memphis, 1860-1865." *Papers of the West Tennessee Historical Society* 3 (1949): 39-89.

(96) Williams, Beverly S. "Anti-Semitism and Shreveport, LA: The Situation in the 1920s." *Louisiana History* 21 (1980): 387-98.

IV. JUDAISM IN THE SOUTH:
BIOGRAPHICAL AND AUTOBIOGRAPHICAL STUDIES

(97) Blumberg, Janice R. *One Voice: Rabbi Jacob M. Rothschild and the Troubled South*. Macon GA: Mercer University Press, 1985.

(98) Cohen, Anne M., and Harry I. Cohen. *The Man Who Stayed in Texas: The Life of Rabbi Henry Cohen.* New York: McGraw-Hill, 1941.

(99) Elzas, Barnett A. *Edwin Warren Moise: In Memoriam, 1832-1903.* Charleston: Daggett Printing, 1903.

(100) _____. *In Memoriam: Marian Moise, Born, June 14, 1855, Died, January 30, 1910.* [Charleston]: n.p., 1910.

(101) _____. *Joseph Salvador: Jewish Merchant Prince Who Came to South Carolina.* Charleston: Daggett Printing, [1903].

(102) _____. *Moses Lindo: A Sketch of the Most Prominent Jew in Charleston in Provincial Days.* Charleston: Daggett Printing, 1903.

(103) Fairbanks, George R. "Moses Elias Levy Yulee." *Florida Historical Quarterly* 19 (1940): 165-67.

(104) Fasman, Oscar Z. "After Fifty Years, an Optimist." *American Jewish History* 69 (1979): 159-73.

(105) Geffen, David. "The Literary Legacy of Rabbi Tobias Geffen in Atlanta, 1910-1970." *Atlanta Historical Journal* 23 (1979): 84-90.

(106) Huhner, Leon. "Moses Elias Levy, Florida Pioneer." *Florida Historical Quarterly* 20 (1941): 319-45.

(107) Kaganoff, Nathan M. "An Orthodox Rabbinate in the South: Tobias Geffen, 1870-1970." *American Jewish History* 73 (September 1983): 56-70.

(108) Kalin, Berkley. "Rabbi William H. Fineshriber: The Memphis Years." *West Tennessee Historical Society Papers* 25 (1971): 47-62.

(109) Korn, Bertram W. "An American Jewish Religious Leader in 1860 Voices His Frustration." *Michael: On the History of the Jews in the Diaspora* 3 (1975): 42-47.

(110) Kramer, William M., and Reva Klar. "Rabbi Abraham Blum: From Alsace to New York by Way of Texas and California." *Western States Jewish Historical Quarterly* 12 (1979): 73-88, 170-84, 266-81.

(111) Levy, B. H. "Joseph Solomon Ottolenghi: Kosher Butcher in Italy, Christian Missionary in Georgia." *Georgia Historical Quarterly* 66 (1982): 119-44.

(112) Mantinband, Charles. "From the Diary of a Mississippi Rabbi." *American Judaism* 13 (1958): 35-46.

(113) Moise, Harold. *The Moise Family of South Carolina.* Columbia SC: Printed by R. L. Bryan, 1961.

(114) Morgan, David T. "The Sheftalls of Savannah." *American Jewish Historical Quarterly* 62 (1973): 348-61.

(115) Rosenwaike, Ira. "Leon Dyer: Baltimore and San Francisco Jewish Leader." *Western Jewish Historical Quarterly* 9 (1977): 135-43.

(116) "The Schirmer Diary." *South Carolina Historical Magazine* 67 (1966): 167-71, 229-33; 68 (1967): 37-41, 97-100; 69 (1968): 59-65, 139-44, 204-208, 262-66; 70 (1969): 59-63, 122-25, 196-99; 72 (1971): 115-17, 236-37; 73 (1972): 39-40, 103-104, 170-72, 311-14; 74 (1973): 50-52, 121-22, 187-88, 249-51; 75 (1974): 35-37, 87-88, 171-73, 250-52; 78 (1977): 264; 79 (1978): 72-74, 166, 250-52; 80 (1979): 88-90, 192, 265-66; 81 (1980): 92-93.

(117) Shook, Robert W. "Abraham Levi: Founder of Victoria [TX] Jewry." *Western States Jewish Historical Quarterly* 9 (1977): 144-54.

(118) Stern, Malcolm H., ed. "Growing Up in Pioneer Savannah." *Publications of the Diaspora Research Institute* Book 11: 15-22.

(119) _____. "Moses Myers and the Early Jewish Community of Norfolk." *Journal of the Southern Jewish Historical Society* 1 (1958): 5-13.

(120) _____, ed. "The Sheftall Diaries: Vital Records of Savannah Jewry (1733-1808)." *American Jewish Historical Quarterly* 54 (1965): 243-77.

7 Anglican and Episcopal Traditions in the South

FROM THE SETTLEMENT of the first permanent English colony at James-town, Virginia, in 1607 to the present, the Church of England and its suc-cessor denomination, the Protestant Episcopal Church, have been vital parts of Southern religious life. Until the era of the War for Independence, the Church of England enjoyed the status of an established church in the English colonies in the South, although that establishment was perhaps the strongest in Virginia and weakest in North Carolina. Dissent, however, was early present and grew in strength with the revivals of the Great Awakening noted in chapter 2. During the colonial period, the Church of England confronted a situation unlike that in the mother country: a shortage of clergy, but strong vestries and a tradition of lay control of parishes. Anticlericalism was not un-common. Like others, Anglicans faced the dilemma of slavery, and the few Anglican efforts to minister to the slaves and the few scattered attempts to convert the Indians are noted in chapters 4 and 3. Ties to Britain left the Church in disarray in the Revolutionary era, although many of the Anglican clergy supported independence. The effort to rebuild, compounded by disestablish-ment, consumed much time and energy between the formal organization of the Protestant Episcopal Church in 1789 and the coming of the Civil War.

Although Southern Episcopalians for three years maintained a regional Protestant Episcopal Church in the Confederate States of America, the de-nomination did not divide officially over sectional issues as did many others. But the rising tide of evangelicalism, apparent by the mid-eighteenth century, left the Episcopal Church identified more with an elite cluster of persons in the Southern states than with the common people, an image perpetuated even today. The association with an educated upper class constituency meant that the denomination was not troubled to the same extent by many of the currents that caused controversy in religious circles in the postbellum New South and opening decades of the twentieth century. For example, as noted in works cited in chapters 20 and 21, fundamentalism made few inroads in Southern Episcopalianism. Episcopalians did, however, have to deal with issues of racial discrimination and the like that generated turmoil in most Southern (and national) religious circles, as seen in chapter 20. In some areas, the Episcopal Church may be construed as a conservator of old Southern tradition. The denomination's University of the South in Sewanee, Tennessee, for example, long served as a bulwark of antebellum values and traditions, as noted in some of the works listed in the bibliography for chapters 18 and 21. At the same time, again perhaps because of its elite character, the Protestant Episcopal Church is popularly perceived as a "liberal" denomination. Its style of liturgical worship has also distinguished it from most evangelical bodies, although an evangelical strain has penetrated the Southern church.

There are no critical regional histories of the Anglican and Episcopal tradition in the South. The large number of studies that center on individual colonies and states and a considerable biographical literature, however, more than make up for this lack. Indeed, for the colonial period, the studies of the Church of England in particular colonies provide a good view of the denomination's development throughout the South. Still indispensable is George M. Brydon, *Virginia's Mother Church and the Political Conditions Under Which It Grew* (42). This two-volume work, admirable for its detail, has a particularly solid discussion of the work of James Blair, one of the Church of England commissaries whose work will be noted in greater detail. Complementing Brydon's study is Jerome W. Jones's doctoral dissertation, "The Anglican Church in Colonial Virginia" (70). Sidney Charles Bolton, *Southern Anglicanism: The Church of England in Colonial South Carolina* (34) is a generally reliable cognate volume, particularly valuable for the way in which it details how the Church functioned as the major cultural force in South Carolina (as well as the established religious body), although it tends to exaggerate the nature and degree of religious dissent in that colony.

Laying the groundwork for Anglican growth in the South was largely the work of Alexander Whitaker (1585-1616/17), popularly dubbed the "Apostle to Virginia." While Whitaker did not have a lengthy association with Virginia, he made his way into the region's folklore when he baptized Pocahontas. Two articles survey Whitaker's work: Harry C. Porter, "Alexander Whitaker: Cambridge Apostle to Virginia" (215), and William H. Littleton, "Alexander Whitaker (1585-1617): The 'Apostle of Virginia' " (194).

Since there was no Anglican bishop resident in the colonies, the Bishop of London (under whose jurisdiction the colonial churches fell) appointed representatives who carried the title of commissary. Of the colonial commissaries, none made a more substantial contribution than James Blair (1655-1743), who exercised considerable political as well as religious influence and who also founded the College of William and Mary. The most recent biography is Parke Rouse, Jr., *James Blair, King-Maker of Virginia* (221). Rouse offers a brief overview in "James Blair of Virginia" (222). Still worth consulting are two older studies: Daniel E. Motley, *Life of Commissary James Blair, Founder of William and Mary College* (203), and Samuel R. Mohler's dissertation, "Commissary James Blair, Churchman, Educator, and Politician of Colonial Virginia" (201). P.G. Scott, "James Blair and the Scottish Church: A New Source" (223), adds a new dimension in the traditional interpretation of Blair, for Scott demonstrates decisively that this devoted Anglican had an early Presbyterian background.

Much of the strength of the Church of England in Maryland derived from the efforts of Thomas Bray (1656-1730), who was also instrumental in the founding of the Society for Promoting Christian Knowledge (1699) and the Society for the Propagation of the Gospel in Foreign Parts (1701). Later, trust funds earmarked for promoting the conversion of slaves and Indians supported the work of the Associates of Dr. Bray. The most recent study emphasizes Bray's commitment to learning: Charles T. Laugher, *Thomas Bray's Grand Design: Libraries of the Church of England in America, 1695-1785* (14). Still the standard biographical treatments are Henry P. Thompson, *Thomas Bray* (232), and the older work edited by Bernard C. Steiner, *Rev. T. Bray: His Life and Selected Works Relating to Maryland* (227).

In South Carolina, Anglican developments owe much to the work of Commissary Alexander Garden (1585-1756). Garden astutely recognized that the way in which the evangelicalism promoted by George Whitefield and other awakeners of the mid-eighteenth century had the potential to undermine Anglican dominance and the Anglican approach to things religious. Accordingly, he devoted considerable energy to attacking Whitefield and his revivals. There is no full-length treatment of Garden. The most thorough study, albeit somewhat dated, is Edgar L. Pennington's two-part "The Reverend Alexander Garden" (211). Garden, as other commissaries, frequently had to contend with a laity sometimes apathetic and sometimes contentious when outside authority and leadership were asserted. See Quentin B. Keen, "Problems of a Commissary: The Rev. Alexander Garden of South Carolina" (188). On Whitefield, see the listing for chapter 2. Colonial South Carolina Anglicanism also benefited from the labors of Francis LeJau (1665-1717), who was committed to ministry with both blacks and Indians. Some of the materials discussing his work are found in the listings in chapters 3 and 4, but also see S. C. Bolton, "South Carolina and the Reverend Doctor Francis LeJau: Southern Society and the Conscience of an Anglican Missionary" (153).

Not all colonial Anglicans were as hostile to the evangelical style as was Alexander Garden. In particular, Virginia's Devereux Jarratt (1733-1801) supported the revivals and consequently stamped the Anglican and later Episcopal traditions in that area with a greater openness to evangelical ways than is generally the case elsewhere in the South. Jarratt's autobiography, *The Life of the Reverend Devereux Jarratt, Rector of Bath Parish, Dinwiddie County, Virginia* (185), remains a valuable source for understanding the dynamics of eighteenth-century evangelicalism within Anglican circles. David L. Holmes, "Devereux Jarratt: A Letter and a Revelation" (175), suggests that Jarratt was a more complex individual than previous interpreters have realized, while Harry G. Rabe, "Reverend Devereux Jarratt and the Virginia Social Order" (216), begins to explore the challenges presented by the Awakening to established political and religious structures. On this latter point especially, one must not fail to examine the work of Rhys Isaac noted in chapter 2.

Scholars have devoted considerable attention to the rise of the vestry as both a religious and political unit in Southern colonial Anglicanism and the extent of power exerted by the vestry over clergy. The traditional view held that the vestries dominated the clergy through their control of the purse, although this interpretation has been challenged in recent scholarship. Joan Reznes Gunderson, for example, in "The Myth of the Independent Virginia Vestry" (57), argued that Commissary James Blair was able to work with the governor to challenge vestry control and was sufficiently successful so that by the mid-eighteenth century vestries were rarely able to depose incompetent clergy. Bradford Spangenburg, "Vestrymen in the House of Burgesses: Protection of Local Vestry Autonomy During James Blair's Term as Commissary" (98), offers a contrasting interpretation. Also see William H. Seiler, "The Anglican Parish Vestry in Colonial Virginia" (93). The most comprehensive studies center on Maryland and stem from the work of Gerald E. Hartdagen. He has addressed conflict between "Vestry and Clergy in the Anglican Church of Colonial Maryland" (64) and discussed the impact of the vestry on ethical attitudes and behavior in "The Vestries and Morals in Colonial Maryland" (63). His "The Anglican Vestry in Colonial Maryland: Organizational Structure and Problems" (62) and "The Anglican Vestry in Colonial Maryland: A Study in Corporate Responsibility" (61) look at the vestry primarily as a religious institution, while he turns to the more overt political responsibilities and influence of the vestry in "The Vestry as a Unit of Local Government in Colonial Maryland" (65).

In mid-eighteenth century Virginia Anglicanism a controversy erupted that flared off and on for roughly two decades. Known as the Parson's Cause, the conflict centered around payment of clerical salaries in tobacco. But that was only the surface issue. Deeper layers reflected a rising strain of anticlericalism in the colony's religious life and lay resentment of the clergy's efforts to

secure prerogatives that would diminish lay control. For a brief overview, see
A. Shrady Hill, "The Parson's Cause" (69). Another source of strife, which
affected the Church of England throughout the colonies, centered around pro-
posals to have a resident bishop who could confirm, ordain, and carry out
other functions that the tradition assigned only to those who held episcopal
office. Dissenters resented the notion, for they feared that an Anglican bishop
in the colonies might have political as well as religious responsibilities as was
the case in Britain. Many Anglican laity were also suspicious, for they sensed
that the presence and power of a bishop could diminish the control that vestries cherished and struggled to maintain. The most recent monograph that
probes the "episcopal controversy" and its impact on the later structure of
the American Episcopal church is Frederick V. Mills, *Bishops by Ballot* (20).
Also valuable is Carl D. Bridenbaugh, *Mitre and Sceptre* (3), and still worth
consulting is the much older study by Arthur M. Cross, *The Anglican Episcopate and the American Colonies* (6). For a brief study of two opponents of
the proposal to have an American bishopric, see Ray Hiner, Jr., "Samuel
Henley and Thomas Gwatkin: Partners in Protest" (11).

These episodes, together with the various clashes over the power of the
vestries, do suggest that Church of England clergy represented an enduring
influence in the political sector. Perhaps the best overall study of the political
involvement of both church and clergy is Alan K. Austin's doctoral dissertation, "The Role of the Anglican Church and Its Clergy in the Political Life
of Colonial Virginia" (30). On South Carolina, see John W. Brinsfield, *Religion and Politics in Colonial South Carolina* (2:105).

The American War for Independence had a disastrous effect on Southern
Anglicanism. In many instances, the identification of the Church of England
with royal power (and perceived royal despotism) placed the church in a pre-
carious position even before hostilities erupted. Such was clearly the case in
North Carolina, where establishment may well have been the weakest and the
influence of Presbyterian and Baptist dissenters was strong. Gary Freeze presents such a case in "Like a House Built upon Sand: The Anglican Church
and Establishment in North Carolina, 1765-1776" (53). While probably the
majority of the Southern Anglican clergy identified with the independence
cause, many were suspect and some were well-known Tory sympathizers.
Perhaps the most well-known Tory was Maryland's Jonathan Boucher (1738-
1804). Three articles provide an introduction to the political style of this Anglican priest: Carol R. Berkin, "Jonathan Boucher: The Loyalist as Rebel"
(152); Richard M. Gummere, "Jonathan Boucher, Toryissimus" (173); and
Robert G. Walker, "Jonathan Boucher: Champion of the Minority" (236).
The war not only decimated the ranks of the clergy, but it left American Anglicanism without any formal structure and without the security of legal establishment. Between the close of the war and the official organization of the

Protestant Episcopal Church in 1789, at times it seemed that the Anglican enterprise would simply fold. The best presentation of the many dimensions of possible collapse and successful endurance form the basis of Frederick V. Mills, "The Protestant Episcopal Church in the United States, 1783-1789: Suspended Animation or Remarkable Recovery?" (22). More popular, but still generally reliable, is Clara O. Loveland, *The Critical Years: The Reconstruction of the Anglican Church in the United States of America, 1780-1789* (15). That the situation in some cases continued to be quite bleak may be seen in Sarah McCulloch Lemmon, "Nathaniel Blount: Last Clergyman of the 'Old Church' " (191). Blount (1748-1816) was an Anglican priest in Beaufort County, North Carolina, who had supported the patriot cause. But when he died in 1816 the state lost its last resident Episcopal clergyman.

The work of rebuilding consumed much energy. In Virginia, the recovery of Anglican strength owed much to the ministry of Richard Channing Moore (1762-1841). For a good assessment of his contribution, see Lawrence L. Brown, "Richard Channing Moore and the Revival of the Southern Church" (156). Moore's work in Virginia was carried on valiantly by William Meade (1789-1862), who became a bishop in 1829. On Meade's earlier years, see the superbly crafted dissertation by David L. Holmes, "William Meade and the Church of Virginia, 1789-1829" (176). The two standard biographies of Meade were both published more than a century ago, but they remain the basic place to begin: John Johns, *A Memoir of the Life of the Right Rev. William Meade, D.D., Bishop of the Protestant Episcopal Church in the Diocese of Virginia* (187), and Robert Nelson, *Reminiscences of the Rt. Rev. William Meade, D.D., Bishop of the Prot. Epis. Church in Virginia, from Aug. 19th, 1829, to March 14th, 1862* (204).

In Georgia, the Episcopal Church benefited greatly from the labors of Stephen Elliott (1806-1866), the state's first Episcopal bishop. In time, Elliott was also a prime mover behind the short-lived Protestant Episcopal Church in the Confederate States of America. The only published biography is Herbert B. Owens, *Georgia's Planting Prelate* (207). A brief study is found in Edgar L. Pennington's older essay, "Stephen Elliott, First Bishop of Georgia" (213). However both of these need to be supplemented by Virgil S. Davis's doctoral dissertation, "Stephen Elliott: A Southern Bishop in Peace and War" (165).

Also prominent in the growth and extension of the Episcopal church in the South in the immediate antebellum period, in organizing the Confederate body, in promoting the establishment of the University of the South as a regional school for the Southern aristocracy, and in devoting himself to the Confederate military effort as a general was Louisiana's Leonidas Polk (1806-1864). One standard study, admirable in its detail and perhaps overexuberant in its appreciation of Polk's achievements, is William M. Polk's two-volume

Leonidas Polk, Bishop and General (214). More balanced, but too much taken by Polk's military involvement, is Joseph H. Parks, *General Leonidas Polk, C.S.A.: The Fighting Bishop* (208). Timothy Reilly, "Genteel Reform versus Southern Allegiance: Episcopal Dilemma in Old New Orleans" (218), makes the important point that even though Polk was identified with the Confederate cause and the culture of the Old South, he did support calls for education of the slaves and even the eventual gradual elimination of the slave labor system.

While the Protestant Episcopal Church in the United States of America did not formally divide into regional bodies over the questions surrounding slavery, its Southern churches, primarily at the prodding of Elliott and Polk, did organize the Protestant Episcopal Church in the Confederate States of America in 1862. On the rationale for having a separate regional body, see Edgar L. Pennington, "The Organization of the Protestant Episcopal Church in the Confederate States of America" (24). When the Civil War ended in 1865, the Southern body dissolved and again became part of the national denomination. The brief history of the regional church is recounted in an older study by Joseph B. Cheshire, *The Church in the Confederate States: A History of the Protestant Episcopal Church in the Confederate States* (5). Other titles on the church in the era of the Confederacy are found in the listing for chapter 20.

The bulk of scholarship probing the story of the Anglican and Episcopal tradition has concentrated heavily on the colonial and antebellum periods. Several studies, however, trace later developments along diocesan and/or state lines, though many of them are popular rather than academic works, occasionally bordering on the filiopietism that marks much denominational history. The most thorough treatment focuses on the Episcopal Church in Florida, Joseph D. Cushman's semipopular and rather traditional *A Goodly Heritage: The Episcopal Church in Florida, 1821-1892* (47), and his *The Sound of Bells: The Episcopal Church in South Florida, 1892-1969* (48). The standard work on the denomination in South Carolina during the colonial period is Frederick Dalcho, *An Historical Account of the Protestant Episcopal Church in South Carolina, from the First Settlement of the Province, to the War of the Revolution* (49), commendable for its thoroughness. It has been continued by Albert S. Thomas, *A Historical Account of the Protestant Episcopal Church in South Carolina, 1820-1957, Being a Continuation of Dalcho's Account, 1670-1820* (99). Henry T. Malone, *The Episcopal Church in Georgia, 1733-1957* (75), and Eleanor Meyer Hamilton, *The Flair and the Fire: The Story of the Episcopal Church in West Virginia, 1877-1977* (60), are both popular accounts for their respective states.

W. Robert Insko has offered an appraisal of early Episcopal developments in Kentucky in a series of articles on the career of Benjamin Bosworth

Smith (177-182). Two works by Ellen Davies-Rodgers recount the story in Tennessee in popular fashion: *Heirs Through Hope: The Episcopal Diocese of West Tennessee* (50) and *The Romance of the Episcopal Church in West Tennessee, 1832-1964* (51). Seven articles by Charles F. Rehkopf appearing over a decade's time in the *Bulletin of the Missouri Historical Society* (82-88) give a summary of Episcopal history in Missouri. For Lousiana, there is one older study that is particularly valuable for its inclusion of historical material about individual parishes: Herman C. Duncan, *The Diocese of Louisiana: Some of Its History, 1838-1888* (52). More popular is Hodding Carter and Betty W. Carter, *So Great a Good: A History of the Episcopal Church in Louisiana and of Christ Church Cathedral, 1805-1955* (43). But the most academic presentation of the Episcopal heritage in Louisiana, limited in scope to the antebellum period, is found in Robert C. Witcher's doctoral dissertation, ''The Episcopal Church in Louisiana, 1805-1861'' (103). Also academic in approach is Samuel L. Botkin, *The Episcopal Church in Oklahoma* (35). Two other popular, but uncritical, studies merit mention: Margaret S. McDonald, *White Already to Harvest: The Episcopal Church in Arkansas, 1838-1971* (74), and Lawrence L. Brown, *The Episcopal Church in Texas, 1835-1874* (40).

To the Southern evangelical mind, the Episcopal Church remains popularly linked to a socioeconomic elite, largely because from the colonial period on the tradition drew many adherents from the plantation aristocracy and those in circles of political power. In some ways, too, the church became associated with those who sought to perpetuate the Lost Cause, to conserve and preserve the values and style perceived to flourish in antebellum Southern culture. This matter will be examined in greater detail in chapter 21. At the same time, the denomination has acquired a liberal reputation in matters of theological doctrine and social practice. In an ethos permeated by a more theologically and socially conservative evangelical Protestantism, this stance has—as Wade C. Roof, *Community and Commitment: Religious Plausibility in a Liberal Protestant Church* (90), demonstrated in the case of North Carolina—generated ongoing problems of legitimation as the Episcopal Church continues to fashion a place for itself in the Southern religious landscape. The response of the Episcopal Church to the many social issues that have left a deep imprint on Southern religion is analyzed in many of the works cited in chapter 20. From the privileged establishment of the colonial era to the minority denomination of today, the Anglican and Episcopal traditions have been integral to the development of Southern religious life.

The bibliography that follows, like the others in the chapters focusing on individual denominations, first lists general and topical studies, then state and local studies, and finally biographical and autobiographical studies. Attention should also be called to two periodical publications that regularly contain material valuable to the study of the Episcopal Church in the South: *Historical Magazine of the Protestant Episcopal Church* and the *Episcopal Church Annual*.

BIBLIOGRAPHY

Numerous titles in chapters 1, 2, 3, 4, 17, 18, 19, 20, and 21 are also relevant to the study of the Anglican and Episcopal traditions in the South.

I. THE ANGLICAN AND EPISCOPAL TRADITIONS IN THE SOUTH: GENERAL AND TOPICAL STUDIES

(1) Addison, James T. *The Episcopal Church in the United States, 1789-1931*. New York: Scribner's, 1951.

(2) Albright, Raymond W. *A History of the Protestant Episcopal Church*. New York: Macmillan, 1964.

(3) Bridenbaugh, Carl. *Mitre and Sceptre: Transatlantic Faiths, Ideas, Personalities, and Politics, 1689-1775*. New York: Oxford University Press, 1962.

(4) Cameron, Kenneth W. *American Episcopal Clergy: Registers of Ordinations in the Episcopal Church in the United States from 1785 through 1904*. Hartford: Transcendental Books, 1970.

(5) Cheshire, Joseph B. *The Church in the Confederate States: A History of the Protestant Episcopal Church in the Confederate States*. New York: Longmans, Green, 1912.

(6) Cross, Arthur L. *The Anglican Episcopate and the American Colonies*. New York and London: Longmans, Green, 1902.

(7) Deloria, Vine. "G[eneral] C[onvention] S[pecial] P[rogram]: The Demons at Work." *Historical Magazine of the Protestant Episcopal Church* 49 (1979): 83-92.

(8) DeMille, George E. *The Episcopal Church Since 1900: A Brief History*. New York: Morehouse-Gorham, 1955.

(9) Dunstan, William E. III. "The Episcopal Church in the Confederacy." *Virginia Cavalcade* 19 (1970): 5-15.

(10) Goodfellow, Guy F. "200 Years: An Address Commemorating the 200th Anniversary of the Convention of 1780, 8 November 1980, at Washington College." *Historical Magazine of the Protestant Episcopal Church* 51 (1982): 231-40.

(11) Hiner, Ray, Jr. "Samuel Henley and Thomas Gwatkin: Partners in Protest." *Historical Magazine of the Protestant Episcopal Church* 37 (1968): 39-50.

(12) Hodges, George, and Powell M. Dawley. *A Short History of the Episcopal Church*. Cincinnati: Forward Movement Publications, 1967.

(13) Holzhammer, Robert E. "The Domestic and Foreign Mission Society: The Period of Expansion and Development." *Historical Magazine of the Protestant Episcopal Church* 40 (1971): 367-97.

(14) Laugher, Charles T. *Thomas Bray's Grand Design: Libraries of the Church of England in America, 1695-1785*. Chicago: American Library Association, 1973.

(15) Loveland, Clara O. *The Critical Years: The Reconstruction of the Anglican Church in the United States of America, 1780-1789*. Greenwich: Seabury Press, 1956.

(16) McCarriar, Herbert G., Jr. "A History of the Missionary Jurisdiction of the South of the Reformed Episcopal Church, 1874-1970." *Historical Magazine of the Protestant Episcopal Church* 41 (1972): 197-220, 287-315.

(17) Manross, William W. *The Episcopal Church in the United States, 1800-1840: A Study of Church Life*. New York: Columbia University Press, 1938.

(18) _____. *A History of the American Episcopal Church*. 2d ed. New York: Morehouse-Gorham, 1950.

(19) Mills, Frederick V. "Anglican Expansion in Colonial America, 1761-1775." *Historical Magazine of the Protestant Episcopal Church* 39 (1970): 315-24.

(20) _____. *Bishops by Ballot: An Eighteenth Century Ecclesiastical Revolution*. New York: Oxford University Press, 1978.

(21) _____. "The Internal Anglican Controversy over an American Episcopate, 1763-1775." *Historical Magazine of the Protestant Episcopal Church* 44 (1975): 257-76.

(22) _____. "The Protestant Episcopal Church in the United States, 1783-1789: Suspended Animation or Remarkable Recovery?" *Historical Magazine of the Protestant Episcopal Church* 46 (1977): 151-70.

(23) Monk, Robert C. "Unity and Diversity among Eighteenth Century Colonial Anglicans and Methodists." *Historical Magazine of the Protestant Episcopal Church* 38 (1969): 51-69.

(24) Pennington, Edgar L. "The Organization of the Protestant Episcopal Church in the Confederate States of America." *Historical Magazine of the Protestant Episcopal Church* 17 (1948): 308-38.

(25) Posey, Walter B. "The Protestant Episcopal Church: An American Adaptation." *Journal of Southern History* 25 (1959): 3-30. Reprinted in George B. Tindall, ed. *The Pursuit of Southern History*. Baton Rouge: Louisiana State University Press, 1964.

(26) Robbins, Roy S. "Crusade in the Wilderness, 1750-1830." *Indiana Magazine of History* 46 (1950): 121-32.

(27) Shepherd, Massey H. *The Worship of the Church*. Greenwich: Seabury Press, 1952.

(28) White, William. *Memoirs of the Protestant Episcopal Church in the United States of America*. 3d ed. New York: E. P. Dutton, 1880.

(29) Woolverton, John F. *Colonial Anglicanism in North America, 1607-1776*. Detroit: Wayne State University Press, 1984.

II. THE ANGLICAN AND EPISCOPAL TRADITIONS IN THE SOUTH: STUDIES BY STATE

(30) Austin, Alan K. "The Role of the Anglican Church and Its Clergy in the

Political Life of Colonial Virginia." Ph.D. dissertation, University of Georgia, 1969.

(31) Bailey, Raymond C. "Popular Petitions and Religion in Eighteenth Century Virginia." *Historical Magazine of the Protestant Episcopal Church* 46 (1977): 419-28.

(32) Berkeley, Edmund, and Dorothy S. Berkeley, eds. "Another 'Account of Virginia': By The Reverend John Clayton." *Virginia Magazine of History and Biography* 76 (1968): 415-36.

(33) Bessly, Claude. A. *The Episcopal Church in Northern Texas*. Wichita Falls: Dallas Diocese, 1952.

(34) Bolton, Sidney C. *Southern Anglicanism: The Church of England in Colonial South Carolina*. Westport: Greenwood Press, 1982.

(35) Botkin, Samuel L. *The Episcopal Church in Oklahoma*. Oklahoma City: American Bond Printing, 1958.

(36) _____. "The Protestant Episcopal Church in Oklahoma, 1835-1941." Ph.D. dissertation, University of Oklahoma, 1958.

(37) Brewster, Lawrence F. *A Short History of the Diocese of East Carolina, 1883-1972*. Wilmington NC: Diocese of East Carolina, 1975.

(38) Brown, Katharine L. *Hills of the Lord: Background of the Episcopal Church in Southwest Virginia, 1738-1938*. Roanoke: Diocese of Southwestern Virginia, 1979.

(39) Brown, Lawrence L. *A Brief History of the Church in West Texas*. Austin: Seminary of the Southwest, 1959.

(40) _____. *The Episcopal Church in Texas, 1835-1874*. Austin: Church Historical Society, 1963.

(41) _____. "Texas Bishop Vetoes Women Council Delegates in 1921." *Historical Magazine of the Protestant Episcopal Church* 48 (1979): 93-102.

(42) Brydon, George M. *Virginia's Mother Church and the Political Conditions Under Which It Grew*. 2 vols. Richmond: Virginia Historical Society, 1947-1952.

(43) Carter, Hodding, and Betty W. Carter. *So Great a Good: A History of the Episcopal Church in Louisiana and of Christ Church Cathedral, 1805-1955*. Sewanee: University Press, 1955.

(44) Cocke, Charles F. *Parish Lines, Diocese of Southwestern Virginia*. Richmond: Virginia State Library, 1960.

(45) Conklin, Paul. "The Church Establishment in North Carolina, 1765-1776." *North Carolina Historical Review* 31 (1955): 1-30.

(46) Crane, Verner W. "Dr. Thomas Bray and the Charitable Colony Project." *William and Mary Quarterly*, 3d series 19 (1962): 49-63.

(47) Cushman, Joseph D., Jr. *A Goodly Heritage: The Episcopal Church in Florida, 1821-1892*. Gainesville: University of Florida Press, 1965.

(48) _____. *The Sound of Bells: The Episcopal Church in South Florida, 1892-1969*. Gainesville: University of Florida Press, 1976.

(49) Dalcho, Frederick. *An Historical Account of the Protestant Episcopal Church in South Carolina, from the First Settlement of the Province, to the War of the Revolution*. New York: Arno Press, 1972. First published 1820.

(50) Davies-Rodgers, Ellen. *Heirs Through Hope: The Episcopal Diocese of West Tennessee*. Memphis: Plantation Press, 1983.

(51) _____. *The Romance of the Episcopal Church in West Tennessee, 1832-1964*. Memphis: Plantation Press, 1964.

(52) Duncan, Herman C. *The Diocese of Louisiana: Some of Its History, 1838-1888*. New Orleans: A. W. Hyatt, 1888.

(53) Freeze, Gary. "Like a House Built upon Sand: The Anglican Church and Establishment in North Carolina, 1765-1776." *Historical Magazine of the Protestant Episcopal Church* 48 (1979): 405-32.

(54) Friedlander, Amy, ed. "Commissary Johnson's Report, 1713." *South Carolina Historical Magazine* 83 (1982): 259-71.

(55) Gage, Thomas E. "The Established Church in Colonial Virginia, 1689-1785." Ph.D. dissertation, University of Missouri, 1974.

(56) Greatwood, Richard N. "Charles Todd Quintard (1824-1898): His Role and Significance in the Development of the Protestant Episcopal Church in the Diocese of Tennessee and in the South." Ph.D. dissertation, Vanderbilt University, 1977.

(57) Gundersen, Joan Reznes. "The Myth of the Independent Virginia Vestry." *Historical Magazine of the Protestant Episcopal Church* 44 (1975): 133-41.

(58) _____. "The Non-Institutional Church: The Religious Role of Women in Eighteenth-Century Virginia." *Historical Magazine of the Protestant Episcopal Church* 51 (1982): 347-58.

(59) Hall, William McL. "A Century of Missionary Work in the Diocese of Florida: A Comparative Study." D.Min. dissertation, University of the South, 1980.

(60) Hamilton, Eleanor Meyer. *The Flair and the Fire: The Story of the Episcopal Church in West Virginia, 1877-1977*. Charleston WV: Diocese of West Virginia, 1977.

(61) Hartdagen, Gerald E. "The Anglican Vestry in Colonial Maryland: A Study in Corporate Responsibility." *Historical Magazine of the Protestant Episcopal Church* 40 (1971): 315-35, 461-79.

(62) _____. "The Anglican Vestry in Colonial Maryland: Organizational Structure and Problems." *Historical Magazine of the Protestant Episcopal Church* 38 (1969): 349-60.

(63) _____. "The Vestries and Morals in Colonial Maryland." *Maryland Historical Magazine* 63 (1968): 360-78.

(64) _____. "Vestry and Clergy in the Anglican Church of Colonial Maryland." *Historical Magazine of the Protestant Episcopal Church* 37 (1968): 371-96.

(65) _____. "The Vestry as a Unit of Local Government in Colonial Maryland." *Maryland Historical Magazine* 67 (1972): 363-88.

(66) Haw, James. "The Patronage Follies: Bennet Allen, John Morton Jordan, and the Fall of Horatio Sharpe." *Maryland Historical Magazine* 71 (1976): 134-58.

(67) Hawks, Francis L. *Contributions to the Ecclesiastical History of the United States.* 1: *A Narrative of Events Connected with the Rise and Progress of the Protestant Episcopal Church in Virginia.* 2: *A Narrative of Events Connected with the Rise and Progress of the Protestant Episcopal Church in Maryland.* New York: Taylor, 1836-1839.

(68) Heyward, Marie H. *The Diocese of South Carolina.* Charleston SC: n.p., 1938.

(69) Hill, A. Shrady. "The Parson's Cause." *Historical Magazine of the Protestant Episcopal Church* 46 (1977): 5-35.

(70) Jones, Jerome W, "The Anglican Church in Colonial Virginia, 1690-1760." Ph.D. dissertation, Harvard University, 1960.

(71) Kimball, Howard E. "Gideon Johnston, the Bishop of London's Commissary to South Carolina, 1707-1716." *Historical Magazine of the Protestant Episcopal Church* 42 (1973): 5-35.

(72) Lemmon, Sarah McCulloh. "The Genesis of the Protestant Episcopal Diocese of North Carolina, 1701-1823." *North Carolina Historical Review* 28 (1951): 426-62.

(73) McCants, David A. "The Authenticity of James Maury's Account of Patrick Henry's Speech in the Parsons' Cause." *Southern Speech Communication Journal* 42 (1976): 20-34.

(74) McDonald, Margaret S. *White Already to Harvest: The Episcopal Church in Arkansas, 1838-1971.* N.p.p.: Episcopal Diocese of Arkansas, 1975.

(75) Malone, Henry T. *The Episcopal Church in Georgia, 1733-1957.* Atlanta: The Protestant Episcopal Church in the Diocese of Atlanta, 1960.

(76) Meade, [Bishop] William. *Old Churches, Ministers, and Families of Virginia.* 2 vols. Philadelphia: J. B. Lippincott, 1857.

(77) Middleton, Arthur P. "The Colonial Virginia Parish." *Historical Magazine of the Protestant Episcopal Church* 40 (1971): 431-46.

(78) Murphy, DuBose. *A Short History of the Protestant Episcopal Church in Texas.* Dallas: Turner, 1935.

(79) Noll, Arthur H. *History of the Church in the Diocese of Tennessee.* New York: James Pott, 1900.

(80) Oliver, David D. "The Society for the Propagation of the Gospel in the Province of North Carolina." *James Sprunt Historical Publications* 9 (1910): 5-23. Also published separately, Raleigh: North Carolina Historical Society, 1910.

(81) Perry, William S. *Historical Collections Relating to the American Colonial Church.* 1: *Virginia,* 4: *Maryland.* [Hartford]: Printed for the Subscribers, 1870-1878.

(82) Rehkopf, Charles F. "The Beginnings of the Episcopal Church in Missouri, 1819-1844." *Bulletin of the Missouri Historical Society* 11 (1955): 265-78.

(83) _____. "The Episcopate of Bishop Charles F. Robertson." *Bulletin of the Missouri Historical Society* 17 (1961): 215-38.

(84) _____. "The Episcopate of Bishop Hawks." *Bulletin of the Missouri Historical Society* 13 (1957): 367-80.

(85) _____. "The Episcopate of Bishop Johnson." *Bulletin of the Missouri Historical Society* 19 (1963): 231-46.

(86) _____. "The Episcopate of Bishop Tuttle." *Bulletin of the Missouri Historical Society* 18 (1962): 207-30.

(87) _____. "The Episcopate of William Scarlett." *Bulletin of the Missouri Historical Society* 20 (1964): 193-217.

(88) _____. "The Missouri Episcopate of Arthur Lichtenberger." *Bulletin of the Missouri Historical Society* 21 (1965): 45-60.

(89) Rightmyer, Nelson W. *Maryland's Established Church.* Baltimore: Church Historical Society of the Diocese of Maryland, 1956.

(90) Roof, Wade C. *Community and Commitment: Religious Plausibility in a Liberal Protestant Church.* New York: Elsevier, 1978.

(91) _____, and Richard B. Perkins. "On Conceptualizing Salience in Religious Commitment." *Journal for the Scientific Study of Religion* 14 (1975): 111-28.

(92) Seabrook, John H. "The Establishment of Anglicanism in Colonial Maryland." *Historical Magazine of the Protestant Episcopal Church* 39 (1970): 287-94.

(93) Seiler, William H. "The Anglican Parish Vestry in Colonial Virginia." *Journal of Southern History* 22 (1956): 310-37.

(94) Sharber, Patricia F. "Social History of Tennessee Episcopalians, 1865-1935." Ph.D. dissertation, Middle Tennessee State University, 1973.

(95) Sill, James B. *Historical Sketches of Churches in the Diocese of Western North Carolina: Episcopal Church.* Asheville NC: Church of the Redeemer, 1955.

(96) Simpson, Marcus B., and Sallie W. Simpson. "The Reverend John Clayton's Letters to the Royal Society of London, 1693-1694: An Important Source for Dr. John Brickell's *Natural History of North Carolina,* 1737." *North Carolina Historical Review* 54 (1977): 1-16.

(97) Spalding, Phinizy. "Some Sermons Before the Trustees of Georgia." *Georgia Historical Quarterly* 57 (1973): 332-46.

(98) Spangenburg, Bradford. "Vestrymen in the House of Burgesses: Protection of Local Vestry Autonomy during James Blair's Term as Commissary (1690-1734)." *Historical Magazine of the Protestant Episcopal Church* 32 (1963): 77-99.

(99) Thomas, Albert S. *A Historical Account of the Protestant Episcopal Church in South Carolina, 1820-1957, Being a Continuation of Dalcho's Account, 1670-1820.* Columbia: R. L. Ryan, 1957.

(100) Watson, Alan D. "The Anglican Parish in Royal North Carolina, 1729-1775." *Historical Magazine of the Protestant Episcopal Church* 48 (1979): 303-19.

(101) Whitaker, Walter C. *History of the Protestant Episcopal Church in Alabama, 1763-1891*. Birmingham: Roberts & Son, 1898.

(102) Williams, George W., ed. "Letters to the Bishop of London from the Commissaries in South Carolina." *South Carolina Historical Magazine* 78 (1977): 1-31, 120-47, 213-47, 286-317.

(103) Witcher, Robert C. "The Episcopal Church in Louisiana, 1805-1861." Ph.D. dissertation, Louisiana State University, 1969.

(104) Woodmason, Charles. *The Carolina Backcountry on the Eve of the Revolution*. Chapel Hill: University of North Carolina Press, for the Institute of Early American History and Culture, 1953.

III. THE ANGLICAN AND EPISCOPAL TRADITIONS IN THE SOUTH: LOCAL STUDIES

(105) Abercrombie, Lelia. "Early Churches of Pensacola." *Florida Historical Quarterly* 37 (1959): 446-62.

(106) Allen, Ethan. *The Garrison Church: Sketches of St. Thomas' Parish, Garrison Forest, Baltimore County, Maryland, 1742-1852*. New York: J. Pott, 1898.

(107) Burger, Nash K. "A Side-Light on an Ante-Bellum Plantation Chapel." *Historical Magazine of the Protestant Episcopal Church* 12 (1943): 69.

(108) Coke, Fletch. "Christ Church, Episcopal, Nashville." *Tennessee Historical Quarterly* 38 (1979): 141-57.

(109) Corbin, Gawin L. "The First List of Pew Holders of Christ-Church, Savannah." *Georgia Historical Quarterly* 50 (1966): 74-86.

(110) Davis, Richard B. "A Sermon Preached at James City in Virginia the 23rd of April 1686 by Deuel Plad." *William and Mary Quarterly* 3d series 17 (1960): 371-94.

(111) Dugas, Vera Lee. "Episcopalian Expansion into the Lower Mississippi Valley." *Louisiana Historical Quarterly* 38 (1955): 57-74.

(112) _____, ed. "A Virginia Colonial Frontier Parish's 'Poor' Petition for a Priest." *Historical Magazine of the Protestant Episcopal Church* 35 (1966): 87-98.

(113) Fraser, Walter J., Jr. "Controlling the Poor in Colonial Charles Town." *Proceedings of the South Carolina Historical Association* 50 (1980): 13-30.

(114) Garland, John M. "The Nonecclesiastical Activities of an English and a North Carolina Parish: A Comparative Study." *North Carolina Historical Review* 50 (1973): 32-51.

(115) Garrett, Jill K. "St. John's Church, Ashwood." *Tennessee Historical Quarterly* 29 (1970): 3-23.

(116) Gearhart, Edward B. "St. Paul's Church in Quincy, Florida, During the Territorial Period." *Florida Historical Quarterly* 34 (1956): 339-65.

(117) Geiger, Florence Gambrill. "St. Bartholomew's Parish as Seen by Its Rectors, 1713-1761." *South Carolina Historical Magazine* 50 (1949): 173-203.

(118) Gerrard, Ginny. "A History of the Protestant Episcopal Church in Shreveport, Louisiana, 1839-1916." *North Louisiana Historical Association Journal* 9 (1978): 193-203.

(119) Goodwin, William A. R. *Bruton Parish Church Restored and Its Environments.* Petersburg VA: Franklin Printing, 1907.

(120) _____. *Historical Sketch of Bruton Church, Williamsburg, Virginia.* Petersburg VA: Franklin Printing, 1903.

(121) "Henry Ward Beecher and St. Michael's." *South Carolina Historical Magazine* 60 (1959): 145-46.

(122) Hitz, Alex M. "The Origin and Distinction between the Two Protestant Episcopal Churches Known as St. Luke's, Atlanta." *Atlanta Historical Quarterly* 34 (1950): 1-7.

(123) Lale, Max S. "Trinity Episcopal Church: Marshall, Texas." *East Texas Historical Journal* 12 (1974): 3-16.

(124) Lewis, Henry W. *Northampton Parishes.* Jackson NC: n.p., 1951.

(125) McCrady, Edward. *An Historic Church, The Westminster Abbey of South Carolina: A Sketch of St. Philip's Church, Charleston, S.C.* Charleston: Lucas & Richardson, 1897.

(126) Mason, George C. "The Colonial Churches of Spotsylvania and Caroline Counties, Virginia." *Virginia Magazine of History and Biography* 58 (1950): 442-72.

(127) _____. "A Supplement to 'Colonial Churches of Tidewater Virginia'." *Virginia Magazine of History and Biography* 66 (1958): 167-77.

(128) Morgan, Philip D., ed. "A Profile of a Mid-Eighteenth Century South Carolina Parish: The Tax Return of Saint James', Goose Creek." *South Carolina Historical Magazine* 81 (1980): 51-65.

(129) Morrow, Sara Sprott. "St. Paul's Church, Franklin." *Tennessee Historical Quarterly* 34 (1975): 3-18.

(130) Norton, Barbara. "A Sketch of St. Paul's Church, Pendleton." *South Carolina Historical Magazine* 63 (1962): 42-51.

(131) Owsley, Harriet C. "The Rugby Papers: A Bibliographical Note." *Tennessee Historical Quarterly* 27 (1968): 225-28.

(132) Pinckney, Elise. "Register of St. John-in-the-Wilderness, Flat Rock." *South Carolina Historical Magazine* 63 (1962): 105-11, 175-81, 232-37.

(133) Rehkopf, Charles F. "Reactions to Events of the '60's and '70's." *Historical Magazine of the Protestant Episcopal Church* 47 (1978): 453-62.

(134) Reynierse, Peter J. "A History of St. John's Church, Versailles, Kentucky." *Historical Magazine of the Protestant Episcopal Church* 45 (1976): 47-55.

(135) Spencer, William M. "St. Andrew's Church, Prairieville." *Alabama Review* 14 (1961): 18-30.

(136) Stagg, Brian L. "Tennessee's Rugby Colony." *Tennessee Historical Quarterly* 27 (1968): 209-34.

(137) Stitt, Susan. "The Will of Stephen Charlton and Hungars Parish Glebe." *Virginia Magazine of History and Biography* 77 (1969): 259-76.

(138) Swinford, Frances K., and Rebecca S. Lee. *The Great Elm Tree: Heritage of the Episcopal Diocese of Lexington.* Lexington: Faith House Press, 1969.

(139) Taylor, Georgia Fairbanks. "The Early History of the Episcopal Church in New Orleans, 1805-1840." *Louisiana Historical Quarterly* 22 (1939): 428-77.

(140) Ulmer, Barbara. "Benevolence in Colonial Charleston." *Proceedings of the South Carolina Historical Association* 50 (1980): 1-12.

(141) Williams, George W. "Early Organists at St. Philip's, Charleston." *South Carolina Historical Magazine* 54 (1953): 83-87.

(142) _____. "Eighteenth-Century Organists of St. Michael's, Charleston." *South Carolina Historical Magazine* 53 (1952): 146-54, 212-22.

(143) _____. *St. Michael's Charleston, 1751-1951.* Columbia: University of South Carolina Press, 1951.

(144) Wroten, William H., Jr. "The Protestant Episcopal Church in Dorchester County, 1692-1860." *Maryland Historical Magazine* 45 (1950): 104-25.

IV. THE ANGLICAN AND EPISCOPAL TRADITIONS IN THE SOUTH: BIOGRAPHICAL AND AUTOBIOGRAPHICAL STUDIES

(145) Allen, Ethan. *Clergy of Maryland of the Protestant Episcopal Church Since the Independence of 1783.* Baltimore: J. S. Waters, 1860.

(146) Armentrout, Donald S. *James Hervey Otey: First Bishop of Tennessee.* Knoxville: Episcopal Diocese of Tennessee, 1984.

(147) Ashdown, Paul G. "Samuel Ringgold: A Missionary in the Tennessee Valley, 1860-1911." *Tennessee Historical Quarterly* 38 (1979): 203-13.

(148) _____. "Samuel Ringgold: An Episcopal Clergyman in Kentucky and Tennessee during the Civil War." *Filson Club Historical Quarterly* 53 (1979): 231-38.

(149) Bailey, Hugh C. *Edgar Gardner Murphy: Gentle Progressive.* Coral Gables: University of Miami Press, 1968.

(150) Batterson, Hermon G. *A Sketch-book of the American Episcopate.* 3d ed. Philadelphia: J. B. Lippincott, 1891.

(151) Beirne, Rosamund Randall. "Reverend Thomas Chase: Pugnacious Parson." *Maryland Historical Magazine* 59 (1964): 1-14.

(152) Berkin, Carol R. "Jonathan Boucher: The Loyalist as Rebel." *West Georgia College Studies in the Social Sciences* 15 (1976): 65-78.

(153) Bolton, S. C. "South Carolina and the Reverend Doctor Francis LeJau: Southern Society and the Conscience of an Anglican Missionary." *Historical Magazine of the Protestant Episcopal Church* 40 (1971): 63-79.

(154) Bowler, Clara Ann. "The Litigious Career of William Cotton, Minister." *Virginia Magazine of History and Biography* 86 (1978): 281-94.

(155) Brewster, Lawrence F. "Alfred Augustine Watson: Episcopal Clergyman of the New South." *East Carolina College Publications in History* 3 (1966): 1-23.

(156) Brown, Lawrence L. "Richard Channing Moore and the Revival of the Southern Church." *Historical Magazine of the Protestant Episcopal Church* 35 (1966): 3-63.

(157) Burger, Nash K. "The Right Rev. William Mercer Green, First Episcopal Bishop of Mississippi." *Journal of Mississippi History* 12 (1950): 3-27.

(158) _____. "Some Notes on Hugh Miller Thompson, Second Episcopal Bishop of Mississippi." *Journal of Mississippi History* 19 (1957): 31-37.

(159) Cargill, John, and Helen Cargill. "The Reverend John Cargill of Colonial Virginia." *Virginia Magazine of History and Biography* 70 (1962): 420-33.

(160) Carpenter, Charles, ed. "Henry Dana Ward: Early Diarist of the Kanawha Valley." *West Virginia History* 37 (1975): 34-48.

(161) Chorley, E. C. "Correspondence between the Right Reverend John Skinner, Jr., and the Reverend Jonathan Boucher, 1786." *Historical Magazine of the Protestant Episcopal Church* 10 (1941): 163-75.

(162) Crow, Charles. "Bishop James Madison and the Republic of Virtue." *Journal of Southern History* 30 (1964): 58-70.

(163) _____. "The Reverend James Madison in Williamsburg and London, 1768-1771." *West Virginia History* 25 (1963-1964): 270-78.

(164) _____. "The War of 'Pure Republicanism' against Federalism, 1794-1801: Bishop James Madison on the American Political Scene." *West Virginia History* 24 (1962-63): 355-62.

(165) Davis, Virgil S. "Stephen Elliott: A Southern Bishop in Peace and War." Ph.D. dissertation, University of Georgia, 1964.

(167) Detweiler, Robert. "Robert Rose, 1704-1751: Effective and Popular Minister of Colonial Virginia." *Historical Magazine of the Protestant Episcopal Church* 41 (1972): 153-62.

(167) Donald, James M. "Bishop Hopkins and the Reunification of the Church." *Historical Magazine of the Protestant Episcopal Church* 47 (1978): 73-91.

(168) Dresbeck, Sandra Ryan. "The Episcopal Clergy in Maryland and Virginia, 1765-1805." Ph.D. dissertation, University of California at Los Angeles, 1976.

(169) Evans, David, ed. "Price Davies, Rector of Blisland Parish: Two Letters, 1763, 1765." *Virginia Magazine of History and Biography* 79 (1971): 153-61.

(170) French, Warren. "A Sketch of the Life of Joseph Holt Ingraham." *Journal of Mississippi History* 11 (1949): 155-71.

(171) Gailor, Thomas F. *Some Memories.* Kingsport TN: Southern Publishers, 1937.

(172) Gregg, Wilson. *Alexander Gregg, First Bishop of Texas.* Arthur H. Knoll, ed. Sewanee: The University Press, 1912.

(173) Gummere, Richard M. "Jonathan Boucher, Toryissimus." *Maryland Historical Magazine* 55 (1960): 138-45.

(174) Heintze, James R. "Alexander Malcolm: Musician, Clergyman, and Schoolmaster." *Maryland Historical Magazine* 73 (1978): 226-35.

(175) Holmes, David L. "Devereux Jarratt: A Letter and a Revelation." *Historical Magazine of the Protestant Episcopal Church* 47 (1978): 37-49.

(176) _____. "William Meade and the Church of Virginia, 1789-1829." Ph.D. dissertation, Princeton University, 1971.

(177) Insko, W. Robert. "Benjamin Bosworth Smith, a Pioneer Kentucky Bishop." *Filson Club Historical Quarterly* 39 (1965): 135-46.

(178) _____. "Benjamin Bosworth Smith, Early Kentucky Clergyman." *Register of the Kentucky Historical Society* 49 (1951): 175-92.

(179) _____. "Benjamin Bosworth Smith: Kentucky Pioneer Clergyman and Educator." *Register of the Kentucky Historical Society* 69 (1971): 37-86.

(180) _____. "Kentucky Bishop: A Picturelog." *Register of the Kentucky Historical Society* 54 (1956): 339-47.

(181) _____. "A Pioneer Educator on Horseback: Kentucky's Third Superintendent of Public Instruction." *Filson Club Historical Quarterly* 32 (1958): 285-94.

(182) _____. "The Trial of a Kentucky Bishop." *Filson Club Historical Quarterly* 35 (1961): 141-58.

(183) Ives, Levi S. *The Trials of a Mind in Its Progress to Catholicism: A Letter to His Old Friends.* Boston: P. Donahoe, 1854.

(184) Jackson, Harry F. "Bishop Madison's Speculations on the Mounds." *West Virginia History* 24 (1962-1963): 363-69.

(185) Jarratt, Devereux. *The Life of the Reverend Devereux Jarratt, Rector of Bath Parish, Dinwiddie County, Virginia.* Baltimore: Warner and Hanna, 1806.

(186) Jennings, John M. "Further Notes on the Reverend Price Davies." *Virginia Magazine of History and Biography* 79 (1971): 162-66.

(187) Johns, John. *A Memoir of the Life of the Right Rev. William Meade, D.D., Bishop of the Protestant Episcopal Church in the Diocese of Virginia.* Baltimore: Innes, 1867.

(188) Keen, Quentin B. "Problems of a Commissary: The Reverend Alexander Garden of South Carolina." *Historical Magazine of the Protestant Episcopal Church* 20 (1951): 136-55.

(189) Kyser, John L. "The Deposition of Bishop William Montgomery Brown in New Orleans, 1925." *Louisiana History* 8 (1967): 35-52.

(190) Lemay, J. A. L. "Franklin's 'Dr. Spence': The Reverend Archibald Spencer, M.D." *Maryland Historical Magazine* 59 (1964): 199-216.

(191) Lemmon, Sarah McCulloh. "Nathaniel Blount: Last Clergyman of the 'Old Church'." *North Carolina Historical Review* 50 (1973): 351-64.

(192) Levine, Daniel. "Edgar Gardner Murphy: Conservative Reformer." *Alabama Review* 15 (1962): 100-116.

(193) Lewis, James. *West Virginia Pilgrim.* New York: Seabury Press, 1976.

(194) Littleton, William H. "Alexander Whitaker (1585-1617): 'The Apostle of Virginia'." *Historical Magazine of the Protestant Episcopal Church* 29 (1960): 325-48.

(195) London, Lawrence F. *Bishop Joseph Blount Cheshire: His Life and Work.* Chapel Hill: University of North Carolina Press, 1941.

(196) Luker, Ralph E. "The Crucible of Civil War and Reconstruction in the Experience of William Porcher DuBose." *South Carolina Historical Magazine* 83 (1982): 50-71.

(197) _____. "God, Man, and the World of James Warley Miles, Charleston's Transcendentalist." *Historical Magazine of the Protestant Episcopal Church* 39 (1970): 101-36.

(198) McCulloch, Samuel C. "The Fight to Depose Governor Francis Nicholson: James Blair's Affidavit of June 7, 1704." *Journal of Southern History* 12 (1946): 403-22.

(199) Malone, Michael T. "Sketches of Anglican Clergy Who Served in North Carolina during the Period, 1765-1776." *Historical Magazine of the Protestant Episcopal Church* 39 (1970): 137-61, 399-438.

(200) Martin, Junius J. "Georgia's First Minister: The Reverend Dr. Henry Herbert." *Georgia Historical Quarterly* 66 (1982): 113-18.

(201) Mohler, Samuel R. "Commissary James Blair: Churchman, Educator, and Politician of Colonial Virginia." Ph.D. dissertation, University of Chicago, 1941.

(202) Morton, Richard L. "The Reverend Hugh Jones: Lord Baltimore's Mathematician." *William and Mary Quarterly* 3d series 7 (1950): 107-15.

(203) Motley, Daniel E. *Life of Commissary James Blair, Founder of William and Mary College.* Johns Hopkins University Studies in History and Political Science, Series 19, number 10. Baltimore: Johns Hopkins University Press, 1901.

(204) Nelson, Robert. *Reminiscences of the Rt. Rev. William Meade, D.D., Bishop of the Prot. Epis. Church in Virginia, from Aug. 19th, 1829, to March 14th, 1862.* Shanghai: "Ching-Foong" General Printing Office, 1873.

(205) Noll, Arthur H. "Bishop Otey as Provisional Bishop of Mississippi." *Publications of the Mississippi Historical Society* 3 (1900): 139-45.

(206) _____, ed. *Doctor Quintard, Chaplain C.S.A. and Second Bishop of Tennessee: Being His Story of the War (1861-1865).* Sewanee: The University Press, 1905.

(207) Owens, Hubert B. *Georgia's Planting Prelate.* Athens: University of Georgia Press, 1945.

(208) Parks, Joseph H. *General Leonidas Polk, C.S.A: The Fighting Bishop.* Baton Rouge: Louisiana State University Press, 1962.

(209) Parramore, Thomas C. "John Alexander, Anglican Missionary." *North Carolina Historical Review* 43 (1966): 304-15.

(210) Pennington, Edgar L. "The Ministry of Joseph Holt Ingraham in Mobile, Alabama." *Historical Magazine of the Protestant Episcopal Church* 27 (1958): 344-60.

(211) _____. "The Reverend Alexander Garden." *Historical Magazine of the Protestant Episcopal Church* 2 (1933): 178-94, 3 (1934): 111-19.

(212) _____. "The Reverend Samuel Quincy, S.P.G. Missionary." *Georgia Historical Quarterly* 11 (1927): 157-65.

(213) _____. "Stephen Elliott, First Bishop of Georgia." *Historical Magazine of the Protestant Episcopal Church* 7 (1938): 203-63.

(214) Polk, William M. *Leonidas Polk, Bishop and General*. New York: Longmans, Green, 1893.

(215) Porter, Harry C. "Alexander Whitaker: Cambridge Apostle to Virginia." *William and Mary Quarterly* 3d series 14 (1957): 317-43.

(216) Rabe, Harry G. "Reverend Devereux Jarratt and the Virginia Social Order." *Historical Magazine of the Protestant Episcopal Church* 33 (1964): 299-306.

(217) Read, Allen W. "Boucher's Linguistic Pastoral of Colonial Maryland." *Dialect Notes* 6 (1933): 353-63.

(218) Reilly, Timothy. "Genteel Reform versus Southern Allegiance: Episcopal Dilemma in Old New Orleans." *Historical Magazine of the Protestant Episcopal Church* 44 (1975): 437-50.

(219) Rightmyer, Thomas N. "The Holy Orders of Peter Muhlenburg." *Historical Magazine of the Protestant Episcopal Church* 30 (1961): 183-97.

(220) Robertson, Heard. "The Reverend James Seymour, Frontier Parson, 1771-1783." *Historical Magazine of the Protestant Episcopal Church* 45 (1976): 145-53.

(221) Rouse, Parke, Jr. *James Blair, King-Maker of Virginia*. Chapel Hill: University of North Carolina Press, 1971.

(222) _____. "James Blair of Virginia." *Historical Magazine of the Protestant Episcopal Church* 43 (1974): 189-93.

(223) Scott, P. G. "James Blair and the Scottish Church: A New Source." *William and Mary Quarterly* 3d series 33 (1976): 300-308.

(224) Skaggs, David C., and F. Garner Ranney. "Thomas Cradock Sermons." *Maryland Historical Magazine* 67 (1972): 179-80.

(225) _____. "Thomas Cradock's Sermon on the Governance of Maryland's Established Church." *William and Mary Quarterly* 3d series 27 (1970): 630-53.

(226) Starin, Mary M. "The Reverend Doctor John Gordon, 1717-1790." *Maryland Historical Magazine* 75 (1980): 167-91.

(227) Steiner, Bernard C., ed. *Rev. T. Bray: His Life and Selected Works Relating to Maryland*. Baltimore: J. Murphy, 1901.

(228) Stokes, Durward T. "Adam Boyd, Publisher, Preacher, Patriot." *North Carolina Historical Review* 49 (1972): 1-21.

(229) Sydnor, William. "David Griffith: Chaplain, Surgeon, Patriot." *Historical Magazine of the Protestant Episcopal Church* 44 (1975): 247-56.

(230) _____. "Doctor Griffith of Virginia: Emergence of a Church Leader, March, 1779-June 3, 1786." *Historical Magazine of the Protestant Episcopal Church* 45 (1976): 5-24.

(231) _____. "Dr. Griffith of Virginia: The Breaking of a Church Leader, September 1786-August 3, 1789." *Historical Magazine of the Protestant Episcopal Church* 45 (1976): 113-32.

(232) Thompson, Henry P. *Thomas Bray.* London: SPCK, 1954.

(233) Tsuruta, Toshiko. "William Stith, Historian of Colonial Virginia." Ph.D. dissertation, University of Washington, 1957.

(234) Vaughn, Gerald F., and Patricia A. Vaughn. "The Life and Ministry of William Murray Stone, D.D., Bishop of the Protestant Episcopal Diocese of Maryland—1830-1838." *Historical Magazine of the Protestant Episcopal Church* 35 (1966): 313-42.

(235) Vivian, James F., and Jean H. Vivian. "The Reverend Isaac Campbell: An Anti-Lockean Whig." *Historical Magazine of the Protestant Episcopal Church* 39 (1970): 71-89.

(236) Walker, Robert G. "Jonathan Boucher: Champion of the Minority." *William and Mary Quarterly* 3d series 2 (1945): 3-14.

(237) Wall, Bennett H. "Charles Pettigrew, First Bishop-Elect of the North Carolina Episcopal Church." *North Carolina Historical Review* 28 (1951): 15-46.

(238) Willams, George W. *Early Ministers of St. Michael's.* Charleston: Dalcho Historical Society, 1961.

(239) _____. *The Reverend James Warley Miles.* Charleston: Dalcho Historical Society, 1954.

(240) Wilson, Charles Reagan. "Bishop Thomas Frank Gailor: Celebrant of Southern Tradition." *Tennessee Historical Quarterly* 39 (1979): 322-31.

(241) Wood, Lillian F. "The Reverend John LaPierre." *Historical Magazine of the Protestant Episcopal Church* 40 (1971): 407-30.

(242) Wood, Sandra Tyler. "The Reverend John Urmstone—A Portrait of North Carolina." *Historical Magazine of the Protestant Episcopal Church* 41 (1972): 263-85.

(243) Wynes, Charles E. "The Reverend Quincy Ewing: Southern Radical Heretic in the 'Cajun' Country." *Louisiana History* 7 (1966): 221-28.

8 Presbyterianism in the South

PREACHERS OF PRESBYTERIAN PERSUASION, many initially part of the Scotch-Irish movement into the Southern hill country in the eighteenth century, successfully planted American Calvinism's most well-known denomination in the South. Even earlier, Francis Makemie had been instrumental in organizing Presbyterian congregations in Maryland and Virginia as well as helping set up the Presbytery of Philadelphia. Today members of the various Presbyterian groups account for the third largest cluster of Southern Protestants. Much of the early story of Presbyterianism in the South is connected with the evangelical surge associated with the Great Awakening and the ministry of Samuel Davies, both of which are discussed in chapter 2.

For many years, Presbyterians in the South shared a common history with Presbyterians throughout the new nation, but in time issues of concern to many American Protestant groups also brought differences of conviction among Presbyterians. Some were primarily concerned with matters of theology, particularly adherence to notions of election. These ultimately raised questions about the nature of conversion in the revival experience, for calls for conversion seemed to undercut the notion that salvation depended on God's election alone. Others became uneasy about the cooperative alliance established with Congregationalists in 1801 (the Plan of Union of 1801) designed to facilitate evangelization of newer areas of settlement as Americans moved over westward. Here the major bone of contention was polity, for Presbyterians and Congregationalists differed over the authority over local congregations of larger administrative bodies. Yet others became concerned about the relationship between the churches and the political order, particularly as a passion for social reform swept through much of American evangelical Protestantism. Some kinds of involvement in social reform quite simply appeared as meddling in politics, as tampering with a realm God had ordained to maintain order and hence one with an authority of its own. All three interacted to promote divisions within the Presbyterian family that ultimately issued in a Southern Presbyterianism with a regional consciousness of its own.

While the issues regarding polity may have steered Presbyterians into forming their own denominational groupings, controversy over use of revival techniques and the voluntary societies bent on social reform that emerged from early nineteenth-century revivalism brought schism within the Presbyterian family. The division of the parent Presbyterian body in the 1830s into Old School and New School groups, depending on whether one supported revivalism and religious ventures in social reform, was only one split that has marked Presbyterian history, for as abolitionist sentiment grew in the North and proslavery defensiveness correspondingly grew in the South, a regional division also ensued, ultimately bringing Old and New School Presbyterians together, but along regional lines. The split over slavery was directly responsible for the creation of what was to become the South's leading Presbyterian denomination, the Presbyterian Church in the United States (originally designated the Presbyterian Church in the Confederate States of America). Many Southerners, though, rejected the idea that slavery had caused the division, arguing instead that the church had become involved too much in politics to remain a genuinely spiritual enterprise. They saw the break as a way to maintain the purity of the church. Hence the Southern body augmented traditional Presbyterian teaching by emphasizing the "spirituality" of the church, a tenet that eschewed involvement of religious bodies in political and social controversy. This concern should be seen as a theological rationale designed at first to allow Presbyterians to avoid wrestling with the moral and religious issues central to the slavery crisis. It has meant, however, that Southern Presbyterians have had somewhat greater difficulty in dealing with social issues over the years, a matter that will be noted in chapter 20.

All these matters remain areas of scholarly inquiry and differences of interpretation. Presbyterians, however, were actively involved in various forms of ministry to Afro-Americans, both before and after the Civil War, and in Indian missions, as the bibliographies to chapters 3 and 4 testify. In addition, Presbyterian thinkers have also been in the forefront of theological developments in the South, as noted in chapter 21. Not until 1983 were merger plans implemented to reunite the major Northern and Southern Presbyterian bodies. Unfortunately, there is a dearth of interpretive and analytical literature about the many smaller Presbyterian denominations that have also found a home in Dixie: the Presbyterian Church in America, the Orthodox Presbyterian Church, the Associate Reformed Presbyterian Church, the Cumberland Presbyterian Church, and others.

Numerous studies place Southern developments within the larger Presbyterian picture. Leonard Trinterud, *The Forming of an American Tradition* (36), remains an important work on the beginnings of Presbyterianism in the United States. Much material in Julius Melton, *Presbyterian Worship in America* (18), pertains to liturgical developments in the South. Elwyn Smith, *The Presbyterian Ministry in American Culture* (28), also includes much of interest to students of the Southern tradition. On topics of more contemporary concern, Lois A. Boyd and R. Douglas Brackenridge, *Presbyterian Women in America* (8), note the vital role of women in Southern Presbyterian circles. There is as well a vast literature that addresses more specifically regional matters.

Ernest Trice Thompson's monumental three-volume work, *Presbyterians in the South* (34), is the basic starting point for any exploration of the contours of Southern Presbyterianism. Thompson, for more than forty years professor of church history at the Presbyterian Union Theological Seminary in Richmond, exemplifies the best of traditional church history in his study, providing not only a massive amount of detailed information, but also a sensitivity to the cultural context that nurtured the denomination. Thompson's awareness of the ways in which Southern culture had deeply influenced the course of Presbyterianism is central to his *The Changing South and the Presbyterian Church in the United States* (33), while his recognition that Southern Presbyterians shared a common religious heritage with fellow denominationalists in the North is seen in his "Presbyterians North and South—Efforts Toward Reunion" (35). An appreciation of Thompson's Herculean contributions to tracing the course of Southern Presbyterianism and examining its nuances is Edgar C. Mayse, "Ernest Trice Thompson: Presbyterian of the South" (103).

There are numerous other studies of the Southern Presbyterian adventure worthy of note. One of the earliest, still worth careful perusal, is Thomas C. Johnson, *History of the Southern Presbyterian Church* (14), part of the American Church History Series edited by Philip Schaff in the 1890s. Johnson's work, however, is frequently more defensive than critical, arguing for the necessity of maintaining a separate Southern church. Margaret B. DesChamps's doctoral dissertation. "The Presbyterian Church in the South Atlantic States, 1801-1861" (9), focuses on the early history prior to the regional division, while Walter B. Posey, *The Presbyterian Church in the Old Southwest, 1778-1838* (26), chronicles developments down to the Old School-New School split. T. Watson Street, *The Story of Southern Presbyterians* (32), is written in a popular vein and lacks the critical acumen of most of the studies noted above. Harold M. Parker, Jr., *Studies in Southern Presbyterian His-*

tory (25), offers a collection of essays on various topics and themes that have shaped Presbyterianism's life in the South, while Morton H. Smith, *Studies in Southern Presbyterian Theology* (30), is a valuable introduction to that topic, written from a conservative perspective.

The impetus toward defining the "spirituality" of the church and its consequences particularly for individual and social ethics informs William D. Blanks, "Ideal and Practice: A Study of the Conception of the Christian Life Prevailing in the Presbyterian Churches of the South During the Nineteenth Century" (7), a doctoral dissertation. The internal debates over revivalism and the voluntary societies that issued in the division of 1837-1838 have been treated in several works. The best overall study of the voluntary societies and their Southern endeavors is John Kuykendall, *"Southern Enterprize"* (20:21). But also see Lois W. Banner, "Presbyterians and Voluntarism in the Early Republic" (2). That apprehension about the impact of religious social reform on the South's "peculiar institution" was central to the Old School/New School controversy is a major theme articulated by Edmund A. Moore, *Robert J. Breckenridge and the Slavery Aspect of the Presbyterian Schism of 1837* (20). A careful study of the other ways in which a regional consciousness propelled division into Old School/New School camps is Elwyn A. Smith, "The Role of the South in the Presbyterian Schism of 1837-1838" (29). Two "case studies" by Harold M. Parker, Jr., however, suggest that this division masked fundamental agreement on many issues, particularly those touching on slavery: "The New School Synod of Kentucky" (60) and "Synod of Kentucky: From Old School to the Southern Church" (61). A pre-Civil War attempt to form a regional denomination that was based in Georgia is the subject of another essay by Parker: "The Cassville Convention: Aborted Birth of a Southern Presbyterian Church" (22). However, the onset of the North-South struggle did provide that impetus but did not mean that all Presbyterians in the region were anti-Union, as seen in Haskell Monroe, "Southern Presbyterians and the Secession Crisis" (19).

There are many nineteenth- and early twentieth-century studies of the development of Presbyterianism in individual Southern states. Most are admirable in their attention to detail, marked by a filiopietistic tone, and short on critical analysis. They will not be noted here, but most are included in the bibliographical listings at the end of this chapter. Of the recent more scholarly studies, many are theses, dissertations, or articles. Thomas C. Cannon, "Founders of Missouri Presbyterianism" (43), looks at early developments in that state. Cooper C. Kirk's doctoral dissertation, "A History of the Southern Presbyterian Church in Florida, 1821-1891" (54), provides an introduction to the important nineteenth-century developments there, while George W. Troxler, "The Story of Presbyterianism in North Carolina" (69), a master's thesis, offers a solid survey of the early days in a state where Presbyterians have exhibited particular strength. Richard B. Hughes's dissertation, "Old School Presbyterians in Texas, 1830-1861" (52), and the article derived from it, "Old School Presbyterians: Eastern Invaders of Texas, 1830-1865" (51), offer judicious insight into Lone Star Presbyterianism. Of course, the Northern Presbyterians maintained a Southern presence even after the regional division that gave birth to the Southern church. The Northern Presbyterian experience in Texas is summarized in George H. Paschal, Jr., and Judith A. Benner, *One Hundred Years of Challenge and Change: A History of the Synod of Texas of the United Presbyterian Church in the U.S.A.* (63), a work complemented by Paschal's dissertation, "The History of the U.S.A. Presbyterian Church in Texas and Louisiana, 1868-1920" (62). A popular history of Louisiana Presbyterians, grounded in good historical research, is C. Penrose St. Amant, *A History of the Presbyterian Church in Louisiana* (66). William Foote has offered important studies of Virginia Presbyterianism in *An Index to Sketches of Virginia* (46). Also see Patricia Aldridge, ed., *Virginia Presbyterians in American Life, Hanover Presbytery (1755-1980)* (39), which provides an entree into regional developments in the area of Virginia where Presbyterians first gained a strong constituency. Howard Wilson, *The Tinkling Spring, Headwater of Freedom* (83), describes the history of one valley congregation to the present.

A number of biographical and autobiographical studies merit mention here, and the listing which follows should be complemented by relevant titles in chapters 2, 4, 19, and 21. On the late seventeenth- and early eighteenth-century work of Francis Makemie, see Boyd D. Schlenther, ed., *The Life and Writings of Francis Makemie* (120). Prominent among Georgia Presbyterians in the eighteenth century was Savannah pastor and Swiss immigrant John Joachim Zubly. Zubly rose to prominence during the era of the American Revolution because, although he denounced British pre-Revolutionary colonial policy, he nevertheless regarded the bond between colonies and mother country as inviolate. He was, therefore, perceived as a Loyalist and consequently imprisoned for a time. Three articles provide brief surveys of his life and career: Leo Schelbert, "The American Revolution, A Lesson in Dissent: The Case of John Joachim Zubly" (119); William E. Pauley, Jr., "Tragic Hero: Loyalist John J. Zubly" (115); and Roger A. Martin, "John J. Zubly Comes to America" (100). For a selection of Zubly's pamphlets with a critical introduction and bibliography, see Randall M. Miller, ed., *"A Warm and Zealous Spirit"* (108).

Several nineteenth-century Presbyterians not only offered leadership to their own denomination—many helping to form the Southern denomination in the 1860s—but also made notable contributions to religious thought in the South, as will be noted in chapter 21. Among these is Robert Lewis Dabney (1820-1898), pastor and professor at Union Theological Seminary (now located in Richmond) whose commitment to Southern mores was so strong that he not only declined pastoral and professorial appointments in the North, he also advocated Southern emigration to South America after the Confederate defeat. The two standard biographies are Thomas C. Johnson, *The Life and Letters of Robert Lewis Dabney* (98), and David H. Overy's dissertation, ''Robert L. Dabney: Apostle of the South'' (113). Charles Reagan Wilson, ''Robert Lewis Dabney: Religion and the Southern Holocaust'' (125), looks particularly at Dabney's promotion of South American emigration. John Holt Rice, first administrative head of Union Seminary, also had a keen interest in revivalism and evangelical social reform, which he promoted in the pages of several periodicals he edited, including the *Virginia Evangelical and Literary Magazine*. Two biographies and one master's thesis provide an overview of his distinguished contributions to Southern Presbyterianism: Philip B. Price, *The Life of the Reverend John Holt Rice, D.D.* (116), reprinted in 1963; William Maxwell, *A Memoir of the Rev. John H. Rice, D.D., First Professor of Christian Theology in Union Theological Seminary, Virginia* (102); and Julius W. Melton, Jr., ''Pioneering Presbyter: A Collection and Analysis of the Letters of John Holt Rice'' (105). Benjamin Morgan Palmer (1818-1902) was an ardent advocate of Southern secession, prominent pastor, founder of the *Southern Presbyterian Review,* and first moderator of the Southern Presbyterian church. The major published biography is Thomas C. Johnson, *The Life and Letters of Benjamin Morgan Palmer* (97), but also see Doralyn J. Hickey's doctoral dissertation, ''Benjamin Morgan Palmer: Churchman of the Old South'' (93). Irish immigrant Thomas Smyth (1808-1873) gained prominence as a Charleston pastor and as an adamant defender of Presbyterian polity. His career deserves more careful scrutiny; T. Erskine Clarke's dissertation, ''Thomas Smyth: Moderate of the Old South'' (89), is a good beginning. Perhaps the most important theologian of antebellum Presbyterianism was James Henley Thornwell (1812-1862), who forcefully articulated the notion of the ''spirituality'' of the church basic to the formation of the Southern Presbyterian church. Benjamin Morgan Palmer, *Life and Letters of James Henley Thornwell* (114), is an appreciative, if uncritical, study. The most trenchant analysis is H. Shelton Smith, ''The Church and the Social Order as Interpreted by James Henley Thornwell'' (123), but also see Paul Garber, ''A Centennial Appraisal of James Henley Thornwell'' (91) and the several titles concerning Thornwell's theological thought in the bibliography to chapter 20. Another Presbyterian dedicated to the ''Lost Cause'' was Moses Drury Hoge (1819-1899), pastor of Richmond's Second Presbyterian Church for fifty-four years. His nephew, Peyton H. Hoge, has written *Moses Drury Hoge: Life and Letters* (94). Not all leading Presbyterians in the South in the nineteenth century supported the Confederate cause. Among the ardent Unionists was Kentucky pastor and educator Robert Jefferson Breckenridge (1800-1871). On his life and career, see Edgar C. Mayse's unpublished dissertation, "Robert Jefferson Breckenridge: American Presbyterian Controversialist" (104).

In the late nineteenth and early twentieth centuries when all Protestant denominations wrestled with the competing claims of "fundamentalism" and "modernism," one son of the South gained prominence as an outspoken advocate of fundamentalism, but a fundamentalism grounded in rigorous analysis: J. Gresham Machen. While Machen's career was centered in the north, C. Allyn Russell, "J. Gresham Machen, Scholarly Fundamentalist" (118), argues convincingly that one cannot understand Machen's deep commitment to fundamentalism without acknowledging his Southern roots. By contrast, Presbyterian layman Francis P. Miller of Virginia in the twentieth century offered a liberal approach to matters of race grounded in deep religious convictions, contributed much to the ecumenical movement locally, nationally, and internationally, and for a time was a force in Virginia politics. His autobiography, *Man from the Valley: Memoirs of a Twentieth Century Virginian* (106), is a compelling account of one individual's struggle with the social and religious forces of the twentieth century that ultimately brought change to a South that still harbored antebellum ideals.

Some studies of other Presbyterian bodies, though few in number overall, deserve mention. The Associate Reformed Presbyterian Church—formed in 1822 by descendants of Scottish Presbyterian immigrants who had broken away from the Church of Scotland and today are concentrated largely in upstate South Carolina and the area around Charlotte, North Carolina—has its story told in a work that combines popular and academic styles: *A History of the Associate Reformed Presbyterian Church* by Ray A. King (15). Earlier, in 1810, the Cumberland Presbyterian Church arose in Tennessee, although it did not begin formal organization until 1813. Cumberland Presbyterians dissented from some of the tenets of a "strict" Calvinism and attempted to combine principles reflecting both moderate Calvinism and moderate Arminianism in their confessional statements. While most Cumberland Presbyterians reunited with the Presbyterian Church in the United States of America in 1906, those who did not continued in a denomination which retained the Cumberland name. Ben M. Barrus explores "Factors Involved in the Origin of the Cumberland Presbyterian Church" (3) in an article by that title, and with others has written the standard history, *A People Called Cumberland Presbyterians* (4). These works supplement B. W. McDonnold's two volume *History of the Cumberland Presbyterian Church* (17), published in the late nineteenth century, and Robert V. Foster's contribution to the American Church History Series of 1894, *A Sketch of the History of the Cumberland Presbyterian Church* (10). On the reunion with the parent denomination, see John T. Ames, "Cumberland Liberals and the Union of 1906" (1).

The bibliography that follows presents first regional and topical studies of Southern Presbyterianism. It then lists numerous state and local studies, concluding with works of a biographical or autobiographical nature. Articles of interest to students of Southern Presbyterians appear regularly in periodicals such as the *Journal of Presbyterian History* and *Presbyterian Survey*.

BIBLIOGRAPHY

Several titles in the listings for chapters 1, 2, 3, 4, 18, 19, 20, and 21 are also relevant to the study of Presbyterianism in the South.

I. SOUTHERN PRESBYTERIANS: GENERAL AND TOPICAL STUDIES

(1) Ames, John T. "Cumberland Liberals and the Union of 1906." *Journal of Presbyterian History* 52 (1974): 3-18.

(2) Banner, Lois W. "Presbyterians and Voluntarism in the Early Republic." *Journal of Presbyterian History* 50 (1972): 187-205.

(3) Barrus, Ben M. "Factors Involved in the Origin of the Cumberland Presbyterian Church." *Journal of Presbyterian History* 45 (1967): 273-89.

(4) _____, et al. *A People Called Cumberland Presbyterians.* Memphis: Frontier Press, 1972.

(5) Batchelor, Alexander R. *Jacob's Ladder: Negro Work of the Presbyterian Church in the United States.* Atlanta: Presbyterian Church in the United States Board of Church Extension, 1953.

(6) Blanks, W. D. "Corrective Church Discipline in the Presbyterian Churches of the Nineteenth Century South." *Journal of Presbyterian History* 44 (1966): 89-105.

(7) _____. "Ideal and Practice: A Study of the Conception of the Christian Life Prevailing in the Presbyterian Churches of the South During the Nineteenth Century." Th.D. dissertation, Union Theological Seminary (VA), 1960.

(8) Boyd, Lois A., and R. Douglas Brackenridge. *Presbyterian Women in America: Two Centuries of a Quest for Status.* Westport CT: Greenwood Press, 1983.

(9) DesChamps, Margaret B. "The Presbyterian Church in the South Atlantic States, 1801-1861." Ph.D. dissertation, Emory University, 1952.

(10) Foster, Robert V. *A Sketch of the History of the Cumberland Presbyterian Church.* American Church History Series 11. New York: Christian Literature, 1894.

(11) Fraser, William H. "Why I Favor Preserving the Southern Church." *Southern Presbyterian Journal* 11 (1952).

(12) Green, Ashbel. *A Historical or Compendious View of the Domestic and Foreign Missions in the Presbyterian Church of the United States of America.* Philadelphia: W. S. Martien, 1838. Reprinted as *Presbyterian Missions.* John C. Lowrie, ed. New York: A. D. F. Randolph, 1893.

(13) Hollis, Daniel W., and Carl Julien. *Look to the Rock: One Hundred Antebellum Presbyterian Churches of the South.* Richmond: John Knox Press, 1961.

(14) Johnson, Thomas C. *History of the Southern Presbyterian Church.* American Church History Series 11. New York: Christian Literature, 1894.

(15) King, Ray A. *A History of the Associate Reformed Presbyterian Church.* Charlotte NC: Board of Christian Education of the Associate Reformed Presbyterian Church, 1967.

(16) Klett, Guy S., ed. *Minutes of the Presbyterian Church in America, 1706-1788.* Philadelphia: Presbyterian Historical Society, 1976.

(17) McDonnold, B. W. *History of the Cumberland Presbyterian Church.* 2d ed. Nashville: Board of Publication of the Cumberland Presbyterian Church, 1888.

(18) Melton, Julius. *Presbyterian Worship in America: Changing Patterns since 1787.* Richmond: John Knox Press, 1967.

(19) Monroe, Haskell. "Southern Presbyterians and the Secession Crisis." *Civil War History* 6 (1960): 351-60.

(20) Moore, Edmund A. *Robert J. Breckenridge and the Slavery Aspect of the Presbyterian Schism of 1837.* Chicago: Private edition distributed by the University of Chicago Libraries, 1935.

(21) Morrow, Herbert W. "Admission of the Cumberland Presbyterian Church to the Wren Alliance of Reformed Churches." *Journal of Presbyterian History* 51 (1973): 59-73.

(22) Parker, Harold M., Jr. "The Cassville Convention: Aborted Birth of a Southern Presbyterian Church." *Historian* 42 (1980): 612-30.

(23) _____. "The Independent Presbyterian Church and Reunion in the South, 1813-1863." *Journal of Presbyterian History* 50 (1972): 89-110.

(24) _____. "Southern Ecumenicism: Six Successful Unions." *Journal of Presbyterian History* 56 (1978): 91-106.

(25) _____. *Studies in Southern Presbyterian History.* Gunnison CO: B & B Printers, 1979.

(26) Posey, Walter B. *The Presbyterian Church in the Old Southwest, 1778-1838.* Richmond: John Knox Press, 1952.

(27) Scott, Eugene C. *Ministerial Directory of the Presbyterian Church, U.S., 1861-1941.* Revised and supplemented, 1942-1950. Atlanta: Hubbard Printing, 1950.

(28) Smith, Elwyn A. *The Presbyterian Ministry in America: A Study in Changing Concepts, 1700-1900.* Philadelphia: Westminster Press for the Presbyterian Historical Society, 1962.

(29) _____. "The Role of the South in the Presbyterian Schism of 1837-1838." *Church History* 29 (1960): 44-63.

(30) Smith, Morton H. *Studies in Southern Presbyterian Theology.* Jackson MS: Presbyterian Reformation Society, 1962. Also Amsterdam: J. Van Campen, 1962.

(31) Street, T. Watson. "Southern Presbyterians and Evangelicalism." *Christianity Today* 5 (2 January 1961): 23-24.

(32) _____. *The Story of Southern Presbyterians*. Richmond: John Knox Press, 1960.

(33) Thompson, Ernest Trice. *The Changing South and the Presbyterian Church in the United States*. Richmond: John Knox Press, 1950.

(34) _____. *Presbyterians in the South*. 3 vols. Richmond: John Knox Press, 1963-1973.

(35) _____. "Presbyterians North and South—Efforts Toward Reunion." *Journal of Presbyterian History* 43 (1965): 1-15.

(36) Trinterud, Leonard J. *The Forming of an American Tradition: A Re-examination of Colonial Presbyterianism*. Freeport NY: Books for Libraries, 1970. First published 1949.

(37) VanderVelde, Lewis G. *The Early Presbyterian Churches and the Federal Union, 1861-1869*. Cambridge: Harvard University Press, 1932.

(38) Weeks, Louis F., and James C. Hickey. " 'Implied Trust' for Connectional Churches: *Watson v. Jones* Revisited." *Journal of Presbyterian History* 54 (1976): 459-70.

II. SOUTHERN PRESBYTERIANS: STUDIES BY STATE

(39) Aldridge, Patricia, ed. *Virginia Presbyterians in American Life: Hanover Presbytery (1755-1980)*. Richmond: Hanover Presbytery, 1982.

(40) Alexander, John E. *A Brief History of the Synod of Texas, from 1817 to 1887*. Philadelphia: MacCalla, 1890.

(41) Brackenridge, R. Douglas, et al. "Presbyterian Missions to Mexican Americans in Texas in the Nineteenth Century." *Journal of Presbyterian History* 49 (1971): 103-32.

(42) _____. *Voice in the Wilderness: A History of the Cumberland Presbyterian Church in Texas*. San Antonio: Trinity University Press, 1968.

(43) Cannon, Thomas C. "Founders of Missouri Presbyterianism." *Journal of Presbyterian History* 46 (1968): 197-218.

(44) Davidson, Robert. *History of the Presbyterian Church in the State of Kentucky: With a Preliminary Sketch of the Churches in the Valley of Virginia*. Greenwood SC: Attic Press, 1974. First published 1847.

(45) DeLozier, Mary Jean. "A Presbyterian Property Dispute Before the Tennessee Supreme Court." *Journal of Presbyterian History* 45 (1967): 193-202.

(46) Foote, William H. *An Index to Sketches of Virginia, Historical and Biographical*. Richmond: Union Theological Seminary in Virginia Library, 1966.

(47) _____. *Sketches of North Carolina, Historical and Biographical, Illustrative of a Portion of Her Early Settlers*. 3d ed. Raleigh: H. J. Dudley, for the Committee on Historical Matters of the Synod of North Carolina, Presbyterian Church in the U.S., 1965.

(48) Graves, Fred R., comp. *The Presbyterian Work in Mississippi*. Sumner MS: Sentinel Press, 1927.

(49) Heiskell, Carrick W., et al.: *Pioneer Presbyterianism in Tennessee*. Richmond: Presbyterian Committee of Publication, 1898.

(50) Howe, George. *History of the Presbyterian Church in South Carolina*. Columbia: Duffie and Chapman, 1870.

(51) Hughes, Richard B. "Old School Presbyterians: Eastern Invaders of Texas, 1830-1865." *Southwestern Historical Quarterly* 74 (1971): 324-36.

(52) _____. "Old School Presbyterians in Texas, 1830-1861." Ph.D. dissertation, University of Texas at Austin, 1963.

(53) Jones, Frank D., and W. H. Mills, eds. *History of the Presbyterian Church in South Carolina since 1850*. Columbia: R. L. Bryan, 1926.

(54) Kirk, Cooper C. "A History of the Southern Presbyterian Church in Florida, 1821-1891." Ph.D. dissertation, Florida State University, 1966.

(55) McIlvain, James William. *Early Presbyterianism in Maryland*. Baltimore: Johns Hopkins University Press, 1890.

(56) McIlwain, William E. *The Early Planting of Presbyterianism in West Florida*. Pensacola: Mayes Printing, 1926.

(57) Monroe, Haskell. "South Carolina and the Formation of the Presbyterian Church in the Confederate States of America." *Journal of Presbyterian History* 42 (1964): 219-43.

(58) Parker, Harold M., Jr. "The Kentucky Presbytery of the Associate Reformed Presbyterian Church." *Filson Club Historical Quarterly* 47 (1972): 322-39.

(59) _____. "Much Wealth and Intelligence: The Presbytery of Patapsco." *Maryland Historical Magazine* 60 (1965): 160-74.

(60) _____. "The New School Synod of Kentucky." *Filson Club Historical Quarterly* 50 (1976): 52-59.

(61) _____. "Synod of Kentucky: From Old School to the Southern Church." *Journal of Presbyterian History* 41 (1963): 14-36.

(62) Paschal, George H. "The History of the U.S.A. Presbyterian Church in Texas and Louisiana, 1868-1920." Ph.D. dissertation, Louisiana State University, 1967.

(63) _____, and Judith A. Benner. *One Hundred Years of Challenge and Change: A History of the Synod of Texas of the United Presbyterian Church in the U.S.A.* San Antonio: Trinity University Press, 1968.

(64) Red, William Stuart. *A History of the Presbyterian Church in Texas*. Austin: Steck, 1936.

(65) Rumple, Jethro. *The History of Presbyterianism in North Carolina*. Richmond: Union Theological Seminary Library, 1966. First published 1878-1887.

(66) St. Amant, C. Penrose. *A History of the Presbyterian Church in Louisiana*. [New Orleans?]: Synod of Louisiana, 1961.

(67) Stacy, James. *A History of the Presbyterian Church in Georgia.* Elberton GA: Press of the Star, 1912.

(68) Stone, William J., Jr. "Texas' First Church Newspaper: The Texas Presbyterian, 1846-1856." *Texana* 11 (1973): 239-47.

(69) Troxler, George W. "The Story of Presbyterianism in North Carolina". M.A. thesis, University of North Carolina in Chapel Hill, 1966.

III. SOUTHERN PRESBYTERIANS: LOCAL STUDIES

(70) Allison, Patrick. *First Presbyterian Church, Baltimore, Md.: Rise and Progress (1793).* Baltimore: C. S. Stirling, 1895.

(71) Blanton, Wyndham B. *The Making of a Downtown Church: The History of the Second Presbyterian Church, Richmond, Virginia, 1845-1945.* Richmond: John Knox Press, 1945.

(72) Byars, Patti W. "Jonesboro Presbyterians Celebrate Centennial." *Georgia Life* 6 (1979): 34-35.

(73) Cooper, James F. "An Historical Sketch of the Indiantown Presbyterian Church." Manuscript, South Caroliniana Library, 1957.

(74) Fayetteville Presbytery. *One Hundred and Twenty-Fifth Anniversary Addresses, Fayetteville Presbytery.* [Fayetteville?]: n.p., [1938?].

(75) *A History of the First Presbyterian Church of Tulsa, Oklahoma, 1885-1960.* Tulsa: n.p., 1960.

(76) Lytch, William E. *History of Bethesda Presbyterian Church, 1765-1965, Caswell County, North Carolina.* Yanceville NC: n.p., 1965.

(77) Mecklenberg Presbytery. *The Semi-Centennial of Mecklenberg Presbytery, 1869-1919.* [Charlotte?]: n.p., 1919.

(78) Martin, Carrie D. *The Story of the Sixty-Six Years on This Corner: Highland Presbyterian Church, Louisville, Kentucky.* Louisville: n.p., 1942.

(79) Stietentroth, Charles W. *One Hundred Years of "Old Trinity" Church, Natchez.* Natchez MS: Natchez Printing and Stationery, 1922.

(80) Stone, Robert H. *A History of the Orange Presbytery, 1770-1970.* Greensboro NC: n.p., 1970.

(81) Sykes, James Lundy. *A History of Saint John's Parish, Aberdeen, Maryland.* N.p.p.: n.p., n.d.

(82) Vernon, Dodd. "The Associate Reformed Presbyterians in Lamar City, Texas." *East Texas Historical Journal* 6 (1968): 33-55.

(83) Wilson, Howard M. *The Tinkling Spring, Headwater of Freedom: A Study of the Church and Her People, 1732-1952.* Fishersville VA: Tinkling Spring and Hermitage Presbyterian Churches, 1954. Reprinted, 1974.

IV. SOUTHERN PRESBYTERIANS: BIOGRAPHICAL AND AUTOBIOGRAPHICAL STUDIES

Works examining the life and work of Samuel Davies are included primarily in chapter 2, although scattered titles appear elsewhere, while those treating Charles Colcock Jones are listed in chapter 4.

(84) Blackburn, George Andrew. *The Life Work of John L. Girardeau, D.D.* Columbia: State, 1916.

(85) Boyd, Lois A., and R. Douglas Brackenridge. "Rachel Henderlite: Women and Church Union." *Journal of Presbyterian History* 56 (1978): 10-18.

(86) Brackenridge, R. Douglas. "Sumner Beacon: 'The Apostle of Texas'." *Journal of Presbyterian History* 45 (1967): 247-55.

(87) Briceland, Alan V. "Daniel McCalla, 1748-1809: New Side Revolutionary and Jeffersonian." *Journal of Presbyterian History* 56 (1978): 252-69.

(88) Brown, Douglas S. "Charles Cummings: The Fighting Parson of Southwest Virginia." *Virginia Cavalcade* 28 (1979): 138-43.

(89) Clarke, T. Erskine. "Thomas Smyth: Moderate of the Old South." Th.D. dissertation, Union Theological Seminary (VA), 1970.

(90) Converse, Amasa. "Autobiography of the Rev. Amasa Converse." *Journal of Presbyterian History* 43 (1965): 197-218, 254-63.

(91) Garber, Paul. "A Centennial Appraisal of James Henley Thornwell." In *A Miscellany of American Christianity*. Stuart C. Henry, ed. Durham: Duke University Press, 1963.

(92) Hartwell, Mrs. Charles K. "Mobile to China: A Valiant Woman's Mission." *Alabama Review* 31 (1978): 243-55.

(93) Hickey, Doralyn J. "Benjamin Morgan Palmer: Churchman of the Old South." Ph.D. dissertation, Duke University, 1962.

(94) Hoge, Peyton H. *Moses Drury Hoge: Life and Letters*. Richmond: Presbyterian Committee of Publication, 1899.

(95) Hughes, Richard B. "Sumner Beacon, Frontier Apostle and Legend." *Texas* 4 (1966): 93-103.

(96) Hutchison, John R. *Reminiscences, Sketches, and Addresses, Selected from My Papers during a Ministry of Forty-Five Years in Mississippi, Louisiana, and Texas*. Houston: Cushing, 1874.

(97) Johnson, Thomas C. *The Life and Letters of Benjamin Morgan Palmer*. Richmond: Presbyterian Committee of Publication, 1906.

(98) ———. *The Life and Letters of Robert Lewis Dabney*. Richmond: Presbyterian Committee of Publication, 1903.

(99) Jones, Walter L. "Francis Mackemie, Disturbing Dissenter." *Virginia Cavalcade* 17 (1967): 27-31.

(100) Martin, Roger A. "John J. Zubly Comes to America." *Georgia Historical Quarterly* 61 (1977): 125-39.

(101) ———. "John J. Zubly: Preacher, Planter, and Politician." Ph.D. dissertation, University of Georgia, 1976.

(102) Maxwell, William. *A Memoir of the Rev. John H. Rice, D.D., First Professor of Christian Theology in Union Theological Seminary, Virginia*. Philadelphia: J. Whetham, 1835.

(103) Mayse, Edgar C. "Ernest Trice Thompson: Presbyterian of the South." *Journal of Presbyterian History* 56 (1978): 36-46.

(104) _____. "Robert Jefferson Breckenridge: American Presbyterian Contro-versialist." Thesis, Union Theological Seminary (VA), 1974.

(105) Melton, Julius W., Jr. "Pioneering Presbyter: A Collection and Analysis of the Letters of John Holt Rice." Th.M. thesis, Union Theological Seminary (VA), 1959.

(106) Miller, Francis P. *Man from the Valley: Memoirs of a Twentieth Century Virginian.* Chapel Hill: University of North Carolina Press, 1971.

(107) Miller, Mark E. "David Caldwell: The Forming of a Southern Educator." Thesis, University of North Carolina in Chapel Hill, 1979.

(108) Miller, Randall M., ed. *"A Warm and Zealous Spirit": John J. Zubly and the American Revolution, A Selection of His Writings.* Macon GA: Mercer University Press, 1982.

(109) Monroe, Haskell. "Bishop Palmer's Thanksgiving Day Address." *Louisiana History* 4 (1963): 105-18.

(110) Moore, Walter W. *Appreciations and Historical Addresses.* Richmond: Presbyterian Committee of Publication, [1914?].

(111) Mulder, John M. "Joseph Ruggles Wilson: Southern Presbyterian Patri-arch." *Journal of Presbyterian History* 52 (1974): 245-71.

(112) Opie, John. "The Melancholy Career of 'Father' David Rice." *Journal of Presbyterian History* 47 (1969): 295-319.

(113) Overy, David H. "Robert L. Dabney: Apostle of the South." Ph.D. dis-sertation, University of Wisconsin, 1967.

(114) Palmer, Benjamin Morgan. *Life and Letters of James Henley Thornwell.* Richmond: Whittet and Shepperson, 1875.

(115) Pauley, William E., Jr. "Tragic Hero: Loyalist John J. Zubly." *Journal of Presbyterian History* 44 (1976): 61-81.

(116) Price, Philip B. *The Life of the Reverend John Holt Rice, D.D.* Richmond: Union Theological Seminary in Virginia Library, 1963. First published 1886-1887.

(117) Rogers, Tommy W. "Frederick A. Ross: Huntsville's Belligerent Clergy-man." *Alabama Review* 22 (1969): 53-67.

(118) Russell, C. Allyn. "J. Gresham Machen, Scholarly Fundamentalist." *Journal of Presbyterian History* 5 (1973): 41-69.

(119) Schelbert, Leo. "The American Revolution, A Lesson in Dissent: The Case of John Joachim Zubly." *Swiss American Historical Society Newsletter* 12 (1976): 3-11.

(120) Schlenther, Boyd S. *The Life and Writings of Francis Makemie.* Philadel-phia: Presbyterian Historical Society, 1971.

(121) Seamon, Janice Louise. "John Joachim Zubly: A Voice for Liberty and Principle." M.A. thesis, University of South Carolina at Columbia, 1982.

(122) Skemer, Don C. "The Papers of William A. McDowell: A New Jersey Presbyterian in Charleston." *South Carolina Historical Magazine* 79 (1978): 19-22.

(123) Smith, H. Shelton. "The Church and the Social Order as Interpreted by James Henley Thornwell." *Church History* 7 (1938): 45-124.

(124) Stokes, Durward T. "Henry Pattillo in North Carolina." *North Carolina Historical Review* 44 (1967): 373-91

(125) Wilson, Charles Reagan. "Robert Lewis Dabney: Religion and the Southern Holocaust." *Virginia Magazine of History and Biography* 89 (1981): 79-89.

(126) Woodruff, Stephen A. "William H. Black: Missouri Leader in the Ecumenical Movement." *Missouri Historical Review* 67 (1972): 75-97.

9 Baptists in the South

THE BAPTIST PRESENCE has virtually dominated Southern mainstream Protestantism for more than a century, to such an extent that in some circles critics cavalierly refer to Dixie as the region "where there are more Baptists than people." Among Southern white Baptists, the Southern Baptist Convention represents the largest group of the Baptist family, a matter that occasions little surprise as the SBC is likewise the numerically largest Protestant denomination in the United States. Indeed, many of the studies noted in chapter 2 that provide an interpretive overview of Southern religion base much of their analysis on the influence of Baptists on the region's religious life. Today it is easy to forget that Baptists were once a minority in the South, as elsewhere, and that they faced a long struggle against established religious, political, social, and economic interests before they secured their place in Southern culture. Also as noted in chapter 2, the revivals of the Great Awakening and the camp meetings of the frontier, coupled with migration to inland areas and then westward across the mountains, were largely responsible for nurturing Baptist growth in the eighteenth and nineteenth centuries. Prior to denominational divisions over slavery that gave birth to—among others—the Southern Baptist Convention, Baptists in the South did not regard themselves as a distinctively regional body, but as part of that evangelical Protestantism that exercised a near hegemony nationally. Of course, not all white Baptists in the South belong to churches affiliated with the Southern Baptist Convention. Countless "independent" Baptist churches dot rural regions in the South and also may be found in many towns and cities. Jerry Falwell's well-known Thomas Road Baptist Church in Lynchburg, Virginia, for example, is an "independent" Baptist congregation. There are numerous smaller Baptists bodies as well, such as the Free Will Baptists, Primitive Baptists, and others. Relatively little secondary literature exists about these smaller Baptist bodies, although a few titles will be noted here. For a solid introduction to the Baptist ethos that sheds light on many of these developments, see Brooks Hays and John E. Steely, *The Baptist Way of Life* (39). Attention should also be called to the *Encyclopedia of Southern Baptists* (1:103) and the *Encyclopedia of Religion in the South* (1:112) as well as other relevant titles in chapter 1 and also *Religion in the Southern States* (2:34).

The best general history of the Southern Baptist Convention is Robert A. Baker, *The Southern Baptist Convention and Its People, 1607-1972* (4), although it occasionally lapses into a filiopietistic paean. It supplants the earlier work by William W. Barnes, *The Southern Baptist Convention, 1845-1953* (6). A history of Southern Baptists grounded in critical scholarship remains to be written, as is the case with most denominations. One beginning effort in this direction is Steve McNeely, "Early Baptists in the South: The Formation of a 'Folk Religion' " (70), which suggests some of the intricate ways the Baptist heritage has been intertwined with Southern culture since the eighteenth century. Here, too, one should see again the work of Rhys Isaac, noted in chapter 2, which provides a model for the ways in which the study of Baptists in the colonial era should proceed. An intriguing effort to explain who Southern Baptists are and what they represent is Claude U. Broach, "Introducing Southern Baptists" (11), written after the election of Georgia's Jimmy Carter to the presidency of the United States. Carter's unabashed self-identification as a Southern Baptist meant at least that it would no longer be possible to dismiss the denomination as a bulwark of an outmoded traditionalism as, for example, H. L. Mencken had done half a century earlier.

Many studies have treated the Baptist story along state lines, reflecting the way in which the denomination itself has been structured. Few of these studies, however, exhibit critical analysis; most have been sponsored by various Baptist state agencies and accordingly tend to lavish praise on denominational growth and development. An exception is the now dated study by Leah Townsend, *South Carolina Baptists, 1670-1805* (195), a revised doctoral dissertation, much of which has been incorporated with additional material in Joe M. King, *History of South Carolina Baptists* (159). Two other South Carolina studies should be noted. Wood Furman, *A History of the Charleston Association of Baptist Churches in the State of South-Carolina* (145), merits mention as the first denominational history to be published in that state. It is now more valuable as a primary source than as secondary analysis. An example of the uncritical study, which nevertheless offers a multitude of factual information, is Loulie L. Owens, *Saints of Clay: The Shaping of South Carolina Baptists* (173). Another older study, Garnett Ryland, *The*

Baptists of Virginia, 1699-1926 (183), is akin to Townsend's work on South Carolina as a scholarly narrative, but must be complemented by the previously noted works of Rhys Isaac for the colonial period. E. Glenn Hinson, *A History of Baptists in Arkansas, 1818-1878* (151), also is grounded in the standard methods of historical interpretation. Remarkable for its detail, if not for its critical depth, is the two-volume work, *History of North Carolina Baptists,* by George W. Paschal (174). C. Penrose St. Amant, *A Short History of Louisiana Baptists* (184), is a brief, popularly written study based as well on "church history" methods. The national bicentennial stimulated preparation of numerous denominational histories. Among the better ones dealing with the South is Leo Crismon, ed., *Baptists in Kentucky, 1776-1976: A Bicentennial History* (136), though most of the genre glibly blend patriotism and piety.

Among the more insightful commentators on the Southern Baptist story is Walter B. Shurden, who has written a number of popular and academic pieces about the group. His brief *Not a Silent People: Controversies That Have Shaped Southern Baptists* (101) argues that points of contention within the Baptist communion have been the most significant in creating a denominational identity, if not a raison d'etre. His thesis is suggestive, for one could build a case that from the debates over the revivals of the Great Awakening down to the civil rights movement of the twentieth century, controversies within the denomination or within society at large form the parameters of Southern Baptist history. The dilemmas around the Awakening, around slavery and whether to offer religious instruction to slaves, and around missions to native American Indians have already been noted. Many other titles on social and religious controversies are included in the listing for chapter 20, but attention should be called here to three of them: John L. Eighmy, *Churches in Cultural Captivity: A History of the Social Attitudes of Southern Baptists* (20:11); Rufus B. Spain, *At Ease in Zion: A Social History of the Southern Baptists, 1865-1900* (20:32); and James J. Thompson, Jr., *"Tried as by Fire": Southern Baptists and the Religious Controversies of the 1920s* (20:36).

In the early decades of the nineteenth century, perhaps the most important additional controversy is what has been dubbed the "antimission" movement. While this protest did oppose the expansion of benevolent societies and missionary groups, it was also rooted in the economic changes coincident with increasing agricultural commercialization in some areas (with the consequent continuation of relatively isolated subsistence farming elsewhere) and the transformation that issued in the emergence of stronger Baptist denominational structures. The story is told from the religious perspective, now seen as only one of a complex of factors generating "antimission" sentiment, in B. H. Carroll's outdated *The Genesis of American Anti-Missions* (14). More recent lines of interpretation are offered in Bertram Wyatt-Brown, "The Antimission Movement in the Jacksonian South: A Study in Regional Folk Culture'' (119), and in Keith R. Burich, ''The Primitive Baptist Schism in North Carolina: A Study of the Professionalism of the Baptist Ministry'' (13).

Around the middle of the nineteenth century, in addition to the growing controversy over slavery, Southern Baptists confronted what has become known as the Landmark Movement. Motivated in part by a radical concern for religious purity, particularly in areas of doctrine and the ritual of baptism, and based on the premise that one could trace a direct line from the ''pure'' Baptists of the day back to the Christianity of the first century—''landmarks'' of authentic belief—the movement found particularly fertile ground in parts of Alabama and Kentucky and in much of the old Southwest. Its origins in Tennessee are recounted by Teddy H. Evans, ''The Big Hatchie Baptist Association'' (144). The overall story in theological context is best told in James E. Tull, *A History of Southern Baptist Landmarkism in the Light of Historical Baptist Ecclesiology* (114), while the continuing impact of the movement— which had lost most of its steam by the early twentieth century—is the focus of W. Morgan Patterson, ''The Influence of Landmarkism Among Baptists'' (86). The three major figures behind the movement, the so-called ''Great Triumvirate,'' were James R. Graves, James M. Pendleton, and A. C. Dayton. None has been the subject of a critical monograph. Among more recent articles, two offer good introductions to two of the three: Bob Compton, ''J. M. Pendleton: A Nineteenth-Century Baptist Statesman'' (218), which demonstrates that other concerns were also important to Pendleton, and Harold S. Smith, ''The Life and Work of J. R. Graves'' (249).

Southern Baptist encounters with fundamentalism, which affected all of Southern Protestantism, will be noted in chapters 20 and 21. But parallel with that movement came one internal to the Southern Baptist ranks that eventuated in a schism of sorts. The central figure, J. Frank Norris, was not only a thoroughgoing fundamentalist and political conservative, but also an opponent of the growing ecclesiasticism that many thought had infected the denomination. Norris's early criticism of tightening denominational authority is told in James J. Thompson, Jr., ''A Free-and-Easy Democracy: Southern Baptists and Denominational Structure in the 1920's'' (109), while the sometimes morbid results of Norris's combination of fundamentalism and political conservatism are the focus of C. Allyn Russell, ''J. Frank Norris: Violent Fundamentalist'' (248). Various Baptist associations, tired of Norris's vitriolic attacks, finally expelled him, though thousands of his supporters remained loyal. On this point, see Mark G. Toulouse, ''A Case Study in Schism: J. Frank Norris and the Southern Baptist Convention'' (113). A brief overview, noting ways in which the furor over Norris has left contemporary traces, is Bobby D. Compton, ''J. Frank Norris and Southern Baptists'' (219). There are two noteworthy studies of Norris's life. E. Ray Tatum, *Conquest or Fail-*

ure? Biography of J. Frank Norris (251), approaches Norris from a psychological vantage point, while Ray E. Falls, *A Biography of J. Frank Norris* (229), is presented from a position of such total devotion to Norris and his principles as to be virtually useless in understanding either the man or the controversies he provoked.

More recent controversy, but not nearly as heated as that which surrounded Norris, has focused on the ecumenical movement, particularly Southern Baptist refusal to participate in agencies such as the National Council of Churches. On the one hand, such aloofness from ecumenical structures reflects the traditional Baptist reluctance to endow any institution beyond the local congregation with real authority (although, ironically, the Southern Baptist Convention itself has accrued much authority). But it also signals dissatisfaction with the orientation of many ecumenical bodies toward social concerns, which goes beyond the individualism that marks traditional Baptist ethics and religious experience, and the sense that most take positions regarded as too "liberal" for Southern Baptists to espouse. Some particular social issues will be noted in chapter 20. Southern Baptists, however, do not necessarily lack a commitment to Christian unity, but insist on relatively narrow doctrinal standards for unity. When Baptists have engaged in formal ecumenical ventures, they have generally entered into cooperative arrangements with other groups in the Baptist family more than with other denominations. William R. Estep, Jr., *Baptists and Christian Unity* (28), and E. Glenn Hinson, "Southern Baptists and Ecumenism: Some Contemporary Patterns" (45), summarize the Baptist position, although both studies are somewhat dated. A more recent appraisal is Glenn A. Iglehart, "Ecumenical Concerns among Southern Baptists" (52).

Ecumenical matters have assumed greater importance as the Southern Baptist Convention has experienced rapid growth in the past four decades, much of it outside the South. Two articles provide a good overview of the way in which growth has challenged Southern Baptists: Leon McBeth, "Expansion of the SBC to 1951" (61), and G. Thomas Halbrooks, "Growing Pains: The Impact of Expansion on Southern Baptists Since 1942" (36). Tom J. Nettles, "Southern Baptists: Regional to National Transition" (80), notes the ways in which expansion has required the Southern Baptist Convention to rethink its identity as a national body, a point also explored in W. R. Estep, "Southern Baptists in Search of an Identity" (29). But geographic expansion is not the only kind of growth that has confronted Southern Baptists. J. Wayne Flynt calls attention to another important dimension of expansion and change in "Southern Baptists: Rural to Urban Transition" (32). Some of the shift to a more urban and more national character has resulted from the movement of Southerners to Northern urban areas, but once planted outside the South, Southern Baptist churches have also gained many converts from other groups.

The resulting challenges are primarily twofold. Outside the South, Southern Baptists face a more religiously pluralistic context and cannot automatically assume a position of cultural dominance. In addition, expansion has brought an end to ideological homogeneity within the denomination. The first is the subject of T. Edwin Boling, "Southern Baptist Migrants and Converts: A Study of Southern Religion in the Urban North" (9), and his "Denominational Sectarianism: Preserving the Mystique" (8). Several studies have looked at the second challenge. Larry McSwain and Walter B. Shurden, in "Changing Values of Southern Baptists, 1900-1980" (71), argue that some of the ideological shifts antedate the rapid growth that followed World War II, for they document a declining emphasis on evangelism and revival techniques before that time and thus introduce a third challenge: fewer new members of Baptist churches have experienced a dramatic evangelical conversion but present themselves for baptism almost as a matter of course. Albert Mc-Clellan, "The Shaping of the Southern Baptist Mind" (67), claims that any homogeneity has already disappeared, a point that finds supports as well in William E. Hull, "Pluralism in the Southern Baptist Convention" (51). The need to face these problems lies behind Walter B. Shurden, "The Southern Baptist Synthesis: Is It Cracking?" (104).

As intimated, the traditional Baptist position that only the local congregation is the proper locus of religious authority within the denomination has allowed much pluralism to infect the ranks. Associations and conventions cannot directly impose their will on local congregations. But as LeRoy Moore argued in "Crazy Quilt: Southern Baptist Patterns of the Church" (78), the Southern Baptist response has been in part to erect one of the nation's most rigid and authoritarian denominational structures. The conflict over increasing denominational authority, of course, was one bone of contention in the controversy surrounding J. Frank Norris. But it remains a lively issue, as Paul D. Brewer has shown in "The State Convention: Is It Headquarters?" (10). The expectation that denominational leaders will exercise some authority has been probed by Wayne Dehoney, "The Role of the SBC President as Denominational Leader" (26), and Bill J. Leonard, "The Southern Baptist Denominational Leader as Theologian" (56).

Good case studies of the way in which individuals can influence the entire denomination could be found in the career of George W. Truett, pastor of First Baptist Church in Dallas from 1897 to 1944 and one-time president of both the Southern Baptist Convention and the Baptist World Alliance, and that of W. A. Criswell, former president of the Southern Baptist Convention (1968-1970) and Truett's successor as pastor of Dallas's First Baptist Church, with its more than 20,000 members, since 1944. On Truett see Powhatan W. James, *George W. Truett: A Biography* (237). Unfortunately, no scholarly study of Criswell yet exists, but suggestive materials are found in Billy Keith,

W. A. Criswell: The Authorized Biography (238), Leon McBeth, *The First Baptist Church of Dallas* (164), and the dissertation by Gene M. Adams (2:5).

Prior to the emergence of the "denominational leader" such as Truett or Criswell and the assumption of a great deal of authority by state associations and the Convention itself, the strongest cohesive force among Southern Baptists stemmed from the religious papers published by various state associations or conventions. By disseminating denominational news and promoting official programs endorsed by the Convention, the newspapers exerted great influence in securing denominational allegiance and identity. On this matter, see Erwin L. McDonald, "Southern Baptist State Papers, 1845-1970" (69).

As Southern Baptists have assumed national stature, they have been affected by religious currents that cut across regional and denominational lines. Among the more important in the recent past is the evangelical resurgence and the rise of the "new" religious right often associated with independent churches and clergy such as Jerry Falwell. In Southern Baptist circles, this has led to other questions of identity that come into sharp relief in James Leo Garrett, et al., *Are Southern Baptists "Evangelicals"?* (34). While Garrett wishes to maintain the appropriateness of the label, his main contender in the debate, E. Glenn Hinson, does not. Hinson's view, expressed in that work and others ("Baptists and Evangelicals: What Is the Difference? [43], and "Southern Baptists: A Concern for Experiential Conversion" [44]), is that personal religious experience, not the new evangelicalism, is at the heart of Baptist identity and that Baptists have traditionally looked to missionary endeavors and personal evangelism as means to foster that experience. Another contemporary current that has left an imprint on Southern Baptists is the charismatic movement, which regards the experience of the gifts of the Spirit, especially glossolalia, as confirming salvation. Once associated primarily with Pentecostal groups, this strand has penetrated all of the Christian denominations. On its impact on Southern Baptists, see Claude L. Howe, "The Charismatic Movement in Southern Baptist Life" (49).

Another vital contemporary issue concerns the ordination of women and the role of women within the Southern Baptist Convention. Two works by Leon McBeth provide a historical perspective and an outline of the points of controversy: *Women in Baptist Life* (63) and "The Role of Women in Southern Baptist History" (62).

Few scholarly biographies of individuals who have been in the forefront of Southern Baptist developments exist. For example, for many years the only monograph examining the life of Richard Furman—a central figure in early Baptist developments in South Carolina and the United States—was written in 1913 (221) and lacks solid critical assessment. Fortunately a more thorough treatment is now available in James Rogers, *Richard Furman: Life and Legacy* (246). Some of the articles and books treating individuals involved in

activities such as Indian missions have been noted elsewhere, and those dealing with persons associated with particular controversies have been indicated
above. There are as well some materials dealing with two other figures whose
work helped mold Southern Baptist history. Basil Manly, Jr. (1825-1892),
devoted most of his career to building the Southern Baptist Theological Seminary, now in Louisville, but he was also influential in promoting the Sunday
School movement among Southern Baptists and in writing hymns and com-
piling hymnals for use by Baptists. The best general work about Manly is Joseph P. Cox's unpublished dissertation, "A Study of the Life and Work of
Basil Manly, Jr." (222), but also see Jonathan A. Lindsey, "Basil Manly:
Nineteenth Century Protean Man" (241). Edgar Young Mullins (1860-1928)
likewise was long associated with the Southern Baptist Theological Seminary, of which he was elected president in 1899, but also caught up in the
conflict over evolution in the 1920s. A moderate with a national reputation,
Mullins grew increasingly conservative particularly in the evolution controversy, but his stature was such that he served as president of the Southern
Baptist Convention (1921-1924) and later of the Baptist World Alliance. The
best short study is William E. Ellis, "Edgar Young Mullins and the Crisis of
Moderate Southern Baptist Leadership" (227). This work is considerably expanded in Ellis's *E. Y. Mullins and the Crisis of Moderate Southern Baptist
Leadership* (228), now in press. Also see Archibald T. Robertson, "A Sketch
of the Life of President Mullins" (245), and the appreciative memoir by Isla
May Mullins, *Edgar Young Mullins: An Intimate Biography* (242).

Southern Baptists, now numbering nearly 14,000,000 persons, are at a
crossroads. The ways in which denominational identity is intertwined with
the fabric of Southern culture and may reflect that culture as much as a distinctive religious stance (see C. Penrose St. Amant, "Southern Baptists and
Southern Culture" [97]) have been challenged by growth and expansion. The
pluralism that marks the denomination today has led to sometimes bitter
struggles for power between moderates and conservatives at meetings of state
associations and the Convention. It has likewise challenged the traditional
Southern Baptist—some would say simply Southern—insistence that society
and religion represent two distinct arenas of human life and that ethics are a
matter of individual rather than social concern (see Samuel S. Hill, Jr., "The
Southern Baptists: Need for Reformation, Redirection" [42]). The Baptist
response to these challenges in the next few decades may well determine how
long the denomination will dominate not only Southern religion, but Protestantism in the United States.

Among works about other Baptist bodies, Damon C. Dodd, *The Free Will
Baptist Story* (27), provides a popular introduction to the distinctive heritage
and views of that body. Also see his "Freewill Baptists in Georgia" (140)
for a capsule history of this Arminian body, which traces the eighteenth-cen-

tury expansion of the movement from North Carolina through South Carolina, Alabama, Florida, and Georgia and then concentrates on Georgia developments. Two other standard works are Norman Baxter, *History of the Free Will Baptists* (7), and William Davidson, *An Early History of Free Will Baptists* (25). Brett Sutton, "In the Good Old Way: Primitive Baptist Traditions" (108), provides a nice introduction to the major distinctive motifs of this group such as reliance on oral testimony and extensive use of lay preaching. The origins of the denomination in North Carolina in the antimission sentiment of the nineteenth century are traced in Cushing B. Hassell and Sylvester Hassell, *History of the Church of God from the Creation to A.D. 1885: Including Especially the History of the Kehukee Primitive Baptist Association* (150).

The bibliography that follows is divided into three sections. The first lists studies that focus on the denomination as a whole, on its development regionally, and on general topics affecting the denomination. The second part deals with works that treat the South's Baptists within particular Southern states or in local areas in the South. The final section notes biographical or autobiographical studies of individuals important in Baptist history in the South. In addition, *Baptist History and Heritage* carries many articles of interest to students of the Baptist tradition in the Southern states, as does *Review & Expositor,* the journal of Southern Baptist Theological Seminary in Louisville.

BIBLIOGRAPHY

Many titles included in the listings for chapters 1, 2, 3, 4, 15, 18, 19, 20, and 21 are relevant to the story of Baptists in the South.

I. BAPTISTS IN THE SOUTH:
GENERAL AND TOPICAL STUDIES

(1) Baker, James T. "Southern Baptists in the Seventies." *Christian Century* 90 (1973): 699-703.

(2) Baker, Robert A. *A Baptist Source Book, with Particular Reference to Southern Baptists.* Nashville: Broadman Press, 1966.

(3) _____. "The Magnificent Years (1917-1931)." *Baptist History and Heritage* 8 (1973): 144-57, 167.

(4) _____. *The Southern Baptist Convention and Its People, 1607-1972.* Nashville: Broadman Press, 1974.

(5) _____. "The Southern Baptist Convention, 1845-1970." *Review and Expositor* 67 (1970): 125-39.

(6) Barnes, William W. *The Southern Baptist Convention, 1845-1953.* Nashville: Broadman Press, 1954.

(7) Baxter, Norman. *History of the Free Will Baptists.* Rochester NY: American Baptist Historical Society, 1957.

(8) Boling, T. Edwin. "Denominational Sectarians: Preserving the Mystique." *Foundations* 21 (1978): 365-72.

(9) _____. "Southern Baptist Migrants and Converts: A Study of Southern Religion in the Urban North." *Sociological Analysis* 33 (1972): 188-95.

(10) Brewer, Paul D. "The State Convention: Is It Headquarters?" *Baptist History and Heritage* 14 (1979): 41-51.

(11) Broach, Claude U. "Introducing Southern Baptists." *Greek Orthodox Theological Review* 22 (1977): 367-75.

(12) Brown, Archie E. *A Million Men for Christ: The History of the Baptist Brotherhood.* Nashville: Convention Press, 1956.

(13) Burich, Keith R. "The Primitive Baptist Schism in North Carolina: A Study of the Professionalism of the Baptist Ministry." M.A. thesis, University of North Carolina in Chapel Hill, 1973.

(14) Carroll, B. H., Jr. *The Genesis of American Anti-Missions.* Louisville: Baptist Book Concern, 1902.

(15) Carter, James E. "The Fraternal Address of Southern Baptists." *Baptist History and Heritage* 12 (1977): 211-18.

(16) _____. "Outreach Theology: A Comparison of Southern Baptist Thought and the Christian Growth Movement." *Baptist History and Heritage* 15 (1980): 33-42, 56.

(17) _____. "A Review of Confessions of Faith Adopted by Major Southern Baptist Bodies in the United States." *Baptist History and Heritage* 12 (1977): 75-91.

(18) Cauthen, Baker James, et al. *Advance: A History of Southern Baptist Foreign Missions.* Nashville: Broadman Press, 1970.

(19) Chandler, Russell. "Southern Baptists: Besides Still Waters." *Christianity Today* 17 (6 July 1973): 48-49.

(20) Childers, J. S., ed. *A Way Home: The Baptists Tell Their Story.* Atlanta: Tupper and Love, 1964.

(21) Clemmons, William. "Voluntary Missions Among Twentieth Century Southern Baptists." *Baptist History and Heritage* 14 (1979): 37-49.

(22) Cooper, Owen. *The Future Is Before Us.* Nashville: Broadman Press, 1973.

(23) Cross, Irvie K. *The Truth About Conventionism: The Southern Baptist Convention, a New Denomination.* 2d ed. Little Rock: Seminary Press, 1956.

(24) Culpepper, Hugo H. "Bold Missions Personified: Missionaries Who Have Led the Way." *Baptist History and Heritage* 14 (1979): 50-57.

(25) Davidson, William. *An Early History of Free Will Baptists.* Nashville: Randall House Publishers, 1974.

(26) Dehoney, Wayne. "The Role of the SBC President as Denominational Leader." *Baptist History and Heritage* 15 (1980): 49-56.

(27) Dodd, Damon C. *The Free Will Baptist Story.* Nashville: Executive Department of the National Association of Free Will Baptists, 1956.

(28) Estep, William R., Jr. *Baptists and Christian Unity*. Nashville: Broadman Press, 1966.

(29) _____. "Southern Baptists in Search of an Identity." *The Lord's Free People in a Free Land*. W. R. Estep, ed., 145-70. Fort Worth: Faculty of the School of Theology, Southwestern Baptist Theological Seminary, 1976.

(30) Fletcher, Jesse C. "A History of the Foreign Missions Board of the Southern Baptist Convention During the Civil War." *Baptist History and Heritage* 10 (1975): 204-19.

(31) Flynt, J. Wayne. "The Impact of Social Factors on Southern Baptist Expansion, 1800-1914." *Baptist History and Heritage* 17 (1982): 20-31.

(32) _____. "Southern Baptists: Rural to Urban Transition." *Baptist History and Heritage* 16 (1981): 24-34.

(33) Garrett, James L., ed. *Baptist Relations with Other Christians*. Valley Forge: Judson Press, 1974.

(34) _____, et al. *Are Southern Baptists "Evangelicals"?* Macon GA: Mercer University Press, 1983.

(35) Halbrooks, G. Thomas. "Church Membership Trends in the Twentieth Century." *Baptist History and Heritage* 16 (1981): 35-44.

(36) _____. "Growing Pains: The Impact of Expansion on Southern Baptists Since 1942." *Baptist History and Heritage* 17 (1982): 44-54.

(37) Hastey, Stanley L. "A History of the Baptist Joint Committee on Public Affairs, 1946-1971." Th.D. dissertation, Southern Baptist Theological Seminary, 1973.

(38) Hastings, Robert J. "Communicating History through Baptist Newspapers." *Baptist History and Heritage* 12 (1977): 166-69.

(39) Hays, Brooks, and John E. Steely. *The Baptist Way of Life*. 2d ed. Macon GA: Mercer University Press, 1981.

(40) Hearne, Erwin M., Jr. "Illustrating Baptist History." *Baptist History and Heritage* 12 (1977): 135-41.

(41) Hill, Samuel S., Jr., and Robert G. Torbet. *Baptists: North and South*. Valley Forge: Judson Press, 1964.

(42) _____. "The Southern Baptists: Need for Reformation, Redirection." *Christian Century* 80 (1973): 39-42.

(43) Hinson, E. Glenn. "Baptists and Evangelicals: What Is the Difference?" *Baptist History and Heritage* 16 (1981): 20-32.

(44) _____. "Southern Baptists: Concern for Experiential Conversion." In *Where the Spirit Leads: American Denominations Today*. Martin E. Marty, ed., 137-48. Atlanta: John Knox Press, 1980.

(45) _____. "Southern Baptists and Ecumenism: Some Contemporary Patterns." *Review and Expositor* 66 (1969): 287-98.

(46) Hobbs, Herschel H. *The Baptist Faith and Message*. Nashville: Convention Press, 1971.

(47) _____. "The Baptist Faith and Message—Anchored but Free." *Baptist History and Heritage* 13 (1978): 33-40, 62.

(48) _____. "Southern Baptists and Confessionalism: A Comparison of the Origins and Contents of the 1925 and 1973 Confessions." *Review and Expositor* 76 (1979): 55-68.

(49) Howe, Claude L. "The Charismatic Movement in Southern Baptist Life." *Baptist History and Heritage* 13 (1978): 20-27, 65.

(50) Hudson, Withrop S. "Divergent Careers of Southern and Northern Baptists: A Study in Growth." *Foundations* 16 (1973): 171-83.

(51) Hull, William E. "Pluralism in the Southern Baptist Convention." *Review and Expositor* 79 (1982): 121-46.

(52) Iglehart, Glenn A. "Ecumenical Concerns among Southern Baptists." *Baptists and Ecumenism*. William J. Boney and Glenn A. Iglehart, eds. Valley Forge: Judson Press, 1980. Special issue of the *Journal of Ecumenical Studies* 17,2 (1980).

(53) _____. "The Baptist Experience in North America." *American Baptist Quarterly* 1 (1982): 121-29.

(54) Kelsey, George D. *Social Ethics among Southern Baptists, 1917-1969*. Metuchen NJ: Scarecrow Press, 1972.

(55) Lambert, Byron C. *The Rise of the Anti-Mission Baptists: Sources and Leaders, 1800-1840*. Chicago: University of Chicago Library Department of Photographic Reproductions, 1957.

(56) Leonard, Bill J. "The Southern Baptist Denominational Leader as Theologian." *Baptist History and Heritage* 15 (1980): 23-32, 61.

(57) _____. "Types of Confessional Doctrines Among Baptists." *Review and Expositor* 76 (1979): 29-42.

(58) Letsinger, Norman H. "The Status of Women in the Southern Baptist Convention in Historical Perspective." *Baptist History and Heritage* 12 (1977): 37-44, 51.

(59) Liggin, Edna. "A Short Concise History of the Concord Baptist Association." *North Louisiana Historical Association Journal* 7 (1976): 101-103.

(60) Lumpkin, W. L. *Baptist Foundations in the South*. Nashville: Broadman Press, 1961.

(61) McBeth, Leon. "Expansion of the Southern Baptist Convention to 1951." *Baptist History and Heritage* 17 (1982): 32-43.

(62) _____. "The Role of Women in Southern Baptist History." *Baptist History and Heritage* 12 (1977): 3-25.

(63) _____. *Women in Baptist Life*. Nashville: Broadman Press, 1979.

(64) McCall, Duke K., ed. *What Is the Church? A Symposium of Baptist Thought*. Nashville: Broadman Press, 1958.

(65) McClellan, Albert. "Bold Mission Thrust of Baptists: Past and Present." *Baptist History and Heritage* 14 (1979): 3-15.

(66) _____. "The Origin and Development of the Southern Baptist Convention Cooperative Program." *Baptist History and Heritage* 10 (1975): 69-78.

(67) _____. "The Shaping of the Southern Baptist Mind." *Baptist History and Heritage* 13 (1978): 2-11.

(68) _____. "Southern Baptist Roots in Practice and Polity." *Review and Expositor* 75 (1978): 279-93.

(69) McDonald, Erwin L. "Southern Baptist State Papers, 1845-1970." *Review and Expositor* 67 (1970): 203-17.

(70) McNeely, Steve. "Early Baptists in the South: The Formation of a 'Folk Religion'." *The Quarterly Review* 35 (1974): 65-72.

(71) McSwain, Larry, and Walter B. Shurden. "Changing Values of Southern Baptists, 1900-1980." *Baptist History and Heritage* 16 (1981): 45-54.

(72) Martin, Sandy Dwayne. "The Baptist Foreign Mission Convention, 1880-1894." *Baptist History and Heritage* 16 (1981): 13-25.

(73) Masters, Victor I. *Baptist Missions in the South*. Atlanta: Home Mission Board of the Southern Baptist Convention, 1915.

(74) May, Lynn E., Jr. "The Role of Associations in Baptist History." *Baptist History and Heritage* 12 (1977): 69-74.

(75) _____. "The Sunday School: A Two-Hundred-Year Heritage." *Baptist History and Heritage* 15 (1980): 3-11.

(76) Measures, Royce. "Men and Movements Influenced by J. Frank Norris." Th.D. dissertation, Southwestern Baptist Theological Seminary, 1976.

(77) Moody, Dale. "The Shaping of Southern Baptist Polity." *Baptist History and Heritage* 14 (1979): 2-11.

(78) Moore, LeRoy. "Crazy Quilt: Southern Baptist Patterns of the Church." *Foundations* 20 (1977): 12-35.

(79) Nettles, Tom J. "Patterns of Financial Giving for Missions Support among Baptists." *Baptist History and Heritage* 14 (1979): 27-46.

(80) _____. "Southern Baptists: Regional to National Transition." *Baptist History and Heritage* 16 (1981): 13-23.

(81) _____. "Themes for Research in Southern Baptist History." *Baptist History and Heritage* 14 (April 1979): 15-19.

(82) Newsome, Jerry. " 'Primitive Baptists': A Study in Name Formation or What's in a Word." *Viewpoints: Georgia Baptist History* 6 (1978): 63-70.

(83) Newton, Louie D. *Why I Am a Baptist*. Boston: Beacon Press, 1965.

(84) Patterson, W. Morgan. "Baptist Growth in America: Evaluation of Trends." *Baptist History and Heritage* 14 (January 1979): 16-26.

(85) _____. *Baptist Successionism: A Critical View*. Valley Forge: Judson Press, 1969.

(86) _____. "The Influence of Landmarkism Among Baptists." *Baptist History and Heritage* 10 (1975): 44-55.

(87) Patton, Richard D. "Baptists and Regenerate Church Membership: Historical Perspective and Present Practice." *Baptist History and Heritage* 13 (1978): 28-32.

(88) Peacock, James L. "Weberian, Southern Baptist, and Indonesian Muslim Conceptions of Belief and Action." In *Symbols and Society: Essays on Belief Systems in Action*. Carole E. Hill, ed., 82-92. *Proceedings of the Southern Anthropological Society* 9 (1975).

(89) Posey, Walter B. *The Baptist Church in the Lower Mississippi Valley, 1776-1845*. Lexington: University of Kentucky Press, 1957.

(90) _____. "The Early Baptist Church in the Lower South West." *Journal of Southern History* 10 (1944): 161-73.

(91) Ranck, George W. " 'The Travelling Church': An Account of the Baptist Exodus from Virginia to Kentucky in 1781." *Register of the Kentucky Historical Society* 79 (1981): 240-65.

(92) Renault, James O. "The Changing Patterns of Separate Baptist Religious Life, 1803-1977." *Baptist History and Heritage* 14 (1979): 16-25, 36.

(93) Riley, Benjamin F. *A History of the Baptists in the Southern States East of the Mississippi*. Philadelphia: American Baptist Publication Society, 1898.

(94) Routh, Porter. "The Role of the Executive Committee of the Southern Baptist Convention." *Baptist History and Heritage* 11 (1976): 194-203, 229.

(95) _____. "The Southern Baptist Convention Presidency, 1845-1870." *Review and Expositor* 67 (1970): 153-66.

(96) Roy, Ralph Lord. *Apostles of Discord: A Study of Organized Bigotry and Disruption on the Fringes of Protestantism*. Boston: Beacon Press, 1953.

(97) St. Amant, C. Penrose. "Southern Baptists and Southern Culture." *Review and Expositor* 67 (1970): 141-52.

(98) Shriver, George. "Southern Baptists: Sect or Denomination?" *Christian Century* 77 (1970): 1093-94.

(99) _____. "When Conservatism Is Liberalism." *Christian Century* 76 (1969): 1040-41.

(100) Shurden, Walter B. "The Historical Background of Baptist Associations." *Review and Expositor* 77 (1980): 161-75.

(101) _____. *Not a Silent People: Controversies That Have Shaped Southern Baptists*. Nashville: Broadman Press, 1972.

(102) _____. "The Problem of Authority in the Southern Baptist Convention." *Review and Expositor* 75 (1978): 219-33.

(103) _____. "Southern Baptist Responses to Their Confessional Statements." *Review and Expositor* 76 (1979): 69-84.

(104) _____. "The Southern Baptist Synthesis: Is It Cracking?" *Baptist History and Heritage* 16 (1981): 2-11.

(105) Slaght, Lawrence T. *Multiplying the Witness: 150 Years of American Baptist Educational Ministries*. Valley Forge: Judson Press, 1974.

(106) "Southern Baptist Churches 200 Years Old or Older." *Baptist History and Heritage* 11 (1976): 232-34.

(107) Sullivan, James L. "Polity Developments in the Southern Baptist Convention (1900-1977)." *Baptist History and Heritage* 14 (1979): 22-31.

(108) Sutton, Brett. "In the Good Old Way: Primitive Baptist Traditions." *Southern Exposure* 5 (1977): 97-104.

(109) Thompson, James J., Jr. "A Free-and-Easy Democracy: Southern Baptists and Denominational Structure in the 1920's." *Foundations* 22 (1979): 43-50.

(110) _____. "Southern Baptist City and Country Churches in the Twenties." *Foundations* 17 (1974): 351-63.

(111) Tonks, A. Ronald. "The Home Missions Board: The Expectant but Anxious Years, 1845-1860." *Baptist History and Heritage* 8 (1973): 168-87.

(112) Torbet, Robert G. *A History of the Baptists*. Philadelphia: Judson Press, 1950.

(113) Toulouse, Mark G. "A Case Study in Schism: J. Frank Norris and the Southern Baptist Convention." *Foundations* 24 (1981): 32-53.

(114) Tull, James E. *A History of Southern Baptist Landmarkism in the Light of Historical Baptist Ecclesiology*. New York: Arno Press, 1980.

(115) _____. "The Landmark Movement: An Historical and Theological Appraisal." *Baptist History and Heritage* 10 (1975): 3-18.

(116) _____. *Shapers of Baptist Thought*. Valley Forge: Judson Press, 1972. Reprint, Macon GA: Mercer University Press, 1984.

(117) _____. "A Study of Southern Baptist Landmarkism in the Light of Historical Baptist Ecclesiology." Ph.D. dissertation, Columbia University, 1960.

(118) Wooley, Davis C. "Major Convention Crises over a Century and a Quarter." *Review and Expositor* 67 (1970): 167-82.

(119) Wyatt-Brown, Bertram. "The Antimission Movement in the Jacksonian South: A Study in Regional Folk Culture." *Journal of Southern History* 36 (1970): 501-29.

II. BAPTISTS IN THE SOUTH: STATE AND LOCAL STUDIES

(120) Abner, Maude M. *The Story of the Union Gospel Mission, 1886-1944: Formerly the Holcombe Mission, 1881-1885: Now Owned by the Long Run Association of Baptists*. Louisville: Mayes Printing, 1944.

(121) Alley, Reuben E. *A History of Baptists in Virginia*. Richmond: Virginia Baptist General Board, 1978.

(122) Armour, Rollin S. "Sidelights on Florida Baptist History: The Winter Assembly at Umatilla and a Connection with the Assassination of President Lincoln." *Baptist History and Heritage* 8 (1973): 225-31.

(123) Atchison, Ray M. *Baptists of Shelby County: History of the Shelby Baptist Association of Alabama*. Birmingham: Banner Press, 1964.

(124) Baker, Robert A. "The Contributions of South Carolina Baptists to the Rise and Development of the Southern Baptist Convention." *Baptist History and Heritage* 17 (1982): 2-9, 19.

(125) "Baptists: Where God's Business Is Big Business." *Time* (8 November 1968): 79.

(126) Birkitt, James N. *Carrying Out a Kingdom: Carmel Baptist Church, 1773-1965.* Richmond: Christian Enterprises, 1965.

(127) Bledsoe, W. C. *History of the Liberty (East) Baptist Association of Alabama.* Atlanta: Constitution Job Office, 1886.

(128) Boyd, Jessie L. *A Popular History of the Baptists in Mississippi.* Jackson: Baptist Press, 1930.

(129) Burlington-Alamance County Chamber of Commerce. *Histories of Baptist Chuches in Burlington and Alamance County, North Carolina.* Burlington: Chamber of Commerce, 1963.

(130) [Burns, Jeremiah M.] *History of the Clear Creek Baptist Association, 1874-1957.* [Haleyville AL?]: n.p., [1958?].

(131) Carroll, James M. *A History of Texas Baptists.* J. B. Cranfill, ed. Dallas: Baptist Standard Publishing, 1923.

(132) Christian, John T. *A History of the Baptists of Louisiana.* Shreveport: The Executive Board of the Louisiana Baptist Convention, 1923.

(133) Chumbley, Joe W. *Kentucky Town and Its Baptist Church: Or, Ann Eliza and Pleasant Hill.* Houston TX: D. Armstrong, 1975.

(134) Clayton, J. Glen. "South Carolina Shapers of Southern Baptists." *Baptist History and Heritage* 17 (1982): 10-19.

(135) Conley, Carolyn. " 'Make Full Proof of Thy Ministry': Lamarr Monneyham, the Tri-City Baptist Temple, and the Moral Majority." *South Atlantic Quarterly* 81 (1982): 131-46.

(136) Crismon, Leo, ed. *Baptists in Kentucky, 1776-1976: A Bicentennial History.* Middletown KY: Kentucky Baptist Convention, 1975.

(137) Daniel, W. Harrison. "Virginia Baptists, 1861-1865." Virginia *Magazine of History and Biography* 72 (1964): 94-114.

(138) Dawson, Joseph M. *A Century with Texas Baptists.* Nashville: Broadman Press, 1947.

(139) Deweese, Charles W. "Disciplinary Procedures in Frontier Baptist Churches in Kentucky." *Baptist History and Heritage* 8 (1973): 194-207.

(140) Dodd, Damon C. "Freewill Baptists in Georgia." *Viewpoints: Georgia Baptist History* 6 (1978): 55-62.

(141) Douglass, Robert S. *History of Missouri Baptists.* Kansas City: Western Baptist Publishing, 1934.

(142) Dunn, Mary Franklin Deason. *A History of Zion Hill Missionary Baptist Church.* Henderson TX: n.p., [1968?].

(143) Durham, John P., and John S. Ramond, comps. *Baptist Builders in Louisiana.* Shreveport: Durham-Ramond, 1934.

(144) Evans, Teddy H. "The Big Hatchie Baptist Association." *West Tennessee Historical Society Papers* 32 (1978): 148-57, 33 (1979): 95-102.

(145) Furman, Wood. *A History of the Charleston Association of Baptist Churches in the State of South-Carolina.* Charleston: J. Hoff, 1811.

(146) Garrett, T. H. *A History of the Saluda Baptist Association*. Richmond: B. F. Johnson Publishing, 1896.

(147) Greene, Glen Lee. *A History of the Baptists of Oak Ridge, Louisiana, 1797-1960*. Nashville: Parthenon Press, 1960.

(148) _____. *House Upon a Rock: About Southern Baptists in Louisiana*. Alexandria LA: Executive Board of the Louisiana Baptist Convention, 1973.

(149) Harrison, Thad F., and J. M. Barfield. *History of the Free Will Baptists of North Carolina*. [Ayden NC?]: [Free Will Baptist Press?], [1898?].

(150) Hassell, Cushing B. *History of the Church of God from the Creation to A.D. 1885: Including Especially the History of the Kehukee [NC] Primitive Baptist Association*. Middletown KY: G. Beebe's Sons, 1886.

(151) Hinson, E. Glenn. *A History of Baptists in Arkansas, 1818-1978*. Little Rock: Arkansas Baptist State Convention, 1979.

(152) Howell, Robert B. *The Early Baptists of Virginia*. Philadelphia: Bible and Publication Society, 1876.

(153) Joiner, Edward E. *A History of Florida Baptists*. Jacksonville: Convention Press, 1972.

(154) Jones, Billy W., et al. *History of Ebenezer Missionary Baptist Association [of Georgia], 1814-1964*. [Dry Branch GA?]: n.p., 1965.

(155) Jones, Walter L. "Growing Up in the Flatwoods: Jack Smith's Memories of the 1860s." *Journal of Mississippi History* 42 (1980): 145-51.

(156) Kendall, William Frederick. *A History of the Tennessee Baptist Convention*. Brentwood TN: Executive Board of the Tennessee Baptist Convention, 1974.

(157) King, Spencer Bidwell, Jr. "Baptist Leaders in Early Georgia Politics." *The Quarterly Review* 38 (1977): 76-79.

(158) _____. "Baptist Leaders in Early Georgia Politics." *Viewpoints: Georgia Baptist History* 5 (1976): 45-50.

(159) King, Joe M. *History of South Carolina Baptists*. Columbia: General Board of the South Carolina Baptist Convention, 1964.

(160) Leavell, Zachery T. *A Complete History of Mississippi Baptists*. Jackson: Mississippi Baptist Publishing, 1904.

(161) Lee, Jerry J. "Separation and Crystallization of Northwest Georgia Primitive Baptists." *Viewpoints: Georgia Baptist History* 4 (1974): 39-53.

(162) Lester, James A. *A History of the Georgia Baptist Convention, 1822-1972*. [Atlanta?]: Executive Committee of the Baptist Convention of the State of Georgia, 1972.

(163) Lumpkin, William L. "The Role of Women in 18th Century Virginia Baptist Life." *Baptist History and Heritage* 8 (1973): 158-67.

(164) McBeth, Leon. *The First Baptist Church of Dallas*. Grand Rapids: Zondervan, 1968.

(165) McLemore, Richard A. *Highlights of Mississippi Baptist History*. Clinton MS: Mississippi Baptist Historical Commission, 1968.

(166) _____. *A History of Mississippi Baptists, 1780-1970*. Jackson: Mississippi Baptist Convention Board, 1971.

(167) Mason, Zane Allen. *Frontiersmen of the Faith: A History of Baptist Pioneer Work in Texas, 1865-1885*. San Antonio: Naylor, 1970.

(168) Masters, Frank M. *History of Baptists in Kentucky*. Louisville: Kentucky Baptist Historical Society, 1953.

(169) Mertins, Marshall, and O. P. Joyce. *Blue River Baptist Association, Missouri*. Kansas City: Brown-White-Lowell Press, 1947.

(170) Moore, Luther W. *A History of the Middle District Baptist Association*. Richmond: Virginia Baptist Historical Society, 1886.

(171) Morris, Byron. *A Charge to Keep: History of the First Baptist Church of Kenova, West Virginia*. Parsons WV: McClain Print, 1971.

(172) Owens, Loulie L. *Banners in the Wind: The Story of South Carolina Baptist Women in Missions*. Columbia SC: Women's Missionary Union of South Carolina, 1950.

(173) _____. *Saints of Clay: The Shaping of South Carolina Baptists*. Columbia SC: R. L. Bryan, 1971.

(174) Paschal, George W. *History of North Carolina Baptists*. 2 vols. Raleigh: General Board, North Carolina Baptist State Convention, 1930-55.

(175) Ransome, William L. *History of the First Baptist Church and Some of Her Pastors, South Richmond, Va*. Richmond VA: n.p., 1935.

(176) Reid, Barney F. *A Brief History of Teachers' Training Work as Connected with the Baptist State Sunday School Convention of Kentucky*. Louisville: The Convention, 1928.

(177) [Rice, Martin]. *History of the Blue River Baptist Association of Missouri*. Kansas City: Interstate Publishing, 1890.

(178) Riley, Benjamin F. *History of the Baptists of Texas*. Dallas: For the Author, 1907.

(179) _____. *A Memorial History of the Baptists of Alabama: Being an Account of the Struggles and Achievements of the Denomination from 1808 to 1923*. Philadelphia: Judson Press, 1923.

(180) Roberts, Derrell C. "Kentucky Baptist Aid to Reconstruction Georgia." *Register of the Kentucky Historical Society* 79 (1981): 219-26.

(181) Rogers, James S. *History of Arkansas Baptists*. Little Rock: Executive Board of the Arkansas Baptist State Convention, 1948.

(182) Rosser, John L. *A History of Florida Baptists*. Nashville: Broadman Press, 1949.

(183) Ryland, Garnett. *The Baptists of Virginia, 1699-1926*. Richmond: Virginia Baptist Board of Missions and Education, 1955.

(184) St. Amant, C. Penrose. *A Short History of Louisiana Baptists*. Nashville: Broadman Press, 1948.

(185) Sapp, Phyllis. *Lighthouse on the Corner: A History of the First Baptist Church, Oklahoma City, Oklahoma*. Oklahoma City: Century Press, 1964.

(186) Self, Jerry D., comp. "A Brief History of Union Baptist Church (Old North Church)." *East Texas Historical Journal* 9 (1971): 60-71.

(187) Semple, Robert B. *History of the Baptists in Virginia.* Rev. by G. W. Beale. Cottonport LA: Polyanthos, 1972. First published 1810.

(188) Shackelford, Josephus. *History of the Muscle Shoals Baptist Association from 1820 to 1890.* Trinity AL: By the author, 1891.

(189) Shamburger, William M. "A History of Tarrant County Baptist Association, 1886-1922." Th.D. dissertation, Southwestern Baptist Theological Seminary, 1953.

(190) Spencer, John H. *A History of Kentucky Baptists from 1769 to 1885.* 2 vols. Cincinnati: J. R. Baumes, [1886].

(191) Stakely, Charles A. *History of the First Baptist Church of Montgomery, Alabama, with Sketches of the Other Baptist Churches of the City and County.* Montgomery: The Paragon Press, 1930.

(192) Taylor, John. *A History of Tennessee Baptist Churches.* New York: Arno Press, 1980. First published 1827.

(193) Taylor, Ouvy W. *Early Tennessee Baptists.* Nashville: Tennessee Baptist Convention, 1957.

(194) Tidwell, Donavon D. *A History of the Baptists at Iredell, Texas.* Irving TX: Griffin Graphic Arts, 1968.

(195) Townsend, Leah. *South Carolina Baptists, 1670-1805.* Florence SC: Florence Printing, 1935.

(196) Truex, Harvey E. *Baptists in Missouri.* 2d ed. Columbia: Press of E. W. Stephens, 1904.

(197) Tupper, H. A., ed. *The First Century of the First Baptist Church of Richmond, 1780-1880.* Richmond: C. McCarthy, 1880.

(198) Walker, Charles O. "Georgia Baptist Historical Interests." *Viewpoints: Georgia Baptist History* 4 (1974): 55-66.

(199) Watson, Ellen. *A History of the Bethel Baptist Association.* Spartanburg SC: Spartan Baptist Association, 1968.

(200) Watts, Joseph. *The Rise and Progress of Maryland Baptists.* Baltimore: State Mission Board of the Maryland Baptist Union Association, 1953.

(201) Weishampel, J. F., Jr., et al. *History of Baptist Churches in Maryland Connected with the Maryland Baptist Union Association.* Baltimore: J. F. Weishampel, Jr., 1855.

(202) Wellborn, Charles. "Brann vs. the Baptists: Violence and Southern Religion." *Religion in Life* 47 (1978): 220-29.

(203) White, Blanche S. *A Century of Service: A History of Bainbridge Street Baptist Church, Richmond, Virginia, 1857-1957.* Richmond: Whittet and Shepperson, 1957.

(204) _____. *History of the Baptists on the Eastern Shore of Virginia, 1776-1959.* Baltimore: n.p., 1959.

(205) _____. *The History of the Middle District Association, 1794-1958.* Richmond: Acme Press, 1958.

(206) _____. *Our Heritage: History of the Women's Missionary Union, Auxiliary to the Maryland Baptist Union, 1742-1958*. [Baltimore?]: n.p., [1959?].

(207) _____. *Richmond Baptists Working Together, 1780-1960*. Richmond: Richmond Baptist Association, 1961.

(208) _____. *The Tie That Binds: A Brief History of the Women's Department of the World Baptist Alliance, 1911-1960*. Washington: Women's Department, World Baptist Alliance, 1960.

III. BAPTISTS IN THE SOUTH;
BIOGRAPHICAL AND AUTOBIOGRAPHICAL STUDIES

(209) Aldredge, E. P. "Amazing Achievements of Dr. George W. Truett's Ministry." *The Quarterly Review* 1 (1941): 59-64.

(210) Birdwhitsell, Jack, ed. "Extracts from the Diary of B. F. Hungerford, A Kentucky Baptist Pastor During the Civil War." *Baptist History and Heritage* 14 (1979): 24-31.

(211) Blair, John L. "A Baptist Minister Visits Kentucky: The Journal of Andrew Broaddus." *Register of the Kentucky Historical Society* 71 (1973): 393-425.

(212) Boles, John B. "Henry Holcombe, Southern Baptist Reformer in the Age of Jefferson." *Georgia Historical Quarterly* 54 (1970): 381-407.

(213) Broach, Claude U. *Dr. Frank: An Informal Biography of Frank Leavell, Leader of Baptist Youth*. Nashville: Broadman Press, 1950.

(214) Bruster, Bill, "J. C. Stalcup: Father of the Baptist General Convention of Oklahoma." *Baptist History and Heritage* 8 (1973): 208-12.

(215) Bryan, G. McLeod. *Dissenter in the Baptist Southland: Fifty Years in the Career of William Wallace Finlator*. Macon GA: Mercer University Press, 1985.

(216) Carey, John J. *Carlyle Marney*. Macon GA: Mercer University Press, 1980.

(217) Carroll, James M., ed. *Dr. B. H. Carroll, the Colossus of Baptist History: Pastor First Baptist Church, Waco, Texas, and First President of S.W.B.T. Seminary, Fort Worth, Texas*. Fort Worth: Seminary Hill Press, 1946.

(218) Compton, Bob. "J. M. Pendleton: A Nineteenth-Century Baptist Statesman." *Baptist History and Heritage* 10 (1975): 28-35, 56.

(219) Compton, Bobby D. "J. Frank Norris and Southern Baptists." *Review and Expositor* 69 (1982): 63-84.

(220) Connelly, Thomas L. *Will Campbell and the Soul of the South*. New York: Continuum, 1982.

(221) Cook, Harvey T., ed. *A Biography of Richard Furman*. Greenville SC: Baptist Courier Job Rooms, 1913.

(222) Cox, Joseph P. "A Study of the Life and Work of Basil Manly, Jr." Th.D. dissertation, Southern Baptist Theological Seminary, 1954.

(223) Davis, Hugh C. "Edwin T. Winkler: Baptist Bayard." *Alabama Review* 17 (1964): 33-44.

(224) Dixon, Helen C. A. *A. C. Dixon: A Romance of Preaching*. New York: G. P. Putnam's Sons, 1931.

(225) Dobbins, Gaines S. "William Owen Carver, Missionary Pathfinder." *Baptist History and Heritage* 14 (1978): 2-6, 15.

(226) Duke, David H. "Henry Holcombe Tucker, Outspoken Baptist Journalist." *The Quarterly Review* 38 (1977): 67-76.

(227) Ellis, William E. "Edgar Young Mullins and the Crisis of Moderate Baptist Leadership." *Foundations* 19 (1976): 171-85.

(228) _____. *"A Man of Books and a Man of the People": E. Y. Mullins and the Crisis of Moderate Southern Baptist Leadership*. Macon GA: Mercer University Press, 1985.

(229) Falls, Ray E. *A Biography of J. Frank Norris, 1877-1952*. N.p.p.: n.p., 1975.

(230) Fletcher, Jesse C. *Bill Wallace of China*. Nashville: Broadman Press, 1963.

(231) Flynt, J. Wayne. "Growing Up Baptist in Anniston, Alabama: The Legacy of the Reverend Charles R. Bell, Jr." In *Clearings in the Thicket: An Alabama Humanities Reader*. Jerry Elijah Brown, ed., 147-82. Macon GA: Mercer University Press, 1985.

(232) Francisco, Clyde T. "John R. Sampey: Samuel Redivivus." *Review and Expositor* 63 (1966): 459-68.

(233) Gardner, Robert G. "Spencer Bidwell King, Jr." *Viewpoints: Georgia Baptist History* 6 (1978): 19-24.

(234) Garrett, James Leo, Jr. "Joseph Martin Dawson: Pastor, Author, Denominational Leader, Social Activist." *Baptist History and Heritage* 14 (1979): 7-15.

(235) Harris, Waldo P. III. "Daniel Marshall: Lone Georgia Baptist Revolutionary Pastor." *Viewpoints: Georgia Baptist History* 5 (1976): 51-64.

(236) Holmes, Jack D. L. "Barton Hannon in the Old Southwest." *Journal of Mississippi History* 44 (1982): 69-79.

(237) James, Powhatan W. *George W. Truett: A Biography*. New York: Macmillan, 1939.

(238) Keith, Billy. *W. A. Criswell: The Authorized Biography*. Old Tappan NJ: Fleming H. Revell, 1973.

(239) Kelley, Jeffrey O'Neal. "Edwin McNeill Poteat, Jr.: The Minister as Advocate." *Foundations* 22 (1979): 152-73.

(240) Lawrence, Una Roberts. *Lottie Moon*. Nashville: Sunday School Board of the Southern Baptist Convention, 1927.

(241) Lindsey, Jonathan A. "Basil Manly: Nineteenth Century Protean Man." *Baptist History and Heritage* 8 (1973): 130-43.

(242) Mullins, Isla May. *Edgar Young Mullins: An Intimate Biography*. Nashville: Broadman Press, 1929.

(243) Newman, S. *W. T. Connor: Theologian of the Southwest*. Nashville: Broadman Press, 1964.

(244) Poe, William A. "The Story of a Friendship and a Book: W. E. Paxton and Green W. Hartsfield." *Louisiana History* 22 (1981): 167-82.

(245) Robertson, Archibald T. "A Sketch of the Life of President Mullins." *Review and Expositor* 22 (1925): 7-10.

(246) Rogers, James A. *Richard Furman: Life and Legacy.* Macon GA: Mercer University Press, 1985.

(247) Routh, Porter. *Chosen for Leadership: Sketches of 39 Presidents of the Southern Baptist Convention.* Nashville: Broadman Press, 1976. First published 1953, as *Meet the Presidents.*

(248) Russell, C. Allyn. "J. Frank Norris: Violent Fundamentalist." *Southwestern Historical Quarterly* 75 (1972): 271-302.

(249) Smith, Harold S. "The Life and Work of J. R. Graves (1820-1893)." *Baptist History and Heritage* 10 (1975): 19-27, 55-56.

(250) Sullivan, Clayton. *Called to Preach, Condemned to Survive.* Macon GA: Mercer University Press, 1985.

(251) Tatum, E. Ray. *Conquest or Failure? Biography of J. Frank Norris.* Dallas: Baptist Historical Foundation, 1966.

(252) Taulman, James E. "The Life and Writings of Amons Cooper Dayton (1813-1865)." *Baptist History and Heritage* 10 (1975): 36-43.

(253) Taylor, James B. *Lives of Virginia Baptist Ministers.* 2d ed. 2 vols. New York: Sheldon, 1860. First published 1838.

(254) Thompson, Dorothy Brown. "John Taylor as Biographer of Pioneer Baptist Preachers." *Filson Club Historical Quarterly* 37 (1963): 258-80, 331-58.

(255) Wachs, Ronald. " 'Duty' Against Family: A Vermont Minister Adopts a Slave State." *Vermont History* n.s. 41 (1973): 9-28.

(256) Walter, Arthur L., Jr. "The Major." *Baptist History and Heritage* 9 (1974): 40-47, 54.

(257) Walser, Richard, "Biblio-Biography of Skitt Taliaferro." *North Carolina Historical Review* 55 (1978): 375-95.

(258) Weaver, Oliver C. "Benjamin Lloyd: A Pioneer Primitive Baptist in Alabama." *Alabama Review* 21 (1968): 144-55.

10 METHODISM IN THE SOUTH

THE RISE OF METHODISM in the South is attributable in part to the climate created by the evangelical revivals of the Great Awakening in the eighteenth century. The favorable disposition toward affective religious experience engendered by the revivals was also integral to the Methodist understanding of conversion. But until the late eighteenth century Methodism was at best an inchoate movement, organizing itself nationally in Baltimore in 1784. Methodist growth in the South thereafter was rapid, for the Methodist reliance on the circuit rider system, ready use of campmeeting techniques on the frontier, willingness to accept clergy on the basis of religious conviction rather than formal theological education, and the travels of the indefatigable Francis Asbury gave the emergent Wesleyan tradition flexibility to adjust to the expansion of the Southern frontier and to establish a presence in new areas of settlement. The continuing links of Methodism to revivalism are noted in several works listed in chapter 15.

The aggressive mobility of Methodists brought extensive contact with Indian societies and a considerable ministry to various Indian groups. Works focusing on Methodist missions among native American cultures are noted in chapter 3. The Methodist approach was also particularly appropriate for ministry among Afro-American slaves and over the years also gave birth to several denominations in the Methodist family with predominantly black memberships, as noted in chapter 4. As well, it was the controversy over slavery that ultimately split Methodism into the Methodist Episcopal Church (the Northern branch) and the Methodist Episcopal Church, South, in 1844. Additional works dealing with that division are also noted in chapter 4. Following the Civil War, Northern Methodists launched an aggressive ministry among freed blacks, a matter that would complicate reunion of the Northern and Southern branches and the Methodist Episcopal Church in 1939 and give Methodism a racially segregated administrative structure until the 1970s. The impact of the civil rights movement on Methodism in the South and concerns about racial discrimination are discussed in works identified in chapter 20.

In addition, the later nineteenth century witnessed the formation of numerous smaller groups that separated from mainstream Methodism in order to recapture what they believed to be Methodist founder John Wesley's proper emphasis on scriptural holiness. Several of those with pockets of strength in the South are noted in chapter 12. Later theological controversies, particularly those associated with the emergence of fundamentalism, also left their mark on Methodism in the South. For titles that examine these, see the listings for both chapters 20 and 21. As well, Methodism has long nurtured a concern for social issues. Methodists, for example, were prominent among leaders of the movement advocating prohibition. Works studying social issues are listed in chapter 20. Methodism's traditional commitment to an ethos within which the Christian life could take shape has led to extensive work in education, particularly in the founding of colleges and universities in the South and elsewhere in the nation. On this topic, see the listing for chapter 18.

In 1968, the United Methodist Church was formed from the merger of the Methodist Church and the Evangelical United Brethren Church. The latter body, originally composed primarily of German immigrants with Wesleyan tendencies, had a small membership in the South outside of border states such as Maryland. Today Methodism is both the nation's and the South's second largest Protestant denomination numerically, and regionally the South is home to more Methodists proportionately than any other section of the country.

The standard overview of the Methodist story is Emory S. Bucke, ed., *The History of American Methodism,* a three-volume collection of essays (6). Several essays treat topics germane to Southern Methodism, black and white, each by a different author. As in any collection, the work suffers from an unevenness of style and approach, but it remains the place to begin study. A necessary complement is Frederick A. Norwood, *The Story of American Methodism* (12), which admirably attempts to integrate Northern and Southern as well as black and white developments, and also the Evangelical United Brethren heritage, into a single, coherent narrative. Methodism's rapid growth in the old Southwest is the subject of two works by Walter B. Posey: *The Development of Methodism in the Old South West, 1783-1824* (14), and "The Advance of Methodism into the Lower Southwest" (13). Still valuable for identifying problems peculiar to Southern Methodism after the 1844 separation is Gross Alexander, *History of the Methodist Church, South* (2), which was part of the monumental American Church History Series edited by Philip

Schaff in the early 1890s. On the early days of the Methodist Episcopal Church, South, see also Lucius C. Mattock, "The Methodist Episcopal Church in the Southern States" (10), and W. Harrison Daniel, "A Brief Account of the Methodist Episcopal Church, South, in the Confederacy" (7). But clearly the most judicious study of the transformations that came to Southern Methodism in the years of recovery after the Civil War and its efforts to adjust to the ethos of the "New South" is Hunter D. Farish, *The Circuit Rider Dismounts: A Social History of Southern Methodism, 1865-1900* (9). Two essays provide beginning work on the internal trauma Methodism experienced in the twentieth century efforts to reunite Northern and Southern branches, when the largest obstacle, given the depth of racial prejudice and separation that prevailed in the South, was the presence of hundreds of black congregations in the South that were part of the Northern body: Henry Y. Warnock, "Southern Methodists, the Negro, and Unification: The First Phase" (18), and Kirk Mariner, "The Negro's Place: Virginia Methodists Debate Unification, 1924-1925" (46). The full story of Methodism's ongoing struggle to become a racially "inclusive" church remains to be told, but Charles H. Lippy, "Toward an Inclusive Church: Religion and Race in South Carolina Methodism, 1972-1982" (20:198), points the way.

More than some other denominations, Methodism has spawned countless studies of its history by state or by annual conference, the church's basic structural unit. As might be expected, most of these studies are filiopietistic in nature and rarely self-critical. But many of them are replete with detail and thus provide extensive material on which scholars might draw in writing more academic studies. Tending toward denominational self-praise is Gordon P. Baker, *Those Incredible Methodists: A History of the Baltimore Conference of the United Methodist Church* (21). But particularly valuable for its attention to detail, readability, and attempt at analysis is *Virginia Methodism: A History,* by William Warren Sweet, pioneer scholar of American religious history (61). An old but insightful study recently reprinted is Abel M. Chreitzberg, *Early Methodism in the Carolinas* (31). Three additional works fill out the North Carolina story: the now dated *History of Methodism in North Carolina from 1772 to the Present Time* by William L. Grissom (37); prominent Methodist historian Elmer T. Clark's *Methodism in Western North Carolina* (32), which treats the subregion where Methodism enjoys unusual numerical strength; and Charles F. Grill, *Methodism in the Upper Cape Fear Valley* (36). For South Carolina developments, the standard study, heavy on detail but weak in analysis, remains Albert D. Betts, *History of South Carolina Methodism* (22). George G. Smith, *The History of Methodism in Georgia and Florida from 1785 to 1865* (60), now more than a century old, is still helpful for minor detail, while Marion E. Lazenby, *History of Methodism in Alabama and West Florida, Being an Account of the Amazing March of*

Methodism through Alabama and West Florida (43), is a prime example of the filiopietistic study. Both George E. Clary, ed., *Our Methodist Heritage in South Georgia* (33), and William E. Brooks, ed., *From Saddlebags to Satellites: A History of Florida Methodism* (23), contain some solid essays, but must be used with caution. On Florida, also see William E. Brooks, *History and Highlights of Florida Methodism* (24). A solid local study treating Georgia Methodism is Mary B. Rebisen, "History of the First Methodist Church of Thomasville, Georgia: Early Days, 1838-1866" (83).

Mississippi Methodism has been the focus of several studies that, taken together, provide a comprehensive overview of the denomination's history in that state. All are admirable in attention to detail, but none offers rigorous scholarly interpretation. The period prior to the formation of the Methodist Episcopal Church, South, receives coverage in John G. Jones, *A Complete History of Methodism as Connected with the Mississippi Conference of the Methodist Episcopal Church, South, 1799-1845* (41), and in John B. Cain, *The Cradle of Mississippi Methodism* (25). Cain's *Methodism in the Mississippi Conference, 1846-1870* (26) takes the story to the point when black Methodists who remained in the Southern branch formed the autonomous Colored (now Christian) Methodist Episcopal Church. Continuing the historical chronicle are William B. Jones, *Methodism in the Mississippi Conference, 1870-1894* (42), and J. Allen Lindsey, *Methodism in the Mississippi Conference* (44), which brings the story to 1919. The early period of Tennessee Methodist history is told by Cullen Carter in *Methodism in the Wilderness, 1786-1836* (29). His *History of the Tennessee Conference and a Brief Summary of the General Conferences, the Methodist Church, from the Frontier in Middle Tennessee, to the Present Time* (28) offers a cursory look at later developments down to the mid-1940s.

William E. Arnold's dated two-volume study, *A History of Methodism in Kentucky* (20), is complemented by Roy H. Short, *Methodism in Kentucky* (59), but neither is academic in the strictest sense. More scholarly are two studies by Walter N. Vernon on the Wesleyan heritage in Arkansas: "Beginnings of Methodism in Arkansas" (66) and *Methodism in Arkansas, 1816-1976* (67). Frank C. Tucker, *The Methodist Church in Missouri, 1798-1938* (65), and Robert H. Harper, *Louisiana Methodism* (39), are the standard works for those states. Harper's monograph, however, does contain helpful bibliographic footnotes. Helpful in understanding the Louisiana story is Ray Holder, "Methodist Beginnings in New Orleans, 1813-1814" (74). Macum Phelan concentrated on Methodism in the Lone Star State in two older studies: *A History of Early Methodism in Texas, 1817-1866* (55) and *A History of the Expansion of Methodism in Texas, 1867-1902* (56). But also see the collection of essays of mixed value edited by Olin W. Nail, *Texas Methodism, 1900-1960* (51). Methodism in Texas, more so than Methodism elsewhere, has had to deal with the presence of a significant Mexican-American minority, long administratively subject to non-Hispanic control. The emergence of indigenous Hispanic leadership is briefly recounted in Alfredo Nanez, "The Transition from Anglo to Mexican-American Leadership in the Rio Grande Conference" (52). Much of the story of Oklahoma Methodism is linked to missionary work among the native American tribal groups forced onto reservations. While titles dealing with that aspect of Oklahoma Methodism are noted in chapter 3, two other studies, though not particularly astute in analysis, merit mention: Paul D. Mitchell, *From Tepees to Towers: A History of the Methodist Church in Oklahoma* (49), and Leland Clegg and William B. Oden, *Oklahoma Methodism in the Twentieth Century* (34).

As with other denominations, Methodism numbers several individuals who made substantial contributions to the shape of the Wesleyan heritage in the South. Noteworthy among those in the early years is Freeborn Garrettson (1752-1827), a wealthy convert from Maryland who freed his slaves, became an itinerant preacher who traveled widely during the Revolutionary epoch, and made a lasting mark on Methodist developments in Nova Scotia and New England. The standard biography is Nathan Bangs, *The Life of the Rev. Freeborn Garrettson* (89), but also see the solid essay by Robert D. Simpson ("The Lord's Rebel: Freeborn Garrettson—A Methodist Preacher During the American Revolution" [123]). More notorious for his eccentric ways was exhorter Lorenzo Dow (1777-1834), who has the distinction of preaching the first Protestant sermon in Alabama for which there is record. Charles Coleman Sellers, *Lorenzo Dow: The Bearer of the Word* (121), is a meticulous study, but also see Richard J. Stockman, "Misunderstood Lorenzo Dow" (127). The German Wesleyan strain that issued in the United Brethren in Christ, forerunner of the Evangelical United Brethren component of today's United Methodist Church, owed much of its early leadership to the Otterbein family. Philip Otterbein had some impact in the South, having served as a pastor in Maryland. The best brief study is J. Steven O'Malley, "The Otterbeins: Men of Two Worlds" (114).

Among the leading advocates of a proslavery position within Methodism and one responsible for much early work in Mississippi, including some mission work with the Choctaws, was William Winans (1788-1857). Ray Holder's biography, *William Winans: Methodist Leader in Antebellum Mississippi* (106), is essentially hagiography and of little value other than for chronological details of Winans's life. Holder's "Parson Winans' Pilgrimage to 'The Natchez' Winter of 1810" (105), is some better, but the best study is Rex P. Kyker's doctoral dissertation, "William Winans: Minister and Politician of the Old South" (108). Much of Methodism's successful mission work among slaves resulted from the labors of William Capers (1790-1855), who was designated one of the first bishops of the Methodist Episcopal Church, South, after the 1844 division. The best study of Capers is D. A. Reily's dissertation, "William Capers: An Evaluation of His Life and Thought" (117), but also see W. M. Wightman, *The Life and William Capers* (131). Methodist preacher, governor of Tennessee, and also United States Senator from Tennessee William G. Brownlow is the subject of E. Merton Coulter's rather traditional *William G. Brownlow: Fighting Parson of the Southern Highlands* (96). Another prominent figure in the late nineteenth century is Emory University president, editor, and sometime bishop Atticus Greene Haygood (1839-1896). Haygood, advanced for his time in advocating educational opportunities for Southern blacks, is the focus of Elem F. Dempsey, *Atticus Greene Haygood: He Took the Kingdom by Violence, Matthew 11:12* (98), but a more penetrating study is Harold W. Mann's published dissertation, *Atticus Greene Haygood: Methodist Bishop, Editor, and Educator* (109), which offers much insight on the social history of the Deep South in the decades of transition that followed Reconstruction. Haygood's protégé, Warren Akin Candler (1857-1941), was far more conservative. Mark K. Bauman's careful biography, *Warren Akin Candler: The Conservative as Idealist* (90), chronicles Candler's many contributions to Methodist-related higher education in the South, but also develops the case that this bishop was one who resisted the trends of the times. Much less valuable is Alfred M. Pierce's hagiographic *Giant Against the Sky: The Life of Bishop Warren Akin Candler* (116).

In the early twentieth century no Methodist leader was more notorious than James Cannon, Jr. (1864-1944), elected a bishop of the Southern church in 1919. Cannon became the subject of much controversy when Senator Carter Glass publicized his possible—some would say probable—misuse of church funds and some public monies, as well as his involvement in stock transactions of dubious legality. A staunch advocate of Prohibition, Cannon was also accused of adultery. The most balanced account, though now dated, is Virginius Dabney, *Dry Messiah: The Life of Bishop Cannon* (97). Cannon's difficulties are appraised in Michael S. Patterson, "The Fall of a Bishop: James Cannon, Jr., *versus* Carter Glass, 1909-1934" (115). Cannon sought to exonerate himself in an autobiography, *Bishop Cannon's Own Story: Life As I Have Seen It,* edited by Raymond L. Watson, Jr. (129). One twentieth-century Methodist layman merits mention: Willis D. Weatherford (1875-1970). Active in YMCA work and most widely known for his commitment to ministry in Appalachia, Weatherford was also a major spokesman for black human rights in a day when it was unfashionable for white Southerners to take such a stand. There is an appreciative memoir, Wilma Dykeman's *Prophet of Plenty: The First Ninety Years of W. D. Weatherford* (101), but there is no scholarly biography. Other works that discuss Weatherford or were written by him are included in the listings for chapters 4 and 13.

The bibliography that follows includes listings of general and topical studies, works that treat Southern Methodism by state, the many local studies of individual congregations, and selected biographies and autobiographies. Attention should also be directed to *Methodist History,* a quarterly that frequently carries articles of interest to students of Methodism in the South.

BIBLIOGRAPHY

Numerous titles in the listings for chapters 1, 2, 3, 4, 12, 15, 18, 19, 20, and 21 are relevant to the study of Methodism in the South.

I. METHODISM IN THE SOUTH: GENERAL AND TOPICAL STUDIES

(1) Albert, Aristides E. "The Church in the South." *Methodist Review* 74 (1892): 229-40.

(2) Alexander, Gross. *History of the Methodist Church, South.* American Church History Series 11. New York: Christian Literature, 1894.

(3) Andrews, Stuart. "John Wesley and America." *History Today* 26 (1976): 353-59.

(4) Atkins, D. "The Unification of the Methodist Episcopal Church and the Methodist Episcopal Church, South." *Methodist Quarterly Review* 73 (1924): 276-99.

(5) Baker, Frank. "John Wesley's Last Visit to Charleston." *South Carolina Historical Magazine* 78 (1977): 265-71.

(6) Bucke, Emory S., ed. *The History of American Methodism.* 3 vols. New York: Abingdon Press, 1964.

(7) Daniel, W. Harrison. "A Brief Account of the Methodist Episcopal Church, South, in the Confederacy." *Methodist History* 6 (1968): 27-41.

(8) Deems, Charles F. *Annals of Southern Methodism.* New York: J. A. Gray's Printing Office, 1865.

(9) Farish, Hunter D. *The Circuit Rider Dismounts: A Social History of Southern Methodism, 1865-1900.* Richmond: Dietz Press, 1938.

(10) Mattock, Lucius C. "The Methodist Episcopal Church in the Southern States." *Methodist Quarterly Review* 54 (1872): 103-26.

(11) Morgan, David T. "John Wesley's Sojourn in Georgia Revisited." *Georgia Historical Quarterly* 64 (1980): 253-62.

(12) Norwood, Frederick A. *The Story of American Methodism: A History of the United Methodists and Their Relations.* Nashville: Abingdon Press, 1974.

(13) Posey, Walter B. "The Advance of Methodism into the Lower Southwest." *Journal of Southern History* 2 (1936): 439-52.

(14) _____. *The Development of Methodism in the Old South West, 1783-1824.* Tuscaloosa: Weatherford Printing, 1933.

(15) Shankman, Arnold. "Dorothy Tilly, Civil Rights, and the Methodist Church." *Methodist History* 18 (1980): 95-108.

(16) Smith, John A. "How Methodism Became a National Church in the United States." *Methodist History* 20 (1981): 13-28.

(17) Smith, Warren T. "Thomas Coke's First Trip to America, 1784-1785." *Wesleyan Quarterly Review* 2 (1965): 125-37.

(18) Warnock, Henry Y. "Southern Methodists, the Negro, and Unification: The First Phase." *Journal of Negro History* 52 (1967): 287-304.

II. METHODISM IN THE SOUTH: STUDIES BY STATE

(19) Armstrong, James E. *History of the Old Baltimore Conference from the Planting of Methodism in 1773 to the Division of the Conference in 1857*. Baltimore: King Brothers, 1907.

(20) Arnold, William E. *A History of Methodism in Kentucky*. 2 vols. Louisville: Herald Press, 1935-36.

(21) Baker, Gordon P. *Those Incredible Methodists: A History of the Baltimore Conference of the United Methodist Church*. Baltimore: The Baltimore Conference, 1972.

(22) Betts, Albert D. *History of South Carolina Methodism*. Columbia: Advocate Press, 1952.

(23) Brooks, William E., ed. *From Saddlebags to Satellites: A History of Florida Methodism*. Nashville: Printed by the Parthenon Press, 1969.

(24) _____. *History and Highlights of Florida Methodism*. Ft. Lauderdale: Tropical Press, 1965.

(25) Cain, John B. *The Cradle of Mississippi Methodism*. Natchez MS: n.p., 1920.

(26) _____. *Methodism in the Mississippi Conference, 1846-1870*. Jackson MS: The Hawkins Foundation, Mississippi Conference Historical Society, 1939.

(27) Carter, Cullen T. *History of Methodist Churches and Institutions in Middle Tennessee, 1787-1956*. Nashville: Parthenon Press, 1956.

(28) _____. *History of the Tennessee Conference and a Brief Summary of the General Conferences, the Methodist Church, from the Frontier in Middle Tennessee, to the Present Time*. Nashville: n.p., 1948.

(29) _____. *Methodism in the Wilderness, 1786-1836*. Nashville: Parthenon Press, 1960.

(30) *Century of Progress, 1846-1946*. Hopkinsville KY: Published by the Historical Society, Louisville Annual Conference, 1946.

(31) Chreitzberg, Abel M. *Early Methodism in the Carolinas*. Nashville: Publishing House of the Methodist Episcopal Church, South, 1897. Reprint, Spartanburg SC: Reprint, 1972.

(32) Clark, Elmer T. *Methodism in Western North Carolina*. Nashville: Western North Carolina Conference, Methodist Church, 1966.

(33) Clary, George E., ed. *Our Methodist Heritage in South Georgia*. Savannah: n.p., 1960.

(34) Clegg, Leland, and William B. Oden. *Oklahoma Methodism in the Twentieth Century*. Nashville: Printed by the Parthenon Press, 1968.

(35) Graham, John H. *Mississippi Circuit Riders, 1865-1965*. Nashville: Parthenon Press, 1967.

(36) Grill, Charles F. *Methodism in the Upper Cape Fear Valley*. Nashville: Parthenon Press, 1966.

(37) Grissom, William L. *History of Methodism in North Carolina from 1772 to the Present Time*. Nashville: Publishing House of the Methodist Episcopal Church, South, 1905.

(38) Hamrick, William L. *The Mississippi Conference of the Methodist Protestant Church (1829-1939)*. Jackson: Hawkins Foundation, 1957.

(39) Harper, Robert H. *Louisiana Methodism*. Washington: Kaufmann Press, 1949.

(40) Higginbotham, Don. "Methodism Moves East: Annual Conference, New Bern, North Carolina, 1807." *Wesleyan Quarterly Review* 1 (1964): 38-42.

(41) Jones, John G. *A Complete History of Methodism as Connected with the Mississippi Conference of the Methodist Episcopal Church, South, 1799-1845*. 2 vols. Nashville: Southern Methodist Publishing House, 1887. Reprint, Baton Rouge: Claitors Book Store, 1966.

(42) Jones, William B. *Methodism in the Mississippi Conference, 1870-1894*. Jackson: Hawkins Foundation, Mississippi Conference Historical Society, 1951.

(43) Lazenby, Marion E. *History of Methodism in Alabama and West Florida, Being an Account of the Amazing March of Methodism through Alabama and West Florida*. [Nashville?]: n.p., 1960.

(44) Lindsey, J. Allen. *Methodism in the Mississippi Conference, 1894-1919*. Nashville: Parthenon Press, 1964.

(45) McFerrin, John B. *History of Methodism in Tennessee*. Nashville: Southern Methodist Publishing House, 1879.

(46) Mariner, Kirk. "The Negro's Place: Virginia Methodists Debate Unification, 1924-1925." *Methodist History* 18 (1980): 155-70.

(47) Martin, Isaac P. *Methodism in Holston*. Knoxville: Methodist Historical Society of Holston Conference, 1945.

(48) Miller, Gene R. *A History of North Mississippi Methodism, 1820-1900*. Nashville: Parthenon Press, 1966.

(49) Mitchell, Paul D. *From Tepees to Towers: A History of the Methodist Church in Oklahoma*. Verden OK: n.p., 1947.

(50) Nail, Olin W. *The First Hundred Years of the Southwest Texas Conference of the Methodist Church, 1859-1958*. San Antonio: Southwest Texas Conference, Methodist Church, 1958.

(51) _____, ed. *Texas Methodism, 1900-1960*. Austin: Capital Printing, 1961.

(52) Nanez, Alfredo. "The Transition from Anglo to Mexican-American Leadership in the Rio Grande Conference." *Methodist History* 16 (1978): 67-74.

(53) *North Texas Methodism: History of the North Texas Conference and the Dallas District.* Dallas: Southern Methodist Historical, 1926.

(54) Norton, Wesley. "The Methodist Episcopal Church and the Civil Disturbances in North Texas in 1859 and 1860." *Southwestern Historical Quarterly* 67 (1964): 317-41.

(55) Phelan, Macum. *A History of Early Methodism in Texas, 1817-1866.* Nashville: Cokesbury Press, 1924.

(56) _____. *A History of the Expansion of Methodism in Texas, 1867-1902.* Dallas: Mathis, Van Nort, 1937.

(57) Pierce, Alfred M. *A History of Methodism in Georgia, February 5, 1746-June 14, 1955.* Atlanta: Georgia Conference Historical Society, [1956].

(58) Redford, A. H. *The History of Methodism in Kentucky.* 3 vols. Nashville: Southern Methodist Publishing House, 1868-70.

(59) Short, Roy H. *Methodism in Kentucky.* Rutland VT: Academy Books, 1979.

(60) Smith, George G. *The History of Methodism in Georgia and Florida from 1785 to 1865.* Macon GA: J. W. Burke, 1877.

(61) Sweet, William Warren. *Virginia Methodism: A History.* Richmond VA: Whittet and Shepperson, 1955.

(62) Thrall, Homer S. *A Brief History of Methodism in Texas.* Nashville: Publishing House of the Methodist Episcopal Church, South, 1894.

(63) _____. *History of Methodism in Texas.* Houston: Cushing, 1872.

(64) Thrift, Charles T. *On the Trail of the Florida Circuit Rider: An Introduction to the Rise of Methodism in Middle and East Florida.* Lakeland FL: Florida Southern College Press, 1944.

(65) Tucker, Frank C. *The Methodist Church in Missouri, 1798-1938.* Nashville: Parthenon Press, 1966.

(66) Vernon, Walter N. "Beginnings of Methodism in Arkansas." *Arkansas Historical Quarterly* 31 (1972): 356-72.

(67) _____. *Methodism in Arkansas, 1816-1976.* Little Rock: Joint Committee for the History of Arkansas Methodism, 1976.

(68) _____. *Methodism Moves Across North Texas.* Nashville: Parthenon Press, 1967.

(69) Wasson, Margaret. "Texas Methodism's Other Half." *Methodist History* 18 (1981): 206-33.

(70) West, Anson. *A History of Methodism in Alabama.* Nashville: Publishing House of the Methodist Episcopal Church, South, 1893.

(71) West, C. A., ed. *Texas Conference Methodism on the March, 1814-1960.* Nashville: Parthenon Press, 1960.

III. METHODISM IN THE SOUTH: LOCAL STUDIES

(72) Carter, Cullen T. *History of the Columbia District of the Tennessee Conference of the Methodist Church.* Nashville: Parthenon Press, [1962?].

(73) Gundersen, Joan Reznes. "A Petition of Early Norfolk County, Virginia, Methodists to the Bishop of London Urging the Ordination of Joseph Pilmoor." *Virginia Magazine of History and Biography* 83 (1975): 412-21.

(74) Holder, Ray. "Methodist Beginnings in New Orleans, 1813-1814." *Louisiana History* 18 (1977): 171-87.

(75) Ironmonger, Elizabeth Hogg. *A History of Zion Methodist Church of Seaford, York County, Virginia*. [Seaford VA?]: n.p., 1967.

(76) _____. *Methodism in York County, Virginia*. [Richmond VA?]: n.p., 1959.

(77) Kirby, James E. "The McKendree Chapel Affair." *Tennessee Historical Quarterly* 25 (1966): 360-70.

(78) Laney, Mrs. Alberta. *Sketch of the Methodist Church, Perote, Alabama, 1839-1908*. Montgomery: Paragon Press, 1908.

(79) Martin, Isaac P. *Church Street Methodists, Children of Francis Asbury: A History of Church Street Methodist Church, Knoxville, Tennessee, 1816-1947*. Knoxville: Methodist Historical Society of Holston Conference, 1947.

(80) *The Methodist Church of Union Springs, Alabama*. Union Springs AL: Alabama Conference Historical Society, Methodist Episcopal Church, South, 1908.

(81) *The Methodist Churches of Mobile*. Mobile: Alabama Conference Historical Society, Methodist Episcopal Church, South, 1908.

(82) Owen, Thomas M. *The Methodist Churches of Montgomery*. [Montgomery]: Paragon Press, 1908.

(83) Rebisen, Mary P. "History of the First Methodist Church of Thomasville, Georgia: Early Days, 1838-1866." *Wesleyan Quarterly Review* 1 (1964): 164-82.

(84) Shankin, Thomas L., and Kenneth E. Rowe, eds. "David Creamer and the Baltimore Mob Riot, April 19, 1861." *Methodist History* 13 (1975): 61-64.

(85) Stokes, Bess D., and Elizabeth F. Duncan. *Methodism in Wayne County, Kentucky, 1802-1974*. Somerset KY: Commonwealth-Journal Print, n.d.

(86) Vernon, Walter N. "Methodist Pioneers Along the Great Bend of Red River." *Red River Valley Historical Review* 6 (1981): 46-57.

(87) Wiley, E. E., Jr., et al. *Centenary . . . The Story of a Church*. Chattanooga: n.p., 1962.

IV. METHODISM IN THE SOUTH: BIOGRAPHICAL AND AUTOBIOGRAPHICAL STUDIES

(88) Anders, Leslie. "His 'Radical Reverence' John H. Cox." *Missouri Historical Review* 65 (1970): 139-58.

(89) Bangs, Nathan. *The Life of the Rev. Freeborn Garrettson*. 4th ed., rev. and corr. New York: T. Mason and G. Lane, 1838.

(90) Bauman, Mark K. *Warren Akin Candler: The Conservative as Idealist*. Metuchen NJ: Scarecrow Press, 1981.

(91) Bennett, John B. "Albert Taylor Bledsoe: Social and Religious Controversialist of the Old South." Ph.D. dissertation, Duke University, 1942.

(92) Boles, John B. "John Hersey: Dissenting Theologian of Abolitionism, Perfectionism, Millennialism." *Methodist History* 14 (1976): 215-34.

(93) Brown, Douglas S. "Elizabeth Henry Campbell Russell: Patroness of Early Methodism in the Highlands of Virginia." *Virginia Calvalcade* 30 (1981): 110-17.

(94) Cannon, William R. "The Pierces: Father and Son." *Methodist History* 17 (1978): 3-15.

(95) Carter, Cullen T. *Methodist Leaders in the Old Jerusalem Conference, 1812-1962*. Nashville: Parthenon Press, 1961.

(96) Coulter, E. Merton. *William G. Brownlow: Fighting Parson of the Southern Highlands*. Chapel Hill: University of North Carolina Press, 1937.

(97) Dabney, Virginius. *Dry Messiah: The Life of Bishop Cannon*. New York: Knopf, 1949.

(98) Dempsey, Elem F. *Atticus Green Haygood: He Took the Kingdom by Violence, Matthew 11:12*. Nashville: Parthenon Press, 1940.

(99) _____. *Life of Bishop Dickey, Bishop of the Methodist Episcopal Church, South*. Nashville: Publishing House of the Methodist Episcopal Church, South, 1937.

(100) _____, ed. *Wit and Wisdom of Warren Akin Candler*. Nashville: Publishing House of the Methodist Episcopal Church, South, 1922.

(101) Dykeman, Wilma. *Prophet of Plenty: The First Ninety Years of W. D. Weatherford*. Knoxville: University of Tennessee Press, 1966.

(102) Earl, J. A. "A Huntington Bishop with Office in His Hat." *West Virginia History* 32 (1971): 108-14.

(103) Hites, Margaret Ann. "Peter Doub, 1796-1869, His Contribution to the Religious and Educational Development of North Carolina." *Methodist History* 11 (1972): 19-45.

(104) Hohner, Robert A., ed. "From the Methodist Parsonage in Charlottesville: Bernard F. Lipscomb's Letters to James Cannon, Jr., 1889-1892." *Virginia Magazine of History and Biography* 83 (1975): 428-74.

(105) Holder, Ray. "Parson Winans' Pilgrimage to 'The Natchez' Winter of 1810." *Journal of Mississippi History* 44 (1982): 47-67.

(106) _____. *William Winans: Methodist Leader in Antebellum Mississippi*. Jackson MS: University Press of Mississippi, 1977.

(107) Holmes, Marjorie M. "The Life and Diary of the Reverend John Jeremiah Jacob (1757-1839)." M.A. thesis, Duke University, 1941.

(108) Kyker, Rex P. "William Winans: Minister and Politician of the Old South." Ph.D. dissertation, University of Florida, 1957.

(109) Mann, Harold W. *Atticus Greene Haygood: Methodist Bishop, Editor, and Educator*. Athens: University of Georgia Press, 1965.

(110) Martin, Isaac P. *Elijah Embree Hoss, Ecumenical Methodist*. Nashville: Parthenon Press, 1942.

(111) _____. *A Minister in the Tennessee Valley, Sixty-Seven Years*. Nashville: Methodist Historical Society of Holston Conference, 1954.

(112) May, James W. "Francis Asbury and Thomas White: A Refugee Preacher and His Tory Patron." *Methodist History* 14 (1976): 141-64.

(113) Miller, Rush G. "John G. Jones: Pioneer Circuit Rider and Historian." *Journal of Mississippi History* 39 (1977): 17-39.

(114) O'Malley, J. Steven. "The Otterbeins: Men of Two Worlds." *Methodist History* 15 (1976): 3-21.

(115) Patterson, Michael S. "The Fall of a Bishop: James Cannon, Jr., *versus* Carter Glass, 1909-1934." *Journal of Southern History* 39 (1973): 493-518.

(116) Pierce, Alfred M. *Giant Against the Sky: The Life of Bishop Warren Akin Candler*. New York: Abingdon-Cokesbury, 1948.

(117) Reily, D. A. "William Capers: An Evaluation of His Life and Thought." Ph.D. dissertation, Emory University, 1972.

(118) Rice, John A. *I Came Out of the Eighteenth Century*. New York: Harper and Brothers, 1942.

(119) Rives, Ralph H. "Nicholas Snethen: Methodist Protestant Pioneer." *Methodist History* 17 (1979): 78-89.

(120) Rogers, Tommy W. "T. C. Thornton: A Methodist Educator of Antebellum Mississippi." *Journal of Mississippi History* 44 (1982): 136-46.

(121) Sellers, Charles Coleman. *Lorenzo Dow: The Bearer of the Word*. New York: Minton, Balch, 1928.

(122) Simmons, Darlene S. "Rev. Herbert Spencer: Roane County Preacher." *Goldenseal* 2 (1976): 31-34.

(123) Simpson, Robert D. "The Lord's Rebel: Freeborn Garrettson—A Methodist Preacher During the American Revolution." *Wesleyan Quarterly Review* 2 (1965): 194-211.

(124) Steele, David L. "The Autobiography of the Reverend John Young, 1747-1837." *Methodist History* 13 (1974): 17-40.

(125) Stein, Stephen J. "A Note on Anne Dutton, Eighteenth-Century Evangelical." *Church History* 44 (1975): 484-91.

(126) Stevenson, Arthur L. *Native Methodist Preachers of Norfolk and Princess Anne Counties, Virginia*. Brevard NC: Stevenson, 1975.

(127) Stockman, Richard J. "Misunderstood Lorenzo Dow." *Alabama Review* 16 (1963): 20-34.

(128) Stokes, Durward T. "Jeremiah Norman, Pioneer Methodist Minister in Augusta and His Diary." *Richmond County History* 10 (1978): 20-35.

(129) Watson, Raymond L., Jr., ed. *Bishop Cannon's Own Story: Life As I Have Seen It*. Durham: Duke University Press, 1955.

(130) West, Earl I. "Religion in the Life of James K. Polk." *Tennessee Historical Quarterly* 26 (1967): 357-71.

(131) Wightman, W. M. *The Life of William Capers*. Nashville: Southern Methodist Publishing House, 1859. First published 1856.

(132) _____. *Lovick Pierce: A Sketch*. Nashville: Southern Methodist Publishing House, 1880.

11 CAMPBELLITE AND RESTORATIONIST TRADITIONS IN THE SOUTH

THE FRENZIED EXCITEMENT of nineteenth-century frontier revivalism not only helped to imprint the evangelical style on much of Southern religion, but also led to the emergence of an interest in returning to the practices of primitive Christianity. Both commonsense rationalists and emotional revivalists sought to return to a presumably more pure Christian practice untainted by the accretions of time that had corrupted authentic Christianity. While this restorationist impulse attracted many campmeeting advocates, including Barton W. Stone, in time it coalesced around Alexander Campbell (1788-1866). Restorationists discarded denominational labels at first as signs of division within the one church, preferring to call themselves simply "Christians." In time, however, the followers of Alexander Campbell grew into one of the first indigenous denominations in the United States, the Disciples of Christ or the Christian Church.

As the movement grew, it enlarged its vision to include a conviction that American society itself could be transformed into a culture replicating the pure simplicity of New Testament Christian communities even as it extended its following into both the North and the South. For many years Campbell maintained an unofficial headquarters in Bethany, West Virginia. As with other groups, the sectional divisions over slavery brought tension to the movement, which combined with disagreement over religious practices (such as the use of musical instruments in worship, the support of ecumenical missionary societies, and the like) to split the developing denomination in two by 1906, though for all practical purposes the emerging schism was obvious at least two decades earlier. The more "conservative" group adopted the name Churches of Christ and still maintains its base of strength in the South. By the time of the formal division, it was also clear that the Disciples of Christ had come to place more emphasis on ecumenical and cooperative ventures than on restorationist principles. Hence the restorationist impulse has been more closely associated with the Churches of Christ as the twentieth century progressed. Differences regarding methods of biblical interpretation also entered into the controversy. Later internal disputes over requiring baptism by immersion for admission into fellowship led the more adamant proimmersion party of the Disciples in 1927 to become popularly known as the Christian Churches and Churches of Christ, though allied congregations have eschewed denominational structures and still regard themselves more as a federation of independent congregations.

A significant body of literature has appraised the history and development of these groups and their leaders, whose stories are intertwined for nearly a century and often treated together. For many years, the work of church historian Winfred Ernest Garrison dominated the field. His early study, *Alexander Campbell's Theology: Its Sources and Setting* (10), attempted to locate the movement's ideology within the broader theological tradition as well as within the American context of frontier revivalism. Garrison's conviction that the religious style of the frontier was essential to understanding the contours of the Campbellite thrust formed the thesis of his *Religion Follows the Frontier: A History of the Disciples of Christ* (13), while its corollary, the specifically American context that gave birth to the movement, is developed in his *An American Religious Movement: A Brief History of the Disciples of Christ* (11). His most synoptic study was coauthored with A. T. DeGroot: *The Disciples of Christ: A History* (12). But Garrison's work, as others of the "church history" genre, is hardly critical, representing the "institutional triumphalism" school of Disciples history, although it is grounded in traditional historical method. More recently, William Tucker and Lester G. McAllister, *Journey in Faith: A History of the Christian Church (Disciples of Christ)* (43) has become the basic Disciples denominational history. A more popular study, lacking rigorous analysis, is Louis Cochran and Bess White Cochran, *Captives of the Word* (6).

The standard denominational history for the Churches of Christ is the three-volume work of Earl Irvin West, *Search for the Ancient Order* (46). West works from an "issues and answers" perspective, but does not bring critical analysis to his study. Different in approach is William S. Banowsky, *The Mirror of a Movement* (4), which looks at themes characterizing the more conservative Churches of Christ and vignettes in that group's history as they have been articulated through a recurring lecture series at the denomination's

Abilene Christian College (now University). A recent comparison of differences in ideological styles between the Churches of Christ and the Disciples of Christ is F. Maurice Ethridge and Joe R. Feagin, "Varieties of 'Fundamentalism': A Conceptual and Empirical Analysis of Two Protestant Denominations" (8), based on a 1972 study of Texas congregations. For the Christian Churches and Churches of Christ, or Independent Christian Churches, see James DeForest Murch, *Christians Only* (36).

By far the most penetrating portrayal of the Disciples and Churches of Christ, particularly before the formal separation in 1906, is found in the work of David Edwin Harrell, Jr. Harrell, a member of the "noncooperation" wing of the Churches of Christ, leaves behind all traces of the filiopietism that marks most studies of denominations written by adherents and also the simple chronicling of names, dates, and events characteristic of most traditional denominational histories written by scholars, though Harrell has mastered such "facts." Aware of tenets advanced by sociologists of knowledge concerning how ideas are absorbed and transformed into systems for understanding the whole of empirical reality, Harrell is also keenly sensitive to the way cultural and religious forces interact and mutually influence each other. Harrell's two volumes on the Disciples of Christ (which include coverage of the tensions that eventuated in the emergence of the separate Churches of Christ), *Quest for a Christian America: The Disciples of Christ and American Society to 1866* (18) and *The Social Sources of Division in the Disciples of Christ, 1865-1900* (22), unravel precisely how a religious world view becomes a way of constructing social reality, which in turn becomes a blueprint for society and social behavior. In several articles, Harrell has treated specific themes, some of which are also covered in his monographs: "The Significance of Social Forces in Disciples History" (21), "From Consent to Dissent: The Emergence of the Churches of Christ in America" (17). "The Sectional Pattern: The Divisive Impact of Slavery on the Disciples of Christ" (20), "The Sectional Origins of the Churches of Christ" (19), "The Disciples of Christ and Social Forces in Tennessee, 1865-1900" (62), and "The Agrarian Myth and the Disciples of Christ in the Nineteenth Century" (16). The Harrell corpus remains a model for a solid, scholarly, and insightful approach to denominational studies.

The differences of opinion over biblical criticism that were part of the schism between the Disciples and the Churches of Christ come into focus in Anthony L. Ash, "Attitudes Toward the Higher Criticism of the Old Testament Among the Disciples of Christ, 1850-1905" (1). Ash has published a series of four articles in *Restoration Quarterly* based on this dissertation (2). Numerous other works have attempted to identify other ideas, ranging from the presumed isolation of churches in the South during the era of the Civil War to the belief that restorationism inherently breeds division, as the fundamental cause of division, though none has been successful in making a convincing case. Representative of studies of this ilk are Arthur V. Murrell, "The Effects of Exclusivism in the Separation of the Churches of Christ from the Christian Church" (37), and Leroy Garrett, *The Stone-Campbell Movement: An Anecdotal History of Three Churches* (9).

Numerous works treat the Campbellite-Restorationist tradition along state lines, though most of these are semipopular in style and avoid sharp critical analysis. Among more recent studies in this genre are Herman A. Norton, *Tennessee Christians: A History of the Christian Churches (Disciples of Christ) in Tennessee* (72), and Wilbur H. Cramblet, *The Christian Church (Disciples of Christ) in West Virginia: A History of Its Co-Operative Work.* (53). H. Jackson Darst explores early and mid-nineteenth-century Campbellite developments in Virginia in *Ante-Bellum Virginia Disciples: An Account of the Emergence and Early Development of the Disciples of Christ in Virginia* (55), while Carter E. Boren traces a parallel story for Texas in his *Religion on the Texas Frontier* (49). Charles C. Ware has written several short monographs of a popular sort on Campbellite history in Carolinas, including histories of three individual North Carolina Disciples of Christ churches (79, 80, 82). His two more synoptic studies are the now dated *North Carolina Disciples of Christ: A History of Their Rise and Progress, and of Their Contributions to Their General Brotherhood* (81), which appeared in 1927, and *South Carolina Disciples of Christ: A History* (83). William J. Barber, *The Disciples' Assemblies of Eastern North Carolina* (48), is notable for its inclusion of the denomination's work, albeit limited, among its black adherents. On the coming of the Disciples to Oklahoma, see Stephen J. England, *Oklahoma Christians: A History of Christian Churches and of the Start of the Christian Church (Disciples of Christ) in Oklahoma* (57). An important study for the Churches of Christ is William Woodson, *Standing for Their Faith: A History of Churches of Christ in Tennessee, 1900-1950* (87). Woodson's study, an outgrowth of a doctoral dissertation, appreciatively but objectively chronicles the denomination's development in the state that was of strategic importance in the evolution of the Churches of Christ, paying particular attention to the emergence of a distinctive denominational identity.

The standard biography of Disciples founder Alexander Campbell remains Robert Richardson's two-volume *Memoirs of Alexander Campbell* (108), published more than a century ago. Most later biographers have relied heavily on Richardson's work. More recently Campbell's life and thought have received attention in several articles by John F. Morrison that deserve wider circulation than they have witnessed to date: "A Rational Voice Crying in an Emotional Wilderness" (104), "The Centrality of the Bible to Alexander Campbell's Life and Thought" (103), "Alexander Campbell: Moral Educator of the Middle Frontier" (102), and "Alexander Campbell: Freedom Fighter of the Middle Frontier" (101). Perry E. Gresham, ed., *The Sage of*

Bethany (93) contains essays by several prominent historians, including Arthur Schlesinger, Jr., and Roland Bainton. Also valuable in delineating Campbell's understanding of the nation and his vision of America is Harold L. Lunger, *The Political Ethics of Alexander Campbell* (98). On this subject for the Churches of Christ, see Royce L. Money, "Church-State Relations in the Churches of Christ since 1945: A Study in Religion and Politics" (32), which emphasizes the role of anti-Catholicism and anti-Communism in determining this denomination's position on church-state issues. Views on other social, ethical, and theological issues advanced by Campbell and by the denominations that have evolved from his teaching are the subject of several works identified in chapters 4, 18, 19, 20, and 21.

A vital influence on Alexander Campbell and on the spirit of ecumenicity associated with Campbell and the Disciples was his father, Thomas Campbell. Alexander Campbell, ed., *Memoirs of Elder Thomas Campbell, Together with a Brief Memoir of Mrs. Jane Campbell* (90), remains fundamental because of its inclusion of important primary material on both father and son. Two later biographies also merit mention: William H. Hanna, *Thomas Campbell: Seceder and Christian Union Advocate* (94); and Lester G. McAllister, *Thomas Campbell: Man of the Book* (99).

Two individuals prominent in the early growth of the Disciples who later exerted strong leadership in the conservative wing of the denomination that became the Churches of Christ were Tolbert Fanning (1810-74) and David Lipscomb (1831-1917). Neither has been the subject of a critical biography. James R. Wilburn, *The Hazard of the Die: Tolbert Fanning and the Restoration Movement* (116), is the best study to date of this major antebellum Disciples evangelist and critic of Disciples involvement in missionary societies. Similar, popularly written appreciations of Lipscomb, who was baptized by Fanning and had a long tenure as editor of the *Gospel Advocate,* are Robert E. Hooper, *Crying in the Wilderness: A Biography of David Lipscomb* (95), and Earl West, *Life and Times of David Lipscomb* (114). Also see John L. Robinson, *David Lipscomb: Journalist in Texas, 1872* (109).

The bibliography that follows identifies first denominational and topical studies that deal with either the Disciples of Christ or the Churches of Christ or both. Studies that focus on the Campbellite-Restorationist tradition in individual Southern states or communities follow. The final section lists biographical or autobiographical studies of individuals affiliated with either or both groups. Also important is *Restoration Quarterly,* a journal that contains articles of both historical and contemporary interest for this tradition. Sometimes useful for historical studies is *Discipliana,* the publication of the Disciples of Christ Historical Society in Nashville.

BIBLIOGRAPHY

Titles in chapters 1, 2, 4, 15, 18, 19, 20, and 21 are also relevant to the story of the Disciples of Christ and the Churches of Christ in the South.

I. THE CAMPBELLITE AND RESTORATIONIST TRADITIONS IN THE SOUTH: GENERAL AND TOPICAL STUDIES

(1) Ash, Anthony L. "Attitudes Toward the Higher Criticism of the Old Testament Among the Disciples of Christ: 1850-1905." Ph.D. dissertation, University of Southern California, 1966.

(2) _____. "Old Testament Studies in the Restoration Movement." *Restoration Quarterly* 9 (1966): 216-28; 10 (1967): 25-39, 89-98, 149-60.

(3) Bailey, Fred A. "The Status of Women in the Disciples of Christ Movement, 1865-1900." Ph.D. dissertation, University of Tennessee, 1979.

(4) Banowsky, William S. *The Mirror of a Movement: Churches of Christ as Seen Through the Abilene Christian College Lectureship*. Dallas: Christian Publishing, 1965.

(5) Blakemore, W. B., ed. *The Renewal of Church: The Panel Reports*. 3 vols. St. Louis: Bethany Press, 1963.

(6) Cochran, Louis, and Bess White Cochran. *Captives of the Word*. Garden City: Doubleday, 1969.

(7) Ethridge, F. Maurice. "Sect-Denominational Evolution: A Dialectical Model of Organizational Change." Ph.D. dissertation, University of Texas, 1973.

(8) _____, and Joe R. Feagin. "Varieties of 'Fundamentalism': A Conceptual and Empirical Analysis of Two Protestant Denominations." *Sociological Quarterly* 20 (1979): 37-48.

(9) Garrett, Leroy. *The Stone-Campbell Movement: An Anecdotal History of Three Churches*. Joplin: College Press Publishing, 1981.

(10) Garrison, Winfred E. *Alexander Campbell's Theology: Its Sources and Historical Setting*. St. Louis: Christian Publishing, 1900.

(11) _____. *An American Religious Movement: A Brief History of the Disciples of Christ*. St. Louis: Bethany Press, 1960. First published, 1945.

(12) _____, and A. T. DeGroot. *The Disciples of Christ: A History*. St. Louis: Christian Board of Publication, 1948.

(13) _____. *Religion Follows the Frontier: A History of the Disciples of Christ*. New York: Harper and Brothers, 1931.

(14) Gifford, Carey J. "Space and Time as Religious Symbols in Ante-Bellum America." Ph.D. dissertation, Claremont Graduate School, 1980.

(15) Hailey, Homer. *Attitudes and Consequences in the Restoration Movement*. Los Angeles: Citizen Print Shop, 1945.

(16) Harrell, David E., Jr. "The Agrarian Myth and the Disciples of Christ in the Nineteenth Century." *Agricultural History* 41 (1967): 181-92.

(17) _____. "From Consent to Dissent: The Emergence of the Churches of Christ in America." *Restoration Quarterly* 19 (1976): 98-111.

(18) _____. *Quest for a Christian America: The Disciples of Christ and American Society to 1866.* Nashville: Disciples of Christ Historical Society, 1966.

(19) _____. "The Sectional Origins of the Churches of Christ." *Journal of Southern History* 30 (1964): 261-77.

(20) _____. "The Sectional Pattern: The Divisive Impact of Slavery on the Disciples of Christ." *Discipliana* 21 (1961): 26 + .

(21) _____. "The Significance of Social Forces in Disciples History." *Integrity* 9 (1977): 67 + .

(22) _____. *The Social Sources of Division in the Disciples of Christ, 1865-1900.* Atlanta and Athens: Publishing Systems, 1973.

(23) Hatch, Nathan O. "The Christian Movement and the Demand for a Theology of the People." *Journal of American History* 67 (1980): 545-67.

(24) Hensley, Carl W. "Rhetorical Vision and the Persuasion of a Historical Movement: The Disciples of Christ in Nineteenth Century American Culture." *Quarterly Journal of Speech* 61 (1975): 250-64.

(25) Holland, Harold E. "Religious Periodicals in the Development of Nashville, Tennessee as a Regional Publishing Center, 1830-1880." Ph.D. dissertation, Columbia University, 1976.

(26) Hughes, Richard T. "Civil Religion, the Theology of the Republic, and the Free Church Tradition." *Journal of Church and State* 22 (1980): 75-87.

(27) _____. "A Comparison of the Restitution Motifs of the Campbells (1809-1830) and the Anabaptists (1524-1560)." *Mennonite Quarterly Review* 45 (1971): 312-30.

(28) _____. "From Civil Dissent to Civil Religion—and Beyond." *Religion in Life* 49 (1980): 268-88.

(29) _____. "From Primitive Church to Civil Religion: The Millennial Odyssey of Alexander Campbell." *Journal of the American Academy of Religion* 44 (1976): 87-103.

(30) Humble, B. J. *The Story of the Restoration.* Austin: Firm Foundation Publishing House, 1969.

(31) Major, James B. "The Role of Periodicals in the Development of the Disciples of Christ, 1850-1910." Ph.D. dissertation, Vanderbilt University, 1966.

(32) Money, Royce L. "Church-State Relations in the Churches of Christ since 1945: A Study in Religion and Politics." Ph.D. dissertation, Baylor University, 1975.

(33) Moore, W. T. *A Comprehensive History of the Disciples of Christ.* New York: Fleming H. Revell, 1909.

(34) Moorhouse, William M. "The Restoration Movement: The Rhetoric of Jacksonian Restorationism in a Frontier Religion." Ph.D. dissertation, Indiana University, 1967.

(35) Muncy, Raymond Lee. "Restitution and the Communal Impulse in America." *Restoration Quarterly* 19 (1976): 84-97.

(36) Murch, James DeForest. *Christians Only*. Cincinnati: Standard Publishing, 1962.

(37) Murrell, Arthur V. "The Effects of Exclusivism in the Separation of the Churches of Christ from the Christian Church." Ph.D. dissertation, Vanderbilt University, 1972.

(38) Phillips, Myer. "A Historical Study of the Attitude of the Churches of Christ toward Other Denominations." Ph.D. dissertation, Baylor University, 1983.

(39) Scarboro, Charles Allen. "A Sectarian Religious Organization in Heterogeneous Society: The Churches of Christ and the Plain-Folk of the Transmontane Mid-South." Ph.D. dissertation, Emory University, 1976.

(40) Sechler, Earl T. *Our Religious Heritage: Church History of the Ozarks, 1806-1906*. Springfiled MO: Westport Press, 1961.

(41) Spencer, Justina K., comp. *A Synoptic History (One Half Century) of the Christian Church*. Roanoke VA: Printed by the Roanoke Tribune, 1959.

(42) Tiffin, Gerald C. "The Interaction of the Bible College Movement and the Independent Disciples of Christ Denomination." Ph.D. dissertation, Stanford University, 1968.

(43) Tucker, William, and Lester G. McAllister. *Journey in Faith: A History of the Christian Church (Disciples of Christ)*. St. Louis: Bethany Press, 1975.

(44) VanKirk, Hiram. *The Rise of the Current Reformation: or, A Study in the History of Theology of the Disciples of Christ*. St. Louis: Christian Publishing, 1907.

(45) Webb, Henry E. "Sectional Conflict and Schism within the Disciples of Christ Following the Civil War." In *Essays on New Testament Christianity*, 115ff. Cincinnati: Standard Publishing, 1978.

(46) West, Earl I. *Search for the Ancient Order*. 3 vols. 1, Nashville: Gospel Advocate, 1949; 2-3, Indianapolis: Religious Book Service, 1950-1979.

(47) Zenor, Charles W. "A History of Biblical Interpretation in the Church of Christ: 1901-1976." Th.D. dissertation, Iliff School of Theology, 1976.

II. THE CAMPBELLITE AND RESTORATIONIST TRADITIONS IN THE SOUTH: STATE AND LOCAL STUDIES

(48) Barber, William J. *The Disciples' Assemblies of Eastern North Carolina*. St. Louis: Bethany Press as a private edition, 1966.

(49) Boren, Carter E. *Religion on the Texas Frontier*. San Antonio: Naylor, 1968.

(50) Brinson, Marion B., et al., eds. *A Century with Christ: A Story of the Christian Church in Richmond*. Richmond VA: Whittet and Shepperson, 1932.

(51) Cannon, John H., Jr. *Where There Is Vision: A History of the Lamar Avenue Church of Christ, 1869-1980*. Paris TX: Lamar Avenue Church of Christ, 1981.

(52) Casey, Mike. "An Era of Controversy and Division: The Origins of the Broadway Church of Christ, Paducah, Kentucky." *Restoration Quarterly* 27 (1984): 3-22.

(53) Cramblet, Wilbur H. *The Christian Church (Disciples of Christ) in West Virginia: A History of Its Co-operative Work.* St. Louis: Bethany Press, 1971.

(54) Dains, Mary K. "Alexander Campbell and the Missouri Disciples of Christ." *Missouri Historical Review* 77 (1982): 13-46.

(55) Darst, H. Jackson. *Ante-Bellum Virginia Disciples: An Account of the Emergence and Early Development of the Disciples of Christ in Virginia.* Richmond: Virginia Christian Mission Society, 1959.

(56) Eckstein, Stephen D. *History of the Churches of Christ in Texas, 1824-1950.* Austin: Firm Foundation Publishing House, 1963.

(57) England, Stephen J. *Oklahoma Christians: A History of Christian Churches and of the Start of the Christian Church (Disciples of Christ) in Oklahoma.* N.p.p.: Christian Church in Oklahoma, 1975.

(58) Fortune, Alonzo W. *The Disciples in Kentucky.* Lexington: Convention of the Christian Churches in Kentucky, 1932.

(59) Haley, Thomas P. *Historical and Biblical Sketches of the Early Churches and Pioneer Preachers of the Christian Church in Missouri.* St. Louis: Christian Publishing, 1888.

(60) Hall, Colby D. *Texas Disciples.* Fort Worth: Texas Christian University Press, 1953.

(61) Harmon, Marion F. *A History of the Christian Churches in Mississippi.* Aberdeen MS: n.p., 1929.

(62) Harrell, David E., Jr. "The Disciples of Christ and Social Forces in Tennessee, 1865-1900." East Tennessee Historical Society *Publications* 38 (1966): 48-61.

(63) Hawley, Monroe E. "Controversy in St. Louis." *Restoration Quarterly* 27 (1984): 49-64.

(64) Haymes, Don. "Hall Calhoun and His 'Nashville Brethren,' 1897-1935." *Restoration Quarterly* 27 (1984): 37-48.

(65) Hodge, Frederick A. *The Plea and the Pioneers in Virginia: A History of the Rise and Early Progress of the Disciples of Christ in Virginia.* Richmond VA: Everett Waddy, 1895.

(66) Hooper, Robert E. *A Call to Remember: Chapters in Nashville Restoration History.* Nashville: Gospel Advocate, 1977.

(67) Hughes, Richard T., et al. *Called to Serve: A Biography of the South National Church of Christ, Springfield, Missouri.* Springfield MO: Gospel Publishing House, 1967.

(68) Lucas, Charles H. "History of the Church of Christ in Mississippi." M.A. thesis, Mississippi College, 1964.

(69) McPherson, Chalmers. *Disciples of Christ in Texas.* Cincinnati: Standard Publishing, 1920.

(70) Moseley, Joseph E. *Disciples of Christ in Georgia*. St. Louis: Bethany Press, 1954.

(71) Nance, Ellwood C. *Florida Christians: Disciples of Christ*. Winter Park FL: The College Press, 1941.

(72) Norton, Herman A. *Tennessee Christians: A History of the Christian Church (Disciples of Christ) in Tennessee*. Nashville: Reed, 1971.

(73) Nunnelly, Donald A. "The Disciples of Christ in Alabama, 1860-1910." M.A. thesis, College of the Bible, 1954.

(74) Peters, George L. *The Disciples of Christ in Missouri: Celebrating One Hundred Years of Co-Operative Work*. Kansas City: The Centennial Commission, 1937.

(75) Pierson, Roscoe M. *The Disciples of Christ in Kentucky: A Finding List of the Histories of Local Congregations of Christian Churches*. Lexington: College of the Bible Library, 1962.

(76) Sechler, Earl. *Brief History of Christian Churches (Disciples of Christ) in Cedar County and St. Clair County, Missouri, 1852-1952*. Heritage MO: The Index, 1953.

(77) _____. *History of Dade County, Missouri, Christian Churches, 1839-1958*. Springfield MO: By the author, 1960.

(78) _____. *History of Hickory County, Missouri, Christian Churches (Disciples of Christ)*. Hermitage MO: n.p., [1951?].

(79) Ware, Charles C. *Hookerton History*. Wilson NC: By the author, 1960.

(80) _____. *Pamlico Profile*. Wilson NC: By the author, 1961.

(81) _____. *North Carolina Disciples of Christ: A History of Their Rise and Progress, and of Their Contributions to Their General Brotherhood*. St. Louis: Christian Board of Publication, 1927.

(82) _____. *Rountree Chronicle, 1827-1840: Documentary Primer of a Tar Heel Faith*. Wilson NC: North Carolina Christian Missionary Convention, 1947.

(83) _____. *South Carolina Disciples of Christ: A History*. Charleston: Christian Churches of South Carolina, 1967.

(84) Watson, George H., and Mildred B. Watson. *History of the Christian Churches in the Alabama Area*. St. Louis: Private edition by Bethany Press, 1965.

(85) Wilson, Michael L. "A History of the Church of Christ in Little Rock, Arkansas, 1900-1925." M.A. thesis, Harding Graduate School of Religion, 1980.

(86) Woodson, William E. "An Analytical History of Churches of Christ in Tennessee (1906-1960)." Th.D. dissertation, New Orleans Baptist Theological Seminary, 1975.

(87) _____. *Standing for Their Faith: A History of Churches of Christ in Tennessee, 1900-1950*. Henderson TN: J & W Publications, 1979.

III. THE CAMPBELLITE AND RESTORATIONIST
TRADITIONS IN THE SOUTH:
BIOGRAPHICAL AND AUTOBIOGRAPHICAL STUDIES

(88) Boles, H. Leo. *Biographical Sketches of Gospel Preachers.* Nashville: Gospel Advocate, 1932.

(89) Brewer, G. C. *Autobiography of G. C. Brewer.* Murfreesboro TN: Dehoff Publications, 1957.

(90) Campbell, Alexander, ed. *Memoirs of Elder Thomas Campbell, Together with a Brief Memoir of Mrs. Jane Campbell.* Cincinnati: H. S. Bosworth, 1861.

(91) Choate, Julian E. *The Anchor That Holds: A Biography of Benton Cordell Goodpasture.* Nashville: Gospel Advocate, 1971.

(92) _____. *Roll, Jordan, Roll: A Biography of Marshall Keeble.* Nashville: Gospel Advocate, 1968.

(93) Gresham, Perry E., ed. *The Sage of Bethany.* St. Louis: Bethany Press, 1960.

(94) Hanna, William H. *Thomas Campbell: Seceder and Christian Union Advocate.* Cincinnati: Standard Publishing, 1935.

(95) Hooper, Robert E. *Crying in the Wilderness: A Biography of David Lipscomb.* Nashville: David Lipscomb College, 1979.

(96) Hopson, Ella Lord. *Memoirs of Dr. Winthrop Hartly Hopson.* Cincinnati: Standard Publishing, 1887.

(97) Kellems, Jesse R. *Alexander Campbell and the Disciples.* New York: R. R. Smith, 1930.

(98) Lunger, Harold L. *The Political Ethics of Alexander Campbell.* St. Louis: Bethany Press, 1954.

(99) McAllister, Lester G. *Thomas Campbell: Man of the Book.* St. Louis: Bethany Press, 1954.

(100) _____. *Z. T. Sweeney: Preacher and Peacemaker.* St. Louis: Christian Board of Publication, 1968.

(101) Morrison, John L. "Alexander Campbell: Freedom Fighter of the Middle Frontier." *West Virginia History* 37 (1976): 291-308.

(102) _____. "Alexander Campbell: Moral Educator of the Middle Frontier." *West Virginia History* 36 (1975): 187-201.

(103) _____. "The Centrality of the Bible in Alexander Campbell's Thought and Life." *West Virginia History* 35 (1974): 185-204.

(104) _____. "A Rational Voice Crying in an Emotional Wilderness." *West Virginia History* 34 (1973): 125-40.

(105) Morrison, Matthew C. *Like a Lion: Daniel Sommer's Seventy Years of Preaching.* Murfreesboro: Dehoff Publications, 1975.

(106) Pearson, Samuel C., Jr. "Rationalist in an Age of Enthusiasm: The Anomalous Career of Robert Cave." *Bulletin of the Missouri Historical Society* 35 (1979): 99-108.

(107) Powell, James M., and Mary Nelle Hardeman Powers. *N. B. H.: A Biography of Nicholas Brodie Hardeman*. Nashville: Gospel Advocate, 1970.

(108) Richardson, Robert. *Memoirs of Alexander Campbell*. 2 vols. Philadelphia: J. B. Lippincott, 1868-1870.

(109) Robinson, John L. *David Lipscomb: Journalist in Texas, 1872*. Wichita Falls: Nortex, 1973.

(110) Sechler, Earl T. *Four Women Pastors of Missouri Christian Churches*. Appleton City MO: n.p., [1957?].

(111) _____. *Sadie McCoy Crank (1863-1948): Pioneer Woman Preacher in the Christian Church (Disciples)*. [Springfield MO?]: n.p., 1950.

(112) Tant, Fanning Yater. *J. D. Tant—Texas Preacher: A Biography*. Lufkin TX: Gospel Guardian, 1958.

(113) Tucker, William E. *J. H. Garrison and the Disciples of Christ*. St. Louis: Bethany Press, 1964.

(114) West, Earl. *Life and Times of David Lipscomb*. Henderson TN: Religious Book Service, [1954].

(115) West, John W., comp. *Sketches of Our Mountain Pioneers*. Lynchburg VA: J. W. West, 1939.

(116) Wilburn, James R. *The Hazard of the Die: Tolbert Fanning and the Restoration Movement*. Austin: Sweet Publishing, 1969.

(117) Woehrmann, Paul, ed. "The Autobiography of Abraham Snethen, Frontier Preacher." *Filson Club Historical Quarterly* 51 (1977): 315-35.

12 Holiness and Pentecostal Religion in the South

ALONGSIDE THE MAINLINE religious groupings, countless sectarian movements have also found the religious climate of the South hospitable. Because many of these smaller clusters draw primarily from a rural constituency and because many of them lack the bureaucratic machinery that delights in counting members, their importance in the overall Southern religious landscape has often gone unnoticed or has been mentioned only in passing. Many of these groups are short-lived, enduring only while a charismatic founder figure is alive to provide inspirational guidance. Others, however, are enduring, and many are linked to national associations of one sort or another. But for the majority, there is a dearth of secondary scholarly literature, particularly monographs, that analyze their respective stories. Many receive treatment only in works that survey "sects" or smaller religious groups.

A good number of Protestant sectarian groups, whether predominantly black or predominantly white or in some cases racially mixed, owe their genesis to the evangelical revivals of the nineteenth century that issued in the Holiness movement and then, towards the end of the century, in the Pentecostal movement. For the most part, they are the offspring of mainline bodies, especially Methodism (which has its own brand of holiness and perfectionism as part of its heritage). Holiness groups have sought in a variety of ways to maintain the affective pitch of a dramatic conversion by encouraging adherents to pursue ever deeper religious experiences that will ultimately eliminate sin from human life and render the individual perfectly holy. The link to Pentecostalism comes in the identification of postconversion religious experiences with the "gifts of the Spirit," particularly glossolalia and healing, although the experience of religious power manifested in the snake-handling groups noted in chapter 13 should perhaps be included here as well. It is important to note, however, that Holiness groups do not see possession of such spiritual gifts as a necessary part of authentic religious experience, while Pentecostal groups tend to regard possession of charismatic gifts, especially tongues and healing, as the sign of genuine religious experience.

Among Holiness and Pentecostal groups founded, once existing, or flourishing in the South about which there is no analytic material are the Alpha and Omega Pentecostal Church, Christ's Sanctified Holy Church, the Sought Out Church of God in Christ and Spiritual House of Prayer, the Christian Purities Fellowship, the Original United Holy Church International, the Pentecostal Full Gospel Church, the Macedonia Churches of Virginia, the General Assembly and Church of the Firstborn, and dozens of others. Countless independent evangelistic and missionary agencies, often established to promote the work of individual Holiness and/or Pentecostal preachers, have penetrated the Southern religious landscape. To this mix should also be added many sectarian bodies that lie outside the Holiness and Pentecostal orbits. The Christadelphians, for example, are a rather sophisticated adventist group founded in Richmond, Virginia, in the mid-nineteenth century with contemporary pockets of strength in Virginia, Arkansas, and Florida. Clearly scholarly work on Southern sectarianism is only in its initial stages, and the academy awaits work that will incorporate the range of sectarian options into historical and current analysis of the Southern religious scene.

A solid study of the religious and cultural forces undergirding Holiness and Pentecostal groups not only in the South but in the nation as a whole is Vinson Synan, *The Holiness-Pentecostal Movement in the United States* (59). Synan, himself a member of the Pentecostal-Holiness Church centered in Oklahoma City (formerly in Franklin Springs, Georgia), brings both scholarly acumen as well as personal appreciation of the movement to his work. Synan also has edited a helpful volume, *Aspects of Pentecostal-Charismatic Origins* (58). Three works provide a good introduction to the Holiness movement: Charles E. Jones, *Perfectionist Persuasion* (35); Timothy L. Smith, *Called Unto Holiness: The Story of the Nazarenes, The Formative Years* (56), which is particularly valuable in locating the emergence of this group within the larger Holiness movement; and the more recent, but less valuable *The Holiness Revival of the Nineteenth Century* by Melvin E. Dieter (20). The broad contours of the Pentecostal movement are ably explored in Robert M. Anderson, *Vision of the Disinherited: The Making of American Pentecostalism* (2). Also see the doctoral dissertation by Robert F. Martin, "The Early Years of American Pentecostalism, 1900-1940: Survey of a Social Movement" (38).

Several studies have a more distinctive regional focus. An older, less rigorous study explores the beginnings of Southern Pentecostalism: Dennis

Rogers, *Holiness Pioneering in the Southland* (52). A more narrowly focused, but careful academic analysis of the surge of interest in pursuing holiness which erupted in the closing years of the nineteenth century is Robert
F. Martin, ''The Holiness-Pentecostal Revival in the Carolinas, 1896-1940''
(74). Less helpful in a scholarly sense, but valuable for conveying the spirit
of the movement is Charles B. Jernigan, *Pioneer Days of the Holiness Movement in the Southwest* (33); its geographic scope spans well beyond Dixie,
but it does include some discussion of Southwestern Arkansas, where the Holiness Baptist Church has found a niche. Klaude Kendrick, *The Promise Fulfilled: A History of the Modern Pentecostal Movement* (36) is a partisan study,
though in many ways a pioneer effort to extend scholarly analysis to Pentecostalism. While limited largely to an exploration of the Assemblies of God,
it does evoke the excitement and enthusiasm that penetrate this strand of
Southern Christianity. Still useful as a ready guide to the numerous groups
that compose the Pentecostal-Holiness thrust, though in need of updating to
account for the demise of some groups and the emergence of others, is Everett L. Moore's master's thesis, ''Handbook of Pentecostal Denominations
in the United States'' (42). Moore's work provides brief summaries of both
the history and peculiar doctrinal emphases of the most prominent Holiness
and Pentecostal bodies. As a bibliographical tool, however, Moore's thesis
has been superseded by the two volumes of Charles E. Jones noted in chapter
1. The Holiness movement has always provoked controversy since outsiders
often see it as nurturing a hypocritical fanaticism. Academic studies of the
opposition to the Holiness and Pentecostal thrusts are few. Indeed, perhaps
the popular spirit of opposition has best been captured in a fictional portrayal
of a Georgia Methodist Holiness preacher: Atticus G. Haygood, *The Monk
and the Prince* (27), written in 1895 when the movement was making significant gains in the South. Also see Horace R. Ward, ''The Anti-Pentecostal
Argument,'' in the collection edited by Synan (58).

The vital links among the Holiness and Pentecostal strands of Christianity, interest in faith healing, and charismatic phenomena are the subject of
David Edwin Harrell, Jr.'s sensitive but critical *All Things are Possible: The
Healing and Charismatic Revivals in Modern America* (24). Like Synan's
study noted above (59), Harrell's is not restricted to the South, but provides
a good appraisal of the broader context within which Southern developments
have transpired. The ethos that surrounds the conviction that authentic faith
generates great healing powers is perhaps best evoked in ''The Ugliest Pilgrim,'' a short story by Doris Betts (3). While adherents readily attribute
healing power and other gifts of the Spirit to the miraculous work of God,
analysts have noted that there are ritual forms that set the stage for their presence and ritual forms that generate the conviction of results. On this point,
see William C. Clements, ''Ritual Expectation in Pentecostal Healing Ex-

perience'' (13), and Troy D. Abell, *Better Felt than Said: The Holiness-Pentecostal Experience in Southern Appalachia* (1).

If those who espouse Pentecostal or Holiness views stand apart from others in their belief that they have direct access to divine power, they are not unlike other Southerners, particularly those who would identify themselves as evangelicals, in other ways. Marion V. Dearmon, first in a doctoral dissertation (''Do Holiness Sects Socialize in Dominant Values?'' [19]) and then in an article based on it (''Christ and Conformity: A Study of Pentecostal Values'' [18], used the predominantly white United Pentecostal Church International as a case study and found that Southern Pentecostal-Holiness advocates tend to affirm traditional, conservative values in other areas of life. David Edwin Harrell, Jr., in *White Sects and Black Men in the Recent South* (25), found that sectarian adherents, including particularly those associated with Holiness and Pentecostal groups, retained a more conservative perspective on race than did other Southerners. Indeed, Harrell found a strident racism in many of these groups.

But what attracts individuals to these groups? For many years, it was fashionable to attribute Holiness or Pentecostal allegiance to deprivation. That is, persons were drawn to such groups because they found in them the sense of power and fulfillment of which they were deprived in the empirical realm. Many were poor and numbered among those H. Richard Niebuhr once called the ''disinherited.'' Experiencing the gifts of the Spirit or reaping the benefits of holiness, according to deprivation theory, functioned as a compensation for the security as well as the power denied persons in their lives within society. This perspective received classic statement in two articles by Anton T. Boisen: ''Economic Distress and Religious Experience: A Study of the Holy Rollers'' (4) and ''Religion and Hard Times: A Study of the Holy Rollers'' (5). Recently, that approach has found many challengers. Harvey K. Clow, ''Ritual, Belief, and the Social Context: An Analysis of a Southern Pentecostal Sect,'' a Duke University doctoral dissertation (14), used anthropological constructs to demolish deprivational-functional interpretation. Working from a more traditional historical framework, Charles E. Jones (''Disinherited or Rural? A Historical Case Study in Urban Holiness Religion'' [72]) examined Church of the Nazarene and Church of God (Holiness) groups in Missouri and also concluded that deprivation theory was from from adequate to account for the attractiveness of the Pentecostal or Holiness world view. Rather, as the title suggests, he found a greater correlation between Holiness affiliation and a rural background. The rural ethos, sensitive to the rhythm and pulse of nature, was simply more logically resonant with the Pentecostal ethos that likewise saw the world as embued with power, but power that could be harnessed through faith. Also see the important theoretical essay by Virginia H. Hine, "The Deprivation and Disorganization Theories of Social Movements" (28).

Few studies of individual Pentecostal-Holiness groups are of a scholarly nature. As with similar works on mainline groups, they tend to be filiopietistic and uncritical. But they are also important in offering scholars the insider's view and providing a sense of the conviction and spirit that permeate these groups. An example is Joseph E. Campbell, *The Pentecostal Holiness Church, 1898-1948: Its Background and History* (9). It should be supplemented by one of the better studies grounded in careful research: Vinson Synan, *The Old-Time Power* (60), which is also a history of the Pentecostal Holiness Church. A sizeable group, numbering nearly one-half million members throughout the United States in 1983, but with Southern origins and headquarters, is the Church of God (Cleveland, Tennessee). Founded in 1886, this Pentecostal body lacks a critical history, but two "in house" studies begin to chronicle its story: Charles W. Conn, *Like a Mighty Army: A History of the Church of God, 1886-1976* (15), and the more restricted *Church of God of North Carolina: A History of the Church of God of North Carolina, 1886-1978* by Douglas W. Slocumb (82). Another Pentecostal body centered in Cleveland, Tennessee, is the Church of God of Prophecy, based on the charismatic ministry and teachings of Homer Tomlinson. While it, too, lacks a scholarly history, those interested may consult James Stone, *The Church of God of Prophecy: History and Polity* (57).

Among those groups having roots in the Methodist heritage, perhaps the strongest in the South is the Wesleyan Church of America, formed in 1968 by the merger of the Wesleyan Methodist Church of America and the Pilgrim Holiness Church. Neither parent group was restricted to a Southern constituency, but both had separated from mainstream Methodism in the nineteenth century in order to reclaim John Wesley's emphases on seeking Christian perfection and scriptural holiness. Each of the parent bodies has a detailed but not very critical history: Ira F. McLeister and Roy S. Nicholson, *Conscience and Commitment: The History of the Wesleyan Methodist Church of America* (37), and Paul Westphal Thomas and Paul William Thomas, *The Days of Our Pilgrimage: The History of the Pilgrim Holiness Church* (61). For the story in South Carolina, where the Wesleyans maintain a college (Central Wesleyan College), see James B. Hilson's popularly written *History of the South Carolina Conference of the Wesleyan Methodist Church of America: Fifty-five Years of Wesleyan Methodism in South Carolina* (69).

Two other national bodies, the Assemblies of God (now approaching two million members) and the Church of the Nazarene (nearly five hundred thousand members reported in 1983), also have considerable strength in parts of the South, and both have national offices in Missouri. For the Assemblies of God, the most comprehensive study is William W. Menzies, *Anointed to*

Serve: The Story of the Assemblies of God (39), which supersedes Irvin J. Harrison's 1954 doctoral dissertation, "A History of the Assemblies of God" (26). Also see William W. Menzies's dissertation, "The Assemblies of God, 1941-1967: The Consolidation of a Revival Movement" (40), and Robert L. Bufkin's master's thesis, "The Assembly of God: Movement along the Continuum from Cult to Church" (8). The titles of both of these are suggestive of the internal transformations that this Pentecostal body has experienced as it has grown rapidly in recent decades. A respectable local study is Leroy W. Hawkins's thesis, "A History of the Assemblies of God in Oklahoma: The Formative Years, 1914-1929" (68). On the origins and early years of the Nazarenes, see the study by Timothy L. Smith noted above. For a dated analysis of internal changes that accompanied growth and expansion in the Church of the Nazarene, see Harold M. Reed, "The Growth of a Contemporary Sect-Type Institution as Reflected in the Development of the Church of the Nazarene" (51), a doctoral dissertation. Reliable, but in need of updating, is Maury E. Redford's 1935 master's thesis, "History of the Church of Nazarene in the South" (48). Also see his earlier thesis, "History of the Church of the Nazarene in Tennessee" (81), and a similar study by W. M. Lynch, "The Rise of the Church of the Nazarene in Texas" (73). Less valuable because it lacks critical perspective is Wallace E. Carruth, *A History of the Louisiana District, Church of the Nazarene* (66).

Perhaps the most prominent twentieth-century individual identified with the Holiness and Pentecostal traditions is Oral Roberts, whose multifaceted evangelistic empire is headquartered in Tulsa, Oklahoma. Rising to prominence as a faith healer, Roberts aligned himself with the United Methodist Church in the 1960s, though he is still perceived popularly as a Pentecostal preacher and entrepreneur. David Edwin Harrell's *Oral Roberts: An American Life* (88) at last provides a solid, sensitive scholarly appraisal that supplants the saccharine *Oral: The Warm, Intimate, Unauthorized Portrait of a Man of God* by Wayne A. Robinson (93) and the thoroughly debunking *Give Me That Prime-Time Religion: An Insider's Report on the Oral Roberts Evangelistic Association* by Jerry Sholes (53).

The South has been fertile ground for sectarianism, particularly of the Holiness-Pentecostal variety. But its story remains to be told in solid academic, scholarly fashion.

The bibliography which follows identifies first thematic studies and works that treat Pentecostal-Holiness groups nationally or regionally. It then lists state and local studies and concludes with titles of biographies or autobiographies of some prominent figures in the movement. In addition, two journals frequently contain historical studies that often pertain to Southern developments: *Wesleyan Theological Review* and *Pneuma: Journal of the Society for Pentecostal Studies*.

BIBLIOGRAPHY

Several titles in the listings for chapters 1, 2, 4, 10, and 13 are relevant to this topic.

I. HOLINESS AND PENTECOSTAL RELIGION IN THE SOUTH: GROUP AND THEMATIC STUDIES

(1) Abell, Troy D. *Better Felt than Said: The Holiness-Pentecostal Experience in Southern Appalachia*. Waco: Markham Press, 1982.

(2) Anderson, Robert M. *Vision of the Disinherited: The Making of American Pentecostalism*. New York: Oxford University Press, 1979.

(3) Betts, Doris. "The Ugliest Pilgrim." In *Stories of the Modern South*. Benjamin Forkner and Patrick Samway, eds., 36-58. New York: Bantam Books, 1978.

(4) Boisen, Anton T. "Economic Distress and Religious Experience: A Study of the Holy Rollers." *Psychiatry* 2 (1939): 185-94.

(5) _____. "Religion and Hard Times: A Study of the Holy Rollers." *Social Action* 5 (1939): 8-35.

(6) Brumback, Carl. *Suddenly . . . from Heaven: A History of the Assemblies of God*. Springfield MO: Gospel Publishing House, 1961.

(7) Buckles, Edwin A. *A Brief History: The Church of God of the Apostolic Faith*. Drumright OK: n.p., 1935.

(8) Bufkin, Robert L. "The Assembly of God: Movement along the Continuum from Cult to Church." M.A. thesis, University of Arkansas, 1968.

(9) Campbell, Joseph Enoch. *The Pentecostal Holiness Church, 1898-1948: Its Background and History*. Franklin Springs GA: Publishing House of the Pentecostal Holiness Church, 1951.

(10) Carter, Herbert F., and Mrs. Ruth K. Moore, "History of the Pentecostal Free Will Baptist Church." In *Discipline of the Pentecostal Free Will Baptist Church*, 5-16. Dunn NC: n.p., n.d.

(11) Chapman, James B. *History of the Church of the Nazarene*. Kansas City: Nazarene Publishing House, 1926.

(12) Clanton, Arthur L. *United We Stand: A History of Oneness Organizations*. Hazelwood MO: Pentecostal Publishing House, 1970.

(13) Clements, William C. "Ritual Expectation in Pentecostal Healing Experience." *Western Folklore* 40 (1981): 139-48.

(14) Clow, Harvey K. "Ritual, Belief, and the Social Context: An Analysis of a Southern Pentecostal Sect." Ph.D. dissertation, Duke University, 1976.

(15) Conn, Charles W. *Like a Mighty Army: A History of the Church of God, 1886-1976*. Rev. ed. Cleveland TN: Pathway Press, 1977.

(16) Cowen, Clarence E. *A History of the Church of God (Holiness)*. Ann Arbor: University Microfilms, 1949.

(17) Cox, B. L. *History and Doctrine of the Congregational Holiness Church.* 2d ed. Greenwood SC: Publishing House of the Congregational Holiness Church, 1959.

(18) Dearmon, Marion V. "Christ and Conformity: A Study of Pentecostal Values." *Journal for the Scientific Study of Religion* 13 (1974): 437-53.

(19) _____. "Do Holiness Sects Socialize in Dominant Values?" Ph.D. dissertation, University of Oregon, 1972.

(20) Dieter, Melvin E. *The Holiness Revival of the Nineteenth Century.* Metuchen NJ: Scarecrow Press, 1980.

(21) Elinson, Howard. "The Implications of Pentecostal Religion for Intellectualism, Politics, and Race Relations." *American Journal of Sociology* 70 (1965): 403-15.

(22) Ellis, James B. *Blazing the Gospel Trail.* Plainfield NJ: Logos International, 1976.

(23) Foster, Fred J. *"Think It Not Strange": A History of the Oneness Movement.* St. Louis: Pentecostal Publishing House, 1965.

(24) Harrell, David Edwin, Jr. *All Things are Possible: The Healing and Charismatic Revivals in Modern America.* Bloomington: Indiana University Press, 1975.

(25) _____. *White Sects and Black Men in the Recent South.* Nashville: Vanderbilt University Press, 1971.

(26) Harrison, Irvine J. "A History of the Assemblies of God." Th.D. dissertation, Berkeley Baptist Divinity School, 1954.

(27) Haygood, Atticus G. *The Monk and the Prince.* Atlanta: Foote and Davis, 1895.

(28) Hine, Virginia K. "The Deprivation and Disorganization Theories of Social Movements." In *Religious Movements in Contemporary America.* Irving I. Zaretsky and Mark P. Leone, eds., 646-61. Princeton: Princeton University Press, 1974.

(29) _____. "Pentecostal Glossolalia: Toward a Functional Interpretation." *Journal for the Scientific Study of Religion* 8 (1969): 211-26.

(30) Holt, John B. "Holiness Religion: Cultural Shock and Social Reorganization." *American Sociological Review* 5 (1940): 740-47.

(31) Hoover, Mario G. "Origin and Structural Development of the Assemblies of God." M.A. thesis, Southwest Missouri State College, 1968.

(32) Jennings, Arthur T. *History of American Wesleyan Methodism.* Syracuse: Wesleyan Methodist Publishing Association, 1902.

(33) Jernigan, Charles B. *Pioneer Days of the Holiness Movement in the Southwest.* Kansas City: Nazarene Publishing House, 1919.

(34) Johnson, Guy B. "A Framework for the Analysis of Religious Action, with Special Reference to Holiness and Non-Holiness Groups." Ph.D. dissertation, Harvard University, 1953.

(35) Jones, Charles E. *Perfectionist Persuasion.* Metuchen: Scarecrow Press, 1974.

(36) Kendrick, Klaude. *The Promise Fulfilled: A History of the Modern Pentecostal Movement*. Springfield MO: Gospel Publishing House, 1961.

(37) McLeister, Ira F., and Roy S. Nicholson. *Conscience and Commitment: The History of the Wesleyan Methodist Church of America*. 4th ed. rev. by Lee M. Haines, Jr., and Melvin E. Dieter. Marion IN: Wesley Press, 1976.

(38) Martin, Robert F. "The Early Years of American Pentecostalism, 1900-1940: Survey of a Social Movement." Ph.D. dissertation, University of North Carolina in Chapel Hill, 1975.

(39) Menzies, William W. *Anointed to Serve: The Story of the Assemblies of God*. Springfield MO: Gospel Publishing House, 1971.

(40) _____. "The Assemblies of God, 1941-1967: The Consolidation of a Revival Movement." Ph.D. dissertation, University of Iowa, 1968.

(41) Moon, Elmer L. *The Pentecostal Church: A History and Popular Survey*. New York: Carlton Press, 1966.

(42) Moore, Everett L. "Handbook of Pentecostal Denominations in the United States." M.A. thesis, Pasadena College, 1954.

(43) Muelder, Walter G. "From Sect to Church: Rural Protestant Sects and the Church of the Nazarene." *Christendom* 10 (1945): 450-62.

(44) Nicholson, Roy S. *Wesleyan Methodism in the South: Being the Story of Eight-Six Years of Reform and Religious Activities in the South as Conducted by American Wesleyans*. Syracuse: Wesleyan Methodist Publishing Association, 1933.

(45) Olila, James H. "Pentecostalism: The Dynamics of Recruitment in a Modern Socio-Religious Movement." M.A. thesis, University of Minnesota, 1968.

(46) Perkins, Floyd J. "The Church of the Nazarene and Its Historical Evangelical Heritage." M.A. thesis, University of Kansas City, 1952.

(47) Rawlings, Elden E. "A History of the Nazarene Publishing House." M.A. thesis, University of Oklahoma, 1960.

(48) Redford, Maury E. "History of the Church of the Nazarene in the South." M.A. thesis, Vanderbilt University, 1935.

(49) _____. *The Rise of the Church of the Nazarene*. 1st ed., Kansas City: Nazarene Publishing House, 1948, 1961. Rev. and abridged ed., Kansas City: Beacon Hill Press, 1965.

(50) Reed, David. "Origins and Development of the Theology of Oneness Pentecostalism in the United States." Ph.D. dissertation, Boston University, 1978.

(51) Reed, Harold M. "The Growth of a Contemporary Sect-Type Institution as Reflected in the Development of the Church of the Nazarene." Th.D. dissertation, Graduate School of Religion, University of Southern California, 1943.

(52) Rogers, Dennis. *Holiness Pioneering in the Southland*. Hemet CA: D. Rogers, 1944.

(53) Sholes, Jerry. *Give Me That Prime-Time Religion: An Insider's Report on the Oral Roberts Evangelistic Association*. New York: Hawthorn Books, 1979.

(54) Simmons, Ernest L. *History of the Church of God*. Cleveland TN: Church of God Publishing House, 1938.

(55) Smeeton, Donald D. "Perfection or Pentecost: A Historical Comparison of Charismatic and Holiness Theologies." M.A. thesis, Trinity Evangelical Divinity School, 1971.

(56) Smith, Timothy L. *Called Unto Holiness: The Story of the Nazarenes, The Formative Years*. Kansas City: Nazarene Publishing House, 1962.

(57) Stone, James. *The Church of God of Prophecy: History and Polity*. Cleveland TN: White Wing Publishing, 1977.

(58) Synan, Vinson, ed. *Aspects of Pentecostal-Charismatic Origins*. Plainfield NJ: Logos, 1975.

(59) _____. *The Holiness-Pentecostal Movement in the United States*. Grand Rapids: Eerdmans, 1971.

(60) _____. *The Old-Time Power*. Franklin Springs GA: Advocate Press, n.d.

(61) Thomas, Paul Westphal, and Paul William Thomas. *The Days of Our Pilgrimage: The History of the Pilgrim Holiness Church*. Melvin E. Dieter and Lee M. Haines, eds. Marion IN: Wesley Press, 1976.

(62) Wessels, Roland H. "The Doctrine of the Baptism in the Holy Spirit among the Assemblies of God." Th.D. dissertation, Pacific School of Religion, 1966.

(63) Wood, Dillard L., and William H. Preskitt, Jr. *Baptism with Fire: A History of the Pentecostal Fire-Baptized Holiness Church*. Colbert [Franklin Springs] GA: Advocate Press, 1983.

(64) Wood, William W. *Culture and Personality Aspects of the Pentecostal Holiness Religion*. The Hague: Mouton, 1965.

II. HOLINESS AND PENTECOSTAL RELIGION IN THE SOUTH: STATE AND LOCAL STUDIES

(65) Booher, Geneva T. *Builders Together with God: The People Speak*. Russellville AR: First Assembly of God, 1972.

(66) Carruth, Wallace E. *A History of the Louisiana District, Church of the Nazarene*. Bossier City LA: Touchstone's, 1955.

(67) Gomer, Thelma. "A Mighty Church Moves On." [Nashville] *Nazarene Weekly* 43 (6 May 1973).

(68) Hawkins, Leroy W. "A History of the Assemblies of God in Oklahoma: The Formative Years, 1914-1929." M.A. thesis, Oklahoma State University, 1972.

(69) Hilson, James B. *History of the South Carolina Conference of the Wesleyan Methodist Church of America: Fifty-five Years of Wesleyan Methodism in South Carolina*. Winona Lake IN: Light and Life Press, 1950.

(70) James, Eleanor. "The Sanctification of Belton." *American West* 2 (Summer 1965): 65-73.

(71) Jones, Charles E. "Background of the Church of the Nazarene in Oklahoma." *B-PC Historian of the Bethany-Peniel College Historical Society* 1 (1953-1954): 18-31.

(72) _____. "Disinherited or Rural? A Historical Case Study in Urban Holiness Religion." *Missouri Historical Review* 66 (1972): 395-412.

(73) Lynch, W. M. "The Rise of the Church of the Nazarene in Texas." M.A. thesis, Stephen F. Austin College, 1956.

(74) Martin, Robert F. "The Holiness-Pentecostal Revival in the Carolinas, 1896-1940." *Proceedings of the South Carolina Historical Association* 49 (1979): 59-78.

(75) Mavis, Marion. *In the Beginning: A History of the Free Methodist Church in Kentucky-Tennessee from Its Earliest Beginnings until 1970.* Wilmore KY: n.p., 1970.

(76) Nelson, Walter O. A *History of the Oklahoma Annual Conference of the Free Methodist Church of North America.* Siloam Springs AR: Silent Minister Booklet Press, 1949.

(77) Paul, George H. *The Religious Frontier in Oklahoma: Dan T. Muse and the Pentecostal Holiness Church.* Norman OK: n.p., 1965.

(78) Piepkorn, Arthur C. "Church of God, World Headquarters." *Concordia Theological Monthly* 40 (1969): 622-25.

(79) Rasnake, John S. *Pentecost Fully Come: A History of the Appalachian District of the Assemblies of God.* Bristol TN: Westhighlands Church, 1971.

(80) _____. *Stones by the River: A History of the Tennessee District of the Assemblies of God.* Bristol TN: Westhighlands Church, 1975.

(81) Redford, Maury E. "History of the Church of the Nazarene in Tennessee." B.D. thesis, School of Religion, Vanderbilt University, 1934.

(82) Slocumb, Douglas W. *Church of God of North Carolina: A History of the Church of God of North Carolina, 1886-1978.* Charlotte NC: H. Eaton, 1978.

(83) Spence, Robert H. *The First Fifty Years: A Brief Review of the Assemblies of God in Alabama, 1915-1965.* [Montgomery]: n.p., [1965].

(84) Underwood, Bernard E. *Fiftieth Anniversary History of the Virginia Conference of the Pentecostal Holiness Church: A Sketch.* [Dublin VA]: Virginia Conference of the Pentecostal Holiness Church, 1960.

(85) Yamada, Yutaka. "There Was Something Precious in My Hand: Narratives of Religious Life Experiences Among the Pentecostals of North Carolina." M.A. thesis, University of North Carolina in Chapel Hill, 1980.

III. HOLINESS AND PENTECOSTAL RELIGION IN THE SOUTH: BIOGRAPHICAL AND AUTOBIOGRAPHICAL STUDIES

(86) Breithaupt, Gerald O. "A Study of the Preachment and Practice of the Reverend Mr. Oral Roberts, 1947-1960.'' M. Div. thesis, Asbury Theological Seminary, 1970.

(87) Davidson, Charles T. *W. M. Lowman, Bishop of Virginia*. South Covington VA: Wings of Truth, 1944.

(88) Harrell, David Edwin, Jr. *Oral Roberts: An American Life*. Bloomington: Indiana University Press, 1985.

(89) McLaughlin, Raymond W. ''A Comparison of the Language Structures of the Sermons of Harry Emerson Fosdick and Oral Roberts to Determine Their Intensional-Extensional Orientation.'' Ph.D. dissertation, University of Denver, 1959.

(90) Morgan, David. ''N. J. Holmes and the Origins of Pentecostalism.'' *South Carolina Historical Magazine* 84 (1983): 136-51.

(91) Nelson, Douglas J. ''For a Time as This: The Story of Bishop William J. Seymour and the Azusa Street Revival.'' Ph.D. dissertation, University of Birmingham, 1981.

(92) Roberts, Oral. *The Call: An Autobiography*. Garden City: Doubleday, 1972.

(93) Robinson, Wayne A. *Oral: The Warm, Intimate, Unauthorized Portrait of a Man of God*. Los Angeles: Acton House, 1976.

13 RELIGION IN APPALACHIA AND THE RURAL SOUTH

UNTIL THE GREAT SOCIETY and the War on Poverty "discovered" Appalachia two decades ago, the residents of this region as well as much of the South's rural population, many of them poor whites, were numbered, in J. Wayne Flynt's term, among "Dixie's forgotten people" (2). Now, happily for scholars at least, there is a growing body of literature that explores the religious culture of the Appalachian region, plumbing the similarities to and differences from what might be called "mainstream" Southern religion. Two older studies, the first written for a nonacademic audience, provide a good general survey of Appalachian religion before the recent burst of interest in the Southern mountain life generated new scholarship. They are Willis D. Weatherford and Earl D. C. Brewer, *Life and Religion in Southern Appalachia* (16), and Willis D. Weatherford, ed., *Religion in the Appalachian Mountains: A Symposium* (17).

To appreciate the pulse of religious life in Appalachia, one must follow material in four journals, all of which offer occasional articles on Appalachian religion, many from an "insider" perspective. *Mountain Review,* for example, often contains sermon transcripts from Appalachian clergy and thereby offers rich resources for understanding not simply one means of perpetuating religious belief, but also the relationship between religious affirmation and daily life. *Mountain Life and Work* is likewise not strictly academic, but it does contain materials written by persons living in Appalachia and working in churches there. More sophisticated in both content and style is the *Foxfire* series, which has devoted occasional numbers to dimensions of Appalachian folk religion in its commitment to celebrate all aspects of mountain folk culture. The most academic in approach is *Appalachian Journal*. While it does not restrict its coverage to religion, it has published several scholarly articles on religious topics. Of special interest is the Spring 1974 issue, which contains five essays on the general theme, "God and the Devil in Appalachia" (5), covering topics such as the personal dimension or individualism in Appalachian religion, the snake-handling groups that dot the region, religious folk music indigenous to the area, the continuing presence of witchcraft, and the importance of religious revivals within the culture.

Many of the recent studies have appeared under the auspices of West Virginia University and reflect the commitment of that school to be responsive to its location. Several of these have been guided by John D. Photiadis, but they have been criticized for minimizing the diversity that exists in Appalachia's religious culture and consequently overemphasizing the pervasiveness of an uncritical fundamentalism throughout the region. The most important of these works is a collection of essays edited by Photiadis, *Religion in Appalachia: Theological, Social, and Psychological Dimensions and Correlates* (12), which does contain a helpful bibliography. In an earlier volume, *Religion in an Appalachian State* (11), Photiadis stressed the way in which Appalachian religion alleviates the anxieties concomitant with mountain poverty, while in "Religion: A Persistent Institution in a Changing Appalachia" (10), coauthored with John E. Schnabel, he highlighted the continuing appeal of fundamentalism to many in Appalachia despite the monumental social changes that have come over the past two decades.

Much of the academic discussion has centered on whether the interpretive categories used by scholars to look at religious life in other sectors of American society are adequate for analyzing the situation in Appalachia. For example, Gerald K. Parker, in "Folk Religion in Southern Appalachia" (81), rejected the standard use of church-sect typology in looking at Appalachian religious institutions, arguing instead that the area exhibited a folk religious tradition that rendered ideas of "church" and "sect" useless. Others have questioned whether it is appropriate to use categories of religious belief as barometers of religiosity in Appalachia. A case in point is Charles T. Davis and Richard A. Humphrey, "Appalachian Religion: A Diversity of Consciousness" (1); they claimed that a doctrinal concept of religion was inadequate in describing Appalachian religion not only because it represented the imposition of external categories, but because it failed to account for the range of beliefs or belief systems characteristic of Appalachia. Rather, they argued, one should see the common thread in terms of religious experience, particularly in the widespread regional assumption that an individual experience of conversion or personal rebirth was the basis for the religious life, not the particulars of religious belief. Dallas M. Lee, focusing on Baptists in Eastern Kentucky in "Central Appalachia" (68), noted another way in which standard measurements of religion and religiosity do not apply. He called attention to the fact that Appalachian residents exhibit a lower degree of formal religious affiliation than other Southerners. He attributed this reluctance to assume membership in a religious group to a regional disposition to refrain from joining any groups, but it may as well be one consequence of the highly individualistic nature of the experience of rebirth previously mentioned.

Numerous essays have documented the ways in which programs developed by the nation's religious groups and denominations make little sense when implementation is attempted in Appalachia, largely because they assume a basic middle-class, urban constituency and sensibility. Max E. Glenn, for example, highlighted this problem in "Will the Church Take a Dare in the New Appalachia?" (51). However, the most persistent critic of the approach of mainline groups to ministry in Appalachia has been Jack E. Weller. In "Addressing the Afflicted and the Affluent" (94), he noted that the middle-class theology of much of American Protestantism was singularly ineffective in speaking to the situation of Appalachian poverty, while in "Ministering to Appalachia" (95), he criticized the denominations for concentrating their efforts on improving social and economic conditions in Appalachia and consequently failing to recognize the need to minister to individuals directly. But Weller is not opposed to efforts to reduce poverty and raise the standard of living in much of Appalachia. In two essays, for example, he addressed some of the shortcomings he found in Appalachian religion itself. In "Salvation Is Not Enough" (96), Weller noted that the Appalachian emphasis on personal salvation, emotional experience, and the use of plain language had a long heritage in the region and still persisted because of the area's relative isolation. But he encouraged religious workers in Appalachia to foster among the people a broader understanding of the nature of religion and religious experience. As well, he argued in "Time for Reason" (97) that mountain churches and residents must learn that emotionalism is only one dimension of religion and that formal education is not necessarily the enemy of religious faith that many Appalachian folk have assumed it to be.

Many of the religious programs in Appalachia that seek to effect social and economic change operate under the aegis of CORA, the Commission on Religion in Appalachia, an interdenominational organization. Its focus is summarized in "Commission on Religion in Appalachia: Church and Change in Appalachia" (34) and in *A United Approach to Fulfilling the Church's Mission in Appalachia* (33). But the work of CORA and other mainline groups' mission enterprises has come under sharp criticism, for it seems predicated on the assumption that other cultural ways are inherently superior to those of Appalachia and therefore fails to recognize the integrity and internal coherence of the Appalachian style. Linda Johnson issued a biting indictment of CORA and mainline efforts in "Foot-Washin' Church and the Prayer-Book

Church'' (63), branding their work as a form of imperialism. Most ''outsider'' appraisals, including those of Jack Weller, were condemned by Appalachia's Loyal Jones in ''Mountain Religion: The Outsider's View'' (64). Jones claimed that sociological or journalistic accounts contained a thinly disguised paternalism that directly and indirectly castigated the authenticity of the region's folk religion and culture.

On the work of several mainline denominations and sectarian groups in Appalachia, see Hart M. Nelsen, et al., *Comparison of Religious Groupings in Appalachia: Presbyterian, Episcopalian, Church of God, Holiness. A Study Based on Southern Appalachian Studies Data* (80). Nelsen focused on Presbyterian efforts in *The Appalachian Presbyterian: Some Rural-Urban Differences, A Preliminary Report* (79). Three works provide an introduction to Baptist ministry in Appalachia: Lynn C. Dickerson II, ''The Baptists of the Cumberland Mountains'' (43); Paul M. DeBusman's dissertation, ''Social Factors Affecting Selected Southern Baptist Churches in the Southern Appalachian Region of the United States'' (40); and Samuel W. Thomas, ''The Oneida Albums: Photography, Oral Tradition, and the Appalachian Experience'' (92), which deals with the Oneida Baptist Institute in Kentucky. Labors of the former Wesleyan Methodist Church (now the Wesleyan Church) form the basis of Charles L. Blanchard's older study, *The Wesleyan Work in the Kentucky Mountains* (24).

To many interpreters, as intimated in the comment on the work of John Photiadis above, the distinguishing feature of much Appalachian folk religion is its fundamentalist cast. When used in connection with Appalachia, fundamentalism does not necessarily refer to the same phenomena also given that designation in much of American Protestantism. Here it generally denotes the primacy of the conversion experience, the acceptance of the Bible as the literal word of God, affirmation of a basic supernaturalism that penetrates all aspects of life and frequently borders on fatalism, a rejection of institutional authority, and a tendency to view ethics as an individual rather than social concern. A splendid study that evokes the ethos generated by Appalachian fundamentalism in both narrative and photographic and artistic illustration is Eleanor Dickinson and Barbara Benziger, *Revival!* (44). There are also some important scholarly studies that seek to document the impact and role of this fundamentalism. Gordon F. DeJong and Thomas R. Ford, for example, noted that a disproportionately high percentage of the Appalachian population had some sort of affiliation with fundamentalist religious groups and that a fundamentalist persuasion was inversely correlated with socioeconomic status (41). In another essay, ''Religious Fundamentalism, Socio-Economic Status, and Fertility Attitudes in the Southern Appalachians'' (42), DeJong demonstrated that this fundamentalist affirmation was also correlated with attitudes that supported a high fertility rate. A fundamentalist persuasion also characterizes Appalachian clergy, as evidenced in Lorin A. Baumhover's doctoral dissertation, "Value Orientations of Clergy in Appalachia" (22).

What is important analytically is to discern why this brand of fundamentalism is appealing. Perhaps the most obvious answer is the way in which it structures empirical reality into neatly defined categories—good/evil, right/wrong, God/Devil. In turn, it provides normative standards of thinking and acting and fosters the conviction that social and religious forces that challenge those standards must be resisted lest the world view be rendered unworkable. This aspect of Appalachian fundamentalism comes into sharp relief in Alice L. Cobb's study of sectarian groups in the Upper Mutton community of Harlan County, Kentucky, "Sectarianism, Religion, and Social Change in an Isolated Rural Community of Southern Appalachia" (32). The resistance to change and the tendency to view alternative approaches as threats to the religious world view of Appalachian fundamentalism may also be seen in the highly publicized controversies that erupt periodically over choice of textbooks for use in the public schools. Looking at one such episode in Virginia in 1974, Scott Cummings and others, in "Preachers versus Teachers: Local-Cosmopolitian Conflict over Textbook Censorship in an Appalachian Community" (37), concluded that educators were suspect because they represented a cosmopolitan way of life alien to the Appalachian world view, while their most vocal opponents, local ministers, symbolized to the community the preservation of tradition and accepted/acceptable mores. But see also Robert M. Reinhardt's West Virginia University doctoral dissertation, "Religion and Politics: The Political Behavior of West Virginia Protestant Fundamentalist Sectarians" (86), which argues that there is at best only a partial correlation between fundamentalist sectarian affirmation and styles of political action and concern. Related titles are found in the listing to chapter 20.

Appalachian fundamentalism has made the region fertile ground for sectarian movements that are identified with the Pentecostal-Holiness movement(s) in American Christianity that form the focus of chapter 12. Troy D. Abell, for instance, probed "The Holiness-Pentecostal Experience in Southern Appalachia" in his doctoral dissertation (18), demonstrating that while Appalachian Pentecostals cannot be distinguished from their peers in most attitudes, they do evidence a more positive self-image, in part because the more intense Pentecostal experience, particularly the sense that one has received charismatic gifts of the Spirit, enhances one's status in the cosmos since one has experienced the dynamic power of the divine directly. Two studies, which are basically descriptions of the Kentucky Mountain Holiness Association rather than scholarly analyses, nevertheless capture the spirit of Appalachian Pentecostal religion: Lela G. McConnell, *The Pauline Ministry in the Kentucky Mountains* (71), and her *Faith Victorious in the Kentucky Mountains: The Story of Twenty-Two Years of Spirit-Filled Ministry* (70).

Two features of Appalachian Pentecostalism that have attracted the most attention among students of the area's religious culture are the rituals of foot washing and snake handling. But foot washing ceremonies especially are not exclusively the domain of Pentecostals. Two student workers in Appalachia, Frieda Mullins and Diana Hall, recounted their impressions of "Old Regular Baptist Foot-Washin': July 29, 1973" (77), while John W. Hall, in "An Old Regular Baptist Foot-Washing in the Mountains" (55), noted that the ritual had been part of the religious life, at least in Eastern Kentucky, since the antebellum era. A more recent study, and perhaps the best overview, is Richard A. Humphrey, "Foot Washing in the Southern Appalachians" (59). See as well the bibliographical listing for chapter 12.

The practice of snake handling, often combined with rituals in which strychnine is ingested or cases when Spirit possession manifests itself in glossolalia, has attracted much more attention even among those commentators who find it repugnant to "genuine" religion. Robert W. Pelton and Karen W. Carden dismissed these practices as "bizarre" and not part of authentic Christian belief and practice in *Snake Handlers: God-Fearers? or Fanatics?* (121), while in an article targeted to a mass audience, John Kobler labeled snake handling as "America's Strangest Religion" (117). The most balanced, but occasionally condescending, monographic treatment of the phenomenon is Weston LaBarre, *They Shall Take Up Serpents: Psychology of the Southern Snake-Handling Cult* (118). Yet detractors fail to realize the reasons why snake handling is plausible. Anthropologist Steven M. Kane, in an article, a master's thesis, and a doctoral dissertation (114-116), argued that one must approach snake handling from the perspective of possession states (which are common to many of the world's religious traditions) when one is taken over in ecstasy by sacred power so that one no longer controls his or her body but is a vehicle through which that sacred power is manifested. Kane has also argued conclusively that snake handlers should not be classified as clinically psychotic or severely neurotic; his work has revealed that those who participate actively in a snake-handling group are normal folk, who are well adjusted and well-adapted to their situation.

What purpose, then, does snake handling play for those who practice it as a religious ritual? Will D. Campbell offered one suggestion, that this ritual possession of divine power signals the ability of God and individuals to conquer the evil forces that are part of the supernatural permeation of existence (106). Nathan L. Gerrard, in "The Serpent-Handling Religions of West Virginia" (111), more specifically in the communities of Scrabble Creek and Jolo, claimed that the highly emotional character of the snake-handling experience provided a release or ecstatic alternative to the frustrations of daily life, while Marsha Maguire, "Confirming the Word: Snake-Handling Sects in Southern Appalachia" (120), advanced the idea that the ritual is a means to verify

Scriptural promises (especially those in Mark 16:18) and thus have concrete evidence of one's salvation. Ellen Steckert, "The Snake-Handling Sect of Harlan County, Kentucky: Its Influence on Folk Tradition" (125), linked the ritual with ethics. She argued that while the fundamentalist orientation of the snake-handling groups led to condemnations of such "worldly" phenomena as modern dance and music on the grounds that they reflected an unholy sensuality, the lively use of song, instrumental music, and ritual dance in snake-handling worship represented a sensuality perceived as legitimate because it was induced by the power of God. But perhaps the most provocative interpretation is that offered by Mary L. Daugherty in "Serpent-Handling as Sacrament" (109). Like others, Daugherty stressed the role played by sacred power in the ritual and claimed that it is a celebration of life, death, and resurrection. Those empowered by God are already victors over the forces of Satan in this life, have already symbolically conquered death, and are thereby assured of resurrection—the final triumph.

Outsiders have also been struck by the continuing presence of witchcraft in some areas of Appalachia. Ruth Ann Musick, "Witchcraft and the Devil in West Virginia" (78) catalogued tales told to her by residents about encounters with the "evil eye" and the Devil that convinced many that witchcraft was part of the realm of the supernatural that pervaded human life. But Yvonne J. Milspaw, "Witchcraft in Appalachia: Protection for the Poor" (74) offered a rather different interpretation. Again drawing on work in West Virginia, Milspaw found that numerous elderly women, often regarded as eccentric, claimed to be witches themselves in order to gain a respect grounded in fear of their presumed power within the community. They were thus able to manipulate the public and often received gifts of the basic necessities of life from others to insure that they would not use their power to the detriment of the public welfare.

Not all persons living in Appalachia espouse belief in witchcraft or handle snakes as a ritual practice, but most Appalachian residents would no doubt identify themselves as Protestants. Institutional religious presence among mountain folk, however, has not been limited to Protestant denominations, sects, or groups. Although clearly a minority and often suspect, the Roman Catholic Church has also maintained a ministry in the mountains. A thoughtful study of Roman Catholic work as well as the occasional hostile reception Roman Catholicism has received in Appalachia is Margaret Wolfe, "Aliens in Southern Appalachia: Catholics in the Coal Camps, 1900-1940" (104). Catholic evangelistic endeavors in Woodway and Lee Counties, Virginia, have been appraised in David M. Byars and Bernard Quinn, *Evangelists to the Poor: A Catholic Ministry in Appalachia* (27).

Rural Southerners are by no means confined to the Appalachian region. A quarter of a century and more ago, there was considerable academic interest in studying "the rural church" and identifying its multifaceted social as well as religious roles. Simply put, the rural church was the center of community life, taking on a character among rural whites very similar to that which has been well-documented in the black church following the Civil War. Among the older studies of Southern rural religion, perhaps the best are Gordon W. Blackwell, *Church-Community Relations in Eleven Selected Southern Communities* (130) and Blackwell and others, *Church and Community in the South* (129). The latter offers an excellent overview of the social and economic forces that commingled with religion in the rural communities of the South in the 1940s, summarizes numerous other studies, and provides an extensive bibliography. Also worthy of note among older studies is William E. Garnett, *The Virginia Rural Church and Related Influences, 1900-1950* (134).

In recent years, relatively little attention has been directed to rural religion, perhaps because the rate of urbanization and industrialization that have come to the region since World War II and the sustained interest in Appalachia have lured scholars to other arenas of research. Fresh work, then, is needed on Southern rural religion, for many parts of the South remain predominantly rural. Three recent studies point the way for future work. One is Robert Coles, "God and the Rural Poor" (132), reprinted from his more extensive *Children of Crisis*, vol. 2: *Migrants, Sharecroppers, and Mountaineers*. Another is the collection of essays written from an anthropological perspective, *Holding On to the Land and the Lord: Kinship, Ritual, Land Tenure, and Social Policy in the Rural South*, especially Part II (135). Also worthy of note is Harry Lefever, "The Church and Poor Whites" (140). All three note the continuing vitality of religion in the rural South, the role of religion as a mechanism to cope with poverty, the traditionalism that prevails in religious belief, and the support provided for family solidarity and moral values by religious affirmation. But one hopes that scholars will soon again direct sustained attention to non-Appalachian Southern rural religion.

The bibliography that follows first lists those studies that provide an overview of Appalachian and/or Southern rural religion. It then identifies topical studies of religion in Appalachia, including those that treat fundamentalism, the work of the mainline denominations, dimensions of folk religion, the presence of Pentecostal-Holiness groups, and the like. The next section indicates the many works which describe and interpret snake-handling religious groups in Appalachia. The final section notes studies that have been concerned with rural religious life outside the Appalachian region.

BIBLIOGRAPHY

Several titles listed in chapter 1 are relevant to this chapter, as are occasional titles in the chapters on the various denominations, Holiness and Pentecostal religion, and the social order, and art, architecture, and music.

I. OVERVIEWS OF RELIGION
IN APPALACHIA AND THE RURAL SOUTH

(1) Davis, Charles T., and Richard A. Humphrey. "Appalachian Religion: A Diversity of Consciousness." *Appalachian Journal* 5 (1978): 390-99.

(2) Flynt, J. Wayne. *Dixie's Forgotten People: The South's Poor Whites*. Bloomington: Indiana University Press, 1980.

(3) *Foxfire*. Frequent articles and issues dealing with religion.

(4) Glenn, Max E. *Appalachia in Transition*. St. Louis: Bethany Press, 1970.

(5) "God and the Devil in Appalachia." *Appalachian Journal* 1 (Spring 1974): 243-300. Series of five articles.

(6) Higgs, Robert J., and A. N. Manning, eds. *Voices from the Hills: Selected Readings of Southern Appalachia*. New York: Frederick Ungar, 1975.

(7) Jones, Loyal. "Studying Mountain Religion." *Appalachian Journal* 5 (1977): 125-30.

(8) *Maryknoll* 70 (November 1976): 3-48, 63-64. Special issue on Appalachia highlighting Roman Catholic ministries.

(9) *Mountain Review*. Frequently contains sermon transcripts from Appalachian preachers.

(10) Photiadis, John D., and John E. Schnabel. "Religion: A Persistent Institution in a Changing Appalachia." *Review of Religious Research* 19 (Fall 1977): 32-42.

(11) _____, and Beryl B. Maurer. *Religion in an Appalachian State*. Morgantown: West Virginia University Division of Personal and Family Development, Appalachian Center, 1974.

(12) _____, ed. *Religion in Appalachia: Theological, Social and Psychological Dimensions and Correlates*. Morgantown: West Virginia University Center for Extension and Continuing Education, 1978.

(13) Quinn, Bernard, and Douglas Johnson. *Atlas of the Church in Appalachia: Administrative Units and Boundaries*. Knoxville: Commission on Religion in Appalachia, 1970.

(14) Reid, Melanie Sovine. "On the Study of Religion in Appalachia: A Review Essay." *Appalachian Journal* 6 (1979): 239-44.

(15) Rosenberg, Bruce A. *The Art of the American Folk Preacher*. New York: Oxford University Press, 1970.

(16) Weatherford, Willis D., and Earl D. C. Brewer. *Life and Religion in Southern Appalachia*. New York: Friendship Press, 1962.

(17) _____, ed. *Religion in the Appalachian Mountains: A Symposium*. Berea KY: Berea College, 1955.

II. RELIGION IN APPALACHIA: TOPICAL STUDIES

(18) Abell, Troy D. "The Holiness-Pentecostal Experience in Southern Appalachia." Ph.D. dissertation, Purdue University, 1974.

(19) Albanese, Catherine L. "Citizen Crockett: Myth, History, and Nature Religion." *Soundings* 61 (1978): 87-104.

(20) _____. *King Crockett: Nature and Civility on the American Frontier.* Charlottesville: University Press of Virginia, 1979.

(21) Anderson-Green, Paula H. " 'The Lord's Work': Southern Folk Belief in Signs, Warnings, and Dream-Visions." *Tennessee Folklore Society Bulletin* 43 (1977): 113-27.

(22) Baumhover, Lorin A. "Value Orientations of Clergy in Appalachia." Ph.D. dissertation, Colorado State University, 1976.

(23) Bing, Louise. " 'Soup, Soap and Salvation': 'Brother Pat' Withrow and the Charleston Union Mission." *Goldenseal* 6 (July-September 1980): 25-32.

(24) Blanchard, Charles L. *The Wesleyan Work in the Kentucky Mountains.* Syracuse: Department of Home Missions of the Wesleyan Methodist Church of America, 1950.

(25) Branscombe, James G. "Comparative Demonology." *Katallagete* 4 (1972): 17-20.

(26) Bruere, Martha B., and Robert Bruere. "The Church of the Lean Land." *Outlook* 109 (1915): 987-95.

(27) Byars, David M., and Bernard Quinn. *Evangelists to the Poor: A Catholic Ministry in Appalachia.* Washington: Glenmary Research Center, 1975.

(28) Chapman, Berlin B. "A. M. Grimes: Country Teacher and Itinerant Minister." *West Virginia History* 40 (1979): 287-92.

(29) Clements, William. "The American Folk Church in Northeast Arkansas." *Journal of the Folklore Institute* 15 (1978): 161-80.

(30) _____. "Faith Healing Narratives from Northeast Arkansas." *Indiana Folklore* 9 (1976): 15-40.

(31) Cleveland, Warren M. "The Heavenly Warfare in the War on Poverty." *Mountain Life and Work* 41 (Fall 1965): 30-31.

(32) Cobb, Alice L. "Sectarianism, Religion and Social Change in an Isolated Rural Community of Southern Appalachia." Ph.D. dissertation, Boston University, 1965.

(33) Commission on Religion in Appalachia, Inc. *A United Approach to Fulfilling the Church's Mission in Appalachia.* Knoxville: CORA, 1966.

(34) "Commission on Religion in Appalachia: Church and Change in Appalachia." *Appalachia* 6 (1973): 29-44.

(35) Conference of Southern Mountain Workers. *The Southern Highlands: An Inquiry into Their Needs, and Qualifications Desired in Church, Educational and Social Service Workers in the Mountain Country.* Asheville NC: Inland Press, 1915.

(36) Craig, Edward M. *Highways and Byways of Appalachia.* Kingsport TN: Kingsport Press, 1927.

(37) Cummings, Scott, et al. "Preachers versus Teachers: Local-Cosmopolitan Conflict over Textbook Censorship in an Appalachian Community." *Rural Sociology* 42 (1977): 7-21.

(38) Davids, Richard C. *The Man Who Moved a Mountain*. Philadelphia: Fortress Press, 1970.

(39) Davidson, Perry. "Religious Response in Our Corner of the Mountain." *Mountain Life and Work* 1 (1926): 5-11.

(40) DeBusman, Paul M. "Social Factors Affecting Selected Southern Baptist Churches in the Southern Appalachian Region of the United States." Th.D. dissertation, Southern Baptist Theological Seminary, 1962.

(41) DeJong, Gordon F., and Thomas R. Ford. "Religious Fundamentalism and Denominational Preference in the Southern Appalachian Region." *Journal for the Scientific Study of Religion* 5 (1965): 24-33.

(42) _____. "Religious Fundamentalism, Socio-Economic Status and Fertility Attitudes in the Southern Appalachians." *Demography* 2 (1965): 543-48.

(43) Dickerson, Lynn C. II. "The Baptists of the Cumberland Mountains." *Appalachian Heritage* 3 (1975): 60-67.

(44) Dickinson, Eleanor, and Barbara Benziger. *Revival!*. New York: Harper and Row, 1974.

(45) Doran, Paul E. "Some Church Problems in the Southern Appalachians." *Mountain Life and Work* 5 (April 1929): 11-15.

(46) Drake, Richard B. "The Mission School Era in Southern Appalachia, 1880-1940." *Appalachian Notes* 6 (1978): 1-8.

(47) Fear, Frank A. "Quest for Saliency: Patterns of Jewish Communal Organization in Three Appalachian Small Towns." Ph.D. dissertation, West Virginia University, 1972.

(48) Ford, Thomas R. "Religious Attitudes and Beliefs in the Southern Appalachians as Revealed by an Attitude Survey." *Review of Religious Research* 3 (Summer 1961): 3-20.

(49) _____. "Status, Residence, and Fundamentalist Religious Beliefs in the Southern Appalachians" *Social Forces* 39 (1960): 41-49.

(50) Gibson, Luther. *History of the Church of God, Mountain Assembly, founded Jellico Creek, Kentucky, 1906*. N.p.p.: n.p., 1954.

(51) Glenn, Max E. "Will the Church Take a Dare in the New Appalachia?" *World Call* 49 (November 1967): 17-20.

(52) Griffith, Henrietta M. "A History of Religious Education in the Kentucky Mountains." Thesis, Asbury Theological Seminary, 1950.

(53) Guerrant, Edward O. *The Galex Gatherers: The Gospel Among the Highlanders*. Richmond: Onward Press, 1910.

(54) Halan, Y. C. "The Folklore of the Appalachians." *Indian Journal of American Studies* 7 (1977): 28-40.

(55) Hall, John W. "An Old Regular Baptist Foot-Washing in the Mountains." *Applachian Heritage* 1 (1973): 27-37.

(56) Hartley, Loyde E. "Sectarianism and Social Participation: A Study of the Relation between Religious Attitudes and Involvement in Voluntary Organizations in Seventy-Two Churches in the Southern Appalachian Mountains." Ph.D. dissertation, Emory University, 1968.

(57) Hilbish, Florence M. A. *Tales of a Frontier Preacher*. New York: Pageant, 1959.

(58) Hooker, Elizabeth R. "The Churches of the Highlanders." *Mountain Life and Work* 9 (July 1933): 25-29.

(59) Humphrey, Richard A. "Foot Washing in the Southern Appalachians." *Appalachian Heritage* 5 (1977): 48-52.

(60) _____. "Hope and Promise of the Gospel: Adventist Christians and Primitive Baptists in the Southern Appalachian Mountains." *Appalachian Heritage* 4 (1976): 21-26.

(61) Jackson, Allen K. "Religious Beliefs and Expressions of the Southern Highlander." *Review of Religious Research* 3 (1961): 21-39.

(62) _____. "Religious Beliefs and Social Status: A Study of the Relation Between Religious Beliefs and Social Status Levels in Sixty-One Churches of the Southern Appalachian Mountains." Ph.D. dissertation, Emory University, 1960.

(63) Johnson, Linda. "Foot-Washin' Church and the Prayer-Book Church." *Christian Century* 93 (1976): 952-55.

(64) Jones, Loyal. "Mountain Religion: The Outsider's View." *Mountain Review* 2 (1976): 43-46.

(65) _____. "Old Time Baptists and Mainline Christianity." *An Appalachian Symposium: Essays Written in Honor of Cratis D. Williams*. J. W. Williamson, ed., 120-30. Boone NC: Appalachian State University Press, 1977.

(66) Kelly, L. C. "The Mountain Preacher and the Mountain Problem." *Mountain Life and Work* 9 (April 1933): 11-16.

(67) Lamar, Ralph E. "Fundamentalism and Selected Social Factors in the Southern Appalachian Region." M.A. thesis, University of Kentucky, 1962.

(68) Lee, Dallas M. "Central Appalachia." *Home Missions* 39 (December 1968): 8-23.

(69) Livingston, William J. "Coal Miners and Religion." Unpublished thesis, Union Theological Seminary, 1951.

(70) McConnell, Lela G. *Faith Victorious in the Kentucky Mountains: The Story of Twenty-Two Years of Spirit-Filled Ministry*. Winona Lake IN: Light and Life Press, 1946.

(71) _____. *The Pauline Ministry in the Kentucky Mountains*. 8th ed. Berne IN: Light and Hope Publishing, 1952. First published 1942.

(72) McInnis, Anne, and Debi Fife. "Persimmon's Log Church." *Foxfire* 11 (1977): 119-22.

(73) Meyer, Rose Ann. "Mountain Character: Carved from the Rock of Faith." *Mountain Heritage* 4 (1976): 4-9.

(74) Milspaw, Yvonne J. "Witchcraft in Appalachia: Protection for the Poor." *Indiana Folklore* 11 (1978): 71-86.

(75) Moody, Robert. "The Lord Selected Me." *Southern Exposure* 7 (1979): 4-10.

(76) "Mountain Ministers: The Last Source for Advice?." *Mountain Life and Work* 35 (Fall 1959): 23-37.

(77) Mullins, Frieda, and Diana Hall. "Old Regular Baptist Foot-Washin': July 29, 1973." *Appalachian Heritage* 1 (1973): 20-21.

(78) Musick, Ruth Ann. "Witchcraft and the Devil in West Virginia." *Appalachian Journal* 1 (1974): 271-76.

(79) Nelsen, Hart M. *The Appalachian Presbyterian: Some Rural-Urban Differences, A Preliminary Report.* Research Bulletin 5. Bowling Green: Western Kentucky University Office of Research and Services, 1968.

(80) _____, et al. *Comparison of Religious Groupings in Appalachia: Presbyterian, Episcopalian, Church of God, Holiness. A Study Based on Southern Appalachian Studies Data.* Research Bulletin 6. Bowling Green: Western Kentucky University Office of Research and Services, 1968.

(81) Parker, Gerald K. "Folk Religion in Southern Appalachia." Th.D. dissertation, Southern Baptist Theological Seminary, 1970.

(82) Petosa, John. "Appalachia Revisited: 'Healthy But Slow Ferment' Follows 1975 Pastoral." *National Catholic Reporter* 12 (20 February 1976): 5-6.

(83) Preece, Harold, and Celia Kraft. *Dew on Jordan.* New York: E. P. Dutton, 1946.

(84) "Prospects for Religious Change in the Appalachian South." *Mountain Life and Work* 40 (Winter 1964): 43-46.

(85) Redman, Barbara J. "The Impact of Great Revival Religion on the Personal Characteristics of the Southern Appalachian People." *Southern Studies* 20 (1981): 303-310.

(86) Reinhardt, Robert M. "Religion and Politics: The Political Behavior of West Virginia Protestant Fundamentalist Sectarians." Ph.D. dissertation, West Virginia University, 1974.

(87) Rich, Mark. *Some Churches of Coal Mining Communities of West Virginia.* New York: West Virginia Council of Churches and the Committee for Cooperative Field Research, 1951.

(88) Siler, James H. "Sunday Schools Remembered." *Appalachian Heritage* 4 (Spring 1976): 49-53.

(89) Smathers, Eugene. "Mountain-City Interchange." *Mountain Life and Work* 37 (Winter 1961): 43-45.

(90) Stover, Virginia H. *Angels in the Mountains.* Birmingham AL: Birmingham Printing, 1957.

(91) Tadlock, E. V. "Church Problems in the Mountains." *Mountain Life and Work* 6 (April 1930): 6-8.

(92) Thomas, Samuel W. "The Oneida Albums: Photography, Oral Tradition, and the Appalachian Experience." *Register of the Kentucky Historical Society* 80 (1982): 432-43.

(93) Watkins, Floyd C., and Charles Hubert Watkins. *Yesterday in the Hills.* Athens: University of Georgia Press, 1963.

(94) Weller, Jack E. "Addressing the Afflicted and the Affluent." *Christian Century* 92 (1975): 764-65.

(95) _____. "Ministering to Appalachia." *Christian Century* 82 (1965): 935-36.

(96) _____. "Salvation Is Not Enough." *Mountain Life and Work* 45 (March 1969): 9-13.

(97) _____. "Time for Reason." *Mountain Life and Work* 45 (April 1969): 11-13.

(98) White, Edwin E. "From the Mountain Worker's Point of View: Religion." *Mountain Life and Work* 9 (July 1933): 38-40.

(99) _____. "Religious Ideals in the Highlands." *Mountain Life and Work* 27 (Fall 1951): 26-31; 28 (Winter 1952): 18-21.

(100) Whitt, Hugh P., and Hart M. Nelsen. "Residence, Moral Traditionalism, and Tolerance of Atheists." *Social Forces* 54 (1975): 328-40.

(101) Williams, Claude C. "Pentecostal Churches." *Mountain Life and Work* (Winter 1944): 18-22.

(102) Wilson, Warren H. "The Educational Ministry in the Mountains." *Mountain Life and Work* 6 (April 1930): 20-24.

(103) Wise, James E. The 'Sons of God Message' in the North Carolina Mountains: An Exercise in 'Thick Description'." M.A. thesis, University of North Carolina in Chapel Hill, 1977.

(104) Wolfe, Margaret Ripley. "Aliens in Southern Appalachia: Catholics in the Coal Camps, 1900-1940." *Appalachian Heritage* 6 (Winter 1978): 43-56.

III. APPALACHIAN HOLINESS SNAKE-HANDLING GROUPS

(105) Alther, Lisa. "They Shall Take Up Serpents." *New York Times Magazine* (6 June 1976): 18-20, 28, 35.

(106) Campbell, Will D. "Come: A Study of Appalachian Folk Religion." *Southern Voices* 1 (1974): 41-48.

(107) Carden, Karen Wilson, and Robert W. Pelton. *The Persecuted Prophets.* South Brunswick NJ: A. S. Barnes, 1976.

(108) Crapps, Robert W. "Religion of the Plain Folk in the Southern United States." *Perspectives in Religious Studies* 4 (1977): 37-53.

(109) Daugherty, Mary L. "Serpent-Handling as Sacrament." *Theology Today* 33 (1976): 232-43.

(110) Gerrard, Nathan L. "The Holiness Movement in Southern Appalachia." In *The Charismatic Movement.* Michael P. Hamilton, ed., 159-71. Grand Rapids: Eerdmans, 1975.

(111) _____. "The Serpent-Handling Religions of West Virginia." *Trans-Action* 5 (May 1968): 22-28.

(112) Holliday, Robert K. *Tests of Faith*. Oak Hill WV: Fayette Tribune, 1966.

(113) "The Holy Ghost People." *Contemporary Films* (McGraw-Hill), 1968.

(114) Kane, Steven M. "Aspects of Holy Ghost Religion: The Snake-Handling Sect of the American Southeast." M.A. thesis, University of North Carolina in Chapel Hill, 1973.

(115) _____. "Ritual Possession in a Southern Appalachian Religious Sect." *Journal of American Folklore* 87 (1974): 293-302.

(116) _____. "Snake Handlers of Southern Appalachia." Ph.D. dissertation, Princeton University, 1979.

(117) Kobler, John. "America's Strangest Religion." *Saturday Evening Post* 230 (28 September 1957): 26-27, 153-54, 156.

(118) LaBarre, Weston. *They Shall Take Up Serpents: Psychology of the Southern Snake-Handling Cult*. Rev. ed. New York: Schocken Books, 1969.

(119) Larsen, Egon. *Strange Sects and Cults: A Study of Their Origins and Influence*, 205-206. New York: Hart Publishing, 1972.

(120) Maguire, Marsha. "Confirming the Word: Snake-Handling Sects in Southern Appalachia." *Quarterly Journal of the Library of Congress* 38 (1981): 166-77.

(121) Pelton, Robert W., and Karen W. Carden. *Snake Handlers: God-Fearers? or Fanatics?* Nashville: Thomas Nelson, 1974.

(122) Robertson, Archibald T. *That Old-Time Religion*, 156-81. Boston: Houghton Mifflin, 1950.

(123) Schwarz, Berthold E. "Ordeal by Serpents, Fire, Strychnine: A Study of Some Provocative Psychosomatic Phenomena." *Psychiatric Quarterly* 34 (1960): 405-29.

(124) "Snake Handling." *Appalachian Heritage* 6 (Spring 1978): 29-32.

(125) Steckert, Ellen. "The Snake-Handling Sect of Harlan County, Kentucky: Its Influence on Folk Tradition." *Southern Folklore Quarterly* 27 (1963): 316-22.

(126) "Virginia Mountaineers Handle Snakes to Prove Their Piety." *Life* 17 (3 July 1944): 59-62.

(127) Wigginton, B. Eliot. "Unto the Church of God . . . " *Foxfire* 7,1 (1973): 2-75.

IV. STUDIES OF SOUTHERN RURAL RELIGION

(128) Alexander, Frank D. "Religion in a Rural Community in the South." *American Sociological Review* 6 (1941): 241-51.

(129) Blackwell, Gordon W., et al. *Church and Community in the South*. Richmond VA: John Knox Press, 1949.

(130) _____. *Church-Community Relations in Eleven Selected Southern Communities*. Chapel Hill: Institute for Research in Social Science, 1946.

(131) Brunner, Edmund deS. *Church Life in the Rural South*. New York: George H. Doran, 1923.

(132) Coles, Robert. "God and the Rural Poor." *Psychology Today* 5 (Jan. 1972): 31-41. Excerpted from *Children of Crisis* 2: *Migrants, Sharecroppers, and Mountaineers*. Boston: Little, Brown, 1971.

(133) Fossett, Mildred B. "History of McDowell Churches." *Mountain Living* 7 (Fall 1976): 32-37, 8 (Winter 1977): 24-27.

(134) Garnett, William E. *The Virginia Rural Church and Related Influences, 1900-1950*. Virginia Agricultural Experiment Station Bulletin 479. Blacksburg: Virginia Polytechnic Institute, 1957.

(135) Hall, Robert L., and Carole V. Stack, eds. *Holding On to the Land and the Lord: Kinship, Ritual, Land Tenure, and Social Policy in the Rural South*, esp. Part II. Athens GA: University of Georgia Press, 1982.

(136) Hamilton, Charles H., and William E. Garnett. *Role of the Church in Rural Community Life in Virginia*. Agricultural Experiment Station Bulletin 267. Blacksburg: Virginia Polytechnic Institute, 1929.

(137) Jordan, Terry G. "Forest Folk, Prairie Folk: Rural Religious Culture in Northern Texas." *Southwestern Historical Quarterly* 80 (1976): 135-62.

(138) Kaufman, Harold F. "Rural Churches in Kentucky." Kentucky Agricultural Experiment Station Bulletin 530 (1949).

(139) Ledbetter, Margaret. "The Village Church in North Carolina." Thesis, Duke University, 1931.

(140) Lefever, Harry. "The Church and Poor Whites." *New South* 25 (1970): 20-32.

(141) Masters, Victor I. *Country Church in the South*. Atlanta: Home Missions Board, 1916.

(142) Maurer, Beryl B. "The Rural Church and Organized Community Activity: A Study of Church-Community Activities in Two East Tennessee Communities." Thesis, University of Tennessee, 1953.

(143) Ormond, Jesse M. *The Country Church in North Carolina*. Durham: Duke University Press, 1931.

(144) Suarez, Raleigh A. "Religion in Rural Louisiana." *Louisiana Historical Quarterly* 38 (1955): 55-63.

(145) Wasserman, Ira M. "Religious Affiliations and Homicide: Historical Results from the Rural South." *Journal for the Scientific Study of Religion* (1978): 415-18.

(146) White, Edwin E. "Some Goals for the Rural Church." *Mountain Life and Work* 13 (July 1937): 25-30.

(147) Wilson L. G., et al. "The Church and Landless Men." *University of North Carolina Bulletin* 1 (1 March 1922): 1-27.

(148) Wyatt-Brown, Bertram. "Religion and the Formation of Folk Culture: Poor Whites of the Old South." In *The Americanizing of the Gulf Coast, 1803-1850*. Lucius F. Ellsworth, ed. Pensacola: Historical Pensacola Preservation Board, 1972.

14 OTHER GROUPS AND MOVEMENTS IN THE SOUTH

THE RELIGIOUS PLURALISM characteristic of American society has meant that countless religious groups and movements have flourished in the South alongside the major denominational groupings. Often overlooked because numerically they represent a small proportion of the region's religiously affiliated population, they nevertheless account for a vital minority presence. Some are mainstream denominations whose demographic strength rises and falls in different parts of the nation; others are smaller sectarian movements that have established enclaves here and there in the South; others have emerged in the Southern context because of population movement within the nation or immigration from elsewhere. Unfortunately many of the the smallest bodies have failed to attract the attention of scholars, creating lacunae in the secondary literature analyzing Southern religion.

LUTHERANS

Among the groups linked with mainstream denominations are the various strands of the Lutheran tradition that have found a home in the South. Lutherans can trace their presence in Dixie to the eighteenth century, thanks to the migration of German colonists from Pennsylvania into Virginia and the North Carolina Piedmont and to immigrants, primarily from Germany and Austria, who came first to Charleston and Savannah and then gradually moved inland. A brief general history, in need of updating, is an unpublished thesis: Paul E. Monroe, Jr., "A History of Southern Lutheranism" (78). More limited in scope, but carefully documented is H. George Anderson, *Lutheranism in the Southeastern States, 1860-1886: A Social History* (53). George Fenwick Jones has looked closely at the Salzburger immigration from Austria to Georgia in the 1730s that forms the backdrop for early Lutheran developments in that state. His most comprehensive study is *The Salzburger Saga: Religious Exiles and Other Germans along the Savannah* (73). He has also provided a brief biography of one of the major leaders of this cluster of Lutherans in "In Memoriam: John Martin Boltzius, 1703-1765" (71). Other works written or edited by Jones, including a multivolume documentary account of the Salzburgers, are listed in the bibliography at the close of this chapter.

Several studies, some filiopietistic in tone, provide historical sketches of Lutheran developments in various sections of the South. The oldest Lutheran Synod in the South is that founded in 1803 in North Carolina. H. George Anderson, *The North Carolina Synod through 175 Years* (54), is a solid account of its development. Two older, but still reliable studies are G. D. Bernheim, *History of the German Settlements and of the Lutheran Church in North and South Carolina* (59), and Bernheim and G. H. Cox, *The History of the Evangelical Lutheran Synod and Ministerium of North Carolina, in Commemoration of the Completion of the First Century of Its Existence* (58). Lutheran work in the South during the epoch when the North Carolina Synod was founded owed much to the missionary labors of men such as John Jacob Scherer and Paul Henkel. On Scherer's ministry, see Donald S. Armentrout's doctoral dissertation, "John Jacob Scherer: A Type of Southern Lutheran" (55). Henkel's early labors in Virginia are recounted in the standard Lutheran history for that state: William E. Eisenberg, *The Lutheran Church in Virginia, 1717-1962* (65). Henkel was also a prime mover in the organization of the Tennessee Synod in 1820. See *Life Sketches of Lutheran Ministers, North Carolina and Tennessee Synods, 1773-1965* (77). An older study focusing on areas associated with Henkel but also treating the limited Lutheran presence in parts of Appalachia is Charles W. Cassell, *History of the Lutheran Church in Virginia and East Tennessee* (62). Abdel R. Wentz, *History of the Evangelical Lutheran Synod of Maryland of the United Lutheran Church in America, 1820-1920* (88), looks at developments in that state. For the Lutheran story in some other parts of the South, see Donald R. Poole, *History of the Georgia-Alabama Synod of the United Lutheran Church in America, 1860-1960* (80), and Walter H. Ellwanger, "Lutheranism in Alabama and Other Parts of the South" (66).

During the era of the Civil War, Charleston pastor John Bachman was Southern Lutheranism's most influential leader. A major figure in the formation of the General Synod in the Confederate States of America (1863), Bachman was also influential in the founding of the Lutheran Theological Southern Seminary (Columbia, South Carolina) and Newberry College (Newberry, South Carolina). The best biographical treatment, though unpublished, is Raymond M. Bost, "The Reverend John Bachman and the Development of Southern Lutheranism" (60). On the Confederate denomination, see Gordon W. Ward, Jr., "The Formation of the Lutheran General Synod, South, During the Civil War" (86). Robert W. Frizzell, " 'Killed by Rebels': A Civil War Massacre and Its Aftermath" (67), has called attention to the ways in which the nation's sectional division strengthened the self-identity of another cluster of Lutherans, those German-Americans who formed the Lutheran Church-Missouri Synod. There is a dearth of scholarly studies on recent Lutheran developments in the South.

Lutherans in the South are far from alone in tracing some roots to German immigrants to the region. The United Church of Christ, the Church of the Brethren, the Moravians, and both the Amish and the Mennonites also have links to the arrival of Germans in the South during the colonial era and early national period.

UNITED CHURCH OF CHRIST

In 1957, the denomination known as the United Church of Christ came into existence through merger of the Evangelical and Reformed Church and the Congregational Christian Church. Each of the parent bodies had resulted from earlier mergers. Roots of the United Church of Christ in the South rest largely, but not exclusively, with the followers of James O'Kelly (who broke with the Methodists in the late eighteenth century); German immigrants who settled in frontier regions in the early nineteenth century; Northerners who came South during Reconstruction to labor with the newly freed black population, often under the auspices of the American Missionary Association; and mid-nineteenth-century German immigration to Texas. Concentrated in four pockets (Tidewater Virginia, the North Carolina Piedmont, The Texas hill country, and coastal Florida), the United Church of Christ today claims only about 125,000 Southern adherents. The most complete overall study is Durwood T. Stokes and William T. Scott, *A History of the Christian Churches in the South* (158). The predecessor Evangelical and Reformed Church, which had been composed primarily of the two clusters of German-Americans already noted, has its story told in two popular studies: Jacob C. Leonard, *The Southern Synod of the Evangelical and Reformed Church* (154), and Banks J. Peeler, *A Story of the Southern Synod of the Evangelical and Reformed Church* (155). Those whose heritage may be traced to the schism from the Methodist Episcopal Church led by O'Kelly because of disagreements over ecclesiastical authority have a superb scholarly study of their origins in Nathan O. Hatch, "The Christian Movement and the Demand for a Theology of the People" (151), but see also Charles F. Kilgore, *The James O'Kelly Schism in the Methodist Episcopal Church* (153). Two studies of individual congregations also merit mention. David Ramsay, noted early historian of the

American Revolution, recounted the beginnings of the Congregationalist movement in Charleston, South Carolina, in *The History of the Independent or Congregational Church of Charleston, S.C.* (156). James Stacy, *A History of the Midway Congregational Church in Liberty County, Georgia* (157), looks at a group noted for its work with Southern blacks in the later antebellum period.

CHURCH OF THE BRETHREN

Although numbering only around 50,000 members, the Church of the Brethren dominates the religious scene in one small section of Virginia, the area around Bridgewater, but it also has considerable strength in parts of Maryland. With roots in early eighteenth-century Germany, the group was once popularly known as the Dunkers and in the nineteenth century as German Baptists. Distinguished by celebrating the rite of foot washing along with communion and by the practice of baptism by immersion three times forward, the Brethren today have come to resemble mainline Protestantism. Two scholars, Roger E. Sappington and Donald F. Durnbaugh, are responsible for the best secondary literature and collections of primary materials documenting the history of this group. Two source books edited by Durnbaugh treat the German background of the Brethren and their development in the North American colonies: *European Origins of the Brethren* (32) and *The Brethren in Colonial America* (31). Durnbaugh's doctoral dissertation, "Brethren Beginnings: The Origins of the Church of the Brethren in Early Eighteenth Century Europe" (30), provides insight on the group's background and formative stages. Sappington has focused on early Brethren history in North Carolina in "Dunker Beginnings in North Carolina in the Eighteenth Century" (36) and "Two Eighteenth Century Dunker Congregations in North Carolina" (38). That story is expanded in his *The Brethren in the Carolinas* (33). Sappington appraises early nineteenth-century Brethren growth and expansion in *The Brethren in the New Nation* (34). He has also written a careful study of developments in Virginia in *The Brethren in Virginia* (35) and a solid case study of one local congregation, *History of the Bridgewater, Virginia Church of the Brethren, 1878-1978* (37).

MORAVIANS

With roots in the Unitas Fratrum strand of the Hussite movement of fifteenth-century Bohemia (now part of Czechoslovakia), Moravians came to Georgia in the 1730s by way of Germany. Involved in evangelization work with the Indians around Savannah, these early Moravian settlers finally settled in Pennsylvania in 1740. Attempts later in that decade to establish outposts in Virginia met with limited success, but in 1752, Moravians began to settle on the Wachovia tract in the area around Winston-Salem, North Carolina. The Old Salem tourist center in Winston-Salem today represents a restoration of the Moravian village of Salem, founded in 1766. While Moravians number only around 21,000 now, their enduring presence has given German pietism a rich heritage in Southern religious life. In 1922, Adelaide Fries and her associates began publishing the *Records of the Moravians in North Carolina* (91), an important collection of primary source material for contemporary scholars. The beginnings of settlement on the Wachovia tract are recounted in Kenneth G. Hamilton, "The Moravians and Wachovia" (92). While generally left alone to pursue their lives of simple piety, the Moravians became suspect during the era of the American Revolution because of their pacifism. See Hunter James, *Quiet People of the Land: A Story of the North Carolina Moravians in Revolutionary Times* (93). Also important for further work is the multivolume publication project launched by Old Salem, Inc., in 1974: *The Three Forks of Muddy Creek* (94).

MENNONITES AND AMISH

Two other groups related to each other and also of German ethnic origin have had a small presence in the South, the Amish and the Mennonites. For an older study of Mennonites in one area of the South, see Harry A. Brunk, *History of the Mennonites in Virginia, 1727-1900* (1). Mennonites were also part of the migration into the Plains area, and several enclaves established in Oklahoma continue to flourish and at one time were engaged in mission work with Indian tribal societies on the reservations. Two brief sketches are Ralph A. Felton, "Mennonite Brethren, Corn, Oklahoma" (2), and Marvin Kolker, "Mennonites in the Oklahoma 'Runs' " (3). One group of Amish settlers came to Arkansas. Their story is told all too briefly in Ruth McKnight, "Quaint and Devout: A Study of the Amish at Vilonia, Arkansas" (4). In the later nineteenth century, internal dissension erupted in some Amish circles over the doctrine and practice of baptism. One with liberal views, John Stoltzfus, migrated to Tennessee in 1872. For a short summary of the dispute and Stoltzfus's role in it, see Paton Yoder, ed., and Elizabeth Bender, trans., "Baptism as an Issue in the Amish Division of the Nineteenth Century: 'Tennessee' John Stoltzfus" (6).

HUGUENOTS

Of French origin were the Huguenots, Protestants of a Calvinistic bent who began migrating to South Carolina in 1679 just as the persecution at home that culminated in the revocation of the Edict of Nantes in 1685 was about to get underway. Later groups came to Virginia and North Carolina, but for various reasons they did not endure, and remnants eventually joined the earlier settlements in and around Charleston. But rather quickly, many of the Huguenots in the South (those in the city of Charleston being the major exception) became Anglicans because, according to Robert M. Kingdon ("Why Did the Huguenot Refugees in the American Colonies Become Episcopalian?" [49]), they were as committed to ignoring nonessential differences and emphasizing the common bonds among Protestants as they were to maintaining a distinctive Calvinism. Hence by the nineteenth century, most of the Huguenots had been absorbed into other religious groups. Arthur H. Hirsch, *The Huguenots of Colonial South Carolina* (48), one old but standard study, contains some material on Huguenot religious life and the group's involvement in the American Revolution. But also see William H. Foote, *The Huguenots* (47). Revolutionary activities of Huguenot clergy are also noted in E. G. C. Terry, "The Huguenots of Upper South Carolina" (51). The old Huguenot church in Charleston, which had ceased operations in 1955, recently reopened for regular worship services.

QUAKERS

The Religious Society of Friends, better known as the Quakers, has also been part of Southern life since the seventeenth century, when the first meeting was organized in North Carolina. Still concentrated today in North Carolina, Southern Quakers distinguished themselves historically for their labors in efforts to secure religious toleration and for their longstanding opposition to slavery. J. Floyd Moore, *Friends in the Colonies* (112), includes a discussion of Southern Quakers. Lindsey S. Butler, "The Seventeenth Century Origins of North Carolina Friends" (102), highlights the initial organization of Friends there during the colonial governorship of John Archdale, himself a Quaker. The most complete history of North Carolina Friends is Francis C. Anscombe, *I Have Called You First: The Story of Quakerism in North Carolina* (99), now in need of updating. Kenneth L. Carroll has offered two scholarly studies of Quaker developments in Maryland and Virginia: *Quakerism on the Eastern Shore* (106), and "Quakerism on the Eastern Shore of Virginia" (107). Carroll has also called attention to Quaker efforts to secure religious toleration in Maryland in "Quaker Opposition to the Establishment of a State Church in Maryland" (105). Religious toleration is also the focus of Warren M. Billings, "A Quaker in Seventeenth-Century Virginia: Four Remonstrances by George Wilson" (101). The well-known Quaker antislavery position is discussed in chapter 4. Some titles in chapter 3 detail Quaker work among the native American Indians.

UNITARIANS

Those who characterize Southern religion as a bastion of conservatism ignore the long presence in the region of liberal religion, particularly that espoused by Unitarians and Universalists. Always a minority and frequently suspect because their views did not mesh with those of the evangelical Protestant majority, these groups do have antebellum roots and point to figures such as Thomas Jefferson as ideological compatriots. Thomas Cooper, first president of South Carolina College (now the University of South Carolina), had Unitarian sympathies, though he was more anticlerical than pro-Unitarian in public statements. Unitarians early found a niche in urban coastal areas such as Charleston and New Orleans, while Universalists tended to establish themselves in rural areas. But the two were sufficiently alike in stance that in 1961 they merged to form the Unitarian-Universalist Association. Today Unitarians are still clustered in urban areas, university centers, and regions of the South that have witnessed the largest immigration of residents from the North over the past half century.

One older study provides a survey of Unitarian developments to the beginning of the twentieth century: Arthur A. Brooks, *The History of Unitarianism in the Southern Churches* (124). More academic in tone and probably the best study is Earl W. Cory, "Unitarians and Universalists of the Southeastern United States during the Nineteenth Century," a University of Georgia doctoral dissertation (129). George W. Gibson, "Unitarian Congregations in the Ante-Bellum South" (137), and Clarence Gohdes, "Some Notes on the Unitarian Churches in the Ante-Bellum South: A Contribution to the History of Southern Liberalism " (140), both note that Unitarian growth slowed in the late antebellum period when, many commentators have argued, the South was undergoing conservative retrenchment in an effort to defend slavery in positive terms, in part because Northern Unitarians were thought to be in the vanguard of the antislavery movement. The intellectual sophistication that buttressed Unitarian affirmation found a less congenial environment as evangelicalism, with its emphasis on affective religious experience, came to dominate Southern religion during the same epoch. As a minority movement, many Unitarians in the South either acquiesced to the presence of the region's "peculiar institution" or quietly opposed it, although on occasion class interests and a commitment to maintain social order superseded ideological convictions, drawing a few Unitarians to support slavery. The full story is told by Douglas C. Stange in the several works noted in chapter 4.

Several studies focusing on individual states or local areas offer complementary scholarly appraisal. Two of the better ones deal with Unitarianism in Georgia: George H. Gibson, "Unitarian Congregations in Ante-Bellum Georgia" (136), and Louis D. Becker, "Unitarianism in Post-War Atlanta, 1882-1908" (123). Charleston, South Carolina, boasts one of the oldest Unitarian congregations, subject of Mary Maxine Larisey, *The Unitarian Church in Charleston, South Carolina: A Brief History* (145), and Elias B. Bull, *Founders and Pew Renters of the Unitarian Church in Charleston, S.C., 1817-1874* (125). Also prominent among Southern Unitarian congregations is Baltimore's First Church, the history of which is told in popular fashion by Rebecca Funk in *A Heritage to Hold in Fee, 1817-1917: First Unitarian Church of Baltimore* (135).

Two of nineteenth-century Southern Unitarianism's leading ministers were Samuel Gilman of Charleston (1791-1858) and Theodore Clapp of New Orleans (1792-1866). Neither has received the scholarly attention he deserves. A good, albeit brief, look at Gilman is provided by Daniel Walker Howe in "A Massachusetts Yankee in Senator Calhoun's Court: Samuel Gilman in South Carolina" (141). Another, which notes Gilman's contributions to his collegiate alma mater, is Henry Wilder Foote, "Samuel Gilman, Author of 'Fair Harvard' " (133). The only book-length study appeared the year Gilman died: A. O. Andrews, *Sixteen Years Chaplain, Friend, and Counsellor of the Washington Light Infantry of Charleston, S.C., The Rev. Samuel Gilman, D.D.* (122). Clapp, a strict Calvinist before he developed Universalist leanings, has not fared any better among scholars. The best study is Timothy F. Reilly's article, "Parson Clapp of New Orleans: Antebellum Social Critic, Religious Radical, and Member of the Establishment" (147). But also see John Duffy, ed., *Parson Clapp of the Strangers' Church of New Orleans* (130), and Henry Wilder Foote, "Theodore Clapp" (134). Indeed, all aspects of Southern Unitarianism deserve greater attention from scholars.

GREEK ORTHODOX

Another religious body in the South likewise has a style that distinguishes it from the Western Christianity that undergirds most organized religion in the South, although it does not share the liberal perspective associated with the Unitarian-Universalist tradition. It is the Greek Orthodox strain of Christianity. Since 1980, the headquarters for Greek Orthodox work in the South has been located in Atlanta, although the first Greek Orthodox to arrive in what became the United States came to Florida in 1768 and the first Greek Orthodox parish to be founded in the United States was established in New Orleans in 1866. The initial experience of those who came to Florida was unpleasant, to say the least, since the 500 or so men involved were indigent servants who were part of Andrew Turnbull's New Smyrna settlement and who ultimately had to petition the British Crown for their freedom. Their story is aptly told in Epaminodas P. Panagopoulos, *New Smyrna: An Eighteenth Century Greek Odyssey* (98). There is no comprehensive study of Eastern Christianity in the South. Charles C. DiMichele's master's thesis, "The History of the Eastern Orthodox Church in Mississippi" (97), is virtually the only scholarly secondary treatment of this tradition in the South.

MORMONS

The Greek Orthodox garner most adherents from internal propagation rather than from conversions. One of the faster growing religious movements in the South today, the Mormons, owes much of its growth to converts from other religious groups. The Church of Jesus Christ of Latter-day Saints, the formal name for the Mormons, emerged in the "burned-over" district of New

York in the early 1830s under the leadership of Joseph Smith. Shortly after Smith and his followers migrated to Ohio, missionaries moved into the South, establishing a congregation in West Virginia perhaps as early as 1832. While there soon were handfuls of Mormons to be found in Kentucky, Tennessee, and elsewhere, the Latter-day Saints figure most prominently in Missouri in the antebellum period, for the group briefly located itself around Independence before embarking on the series of movements which culminated in the migration to Utah. Several articles recount the turbulence that marked the stay in Missouri. R. J. Robertson, Jr.'s two-part "The Mormon Experience in Missouri, 1830-1839" (28), is the most complete account. Warren A. Jennings has examined the arrival of the Mormons in Missouri in "The Army of Israel Marches into Missouri" (22) and problems they encountered because of stiff local opposition in "The Expulsion of the Mormons from Jackson County, Missouri" (23). Some of the opposition came from Isaac McCoy, best known as a Baptist missionary to the Indians. See Warren A. Jennings, "Isaac McCoy and the Mormons" (24).

Although now considerably outdated, given the rapid expansion of the Mormons in the South in recent decades, the fifth volume of Brigham H. Roberts, *A Complete History of the Church of Jesus Christ of Latter-day Saints* (27), is the fullest treatment of the Mormon story in the South. Early missionary activities in the region are recounted in LaMar C. Berrett's M.A. thesis, "History of the Southern States Mission, 1831-1861" (12), although this agency of the church that had oversight over work in the South was not formally organized until 1875. Scholarly examination of Mormon activities in the South is also found in Samuel G. Ellsworth, "A History of Mormon Missions in the United States and Canada, 1830-1860" (17). Two articles by David Buice offer insight into the difficulties Mormons often faced in gaining an appreciative hearing when seeking converts: "When the Saints Came Marching In: The Mormon Experience in Antebellum New Orleans, 1840-1855" (15) and "Excerpts from the Diary of Teancum William Heward, Early Mormon Missionary to Georgia" (14). Also valuable, although told from ain "insider" point of view, is Wallace R. Draughon, *History of the Church of Jesus Christ of Latter-day Saints in North Carolina* (16). In the postbellum period, Mormons encountered their greatest opposition in the South, much of it violent, largely because of cultural apprehension over the practice of polygamy. For a general study, see William W. Hatch, *There Is No Law: A History of Mormon Civil Relations in the Southern States, 1865-1905* (20). In Tennessee, an outspoken critic of the Mormons during the epoch was Methodist preacher and politician William Brownlow, whose attacks on the Latter-day Saints are examined in R. B. Lattimore, "A Survey of William Brownlow's Criticism of the Mormons, 1841-1857" (26). In Missouri, Sen. George Graham Vest was an outspoken opponent of the group. See M. Paul

Holsinger, "Senator George Graham Vest and the 'Menace' of Mormonism, 1882-1887" (21). An unusually provocative discussion of the violent nature of much of the opposition to Mormonism is Gene A. Sessions, "Myth, Mormonism, and Murder in the South" (29), who uses the attacks on the Mormons as an entrée to analyze the phenomenon of Southern violence in general. Given Mormon growth in the South over the past several decades, there is need for renewed scholarly appraisal of this group's story.

SHAKERS

Not all religious groups that once found a home in the South still exist today. Among those that have faded is the United Society of Believers in Christ's Second Appearing, better known as the Shakers. Shaker roots in America go back to 1774, when Ann Lee and a group of about a dozen of her followers migrated from England to New York. Committed to the practice of celibacy and separation of the sexes, the Shakers were among the many groups that gained adherents when the campmeetings of Kentucky generated considerable religious enthusiasm along the old Southwestern frontier. Two Shaker communities were established in Kentucky in the early nineteenth century, one at South Hill near the Tennessee border and the other at Pleasant Hill, near Harrodsburg and Lexington. Reliance on conversion rather than internal propagation was only one of the factors that fostered decline in the later nineteenth century, despite efforts at expansion that involved the establishment of short-lived communities in Southwest Georgia in the 1890s. Pleasant Hill disbanded in 1910, followed by South Hill twelve years later. Today, however, Pleasant Hill has been restored and is open to the public. Early Shaker success in Kentucky is the focus of Raymond J. Randles, "Shaker Harvest in Kentucky" (118). Samuel W. Thomas and Mary Lawrence Young have examined "The Development of Shakertown at Pleasant Hill, Kentucky" (120). Although the Shakers generally remained aloof from the sectional division that resulted in the Civil War and the Kentucky communities offered aid to soldiers on both sides, they suffered greatly from plunder and arson during the war years. See Julia Neal, "South Union Shakers during War Years" (116), and Stephen Paterwick, "The Effects of the Civil War on Shaker Societies" (117). The four-year experiment with founding new communities in Georgia is the subject of Russell H. Anderson, "The Shaker Communities in Southwest Georgia" (115).

KORESHAN UNITY

One other attempt at creating a religiously based utopian community in the South merits attention: Koreshan Unity, which opened in Estero, Florida (near Fort Myers), in 1894 and endured until 1961. Revolving around the teachings of Cyrus Read Teed, Koreshan Unity also espoused celibacy. The teachings of Teed and the community itself have escaped the attention of scholars with the exception of one article that treats the group's experiences in Chicago when the plans for the Florida community were being formulated. See Howard D. Fine, "The Koreshan Unity: The Chicago Years of a Utopian Community" (160).

Many of the groups discussed in this chapter are so small numerically as to be nearly insignificant statistically. Others flourished for a time, but no longer exist. Nevertheless their presence and their stories constitute an important dimension of Southern religious life past and present. They reveal that despite the evangelical Protestant hegemony, religious pluralism has long been a dynamic part of Southern religion.

The bibliography that follows lists works treating groups and movements in alphabetical order and then some miscellaneous studies: Amish and Mennonites, Christian Union, Church of Jesus Christ of Latter-day Saints (Mormons), Church of the Brethren (Dunkers), Free Thought, Germanna and German Mystics, Huguenots, Lutheranism and the Lutheran Tradition, Moravians, Orthodox Christianity, Quakers (Society of Friends), Shakers (United Society of Believers in Christ's Second Appearing), Unitarians and Universalists, and the United Church of Christ (Congregationalists).

BIBLIOGRAPHY

Many titles in chapter 2 as well as in those chapters dealing with native American Indians, black religion, religion and education, religion and the social order, and art, architecture, and music are also relevant for the study of several of the groups listed here.

I. AMISH AND MENNONITES IN THE SOUTH

(1) Brunk, Harry A. *History of the Mennonites in Virginia, 1727-1900*. Staunton VA: McClure Printing, 1959.

(2) Felton, Ralph A. "Mennonite Brethren, Corn, Oklahoma." *Mennonite Life* 10 (1955): 121-22.

(3) Kolker, Marvin. "Mennonites in the Oklahoma 'Runs'." *Mennonite Life* 10 (1955): 114-20.

(4) McKnight, Ruth. "Quaint and Devout: A Study of the Amish at Vilonia, Arkansas." *Arkansas Historical Quarterly* 23 (1964): 314-28.

(5) Showalter, Grace I. "The Virginia Mennonite Rhodes Families." *Pennsylvania Mennonite Heritage* 3 (1980): 15-22.

(6) Yoder, Paton, ed., and Elizabeth Bender, trans. "Baptism as an Issue in the Amish Division of the Nineteenth Century: 'Tennessee' John Stoltzfus." *Mennonite Quarterly Review* 53 (1979): 306-23.

II. CHRISTIAN UNION IN THE SOUTH

(7) Brown, Kenneth O. " 'Building Father's House Anew'—James E. Given and the Founding of the Christian Union." *Methodist History* 20 (1982): 209-18.

(8) _____. *The History of the Christian Union Church*. N.p.p.: Published independently by the General Council of the Christian Union, 1981.

(9) Thomas, A. C. "A Brief History of Christian Union." *Christian Union Bible Theology*. Hiram Rathbun, ed. Excelsior Springs MO: Christian Union Herald Printing, 1911.

(10) Wolford, Ralph. *History of the Christian Union Denomination*. N.p.p.: Privately published by the author, 1957.

III. CHURCH OF JESUS CHRIST OF LATTER-DAY SAINTS (MORMONS) IN THE SOUTH

(11) Alexander, Thomas G. "Wilford Woodruff and the Changing Nature of Mormon Religious Experience." *Church History* 45 (1976): 56-69.

(12) Berrett, LaMar C. "History of the Southern States Mission, 1831-1861." M.A. thesis, Brigham Young University, 1960.

(13) Brown, Lisle G. "West Virginia and Mormonism's Rarest Book." *West Virginia History* 39 (1978): 195-99.

(14) Buice, David. "Excerpts from the Diary of Teancum William Heward, Early Mormon Missionary to Georgia." *Georgia Historical Quarterly* 64 (1980): 317-25.

(15) _____. "When the Saints Came Marching In: The Mormon Experience in Antebellum New Orleans, 1840-1855." *Louisiana History* 23 (1982): 221-37.

(16) Draughon, Wallace R. *History of the Church of Jesus Christ of Latter-day Saints in North Carolina*. Durham: Durham Ward of the Church of Jesus Christ of Latter-day Saints, 1974.

(17) Ellsworth, Samuel G. "A History of Mormon Missions in the United States and Canada, 1830-1860." Ph.D. dissertation, University of California at Berkeley, 1951.

(18) "Expulsion of a Poor, Deluded and Miserable Set of Villains: A Contemporary Account." *Dialogue* 11 (1978): 112-17.

(19) Hatch, William W. "A History of Mormon Civil Relations in the Southern States, 1865-1905." M.A. thesis, Utah State University, 1965.

(20) _____. *There Is No Law: A History of Mormon Civil Relations in the Southern States, 1865-1905*. New York: Vantage Press, 1968.

(21) Holsinger, M. Paul. "Senator George Graham Vest and the 'Menace' of Mormonism, 1882-1887," *Missouri Historical Review* 65 (1970): 23-36.

(22) Jennings, Warren A. "The Army of Israel Marches into Missouri." *Missouri Historical Review* 62 (1968): 107-35.

(23) _____. "The Expulsion of the Mormons from Johnson City, Missouri." *Missouri Historical Review* 64 (1969): 41-63.

(24) _____. "Isaac McCoy and the Mormons." *Missouri Historical Review* 61 (1966): 62-82.

(25) _____, ed. "'What Crime Have I Been Guilty Of?': Edward Partridge's Letter to an Estranged Sister." *Brigham Young University Studies* 18 (1978): 520-28.

(26) Lattimore, R. B. "A Survey of William Brownlow's Criticisms of the Mormons, 1841-1857." *Tennessee Historical Quarterly* 27 (1968): 249-56.

(27) Roberts, Brigham H. *A Complete History of the Church of Jesus Christ of Latter-day Saints* Vol. 5. Salt Lake City: Deseret News Press, 1930.

(28) Robertson, R. J., Jr. "The Mormon Experience in Missouri, 1830-1839." *Missouri Historical Review* 68 (1974): 280-98, 393-415.

(29) Sessions, Gene A. "Myth, Mormonism, and Murder in the South." *South Atlantic Quarterly* 75 (1976): 212-25.

IV. CHURCH OF THE BRETHREN (DUNKERS) IN THE SOUTH

(30) Durnbaugh, Donald F. "Brethren Beginnings: The Origins of the Church of the Brethren in Early Eighteenth Century Europe." Ph.D. dissertation, University of Pennsylvania, 1960.

(31) _____. *The Brethren in Colonial America: A Source Book on the Transplantation and Development of the Church of the Brethren in the Eighteenth Century.* Elgin IL: Brethren Press, 1967.

(32) _____, comp. *European Origins of the Brethren: A Source Book on the Beginnings of the Church of the Brethren in the Early Eighteenth Century.* Elgin IL: Brethren Press, 1958.

(33) Sappington, Roger E. *The Brethren in the Carolinas: The History of the Church of the Brethren in the District of North and South Carolina.* Bridgewater VA: n.p., 1971.

(34) _____. *The Brethren in the New Nation.* Elgin IL: Brethren Press, 1976.

(35) _____. *The Brethren in Virginia: The History of the Church of the Brethren in Virginia.* Harrisonburg VA: Committee for Brethren History in Virginia, 1973.

(36) _____. "Dunker Beginnings in North Carolina in the Eighteenth Century." *North Carolina Historical Review* 46 (1969): 214-38.

(37) _____. *History of the Bridgewater, Virginia Church of the Brethren, 1878-1978.* Bridgewater VA: Board of Administration, Bridgewater Church of the Brethren, 1978.

(38) _____. "Two Eighteenth Century Dunker Congregations in North Carolina." *North Carolina Historical Review* 47 (1970): 176-204.

V. FREE THOUGHT IN THE SOUTH

(39) Doepke, Dale K. "*The Western Examiner:* A Chronicle of Atheism in the West." *Bulletin of the Missouri Historical Society* 40 (1973): 29-43.

(40) Hix, Clarence E., Jr. "The Conflict Between Presbyterianism and Free Thought in the South, 1776-1838." Ph.D. dissertation, University of Chicago, 1940.

(41) Miller, Joseph M. "Bob Ingersoll Comes to Louisville." *Filson Club Historical Quarterly* 39 (1965): 311-19.

(42) Tolzmann, Don H. "The St. Louis Free Congregation Library: A Study of German-American Reading Interests." *Missouri Historical Review* 70 (1976): 142-61.

VI. GERMANNA AND GERMAN MYSTICS IN THE SOUTH

(43) Myers, Raymond E. "The Story of Germanna." *Filson Club Historical Quarterly* 48 (1974): 27-42.

(44) West, Klaus G. "German Mystics and Sabbatarians in Virginia, 1700-1764." *Virginia Magazine of History and Biography* 72 (1964): 330-47.

(45) _____. *Saint-Adventurers of the Virginia Frontier: Southern Outposts of Ephrata*. Edinburg VA: Shenandoah History Publications, 1977.

VII. HUGUENOTS IN THE SOUTH

(46) Bennett, Susan Smythe. "Paul Turquand." *Transactions of the Huguenot Society of South Carolina* 32 (1927): 33-35.

(47) Foote, William H. *The Huguenots: or, Reformed French Church, Their Principles Delineated; Their Character Illustrated; Their Sufferings and Successes Recorded*. Richmond: Presbyterian Committee of Publication, 1870.

(48) Hirsch, Arthur H. *The Huguenots of Colonial South Carolina*. Durham: Duke University Press, 1928.

(49) Kingdon, Robert M. "Why Did the Huguenot Refugees in the American Colonies Become Episcopalian?" *Historical Magazine of the Protestant Episcopal Church* 49 (1980): 317-35. Also published as "Pourquoi les refugies huguenots aux colonies americaines sont-ils devenus episcopaliens?" *Bulletin de la Societe de l'historie du protestantisme français* 115 (1969).

(50) Starr, J. Barton. "Campbell Town: French Huguenots in British West Florida." *Florida Historical Quarterly* 54 (1976): 532-47.

(51) Terry, E. G. C. "The Huguenots of Upper South Carolina." *Transactions of the Huguenot Society of South Carolina* 32 (1927): 27-33.

VIII. LUTHERANISM AND THE LUTHERAN TRADITION IN THE SOUTH

(52) Anderson, H. George. "The European Phase of John Ulrich Giessendanner's Life." *South Carolina Historical Magazine* 67 (1966): 129-37.

(53) _____. *Lutheranism in the Southeastern States, 1860-1886: A Social History*. The Hague: Mouton, 1969.

(54) _____. *The North Carolina Synod through 175 Years (1803-1978)*. Salisbury NC: n.p., 1978.

(55) Armentrout, Donald S. "John Jacob Scherer: A Type of Southern Lutheran." Ph.D. dissertation, Vanderbilt University, 1970.

(56) Bachman, Catherine L., ed. *John Bachman, D.D., L.H.D., Ph.D., the Pastor of St. John's Lutheran Church, Charleston*. Charleston: Walker, Evans & Cogswell, 1888.

(57) Bernheim, G. D. *The First Twenty Years of the History of St. Paul's Evangelical Lutheran Church, Wilmington, N.C.* Wilmington NC: S. G. Hall, 1879.

(58) _____, and G. H. Cox. *The History of the Evangelical Lutheran Synod and Ministerium of North Carolina, in Commemoration of the Completion of the First Century of Its Existence*. Philadelphia: Published for the Synod by the Lutheran Publication Society, 1902.

(59) _____. *History of the German Settlements and of the Lutheran Church in North and South Carolina*. Philadelphia: Lutheran Book Store, 1872.

(60) Bost, Raymond M. "The Reverend John Bachman and the Development of Southern Lutheranism." Ph.D. dissertation, Yale University, 1963.

(61) Buettner, George L. "Concordia Publishing House As I Knew It (1888-1955)." *Concordia Historical Institute Quarterly* 47 (1974): 62-69.

(62) Cassell, Charles W. *History of the Lutheran Church in Virginia and East Tennessee*. Strasburg VA: Shenandoah Publishing House, 1930.

(63) Cody, Mary Alice Bull. "The Brazean, Missouri, Scene, 1852-1856: Excerpts from the Diary of Sarah M. McPherson." *Concordia Historical Institute Quarterly* 47 (1974): 3-6.

(64) DeVorsey, Louis, Jr., ed. *DeBrahm's Report of the General Survey in the Southern District of North America*. Columbia: University of South Carolina Press, 1971.

(65) Eisenberg, William E. *The Lutheran Church in Virginia, 1717-1962*. Roanoke: Trustees of the Virginia Synod, Lutheran Church in America, 1967.

(66) Ellwanger, Walter H. "Lutheranism in Alabama and Other Parts of the South." *Concordia Historical Institute Quarterly* 48 (1975): 35-43.

(67) Frizzell, Robert W. " 'Killed by Rebels': A Civil War Massacre and Its Aftermath." *Missouri Historical Review* 71 (1977): 369-95.

(68) Hvidt, Kristian, ed. *Von Reck's Voyage: Drawings and Journal of Philip Georg Friedrich von Reck*. Savannah: Beehive Press, 1980.

(69) Jones, George Fenwick, and Renate Wilson, eds. *Detailed Reports on the Salzburger Emigrants Who Settled in America*. By Samuel Urlsperger. Wormsloe Foundation Publications. Athens: University of Georgia Press, 1968.

(70) _____, ed. and trans. *Henry Newman's Salzburger Letterbooks*. Athens: University of Georgia Press, 1966.

(71) _____. "In Memoriam: John Martin Boltzius, 1703-1765." *Lutheran Quarterly* 17 (1965): 151-66.

(72) _____. "Journal of a Trip from Georgia to South Carolina in 1734." *Lutheran Quarterly* 16 (1964): 168-74.

(73) _____. *The Salzburger Saga: Religious Exiles and Other Germans along the Savannah*. Athens: University of Georgia Press, 1984.

(74) _____, ed. "The Secret Diary of Pastor Johann Martin Boltzius." *Georgia Historical Quarterly* 53 (1969): 78-110.

(75) _____, contr. "Two 'Salzburger' Letters from George Whitefield and Theobold Kiefer II." *Georgia Historical Quarterly* 62 (1978): 50-57.

(76) Lewis, Andrew W., ed. "Henry Muhlenberg's Georgia Correspondence." *Georgia Historical Quarterly* 49 (1965): 424-54.

(77) *Life Sketches of Lutheran Ministers, North Carolina and Tennessee Synods, 1773-1965.* N.p.p.: n.p., [1966?].

(78) Monroe, Paul E., Jr. "A History of Southern Lutheranism." S.T.M. thesis, Hamma Divinity School, n.d.

(79) Nau, John F. "The Lutheran Church in Louisiana." *Concordia Historical Institute Quarterly* 25 (1952): 30-35.

(80) Poole, Donald R. *History of the Georgia-Alabama Synod of the United Lutheran Church in America, 1860-1960.* Birmingham: n.p., 1959.

(81) Rehmer, R. F., ed. "Sheep Without Shepherds: Letters of Two Lutheran Traveling Missionaries, 1835-1837." *Indiana Magazine of History* 71 (1975): 21-84.

(82) Reith, Ferdinand. "A Swedish Pastor among Germans: Niels Albert Wihlborg, 1848-1928." *Concordia Historical Institute Quarterly* 51 (1978): 168-78.

(83) Schlegel, Ronald J. " 'Daddy' Herzberger's Legacy." *Concordia Historical Institute Quarterly* 52 (1979): 50-65.

(84) Snyder, Walter W. "H. D. Wacker, Besucher, Reiseprediger, Pastor in Frontier Texas." *Concordia Historical Institute Quarterly* 53 (1980): 70-83.

(85) Strobel, P. A. *The Salzburgers and Their Descendants: Being the History of a Colony of German (Lutheran) Protestants, Who Emigrated to Georgia in 1734, and Settled at Ebenezer, Twenty-five Miles above the City of Savannah.* Baltimore: T. Newton Kurtz, 1855.

(86) Ward, Gordon W., Jr. "The Formation of the Lutheran General Synod, South, During the Civil War." *Lutheran Quarterly* 13 (1961): 132-54.

(87) Wentz, Abdel R. *History of the Evangelical Lutheran Church of Frederick, Maryland, 1738-1938.* Harrisburg: The Evangelical Press, 1938.

(88) _____. *History of the Evangelical Lutheran Synod of Maryland of the United Lutheran Church in America, 1820-1920.* Harrisburg: The Evangelical Press, 1920.

(89) Wright, Willard E., ed. "The Journals of the Reverend Robert J. Miller, Lutheran Missionary in Virginia, 1811 and 1813." *Virginia Magazine of History and Biography* 61 (1953): 141-66.

IX. MORAVIANS IN THE SOUTH

(90) Frank, Albert H. "George Neisser: An Early Moravian Historian." *Transactions of the Moravian Historical Society* 23 (1979): 1-11.

(91) Fries, Adelaide, et al., eds. *Records of the Moravians in North Carolina*. Vols. 1- . Raleigh: Edwards and Broughton, 1922- .

(92) Hamilton, Kenneth G. "The Moravians and Wachovia." *North Carolina Historical Review* 44 (1967): 144-53.

(93) James, Hunter. *Quiet People of the Land: A Story of the North Carolina Moravians in Revolutionary Times*. Chapel Hill: University of North Carolina Press for Old Salem, 1976.

(94) *The Three Forks of Muddy Creek*. Vols. 1- . Winston-Salem NC: Old Salem, 1974- .

(95) Surratt, Jerry L. *Gottlieb Schober of Salem: Discipleship and Ecumenical Vision in an Early Moravian Town*. Macon GA: Mercer University Press, 1983.

(96) _____. "The Role of Dissent in Community Evolution among Moravians in Salem, 1772-1860." *North Carolina Historical Review* 52 (1975): 235-55.

X. ORTHODOX CHRISTIANITY IN THE SOUTH

(97) DiMichele, Charles C. "The History of the Eastern Orthodox Church in Mississippi." M.A. thesis, Mississippi College, 1968.

(98) Panagopoulos, Epaminodas P. *New Smyrna: An Eighteenth Century Greek Odyssey*. Gainesville: University of Florida Press, 1966.

XI. QUAKERS (SOCIETY OF FRIENDS) IN THE SOUTH

(99) Anscombe, Francis C. *I Have Called You First: The Story of Quakerism in North Carolina*. Boston: Christopher Publishing House, 1959.

(100) Barns, William D. "Status and Sectionalism in West Virginia." *West Virginia History* 34 (1973): 247-72, 360-81.

(101) Billings, Warren M. "A Quaker in Seventeenth-Century Virginia: Four Remonstrances by George Wilson." *William and Mary Quarterly* 3d series 33 (1976): 127-42.

(102) Butler, Lindsey S. "The Seventeenth Century Origins of North Carolina Friends." *Louisburg College Journal of Arts and Science* 2 (1968): 1-11.

(103) Carroll, Kenneth L., ed. "Death Comes to a Quakeress." *Quaker History* 64 (1975): 96-104.

(104) _____. "The Irish Quaker Community at Camden." *South Carolina Historical Magazine* 77 (1976): 69-83.

(105) _____. "Quaker Opposition to the Establishment of a State Church in Maryland." *Maryland Historical Magazine* 65 (1970): 149-70.

(106) _____. *Quakerism on the Eastern Shore*. Baltimore: Maryland Historical Society, 1970.

(107) _____. "Quakerism on the Eastern Shore of Virginia." *Virginia Magazine of History and Biography* 74 (1966): 170-89.

(108) _____, ed. "Robert Pleasants on Quakerism: 'Some Account of the First Settlement of Friends in Virginia . . . .'." *Virginia Magazine of History and Biography* 86 (1978): 3-16.

(109) _____. "Thomas Thurston, Renegade Maryland Quaker." *Maryland Historical Magazine* 62 (1967): 170-92.

(110) Cartland, Fernando G. *Southern Heroes; or, the Friends in War Time.* Cambridge: Riverside Press, 1895.

(111) Joint Committee of Hopewell Friends. *Hopewell Friends History, 1734-1934, Frederick County, Virginia.* Strasburg VA: Shenandoah Publishing House, 1936.

(112) Moore, J. Floyd. *Friends in the Colonies.* High Point: High Point Monthly Meeting of Friends, 1963.

(113) Scott, Ralph C., Jr. "The Quaker Settlement of Wrightsborough, Georgia." *Georgia Historical Quarterly* 56 (1972): 210-23.

(114) Smith, Bruce R. "Benjamin Hallowell of Alexandria: Scientist, Educator, Quaker Idealist." *Virginia Magazine of History and Biography* 85 (1977): 337-61.

XII. SHAKERS (UNITED SOCIETY OF BELIEVERS IN CHRIST'S SECOND APPEARING) IN THE SOUTH

(115) Anderson, Russell H. "The Shaker Communities in Southwest Georgia." *Georgia Historical Quarterly* 49 (1966): 162-72.

(116) Neal, Julia. "South Union Shakers During War Years." *Filson Club Historical Quarterly* 39 (1965): 147-50.

(117) Paterwick, Stephen. "The Effects of the Civil War on Shaker Societies." *Historical Journal of Western Massachusetts* 2 (1973): 6-26.

(118) Randles, Raymond J. "Shaker Harvest in Kentucky." *Filson Club Historical Quarterly* 37 (1963): 38-58.

(119) Stein, Stephen J. "The Conversion of Charles Willing Bird to Shakerism." *Filson Club Historical Quarterly* 56 (1982): 395-414.

(120) Thomas, Samuel W., and Mary Lawrence Young. "The Development of Shakertown at Pleasant Hill, Kentucky." *Filson Club Historical Quarterly* 49 (1975): 231-55.

(121) Whitaker, Thomas. "A Benedictine Link with the Shakers." *Register of the Kentucky Historical Society* 67 (1969): 360-69.

XIII. UNITARIANISM AND UNIVERSALISM IN THE SOUTH

(122) Andrews, A. O. *Sixteen Years Chaplain, Friend, and Counsellor of the Washington Light Infantry of Charleston, S.C., The Rev. Samuel Gilman, D.D.* Charleston: Walker, Evans, and Cogswell, [1858?].

(123) Becker, Louis D. "Unitarianism in Post-War Atlanta, 1882-1908." *Georgia Historical Quarterly* 56 (1972): 349-64.

(124) Brooks, Arthur A. *The History of Unitarianism in the Southern Churches.* Boston: American Unitarian Association, [1906?].

(125) Bull, Elias B. *Founders and Pew Renters of the Unitarian Church in Charleston, S.C., 1817-1874*. Charleston: Unitarian Church in Charleston SC, 1970.

(126) Cheetham, Henry H. *Unitarianism and Universalism: An Illustrated History*. Boston: Beacon Press, 1962.

(127) Clapp, Theodore. *Autobiographical Sketches and Recollections, During a Thirty-Five Years' Residence in New Orleans*. Boston: Phillips, Sampson, 1857.

(128) _____. *Theological Views, Comprising the Substance of Teachings during a Ministry of Thirty-Five Years in New Orleans*. Boston: Abel Tompkins, 1859.

(129) Cory, Earl W. "Unitarians and Universalists of the Southeastern United States during the Nineteenth Century." Ph.D. dissertation, University of Georgia, 1970.

(130) Duffy, John, ed. *Parson Clapp of the Strangers' Church of New Orleans*. Baton Rouge: Louisiana State University Press, 1957.

(131) Eaton, Clement. "Winifred and Joseph Gales, Liberals in the Old South." *Journal of Southern History* 10 (1944): 461-74.

(132) Eliot, Charlotte C. *William Greenleaf Eliot: Minister, Educator, Philanthropist*. Boston: Houghton, Mifflin, 1904.

(133) Foote, Henry Wilder. "Samuel Gilman, Author of 'Fair Harvard'." *Harvard Graduates Magazine* 34 (1916): 610-16.

(134) _____. "Theodore Clapp." *Proceedings of the Unitarian Historical Society* 3,2 (1934): 13-39.

(135) Funk, Rebecca. *A Heritage to Hold in Fee, 1817-1917: First Unitarian Church of Baltimore (Universalist and Unitarian)*. Baltimore: Garamond Press, 1962.

(136) Gibson, George H. "Unitarian Congregations in Ante-Bellum Georgia." *Georgia Historical Quarterly* 54 (1970): 147-68.

(137) _____. "Unitarian Congregations in the Ante-Bellum South." *Proceedings of the Unitarian Historical Society* 21,2 (1959): 53-78.

(138) _____. "The Unitarian-Universalist Church of Richmond." *Virginia Magazine of History and Biography* 74 (1966): 321-35.

(139) Gilman, Caroline. *Recollections of a Southern Matron*. New York: Harper and Brothers, 1838.

(140) Gohdes, Clarence. "Some Notes on the Unitarian Churches in the Ante-Bellum South: A Contribution to the History of Southern Liberalism." In *American Studies in Honor of William Kenneth Boyd*. David C. Jackson, ed. Durham: Duke University Press, 1940.

(141) Howe, Daniel Walker. "A Massachusetts Yankee in Senator Calhoun's Court: Samuel Gilman in South Carolina." *New England Quarterly* 44 (1971): 197-200.

(142) _____. "Samuel Gilman: Unitarian Minister and Public Man." *Proceedings of the Unitarian Historical Society* 17,2 (1973-1975): 45-53.

(143) Hoole, William S. "The Gilmans and the Southern Rose." *North Carolina Historical Review* 11 (1934): 116-28.

(144) Johnson, David A. "Beginnings of Universalism in Louisville." *Filson Club Historical Quarterly* 43 (1969): 173-83.

(145) Larisey, Mary Maxine. *The Unitarian Church in Charleston, South Carolina: A Brief History.* [Charleston?]: n.p., 1967.

(146) Moore, John Hammond, ed. "The Abiel Abbot Journals: A Yankee Preacher in Charleston Society, 1818-1827." *South Carolina Historical Magazine* 68 (1967): 51-73, 115-39, 232-54.

(147) Reilly, Timothy F. "Parson Clapp of New Orleans: Antebellum Social Critic, Religious Radical, and Member of the Establishment." *Louisiana History* 16 (1975): 167-91.

(148) Taggart, Charles M. *Sermons: With a Memoir by John H. Heywood.* Boston: Crosby, Nichols, 1856.

XIV. UNITED CHURCH OF CHRIST (CONGREGATIONAL CHURCH) IN THE SOUTH

(149) Alley, Joe K. *Churches of Christ in Mississippi, 1836-1954.* Booneville MS: By the author, 1953.

(150) Franch, Michael S. "The Congregational Community in the Changing City, 1840-70." *Maryland Historical Magazine* 71 (1976): 367-80.

(151) Hatch, Nathan O. "The Christian Movement and the Demand for a Theology of the People." *Journal of American History* 67 (1980): 545-67.

(152) Jones, Newton B. "Writings of the Reverend William Tennent." *South Carolina Historical Magazine* 61 (1960): 129-45.

(153) Kilgore, Charles F. *The James O'Kelly Schism in the Methodist Episcopal Church.* Mexico City: Casa Unida de Publicaciones, 1963.

(154) Leonard, Jacob C. *The Southern Synod of the Evangelical and Reformed Church.* Raleigh: Edwards and Broughton, 1940.

(155) Peeler, Banks J. *A Story of the Southern Synod of the Evangelical and Reformed Church.* Salisbury NC: Under the Supervision of the Board of Editors and Authorized by the Synod, 1968.

(156) Ramsay, David. *The History of the Independent or Congregational Church of Charleston, S.C.* Philadelphia: J. Maxwell for the author, 1814.

(157) Stacy, James. *A History of the Midway Congregational Church in Liberty County, Georgia.* Rev. ed. Newman GA: S. W. Murray, 1903. First published 1894.

(158) Stokes, Durwood T., and William T. Scott. *A History of the Christian Churches in the South.* Burlington NC: Southern Conference Office of the United Church of Christ, 1973.

XV. OTHER RELIGIOUS GROUPS AND MOVEMENTS IN THE SOUTH

(159) Classis of North Carolina. *Historical Sketch of the Reformed Church in North*

Carolina. Philadelphia: Publication Board of the Reformed Church in the United States, 1908.

(160) Fine, Howard D. "The Koreshan Unity: The Chicago Years of a Utopian Community." *Journal of the Illinois State Historical Association* 68 (1975): 213-27.

(161) Grant, H. Roger. "The Society of Bethel: A Visitor's Account." *Missouri Historical Review* 68 (1974): 223-31.

15 Southern Revivalism and Billy Graham

SINCE THE AGE of the Great Awakening in the eighteenth century, revivalism has been a staple of Southern religion. The campmeetings on the Southern frontier in the early nineteenth century not only helped "bring religion" to newly settled regions of the South, they helped impress the phenomenon of revivalism on the Southern religious consciousness. Later in the nineteenth century, revivals became a major vehicle through which the Holiness-Pentecostal movement garnered a place for itself in Southern religious life. Even today, tent meeting revivals, camp meetings, and protracted "gospel meetings" in town and city churches are regular events in many areas, from the most rural parts of Appalachia to the most densely populated urban centers, occasions when the faithful are revitalized in their commitment and a few of those outside the fold make their way into the churches. While revivals today may lack the spontaneity of their historical predecessors, they remain vital ritual events that signal to the region the continuing importance of affective religious experience. And among the nation's—indeed the world's—evangelists, none has had such an illustrious career as Billy Graham, a Baptist preacher from North Carolina.

Southern revivalism past and present is part of a larger story, that of revivalism in the nation as a whole. Two solid studies by William G. McLoughlin probe the overall picture and provide the context within which Southern revivalism flourishes: *Modern Revivalism* (25) and his more recent *Revivals, Awakenings, and Reform* (26). The latter work especially is distinguished in its attempt to use interpretive constructs drawn from the social sciences to appraise the cycles of revivals and the function of revivalism itself in American religious life. Somewhat more popular in style, but nevertheless a good academic analysis, is Bernard A. Weisberger, *They Gathered at the River* (39). This volume and McLoughlin's *Modern Revivalism* both include discussion of some individual revivalists whose work has been influential in the South.

The revivals of the Great Awakening have been noted in chapter 2, as have those works on the frontier campmeeting revivals that argue that revivals are one of the sources of the evangelical hegemony that yet prevails in many regions of the South. Attention should again be called particularly to the work of Rhys Isaac and John B. Boles noted in that chapter. The standard chronicle of the campmeetings that dominated much of religion on the frontier in the opening decades of the nineteenth century is Charles A. Johnson, *The Frontier Campmeeting: Religion's Harvest Time* (15). As Johnson suggests, the campmeetings were frequently interdenominational in complexion and often combined a high sense of sacramentalism with the fervent preaching and occasional social revelry that dominate popular perception of their character. Dickson D. Bruce, Jr., *And They All Sang Hallelujah: Plain-Folk Campmeeting Religion, 1800-1845* (4) is a brilliant effort to analyze the revivals from an anthropological perspective. Bruce demonstrates how the revivals quickly developed their own ritual frameworks, which were carefully structured in both form and content not only to generate conversions but also to provide opportunities for confirming a sense of identity, ritualizing role reversal, and cementing social cohesion. William M. Clements, "Physical Layout of the Methodist Camp Meeting" (5), lends support to Bruce's emphasis on the attention given to the physical space in which the revivals transpired. Bruce's study has been criticized for emphasizing interpretation at the expense of evidence, but it is provocative in understanding the multifaceted nature of the campmeeting revivals. Bruce notes as well the importance of singing at these gatherings and the ways in which they nurtured a folk hymnody of their own. Ellen J. Lorenz, *Glory, Hallelujah! The Story of the Campmeeting Spiritual* (21), however, falls short of explaining adequately the role or significance of this popular hymnody. Benjamin R. Lacy, *Revivals in the Midst of the Years* (18) is a popular, filiopietistic history of little use to the serious student. The prevalence of revivalism in Southern religion generated a literature of its own, as writers and denominational agencies published guidebooks outlining methods of organization, procedures to follow, and results to expect. An example is George R. Stuart's revival textbook, *Methodist Evangelism* (36).

But precisely what did the early revivals accomplish, other than solidifying the evangelical style as the dominant expression of Protestantism in the South? Donald G. Mathews, whose "The Second Great Awakening as an Organizing Process, 1780-1830: An Hypothesis" (27) is not restricted in scope to the South, suggests that the revivals were one means by which social order and social structure emerged in a nation undergoing rapid transition. Anne C. Loveland, "Presbyterians and Revivalism in the Old South" (22), calls attention to the role these occasions of heightened religious interest played in recruiting new members, identifying candidates for the professional clergy, improving moral standards, and securing loyalty to the republican mores of the day. But Presbyterians were not of one mind in endorsing the revivals and ultimately divided over whether to support them. The difficulty was in part theological, for the revivals were increasingly predicated on the Arminian assumption that humans freely chose to accept salvation, rather than on the Calvinist notion, which lay behind the Presbyterian attitude, that God had predestined to salvation those who were "elect." James S. Dalton's doctoral dissertation, "The Kentucky Camp Meeting Revivals of 1797-1805 as Rites of Initiation" (7) convincingly argues that the evangelical conversion experience was not only a religious event but one in which the individual gained a legitimate place in the social order.

Revivals may be more muted in their impact in the late twentieth-century South, serving more to provoke nostalgia for a religious world view of a bygone era and to enhance the commitment of those already converted than to mark one's entrance into the social order or even to reap harvests of new converts. But the revival and the campmeeting endure. A thoughtful study, though now somewhat dated, is Charles L. Blanchard, "A Study of the Modern Campmeeting" (3). Patricia Anthony Gage, "The Sawdust Trail Lives On at the Hudson River Camp Meeting" (10), describes one contemporary Holiness camp in Louisiana's Winn Parish, which has been in operation since 1899.

Revivalism is usually regarded as a phenomenon of Protestantism, but there is a Roman Catholic parallel. While not restricted to Southern Catholicism, Jay P. Dolan, *Catholic Revivalism: The American Experience, 1830-1907* (9), is a careful study of the ways in which Roman Catholics adapted the techniques of the revival to foster continuing commitment among adherents through parish renewal movements, preaching ventures, and similar activities. In the minds of some scholars, Catholic revivalism played an important role in keeping Catholics within the fold in areas, such as much of the South, where the Catholic population was a small minority whose devotion might easily have been eroded by the emotional pitch and overwhelming presence of an evangelical Protestantism fired by the zeal of revivalism.

As revivalism became an established part of the American religious scene, it brought to prominence many itinerant evangelists who conducted campaigns in cities throughout the country. In the nineteenth century, there was only one Southern evangelist with a national reputation: Samuel Porter Jones (1847-1906), a one-time alcoholic from Alabama whose conversion experience at the time of his father's death led him to become a Methodist preacher. There is no scholarly monograph treating Jones's life, but a good brief overview is Ray C. Rensi, "The Gospel According to Sam Jones" (33). Rensi makes special note of the way in which Jones's style reflected rural Southern values, particularly in condemning "personal vices" such as use of liquor and tobacco, dancing, card playing, sports (especially baseball, which was quite popular in Jones's day), and attending theatrical performances. Indeed, the way in which Jones and others like him emphasized an individualistic ethic contributed to the later perception that Southern religion has lacked a social ethic. Also see the discussions of Sam Jones in the synoptic studies of McLoughlin and Weisberger.

But in the twentieth century, the premier figure in revivalism in the United States and throughout the world has been a son of the South, Billy Graham. Born William Franklin Graham in 1918 in Charlotte, North Carolina, Graham has dominated American revivalism for more than a third of a century. Through preaching crusades, books, radio and television broadcasts, and a newspaper column, Graham has brought his message to more people than any other preacher in history. Moving freely among those prominent in politics and world affairs, Graham made a moderate evangelicalism not only respectable but also virtually normative in the minds of many. Graham has been somewhat eclipsed in recent years by the rise of televangelists such as Jerry Falwell, from whom he has sought to distance himself, and by an increasing reluctance to maintain close ties to public figures since his relationship with Richard Nixon brought criticism during the days leading up to Nixon's resignation from the presidency. The Billy Graham Evangelistic Association, headquartered in Minneapolis, remains a thriving operation, however, and Graham still conducts crusades, though on a smaller scale than previously. In addition, the Billy Graham Center at Wheaton College in Illinois, Graham's alma mater, has established a Center for the Study of American Evangelicalism that has quickly gained academic respectability both for the archival materials it has gathered and for the scholarly conferences it has sponsored.

The literature on Graham is voluminous. For example, Graham and his work were the subject of more than fifty articles in *Newsweek* alone between 1954 and 1974. This chapter's bibliography will not attempt to be all-inclusive, but will note the range of material about Graham, noting several short pieces that have appeared in mass circulation print media. The most recent comprehensive study of Graham and his work is the highly overwritten *Billy Graham: A Parable of American Righteousness* (65) by former journalist Marshall Frady. Frady argues that Graham's major contribution has been to fuse religious and patriotic values into a composite of what the individual ought to be and do if one wishes to be regarded as a moral citizen. Frady is sensitive as well to Graham's Southern roots, particularly the piety that characterized his upbringing in the Associate Reformed Presbyterian tradition (though Graham is today a member of Dallas's First Baptist Church). More academic and in many ways more perceptive is William G. McLoughlin, *Billy Graham: Revivalist in a Secular Age* (89). McLoughlin's work appeared in 1960, when Graham was nearing the zenith of his personal popularity, and the scholarly world would benefit if McLoughlin were to revise his work to take account of the developments in Graham's life and career since that time. Another valuable overview, concentrating more on the conservative orthodoxy at the heart of Graham's preaching and writing, is Joe E. Barnhart, *The Billy Graham Religion* (45). On this matter, also see James L. McAllister, "Evangelical Faith and Billy Graham" (86), an analysis grounded in sociological interpretation. An older popular introduction of merit is the work of Neil Houston that appeared in *Holiday* (76). There have been two sympathetic biographies, both now in need of updating: Stanley High, *Billy Graham: The Personal Story of the Man, His Message, and His Mission* (74), which appeared in the mid-1950s, and John Pollock, *Billy Graham: The Authorized Biography* (103), which was published a decade later. Another uncritical, almost hagiographic study is Curtis Mitchell, *Billy Graham: The Making of a Crusader* (96). Individual studies detailing most of Graham's major crusades around the globe tend to lack scholarly analysis and generally highlight numbers of conversions, unexpected events, organizational matters, and sermon themes that mark a crusade. Several of these are included in the bibliography. The crusade that solidified Graham's position in the front ranks of American revivalism was conducted in New York City in 1957; its story is told uncritically in George Burnham and Lee Fisher, *Billy Graham and the New York Crusade* (53), a work representative of this genre. A noteworthy study of an earlier crusade, worth the attention of scholars, is the unpublished essay by James L. McAllister, "Greensboro and Billy Graham" (87).

Somewhat surprisingly, Billy Graham's crusades have not received extensive analysis within the academy. Much of the work to date has come from sociologists who have been interested in analyzing the structure of the crusade form and the religious orientation and background of those who make a "decision for Christ" in the context of a crusade. Weldon T. Johnson, "The Religious Crusade: Revival or Ritual" (78), notes the reliance on set forms in a Graham campaign, while Ronald C. Wimberley and others, "Conversion in a Billy Graham Crusade: Spontaneous Event or Ritual Performance" (119), as the title suggests, argues that the conversion experience itself is one that transpires according to a fixed pattern more than through an affective cataclysm. Particularly provocative is Donald A. Clelland and others, "In the Company of the Converted: Characteristics of a Billy Graham Crusade Audience" (55). This important essay, based on analysis of a crusade in Knoxville, Tennessee, demonstrates that persons attending a crusade tend to be

better educated, from a higher income level, and employed in more presti-
gious occupations than the average resident of the area where a crusade is held.
As well, the audience is generally composed predominantly of persons who
evidence a higher degree of participation in religious activities and a more
conservative stance in matters of religious belief than the population at large.
Even among those "converted" at a crusade, there is a high incidence of prior
religious affiliation and a low incidence of overt change in religious activity
within one year of the crusade. Hence the authors conclude that at least in
recent years a Billy Graham crusade actually functions more to reaffirm a life-
style perceived as threatened by secular forces than to generate real change.
Charles H. Lippy, "Billy Graham's 'My Answer': Agenda for the Faithful"
(85), makes a similar case in analyzing the role played by Graham's popular
newspaper column: it serves to perpetuate a model of proper behavior and
proper attitudes for the religious person rather than to make an evangelical
appeal.

Graham's links to prominent political figures are well-known, as is his
generally conservative position on issues of controversy in the political arena,
a point emphasized by Frady in his study. On this matter, see as well Edward
B. Fiske, "Closest Thing to a White House Chaplain" (64), and Lowell
Streiker and Gerald S. Strober, *Religion and the New Majority: Billy Graham, Middle America, and the Politics of the 70s* (112). The latter work, especially, notes the correlation between Graham's ideology and that popularly
attributed to the so-called "silent" majority of Americans who are regarded
as basically conservative in both religion and politics.

A final assessment of Graham is, of course, impossible at present since
Graham's own career and convictions are yet evolving. Despite the distance
Graham has kept from "new evangelicals" such as Jerry Falwell, he remains
the South's and the nation's preeminent evangelist.

Revivalism has had a significant impact on the stories of the various denominations in the South. Numerous titles in the chapters discussing the Baptists, Presbyterians, Methodists, Disciples of Christ, and the Churches of
Christ detail the influence of revivals and controversies over their usefulness
in those traditions. As well, revivalism has helped shape the religious life of
Southern blacks. Many titles in chapter 4 highlight that aspect of the overall
story. Chapter 12 includes a listing of works that focus particularly on the
style of revivals identified with the Pentecostal and Holiness movements as
well as on the work of Oral Roberts, perhaps the most well-known evangelist
associated with that strain of Southern religion. Links between fundamentalism and revivalism are noted in several works included in chapter 20. In addition to the titles centering on the role of music in revivals and campmeetings,
some works identified in chapter 17 also discuss the importance of music to
perpetuating the evangelical world view emerging from revivalism. Discus-

sion of revivalism in the context of Appalachian religion may be found in several works listed in chapter 13. The use of techniques associated with revivalism by individuals popularly identified with the Moral Majority or new religious right as well as with preachers whose public ministry revolves around the electronic media are found in both chapter 2 and chapter 20.

The bibliography that follows lists first those studies that focus on the campmeeting and Southern revivalism after the age of the Great Awakening. It then offers a representative sampling of the vast corpus of secondary literature about Billy Graham and his work.

BIBLIOGRAPHY

Many of the titles in chapters 1, 2, 4, 8, 9, 10, 11, 12, 13, 17, and 20 are relevant here.

I. SOUTHERN REVIVALISM AFTER THE GREAT AWAKENING

(1) Baugh, Stanley T. *Camp Grounds and Camp Meetings in the Little Rock Conference, the Methodist Church*. Little Rock: Epworth Press, 1953.

(2) Bauman, Mark K. "Hitting the Sawdust Trial: Billy Sunday's Atlanta Campaign of 1917." *Southern Studies* 19 (1980): 385-99.

(3) Blanchard, Charles L. "A Study of the Modern Campmeeting." Th.M. thesis, Louisville Presbyterian Theological Seminary, 1962.

(4) Bruce, Dickson D., Jr. *And They All Sang Hallelujah: Plain-Folk Campmeeting Religion, 1800-1845*. Knoxville: University of Tennessee Press, 1974.

(5) Clements, William M. "Physical Layout of the Methodist Camp Meeting." *Pioneer America* 5 (1973): 9-15.

(6) Colemon, Robert E., ed. *One Divine Moment*. Old Tappan NJ: Fleming H. Revell, 1970.

(7) Dalton, James S. "The Kentucky Camp Meeting Revivals of 1797-1805 as Rites of Initiation." Ph.D. dissertation, University of Chicago, 1973.

(8) Dickinson, Hoke S., ed. *The Cane Ridge Reader*. 3 vols. in one. Cane Ridge: Cane Ridge Preservation Project, 1972.

(9) Dolan, Jay. *Catholic Revivalism: The American Experience, 1830-1907*. Notre Dame: University of Notre Dame Press, 1978.

(10) Gage, Patricia Anthony. "The Sawdust Trial Lives On at the Hudson River Camp Meeting." *Northern Louisiana Historical Association Journal* 10 (1979): 23-25.

(11) Houchens, Mariam S. "The Great Revival of 1800." *Register of the Kentucky Historical Society* 69 (1971): 216-34.

(12) Humphrey, Richard A. "Mountain Revival Methods." *Appalachian Heritage* 6 (1978): 22-28.

(13) James, Henry C. *Halls Aflame: An Account of the Spontaneous Revivals at Asbury College in 1950 and 1958.* 3d ed. Wilmore KY: Asbury Theological Seminary, 1966. First published 1959.

(14) Kincheloe, Joe L., Jr. "Similarities in Crowd Control Techniques for the Camp Meeting and Political Rally: The Pioneer Role of Tennessee." *Tennessee Historical Quarterly* 37 (1978): 155-69.

(15) Johnson, Charles A. *The Frontier Campmeeting: Religion's Harvest Time.* Dallas: Southern Methodist University Press, 1955.

(16) Johnson, Guion B. "The Camp Meeting in Ante-Bellum North Carolina." *North Carolina Historical Review* 10 (1933): 95-110.

(17) _____. "Revival Moments in Ante-Bellum North Carolina." *North Carolina Historical Review* 10 (1933): 21-43.

(18) Lacy, Benjamin R. *Revivals in the Midst of the Years.* Richmond: John Knox Press, 1943.

(19) Long, Ronald W. "Religious Revivalism in the Carolinas and Georgia, 1740-1805." Ph.D. dissertation, University of Georgia, 1968.

(20) Lord, Clyde W. "The Mineral Springs Holiness Camp Meetings." *Louisiana History* 16 (1975): 257-77.

(21) Lorenz, Ellen J. *Glory, Hallelujah! The Story of the Campmeeting Spiritual.* Nashville: Abingdon Press, 1980.

(22) Loveland, Anne C. "Presbyterians and Revivalism in the Old South." *Journal of Presbyterian History* 57 (1979): 36-49.

(23) McBride, Robert M. "Camp Meeting at Goshen Church." *Tennessee Historical Quarterly* 22 (1963): 137-42.

(24) McKissick, Marvin. "The Function of Music in American Revivals since 1875." *The Hymn* 9,4 (1958): 107-17.

(25) McLoughlin. William G. *Modern Revivalism: Charles Grandison Finney to Billy Graham.* New York: Ronald Press, 1959.

(26) _____. *Revivals, Awakenings, and Reform.* Chicago: University of Chicago Press, 1978.

(27) Mathews, Donald G. "The Second Great Awakening as an Organizing Process, 1780-1830: An Hypothesis." *American Quarterly* 21 (1969): 23-43.

(28) Opie, John, Jr. "James McGready: Theologian of Frontier Revivalism." *Church History* 34 (1965): 445-56.

(29) Parker, Charles A. "The Camp Meeting on the Frontier and the Methodist Religious Resort in the East—Before 1900." *Methodist History* 18 (1980): 179-92.

(30) _____. "Make a Joyful Noise Unto the Lord." *North Carolina Folklore* 15 (1967): 35-40.

(31) Phifer, Edward W. "Religion in the Rain: Cyclone Mack in Burke County, August-September 1920." *North Carolina Historical Review* 48 (1971): 225-44.

(32) Prim, G. Clinton, Jr. "Revivals in the Armies of Mississippi During the Civil War." *Journal of Mississippi History* 44 (1982): 227-34.

(33) Rensi, Ray C. "The Gospel According to Sam Jones." *Georgia Historical Quarterly* 60 (1976): 251-63.

(34) Robertson, James I., Jr. "Revelry and Religion in Frontier Kentucky." *Register of the Kentucky Historical Society* 79 (1981): 354-68.

(35) Shaw, Wayne. "Historians' Treatment of the Cane Ridge Revival." *Filson Club Historical Quarterly* 37 (1963): 249-57.

(36) Stuart, George R. *Methodist Evangelism.* Nashville: Publishing House of the Methodist Episcopal Church, South, 1923.

(37) Tilton, Jeff T. "Some Recent Pentecostal Revivals: A Report in Words and Photographs." *Georgia Quarterly* 32 (1978): 580-605.

(38) Ward, David A. "Toward a Normative Explanation of 'Old Fashioned Revivals'." *Qualitative Sociology* 3 (1980): 3-22.

(39) Weisberger, Bernard A. *They Gathered at the River: The Story of the Great Revivalists and Their Impact on Religion in America.* Boston: Little, Brown, 1958.

(40) Whitaker, Thomas. "The Gasper River Meeting House." *Filson Club Historical Quarterly* 56 (1982): 30-61.

II. SOUTHERN REVIVALISM'S SON:
THE BILLY GRAHAM PHENOMENON

(41) Adler, Bill, ed. *The Wit and Wisdom of Billy Graham.* New York: Random House, 1967.

(42) Allan, Tom, ed. *Crusade in Scotland.* London: Pickering and Inglis, 1955.

(43) *America's Hour of Decision.* Wheaton IL: Van Kampen, 1951.

(44) Ashman, Chuck. *The Gospel According to Billy.* Secaucus NJ: Lyle Stuart, 1977.

(45) Barnhart, Joe E. *The Billy Graham Religion.* Philadelphia: United Church Press, 1972.

(46) Bell, Dr. L. Nelson. "Billy Graham: My Son-in-Law." *Ladies' Home Journal* 78 (October 1958): 103-110.

(47) "Billy Graham: The Man at Home," *Saturday Evening Post* 244 (Spring 1972): 40-47.

(48) "Billy Graham's Plea to President Johnson." *U.S. News and World Report* 63 (7 August 1967): 92.

(49) "Billy Graham's Seattle Campaign." *Christian Century* 69 (1952): 494-96.

(50) Brabham, Lewis F. *A New Song in the South: The Story of the Billy Graham Greenville, S.C., Crusade.* Grand Rapids: Zondervan, 1966.

(51) Burnham, George. *Billy Graham: A Mission Accomplished.* Westwood NJ: Fleming H. Revell, 1955.

(52) ———. *To the Far Corners: With Billy Graham in Asia.* Westwood NJ: Fleming H. Revell, 1956.

(53) ———, and Lee Fisher. *Billy Graham and the New York Crusade.* Grand Rapids: Zondervan, 1957.

(54) _____, and Lee Fisher. *Billy Graham: Man of God*. Westchester IL: Good News Publishers, n.d.

(55) Clelland, Donald A., et al. "In the Company of the Converted: Characteristics of a Billy Graham Crusade Audience." *Sociological Analysis* 35 (1974): 45-56.

(56) Colquhoun, Frank. *Harringay Story: The Official Record of the Billy Graham Greater London Crusade 1954*. London: Hodder and Stoughton, 1955.

(57) Cook, Charles T. *The Billy Graham Story*. Wheaton IL: Van Kampen Press, 1954.

(58) _____. *London Hears Billy Graham*. London: Marshall, Morgan, and Scott, 1954.

(59) Corry, John. "God, Country, and Billy Graham." *Harper's* 248 (February 1969): 33-39.

(60) "Dedicated Deciders in Billy Graham's Crusade." *Life* 43 (1 July 1957): 86-91.

(61) Farrell, Barry. "Billy in the Garden." *Life* 67 (4 July 1969): 2B.

(62) Fisher, Lee. *A Funny Thing Happened on the Way to the Crusade*. Carol Stream IL: Creation House, 1974.

(63) Ferm, Lois. "Billy Graham in Florida." *Florida Historical Quarterly* 60 (1981): 174-85.

(64) Fiske, Edward B. "Closest Thing to a White House Chaplain." *The New York Times Magazine* (8 June 1969): 27+.

(65) Frady, Marshall. *Billy Graham: A Parable of American Righteousness*. Boston: Little, Brown, 1979.

(66) Fritchey, Clayton. "The Issue and Some Miscellaneous Trimmings." *Harper's* 232 (May 1966): 32ff.

(67) Frost, David. *Billy Graham Talks with David Frost*. London: Hodder and Stoughton, 1972.

(68) Gillenson, Lewis. *Billy Graham and Seven Who Were Saved*. New York: Pocket Books, 1968.

(69) "Graham Denounces Dissenters." *Christian Century* 84 (1967): 645.

(70) Hall, Clarence. "The Charisma of Billy Graham." *Reader's Digest* 97 (July 1970): 88-92.

(71) Hall, George F. "Billy Graham in Moshi." *Christian Century* 77 (1960): 366.

(72) Ham, Edward. *Fifty Years on the Battle Front with Christ*. Nashville: The Hermitage Press, 1950.

(73) Heilman, Joan Rattner. "Billy Graham's Daughter Answers His Critics." *Good Housekeeping* 236 (June 1973): 82-83.

(74) High, Stanley. *Billy Graham: The Personal Story of the Man, His Message, and His Mission*. New York: McGraw-Hill, 1956.

(75) "Hiring for God." *The Nation* 208 (26 May 1969): 653.

(76) Houston, Neil. "Billy Graham." *Holiday* 23 (1958): 62-65, 80-81.

(77) Hutchinson, Warner, and Cliff Wilson. *Let the People Rejoice: An Amazing Week in New Zealand.* Wellington, New Zealand: Crusader Bookroom Society, 1959.

(78) Johnson, Weldon T. "The Religious Crusade: Revival or Ritual?" *American Journal of Sociology* 76 (1971): 873-90.

(79) Kahn, E. J. "The Wayward Press." *The New Yorker* (8 June 1957): 117-23.

(80) Kilgore, James E. *Billy Graham the Preacher.* New York: Exposition Press, 1968.

(81) Kooiman, Helen W. *Transformed: Behind the Scenes with Billy Graham.* Wheaton IL: Tyndale House Publishers, 1970.

(82) Lal, P. "Billy Graham in India." *The Nation* 184 (7 April 1957): 276-77.

(83) Larson, Mel. *Young Men on Fire: The Story of Torrey Johnson and Youth for Christ.* Chicago: Youth Publications, 1945.

(84) Levy, Alan. *God Bless You Real Good: My Crusade with Billy Graham.* New York: Essandess Special Editions, 1969.

(85) Lippy, Charles H. "Billy Graham's 'My Answer': Agenda for the Faithful." *Studies in Popular Culture* 5 (1982): 27-34.

(86) McAllister, James L. "Evangelical Faith and Billy Graham." *Social Action* 29 (March 1963).

(87) _____. "Greensboro and Billy Graham." Manuscript, Yale Divinity School, 1952.

(88) McLoughlin, William G. "Billy Graham." *The Nation* 184 (11 May 1957): 403-410.

(89) _____. *Billy Graham: Revivalist in a Secular Age.* New York: Ronald Press, 1960.

(90) _____. "The Revival of Revivalism." *Christian Century* 76 (1959): 743-45.

(91) McMahan, Tom. *Safari for Souls: With Billy Graham in Africa.* Columbia SC: The State-Record, 1960.

(92) Martin, Harold. "Billy Graham." *Saturday Evening Post* 236 (13 April 1963): 17-23.

(93) "Mass Conversions." *Christian Century* 74 (1957): 677-79.

(94) Meyer, Donald. "Billy Graham and Success." *New Republic* (22 August 1955): 8-10.

(95) "Mighty City Hears Billy's Mighty Call." *Life* 42 (27 May 1957): 20-27.

(96) Mitchell, Curtis. *Billy Graham: The Making of a Crusader.* Philadelphia: Chilton Books, 1966.

(97) _____. *Those Who Came Forward: Men and Women Who Responded to the Ministry of Billy Graham.* Philadelphia: Chilton Books, 1966.

(98) Morris, James. *The Preachers.* New York: St. Martin's Press, 1973.

(99) Niebuhr, Reinhold. "Liberalism, Individualism, and Billy Graham." *Christian Century* 73 (1956): 640-42.

(100) Osborne, John. "The Rev. Billy's Day." *New Republic* 169 (30 October 1971): 11-13.

(101) Patterson, Vernon W. "The Prayer Heard Round the World." *Decision* 16 (October 1975): 3.

(102) Pierard, Richard V. "Billy Graham and the U.S. Presidency." *Journal of Church and State* 22 (1980): 107-27.

(103) Pollock, John. *Billy Graham: The Authorized Biography*. New York: McGraw-Hill, 1966.

(104) _____. *A Foreign Devil in China*. Grand Rapids: Zondervan, 1971.

(105) Raney, Linda, and Joan Gage. "Mrs. Billy Graham: Teaching Children to Believe in God." *Ladies' Home Journal* 89 (December 1972): 84ff.

(106) Robertson, R. B. "When Billy Graham Saved Scotland." *The Atlantic* 101 (June 1957): 39-45.

(107) Rovere, Richard. "Letter from Washington." *The New Yorker* 28 (23 February 1952): 78.

(108) Settel, T. S., ed. *The Faith of Billy Graham*. Anderson SC: Droke House, 1968.

(109) Shea, George Beverly, with Fred Bauer. *Then Sings My Soul*. Old Tappan NJ: Fleming H. Revell, 1968.

(110) "Still in Business with the Lord." *The Nation* 208 (30 June 1969): 814ff.

(111) Strober, Gerald. *Graham: A Day in Billy's Life*. Garden City: Doubleday, 1976.

(112) Streiker, Lowell, and Gerald S. Strober. *Religion and the New Majority: Billy Graham, Middle America, and the Politics of the 70s*. New York: Association Press, 1972.

(113) Thorkelson, Willmar L. "Billy Graham Draws Throngs." *Christian Century* 67 (1950): 1270-71.

(114) Tracy, Philip. "Billy Graham Plays the Garden." *Commonweal* 92 (25 July 1969): 457-59.

(115) Watson, W. T. "The Bible School Days of Billy Graham." Dunedin FL: n.p., n.d.

(116) Weiner, Herbert. "Billy Graham: Respectable Evangelism." *Commentary* 26 (September 1957): 257-62.

(117) Whitam, Frederick L. "Revivalism as Institutionalized Behavior: An Analysis of the Social Base of a Billy Graham Crusade." *Social Science Quarterly* 49 (1968): 115-27.

(118) Wills, Garry. "How Nixon Used the Media, Billy Graham, and the Good Lord to Rap with Students." *Esquire* 76 (September 1970): 119ff.

(119) Wimberly, Ronald C., et al. "Conversion in a Billy Graham Crusade: Spontaneous Event or Ritual Performance." *Sociological Quarterly* 16 (1975): 162-70.

(120) Wirt, Sherwood E. *Crusade at the Golden Gate*. New York: Harper and Brothers, 1959.

16 SOUTHERN LITERATURE AND RELIGION

AS ELSEWHERE in those colonies that became the United States, in the South literature and religion enjoyed an intimate relationship in the colonial era. As Jay B. Hubbell noted repeatedly in his *The South in American Literature, 1607-1900* (19), religion has long been one of the more powerful influences giving shape to both the nature and content of much Southern literature. Samuel Davies, who was among the more prolific Southern writers of the eighteenth century, was a clergyman and the bulk of his published writing is religious in nature. But during the antebellum period, the South produced few writers of stature regionally or nationally. Charleston's William Gilmore Simms (1806-1870), one of the South's most well-known antebellum authors, had a wider and more appreciative following outside the region, while Edgar Allan Poe (1809-1849), whose work will be noted below, rarely drew on explicitly Southern contexts in his poetry and fiction. Hence a distinctively Southern literature has emerged only during the past century and a quarter, though a work like Augustus Longstreet Baldwin's *Georgia Scenes, Characters, Incidents, &c.* (23), reveals much of the timbre of antebellum Southern life.

Lewis P. Simpson, "Southern Spiritual Nationalism: Notes on the Background of Modern Southern Fiction" (38), suggested that the presence of slavery had much to do with the lack of a rich literary heritage and that it was not until the postbellum period that there was a coalescence of forces that allowed the artist to develop both a Southern identity and an American identity that fostered creativity and issued in works of literary merit. Since then, many writers of distinction have come from the South—George Washington Cable,

Albion Winegar Tourgee, Mark Twain, John Pendleton Kennedy, William Faulkner, Flannery O'Connor, Walker Percy, Robert Penn Warren, Richard Wright, and numerous others—revealing in their prose and poetry the influences of the region's religious culture. As the following discussion and bibliographical listing will demonstrate, there is now a large and growing corpus of secondary literature sensitive to the religious ethos that has informed the thinking of these writers and alert to the ways in which they draw religious themes into their work. This discussion and the bibliographical listing will highlight these secondary treatments of Southern writers rather than the original works of specific authors. It will not routinely comment on general works of criticism or anthologies of critical essays as a whole. Rather, primary attention will be given to essays and monographs that specifically examine religious themes, ideas, symbols, and the like in the work of Southern writers.

Students who wish to explore what is now a rich regional literary heritage as a way to gain yet another vantage point to scrutinize Southern religion have two important bibliographical aids, in addition to those noted in chapter One, to assist them. George N. Boyd and Lois A. Boyd slightly more than a decade ago compiled *Religion in Contemporary Fiction: Criticism from 1945 to the Present* (5), a work which is by no means restricted to Southern literature and writers. Somewhat more narrow in coverage is Abraham Avni, ''The Influence of the Bible on American Literature: A Review of Research from 1955 to 1965'' (2), which does note research on Edgar Allan Poe, William Faulkner, and Andrew Lytle.

In addition, there are several critical works treating American literature and religion as a whole that include some discussion of individual Southern writers. Among older studies still worth examination is Augustus Hopkins Strong, *American Poets and Their Theology* (40), which deals briefly with Sidney Lanier, William Cullen Bryant, and Poe. Bryant, Poe, and a few others are also noted in Elmer J. Bailey's older *Religious Thought in the Greater American Poets* (3). Rachel Ball's master's thesis, ''A Study of Some American Religion Problem Novels'' (4), has one section on Southern writers, many of whom are not widely known and studied, for she highlights the work especially of Kentucky ''local color'' authors James Lane Allen and T.S. Stribling. Another older master's thesis, Maude Miller Hawkins's ''Religious Aspects of Modern American Fiction'' (18), pays special attention to selected Southern writers, especially Elizabeth Madox Roberts. John J. Lanier, ''The South's Religious Thinkers'' (21), looks to literary figures rather than theologians or clergy and offers a somewhat exaggerated argument that both Sidney Lanier and Edgar Allan Poe espoused theopantism. Robinson Jeffers and William Faulkner are among the authors examined by the distinguished Amos N. Wilder in his *Theology and Modern Literature* (45).

More recently, David W. Noble, *The Eternal Adam and the New World Garden* (31), built the argument that American writers have for a century and a half looked at the American frontier as a new Eden. Among the eighteen novelists whose work he probes are two Southern writers, William Faulkner and Robert Penn Warren. Brief mention of both Faulkner and Warren is also found in Marion A. Fairman, *Biblical Patterns in Modern Literature* (14). John R. May has emphasized both religious and secular visions of the apocalypse in American literature in *Toward a New Earth* (28), drawing on apocalyptic images and symbolism in the work of numerous writers with Southern roots, including John Barth, Ralph Ellison, Faulkner, O'Connor, Mark Twain, Richard Wright, and several others. Perry Westbrook has looked at one classical theological theme, *Free Will and Determinism in American Literature* (44). Highlighting the impact of both Puritanism and naturalism in shaping American attitudes toward free will and determinism, Westbrook deals with three Southern writers in his analysis: Mark Twain, Ellen Glasgow, and Faulkner. The broader influence of Calvinism, in part filtered through Puritanism in the United States, is the subject of William H. Shurr, *Rappaccini's Children* (36). Shurr offers one chapter on ''The Southern Experience'' in which he examines briefly the work of George Washington Cable, Thomas Dixon, Faulkner, O'Connor, Poe, Allen Tate, Mark Twain, John Donald Wade, John Crowe Ransom, and Robert Penn Warren. Also thematic in approach is Ted R. Spivey's recent *The Journey Beyond Tragedy* (39). Arguing that writers with a religious focus or orientation present a less nihilistic view of the world, Spivey draws examples from the work of Faulkner, O'Connor, and Percy. More directly centered on Southern literature is Thomas D. Young, ''Religion, the Bible Belt, and the Modern South'' (47). His essay, albeit brief, includes references to Faulkner, William Hall, Johnson Jones Hooper, O'-Connor, Mark Twain, and Wright. As well, one should not neglect David S. Reynolds, *Faith in Fiction: The Emergence of Religious Literature in American Fiction* (33). Two works that bear on American and Southern literature in the Civil War era, making occasional references to religious aspects, are Edmund Wilson, *Patriotic Gore* (46), and Daniel Aaron, *The Unwritten War* (1). But by far the most trenchant discussion of the impact of religion and religious sensibility on Southern literature has come in monographs and essays that examine individual authors.

EDGAR ALLAN POE

Edgar Allan Poe is the subject of two major critical studies that note both his Southern background and the religious dimensions of his writing. They are Edward Davidson, *Poe: A Critical Study* (268), and Daniel Hoffman, *Poe Poe Poe Poe Poe Poe Poe* (273). Two older studies provide a general discussion of religious themes in Poe's writing: Claire E. Partridge's master's thesis, "Religious Tendencies of Edgar Allan Poe" (277), and Allan G. Halline's essay, "Moral and Religious Concepts in Poe" (270). C. Lecompte, *"L'Homeo-Camelopard* ou la mort de Dieu" (275), looks at the religious implications of Poe's "A Tale of Jerusalem." Jules Zanger, " 'The Pit and the Pendulum' and American Revivalism" (284), has argued that this story, taken together with Poe's critical theory, reflects both the message and techniques of the revivalism associated with the Second Great Awakening in the nineteenth century. David H. Hirsch, "The Pit and the Apocalypse" (272), has drawn attention to Poe's use of biblical allusions in the same story, claiming the allusions raise the story above the realm of pure horror. Poe also drew heavily on the Bible in "The City in the Sea," though more by way of offering a dissenting view to the perspective found in the Revelation of St. John. According to Dwayne Thorpe, "Poe's 'The City in the Sea': Source and Interpretation" (283), whereas the author of the New Testament Apocalypse points to resurrection and immortality, Poe regards death as the final, everlasting end of everything. In a rather different vein, Alice M. Claudel, "Poe as Voyager in 'To Helen' " (264), demonstrated that Poe linked Greek and Christian traditions in this poem.

Poe's relationship to the religious currents of his day and the influence of Puritan thought have also caught the attention of his interpreters. John A. Serio, "From Edwards to Poe" (281), for example, claims that Poe reflects both the Puritan affinities to mysticism and the Puritan concept of human depravity. For many years, scholarship suggested that Poe was generally hostile to the transcendentalism that issued from one strain of Puritanism. Ottavio M. Casale, however, in "Poe on Transcendentalism" (263), makes the case that Poe is not as antitranscendentalist as is usually thought. Some specifically religious themes make their way into Poe's work. Jean S. Stromberg notes that Poe assigns to human beings roles that Christianity gives to Christ in "The Relationship of Christian Concepts to Poe's *Grotesque Tales*" (282). Two articles deal with religious dimensions of Poe's "Ligeia." Walter Garrett, "The 'Moral' of 'Ligeia' Reconsidered" (269), suggests that Ligeia's resurrection effects an allegorical unification of God and the universe, while Kenneth T. Reed, " 'Ligeia': The Story as Sermon" (279), has demonstrated that the story could be structured according to the five-part organizational plan for sermons recommended in standard homiletics textbooks of Poe's time. Contemporary religious currents form at least part of the backdrop for "The Cask of Amontillado" according to Kathryn M. Harris. In her "Ironic Revenge in Poe's 'The Cask of Amontillado' " (271), she sought to show that the conflict between Masons and Roman Catholics that raged in the mid-nineteenth century provided the background for Poe's story. Gary Scharnhorst, "Images of the Millerites in American Literature" (280), briefly discusses Poe's references to this millennialist group. The contention that Poe should be numbered among those writers who view America as the locus of the coming apocalypse forms part of the thesis advanced by Martha Banta in "American Apocalypses: Excrement and Ennui" (262).

SIDNEY LANIER

The poetry of Sidney Lanier (1842-1881) has generally not been held in high regard in critical circles in recent decades. However, several students of his work have called attention to religious concepts in his writing, particularly his idea of nature and the beauty and wonder of the created order that he manifests. Three older master's theses all address religious themes found in Lanier's poetry: Lelia Z. Moore, "The Religious Element in Sidney Lanier's Works" (140); Hortense Watkins, "A Study of the Religious Concepts of Sidney Lanier" (141); and Marguerite Weed, "The Ethical and Religious Beliefs of Sidney Lanier" (142). In addition, there is a brief discussion of Lanier's emphasis on nature in another older study, Edwin Mims, *Great Writers as Interpreters of Religion* (139).

ABRAM J. RYAN

A more popular poet among people of the South was Lanier's contemporary, Abram J. Ryan (1838-1896). Ryan, a Roman Catholic priest, became a zealous advocate of Southern nationalism and the Confederate cause, producing many poems that reflected a Confederate patriotism as well as some—albeit lesser known—that advanced religious themes. Gordon Weaver, ed., *Selected Poems of Father Ryan* (300), includes several of the religious poems in this collection. L. Moody Simms, Jr., "Father Abram Joseph Ryan: Poet of the Lost Cause" (298), briefly sketches Ryan's career as a poet. Also biographical in focus is Msgr. C. C. Boldrick, "Father Abram J. Ryan: 'The Poet-Priest of the Confederacy' " (293). Oscar H. Lipscomb precedes his "Some Unpublished Poems of Abram J. Ryan" (296) with a short biographical sketch. Several older studies are noted in the bibliography at the conclusion of this chapter. Critics have paid scant attention to Ryan in recent years. No study seriously explores the connection between his Roman Catholicism and his support for the Confederate cause.

JOHN BANISTER TABB

Another poet-priest of the South, one whose work came in the postbellum period, was John Banister Tabb (1845-1909). Again there is a dearth of secondary literature on his poetry and the ways in which his priestly vocation was related to it. Three brief essays that appeared in the popular *Catholic World* more than half a century ago provide only a sketchy introduction: Alice Meynell, "Father Tabb as a Poet" (318); J. B. Kelly, "Poetry of a Priest"

(317); and K. Bregy, "Of Father Tabb" (314). Sr. Mary Paulina Finn, *John Banister Tabb: The Priest-Poet* (315), lacks scholarly rigor. The only study treating religious elements in Tabb's work is Sr. Mary Humiliata, "Religion and Nature in Father Tabb's Poetry" (316), a short essay that also appeared in *Catholic World*.

MARK TWAIN

It was in the postbellum epoch and early twentieth century that Samuel L. Clemens (1835-1910), better known by his pseudonym Mark Twain, produced his immensely popular novels. Always the humorist, Mark Twain brought his wit to bear in comments about religion that have often been regarded as hostile. At the same time, though, he frequently offered trenchant views on religion in his writing, drew on religious sources in his work, and reflected an awareness of the religious currents of the day. Albert B. Paine's three-volume *Mark Twain: A Biography* (354) emphasizes Twain's later religious pessimism, which Van Wyck Brooks, *The Ordeal of Mark Twain* (325), links to Twain's Calvinist heritage. Justin Kaplan, particularly in *Mr. Clemens and Mark Twain* (343) but to some extent also in his *Mark Twain and His World* (342), downplays this pessimism in his argument that Twain's life as a full and complete human being really ended a decade before his physical death. More recently, Hamlin Hill in *Mark Twain: God's Fool* (337), carefully explored this religious pessimism, suggesting in part that it appears to loom so large because later generations have harbored an overly optimistic view of Victorian culture. Henry Nash Smith, *Mark Twain: The Development of a Writer* (359), shifts the focus to the kind of genteel piety that had begun to challenge and replace traditional faith in the South during Twain's early years. Also see Daniel Hoffman, *Form and Fable in American Fiction* (338), for a sensitive analysis of religion, mythology, and superstition in *Huckleberry Finn*.

Maxwell Geismar includes Mark Twain's scattered comments on religion, along with those on race and revolution, in his edited anthology, *Mark Twain and the Three R's* (336). Lloyd A. Hunter, "Mark Twain and the Southern Evangelical Mind" (340), notes that while Mark Twain found much of Southern evangelical religion repugnant because he found it intolerant of individual conscience and repressive of individual humanitarian impulses—criticisms shared by other writers and analysts—he could not avoid it in his writing. What troubled Mark Twain in part was that Southern evangelicalism was ineffective in providing a comprehensive view of the real world. Joseph J. Feeney develops this point with reference to Tom Sawyer's apparent hostility to religion in "Darkness at Morning: The Bitterness in Mark Twain's Early Novel *Tom Sawyer*" (334). Such ineffectiveness, to Mark Twain, produced a hypocrisy, particularly in the disjunction between behavior and espoused ideals. Thomas Werge has suggested that this disdain for hypocrisy echoes that of Dante in his "The Sin of Hypocrisy in 'The Man That Corrupted Hadleyburg' and 'Inferno XXIII' " (362). That Mark Twain came to regard organized religion as advocating an abstract behavioral code rather than concrete human values forms the basis of James D. Wilson's discussion in "*Adventures of Huckleberry Finn:* From Abstraction to Humanity" (363). But as Elmo Howell argued in "Tom Sawyer's Mock Funeral: A Note on Mark Twain's Religion" (339), at heart Mark Twain did accept old cultural verities. As well, Mark Twain, according to some interpreters, also affirmed a rather traditional concept of virtue and the necessity of maintaining virtue. Arthur A. Bendixen, "Huckleberry Finn and Pilgrim's Progress" (320), for example, claims that Huck rejects the world and appears antisocial precisely in order to affirm virtue. Virtue, of course, raises the problem of moral choice and determinism. Mary E. Rucker addresses this dilemma in "Moralism and Determinism in 'The Man That Corrupted Hadleyburg' " (355). At times, though, Mark Twain seems to adopt a deterministic perspective that, John T. Frederick claims in *The Darkened Sky: Nineteenth Century American Novelists and Religion* (335), resulted from the influence of evolutionary science on his thinking.

Mark Twain's attitudes toward and use of the Bible have attracted much critical attention. The most comprehensive study of this topic is Allison Ensor, *Mark Twain and the Bible* (332). John F. McDermott, "Mark Twain and the Bible" (347), points to a letter Mark Twain wrote in which he admitted that he had made up quotations that he then attributed to the Bible. Yet authentic Biblical myth and story did shape some of Mark Twain's writing. Allison Ensor, "Mark Twain's Yankee and the Prophets of Baal" (333), notes that Hank Morgan's contest with Merlin is a parallel to the story of Elijah's confrontation with the prophets of Baal recorded in 1 Kings 18. The Bible also figures prominently in *Huckleberry Finn*. For a general study, see Joseph B. McCullough, "Uses of the Bible in *Huckleberry Finn*" (346). More particularly, Robert D. Arner, "Acts Seventeen and *Huckleberry Finn:* A Note on Silas Phelps' Sermon" (319), demonstrates how Mark Twain uses Acts 17:29 to highlight the immoral and unChristian center of Huck's world.

Many analysts have emphasized Mark Twain's adept use of the Adamic myth. Thomas Werge, "Mark Twain and the Fall of Adam" (361), finds the Adamic myth especially prominent in both *Huckleberry Finn* and "The Man That Corrupted Hadleyburg." Henry B. Rule suggests that Hadleyburg was an ironic Eden because of corruption and hypocrisy, with the "mysterious stranger" functioning as the equivalent of Satan. See his "The Role of Satan in 'The Man That Corrupted Hadleyburg' " (356). Stanley Brodwin has written three studies discussing Mark Twain's fascination with the Adamic myth. In "The Theology of Mark Twain: Banished Adam and the Bible"

(324), he argued that the myth of Adam's fall is central to Mark Twain's personal theological viewpoint. He also claims that the Adam story is basic to the theological roots of Mark Twain's cosmic sense in "The Humor of the Absurd: Mark Twain's Adamic Diaries" (322). Finally, Brodwin describes *Pudd'nhead Wilson* as a theological study of human nature patterned on the story of the Fall of Adam in his "Blackness and the Adamic Myth in Twain's *Pudd'nhead*" (321). The human condition after Adam's fall figures prominently in the hymnody of Isaac Watts, and two studies by John R. Byers, Jr., suggest that Mark Twain was influenced by Watts: "Miss Emmeline Grangerford's Hymn Book" (326), and "The Pokeville Preacher's Invitation in *Huckleberry Finn*" (327). Joseph R. Millichap pursues a different approach in suggesting that "Calvinistic Attitudes and Pauline Imagery in *Huckleberry Finn*" (352) point the way to clarifying what is otherwise the puzzling ambiguity of the novel's conclusion. Scholars directing attention to the unfinished manuscripts of the posthumously published *The Mysterious Stranger* have appraised Mark Twain's use of Christ imagery. Differences in Christ imagery, based on an examination of three unfinished manuscripts, provide the focus of Paul Delaney, "The Avatars of the Mysterious Stranger: Mark Twain's Images of Christ" (330). Bruce Michelson, "Dens Ludens: The Shaping of Mark Twain's Mysterious Stranger" (350), is convinced from his reading of the manuscripts that Mark Twain was attempting to create an image of God as a divine, omnipotent, but yet playful Tom Sawyer.

Subjects of much controversy in American religious circles in Mark Twain's day were the Mormons, the practice of spiritualism, and espousal of free thought. Mark Twain, clearly unsympathetic to the Mormon cause, did distort Mormon belief and practice in his humorous jabs at the movement. His techniques in poking fun at the Mormons are the subject of Herman Nibbelink, "Mark Twain and the Mormons" (353). Mark Twain's misconceptions of the Mormon enterprise are demonstrated in two essays by Richard H. Cracroft: "The Gentle Blasphemer: Mark Twain, Holy Scripture and the Book of Mormon" (329), and "Distorting Polygamy for Fun and Profit: Artemus Ward and Mark Twain Among the Mormons" (328). Howard Kerr briefly notes the influence of late nineteenth-century spiritualism on Mark Twain in *Mediums, and Spirit-Rappers, and Roaring Radicals: Spiritualism in American Literature, 1850-1900* (344). The impact of free thought on Mark Twain is discussed by Thomas D. Schwartz, "Mark Twain and Robert Ingersoll: The Freethought Connection" (357).

WILLIAM FAULKNER

Criticism of twentieth-century Southern authors has produced a vast secondary literature discussing religious themes, religious symbolism, and views about religion in the work of William Faulkner (1897-1962). Cleanth Brooks has provided three critical studies of Faulkner that treat Faulkner's portrayal of Southern religion as well as the religious ideas Faulkner expresses: *Wil-

liam Faulkner: The Yoknapatawpha Country (67), *William Faulkner: Toward Yoknapatawpha and Beyond* (68), and *William Faulkner: First Encounters* (66). Both John W. Hunt, *William Faulkner: Art in Theological Tension* (96), and David L. Minter, *William Faulkner: His Life and Work* (110), call attention to Faulkner's religious sensibilities.

Martin Jarrett-Kerr emphasizes Faulkner's use of religious ideas and images in *William Faulkner: A Critical Essay* (100), a volume in the Eerdmans Contemporary Writers in Christian Perspective series. Another overview is found in J. Robert Barth, ed., *Religious Perspectives in Faulkner's Fiction* (61). Cleanth Brooks, "William Faulkner: Vision of Good and Evil" (69), makes the case that Faulkner is a religious writer whose works cannot be understood outside of a Christian frame of reference, while Margaret M. Culley, "Judgment in Yoknapatawpha Fiction" (78), highlights the prevalence of Biblical imagery and mythology in Faulkner's novels. The most recent comprehensive study in this area is Jessie A. Coffee, *Faulkner's Un-Christlike Christians: Biblical Allusions in the Novels* (76).

Many commentators have noted that Faulkner is critical of formal religion and of rigid religious styles. Stephen L. Tanner, for example, claimed that *Light in August,* sometimes perceived to be antireligious in tone, is really an attack on a narrow concept of religion and advocates instead a more comprehensive and humane understanding of what religion is about (128). William V. O'Connor, "Protestantism in Yoknapatawpha County" (113), looks more specifically at Faulkner's concern for Southern religion, noting as well that Faulkner severely criticizes the sanctimony and cruel righteousness that permeate popular Southern evangelical Protestantism and result in a church devoid of compassion and forgiveness. Like Tanner, O'Connor claims that Faulkner's critique is also advocacy of a "genuine" religion. Joshua McClennen, "William Faulkner and Christian Complacency" (105), addresses a similar concern, particularly in Faulkner's contrast between black and white religion. McClennen argues that Faulkner, while affirming that the good life is impossible without spiritual religion, condemns white religion for its complacency and false sense of superiority and regards black religion as retaining authentic spirituality. Elmo Howell, "Faulkner's Country Church: A Note on 'Shingles for the Lord' " (94), suggests that Faulkner's distaste for formal religion hampers his ability to portray rural people engaged in religious activities as skillfully as he depicts them otherwise. William H. Nolte, "Mencken, Faulkner and Southern Moralism" (112), seeks to demonstrate that Faulkner's criticism of Southern religious hypocrisy parallels that of Mencken (which was noted in chapter 2).

Several critics have focused on Faulkner's treatment of Calvinism. Robert L. Johnson, for example, argues that Faulkner's experiences with Southern Presbyterians helped generate his castigation of Calvinism as a rigid, doctrinaire tradition in *Light in August* (101), a point echoed by Benjamin Griffith in "Calvinism in Faulkner's *Light in August*" (88). Griffith analyzes the character of Joe Christmas, noting that his need for rigidity in life leads him to become a representative of a rigid Calvinist extreme. The narrowness, harshness, and bigotry that Faulkner attributes to Calvinism and religious fanaticism in *Light in August* makes the novel, according to Glenn O. Carey in "*Light in August* and Religious Fanaticism" (73), Faulkner's strongest criticism of religion. Mary Dell Fletcher, "William Faulkner and Residual Calvinism" (83), extends the discussion to include *Absalom, Absalom!*. Also see Harold J. Douglas and Robert Daniel, "Faulkner and the Puritanism of the South" (80), and especially Ilse Dusoir Lind, "The Calvinistic Burden of 'Light in August' " (104). Despite Faulkner's condemnation of much popular religiosity, Elmo Howell, "William Faulkner, the Substance of Faith" (95), claimed that Faulkner's works represent one of American literature's strongest affirmations of religious faith.

Richard J. O'Dea, "Faulkner's Vestigial Christianity" (114), shifts the focus away from Faulkner's criticism of certain styles and forms of religion to the constructive dimensions of a positive view of religion. O'Dea claims that Faulkner advocates a Christianity rooted in virtue, rather than in dogma or symbol. In "Faulkner and the Adamic Myth" (124), Herman E. Spivey advanced the view that Faulkner's constructive notion of religion revolved around his rejection of most popular understanding of the human condition as encapsulated in the Adamic myth. Instead, according to Spivey, Faulkner accented only that part of it that portrays a lonely humanity as occasionally achieving strength and maturity through contact with evil. Peter Swiggert's essay, "Moral and Temporal Order in *The Sound and the Fury*" (127), however, notes that while the virtue of love endows those who have experienced salvation with insight into the true nature of human experience, that virtue can readily degenerate into the moral complacency Faulkner abhorred. In an older article, "The Hero in the New World: William Faulkner's *The Bear*" (103), R. W. B. Lewis showed how Faulkner's characters live in a world created after the Incarnation in which one must suffer the humiliation of Christ if one hopes to gain redemption and virtue. Hence R. C. Carpenter, "Faulkner's *Sartoris*" (74), argues that the central themes of this work are the myths of sin, guilt, and redemption, while James R. Giermanski, "William Faulkner's Use of the Confessional" (85), explores how Faulkner uses the recounting of sins as a form of penance and expiation through suffering. A somewhat different, yet compatible thesis is advanced in Joseph Gold's analysis of *As I Lay Dying,* "'Sin, Salvation and Bananas'" (86). Gold's point is that this novel contrasts faith and works, doing and saying, life and death and that Addie represents the forces of "'anti-life'" that must be overcome before life can be celebrated. The emphasis on suffering as the path to virtue naturally leads to discussion of Faulkner's use of the Christ image, which comes to the fore particularly in *A Fable*. A general appraisal of Faulkner's use of the Christ story in this work is Kathryn A. Chittick, "The Fables in William Faulkner's *A Fable*" (75). Julian N. Hartt, "Some Reflections on Faulkner's Fable" (90), suggests that Faulkner's attempt to answer the question "Who is Christ?" is linked to Faulkner's insistence that religion go beyond petty moralism to a broader belief in humanity and hence reflects his concern for authentic virtue. But it may also be the human quest to wrestle with the vicissitudes of life that points toward the holy. Such a case has been advanced by Stuart James, " 'I Lay My Hand on My Mouth': Religion in *Yoknapatawpha County*" (99), while Robert R. Sanderlin, "*As I Lay Dying:* Christian Symbols and Thematic Implications" (121), claims that this novel is fundamentally concerned with a family's attempts to cope with the realities of life and death, a struggle enriched by the use of Biblical allusion.

In a more philosophical vein, George C. Bedell, *Kierkegaard and Faulkner: Modalities of Existence* (62), attempts to elucidate the Danish philosopher-theologian's aesthetic, ethical, and religious ways of existence with reference to Faulkner's characters, noting that the genuinely religious path is not only the highest, but the most rarely attained. In the end, Faulkner's characters are simply humans who believe or do not believe, who have genuine faith or lack it. As Donald Palumbo argued in "The Concept of God in Faulkner's *Light in August, The Sound and the Fury, As I Lay Dying,* and *Absalom, Absalom!*" (115), Faulkner's God reveals the divine self to those who believe such revelation possible and remains absent from those who do not believe in such revelation.

FLANNERY O'CONNOR

The work of Flannery O'Connor (1925-1964) has likewise generated considerable critical interest since O'Connor wrote as one who was both a Catholic and a Southerner dealing quite explicitly with matters of faith and belief. Robert Drake, "Flannery O'Connor" (163), for example, claims that O'Connor is an uncompromising worker of Christian themes in her novels and stories. Drake earlier presented a fuller case for his thesis in *Flannery O'Connor: A Critical Essay* (164), one of the Eerdmans Contemporary Writers in Christian Perspective series. Preston M. Browning's monograph, *Flannery O'Connor* (149), builds the case that the tension between unbelief and the necessity of belief forms the basis for the religious motifs O'Connor weaves into her fiction, while Stanley Hyman's *Flannery O'Connor* (177), one of the University of Minnesota Pamphlets on American Writers series, declares that O'Connor is the "most radical Christian dualist since Dostoevski." A different dimension is noted by David Eggenschwiler, *The Christian Humanism of Flannery O'Connor* (166), who argues that the religious themes

O'Connor develops are the same as the major themes explored by modern psychologists as well as theologians. Kathleen M. Feeley, *Flannery O'Connor: Voice of the Peacock* (167), emphasizes not only O'Connor's reading and use of theology, but also her interest in philosophy as one key to appreciating her work. The link between O'Connor's use of irony, seen as the basis of her style and technique, and the Christian vision behind her stories and novels forms the subject of Dorothy T. McFarland's *Flannery O'Connor* (190). In a similar vein Thomas M. Lorch, "Flannery O'Connor: Christian Allegorist" (185), sees her use of allegory as the means of bringing O'Connor's religious beliefs and art together. Henry McDonald, "The Moral Meaning of Flannery O'Connor" (189), notes the religious underpinnings of O'Connor's work and insists that her thought is similar to that of Nietzsche.

But of particular interest to critics in examining O'Connor's work has been the influence of both her Roman Catholic religious identification and her Southern heritage. Patric Choffrut-Faure, "Flannery O'Connor ou la Vision Eclatee" (155), for example, argues that Roman Catholicism and the defeated South gave shape to O'Connor's views. The two also come together in Chrysostom Kim's contention in "A Do-It-Yourself Religion and the Grimly Comic in Flannery O'Connor" (181) that O'Connor's attraction to Christian mysteries and her use of the "grimly comic" emerge from her life as a Catholic and a Southerner. Robert Regan, "The Legitimate Sources of Depravity in Flannery O'Connor" (210), suggests that O'Connor's genius lies in fusing Southern life and character, Roman Catholic concepts of grace, and influences from nineteenth-century American fiction into a single whole. A more sustained argument regarding O'Connor's orthodox Catholicism and her use of the American grotesque tradition in literature is found in Gilbert H. Muller's unusually thoughtful study, *Nightmares and Visions: Flannery O'-Connor and the Catholic Grotesque* (203). Gene Kellogg, in a monograph entitled *The Vital Tradition: The Catholic Novel in a Period of Convergence* (179) and an article titled "The Catholic Novel in Convergence" (178), emphasizes the impact of O'Connor's Catholic background, but also claims that O'Connor's firm Catholicism is the force that allows her to become a critic of both Catholicism and secularism.

O'Connor's commitment to Catholic sacramentalism, with its implicit criticism of Southern evangelicalism, forms the core of Suzanne Allen's essay, "Memories of a Southern Catholic Girlhood: Flannery O'Connor's 'A Temple of the Holy Ghost' " (143). Three essays in Melvin A. Friedman, Jr., and Lewis A Lawson, eds., *The Added Dimension: The Art and Mind of Flannery O'Connor* (169), also seek to unravel O'Connor's relation to and use of themes emerging from her self-identity as a Southerner and a Catholic: Frederick J. Hoffman, "The Search for Redemption: Flannery O'Connor's Fiction"; Louis D. Rubin, "Flannery O'Connor and the Bible Belt"; and

Nathan A. Scott, Jr., "Flannery O'Connor's Testimony: The Pressure of Glory." O'Connor's combination of images and themes rooted in Southern agrarian culture with those identified as Christian is the subject of Elmo Howell, "Flannery O'Connor and the Home Country" (175). William Koon, in " 'Help Me Not to Be So Mean': Flannery O'Connor's Subjectivity" (183), argues that O'Connor's religious stance leads her to rework traditional Southern themes in order to present a sternly Catholic orthodoxy. Also see A. R. Coulthard, "The Christian Writer and the New South: Or, Why Don't You Like Flannery O'Connor?" (156).

The Christian notion of grace figures prominently in O'Connor's writing. In *The True Country: Themes in the Fiction of Flannery O'Connor* (193), Carter W. Martin suggested that the Christian doctrines of grace and redemption were the central ideas developed by O'Connor. On this point, also see Sr. Bernice Bergup, "Themes of Redemptive Grace in the Works of Flannery O'Connor" (147). The most recent comprehensive study of this idea is found in Lorine M. Getz, *Nature and Grace in Flannery O'Connor's Fiction* (170). The title of Jonathan Baumback's essay, "The Acid of God's Grace: *Wise Blood* by Flannery O'Connor" (145), suggests, however, that redemptive grace has a hard side to it. In "Paradise Not Regained: Flannery O'Connor's Unredeemed Pilgrims in the Garden of Evil" (186), Mary McBride argues that for O'Connor the suffering of the innocent at the hands of often violent (and vile) aggressors becomes a source for grace, for the vision that takes human imperfection and molds it into the raw material of the good. In a comparative study, "Graham Greene's Pinkie Brown and Flannery O'Connor's Misfit: The Psychopathic Killer and the Mystery of God's Grace" (180), Carola Kaplan claims that O'Connor is successful in using human evil as a means to point the way to eternal truth, to the experience of grace. This basic notion is echoed in Robert H. Brinkmeyer's thesis in "Borne Away by Violence: The Reader and Flannery O'Connor" (148), that O'Connor uses violence to communicate her basic religious vision. So, too, Marlene Spencer demonstrates that O'Connor's characters tend to acknowledge both the presence of God and the manifestations of God's grace as a result of experiencing violence and its consequences in her essay, "The Sacred and the Profane in Flannery O'Connor's 'The Comforts of Home' " (218). Thelma J. Shinn, "Flannery O'Connor and the Violence of Grace" (214), links this association of grace and violence with O'Connor's fusion of Roman Catholic belief and the Southern grotesque, arguing that this fusion resulted from O'Connor's conviction that the violence of rejection in the modern world demanded an equal violence of redemption. James M. Mellard, in another comparative study, finds a similar connection between violence and grace in the work of Mauriac ("Violence and Belief in Mauriac and O'Connor" [195]). But it may also be the case, as Paul W. Nisly suggested in "Wart Hogs from

Hell: The Demonic and the Holy in Flannery O'Connor's Fiction'' (204), that O'Connor simply believed that without a genuine knowledge of the demonic (violence), it was difficult, if not impossible, to recognize the holy (grace). Other studies that focus on O'Connor's use of the doctrine of grace include Marion Montgomery, ''Grace: A Tricky Fictional Agent'' (199); Walter Sullivan, ''Flannery O'Connor, Sin, and Grace: *Everything That Rises Must Converge*'' (222); and Miles D. Orvell, ''Flannery O'Connor'' (208).

But O'Connor's Southern heritage included as well a rich exposure to evangelical Protestantism. It is therefore not surprising that critics have also found certain more distinctively Protestant religious ideas in her work and the influence of Protestant notions in images she employs. Robert Milder, for example, in ''The Protestantism of Flannery O'Connor'' (196), notes that two recurring ideas in O'Connor's fiction—the irremediable corruption of natural man and the exaltation of private religious experience—reflect an essentially Protestant approach to religion. More specifically, Joseph R. Millichap argues that O'Connor maintained a basically Calvinist view of human nature, of humanity constrained by the race's heritage, in his ''The Pauline 'Old Man' in Flannery O'Connor's 'The Comforts of Home' '' (197). Michael Bellamy has claimed in ''Everything Off Balance: Protestant Election in Flannery O'-Connor's 'A Good Man Is Hard to Find' '' (146) that O'Connor is also influenced by the Calvinist doctrine of predestination in her portrayal of the grandmother in this story. Distinguished comparative literature critic Albert Sonnenfeld has pushed these ideas further in seeking to demonstrate that the prevalence of fundamentalist extremists in the Southern culture that nurtured O'Connor may have led her to see salvation as a stormy, violent process. See his ''Flannery O'Connor: The Catholic Writer as Baptist'' (217). O'Connor's own awareness of the impact of Protestantism on her Catholic affirmation is revealed particularly in letters to her Protestant friends. Those letters form the basis of Thomas F. Gossett's study, ''No Vague Believer: Flannery O'Connor and Protestantism'' (173).

But there are dissenting voices, some critical of O'Connor's religious stance and some concerned that overemphasis on the religious dimensions of her works detracts from regarding them from a more authentic literary perspective. Louis D. Rubin, ''Flannery O'Connor's Company of Southerners: or, 'The Artificial Nigger' Read as Fiction Rather than Theology'' (211), makes a strong case that one should read O'Connor's fiction just as fiction and not as an exercise in religious thought. Marion Montgomery, ''Miss O'-Connor and the Christ-Haunted'' (200), verges on the polemical in her attack on O'Connor's religious views from an essentially conservative Christian theological perspective. Finally, John T. O'Brien, ''The Un-Christianity of Flannery O'Connor'' (205), proclaims that one should forget both O'Connor's Catholic background and her Southern background since, in his view, she followed no particular creed, but fashioned an idiosyncratic religious vision.

WALKER PERCY

The influence of Southern culture and the Catholic heritage on another writer, Walker Percy (1916-), has also intrigued literary critics. Indeed, several commentators have attempted to show similarities between O'Connor and Percy because of their common identity as Southern Catholics. Lawrence Cunningham, for example, in his "Catholic Sensibility and Southern Writers" (238), finds points of similarity in O'Connor's and Percy's "premodern" concept of the world, that is of the world as a sign from God and the arena of God's activity. On the other hand, Susan S. Kissel, "Voices in the Wilderness: The Prophets of O'Connor, Percy, and Powers" (247), finds that the Catholic affiliation of both leads to similar views of both the Catholic Church and American society. But Percy and O'Connor are not cut from the same mold. In particular, as many analysts have pointed out, Percy has a far deeper affinity for themes and ideas emerging from existentialist philosophy and theology than O'Connor.

Robert Coles, *Walker Percy: An American Search* (236), contends that Percy essentially transforms existentialism in its traditional European, Christian, and secular modes into a contemporary American entity balanced with pragmatism and empiricism. Much of existentialist thought derives from the work of the nineteenth-century Danish philosopher Søren Kierkegaard, whose influence on his own thinking Percy has acknowledged. Two interviews, for example, include Percy's own statements about his appreciation for Kierkegaard: Jan Nordby Gretlund, "Interview with Walker Percy" (244), and Bradley R. Dewey, "Walker Percy Talks about Kierkegaard: An Annotated Interview" (240). Thomas LeClair, "The Eschatological Vision of Walker Percy" (251), also sees existentialism as the key to interpreting Percy's work, even in Percy's depiction of evil. On this point, see LeClair's essay, "Walker Percy's Devil" (252). Anthony Quagliano, "Existential Modes in *The Moviegoer*" (254), examines this one novel from an existentialist perspective, noting that critics need to study Percy's essay on philosophy and psychology in order to understand the existential dynamic operating in his fiction. Percy's brand of Christian existentialism has also been seen by some to be at the heart of *Lancelot* and "Message in a Bottle." See, for example, Rainulf A. Stelzmann, "Das Schwert Christi: Zwei Versuche Walker Percys" (257). John F. Zeugner has argued that the later existentialism advocated by Gabriel Marcel is at least as important as the earlier form developed by Kierkegaard in "Walker Percy and Gabriel Marcel: The Castaway and the Wayfarer" (261). But some are reluctant to transform Percy into a contemporary existentialist philosopher. In "Walker Percy's Christian Vision" (243), William L. Godshalk has claimed that Percy is far more the Christian commentator on the nature of human being than an existentialist philosopher, while Anselm Atkins, "Walker Percy and Post-Christian Search" (232), a study of *The Moviegoer,* suggests that the philosophical and theological framework that supports Percy's characters moves well beyond even twentieth-century Christian existentialism.

The links to existentialism are perhaps most obvious in Percy's frequent depiction of characters who find themselves alienated from the world around them. Thomas Griffith, "Moral Tales for a Depraved Age" (245), claims that it is Percy's hatred for his own age, a hatred erupting from a religiously tormented inner self, that impels such characterizations. But to Ellen Douglas, *Walker Percy's The Last Gentleman* (241), Percy's genius lies in the way he confronts the spiritual dilemma that itself emerges from the modern age. One of the briefer yet more provocative studies of the theme of alienation is Robert H. Brinkmeyer, Jr., "Percy's Bludgeon: Message and Narrative Strategy" (234). Brinkmeyer seeks to demonstrate that Percy addressed both *The Moviegoer* and *The Last Gentleman* to those who recognize their own alienation and *Love in the Ruins* and particularly *Lancelot* to those who do not in order to shock both types into a rejection of ordinary secularity and then into a turn toward God. But as Robert D. Daniel, "Walker Percy's *Lancelot:* Secular Raving and Religious Salience" (239), argues, *Lancelot* is both a satire on secularism and its inadequacy and a criticism of much contemporary religion that shuns an active ethical response to the world's problems. This latter issue is also the focus of Deborah J. Barrett, "Discourse and Intercourse: The Conversion of the Priest in Percy's *Lancelot*" (233). However, Lewis A. Lawson, "The Fall of the House of Lamar" (249), makes the case that a Southern stoicism competes with a Christian view of the world for Percy's allegiance (parallels, to an extent, with what Daniel labels secularism and religion) and that while the Christian emerges as superior, the stoic is never fully vanquished. Regardless, whatever positive spiritual identity comes to Percy's characters comes through encounters with persons and objects in the world around them, a viewpoint that Patrick Samway, "A Rahnerian Backdrop to Percy's *The Second Coming*" (255), finds more directly developed in the writings of twentiety-century Roman Catholic theologian Karl Rahner. The point ultimately for Percy is that despite experiences of alienation on the part of humans, God remains very much present in all of life. For a fuller treatment of this matter, see R. E. Lauder, "The Catholic Novel and the 'Insider God' " (248), a comparison of Percy with Graham Greene.

Other essays have focused more on the treatment of particular Christian doctrines in Percy's work. Lewis A. Lawson, "Tom More: Cartesian Physician" (250), finds in *Love in the Ruins* a statement of how a gnostic view of the world must finally recognize the need for atonement. The doctrine of salvation or redemption is the basis for Richard Lehan's appraisal in "The Way Back: Redemption in the Novels of Walker Percy" (253). Finally, Paul L. Gaston, "The Revelation of Walker Percy" (242), calls attention to the strains of millennialism that weave in and out of Percy's fiction.

CAROLINE GORDON

Several studies center on the work of Caroline Gordon (1895-1981). James E. Rocks, "The Christian Myth as Salvation: Caroline Gordon's *The Strange Children*" (137), argues that this novel demonstrates Gordon's transition from reliance on the agrarian myth to use of the Christian myth. But Larry Rubin, "Christian Allegory in Caroline Gordon's 'The Captive' " (138), finds a Christian orientation in that story, a work written earlier than those in which critics have generally acknowledged a Christian backdrop in Gordon's work. The human situation in Gordon's writing is appraised by Louise Cowan in "Nature and Grace in Caroline Gordon" (135), while Brainard Cheney looks at "Caroline Gordon's Ontological Quest" (134). As is the case with many Southern writers, Gordon has been compared with Dante. See Ashley Brown's study of Gordon's *The Malefactor* and Dante's *Purgatorio,* "The Novel as Christian Comedy" (133).

ERSKINE CALDWELL

Erskine Caldwell (1903–), son of an Associate Reformed Presbyterian minister, offered a personal perspective on Southern religion in the collection of essays published as *Deep South* (2:11). This intimate exposure to the dynamics and hypocrisy of Southern religion in the earlier twentieth century meant that Caldwell treats religion more fully and more carefully than many other writers, according to James J. Thompson, Jr., "Erskine Caldwell and Southern Religion" (56). Thompson finds Caldwell highlighting three basic themes in his portrayal of Southern religion, themes that critics of Southern evangelicalism have often identified as weaknesses of the region's dominant religious style: an underlying fatalism, a preoccupation with sexuality, and the absence of a viable social ethic. Other features of Caldwell's presentation of Southern religion have been identified by Benjamin W. Farley, "Erskine Caldwell: Preacher's Son and Southern Prophet" (53). Farley notes how Caldwell depicts Southern religion as a social front that masks hypocrisy, as a presumed panacea for all personal and social ills, and as an ethical code with ramifications only for individual behavior. Caldwell's occasionally bitter statements about the South's religious culture have led some to conclude that he was hostile to religion. But Jac Tharpe, "Interview with Erskine Caldwell" (55), concludes that Caldwell's experience left him indifferent to organized religion rather than hostile to it. Harvey Klevar, "Some Things Holy in a Forsaken Land" (54), finds that Caldwell's perspective changed from his earlier writing to his later works. In the early materials, Klevar argues that Caldwell tended to emphasize the tragic dimension of life for those who were seeking God in a land that had forsaken genuine religion, but that in the later works Caldwell tempts his readers to bemoan what might have been had the religious life of the South been different.

ROBERT PENN WARREN

The poetry and fiction of Robert Penn Warren (1905-) reveals Warren's sensitivity to Southern culture and its religiosity as well as his association with the "Fugitives," a group of poets that included John Crowe Ransom, Allen Tate, Donald Davidson, and others. Often compared with Faulkner, Warren is more academic and cosmopolitan in his work than Faulkner. Louis D. Rubin, Jr., offers an overview of religious ideas in Warren's poetry in his "The Eye of Time: Religious Themes in Robert Penn Warren's Poetry" (370). Allen Shepherd, appraising Warren's fiction, emphasizes Warren's concern for values in "Robert Penn Warren as a Philosophical Novelist" (371). Warren's mystical sensibility has caught the attention of several critics. See, for example, A. L. Clements, "Sacramental Vision: The Poetry of Robert Penn Warren" (366), and Victor H. Strandberg's more sustained study, *The Poetic Vision of Robert Penn Warren* (372). L. Hugh Moore, Jr., has called attention to affinities between Warren and Dante in "Robert Penn Warren and the Terror of Answered Prayer" (368).

JOHN CROWE RANSOM

Emory B. Elliott, Jr., has looked at the work of another of the Fugitives, John Crowe Ransom (1888-1974), and found subtle interconnections between Ransom's religious views and his agrarian stance. See Elliott's "Theology and Agrarian Ideology in the Critical Theory of John Crowe Ransom" (288). Wayne A. Knoll, "Ransom as Religionist" (289), focuses on Ransom's reinterpretation of Southern fundamentalism, arguing that Ransom ultimately portrays fundamentalism more as an aestheticism than as a religion.

RICHARD WRIGHT

Mississippi's Richard Wright (1908-1960) ranks among the more prominent black Southern writers of the twentieth century. John Killinger, *The Fragile Presence: Transcendence in Modern Literature* (387), briefly discusses Wright's work in a section on religion in the writing of black authors. Nathan A. Scott, Jr., calls attention to Wright's portrayal of the religious quest in "Search for Beliefs: Fiction of Richard Wright" (392). Lewis A. Lawson, "Cross Demon: Kierkegaardian Man of Dread" (388), claims that Wright offers a distinctively Christian perspective in *The Outsider* rather than an aesthetic or existential one. But Raman K. Singh, "Christian Heroes and Anti-Heroes in Richard Wright's Fiction" (393), has found a marked change in religious attitudes between Wright's early novels and his later ones. According to Singh, the heroes of the earlier novels reflect an acceptance of Christianity, while those of the later novels reflect a negation of Christianity. Jerold J. Savory, "Descent and Baptism in *Native Son, Invisible Man,* and *Dutchman*" (391), looks at two particular religious symbols, the descent into hell and baptism by fire, and finds these as interpretive keys to understanding the experience of the main characters in each of these novels.

JAMES AGEE

Mark A. Doty's biography of critic-author James Agee (1909-1955), *Tell Me Who I Am: James Agee's Search for Selfhood* (48), emphasizes the several works of Agee that are preoccupied with the problem of self-identity in both theological and psychological senses and concludes that Agee's childhood grief over the loss of his own parents provides the key to understanding them. Agee's lifelong concern for the role of religion in life is also seen to lie behind the theme of "Belief and Unbelief in *A Death in the Family*," according to Gayle Whittier (51). Victor A. Kramer, "James Agee's Unpublished Manuscript and His Emphasis on Religious Emotion in *The Morning Watch*" (49), notes that the published work has a different beginning and a different conclusion than the unpublished manuscript. The unpublished version, he notes, contains a greater emphasis on the difficulty adults encounter in maintaining religious fervor. Such a dilemma is common to the evangelical style that permeates much Southern religion. On Agee, also see William Stott, *Documentary Expression and Thirties America* (50).

TENNESSEE WILLIAMS

The work of playwright Tennessee Williams (1912-1983) is more problematic, for as F. L. Kunkel argued in "Tennessee Williams and the Death of God" (382), Williams's art is decadent and his characters remain basically indifferent to human suffering in a quest for salvation in sex rather than in religion. Consequently, Sr. M. Carol Blitgen, "Tennessee Williams: Modern Idolater" (380), castigates Williams for having an "Old Testament mindset" that portrays God as wrathful and judgmental. Neal B. Houston, "Meaning by Analogy in *Suddenly Last Summer*" (381), finds in the play a startling allegory of a malevolent God. But Thomas P. Adler, "The Search for God in the Plays of Tennessee Williams" (379), attempted to demonstrate that Williams himself did not share his characters' view of God as threatening and vengeful.

WILLIAM STYRON

Critics have also found religious themes and images in the work of William Styron (1925-), who was born in Newport News, Virginia, and was graduated from Duke University. Robert H. Fossum's contribution to the Eerdmans Contemporary Writers in Christian Perspective series, *William Styron: A Critical Essay* (303), argues that Styron's works capture the spiritual vacuity of the present age and the often desperate efforts to fill it. Scholars have directed particular attention to Styron's *The Confessions of Nat Turner*. Patricia R. Cannon, "Nat Turner: God, Man, or Beast?" (302), claims that Styron portrays Nat Turner as a Christ-figure, but an ambiguous one at best. William J. McGill, "William Styron's Nat Turner and Religion" (308), also notes parallels between Nat Turner and Jesus, arguing that Turner is not an avenging Black Messiah, but a genuinely human, faithful, sensitive person more akin to the Biblical Jesus than to an aggressive Hebrew prophet such as Ezekiel. William J. Swanson, "Religious Implications in *The Confessions of Nat Turner*" (311), takes a different approach, suggesting that Margaret Whitehead functions as a Beatrice to Nat Turner's Dante. Finally, John Lang, "The Alpha and the Omega: Styron's *The Confessions of Nat Turner*" (305), not only emphasizes the religious themes of the novel, but points out the possibility of their being obscured in papercover reprint editions that omit the alpha and omega symbols (a Christ referent) that appeared on the hardcover editions.

OTHER AUTHORS

A smattering of titles treats religion in the writing of numerous other authors. Joseph Holt Ingraham penned some of the South's most popular religious best-sellers. Robert W. Weatherby, "J. H. Ingraham and Tennessee: A Record of Social and Literary Contributions" (422), notes that Ingraham (1809-1860) studied theology in Nashville and began to write his best-sellers there, but that he was also concerned with social issues such as tax-supported public schools and prison reform. Warren French appraises the impact of one of Ingraham's best-sellers, *The Prince of the House of David,* in "One Hundred Years of a Religious Best-Seller" (404). Benjamin W. Farley examines the influence of the sermons of Presbyterian clergyman Benjamin Morgan Palmer on George Washington Cable (1844-1925) and also calls attention to Mark Twain's criticism of Cable's Sabbatarian habits in "George W. Cable: Presbyterian Romancer, Reformer, Bible Teacher" (402). The influence of Dante and T. S. Eliot on the view of hell espoused by Katherine Anne Porter (1890-1980) is discussed by Leon Gottfried in "Death's Other Kingdom: Dantesque and Theological Symbolism in 'Flowering Judas' " (285). Clinton W. Trowbridge, "The Word Made Flesh: Andrew Lytle's *The*

Velvet Horn'' (420), makes the case that this book is deeply Christian, that Lytle (1902-) focuses on the paradox of fallen humanity yearning for Eden while simultaneously wishing to forget Eden ever existed, as well as on the contrast between paganism and Christianity. Neil D. Isaacs, *Eudora Welty* (377), provides a broad study by no means exclusively devoted to religion in the works of Welty (1909-), although he does call attention to religious myth and ritualism in her writing. Frank Durham probes God symbolism in one well-known novel by Carson McCullers (1917-1967) in his ''God and No God in *The Heart Is a Lonely Hunter*'' (401).

As religion has penetrated the fabric of Southern culture, so it has permeated the writing of authors whose lives were shaped by that culture. From criticism of the dominant religious style of the South to affirmation of religious belief as the source of meaning in life, Southern literature presents countless examples of the way in which religion, art, and life are inextricably intertwined for those writers who come from Dixie.

The bibliography that follows starts with a listing of general and topical works dealing with Southern literature and religion. Individual sections follow, identifying secondary literature treating these authors in alphabetical order: James Agee, Erskine Caldwell, William Faulkner, Caroline Gordon, Sidney Lanier, Flannery O'Connor, Walker Percy, Edgar Allen Poe, Katherine Anne Porter, John Crowe Ransom, Abram J. Ryan, William Styron, John Banister Tabb, Mark Twain, Robert Penn Warren, Eudora Welty, Tennessee Williams, Thomas Wolfe, and Richard Wright. The final section includes titles that highlight religious themes, images, and background of numerous other Southern authors.

BIBLIOGRAPHY

Several of the titles in chapters 1 and 2 are also relevant to a discussion of religion and Southern literature.

I. SOUTHERN LITERATURE AND RELIGION: GENERAL AND TOPICAL STUDIES

(1) Aaron, Daniel. *The Unwritten War: American Writers and the Civil War*. New York: Knopf, 1973.

(2) Avni, Abraham. ''The Influence of the Bible on American Literature: A Review of Research from 1955 to 1965.'' *Bulletin of Bibliography* 27 (1970): 101-106.

(3) Bailey, Elmer J. *Religious Thought in the Greater American Poets*. Boston and Chicago: Pilgrim Press, 1922.

(4) Ball, Rachel. ''A Study of Some American Religion Problem Novels.'' M.A. thesis, Southern Methodist University, 1930.

(5) Boyd, George N., and Lois A. Boyd, comps. *Religion in Contemporary Fiction: Criticism from 1945 to the Present*. San Antonio: Trinity University Press, 1973.

(6) Cable, George Washington. *The Grandissimes: A Story of Creole Life*. New York: Charles Scribner's Sons, 1880.

(7) Campbell, Harry M. "Notes on Religion in the Renascence." *Shenandoah* 6 (Summer 1955): 10-18.

(8) Chesnut, Mary B. *A Diary from Dixie*. Ben A. Williams, ed. Cambridge MA: Harvard University Press, 1980.

(9) Cowan, Louise. "The Pietas of Southern Poetry." In *South: Modern Southern Literture in Its Cultural Setting*. Louis D. Rubin and Robert D. Jacobs, eds., 95-114. Garden City: Doubleday, 1961.

(10) Davis, Richard B. "The Colonial Virginia Satirist: Mid-Eighteenth Century Commentaries on Politics, Religion, and Society." *Transactions of the American Philosophical Society* new series 57 (1967): Part 1.

(11) ———. *Literature and Society in Early Virginia: 1608-1840*. Baton Rouge: Louisiana State University Press, 1973.

(12) Detwiler, Robert. *Four Spiritual Crises in Mid-Century American Fiction*. Freeport NY: Books for Libraries Press, 1970.

(13) ———. "The Moment of Death in Modern Fiction." *Contemporary Literature* 13 (1972): 269-94.

(14) Fairman, Marion A. *Biblical Patterns in Modern Literature*. Cleveland: Dillion/Liederbach, 1972.

(15) Gross, Seymour, and Rosalie Murphy. "From Stephen Crane to William Faulkner: Some Remarks on the Religious Sense in American Literature." *Cithara* 16 (1977): 90-108.

(16) Grumbach, Doris. "Christianity and Black Writers." *Renascence* 23 (1971): 198-212.

(17) Hassan, Ihab H. "The Victim: Images of Evil in Recent American Fiction." *College English* 21 (1959): 140-46.

(18) Hawkins, Maude Miller. "Religious Aspects of Modern American Fiction." M.A. thesis, University of South Carolina at Columbia, 1932.

(19) Hubbell, Jay B. *The South in American Literature, 1607-1900*. Durham: Duke University Press, 1954.

(20) Jackson, George B. "Faith Without Works in Negro Literature." *Phylon* 12 (1951): 378-88.

(21) Lanier, John J. "The South's Religious Thinkers." *Southern Literary Messenger* 2 (1940): 19-24.

(22) Lawson, Lewis A. "Kierkegaard and the Modern American Novel." In *Essays in Memory of Christine Burleson: In Language and Literature by Former Colleagues and Students*. Thomas G. Burton, ed. Johnson City TN: Research Advisory Council, East Tennessee State University, 1969.

(23) Longstreet, Augustus B. *Georgia Scenes, Characters, Incidents, &c., in the First Half Century of the Republic*. 2d ed. New York: Harper and Brothers, 1840.

(24) Luccock, Halford A. *American Mirror: Social, Ethical, and Religious Aspects of American Literature, 1930-1940*. New York: Macmillan, 1940.

(25) _____. *Contemporary American Literature and Religion*. Chicago: Willett, Clark, 1934.

(26) _____, and Francis Brentano, eds. *The Questing Spirit: Religion in the Literature of Our Times*. New York: Coward-McCann, 1947.

(27) Luker, Ralph E. "To Be Southern/To Be Catholic: An Interpretation of the Thought of Five American Writers." *Southern Studies* 23 (1984).

(28) May, John R. *Toward a New Earth: Apocalypse in the American Novel*. Notre Dame: University of Notre Dame Press, 1972.

(29) Miller, Perry. "Religion and Society in the Early Literature of Virginia." In *Errand into the Wilderness*, 99-140. Cambridge: Harvard University Press, 1956.

(30) Nance, William L. "Eden, Oedipus, and Rebirth in American Fiction." *Arizona Quarterly* 31 (1975): 353-65.

(31) Noble, David W. *The Eternal Adam and the New World Garden: The Central Myth in the American Novel since 1830*. New York: George Braziller, 1968.

(32) Redding, Jay S. *To Make a Poet Black*. Chapel Hill: University of North Carolina Press, 1939.

(33) Reynolds, David S. *Faith in Fiction: The Emergence of Religious Literature in American Fiction*. Cambridge MA: Harvard University Press, 1981.

(34) Rubin, Louis D., ed. *The American South*. Baton Rouge: Louisiana State University Press, 1980.

(35) _____. "Second Thoughts on the Old Gray Mare: The Continuing Relevance of Southern Literary Issues." In *Southern Fiction Today*. George Core, ed. Athens: University of Georgia Press, 1969.

(36) Shurr, William H. *Rappaccini's Children: American Writers in a Calvinist World*. Lexington: University Press of Kentucky, 1981.

(37) Simpson, Lewis P. *The Man of Letters in New England and the South: Essays on the History of the Literary Vocation in America*. Baton Rouge: Louisiana State University Press, 1973.

(38) _____. "Southern Spiritual Nationalism: Notes on the Background of Modern Southern Fiction." In *The Cry of Home: Cultural Nationalism and the Modern Writer*. H. Ernest Lewald, ed., 189-210. Knoxville: University of Tennessee Press, 1972.

(39) Spivey, Ted R. *The Journey Beyond Tragedy: A Study of Myth and Modern Fiction*. Orlando: University Presses of Florida, 1980.

(40) Strong, Augustus Hopkins. *American Poets and Their Theology*. Philadelphia: Griffin and Rowland Press, 1916.

(41) Tischler, Nancy M. *Black Masks: Negro Characters in Modern Southern Fiction,* chap. 6. University Park: Pennsylvania State University Press, 1969.

(42) Wages, Jack D. *Seventy-Five Writers of the Colonial South.* Boston: G. K. Hall, 1979.

(43) Wagner, Jean-Michel. *Les Poetes Negres des Etats Unis.* Paris: Librairie Istra, 1963.

(44) Westbrook, Perry. *Free Will and Determinism in American Literature.* Cranbury NJ: Associated University Presses, 1979.

(45) Wilder, Amos N. *Theology and Modern Literature.* Cambridge MA: Harvard University Press, 1958.

(46) Wilson, Edmund. *Patriotic Gore: Studies in the Literature of the American Civil War.* Corrected ed. New York: Oxford University Press, 1966.

(47) Young, Thomas D. "Religion, the Bible Belt, and the Modern South." In *The American South: Portrait of a Culture.* Louis D. Rubin, ed., 110-17. Baton Rouge: Louisiana State University Press, 1980.

II. SOUTHERN LITERATURE AND RELIGION: THE WORK OF JAMES AGEE

(48) Doty, Mark A. *Tell Me Who I Am: James Agee's Search for Selfhood.* Baton Rouge: Louisiana State University Press, 1981.

(49) Kramer, Victor A. "James Agee's Unpublished Manuscript and His Emphasis on Religious Emotion in *The Morning Watch.*" *Tennessee Studies in Literature* 17 (1972): 159-64.

(50) Stott, William. *Documentary Expression and Thirties America.* New York: Oxford University Press, 1973.

(51) Whittier, Gayle. "Belief and Unbelief in *A Death in the Family.*" *Renascence* 31 (1979): 177-92.

III. SOUTHERN LITERATURE AND RELIGION: THE WORK OF ERSKINE CALDWELL

(52) Erskine Caldwell Papers. Baker Library, Dartmouth College, Hanover NH.

(53) Farley, Benjamin W. "Erskine Caldwell: Preacher's Son and Southern Prophet." *Journal of Presbyterian History* 56 (1978): 202-17.

(54) Klevar, Harvey. "Some Things Holy in a Forsaken Land." *Pembroke Magazine* 11 (1979): 65-76.

(55) Tharpe, Jac. "Interview with Erskine Caldwell." *Southern Quarterly* 20 (1981): 64-74.

(56) Thompson, James J., Jr. "Erskine Caldwell and Southern Religion." *Southern Humanities Review* 5 (1971): 33-44.

IV. SOUTHERN LITERATURE AND RELIGION: THE WORK OF WILLIAM FAULKNER

(57) Alsen, Eberhard. "An Existentialist Reading of Faulkner's 'Pantaloon in Black'." *Studies in Short Fiction* 14 (1977): 169-78.

(58) Asals, Frederick. "Faulkner's *Light in August*." *Explicator* 26 (1965): Item 74.

(59) Baker, Carlos. "The Doomed and the Damned: Faulkner's Young Rebels." In *The Young Rebel in American Literature*. Carl Bode, ed., 145-69. New York: Praeger, 1960.

(60) _____. "The Place of the Bible in American Fiction." In *Religious Perspectives in American Culture*. James Ward Smith and A. Leland Jamison, eds., 243-72. Princeton: Princeton University Press, 1961.

(61) Barth, J. Robert, ed. *Religious Perspectives in Faulkner's Fiction: Yoknapatawpha and Beyond*. Notre Dame: University of Notre Dame Press, 1972.

(62) Bedell, George C. *Kierkegaard and Faulkner: Modalities of Existence*. Baton Rouge: Louisiana State University Press, 1972.

(63) Beebe, Maurice. "Criticism of William Faulkner: A Selected Checklist." *Modern Fiction Studies* 13 (1967): 115-61.

(64) Bjork, Lennart. "Ancient Myths and the Moral Framework of *Absalom, Absalom!*." *American Literature* 35 (1963): 196-204.

(65) Brooks, Cleanth. *The Hidden God: Studies in Hemingway, Faulkner, Yeats, Eliot, and Warren*. New Haven: Yale University Press, 1963.

(66) _____. *William Faulkner: First Encounters*. New Haven: Yale University Press, 1983.

(67) _____. *William Faulkner: The Yoknapatawpha Country*. New Haven: Yale University Press, 1963.

(68) _____. *William Faulkner: Toward Yoknapatawpha and Beyond*. New Haven: Yale University Press, 1978.

(69) _____. "William Faulkner: Vision of Good and Evil." In *Religion and Modern Literature*. G. B. Tennyson and E. E. Ericson, eds., 310-15. Grand Rapids: William B. Eerdmans, 1975.

(70) Burton, Dolores M. "Intonation Patterns of Sermons in Seven Novels." *Language and Style* 3 (1970): 205-20.

(71) Cabaniss, Allen. *Liturgy and Literature: Selected Essays*. University AL: University of Alabama Press, 1970.

(72) Campbell, Harry M., and Ruel E. Foster. *William Faulkner: A Critical Appraisal*. Norman: University of Oklahoma Press, 1951.

(73) Carey, Glenn O. "*Light in August* and Religious Fanaticism." *Studies in the Twentieth Century* 10 (1972): 101-13.

(74) Carpenter, R. C. "Faulkner's *Sartoris*." *Explicator* 14,7 (1956): Item 41.

(75) Chittick, Kathryn A. "The Fables in William Faulkner's *A Fable*." *Mississippi Quarterly* 30 (1977): 403-15.

(76) Coffee, Jessie A. *Faulkner's Un-Christlike Christians: Biblical Allusions in the Novels*. Ann Arbor: UMI Research Press, 1983.

(77) Cottrell, Buchman W. "Christian Symbolism in 'Light in August'." *Modern Fiction Studies* 2 (1956-57): 207-13.

(78) Culley, Margaret M. ''Judgment in Yoknapatawpha Fiction.'' *Renascence* 28 (1976): 59-70.

(79) Dickerson, Mary Jane. ''Some Sources of Faulkner's Myths in *As I Lay Dying.*'' *Mississippi Quarterly* 19 (1966): 132-42.

(80) Douglas, Harold J., and Robert Daniel. ''Faulkner and the Puritanism of the South.'' *Tennessee Studies in Literature* 2 (1957): 1-13.

(81) Ficken, Carl. ''The Christ Story in *A Fable.*'' *Mississippi Quarterly* 23 (1970): 251-64.

(82) Fletcher, Mary Dell. ''Edenic Images in *The Sound and the Fury.*'' *South Central Bulletin* (Studies by Members of the SCMLA) 40 (1980): 142-44.

(83) _____. ''William Faulkner and Residual Calvinism.'' *Southern Studies* 18 (1979): 199-216.

(84) Fowler, Doreen F. ''Faith As a Unifying Principle in Faulkner's *Light in August.*'' *Tennessee Studies in Literature* 21 (1976): 49-57.

(85) Giermanski, James R. ''William Faulkner's Use of the Confessional.'' *Renascence* 21 (1969): 119-23, 166.

(86) Gold, Joseph. '' 'Sin, Salvation and Bananas': *As I Lay Dying.*'' *Mosaic* 7 (1973): 55-73.

(87) Grant, William E. ''Benjy's Branch: Symbolic Method in Part I of *The Sound and the Fury.*'' *Texas Studies in Literature and Language* 13 (1972): 705-710.

(88) Griffith, Benjamin W. III. ''Calvinism in Faulkner's *Light in August.*'' *Bulletin of the Center for the Study of Southern Culture and Religion* 2 (1978): 8-10.

(89) Hagopian, John V. ''The Biblical Background of Faulkner's *Absalom, Absalom!.*'' *CEA Critic* 36 (1974): 22-24.

(90) Hartt, Julian N. ''Some Reflections on Faulkner's Fable.'' *Religion in Life* 24 (1955): 601-607.

(91) Haury, Beth B. ''The Influence of Robinson Jeffers' 'Tamor' on *Absalom, Absalom!.*'' *Mississippi Quarterly* 25 (1972): 356-68.

(92) Hoffman, Frederick J., and Olga W. Vickery, eds. *William Faulkner: Three Decades of Criticism.* East Lansing: Michigan State University Press, 1960.

(93) Howe, Irving. *William Faulkner: A Critical Study.* New York: Random House, 1952.

(94) Howell, Elmo. ''Faulkner's Country Church: A Note on 'Shingles for the Lord'.'' *Mississippi Quarterly* 21 (1968): 205-210.

(95) _____. ''William Faulkner, the Substance of Faith.'' *Brigham Young University Studies* 9 (1969): 453-62.

(96) Hunt, John W. *William Faulkner: Art in Theological Tension.* Syracuse: Syracuse University Press, 1965.

(97) Ilacqua, Alma A. ''Faulkner's *Absalom, Absalom!:* An Aesthetic Projection of the Religious Sense of Beauty.'' *Ball State University Forum* 21 (1980): 34-41.

(98) _____. "From Purveyor of Perversion to Defender of the Faithful: A Summary of Critical Studies on Faulkner's Theological Vision." *Language Quarterly* 20 (1981): 35-38.

(99) James, Stuart. " 'I Lay My Hand on My Mouth': Religion in *Yoknapatawpha County*." *Illinois Quarterly* 40 (1977): 38-53.

(100) Jarrett-Kerr, Martin. *William Faulkner: A Critical Essay*. Contemporary Writers in Christian Perspective Series. Grand Rapids: William B. Eerdmans, 1970.

(101) Johnson, Robert L. "William Faulkner, Calvinism, and the Presbyterians." *Journal of Presbyterian History* 57 (1979): 66-81.

(102) Levins, Lynn G. *Faulkner's Heroic Design: The Yoknapatawpha Novels*. Athens: University of Georgia Press, 1976.

(103) Lewis, R. W. B. "The Hero in the New World: William Faulkner's *The Bear*." *Kenyon Review* 13 (1951): 641-60.

(104) Lind, Ilse Dusoir. "The Calvinistic Burden of 'Light in August'." *New England Quarterly* 30 (1957): 307-29.

(105) McClennen, Joshua. "William Faulkner and Christian Complacency." *Papers of the Mississippi Academy of Science, Arts, and Letters* 41 (1956): 315-22.

(106) McHaney, Thomas L. "Robinson Jeffers' 'Tamar' and *The Sound and the Fury*." *Mississippi Quarterly* 22 (1969): 261-63.

(107) _____. *William Faulkner: A Reference Guide*. Boston: G. K. Hall, 1976.

(108) Magee, Rosemary M. "*A Fable* and the Gospels: A Study in Contrasts." *Research Studies* 47 (1979): 98-107.

(109) Minter, David L., comp. *Twentieth Century Interpretations of "Light in August": A Collection of Critical Essays*. Englewood Cliffs: Prentice-Hall, 1970.

(110) _____. *William Faulkner: His Life and Work*. Baltimore: Johns Hopkins University Press, 1980.

(111) Morrison, Gail Moore. "Faulkner's Priests and Fitzgerald's 'Absolution'." *Mississippi Quarterly* 32 (1979): 461-65.

(112) Nolte, William H. "Mencken, Faulkner, and Southern Moralism." *South Carolina Review* 4 (1971): 45-61.

(113) O'Connor, William V. "Protestantism in Yoknapatawpha County." *Hopkins Review* 5,3 (1952): 26-42.

(114) O'Dea, Richard J. "Faulkner's Vestigial Christianity." *Renascence* 21 (1968): 44-54.

(115) Palumbo, Donald. "The Concept of God in Faulkner's *Light in August, The Sound and the Fury, As I Lay Dying*, and *Absalom, Absalom!*." *South Central Bulletin* (Studies by Members of the SCMLA) 34 (1979): 142-46.

(116) Penick, Edwin A., Jr. "A Theological Critique of the Interpretation of Man in the Fiction and Drama of William Faulkner, Ernest Hemingway, Jean-Paul Sartre, and Albert Camus." Ph.D. dissertation, Yale University, 1954.

(117) Polk, Noel. "Some Recent Books on Faulkner." *Studies in the Novel* 9 (1976): 201-210.

(118) Rose, Maxine. "Echoes of the King James Bible in the Prose Style of *Absalom, Absalom!*." *Arizona Quarterly* 37 (1981): 137-48.

(119) _____. "From Genesis to Revelation: The Grand Design of William Faulkner's *Absalom, Absalom!*." *Studies in American Fiction* 8 (1980): 219-28.

(120) Rosenberg, Bruce A. "The Oral Quality of Rev. Shegog's Sermon in William Faulkner's *The Sound and the Fury*." *Literatur in Wissenschaft und Unterricht* 2,2 (1969): 73-88.

(121) Sanderlin, Robert R. "*As I Lay Dying:* Christian Symbols and Thematic Implications." *Southern Quarterly* 7 (1969): 155-66.

(122) Seib, Kenneth. "Midrashic Legend in Faulkner's *As I Lay Dying*." *Notes on Modern American Literature* 2 (1977): Item 5.

(123) Smart, George K. *Religious Elements in Faulkner's Early Novels: A Selective Concordance*. Coral Gables FL: University of Miami Press, 1965.

(124) Spivey, Herman E. "Faulkner and the Adamic Myth: Faulkner's Moral Vision." *Modern Fiction Studies* 19 (1973-1974): 497-505.

(125) Strandberg, Victor. "Faulkner's God: A Jamesian Perspective." *Faulkner Studies* 1 (1980): 122-35.

(126) Swanson, William J. "William Faulkner and William Styron: Notes on Religion." *Cimarron Review* 7 (1969): 45-52.

(127) Swiggert, Peter. "Moral and Temporal Order in *The Sound and the Fury*." *Sewanee Review* 61 (1953): 221-37.

(128) Tanner, Stephen L. "*Light in August:* The Varieties of Religious Fanaticism." *Essays in Literature* 7 (1980): 79-90.

(129) Ulbrich, Armand H. "The Trend Toward Religion in the Modern American Novel, 1925-1951." Ph.D. dissertation, University of Michigan, 1953.

(130) Vickery, Olga W. *The Novels of William Faulkner: A Critical Interpretation*. Rev. ed. Baton Rouge: Louisiana State University Press, 1964.

(131) Waggoner, Hyatt H. *William Faulkner: From Jefferson to the World*. Lexington: University of Kentucky Press, 1959.

(132) _____. "William Faulkner's Passion Week of the Heart." In *The Tragic Vision and the Christian Faith*. Nathan A. Scott, ed. New York: Association Press, 1957.

V. SOUTHERN LITERATURE AND RELIGION:
THE WORK OF CAROLINE GORDON

(133) Brown, Ashley. "The Novel as Christian Comedy." In *Reality and Myth: Essays in American Literature in Memory of Richard Croom Beatty*. William E. Walker and Robert L. Walker, eds. Nashville: Vanderbilt University Press, 1964.

(134) Cheney, Brainard. "Caroline Gordon's Ontological Quest." *Renascence* 16 (1963): 3-12.

(135) Cowan, Louise. "Nature and Grace in Caroline Gordon." *Critique* 1 (1956): 11-27. Reprinted in *Studies in Medieval, Renaissance, American Literature: A Festschrift*. Betsy F. Colquitt, ed. Fort Worth: Texas Christian University Press, 1971.

(136) Golden, Robert E., and Mary C. Sullivan. *Flannery O'Connor and Caroline Gordon: A Reference Guide*. Boston: G. K. Hall, 1977.

(137) Rocks, James E. "The Christian Myth as Salvation: Caroline Gordon's *The Strange Children*." *Tulane Studies in English* 16 (1968): 149-60.

(138) Rubin, Larry. "Christian Allegory in Caroline Gordon's 'The Captive'." *Studies in Short Fiction* 5 (1968): 283-89.

VI. SOUTHERN LITERATURE AND RELIGION: THE WORK OF SIDNEY LANIER

(139) Mims, Edwin. *Great Writers as Interpreters of Religion*. New York and Nashville: Abingdon-Cokesbury Press, 1945.

(140) Moore, Lelia Z. "The Religious Element in Sidney Lanier's Works." M.A. thesis, University of Kansas, 1924.

(141) Watkins, Hortense. "A Study of the Religious Concepts of Sidney Lanier." M.A. thesis, Southern Methodist University, 1947.

(142) Weed, Marguerite. "The Ethical and Religious Beliefs of Sidney Lanier." M.A. thesis, Columbia University, 1932.

VII. SOUTHERN LITERATURE AND RELIGION: THE WORK OF FLANNERY O'CONNOR

(143) Allen, Suzanne. "Memories of a Southern Catholic Girlhood: Flannery O'-Connor's 'A Temple of the Holy Ghost'." *Renascence* 31 (1979): 83-92.

(144) Asals, Frederick. "The Double in Flannery O'Connor's Stories." *Flannery O'Connor Bulletin* 9 (1980): 49-86.

(145) Baumback, Jonathan. "The Acid of God's Grace: *Wise Blood* by Flannery O'Connor." In *The Landscape of Nightmares: Studies in the Contemporary American Novel*, 87-100. New York: New York University Press, 1965.

(146) Bellamy, Michael. "Everything Off Balance: Protestant Election in Flannery O'Connor's 'A Good Man Is Hard to Find'." *Flannery O'Connor Bulletin* 8 (1979): 116-24.

(147) Bergup, Sr. Bernice. "Themes of Redemptive Grace in the Works of Flannery O'Connor." *American Benedictine Review* 21 (1970): 169-91.

(148) Brinkmeyer, Robert H., Jr. "Borne Away by Violence: The Reader and Flannery O'Connor." *Southern Review* 15 (1979): 313-21.

(149) Browning, Preston M., Jr. *Flannery O'Connor*. Carbondale: Southern Illinois University Press, 1974.

(150) _____. "Flannery O'Connor and the Grotesque Recovery of the Holy." In *Adversity and Grace: Studies in Recent American Literature*. Nathan A. Scott, Jr., ed. Chicago: University of Chicago Press, 1968.

(151) _____. " 'Parker's Back': Flannery O'Connor's Iconography of Salvation by Profanity." *Studies in Short Fiction* 6 (1969): 525-35.

(152) Burns, Stuart L. "Freaks in a Circus Tent: Flannery O'Connor's Christ-haunted Characters." *Flannery O'Connor Bulletin* 1 (1972): 1-23.

(153) Casper, Leonard. "The Unspeakable Peacock: Apocalypse in Flannery O'-Connor." In *The Shaken Realist: Essays in Modern Literature in Honor of Frederick J. Hoffman.* Melvin J. Friedman and John Vickery, eds., 287-99. Baton Rouge: Louisiana State University Press, 1970.

(154) Chapin, John D. "Flannery O'Connor and the Rich Red River of Jesus' Blood." *Christianity and Literature* 25 (1976): 30-35.

(155) Choffrut-Faure, Patric. "Flannery O'Connor ou la Vision Eclatee." *Delta* 2 (1976): 33-51.

(156) Coulthard, A. R. "The Christian Writer and the New South: Or, Why Don't You Like Flannery O'Connor?" *Southern Humanities Review* 13 (1979): 79-83.

(157) Cunningham, Lawrence. "Catholic Sensibility and Southern Writers." *Bulletin of the Center for the Study of Southern Culture and Religion* 2 (1978): 7-10.

(158) Davies, Horton M. "Anagogical Signals in Flannery O'Connor's Fiction." *Thought* 55 (1980): 428-38.

(159) _____, and Marie-Helene Davies. "The God of Storm and Stillness: The Fiction of Flannery O'Connor and Frederick Buechner." *Religion in Life* 48 (1979): 188-96.

(160) Desmond, John F. "The Mystery of the Word and the Act: *The Violent Bear It Away.*" *American Benedictine Review* 24 (1973): 342-47.

(161) Detweiler, Robert. "The Curse of Christ in Flannery O'Connor's Fiction." *Comparative Literature Studies* 3 (1966): 235-45.

(162) Drake, Robert. " 'The Bleeding Stinking Mad Shadow of Jesus' in the Fiction of Flannery O'Connor." *Comparative Literature Studies* 3 (1966): 183-96.

(163) _____. "Flannery O'Connor." *Religion and Modern Literature.* G. B. Tennyson and E. E. Ericson, Jr., eds., 393-406. Grand Rapids: William B. Eerdmans, 1975.

(164) _____. *Flannery O'Connor: A Critical Essay.* Contemporary Writers in Christian Perspective Series. Grand Rapids: William B. Eerdmans, 1966.

(165) Dula, Martha A. "Evidences of the Prelapsarian in Flannery O'Connor's *Wise Blood.*" *Xavier University Studies* 11 (1972): 1-12.

(166) Eggenschwiler, David. *The Christian Humanism of Flannery O'Connor.* Detroit: Wayne State University Press, 1972.

(167) Feeley, Sr. Kathleen M. *Flannery O'Connor: Voice of the Peacock.* New Brunswick NJ: Rutgers University Press, 1972.

(168) *Flannery O'Connor et le realisme des lointains. Delta* 2 (1976).

(169) Friedman, Melvin J., and Lewis A. Lawson, eds. *The Added Dimension: The Art and Mind of Flannery O'Connor*. New York: Fordham University Press, 1966.

(170) Getz, Lorine M. *Nature and Grace in Flannery O'Connor's Fiction*. Lewiston NY: Edwin Mellen Press, 1982.

(171) Golden, Robert E., and Mary C. Sullivan. *Flannery O'Connor and Caroline Gordon: A Reference Guide*. Boston: G. K. Hall, 1977.

(172) Gordon, Caroline. "Heresy in Dixie." *Sewanee Review* 76 (1968): 262-98.

(173) Gossett, Thomas F. "No Vague Believer: Flannery O'Connor and Protestantism." *Southwest Review* 60 (1975): 256-63.

(174) Hawkins, Peter S. "Problems of Overstatement in Religious Fiction and Criticism." *Renascence* 33 (1980): 36-46.

(175) Howell, Elmo. "Flannery O'Connor and the Home Country." *Renascence* 24 (1972): 171-76.

(176) Hubert, Thomas. Review of *The Habit of Being*. *Christianity and Literature* 29 (1980): 73-74.

(177) Hyman, Stanley. *Flannery O'Connor*. University of Minnesota Pamphlets on American Writers 54. Minneapolis: University of Minnesota Press, 1966.

(178) Kellogg, Gene. "The Catholic Novel in Convergence." *Thought* 45 (1970): 265-96.

(179) _____. *The Vital Tradition: The Catholic Novel in a Period of Convergence*. Chicago: Loyola University Press, 1970.

(180) Kaplan, Carola. "Graham Greene's Pinkie Brown and Flannery O'Connor's Misfit: The Psychopathic Killer and the Mystery of God's Grace." *Renascence* 32 (1980): 116-28.

(181) Kim, Chrysostom. "A Do-It-Yourself Religion and the Grimly Comic in Flannery O'Connor." *American Benedictine Review* 31 (1980): 263-89.

(182) Kissel, Susan S. "Voices in the Wilderness: The Prophets of O'Connor, Percy, and Powers." In *Walker Percy: Art and Ethics*. Jac Tharpe, ed., 91-98. Jackson: University Press of Mississippi, 1980. Also in *Southern Quarterly* 18 (1980): 91-98.

(183) Koon, William. " 'Help Me Not to Be So Mean': Flannery O'Connor's Subjectivity." *Southern Review* 15 (1979): 322-32.

(184) Lesgoirres, Daniel. "*The Displaced Person* ou 'Le Christ Recrucife'." *Delta* 2 (1976): 75-87.

(185) Lorch, Thomas M. "Flannery O'Connor: Christian Allegorist." *Critique* 10,2 (1968): 69-80.

(186) McBride, Mary. "Paradise Not Regained: Flannery O'Connor's Unredeemed Pilgrims in the Garden of Evil." *South Central Bulletin* (Studies by Members of SCMLA) 40 (1980): 154-56.

(187) McCullagh, James C. "Aspects of Jansenism in Flannery O'Connor's *Wise Blood*." *Studies in the Humanities* 3 (1972): 12-16.

(188) _____. "Symbolism and the Religious Aesthetic: Flannery O'Connor's *Wise Blood*." *Flannery O'Connor Bulletin* 2 (1973): 43-58.

(189) McDonald, Henry. ''The Moral Meaning of Flannery O'Connor.'' *Modern Age* 24 (1980): 274-83.

(190) McFarland, Dorothy T. *Flannery O'Connor*. New York: Frederick Ungar, 1976.

(191) McGown, James H. ''Remembering Flannery O'Connor.'' *America* 141 (1979): 86-88.

(192) Mallon, Anne Marie. ''Mystic Quest in *The Violent Bear It Away*.'' *Flannery O'Connor Bulletin* 10 (1981): 54-69.

(193) Martin, Carter W. *The True Country: Themes in the Fiction of Flannery O'-Connor*. Nashville: Vanderbilt University Press, 1969.

(194) May, John R. *The Pruning Word: The Parables of Flannery O'Connor*. Notre Dame: University of Notre Dame Press, 1976.

(195) Mellard, James M. ''Violence and Belief in Mauriac and O'Connor.'' *Renascence* 26 (1974): 158-68.

(196) Milder, Robert. ''The Protestantism of Flannery O'Connor.'' *Southern Review* 11 (1975): 802-19.

(197) Millichap, Joseph R. ''The Pauline 'Old Man' in Flannery O'Connor's 'The Comforts of Home'.'' *Studies in Short Fiction* 11 (1974): 96-99.

(198) Montgomery, Marion. ''Flannery O'Connor and the Jansenist Problem in Fiction.'' *Southern Review* 14 (1978): 438-48.

(199) _____. ''Grace: A Tricky Fictional Agent.'' *Flannery O'Connor Bulletin* 9 (1980): 19-29.

(200) _____. ''Miss O'Connor and the Christ-Haunted.'' *Southern Review* 4 (1968): 665-72.

(201) _____. ''O'Connor and Teilhard de Chardin: The Problem of Evil.'' *Renascence* 22 (1969): 34-42.

(202) Mooney, Harry J., Jr. ''Moments of Eternity: A Study in the Short Stories of Flannery O'Connor.'' In *The Shapeless God: Essays on Modern Fiction*. Harry J. Mooney, Jr., and Thomas F. Staley, eds., 117-38. Pittsburgh: University of Pittsburgh Press, 1968.

(203) Muller, Gilbert H. *Nightmares and Visions: Flannery O'Connor and the Catholic Grotesque*. Athens: University of Georgia Press, 1972.

(204) Nisly, Paul W. ''Wart Hogs from Hell: The Demonic and the Holy in Flannery O'Connor's Fiction.'' *Ball State University Forum* 22 (1982): 45-50.

(205) O'Brien, John T. ''The Un-Christianity of Flannery O'Connor.'' *Listening* 5 (1971): 71-82.

(206) _____. ''Novelist and Believer.'' *Religion and Modern Fiction*. G. B. Tennyson and E. E. Ericson, Jr., eds. Grand Rapids: William B. Eerdmans, 1975.

(207) Oppegard, Susan H. ''Flannery O'Connor and the Backwards Prophets.'' *Americana-Norvegica* 4 (1973): 305-25.

(208) Orvell, Miles D. ''Flannery O'Connor.'' *Sewanee Review* 78 (1970): 184-92.

(209)   _____. *Invisible Parade: The Fiction of Flannery O'Connor*. Philadelphia: Temple University Press, 1972.

(210)   Regan, Robert. "The Legitimate Sources of Depravity in Flannery O'Connor." *Delta* 2 (1976): 53-59.

(211)   Rubin, Louis D. "Flannery O'Connor's Company of Southerners: or, 'The Artificial Nigger' Read as Fiction Rather than Theology." *Flannery O'-Connor Bulletin* 4 (1977): 47-71.

(212)   Scouten, Kenneth. " 'The Artificial Nigger': Mr. Head's Ironic Salvation." *Flannery O'Connor Bulletin* 9 (1980): 87-97.

(213)   Shields, John C. "Flannery O'Connor's 'Greenleaf' and the Myth of Europa and the Bull." *Studies in Short Fiction* 18 (1978): 421-31.

(214)   Shinn, Thelma J. "Flannery O'Connor and the Violence of Grace." *Contemporary Literature* 9 (1968): 58-73.

(215)   Slattery, Dennis P. "Faith in Search of an Image: The Iconic Dimension of Flannery O'Connor's 'Parker's Back'." *South Central Bulletin* (Studies by Members of SCMLA) 41 (1981): 120-33.

(216)   Smith, Francis J. "O'Connor's Religious Viewpoint in *The Violent Bear It Away. Renascence* 22 (1970): 108-12.

(217)   Sonnenfeld, Albert. "Flannery O'Connor: The Catholic Writer as Baptist." *Contemporary Literature* 13 (1972): 445-57.

(218)   Spencer, Marlene. "The Sacred and the Profane in Flannery O'Connor's 'The Comforts of Home'." *Bulletin of the Center for the Study of Southern Culture and Religion* 4 (1980): 32-34.

(219)   Spivey, Ted R. "Flannery O'Connor's View of God and Man." *Studies in Short Fiction* 1 (1964): 200-206.

(220)   _____. "Religion and Reintegration of Man in Flannery O'Connor and Walker Percy." *Spectrum* 2 (1972): 67-179.

(221)   Stephens, Martha. "Flannery O'Connor and the Sanctified-Sinner Tradition." *Arizona Quarterly* 24 (1968): 223-39.

(222)   Sullivan, Walter. "Flannery O'Connor, Sin, and Grace: *Everything That Rises Must Converge." Hollins Criticism* 2,4 (1965): 1-8, 10.

(223)   Tolomeo, Diane. "Flannery O'Connor's 'Revelation' and the Book of Job." *Renascence* 30 (1978): 78-90.

(224)   Trowbridge, Clinton W. "The Symbolic Vision of Flannery O'Connor: Patterns of Imagery in *The Violent Bear It Away." Sewanee Review* 76 (1968): 298-319.

(225)   Vande Kieft, Ruth. "Judgment in the Fiction of Flannery O'Connor." *Sewanee Review* 76 (1968): 337-56.

(226)   Walden, Daniel, and Jane Salvia. "Flannery O'Connor's Dragon Vision in 'A Temple of the Holy Ghost'." *Studies in American Fiction* 4 (1976): 230-35.

(227)   Walters, Dorothy. *Flannery O'Connor*. Twayne's U.S. Author's Series 216. New York: Twayne, 1973.

(228) Wasserman, Renata R. "Backwards to Nineveh." *Renascence* 32 (1979): 21-32.

(229) Weaver, Mary Jo. "Thomas Merton and Flannery O'Connor: The Urgency of Vision." *Religion in Life* 48 (1979): 449-61.

(230) Wood, Ralph C. "The Heterodoxy of Flannery O'Connor's Book Reviews." *Flannery O'Connor Bulletin* 5 (1976): 3-29.

(231) Zaidman, Laura M. "Varieties of Religious Experience in O'Connor and West." *Flannery O'Connor Bulletin* 7 (1978): 26-46.

VIII. SOUTHERN LITERATURE AND RELIGION: THE WORK OF WALKER PERCY

(232) Atkins, Anselm. "Walker Percy and Post-Christian Search." *Centennial Review* 12 (1968): 73-95.

(233) Barrett, Deborah J. "Discourse and Intercourse: The Conversion of the Priest in Percy's *Lancelot*." *Critique* 23,2 (1981-1982): 5-12.

(234) Brinkmeyer, Robert H., Jr. "Percy's Bludgeon: Message and Narrative Strategy." In *Walker Percy: Art and Ethics*. Jac Tharpe, ed., 80-90. Jackson: University Press of Mississippi, 1980. Also *Southern Quarterly* 18 (1980): 80-90.

(235) Cashin, Edward J. "History as Mores: Walker Percy's *Lancelot*." *Georgia Review* 31 (1977): 875-80.

(236) Coles, Robert. *Walker Percy: An American Search*. Boston: Little, Brown, 1978.

(237) Cunningham, John. " 'The Thread in the Labyrinth': *Love in the Ruins* and One Tradition of Comedy." *South Carolina Review* 13 (1981): 28-34.

(238) Cunningham, Lawrence. "Catholic Sensibility and Southern Writers." *Bulletin of the Center for the Study of Southern Culture and Religion* 2 (1978): 7-10.

(239) Daniel, Robert D. "Walker Percy's *Lancelot*: Secular Raving and Religious Salience." *Southern Review* 14 (1978): 186-94.

(240) Dewey, Bradley R. "Walker Percy Talks about Kierkegaard: An Annotated Interview." *Journal of Religion* 54 (1974): 273-98.

(241) Douglas, Ellen. *Walker Percy's The Last Gentleman*. Religious Dimensions in Literature, Seabury Reading Program. New York: Seabury Press, 1969.

(242) Gaston, Paul L. "The Revelation of Walker Percy." *The Colorado Quarterly* 20 (1972): 459-70.

(243) Godshalk, William L. "Walker Percy's Christian Vision." *Louisiana Studies* 13 (1974): 130-41.

(244) Gretlund, Jan Nordby. "Interview with Walker Percy." *South Carolina Review* 13 (1981): 3-12.

(245) Griffith, Thomas. "Moral Tales for a Depraved Age." *Atlantic Monthly* 240 (1977): 20-21.

(246) Hawkins, Peter S. "Problems of Overstatement in Religious Fiction and Criticism." *Renascence* 33 (1980): 36-46.

(247) Kissel, Susan S. "Voices in the Wilderness: The Prophets of O'Connor, Percy, and Powers." *Walker Percy: Art and Ethics*. Jac Tharpe ed., 91-98. Jackson: University Press of Mississippi, 1980. Also in *Southern Quarterly* 18 (1980): 91-98.

(248) Lauder, R. E. "The Catholic Novel and the 'Insider God'." *Commonweal* 51 (25 October 1974): 78-81.

(249) Lawson, Lewis A. "The Fall of the House of Lamar." In *The Art of Walker Percy*. Panthea Reid Broughton, ed., 219-44. Baton Rouge: Louisiana State University Press, 1979.

(250) _____. "Tom More: Cartesian Physician." *Delta* 13 (1981): 67-82.

(251) LeClair, Thomas. "The Eschatological Vision of Walker Percy." *Renascence* 26 (1974): 1115-22.

(252) _____. "Walker Percy's Devil." *Southern Literary Journal* 10 (1977): 3-13.

(253) Lehan, Richard. "The Way Back: Redemption in the Novels of Walker Percy." *Sewanee Review,* new series 4 (1968): 306-19.

(254) Quagliano, Anthony. "Existential Modes in *The Moviegoer*." *Research Studies* 45 (1977): 214-23.

(255) Samway, Patrick. "A Rahnerian Backdrop to Percy's *The Second Coming*." *Delta* 13 (1981): 127-44.

(256) Spivey, Ted A. "Religion and Reintegration of Man in Flannery O'Connor and Walker Percy." *Spectrum* 2 (1972): 67-179.

(257) Stelzmann, Rainulf A. "Das Schwert Christi: Zwei Versuche Walker Percys." *Stimmen der Zeit* 195 (1977): 641-43.

(258) Tanner, Tony. *The Reign of Wonder: Naivety and Reality in American Literature*. Cambridge: Cambridge University Press, 1965.

(259) "Walker Percy: A Selected Bibliography." *Delta* 13 (1981): 177-87.

(260) Weixlmann, Joe, and Daniel H. Gann. "A Walker Percy Bibliography." *Walker Percy: Art and Ethics*. Jac Tharpe, ed., 137-57. Jackson: University Press of Mississippi, 1980. Also in *Southern Quarterly* 18 (1980): 137-57.

(261) Zeugner, John F. "Walker Percy and Gabriel Marcel: The Castaway and the Wayfarer." *Mississippi Quarterly* 28 (1974-1975): 21-53.

IX. SOUTHERN LITERATURE AND RELIGION: THE WORK OF EDGAR ALLAN POE

(262) Banta, Martha. "American Apocalypses: Excrement and Ennui." *Studies in the Literary Imagination* 7 (1974): 1-30.

(263) Casale, Ottavio M. "Poe on Transcendentalism." *Emerson Society Quarterly* 50 (1968): 85-97.

(264) Claudel, Alice M. "Poe as Voyager in 'To Helen'." *Emerson Society Quarterly* 60 (Fall 1970, Part I, supplement): 33-37.

(265) Dameron, J. Lasley, and Irby B. Cauthen, Jr. *Edgar Allen Poe: A Bibliography of Criticism*. Charlottesville VA: University Press of Virginia, 1974. Supersedes Dameron, *Edgar Allan Poe: A Checklist of Criticism, 1942-1960*. Charlottesville: Bibliographical Society of the University of Virginia, 1966, and Charlottesville: University Press of Virginia, 1968.

(266) _____. "Edgar Allan Poe in the Mid-Twentieth Century: His Literary Reputation in England and America, 1928-1960." Ph.D. dissertation, University of Tennessee, 1961.

(267) Daniel, Robert. "Odes to Dejection." *Kenyon Review* 15 (1953): 129-40.

(268) Davidson, Edward. *Poe: A Critical Study*. Cambridge: Belknap Press of the Harvard University Press, 1957.

(269) Garrett, Walter. "The 'Moral' of 'Ligeia' Reconsidered." *Poe Studies* 4 (1971): 19-20.

(270) Halline, Allan G. "Moral and Religious Concepts in Poe." *Bucknell University Studies* 2 (1951): 126-50.

(271) Harris, Kathryn M. "Ironic Revenge in Poe's 'The Cask of Amontillado'." *Studies in Short Fiction* 6 (1969): 333-35.

(272) Hirsch, David H. "The Pit and the Apocalypse." *Sewanee Review* 76 (1968): 632-52.

(273) Hoffman, Daniel. *Poe Poe Poe Poe Poe Poe Poe*. Garden City: Doubleday, 1972.

(274) Jungman, Robert E., and Charles A. Sweet. "Demonology in 'The Raven'." *Tennessee Folklore Society Bulletin* 43 (1977): 65-66.

(275) Lecompte, C. "*L'Homeo-Camelopard* ou la mort de Dieu." *Delta* 1 (1975): 83-94.

(276) Miller, Perry. *The Raven and the Whale*. New York: Harcourt, Brace, 1956.

(277) Partridge, Claire E. "Religious Tendencies of Edgar Allan Poe." M.A. thesis, Boston University, 1931.

(278) *Poe Studies*. Contains periodic bibliographies of secondary literature.

(279) Reed, Kenneth T. " 'Ligeia': The Story as Sermon." *Poe Studies* 4 (1971): 20.

(280) Scharnhorst, Gary. "Images of the Millerites in American Literature." *American Quarterly* 32 (1980): 19-36.

(281) Serio, John N. "From Edwards to Poe." *Connecticut Review* 6 (1972): 88-92.

(282) Stromberg, Jean S. "The Relation of Christian Concepts to Poe's *Grotesque Tales*." *Gordon Review* 11 (1968): 144-58.

(283) Thorpe, Dwayne. "Poe's 'The City in the Sea': Source and Interpretation." *American Literature* 51 (1979): 394-99.

(284) Zanger, Jules. " 'The Pit and the Pendulum' and American Revivalism." *Religion in Life* 49 (1980): 96-105.

X. SOUTHERN LITERATURE AND RELIGION:
THE WORK OF KATHERINE ANNE PORTER

(285) Gottfried, Leon. "Death's Other Kingdom: Dantesque and Theological

Symbolism in 'Flowering Judas'." *Publications of the Modern Language Association* 84 (1969): 112-24.

(286) Kiernan, Robert F. *Katherine Anne Porter and Carson McCullers: A Reference Guide.* Boston: G. K. Hall, 1976.

(287) Waldrip, Louise, and Shirley Ann Bauer. *A Bibliography of the Works of Katherine Anne Porter and A Bibliography of the Criticism of the Works of Katherine Anne Porter.* Metuchen NJ: Scarecrow Press, 1969.

XI. SOUTHERN LITERATURE AND RELIGION: THE WORK OF JOHN CROWE RANSOM

(288) Elliott, Emory B., Jr. "Theology and Agrarian Ideology in the Critical Theory of John Crowe Ransom." *Xavier University Studies* 10 (1971): 1-7.

(289) Knoll, Wayne A. "Ransom as Religionist." *Mississippi Quarterly* 30 (1976-77): 111-36.

(290) Young, Thomas D. "John Crowe Ransom: A Checklist, 1967-1976." *Mississippi Quarterly* 30 (1976-77): 155-68.

(291) _____. *John Crowe Ransom: An Annotated Bibliography.* New York: Garland Publications, 1982.

(292) _____, ed. *John Crowe Ransom: Critical Essays and a Bibliography.* Baton Rouge: Louisiana State University Press, 1968.

XII. SOUTHERN LITERATURE AND RELIGION: THE WORK OF ABRAM J. RYAN

(293) Boldrick, Msgr. C. C. "Father Abram J. Ryan: 'The Poet-Priest of the Confederacy'." *Filson Club Historical Quarterly* 46 (1972): 201-18.

(294) Heagney, H. J. "Recollections of Father Ryan." *Catholic World* 126 (1928): 497-504.

(295) Kennedy, Thomas. *Father Ryan: The Irish-American Poet-Priest of the Southern States.* Dublin: J. J. Lalor, n.d.

(296) Lipscomb, Oscar H. "Some Unpublished Poems of Abram J. Ryan." *Alabama Review* 25 (1972): 163-77.

(297) Lovett, Howard M. "Father Ryan of the South." *Commonweal* 10 (1929): 503-504.

(298) Simms, L. Moody, Jr. "Father Abram Joseph Ryan: Poet of the Lost Cause." *Lincoln Herald* 73 (1971): 3-7.

(299) Toomey, John D. "Priest, Poet, and Hero." *Columbia* 17 (1938): 10.

(300) Weaver, Gordon, ed. *Selected Poems of Father Ryan.* Jackson: University and College Press of Mississippi, 1973.

(301) White, Kate. "Father Ryan, the Poet-Priest of the South." *South Atlantic Quarterly* 18 (1919): 69-74.

XIII. SOUTHERN LITERATURE AND RELIGION: THE WORK OF WILLIAM STYRON

(302) Cannon, Patricia R. "Nat Turner: God, Man, or Beast?" *Barat Review* 6 (1971): 25-28.

(303) Fossum, Robert H. *William Styron: A Critical Essay*. Contemporary Writers in Christian Perspective Series. Grand Rapids: William B. Eerdmans, 1968.

(304) Kort, Wesley A. *Shriven Selves: Religious Problems in Recent American Fiction*. Philadelphia: Fortress Press, 1972.

(305) Lang, John. "The Alpha and the Omega: Styron's *The Confessions of Nat Turner*." *American Literature* 53 (1981): 499-503.

(306) Lawson, Lewis A. "Cass Kinsolving: Kierkegaardian Man of Despair." *Wisconsin Studies in Contemporary Literature* 3 (1962): 54-66.

(307) Leon, Philip W. *William Styron: An Annotated Bibliography of Criticism*. Westport CT: Greenwood Press, 1978.

(308) McGill, William J. "William Styron's Nat Turner and Religion." *South Atlantic Quarterly* 79 (1980): 75-81.

(309) Morris, Robert K., and Irving Malin, eds. *The Achievement of William Styron*. 2d ed. Athens GA: University of Georgia Press, 1981.

(310) Pinsker, Sanford S. "Christ as Revolutionary/Revolutionary as Christ: The Hero in Bernard Malamud's *The Fixer* and William Styron's *The Confessions of Nat Turner*." *Barat Review* 6 (1971): 29-37.

(311) Swanson, William J. "Religious Implications in *The Confessions of Nat Turner*." *Cimarron Review* 12 (1970): 57-66.

(312) _____. "William Faulkner and William Styron: Notes on Religion." *Cimarron Review* 7 (1969): 45-52.

(313) Via, Dan O., Jr. "Law as Grace in Styron's *Set This House on Fire*." *Journal of Religion* 57 (1971): 125-36.

XIV. SOUTHERN LITERATURE AND RELIGION: THE WORK OF JOHN BANISTER TABB

(314) Bregy, K. "Of Father Tabb." *Catholic World* 114 (1921): 308-18.

(315) Finn, Sr. Mary Paulina. *John Banister Tabb: The Priest-Poet*. Washington: Published for Georgetown Visitation Convent, 1915.

(316) Humiliata, Sr. Mary. "Religion and Nature in Father Tabb's Poetry." *Catholic World* 165 (1947): 330-36.

(317) Kelly, J. B. "Poetry of a Priest." *Catholic World* 103 (1916): 228-33.

(318) Meynell, Alice. "Father Tabb as a Poet." *Catholic World* 90 (1910): 577-82.

XV. SOUTHERN LITERATURE AND RELIGION: THE WORK OF MARK TWAIN

(319) Arner, Robert D. "Acts Seventeen and *Huckleberry Finn:* A Note on Silas Phelps' Sermon." *Mark Twain Journal* 16 (1972): 12.

(320) Bendixen, Arthur A. "Huck Finn and Pilgrim's Progress." *Mark Twain Journal* 18 (1976-1977): 21.

(321) Brodwin, Stanley. "Blackness and the Adamic Myth in Twain's *Pudd'nead*." *Texas Studies in Literature and Language* 15 (1973): 167-76.

(322) _____. "The Humor of the Absurd: Mark Twain's Adamic Diaries." *Criticism* 14 (1972): 49-64.

(323) _____. "Mark Twain's Masks of Satan: The Final Phase." *American Literature* 45 (1973): 206-27.

(324) _____. "The Theology of Mark Twain: Banished Adam and the Bible." *Mississippi Quarterly* 29 (1976): 167-89.

(325) Brooks, Van Wyck. *The Ordeal of Mark Twain*. New York: E. P. Dutton, 1920.

(326) Byers, John R., Jr. "Miss Emmeline Grangerford's Hymn Book." *American Literature* 43 (1971): 259-63.

(327) _____. "The Pokeville Preacher's Invitation in *Huckleberry Finn*." *Mark Twain Journal* 18 (1977): 15-16.

(328) Cracroft, Richard H. "Distorting Polygamy for Fun and Profit: Artemus Ward and Mark Twain Among the Mormons." *Brigham Young University Studies* 14 (1974): 272-88.

(329) _____. "The Gentle Blasphemer: Mark Twain, Holy Scripture and the Book of Mormon." *Brigham Young University Studies* 11 (1971): 119-40.

(330) Delaney, Paul. "The Avatars of the Mysterious Stranger: Mark Twain's Images of Christ." *Christianity and Literature* 24 (1974): 25-38.

(331) Ditsky, John M. "Mark Twain and the Great Dark: Religion in *Letters from the Earth*." *Mark Twain Journal* 17 (1975): 12-19.

(332) Ensor, Allison. *Mark Twain and the Bible*. Lexington: University Press of Kentucky, 1969.

(333) _____. "Mark Twain's Yankee and the Prophets of Baal." *American Literary Realism* 14 (1981): 38-42.

(334) Feeney, Joseph J. "Darkness at Morning: The Bitterness in Mark Twain's Early Novel *Tom Sawyer*." *Mark Twain Journal* 19 (1978-1979): 4-5.

(335) Frederick, John T. *The Darkened Sky: Nineteenth Century American Novelists and Religion*. Notre Dame: University of Notre Dame Press, 1969.

(336) Geismar, Maxwell, ed. *Mark Twain and the Three R's*. Indianapolis: Bobbs-Merrill, 1971.

(337) Hill, Hamlin. *Mark Twain: God's Fool*. New York: Harper and Row, 1973.

(338) Hoffman, Daniel. *Form and Fable in American Fiction*. New York: Oxford University Press, 1961.

(339) Howell, Elmo. "Tom Sawyer's Mock Funeral: A Note on Mark Twain's Religion." *Mark Twain Journal* 16 (1972): 15-16.

(340) Hunter, Lloyd A. "Mark Twain and the Southern Evangelical Mind." *Missouri Historical Society Bulletin* 33 (1977): 246-64.

(341) Kaplan, Justin, comp. *Mark Twain: A Profile*. New York: Hill and Wang, 1968.

(342) _____. *Mark Twain and His World*. New York: Simon and Schuster, 1974.

(343) _____. *Mr. Clemens and Mark Twain: A Biography*. New York: Simon and Schuster, 1966.

(344) Kerr, Howard. *Mediums, and Spirit-Rappers, and Roaring Radicals: Spiritualism in American Literature, 1850-1900*. Urbana: University of Illinois Press, 1972.

(345) McCarthy, Harold T. "Mark Twain's Pilgrim's Progress: *The Innocents Abroad*." *Arizona Quarterly* 26 (1970): 249-58.

(346) McCullough, Joseph B. "Uses of the Bible in *Huckleberry Finn*." *Mark Twain Journal* 19 (1978-1979): 2-3.

(347) McDermott, John F. "Mark Twain and the Bible." *Papers on Literature and Language* 4 (1968): 195-98.

(348) Mark Twain Papers. University of California at Berkeley, Berkeley CA, and University of Virginia, Charlottesville VA.

(349) Marx, Leo. " 'Noble Shit': The Uncivil Response of American Writers to Civil Religion in America." *Massachusetts Review* 14 (1973): 709-39.

(350) Michelson, Bruce. "Dens Ludens: The Shaping of Mark Twain's Mysterious Stranger." *Novel* 14 (1980): 44-56.

(351) Miller, Bruce E. "*Huckleberry Finn:* The Kierkegaardian Dimension." *Illinois Quarterly* 34 (1971): 55-64.

(352) Millichap, Joseph R. "Calvinistic Attitudes and Pauline Imagery in *Huckleberry Finn*." *Mark Twain Journal* 16 (1971-1972): 8-10.

(353) Nibbelink, Herman. "Mark Twain and the Mormons." *Mark Twain Journal* 17 (1973-1974): 1-5.

(354) Paine, Albert B. *Mark Twain, a Biography: The Personal and Literary Life of Samuel Langhorne Clemens*. 3 vols. New York: Harper and Brothers, 1912.

(355) Rucker, Mary E. "Moralism and Determinism in 'The Man That Corrupted Hadleyburg'." *Studies in Short Fiction* 14 (1977): 49-54.

(356) Rule, Henry B. "The Role of Satan in 'The Man That Corrupted Hadleyburg'." *Studies in Short Fiction* 6 (1969): 619-29.

(357) Schwartz, Thomas D. "Mark Twain and Robert Ingersoll: The Freethought Connection." *American Literature* 48 (1976): 183-93.

(358) Smith, Henry Nash, ed. *Mark Twain: A Collection of Critical Essays*. Englewood Cliffs NJ: Prentice-Hall, 1963.

(359) _____. *Mark Twain: The Development of a Writer*. Cambridge MA: Belknap Press of Harvard University Press, 1962.

(360) Walker, Franklin. *Irreverent Pilgrims: Melville, Browne, and Mark Twain in the Holy Land*. Seattle: University of Washington Press, 1974.

(361) Werge, Thomas. "Mark Twain and the Fall of Adam." *Mark Twain Journal* 15 (1970): 5-13.

(362) _____. "The Sin of Hypocrisy in 'The Man That Corrupted Hadleyburg' and 'Inferno XIII'." *Mark Twain Journal* 18 (1975-1976): 17-18.

(363) Wilson, James D. "*Adventures of Huckleberry Finn:* From Abstraction to Humanity." *Southern Review* 10 (1974): 80-94.

(364) _____. "In Quest of Redemptive Vision: Mark Twain's *Joan of Arc*." *Texas Studies in Language and Literature* 20 (1978): 181-98.

XVI. SOUTHERN LITERATURE AND RELIGION: THE WORK OF ROBERT PENN WARREN

(365) Brooks, Cleanth. *The Hidden God: Studies in Hemingway, Faulkner, Yeats, Eliot, and Warren*. New Haven: Yale University Press, 1963.

(366) Clements, A. L. "Sacramental Vision: The Poetry of Robert Penn Warren." *South Atlantic Bulletin* 43 (1978): 47-65.

(367) Longley, John L., Jr. *Robert Penn Warren*. Southern Writers Series 2. Austin: Steck-Vaughn, 1969.

(368) Moore, L. Hugh, Jr. "Robert Penn Warren and the Terror of Answered Prayer." *Mississippi Quarterly* 21 (1967-68): 29-36.

(369) Nakadate: Neil. *Robert Penn Warren: A Research Guide*. Boston: G. K. Hall, 1977.

(370) Rubin, Louis D., Jr. "The Eye of Time: Religious Themes in Robert Penn Warren's Poetry." *Diliman Review* 4 (1958): 215-37.

(371) Shepherd, Allen. "Robert Penn Warren as a Philosophical Novelist." *Western Humanities Review* 24 (1970): 157-68.

(372) Strandberg, Victor H. *The Poetic Vision of Robert Penn Warren*. Lexington: University Press of Kentucky, 1977.

(373) Witte, Flo. "Adam's Rebirth in Robert Penn Warren's *Wilderness*." *Southern Quarterly* 12 (1974): 365-77.

XVII. SOUTHERN LITERATURE AND RELIGION: THE WORK OF EUDORA WELTY

(374) *Eudora Welty Newsletter*. Contains periodic bibliography of secondary materials.

(375) Eudora Welty Manuscripts. Mississippi Department of Archives and History.

(376) Gross, Seymour L. "Eudora Welty: A Bibliography of Criticism and Comment." *Secretary's News Sheet,* Bibliographical Society, University of Virginia, 45 (April 1960): 1-32.

(377) Isaacs, Neil D. *Eudora Welty*. Southern Writers Series 8. Austin: Steck-Vaughn, 1969.

(378) Thompson, Victor H. *Eudora Welty: A Reference Guide*. Boston: G. K. Hall, 1976.

XVIII. SOUTHERN LITERATURE AND RELIGION:
THE WORK OF TENNESSEE WILLIAMS

(379) Adler, Thomas P. "The Search for God in the Plays of Tennessee Williams." *Renascence* 26 (1973): 48-56.

(380) Blitgen, Sr. M. Carol. "Tennessee Williams: Modern Idolater." *Renascence* 22 (1970): 192-97.

(381) Houston, Neal B. "Meaning by Analogy in *Suddenly Last Summer.*" *Notes on Modern American Literature* 4 (1980): Item 24.

(382) Kunkel, F. L. "Tennessee Williams and the Death of God." *Commonweal* 87 (1968): 614-17.

XIX. SOUTHERN LITERATURE AND RELIGION:
THE WORK OF THOMAS WOLFE

(383) Phillipson, John S. *Thomas Wolfe: A Reference Guide*. Boston: G. K. Hall, 1977.

(384) Ribalow, Harold U. "Of Jews and Thomas Wolfe." *Chicago Jewish Forum* 13 (1954-1955): 89-99.

(385) Singh, Hari. "Thomas Wolfe: The Idea of Eternity." *South Carolina Review* 1 (1969): 40-47.

(386) Trotti, John Boone. "Thomas Wolfe: The Presbyterian Connection." *Journal of Presbyterian History* 59 (1981): 517-42.

XX. SOUTHERN LITERATURE AND RELIGION:
THE WORK OF RICHARD WRIGHT

(387) Killinger, John. *The Fragile Presence: Transcendence in Modern Literature*. Philadelphia: Fortress Press, 1973.

(388) Lawson, Lewis A. "Cross Demon: Kierkegaardian Man of Dread." *College Language Association Journal* 14 (1971): 298-316.

(389) May, John R., S.J. "Images of Apocalypse in the Black Novel." *Renascence* 23 (1970): 31-45.

(390) Savory, Jerold J. "Bigger Thomas and the Book of Job: The Epigraph to *Native Son.*" *Negro American Literature Forum* 9 (1975): 55-56.

(391) _____. "Descent and Baptism in *Native Son, Invisible Man,* and *Dutchman.*" *Christian Scholar's Review* 3 (1973): 33-37.

(392) Scott, Nathan A., Jr. "Search for Beliefs: Fiction of Richard Wright." *University of Kansas City Review* 23 (1956): 19-24, 131-38.

(393) Singh, Raman K. "Christian Heroes and Anti-Heroes in Richard Wright's Fiction." *Negro American Literature Forum* 6 (1972): 99-104, 131.

XXI. SOUTHERN LITERATURE AND RELIGION:
THE WORK OF MISCELLANEOUS WRITERS

(394) Adams, Charlotte. "A Hebrew Poet of the South." *The Critic* 9 (28 December 1889).

(395) Allen, Blanche T. "An Analysis and Interpretation of Thirty-one Poems of James Weldon Johnson: Implications for Black Religious Experience." M.A. thesis, Howard University, 1971.

(396) Bregy, K. "Allen Tate, Paradoxical Pilgrim." *Catholic World* 188 (1954): 121-25.

(397) Christ, Carol P. *Diving Deep and Surfacing: Women Writers on Spiritual Quest*. Boston: Beacon Press, 1980.

(398) Chyet, Stanley. "Ludwig Lewisohn: The Years of Becoming." *American Jewish Archives* 12 (October 1959): 26 + .

(399) Cohen, Charles L. "The 'Liberty or Death' Speech: A Note on Religion and Revolutionary Rhetoric." *William and Mary Quarterly* 3d series 38 (1981): 702-17.

(400) Daniel, Robert. "Odes to Dejection." *Kenyon Review* 15 (1953): 129-40.

(401) Durham, Frank. "God or No God in *The Heart Is a Lonely Hunter*." *South Atlantic Quarterly* 56 (1957): 494-99.

(402) Farley, Benjamin W. "George W. Cable: Presbyterian Romancer, Reformer, Bible Teacher." *Journal of Presbyterian History* 58 (1980): 166-81.

(403) Fontenot, Chester J. "Ishmael Reed and the Politics of Aesthetics, or Shake Hands and Come Out Conjuring." *Black American Literature Forum* 12 (1978): 20-23.

(404) French, Warren. "One Hundred Years of a Religious Best-Seller." *Western Humanities Review* 10 (1955-56): 45-54.

(405) Gillis, Adolph. *Ludwig Lewisohn: The Artist and His Message*. New York: Duffield and Green, 1933.

(406) Gundersen, Joan R. "Anthony Gavin's *A Master-Key to Popery:* A Virginia Parson's Best Seller." *Virginia Magazine of History and Biography* 82 (1974): 39-46.

(407) Harby, Lee. "Penina Moise: Woman and Writer." *American Jewish Year Book* 7 (1905-1906): New York: Jewish Publication Society of America, 1906.

(408) Killingsworth, M. Jimmie. "The Reverend Michael Smith's Contribution to Colonial Literary History." *Historical Magazine of the Protestant Episcopal Church* 50 (1981): 369-76.

(409) Leavell, Frank H. Review of *If I Were Seventeen Again and Other Essays*. *Register of the Kentucky Historical Society* 79 (1981): 180-81.

(410) Margolis, Edward. "The Negro Church: James Baldwin and the Christian Vision." In *Native Sons: A Critical Study of Twentieth Century Negro-American Authors*. Philadelphia: J. B. Lippincott, 1969.

(411) Moise, Penina. *Secular and Religious Works of Penina Moise, with a Brief Sketch of Her Life*. Charleston SC: N. G. Duffy, Printer, 1911.

(412) Paul, Jay S. " 'Nests in a Stone Image': Goyen's Surreal Gethsemane." *Studies in Short Fiction* 15 (1978): 415-20.

(413) Ringe, Donald A. "Kindred Spirits: Bryant and Coleridge." *American Quarterly* 6 (1954): 233-44.

(414) Rose, Maxine S. "On Being Born Again: James Dickey's 'May Day Sermon to the Women of Gilmer City, Georgia, by a Woman Preacher Leaving the Baptist Church'." *Research Studies* 46 (1978): 254-58.

(415) Ruffini, Rosalia, ed. "Due Lettere di Conrad Aiken." *Studi Americani* 14 (1969): 451-54.

(416) Sanford, Charles L. "The Concept of the Sublime in the Works of Thomas Cole and William Cullen Bryant." *American Literature* 28 (1947): 434-48.

(417) Schafer, William J. "Cormac McCarthy: The Hard Wages of Original Sin." *Appalachian Journal* 4 (1977): 105-19.

(418) Skaggs, David C. "The Chain of Being in Eighteenth Century Maryland: The Paradox of Thomas Cradock." *Historical Magazine of the Protestant Episcopal Church* 45 (1976): 155-64.

(419) _____. "Thomas Cradock and the Chesapeake Golden Age." *William and Mary Quarterly* 3d series 30 (1973): 93-116.

(420) Trowbridge, Clinton W. "The Word Made Flesh: Andrew Lytle's *The Velvet Horn*." *Critique* 10 (1968): 53-68.

(421) Walhout, Clarence P. "Religion in the Thought and Fiction of Three Ante-Bellum Southerners: Kennedy, Caruthers, and Simms." Ph.D. dissertation, Northwestern University, 1964.

(422) Weatherby, Robert W. II. "J. H. Ingraham and Tennessee: A Record of Social and Literary Contributions." *Tennessee Historical Quarterly* 34 (1975): 264-72.

(423) Weeks, Stephen B. "Clement Hall, the First North Carolina Author, and Thomas Godfrey, the First American Dramatist." *Trinity Archive* 6 (1893): 330-35.

(424) Weixlmann, Joseph. *John Barth: A Descriptive Primary and Annotated Secondary Bibliography*. New York: Garland Publishing, 1976.

17 Southern Religious Art, Architecture, and Music

FROM COLONIAL DAYS to the present, the construction and adornment of houses of worship have been important features of Southern religious life, as has the expression of religious belief and experience in song. For many of their religious buildings, Southerners have usually "borrowed" styles that had already become accepted elsewhere. The familiar colonial style, for example, reflected adaptation and a further Protestantizing of patterns emerging in English culture, while those churches popularly regarded as representing "Southern" style generally emerged from the classical revivalism fostered by Thomas Jefferson and the circle of architects influenced by him. The architectural features of the campmeeting and revival religion so important to much of the South's popular religion have yet to receive sustained scrutiny by architectural specialists. More attention has been paid to some of the distinctive regional contributions of the region to religious music. In particular, the genre of the Black spiritual and its musical cousins, both Black and white "gospel" and white religious folk music—while no longer limited to the South, of course—and the shape note music of the Sacred Harp and the singing schools and conventions it fostered are well-known and the subjects of many studies.

Numerous more general works, however, provide a solid background for appreciating Southern religious architecture. A good general study that, while not restricted to religious architecture, places Southern architecture in context is Marcus Whiffen, *American Architecture Since 1780: A Guide to the Styles* (108). Emphasizing more recent developments and again national rather than regional in scope is *Religious Buildings* (21), put together by the editors of *Architectural Record*. Some comment on Southern religious architecture is provided by Donald Drew Egbert in "Religious Expression in American Architecture" (22). Kenneth Severens, *Southern Architecture: 350 Years of Distinctive American Buildings* (88) does focus more specifically on the regional context and, as the title suggests, builds a case for a distinctive regional heritage, though one linked to movements elsewhere in the nation. An older cognate study, still worth consulting, is Edward and Elizabeth Waugh, *The South Builds* (106).

Concentrating mainly on structures in Virginia and Maryland is Henry Chandlee Forman's highly regarded *The Architecture of the Old South: The Medieval Style, 1585-1850* (27). Looking at much more than religious architecture, Forman emphasizes the English influence on Southern architecture. Lewis Mumford's older *The South in Architecture* (64), notes the impact of Jefferson's ideas and the Classic revivalism he helped nuture. Mumford also notes the influence of Southerners, especially Henry Hobson Richardson, on the nation's architecture, although it must be noted that many of the leading architects with Southern roots, including Richardson, did most of their work elsewhere and are only rarely represented in Dixie by buildings that they actually designed. Joseph C. Farber and Wendell Garrett, in *Thomas Jefferson Redivivus* (24) use both narrative and photographic illustration to demonstrate the regional and national impact of Jefferson's interest and experimentation with classical motifs. One obvious manifestation of that trend came in the development of what has since become known as Greek Revival architecture. See Talbot Hamlin, *Greek Revival Architecture in America* (33).

The pervasive English influence, particularly in the colonial period, forms the focus of Harold W. Rose, *The Colonial Houses of Worship in America: Built in the English Colonies Before the Republic, 1607-1789, and Still Standing* (83), includes some consideration of structures found in the seaboard South. On these, also see Stephen P. Dorsey, *Early English Churches in America, 1607-1807* (16). Many of these examples come from Virginia, where St. Luke's Episcopal Church (1632), Isle of Wight County, is the oldest Protestant church still standing in the United States. The most comprehensive study is James Scott Rawlings and Vernon Perdue-Davis, *Virginia's Colonial Churches: An Architectural Guide, Together with Their Surviving Books, Silver and Furnishings* (79). George Carrington Mason, *Colonial Churches of Tidewater Virginia* (58), notes how the use of brick in construction of many of these churches represented an important adaptation to the resources of the area. A readable, popular study is Henry Irving Brock's older *Colonial Churches in Virginia* (6), which contains a short nonscholarly essay on both the architecture and history of each of the churches treated. Two other popular or semipopular studies of more general than specific interest are Margaret Davis, "Tidewater Churches" (13), and Marcus Binney, "Virginia's

Country Churches'' (2). On some of the decorative art work in these colonial structures, see Milton L. Grigg, ''The Colonial Churches of Virginia'' (32).

Spanish and French influences were prevalent in other parts of the South throughout the colonial period and, in many cases, long after. Artistic representations of selected examples of Spanish-style structures are found in Edward M. Schiwetz, *Six Spanish Missions in Texas: A Portfolio of Paintings* (84). The lingering Spanish influence, but also the frontier ethos, are noted briefly in ''Houses of Worship in Nineteenth-Century Texas'' by Willard B. Robinson (82). Samuel J. Wilson, ''Religious Architecture in French Colonial Louisiana'' (114), analyzes how religious intentions and architecture were subordinate to military needs and structures in the early days of French settlement. Elsewhere a different French influence may still be observed. The French Protestant Huguenots brought their own architectural ideas with them when they arrived in colonial South Carolina, ideas conditioned by their discontent with Catholic styles on theological rather than architectural grounds. A brief sketch is found in Jane Gaston Mahler, ''Our Huguenot Heritage: Homes, Houses of Worship, and Public Buildings'' (56).

Two local studies detail examples which mark the transition from fascination with Classical revival styles to the Gothic, which made deep inroads in Southern architectural tastes as those elsewhere in the nation in the mid-third of the nineteenth century. Drawing on sophisticated analysis but written in a semipopular vein is Nora Miller Turman, ''Trompe L'Oeil in Accomac: St. James Episcopal Church'' (98), a study of the architecture of a church built in 1838 in Accomac, Virginia. The fusion of romantic currents with classicism which is one mark of the transition to Gothic is the focus of James Patrick's discussion of Nashville's First Baptist Church, built in 1837, and its architect: ''The Architecture of Adolphus Herman'' (73).

The shift to Gothic and its overall significance in American architectural development is adeptly analyzed by Calder Loth and Julius Trousdale Sadler in *The Only Proper Way: Gothic Architecture in America* (51). Much of the interest in the Gothic revival was nurtured by Richard Upjohn. His influence, and that of Frank Wills, especially on Episcopal notions of ''what a church should look like,'' is the subject of James Patrick's illustrated essay, ''Ecclesiological Gothic in the Antebellum South'' (74). One example of Gothic revival is Nashville's Episcopal Church of the Holy Trinity, built in 1852-53. See Sara Sprott Morrow, ''The Church of the Holy Trinity: English Countryside Tranquility in Downtown Nashville'' (62). While the South escaped many of the garish architectural trends popular elsewhere in the nation in the decades following the Civil War, most likely because the dire economic situation of the region effectively prohibited any large-scale construction of church edifices for many years, one Virginia example of the combination of Gothic elements with the more lavish High Victorian is appraised in W. L.

Whitwell, "Saint Andrew's Roman Catholic Church: Roanoke's High Victorian Gothic Landmark" (111). As noted previously, one of the nation's
preeminent and innovative architects of the postbellum period was Henry
Hobson Richardson, born in New Orleans. Richardson, never invited to design a church in the South, has left all his monuments elsewhere, but the
Southern regionalism that was part of his style is evident in Mariana Griswold
Van Rensselaer, *Henry Hobson Richardson and His Works* (101).

A few studies that examine architectural trends within various religious
denominations merit attention. James L. McAllister, Jr., "Architecture and
Change in the Diocese of Virginia" (53), discusses how the architecture of
many of the earliest structures reflected the near Puritan orientation of colonial Anglicanism, for the location of the pulpit in the center betrays the obvious emphasis on preaching, and how the emerging sacramentalism in the
Episcopal tradition may be observed in the way the altar became the center
of visual attention, with pulpit moved to the side. A popularly presented volume that makes a good companion to McAllister's article is Norvin C. Duncan, *Pictorial History of the Episcopal Church in North Carolina, 1701-1964*
(19). The more evangelical Baptists found the Classic revival style more appropriate and also experimented with other faddish trends of a later time, including the well-known "Akron plan" design. A good beginning study is J.
B. Nichols's dissertation, "A Historical Study of Southern Baptist Church
Architecture" (69). Presbyterian architectural history also reflects an eclec-
ticism of approaches, as evidenced in James E. Bouldin, *The Presbyterians
of Baltimore: Their Churches and Historic Graveyards* (3). James A. Hoobler, "Karnak on the Cumberland" (35), offers a few comments on the architecture of Nashville's First Presbyterian Church, but his study is more a
local history than exclusively an architectural analysis. Instructive in a different vein and for a different tradition, the Roman Catholic, is Walter K.
Sturges, "A Bishop and His Architect: The Story of the Building of Baltimore Cathedral" (95).

South Carolina contains examples of virtually every genre of religious architecture that has found a home in the South. The story there is put in broader
context in Harlan McClure and Vernon Hodges, *South Carolina Architecture, 1670-1970* (54). A popular and not very academic older study of specifically religious architecture in the Palmetto State is Hazel Crowson Sellers,
Old South Carolina Churches (87); in a similar vein is her *Faith of Our Fathers: A Book of Sketches of Old North Carolina Churches* (86). The coastal
city of Charleston provides a dazzling array of religious structures, including
those that reflect classical revival, Huguenot, Gothic, and other influences
and that span religious traditions ranging from Episcopalian to Unitarian and
Jewish. Some of the older examples may be studied in Albert Simons and
Samuel Lapham, eds. *The Early Architecture of Charleston* (90), but the most

comprehensive is Edward G. Lilly, ed., and Clifford L. Legerton, comp., *Historic Churches of Charleston, South Carolina* (49).

Numerous works focus on the architectural heritage of other individual states and on individual towns and cities. While none of these is devoted solely to religious architecture, each contains some examples of buildings designed for use by religious groups. See, for examples of the former, Mary Wallace Crocker, *Historic Architecture in Mississippi* (11), and John Linely, *Architecture of Middle Georgia: The Oconee Area* (50). Three well-done local studies are Royster Lyle, Jr., and Pamela Hemenway Simpson, *The Architecture of Historic Lexington* (52); Paul S. Dulaney, *The Architecture of Historic Richmond* (18), and S. Allen Chambers, *Lynchburg: An Architectural History* (9).

One religious group noted for its achievements in numerous areas of design, from architecture to furniture, is the Shakers. While most of the Shaker communities that flourished in the mid-nineteenth century were located in Ohio, New York, and New England, the Shaker settlement at Pleasant Hill, Kentucky, was long a prominent community of this utopian movement and one that has been carefully restored and is open to the public today. James C. Thomas, "Shaker Architecture in Kentucky" (97), who calls the group's characteristic style "Shaker Georgian," provides the best brief study. But two accounts of the restoration of the Pleasant Hill settlement are also illuminating for their discussion of the nature of architectural preservation and restoration: Alice Winchester, "Shakertown at Pleasant Hill" (115), and Branley A. Branson, "The Strength of Simplicity" (4). Other smaller groups, such as the German Catholic immigrants who made homes in parts of Missouri, have also left examples of distinctive architecture. Charles van Ravenswaay, for example, discusses the stone churches fashioned by this ethnic community in a careful study, *The Arts and Architecture of German Settlements in Missouri: A Survey of a Vanishing Culture* (100). Glimpses of the folk style that marks rural Appalachia may be seen in Kenneth Murray's photographic essay, "Appalachian Churches" (65).

There are few separate studies of the decorative arts that are part of religious structures in the South as elsewhere. But two are worthy of mention. Sara Sprott Morrow, "St. Paul's Church, Franklin" (63), pays special attention to the Tiffany stained glass windows that adorn this Tennessee Episcopal church completed in 1834, while Joseph R. Kerr, "Memorial Windows: Camp Lejeune's Stained Glass Masterpieces" (44), comments on the windows designed by Lamb Studios in Tenafly, New Jersey, for the Protestant Chapel on this Marine base in North Carolina, constructed in the early 1940s.

A much more extensive and specific literature explores Southern religious music. Leonard W. Ellinwood's older *The History of American Church Music* (135), is still a reliable introduction that places Southern contributions to the overall development of American religious music—the campmeeting folksong, the spiritual, the Sacred Harp—into context. Also useful by way of introduction is Ellinwood's essay, "Religious Music in America" (136). Gilbert Chase, *America's Music: From the Pilgrims to the Present* (124), although in need of updating, likewise contains several chapters treating Southern religious music. Musicologists tend to describe the distinctive Southern developments under the rubric of folk music as a way of suggesting that the region's indigenous music has emerged directly from the life experiences of its people. That such a tradition has a distinguished heritage is evidenced in Austin C. Lovelace, "Early Sacred Folk Music in America" (159). While Lovelace's essay does not focus exclusively on the South, it does contain a valuable bibliography of older works. Arthur L. Stevenson, *The Story of Southern Hymnology* (182), is also worth consulting for a general overview, although its coverage tends to be cursory. While Stevenson does deal with the emergence of "gospel" and the "gospel hymn" as well as with the singing schools associated with the Sacred Harp tradition, he tends to look more at the musical heritage of various denominations.

Among the eighteenth-century European immigrants to the South, primarily to North Carolina, who brought with them a distinctive musical heritage were the Moravians, whose expression of intensely personal religious experience in hymnody lives on even today. While most current studies focus primarily on the enclaves of Moravian descendants who live in the area around Bethlehem, Pennsylvania, there continue to be events, generally around Winston-Salem, North Carolina, that celebrate the Moravian musical heritage. An older but still reliable overview of the influence of the Moravian settlers on American religious music overall is Donald M. McCorkle, "The Moravian Contribution to American Music" (162).

Afro-Americans in the South also developed a distinctive musical heritage that gave birth to the spiritual, helped generate the emergence of "gospel," and also had a decisive impact on the development of the blues. Some of the earliest studies of the music of American blacks came from sociologists. Three-quarters of a century ago, Howard W. Odum launched serious academic study of American black music with his article, "Religious Folk Songs of the Southern Negroes" (171), in which he emphasized the social function of these songs in intensifying emotional experience and consciousness of the supernatural among Southern blacks. His ideas were expanded and reflected in a work coauthored with Guy B. Johnson, *The Negro and His Songs* (170), which appeared half a century ago. Later students of the black religious experience have noted the centrality of what has become known as "the spiritual" to black religion. See, for example, LeRoy Moore, Jr., "The Spiritual: Soul of Black Religion" (169), as well as the many studies giving overviews of black religious life noted in chapter 4. A more sustained study is

John Lovell, Jr., *Black Song: The Forge and the Flame—The Story of How the Afro-American Spiritual Was Hammered Out* (160). Much attention has been devoted to the question of sources or origins of the spiritual. As will be noted in greater detail in comment on the work of George Pullen Jackson, one long-standing interpretation has looked to the religious folksongs emerging from the campmeeting experience as the generative force behind the Black spiritual. However, that explanation today seems simplistic. Current consensus suggests that the search for a single origin may be futile: rather, the complex of the oppressive experience of slavery, the evangelical Protestant Christianity of white missions to the slaves, and the African cultural heritage are also part of the background. Roland Hayes, *My Songs: Aframerican Religious Folk Songs Arranged and Interpreted* (145) offers an early argument for the importance of African influence. Other approaches are advanced in Eileen Southern, ''An Origin for the Negro Spiritual'' (180), and David McD. Simms, ''The Negro Spirituals: Origins and Themes'' (178). An older, but extensive study with an admirable bibliography, which highlights the experience of slavery in generating an indigenous American black music is Miles M. Fisher, *Negro Slave Songs in the United States* (140). Dena J. Epstein's recent *Sinful Tunes and Spirituals: Black Folk Music to the Civil War* (137) rightfully calls attention as well to the secular influences on black music and the fusion of sacred and secular that many scholars see as basic to the world view of the slave.

Henderson S. Davis's older doctoral dissertation, ''The Religious Experience Underlying the Negro Spiritual'' (130), remains a good introduction to the overall piety and belief structure manifested in black songs. But most studies still echo the theses advanced by Howard Thurman a generation ago. In his brief *The Negro Spiritual Speaks of Life and Death* (185), Thurman highlighted the concern for immortality that the lyrics of many spirituals demonstrate, while in *Deep River: Reflections on the Religious Insight of Certain of the Negro Spirituals* (184), he emphasizes how the seemingly ''otherworldly'' focus of many of the spirituals helped provide courage, self-respect, and emotional security first in the struggle to endure the oppression of slavery and then in the struggle to survive in a racist society. The biblical stories that provide the overt content of numerous spirituals come to the fore in L. M. Friedel, *The Bible and the Negro Spirituals* (142). But the apparent otherworldliness of the content of spirituals is misleading. As Joseph R. Washington (*Black Religion* [4:27]) and numerous others have argued, the themes of release from bondage and freedom from the constraints of this world referred as well to release from the bondage of chattel slavery and freedom from its oppression and therefore served as important catalysts in the struggle against slavery.

Spirituals came to the attention of white America outside the South largely through the tours of the Fisk University Jubilee Singers beginning in the 1870s and the initial movement of Southern blacks to the North in the postbellum period. One of the earliest accounts of the impact of the Fisk groups is J. B. T. Marsh, *The Story of the Jubilee Singers: With Their Songs* (163). James H. Cone has forcefully argued that the spirituals are the ideological and musical roots of later "blues" in his *The Spirituals and the Blues* (128).

As already indicated, spirituals may be included in the category of folksong. So, too, may much of the indigenous religious music of Southern whites, particularly those in rural areas and those most influenced by campmeetings and revivals on the nineteenth-century frontier. And, of course, the Black spiritual and the white religious folksong are related, given the way in which the genre of folksong is diffused within any culture. In this area, as so many others, the work of George Pullen Jackson continues to be a basic starting point. See, for example, his "Some Factors in the Diffusion of American Religious Folksongs" (151) for a discussion of the manifold ways in which folksongs spread throughout a culture. His major works, *Spiritual Folk-Songs of Early America* (152) and *Down-East Spirituals, and Others: Three Hundred Songs Supplementary to the Author's Spiritual Folk-Songs of Early America* (150), look especially to revival spirituals, their use and misuse in campmeetings, and the ways in which Southern evangelicals (his evidence concentrates on the Baptists) absorbed them. Jackson's work is particularly valuable not only because of his narrative analysis, but also because of his inclusion of hundreds of tunes and texts along with it. Jackson makes the case that black spirituals are musical descendants of white campmeeting songs most forcefully in *White and Negro Spirituals: Their Life Span and Kinship* (154), but also see his *White Spirituals in the Southern Uplands: The Story of the Fasola Folk, Their Songs, Singing, and "Buckwheat Notes"* (155), which also touches on the Sacred Harp music. Again, he links black and white spirituals and the shape-note tradition of the Sacred Harp in *Another Sheaf of White Spirituals, Collected, Edited, and Illustrated* (149).

Numerous works, some noted in chapter 15 on revivalism, have emphasized the importance of music to the campmeetings. Still reliable is B. St. James Fry, "The Early Camp-Meeting Song Writers" (143). On the function of the campmeeting hymnody, see Dickson Bruce, *And They All Sang Hallelujah* (15:4). Ellen Jane Lorenz, *Glory, Hallelujah!* (15:21), is disappointing in its lack of analysis and perspective. But see Samuel E. Asbury's and H. E. Meyer's older article, "Old-Time White Camp Meeting Spirituals" (118). Frank J. Metcalf, *American Writers and Compilers of Sacred Music* (167), unlike many who concentrate only on music deriving from "high culture," does note the contribution of revival and campmeeting music to the overall story. Later revivals of the nineteenth century may have provided the force that indelibly imprinted the simple "gospel hymn" on the Southern religious mind (and perhaps on the American Protestant religious mind as well). Two works are helpful in appraising the role of the later revivals: James C. Downey's doctoral dissertation, "The Music of American Revivalism" (131), and Sandra S. Sizer, *Gospel Hymns and Social Religion* (179).

Connections and kinship between black and white religious folksongs, as intimated previously, are also important in understanding the emergence of "gospel" as a genre of its own. In addition to George Pullen Jackson's work previously noted, several other studies explore some of the links that gave birth to "gospel." Eugene C. Wylie's master's thesis, "The White Spirituals" (190), also makes connections to the Sacred Harp tradition. D. K. Wilgus, "The Negro-White Spiritual" (189), is valuable in identifying older studies and relevant discography. Among other studies, the most provocative is George R. Ricks, *Some Aspects of the Religious Music of the United States Negro: An Ethnomusicological Study with Special Emphasis on the Gospel Tradition* (175). As the title indicates, Irene V. Jackson, *Afro-American Religious Music: A Bibliography and A Catalogue of Gospel Music* (156) is particularly helpful to the student or scholar for noting work already done in the field.

The most comprehensive study of white "gospel" is found in a doctoral dissertation: Stanley Brobston, "A Brief History of White Southern Gospel Music" (120). More accessible, and treating black "gospel" as well, is Tony Heilbut, *The Gospel Sound: Good News and Bad Times* (146). Lois Blackwell, *The Wings of the Dove: The Story of Gospel Music in America* (119), gives historical perspective as well as an appreciation of the way in which the media helped "gospel" music permeate so much of American popular culture. Also see William H. Tallmadge, "Dr. Watts and Mahalia Jackson: The Development, Decline, and Survival of a Folk Style in America" (183), for an understanding of the relationship between the hymnody emerging from the affective religious experience that came to the fore in the revivals of the Great Awakening in the eighteenth century and contemporary "gospel." Perhaps it goes without saying that the "gospel" tradition would not have survived had it not been for many publishers who make music of this sort available. Among the earliest gospel music publishers in the South was James D. Vaughan, although there have been countless others. Vaughan's pivotal role in perpetuating the gospel tradition is examined in Jo Lee Fleming, "James D. Vaughan, Music Publisher" (141).

Another distinctive musical genre with a long heritage in the South is the shape note music, a capella harmony based on its four-note style, and the ongoing singing schools associated with the Sacred Harp. In the South, the tradition may be traced to Joseph Funk, a Mennonite immigrant from Pennsylvania who settled in Virginia around 1816 and whose descendants organized the first "singing school" in Virginia. The designation "Sacred Harp" derives from the shape-note collection compiled by Benjamin F. White and E. O. King, which was first published in 1844. For many years, the standard study was another work by George Pullen Jackson, *The Story of the Sacred Harp, 1844-1944: A Book of Religious Folk Song as an American Institution* (153). There are now other studies that refine and complement Jackson's analysis. Of these, the most thorough and well-done is Buell E. Cobb, Jr., *The Sacred Harp: A Tradition and Its Music* (126). In two earlier essays, Cobb probed particular facets of the Sacred Harp tradition. His "The Sacred Harp of the South: A Study of the Origins, Practices, and Present Implications" (127), looked at the cultural and folk aspects of the heritage, while his "Fasola Folk: Sacred Harp Singing in the United States" (125) examined its persistence in rural areas, especially among Primitive Baptists, and the singing conventions in scattered places in Dixie, but perhaps concentrated in north Georgia and Alabama, which yet today perpetuate this unusual form of ensemble singing. Also worth examination is Charles L. Ellington's doctoral dissertation, "The Sacred Harp Tradition of the South" (133).

Dorothy Horne, "Shape-Note Hymnals and the Art of Music in Early America" (148), attempts to place the emergence of the Sacred Harp tradition in the broader context of American musical history of the early nineteenth century. "Shape-Note Hymnody in the Shenandoah Valley, 1816-60," a doctoral dissertation by Harry Eskew (139), examines how the tradition took root in the area where shape note singing first gained an enduring foothold. More technical musicologically is Dorothy Horne's "Quartal Harmony in the Pentatonic Folk Hymns of the Sacred Harp" (147). Ways in which the tradition was perpetuated in the mid-twentieth century form the basis of Linda Traywick's article, "Some Contemporary Builders of *The Sacred Harp*" (186). Three recent essays describe and appraise the singing schools held generally on an annual basis that have been the most important vehicle for passing the tradition from generation to generation. Edith B. Card, " 'Saints Bound for Heaven': The Singing School Lives On" (123), comments on the influence of nineteenth-century shape note hymnwriter William Walker as it is manifested in contemporary singing schools in Etowah and Canton, North Carolina. Similar schools held in Kentucky are the subject of Terry E. Miller, "Old Time Shape-Note Singing Schools in Eastern Kentucky" (168), while David H. Stanley focuses on those in Georgia in "The Gospel-Singing Convention in Georgia" (181). The vibrancy of this tradition today testifies to the importance of music as a means to express inner religious experience in much of the rural South since the days of the frontier campmeeting. The Sacred Harp, like black and white spirituals—and black and white "gospel"—remains central to the folk religion of Dixie.

The bibliography that follows is divided into two sections. The first looks at religious art and architecture in the South and includes titles that attempt to identify the Southern contributions to architecture, sacred and secular, to American architecture in general. The second section probes the Southern religious heritage in music. In addition to general titles and those that examine black spirituals, white religious folksongs, the Sacred Harp, this part also notes several recordings of the distinctive religious music of the region.

BIBLIOGRAPHY

I. SOUTHERN RELIGIOUS ART AND ARCHITECTURE

Several of the local studies in the various chapters treating particular religious groups also comment on the architecture of specific religious structures.

(1) Biloxi, City of. *The Buildings of Biloxi: An Architectural Survey*. Biloxi: City of Biloxi, 1976.

(2) Binney, Marcus. "Virginia's Country Churches." *Country Life* 163 (1978): 1138-40.

(3) Boulden, James E. *The Presbyterians of Baltimore: Their Churches and Historic Graveyards*. Baltimore: W. K. Boyle and Son, 1875.

(4) Branson, Branley A. "The Strength of Simplicity." *Americas* 30 (1978): 38-43.

(5) Briggs, Martha Wren. "The Memorial Windows of Blandford Church: A Tribute in Tiffany Glass." *Virginia Cavalcade* 31 (1982): 144-57.

(6) Brock, Henry Irving. *Colonial Churches in Virginia*. Richmond: Dall Press, 1930.

(7) Bush-Brown, Albert. *Louis Sullivan*. New York: G. Braziller, 1960.

(8) Busignani, Alberto. *Gropius*. London: Hamlyn, 1973.

(9) Chambers, S. Allen. *Lynchburg: An Architectural History*. Charlottesville: University of Virginia Press, 1981.

(10) Cooper, Patricia Irvin. "Postscript to 'A Quaker-Plan' House in Georgia." *Pioneer America* 11 (1979): 142-50.

(11) Crocker, Mary Wallace. *Historic Architecture in Mississippi*. Jackson: University and College Press of Mississippi, 1973.

(12) Crowley, Timothy L. *Paintings in St. Louis Bertrand Church, Louisville, Kentucky*. Somerset OH: Rosary Press, 1916.

(13) Davis, Margaret. "Tidewater Churches." *South Atlantic Quarterly* 35 (1936): 86-97.

(14) Dawe, Louise Belote. "Christ Church, Lancaster County: Built and Endowed by Robert 'King' Carter: A Pictorial Essay." *Virginia Cavalcade* 23 (1973): 20-33.

(15) Dorsey, John, and James D. Dilts. *A Guide to Baltimore Architecture*. Cambridge MD: Tidewater Publishers, 1973.

(16) Dorsey, Stephen P. *Early English Churches in America, 1607-1807*. New York: Oxford University Press, 1952.

(17) Drummond, Andrew L. *The Church Architecture of Protestantism: An Historical and Constructive Study*. Edinburgh: T. and T. Clark, 1934.

(18) Dulaney, Paul S. *The Architecture of Historic Richmond*. 2d ed. Charlottesville: University of Virginia Press, 1976.

(19) Duncan, Norvin C. *Pictorial History of the Episcopal Church in North Carolina, 1701-1964*. Asheville: n.p., 1965.

(20) Eberlein, Harold D. *The Architecture of Colonial America*. Boston: Little, Brown, 1913.

(21) Editors of *Architectural Record*. *Religious Buildings*. New York: McGraw-Hill, 1979.

(22) Egbert, Donald Drew. "Religious Expression in American Architecture." In *Religious Perspectives in American Culture*. James Ward Smith and A. Leland Jamison, eds., 361-411. Princeton: Princeton University Press, 1961.

(23) Embury, Aymar II. *Early American Churches*. Garden City: Doubleday, Page, 1914.

(24) Farber, Joseph C., and Wendell Garrett. *Thomas Jefferson Redivivus*. Barre MA: Barre Publishers, 1971.

(25) Feucht, Oscar E. "St. Paul's Lutheran Church, Wartburg, Tennessee." *Concordia Historical Institute Quarterly* 48 (1975): 67-86.

(26) Field, Jean O. "Church Architecture According to Cincinnatus Shyrock." *Filson Club Historical Quarterly* 38 (1964): 342-43.

(27) Forman, Henry Chandlee. *The Architecture of the Old South: The Medieval Style, 1585-1850*. Cambridge: Harvard University Press, 1948.

(28) _____. *Maryland Architecture: A Short History from 1634 through the Civil War*. Cambridge MD: Tidewater Publishers, 1968.

(29) Fox, Wilburn M. *History and Pictures of the Fifty Churches of Christ in Maury County*. Clarence M. Holman, comp. N.p.p.: n.p., [1962?].

(30) Fraser, Charles. *A Charleston Sketchbook, 1796-1806*. Charleston: Carolina Art Association, 1940.

(31) Gray, Sally M. "Joseph Carden's 'Most Perfect Church'." *Chronicles of Oklahoma* 59 (1981): 73-82.

(32) Grigg, Milton L. "The Colonial Churches of Virginia." *Stained Glass* 58 (Summer 1963): 30-37.

(33) Hamlin, Talbot. *Greek Revival Architecture in America*. New York: Oxford University Press, 1944.

(34) Harrell, W. A. "Church Architecture." *Encyclopedia of Southern Baptists*. Nashville: Broadman Press, 1958. 1:56-58, 3:1571-72.

(35) Hoobler, James A. "Karnak on the Cumberland." *Tennessee Historical Quarterly* 35 (1976): 251-62.

(36) Horbach, Charles F. "The Motifs of the First and Second Great Awakenings, Illustrated by Contemporary American Paintings of Texas." Ph.D. dissertation, Temple University, 1972.

(37) Howland, Richard H., and Eleanor P. Spencer. *The Architecture of Baltimore: A Pictorial History*. Baltimore: Johns Hopkins University Press, 1953.

(38) Howlett, William J. "St. Joseph's: The Cathedral Church of the Diocese of Bardstown, Kentucky." *Illinois Catholic Historical Review* 4 (1922): 278-85.

(39) Hutchison, Harold. *Sir Christopher Wren: A Biography*. New York: Stein and Day, 1976.

(40) Jackson, Joseph F. A. *American Colonial Architecture: Its Origin and Development*. Philadelphia: David McKay, 1924.

(41) Jackson, Kathleen Eagen. "Nineteenth Century Moravian Schoolgirl Art." *Art and Antiques* 3,6 (1980): 78-83.

(42) Jeane, D. Gregory, ed. *The Architectural Legacy of the Lower Chattahoochee Valley in Alabama and Georgia*. Tuscaloosa: University of Alabama Press, 1978.

(43) Kalman, Harold, and John de Visser. *Pioneer Churches*. New York: W. W. Norton, 1976.

(44) Kerr, Joseph R. "Memorial Windows: Camp Lejeune's Stained Glass Masterpieces." *Marine Corps Gazette* 64 (1980): 45-48.

(45) Kocher, A. Lawrence, and Howard Dearstyne. *Colonial Williamsburg: Its Buildings and Gardens*. Williamsburg: Colonial Williamsburg, 1949.

(46) Kramer, Gerhardt. "The Saxon Lutheran Memorial: A Case History in Preservation." *Concordia Historical Institute Quarterly* 51 (1978): 155-67.

(47) Lancaster, Clay. *Eutaw: The Builders and Architecture of an Ante-Bellum Southern Town*. Eutaw AL: Greene City Historical Society, 1979.

(48) Lewis, Wilber H. "Artists of Saint Anne's Rock Chapel." *North Louisiana Historical Association Journal* 7 (1976): 64-67.

(49) Lilly, Edward G., ed., and Clifford L. Legerton, comp. *Historic Churches of Charleston, South Carolina*. Charleston: Legerton, 1966.

(50) Linely, John. *Architecture of Middle Georgia: The Oconee Area*. Athens: University of Georgia Press, 1972.

(51) Loth, Calder, and Julius T. Sadler. *The Only Proper Style: Gothic Architecture in America*. Boston: New York Graphic Society, 1975.

(52) Lyle, Royster, Jr., and Pamela Hemenway Simpson. *The Architecture of Historic Lexington*. Charlottesville: Historic Lexington Foundation and University Press of Virginia, 1977.

(53) McAllister, James L., Jr. "Architecture and Change in the Diocese of Virginia." *Historical Magazine of the Protestant Episcopal Church* 45 (1976): 297-323.

(54) McClure, Harlan, and Vernon Hodges. *South Carolina Architecture, 1670-1970*. Columbia: South Carolina Tricentennial Committee, 1970.

(55) McKee, Harley J., comp. *Records of Buildings in Charleston and the South Carolina Low Country.* History of American Buildings Survey, National Park Service. Philadelphia: Eastern Office, U.S. Department of the Interior, 1965.

(56) Mahler, Jane Gaston. "Our Huguenot Heritage: Homes, Houses of Worship, and Public Buildings." *Transactions of the Huguenot Society of South Carolina* 79 (1974): 1-43.

(57) Martin, Thomas L. *Churches of Davie County, North Carolina.* [Charlotte]: n.p., [1957].

(58) Mason, George Carrington. *Colonial Churches of Tidewater Virginia.* Richmond VA: Whittet and Shepperson, 1945.

(59) Millar, John F. *The Architects of the American Colonies: or, Vitruvius Americanus.* Barre MA: Barre Publications, 1968.

(60) Morgan, Williams. *Louisville: Architecture and the Urban Environment.* Dublin NH: William L. Bauhan, Publisher, 1979.

(61) Morrison, Mary L., ed. *Historic Savannah: Survey of Significant Buildings in the Historic and Victorian Districts of Savannah, Georgia.* Savannah: Historic Savannah Foundation and Junior League of Savannah, 1979.

(62) Morrow, Sara Sprott. "The Church of the Holy Trinity: English Countryside Tranquility in Downtown Nashville." *Tennessee Historical Quarterly* 34 (1975): 333-49.

(63) _____. "St. Paul's Church, Franklin." *Tennessee Historical Quarterly* 34 (1975): 3-18.

(64) Mumford, Lewis. *The South in Architecture.* New York: Harcourt, Brace, 1941.

(65) Murray, Kenneth. "Appalachian Churches." *Appalachia* 8 (October-November 1974): 48-53.

(66) New Orleans Chapter, American Institute of Architects. *A Guide to New Orleans Architecture.* New Orleans: New Orleans Chapter, American Institute of Architects, 1974.

(67) Newcomb, Ralph. *Architecture in Old Kentucky.* Urbana IL: University of Illinois Press, 1953.

(68) Nichols, Frederick Doveton. *The Architecture of Savannah.* Savannah: Beehive Press, 1976.

(69) Nichols, J. B. "A Historical Study of Southern Baptist Church Architecture." D.R.Ed. dissertation, Southwestern Baptist Theological Seminary, 1954.

(70) Niederer, Frances J. *The Town of Fincastle, Virginia.* Charlottesville: University Press of Virginia, 1965-66.

(71) O'Neal, William B. *Architecture in Virginia.* New York: Virginia Museum and Walker, 1968.

(72) Patrick, James. *Architecture in Tennessee, 1786-1897.* Knoxville: University of Tennessee Press, 1981.

(73) _____. "The Architecture of Adolphus Herman." *Tennessee Historical Quarterly* 38 (1979): 167-87, 277-95.

(74) _____. "Ecclesiological Gothic in the Antebellum South." *Winterthur Portfolio* 15 (1980): 117-38.

(75) Patton, Helen. "Lucas Bradley: Carpenter, Builder, Architect." *Wisconsin Magazine of History* 58 (1974-1975): 107-25.

76) Pohlkamp, Diomede. "A Franciscan Artist of Kentucky: Johann Schmitt, 1825-1898." *Franciscan Studies* 28 (1947): 147-70.

(77) Priddy, Benjamin J. "Old Churches of Memphis." *West Tennessee Historical Society Papers* 29 (1975): 130-61.

(78) Ravenel, Beatrice St. Julien. *Architects of Charleston*. Charleston: Carolina Art Association, 1945.

(79) Rawlings, James Scott, and Vernon Perdue-Davis. *Virginia's Colonial Churches: An Architectural Guide, Together with Their Surviving Books, Silver and Furnishings*. Richmond: Garrett and Massie, 1963.

(80) Ridgely, Helen West. *The Old Brick Churches of Maryland*. Sophie De-Butts Stewart, illus. New York: A. D. F. Randolph, 1894.

(81) Rines, Edward F. *Old Historic Churches of America: Their Romantic History and Their Traditions*. New York: Macmillan, 1936.

(82) Robinson, Willard B. "Houses of Worship in Nineteenth-Century Texas." *Southwestern Historical Quarterly* 85 (1982): 235-98.

(83) Rose, Harold W. *The Colonial Houses of Worship in America: Built in the English Colonies Before the Republic, 1607-1789, and Still Standing*. New York: Hastings House, 1964.

(84) Schiwetz, Edward M. *Six Spanish Missions in Texas: A Portfolio of Paintings*. Austin: University of Texas Press, 1968.

(85) Scully, Arthur, Jr. *James Dakin, Architect: His Career in New York and the South*. Baton Rouge: Louisiana State University Press, 1973.

(86) Sellers, Hazel Crowson. *Faith of Our Fathers: A Book of Sketches of Old North Carolina Churches*. N.p.p.: n.p., 1940.

(87) _____. *Old South Carolina Churches*. Columbia: Crowson Printing, 1941.

(88) Severens, Kenneth. *Southern Architecture: 350 Years of Distinctive American Building*. New York: Dutton, 1981.

(89) Shear, John Knox. *Religious Buildings for Today*. New York: F. W. Dodge, 1957.

(90) Simons, Albert, and Samuel Lapham, eds. *The Early Architecture of Charleston*. 2d ed. Columbia: University of South Carolina Press, 1970.

(91) Smith, Joseph Frazier. *White Pillars: Early Life and Architecture of the Lower Mississippi Valley*. New York: Bramhall House, 1941.

(92) Souvay, Charles L. *The Cathedrals of St. Louis: An Historical Sketch*. N.p.p.: n.p., n.d.

(93) Spalding, Phinizy. "The Relevance of Local History: Augusta and Sacred Heart." *Richmond County History* 11 (1979): 5-10.

(94) *Story of St. Joseph's Proto-Cathedral and Its Paintings.* Bardstown KY: n.p., 1930.

(95) Sturges, Walter K. "A Bishop and His Architect: The Story of the Building of Baltimore Cathedral." *Liturgical Arts* 17 (1949): 53-64.

(96) Swisher, Bob. "German Folk Art in Harmony Cemetery." *Appalachian Journal* 5 (1978): 313-17.

(97) Thomas, James C. "Shaker Architecture in Kentucky." *Filson Club Historical Quarterly* 53 (1979): 26-36.

(98) Turman, Nora Miller. "Trompe L'Oeil in Accomac: St. James Episcopal Church." *Virginia Cavalcade* 24 (1974): 5-9.

(99) Upjohn, Hobart B. *Churches in Eight American Colonies Differing in Elements of Design.* New York: Russell F. Whitehead, 1929.

(100) van Ravenswaay, Charles. *The Arts and Architecture of German Settlements in Missouri: A Survey of a Vanishing Culture.* Columbia MO: University of Missouri Press, 1977.

(101) Van Rensselaer, Mariane Griswold. *Henry Hobson Richardson and His Works.* New York: Dover Publications, 1969.

(102) Wallington, Nellie Urner. *Historic Churches of America.* New York: Duffield, 1907.

(103) Walters, Jonathan. "A Revolutionary Monastery." *Historical Preservation* 32 (1980): 42-47.

(104) Waterman, Thomas J., and J. A. Barrows. *Domestic Colonial Architecture of Tidewater Virginia.* Chapel Hill: University of North Carolina Press, 1947.

(105) Watterson, Joseph. *Architecture: A Short History.* Rev. ed. New York: W. W. Norton, 1968.

(106) Waugh, Edward, and Elizabeth Waugh. *The South Builds.* Chapel Hill: University of North Carolina Press, 1960.

(107) Welch, Jack. "A Heritage of Regional Landscapes: Appalachian Baptistry Paintings." *Goldenseal* 6 (April-June 1980): 41-45.

(108) Whiffen, Marcus. *American Architecture Since 1780: A Guide to the Styles.* Cambridge: M.I.T. Press, 1969.

(109) _____. *The Public Buildings of Williamsburg, Colonial Capital of Virginia: An Architectural History.* Williamsburg: Colonial Williamsburg, 1958.

(110) Whitwell, W. L., and Lee W. Winborne. *The Architectural Heritage of the Roanoke Valley.* Charlottesville: University of Virginia Press, 1982.

(111) _____. "Saint Andrew's Roman Catholic Church: Roanoke's High Victorian Gothic Landmark." *Virginia Cavalcade* 24 (1975): 124-33.

(112) Wilson, Everett B. *Early Southern Towns.* South Brunswick NJ: A. S. Barnes, 1967.

(113) Wilson, Mabel Ponder, et al. *Some Early Alabama Churches (Established before 1790).* [Birmingham]: Alabama Society, Daughters of the American Revolution, [1973].

(114) Wilson, Samuel J. "Religious Architecture in French Colonial Louisiana." *Winterthur Portfolio* 8 (1973): 63-106.

(115) Winchester, Alice. "Shakertown at Pleasant Hill." *Historic Preservation* 29,4 (1977): 13-20.

II. SOUTHERN RELIGIOUS MUSIC

Some entries in chapter 15 on revivalism are also pertinent here.

(116) American Folklore Recordings, University of North Carolina Press, "Powerhouse for God: Sacred Speech, Chant, and Song in an Appalachian Baptist Church." 2 record set with booklet by Jeff Todd Tilton.

(117) _____. "Primitive Baptist Hymns of the Blue Ridge." 1 record with booklet by Brett Sutton.

(118) Asbury, Samuel E., and H. E. Meyer. "Old-Time White Camp Meeting Spirituals." *Texas Folklore Society Publications* 10 (1932): 169-85.

(119) Blackwell, Lois. *The Wings of the Dove: The Story of Gospel Music in America.* Norfolk VA: Donning, 1978.

(120) Brobston, Stanley. "A Brief History of White Southern Gospel Music." Ph.D. dissertation, New York University, 1977.

(121) Buchanan, Annabel Morris. *Folk Hymns of America, Collected and Arranged.* New York: J. Fischer and Brother, 1938.

(122) Carawan, Guy, ed. *Been in the Storm So Long: Spirituals and Shouts, Children's Game Songs.* Folkways album FS-3842 (1967).

(123) Card, Edith B. " 'Saints Bound for Heaven': The Singing School Lives On." *Southern Quarterly* 15 (1976): 75-87.

(124) Chase, Gilbert. *America's Music: From the Pilgrims to the Present.* New York: McGraw-Hill, 1955. 41-282, 679-706.

(125) Cobb, Buell E., Jr. "Fasola Folk: Sacred Harp Singing in the South." *Southern Exposure* 5 (1977): 48-53.

(126) _____. *The Sacred Harp: A Tradition and Its Music.* Athens GA: University of Georgia Press, 1978.

(127) _____. "The Sacred Harp of the South: A Study of the Origins, Practices, and Present Implications." *Louisiana Studies* 7 (1968): 107-21.

(128) Cone, James. *The Spirituals and the Blues.* New York: Seabury Press, 1972.

(129) Covey, Cyclone. "Religion and Music in Colonial America." Ph.D. dissertation, Stanford University, 1949.

(130) Davis, Henderson S. "The Religious Experience Underlying the Negro Spiritual." Ph.D. dissertation, Boston University, 1950.

(131) Downey, James C. "The Music of American Revivalism." Ph.D. dissertation, Tulane University, 1968.

(132) Eddy, Mary O. "Three Early Hymn Writers." *Southern Folklore Quarterly* 10 (1946): 177-82.

(133) Ellington, Charles Linwood. "The Sacred Harp Tradition of the South." Ph.D. dissertation, Florida State University, 1970.

(134) Ellinwood, Leonard W. *English Influences in American Church Music*. Taunton, Eng.: n.p., 1954.

(135) _____. *The History of American Church Music*. New York: Morehouse-Gorham, 1953.

(136) _____. "Religious Music in America." In *Religious Perspectives in American Culture*. James Ward Smith and A. Leland Jamison, eds., 289-359. Princeton: Princeton University Press, 1961.

(137) Epstein, Dena J. *Sinful Tunes and Spirituals: Black Folk Music to the Civil War*. Urbana: University of Illinois Press, 1977.

(138) Eskew, Harry. "Music in the Baptist Tradition." *Review and Expositor* 69 (1972): 161-75.

(139) _____. "Shape-Note Hymnody in the Shenandoah Valley, 1816-60." Ph.D. dissertation, Tulane University, 1966.

(140) Fisher, Miles M. *Negro Slave Songs in the United States*. Ithaca: Cornell University Press, 1953.

(141) Fleming, Jo Lee. "James D. Vaughan, Music Publisher." S.M.D. dissertation, Union Theological Seminary (VA), 1972.

(142) Friedel, L. M. *The Bible and the Negro Spirituals*. [Bay St. Louis MS]: n.p., 1947.

(143) Fry, B. St. James. "The Early Camp-Meeting Song Writers." *Methodist Quarterly Review* 4th series 11 (1859): 401-13.

(144) [Greene, Archie, ed.] "Babies in the Mill: Carolina Traditional, Industrial, Sacred Songs, Sung by Dorsey, Nancy, and Howard Dixon." Testament album T-3301 (1964).

(145) Hayes, Roland. *My Songs: Aframerican Religious Folk Songs Arranged and Interpreted*. Boston: Little, Brown, 1948.

(146) Heilbut, Tony. *The Gospel Sound: Good News and Bad Times*. New York: Simon and Schuster, 1971.

(147) Horne, Dorothy D. "Quartal Harmony in the Pentatonic Folk Hymns of the Sacred Harp." *Journal of American Folklore* 71 (1958): 564-81.

(148) _____. "Shape-Note Hymnals and the Art of Music in Early America." *Southern Folklore Quarterly* 5 (1941): 251-56.

(149) Jackson, George Pullen. *Another Sheaf of White Spirituals, Collected, Edited, and Illustrated*. Gainesville: University of Florida Press, 1952.

(150) _____. *Down-East Spirituals, and Others: Three Hundred Songs Supplementary to the Author's Spiritual Folk-Songs of Early America*. 2d ed. Locust Valley NY: J. J. Augustin, 1953.

(151) _____. "Some Factors in the Diffusion of American Religious Folk-songs." *Journal of American Folklore* 65 (1952): 365-69.

(152) _____, ed. *Spiritual Folk-Songs of Early America.* 2d ed. Locust Valley NY: J. J. Augustin, 1953.

(153) _____. *The Story of the Sacred Harp, 1844-1944: A Book of Religious Folk Song as an American Institution.* Nashville: Vanderbilt University Press, 1944.

(154) _____. *White and Negro Spirituals: Their Life Span and Kinship.* New York: J. J. Augustin, 1944.

(155) _____. *White Spirituals in the Southern Uplands: The Story of the Fasola Folk, Their Songs, Singing, and "Buckwheat Notes".* Chapel Hill: University of North Carolina Press, 1933.

(156) Jackson, Irene V. *Afro-American Religious Music: A Bibliography and a Catalogue of Gospel Music.* Westport CT: Greenwood Press, 1979.

(157) _____. "Music Among Blacks in the Episcopal Church: Some Preliminary Considerations." *Historical Magazine of the Protestant Episcopal Church* 49 (1980): 21-35.

(158) Johnson, Guy B. *Folk Culture on St. Helena Island, South Carolina.* Chapel Hill: University of North Carolina Press, 1930.

(159) Lovelace, Austin C. "Early Sacred Folk Music in America." *The Hymn* 3 (1952): 11-14, 56-63.

(160) Lovell, John, Jr. *Black Song: The Forge and the Flame—The Story of How the Afro-American Spiritual Was Hammered Out.* New York: Macmillan, 1972.

(161) Lowens, Irving. "John Wyeth's *Repository of Sacred Music, Part Second* (1813): A Northern Precursor of Southern Folk-Hymnody." In *Music and Musicians in Early America*, 138-55. New York: W. W. Norton, 1964.

(162) McCorkle, Donald M. "The Moravian Contribution to American Music." *Music Library Association Notes* 2d series 13 (1956): 597-606.

(163) Marsh, J. B. T. *The Story of the Jubilee Singers: With Their Songs.* Rev. ed. Boston: Houghton, Mifflin, 1881.

(164) Martin, William C. "At the Corner of Glory Avenue and Hallelujah Street." *Harper's* 244 (1972): 95-99.

(165) Mason, Wilton. "The Music of the Waldensians in Valdese, North Carolina." *North Carolina Folklore* 8 (1960): 1-6.

(166) Maurer, Sr. Hermana. "The Musical Life of Colonial America in the Eighteenth Century." Ph.D. dissertation, Ohio State University, 1950.

(167) Metcalf, Frank J. *American Writers and Compilers of Sacred Music.* New York: Abingdon Press, 1925.

(168) Miller, Terry E. "Old Time Shape-Note Singing Schools in Eastern Kentucky." *Southern Quarterly* 60 (1981): 35-45.

(169) Moore, LeRoy, Jr. "The Spiritual: Soul of Black Religion." *American Quarterly* 23 (1971): 658-76.

(170) Odum, Howard, and Guy B. Johnson. *The Negro and His Songs.* Chapel Hill: University of North Carolina Press, 1925.

(171) _____. ''Religious Folk Songs of the Southern Negroes.'' *Journal of Religious Psychology* 3 (1909): 265-365.

(172) ''Original Sacred Harp Singing in the Traditional Style by Sacred Harp Singers.'' Sacred Harp Publishing (Cullman AL) album S.H.-101 (1965).

(173) Owens, William A. ''Anglo-Texan Spirituals.'' *Southwestern Historical Quarterly* 86 (1982): 31-48.

(174) Reynolds, William J. ''Our Heritage of Baptist Hymnody in America.'' *Baptist History and Heritage* 11 (1976): 204-17.

(175) Ricks, George R. *Some Aspects of the Religious Music of the United States Negro: An Ethnomusicological Study with Special Emphasis on the Gospel Tradition.* New York: Arno Press, 1977.

(176) Seeger, Charles. ''Contrapuntal Style in the Three-Voice Shape-Note Hymns.'' *Musical Quarterly* 26 (1940): 483-93.

(177) Seeger, Charles. ''Music and Class Structure in the United States.'' *American Quarterly* 9 (1957): 281-94.

(178) Simms, David McD. ''The Negro Spirituals: Origins and Themes.'' *Journal of Negro Education* 35 (1966): 35-44.

(179) Sizer, Sandra S. *Gospel Hymns and Social Religion: The Rhetoric of Nineteenth-Century Revivalism.* Philadelphia: Temple University Press, 1978.

(180) Southern, Eileen. ''An Origin for the Negro Spiritual.'' *Black Scholar* 4 (1972): 8-13.

(181) Stanley, David H. ''The Gospel-Singing Convention in Georgia.'' *Journal of American Folklore* 95 (1982): 1-32.

(182) Stevenson, Arthur L. *The Story of Southern Hymnology.* Roanoke VA: Stone Printing and Manufacturing, 1931.

(183) Tallmadge, William H. ''Dr. Watts and Mahalia Jackson: The Development, Decline, and Survival of a Folk Style in America.'' *Ethnomusicology* 5 (1961): 95-99.

(184) Thurman, Howard. *Deep River: Reflections on the Religious Insight of Certain of the Negro Spirituals.* Rev. ed. New York: Harper, 1955.

(185) _____. *The Negro Spiritual Speaks of Life and Death.* New York: Harper, 1947.

(186) Traywick, Linda. ''Some Contemporary Builders of *The Sacred Harp.*'' *Tennessee Folklore Society Bulletin* 30 (1964): 57-61.

(187) Troubetzkoy, Ulrich. ''How Virginia Saved the Outlawed English Carols.'' *Historical Magazine of the Protestant Episcopal Church* 30 (1961): 198-202.

(188) West, Edward M. ''History and Development of Music in the American Church.'' *Historical Magazine of the Protestant Episcopal Church* 14 (1945): 15-37.

(189) Wilgus, D. K. ''The Negro-White Spiritual.'' In *Anglo-American Folksong Scholarship Since 1898,* 345-64. New Brunswick: Rutgers University Press, 1959.

(190) Wylie, Eugene C. ''The White Spirituals.'' M.Mus.Ed. thesis, Minneapolis College of Music, 1950.

18 SOUTHERN RELIGION AND EDUCATION

RELIGION AND EDUCATION have been intertwined in American and Southern life since the inception of the European colonial enterprise. Throughout the English colonies, clergy frequently served as schoolteachers, and many of the earliest collegiate ventures stemmed from the educational outreach of the various denominations. Indeed, hundreds of colleges and universities in the South had a religious background. Although several have severed religious connections over the years or been absorbed into state systems, church colleges remain central to the region's higher education endeavors. Some religious groups, particularly the Roman Catholics and the Lutherans, developed extensive parochial school systems to meet the needs of their immigrant constituencies. Even with the rise of public education and the end of massive immigration, many of these parochial schools continue to play important roles in Southern education.

The South's oldest institution of higher learning, Virginia's College of William and Mary, although today a public university, owes its genesis to the work of Church of England Commissary James Blair. Blair's educational leadership is noted in several of the works listed in the bibliography to chapter 7. On the college's founding, also see Jean O'Neill, "Henry Compton, Bishop of London: Guardian of Education and Religion in Colonial Virginia" (42), and J. E. Morpurgo, *Their Majesties' Royall Colledge* (97). The standard histories of William and Mary are Herbert Adams, *The College of William and Mary* (57), and Lyon G. Tyler, *The College of William and Mary in Virginia* (117). Other Anglican educational labors in the colonial South are appraised by John Calam in *Parsons and Pedagogues: The S.P.G. Adventure in Amer-*

ican Education (20). Later educational efforts of the Protestant Episcopal Church, along with an appraisal of the philosophy supporting them, form the basis for Kendig Brubaker Cully, *The Episcopal Church and Education* (23).

As the South expanded westward across the Appalachian mountain chain, virtually all early educational activity emerged under religious auspices. Neal O'Steen, ''Pioneer Education in the Tennessee Country'' (178), notes how all education there in the late eighteenth century was permeated with religion, with the earliest religious missionaries serving as the earliest teachers. H. E. Everman, ''Early Educational Channels of Bourbon County'' (161), demonstrates that virtually all education outside of the home in this area of Kentucky was centered in religiously oriented private schools until the mid-nineteenth century. Further West, a similar story prevails. Ralph E. Glauert, ''An Uncommon Commitment: Clergymen and Their Schools in Frontier Missouri'' (164), argues that prior to 1830 even schools that were primarily secular in focus were staffed by clergy doubling as teachers. William A. Kramer, ''Life in Perry County, Missouri, at the Turn of the Century'' (168), discusses the importance of the Lutheran parochial schools in this area, noting that as late as the beginning of the twentieth century, the normative pattern was to have primary education through the sixth grade based in the Lutheran-run schools.

Higher education in recently settled areas also revolved around denominational institutions. An old but reliable work surveys the emergence of the denominational college in the antebellum period, noting that in many areas of the South, the church college was basically the norm for higher education for many years: Albea Godbold, *The Church College of the Old South* (9). Many parts of the South remained thinly populated until the later nineteenth century, but when population growth generated a need for schools and colleges, the commitment of the churches to education held sway. In Florida, for example, when the population in the Orlando area began to grow significantly in the later nineteenth century, Congregationalists led the way in higher education with the founding of Rollins College in 1885. For this story, see Jack C. Lane. ''Liberal Arts on the Florida Frontier: The Founding of Rollins College, 1885-1890'' (86). Roman Catholics, too, established colleges and seminaries as they expanded on the Southern frontier, for there was a need to provide training for diocesan priests as well as to have visible symbols of the church's commitment to its growing constituency. See, for example, John E. Rybolt, ''Kenrick's First Seminary'' (153).

Numerous studies direct their attention to the educational activities of the various denominations. For example, although now somewhat dated, Charles D. Johnson, *Higher Education of Southern Baptists: An Institutional History, 1826-1954* (31), gives a survey of the various colleges and universities presently or formerly affiliated with that denomination, while Judith Brigham,

A Historical Study of the Educational Agencies of the Southern Baptist Convention, 1845-1945 (18), expands the story to include other types of denominational work in education. Also see Thomas Clark, "A History of Baptist Involvement in Higher Education" (21). Particularly influential within the Southern Baptist Convention in the training of clergy and other church workers has been Southern Baptist Theological Seminary, the oldest of the six theological schools related to the Convention. Founded in 1877 and located in Greenville, South Carolina, before its removal to Louisville, Kentucky, the Seminary has its story told briefly in Duke K. McCall, "The Southern Baptist Theological Seminary" (140), and more fully in William A. Mueller, *A History of Southern Baptist Theological Seminary* (146). Both Duke K. McCall, "The Role of Southern Seminary in Southern Baptist Life" (139), and Inman Johnson, *Of Parsons and Professors* (136), discuss the influence of the Seminary as the center of sophisticated theological reflection within the denomination.

Roman Catholic endeavors in the South are included in two works by Edward J. Power, *Catholic Higher Education in America* (44) and *A History of Catholic Higher Education in the United States* (45), but neither work focuses exclusively on the region. Also see Harold A. Buetow, *Of Singular Benefit: The Story of Catholic Education in the United States* (19). Philip Gleason draws attention to the pivotal role of John Carroll in launching Catholic commitment to educational endeavors. See his "The Main Sheet Anchor: John Carroll and Catholic Higher Education" (30). Michael Kenny, *Catholic Culture in Alabama* (85) not only recounts the early history of Spring Hill College, but also offers useful information on Catholic developments in that state. Various religious orders have been instrumental in carrying out Catholicism's educational ministry. Many studies of the work of these groups are listed in the bibliography to chapter 5 as well as the bibliography for this chapter.

Woodrow Geier, *A Perspective on Methodist Higher Education* (29), while an older study, analyzes the educational philosophy that spurred Methodist interest in education in the South and elsewhere in the nation. Earl P. Barker provides a more specific study in "The Contribution of Methodism to Education in Kentucky" (16). Tennessee's Vanderbilt University, now an independent institution, originally had Methodist connections. The severing of those ties is the subject of John O. Gross, "Bishops Versus Vanderbilt University" (76). Duke and Emory Universities are two of the most well-known Methodist-related schools in Dixie. Much of the early story of Emory is recounted in the biographical studies of Asa Candler noted in the listings for chapter 10. Two articles by Robert F. Durden, "James B. Duke and the Launching of Duke University" (69) and "The Origins of the Duke Endowment and the Launching of Duke University'' (70), trace the transformation of Trinity College in Durham, North Carolina, into Duke University.

Three works offer an introduction to Presbyterian educational concerns: R. T. L. Liston, *The Neglected Educational Heritage of Southern Presbyterians* (34); DeWitt C. Reddick, ed., *Church and Campus: Presbyterians Look to the Future from Their Historic Role in Christian Higher Education* (48); and the more narrowly focused ''Some Presbyterian Contributions to Education in North Carolina'' (28) by Lorton H. Floyd. Kentucky's Berea College, long a leader in cooperative education, owes its genesis to Presbyterian missionary John Gregg Fee, a committed abolitionist. Its story down to the end of its formal religious affiliation is recounted in Malcolm L. Warford, ''The Making and Unmaking of a Radical Tradition: Berea College, 1855-1904'' (121).

A few titles detailing the educational work of other denominational groups deserve mention. The restorationist Churches of Christ have also been active in maintaining colleges and universities. M. Norvel Young's older work, *A History of Colleges Established and Controlled by Members of the Churches of Christ* (56), looks briefly at these institutions. Raymond O. Corvin's now outdated master's thesis, ''History of Education by the Pentecostal Holiness Church in South Carolina and Georgia'' (22), explores collegiate work of that body, while Vinson Synan, *Emmanuel College: The First Fifty Years, 1919-1969* (116), is a carefully crafted exposition of the denomination's major institution in Franklin Springs, Georgia.

Many other histories and studies of individual educational institutions further illuminate the links between religion and education in the South. Most of these works are of little scholarly value, for the bulk are uncritical and intended more to entice alumni support than to present a rigorous academic analysis of a given college or university. A bibliography listing all the historical materials published by individual schools to trumpet their own stories would fill a separate volume; the titles included in the bibliography for this chapter are a representative sampling of the type of literature available and therefore not exhaustive. Some institutions, however, have attracted considerable scholarly attention, perhaps because the religious ideology advanced by the sponsoring group might at first appear at odds with free intellectual inquiry. Lee College in Cleveland, Tennessee, is one such school. Originally a junior college, Lee College stands as the premier educational institution of the Church of God (Cleveland, Tennessee), one of the South's larger indigenous Pentecostal denominations. A self-praising history of the school is Richard T. McBrayer, *Lee College: Pioneer in Pentecostal Education, 1918-1968* (87). More substantive are several graduate theses, projects, and dissertations: E. Gene Horton, ''A History of Lee Junior College, Cleveland, Tennessee'' (80); Bobby G. Johnson, ''The Establishment and Development of Lee College, 1918-1954'' (84); James L. Underwood, ''Historical Development of Lee Junior College'' (118); and Mauldin A. Ray, ''A Study of the History of Lee College, Cleveland, Tennessee'' (105). Changes that came to Lee when it became a four-year rather than two-year institution form the focus of Ray H. Hughes's dissertation, ''The Transition of Church-Related Junior Colleges to Senior Colleges, with Implications for Lee College'' (82). Alexander W. Delk looked at the impact of the school on the town of Cleveland in a master's thesis: ''Lee College and Its Relationship to the Community in Which It Is Located'' (68). The school has also had an impact on its denominational sponsor since the Church of God is also headquartered in Cleveland. Part of that relationship is noted by Ray H. Hughes in a master's thesis, ''The Influence of Lee College on the Development of the World Missions Program of the Church of God'' (81). Lee College students provided the subject matter for Earl J. Gilbert, ''Some Personality Correlates of Certain Religious Beliefs, Attitudes, Practices, and Experiences in Students Attending a Fundamentalist Pentecostal Church College'' (75).

The University of the South in Sewanee, Tennessee, emerging from the vision of Episcopal Bishop and Confederate General Leonidas Polk, for more than a century has been the mainstay of Episcopal higher and theological education in Dixie as well as a symbolic center for preservation of the values and mythology associated with antebellum plantation culture, as noted in Charles Reagan Wilson, *Baptized in Blood* (21:60). The early stages of this school's development are recounted in Arthur B. Chitty, *Reconstruction at Sewanee: The Founding of the University of the South and Its First Administration, 1857-1872* (61), while Donald S. Armentrout traces the genesis of the theological school affiliated with the University in ''The Beginnings of Theological Education at the University of the South: The Role of John Austin Merrick'' (127). Armentrout offers a more complete treatment of the University's work in theological education in *The Quest for the Informed Priest: A History of the School of Theology* (128).

There are also numerous religious institutions in the South that are independent of denominational affiliation or control. Many tend to be fundamentalist in ideology, if not advocates of the more extreme premillennial dispensationalism that has often been allied with fundamentalism in the popular mind. While the designation ''Baptist'' is frequently applied to such universities and seminaries, that label does not denote formal affiliation with the Southern Baptist Convention. One example is the Dallas Theological Seminary in Texas. Although it has been popularly classified as a Baptist school, there was not, as Rudolf A. Reiner demonstrated in his doctoral dissertation, ''A History of Dallas Theological Seminary'' (150), a single member of the Southern Baptist Convention among the school's founders. Another bastion of the more conservative evangelicalism associated with much of Southern

Protestantism is Asbury Theological Seminary in Wilmore, Kentucky, a school that once had links to the Methodist Church. See Howard F. Shipps's now dated study, *A Short History of Asbury Theological Seminary* (155).

In recent years, the question of doctrinal standards has emerged as one with serious ramifications for church-related or church-controlled schools. The rise of the new religious right or the new evangelicalism has fostered concern among some religious leaders about the degree to which faculty at denominational schools espouse and teach views that are perceived to be opposed to beliefs held by the denomination and/or a majority of its members. The Missouri Synod Lutheran Concordia Seminary in St. Louis faced institutional schism in the mid-1970s when the denomination's governing body launched investigations into the orthodoxy of several faculty members. The story is summarized in "Academic Freedom and Tenure: Concordia Seminary" (125). There have also been periodic calls for similar inquiries into the religious orthodoxy of faculty at Southern Baptist institutions. For the background to that story, see Reuben E. Alley, "Southern Baptist Seminaries and Academic Freedom" (126).

The delicate interconnections between religion and Southern culture have also meant that religious concerns have frequently had an impact on the governance and structure of public institutions. At the turn of the century, for example, hostility between Baptists and Methodists over the administration of the University of Georgia was not resolved until one chancellor was forced to resign and a compromise candidate installed in his place. For an exposition of those developments, see Roy Mathis, "Walter B. Hill, A New Chancellor for the University of Georgia" (93). Three-quarters of a century earlier, Boston Unitarian clergyman Horace Holley became president of Transylvania University in Kentucky, much to the consternation of the school's Presbyterian supporters. The ensuing controversy, recounted in William J. McGlothlin, "Rev. Horace Holley: Transylvania's Unitarian President" (90), not only led to Holley's resignation as head of a school that had acquired a rather liberal reputation for the times, but also disrupted the university to such an extent that public control seemed imminent. In the end, however, evangelicals who were hostile to liberal influences and committed to support revivals as a means to secure converts carried the day at Transylvania.

Today, public colleges and universities are experiencing greater influence and higher enrollments than many of their church-related or church-controlled parallel institutions. But the heritage of religious support for education and the number of religiously-affiliated institutions that continue to dot the Southern landscape suggest that religion and education will long remain in partnership in Dixie.

The bibliography that follows identifies first those studies of a general or topical nature. It then lists titles that focus on the educational work of the various denominations. Studies of individual colleges and universities and of particular seminaries or theological schools comprise the next two sections. The final part notes titles dealing with primary and secondary education, parochial schools, and miscellaneous matters.

BIBLIOGRAPHY

Titles dealing with religiously related educational activities among Indian tribal groups are included in the listing for chapter 3. Those treating educational work oriented toward blacks are listed in chapter 4. In addition, numerous titles in the chapters on individual religious groups also deal with education.

I. SOUTHERN RELIGION AND EDUCATION: GENERAL AND TOPICAL STUDIES

(1) Bell, Sadie. *The Church, the State, and Education in Virginia*. Philadelphia: University of Pennsylvania Press, 1930.

(2) Brown, Kenneth I. *Not Minds Alone: Some Frontiers of Christian Education*. New York: Harper, 1954.

(3) Carlson, Edgar M. *The Future of Church-Related Higher Education*. Minneapolis: Augsburg Publishing House, 1977.

(4) Christenbury, Eugene C. "A Study of Teacher Education in Sixteen Pentecostal Colleges in the United States." Ed.D. dissertation, University of Tennessee at Knoxville, 1972.

(5) *Church and College: A Vital Partnership*. 4 vols. Sherman TX: National Congress on Church-Related Colleges and Universities, 1980.

(6) Ferre, Gustave Adolph. "A Concept of Higher Education and Its Relation to the Christian Faith as Evidenced in the Writings of Alexander Campbell." Ph.D. dissertation, Vanderbilt University, 1958.

(7) Franklin, Robert L. "Georgia Baptist Student Union Power: David Bascom Nicholson III." *Viewpoints: Georgia Baptist History* 4 (1974): 67-85.

(8) Geier, Woodrow, ed. *Church Colleges Today*. Nashville: Board of Higher Education and Ministry, United Methodist Church, 1974.

(9) Godbold, Albea. *The Church College of the Old South*. Durham: Duke University Press, 1944.

(10) McCain, William D. "Education in Mississippi in 1860." *Journal of Mississippi History* 22 (1960): 153-67.

(11) McCormick, Leo J. *Church-State Relations in Education in Maryland*. Washington: Catholic University of America Press, 1942.

(12) Moots, Philip R., and Edward McGlynn Gaffney, Jr. *Church and Campus: Legal Issues in Religiously Affiliated Higher Education*. Notre Dame: University of Notre Dame Press, 1974.

(13) Parsonage, Robert R., ed. *Church-Related Higher Education*. Valley Forge PA: Judson Press, 1978.

(14) Solberg, Richard W., and Merton P. Strommen. *How Church-Related Are Church-Related Colleges?* Philadelphia: Board of Publication, Lutheran Church in America, 1978.

II. SOUTHERN RELIGION AND EDUCATION:
DENOMINATIONAL STUDIES

(15) Alberta, Mary. "A Study of the Schools Conducted by the Sisters of St. Joseph in Florida." M.A. thesis, University of Florida, 1940.

(16) Barker, Earl P. "The Contribution of Methodism to Education in Kentucky." Ph.D. dissertation, George Peabody College for Teachers, 1937.

(17) Bowie, Dennis Harold. "A Study of Certain Factors Affecting Non-Enrollment in Selected Church-of-Christ-Related Private Schools." Ed.D. dissertation, Memphis State University, 1968.

(18) Brigham, Judith. *A Historical Study of the Educational Agencies of the Southern Baptist Convention, 1845-1945.* New York: Arno Press, 1972. First published 1951.

(19) Buetow, Harold A. *Of Singular Benefit: The Story of Catholic Education in the United States.* New York: Macmillan, 1970.

(20) Calam, John. *Parsons and Pedagogues: The S.P.G. Adventure in American Education.* New York: Columbia University Press, 1971.

(21) Clark, Thomas. "A History of Baptist Involvement in Higher Education." *Review and Expositor* 64 (1967): 19-30.

(22) Corvin, Raymond O. "History of Education by the Pentecostal Holiness Church in South Carolina and Georgia." M.A. thesis, University of South Carolina at Columbia, 1942.

(23) Cully, Kendig Brubaker. *The Episcopal Church and Education.* New York: Morehouse-Barlow, 1966.

(24) Daniel, W. Harrison. "Southern Baptists and Education, 1865-1900: A Case Study." *Maryland Historical Magazine* 64 (1969): 218-47.

(25) Donaghue, Mary Stanislaus. "History of Catholic Education in Alabama." M.A. thesis, University of Alabama, 1935.

(26) Evans, Warren D. "Educational Expenditures within Liberal Arts Colleges and Colleges Maintained by Members of the Church of Christ." Ed.D. dissertation, Pennsylvania State University, 1963.

(27) Flowers, Ronald B. "The Bible Chair Movement in the Disciples of Christ Tradition: Attempts to Teach Religion in State Universities." Ph.D. dissertation, University of Iowa, 1967.

(28) Floyd, Lorton H. "Some Presbyterian Contributions to Education in North Carolina." M.A. thesis, University of North Carolina at Chapel Hill, 1948.

(29) Geier, Woodrow. *A Perspective on Methodist Higher Education.* Nashville: Commission on Higher Education, Methodist Church, 1960.

(30) Gleason, Philip. "The Main Sheet Anchor: John Carroll and Catholic Higher Education." *Review of Politics* 38 (1976): 576-613.

(31) Johnson, Charles D. *Higher Education of Southern Baptists: An Institutional History, 1826-1954.* Waco: Baylor University Press, 1955.

(32) Kohlbrenner, Bernard J. "Catholic Education in Colonial Maryland." *Maryland Historical Bulletin* 12 (1934): 35-36.

(33) Lavender, Abraham D. "Studies of Jewish College Students: A Review and a Replication." *Jewish Social Studies* 39 (1977): 37-52.

(34) Liston, R. T. L. *The Neglected Educational Heritage of Southern Presbyterians.* Bristol TN: n.p., 1956.

(35) McCully, Bruce T. "Governor Francis Nicholson, Patron *Par Excellence* of Religion and Learning in Colonial America." *William and Mary Quarterly* 3d series 39 (1982): 310-33.

(36) Magruder, Edith C. *A Historical Study of the Educational Agencies of the Southern Baptist Convention, 1845-1945.* New York: Board of Publications, Teachers College, Columbia University, 1951.

(37) Meiring, Bernard J. *Educational Aspects of the Councils of Baltimore, 1829-1884.* New York: Arno Press, 1978.

(38) Middleton, Arthur P. "Anglican Contributions to Higher Education." *Pennsylvania History* 25 (1958): 251-68.

(39) Moran, Alice Frances. "A History of Catholic Education in South Carolina." M.A. thesis, University of South Carolina, 1941.

(40) Ognibene, Richard. "The Baptist Academy Movement of the Late Nineteenth Century." *Foundations* 22 (1979): 246-60.

(41) O'Leary, Mary Rosalia. "The History of Catholic Education in Nelson County [KY], 1805-1934." M.A. thesis, University of Kentucky, 1934.

(42) O'Neill, Jean. "Henry Compton, Bishop of London: Guardian of Education and Religion in Colonial Virginia." *Virginia Cavalcade* 29 (1979): 88-95.

(43) O'Neill, Sr. Mary Roselina. "History of the Contribution of the Sisters of the Holy Names of Jesus and Mary to the Cause of Education in Florida." M.A. thesis, Fordham University, 1941.

(44) Power, Edward J. *Catholic Higher Education in America.* New York: Appleton-Century Crofts, 1972.

(45) _____. *A History of Catholic Higher Education in the United States* . Milwaukee: Bruce Publishing, 1958.

(46) Purcell, Richard J. "Education and Irish Schoolmasters in Maryland's National Period." *Catholic Educational Review* 32 (1934): 198-207.

(47) _____. "Education and Irish Teachers in Colonial Maryland." *Catholic Educational Review* 32 (1934): 143-53.

(48) Reddick, DeWitt C., ed. *Church and Campus: Presbyterians Look to the Future from Their Historic Role in Christian Higher Education.* Richmond VA: John Knox Press, 1956.

(49) Repetti, W. C. "Catholic Schools in Colonial Maryland." *Woodstock Letters* 81 (1952): 123-34.

(50) Reynolds, Margaret Mary. "The History of Catholic Higher Education in Kentucky." M.A. thesis, University of Kentucky, 1927.

(51) Ross, M. Luperta. "Catholic Education among the Negroes in Mississippi, 1841-1951." M.A. thesis, St. Louis University, 1951.

(52) Smiley, David L. "Educational Attitudes of North Carolina Baptists." *North Carolina Historical Review* 35 (1958): 316-27.

(53) Watts, Fred G. "A Brief History of Early Higher Education among the Baptists of Oklahoma." *Chronicles of Oklahoma* 17 (1939): 26-34.

(54) Watts, John D. W. "Higher Education in Southern Baptist Foreign Missions." *Baptist History and Heritage* 11 (1976): 218-31.

(55) Yeakel, Sr. Mary A. *The Nineteenth Century Educational Contributions of the Sisters of Charity of Saint Vincent de Paul in Virginia.* Baltimore: Johns Hopkins University Press, 1939.

(56) Young, M. Norvel. *A History of Colleges Established and Controlled by Members of Churches of Christ.* Kansas City: Old Paths Book Club, 1949.

III. SOUTHERN RELIGION AND EDUCATION: STUDIES OF INDIVIDUAL COLLEGES AND UNIVERSITIES

(57) Adams, Herbert B. *The College of William and Mary: A Contribution to the History of Higher Education.* Washington: Government Printing Office, 1887.

(58) Anderson, Tony M., ed. *Our Holy Faith.* Kansas City: Printed for Asbury College by Beacon Hill Press, 1966.

(59) Banowsky, William S. "A Historical Study of the Speech-making at the Abilene Christian College Lectureship, 1918-1961." Ph.D. dissertation, University of Southern California, 1963.

(60) Cantrell, Roy H. "A History of Bethany Nazarene College." D.R.E. dissertation, Southwestern Baptist Theological Seminary, 1955.

(61) Chitty, Arthur B. *Reconstruction at Sewanee: The Founding of the University of the South and Its First Administration, 1857-1872.* Sewanee: The University Press, 1954.

(62) _____. "Sewanee: Then and Now." *Tennessee Historical Quarterly* 38 (1979): 383-400.

(63) Corvin, Raymond O. "Religious and Educational Backgrounds in the Founding of Oral Roberts University." Ph.D. dissertation, University of Oklahoma, 1967.

(64) Cosgrove, Owen. "The Administration of Don Heath Morris at Abilene Christian College." Ed.D. dissertation, North Texas State University, 1976.

(65) Crowson, E. T. "Samuel Stanhope Smith: A Founder of Hampden-Sydney College." *Virginia Cavalcade* 24 (1974): 52-61.

(66) Daniel, W. Harrison. "The Genesis of Richmond College, 1843-1860." *Virginia Magazine of History and Biography* 83 (1975): 131-49.

(67) Davis, Mollie C. "George Whitefield's Attempt to Establish a College in Georgia." *Georgia Historical Quarterly* 55 (1971): 459-76.

(68) Delk, Alexander W. "Lee College and Its Relationship to the Community in Which It Is Located." M.S. thesis, University of Tennessee at Knoxville, 1959.

(69) Durden, Robert F. "James B. Duke and the Launching of Duke University." *South Atlantic Quarterly* 74 (1975): 143-63.

(70) _____. "The Origins of the Duke Endowment and the Launching of Duke University." *North Carolina Historical Review* 52 (1975): 130-46.

(71) Faupel, Charles E. "Bridge-Burning: A Factor Contributing to Religiosity." M.A. thesis, Central Michigan University, 1978.

(72) Fletcher, Charlotte. "1784: The Year St. John's College Was Named." *Maryland Historical Magazine* 74 (1979): 133-51.

(73) Garber, Paul N. *John Carlyle Kilgo: President of Trinity College, 1894-1910.* Durham: Duke University Press, 1937.

(74) Gardner, Robert G. "Woodland Female College." *Viewpoints: Georgia Baptist History* 6 (1978): 71-82.

(75) Gilbert, Earl J. "Some Personality Correlates of Certain Religious Beliefs, Attitudes, Practices, and Experiences in Students Attending a Fundamentalist Pentecostal Church College." Ed.D. dissertation, University of Tennessee at Knoxville, 1972.

(76) Gross, John O. "Bishops Versus Vanderbilt University." *Tennessee Historical Quarterly* 22 (1963): 53-65.

(77) Holder, Ray. "Centenary: Roots of a Pioneer College, 1638-1844." *Journal of Mississippi History* 42 (1980): 77-98.

(78) Holland, Dorothy Garesche. "Maryville—The First Hundred Years." *Missouri Historical Society Bulletin* 29 (1973): 145-62.

(79) Hollow, Elizabeth Patton. "Development of the Brownsville Baptist Female College: An Example of Female Education in the South, 1850-1910." *West Tennessee Historical Society Papers* 32 (1978): 48-59.

(80) Horton, E. Gene. "A History of Lee Junior College, Cleveland, Tennessee." M.Ed. thesis, University of South Dakota, 1953.

(81) Hughes, Ray H. "The Influence of Lee College on the Development of the World Missions Program of the Church of God." M.S. thesis, University of Tennessee at Knoxville, 1964.

(82) _____. "The Transition of Church-Related Junior Colleges to Senior Colleges, with Implications for Lee College." Ed.D. dissertation, University of Tennessee at Knoxville, 1966.

(83) Humphries, Jack W. "The Law Department at Old Austin College." *Southwestern Historical Quarterly* 83 (1980): 371-86.

(84) Johnson, Bobby G. "The Establishment and Development of Lee College, 1918-1954." M.A. research project, Memphis State University, 1955.

(85) Kenny, Michael. *Catholic Culture in Alabama: Centenary Story of Spring Hill College, 1830-1930.* New York: America Press, 1931.

(86) Lane, Jack C. "Liberal Arts on the Florida Frontier: The Founding of Rollins College, 1885-1890." *Florida Historical Quarterly* 59 (1980): 144-64.

(87) McBrayer, Richard T. *Lee College: Pioneer in Pentecostal Education, 1918-1968*. Cleveland TN: n.p., 1968.

(88) McCaul, Robert L. "Whitefield's Bethesda College Projects and Other Major Attempts to Found Colonial Colleges." *Georgia Historical Quarterly* 44 (1960): 263-77.

(89) McConnell, Leona Bellew. "A History of the Town and College of Bethany, Oklahoma." M.A. thesis, University of Oklahoma, 1935.

(90) McGlothlin, William J. "Rev. Horace Holley: Transylvania's Unitarian President." *Filson Club Historical Quarterly* 51 (1977): 234-48.

(91) McKee, Earl S. "The Early History of Asbury College (1890-1910)." M.A. thesis, University of Kentucky, 1926.

(92) Maitrugues, J. B. "St. Charles College, Grand Coteau, La." *Woodstock Letters* 5 (1876): 16-29.

(93) Mathis, Roy. "Walter B. Hill, A New Chancellor for the University of Georgia." *Georgia Historical Quarterly* 57 (1973): 76-84.

(94) Mayo, Janet. "The Authority to Govern and the Right to Dance on Campus at Centenary College." *North Louisiana Historical Association Journal* 9 (1978): 205-18.

(95) Meline, Mary M. "The Beginnings of Mount St. Mary's." *Catholic World* 45 (1887): 690-97.

(96) Melton, Culbreth Y. "A Study of the Students Who Enrolled in Emmanuel College from September 1952 through September 1955." M.A. thesis, University of North Carolina in Chapel Hill, 1956.

(97) Morpurgo, J.E. *Their Majesties' Royall Colledge: William and Mary in the Seventeenth and Eighteenth Centuries*. Williamsburg: College of William and Mary in Virginia, 1976.

(98) Morrison, Betty L. *A History of Our Lady of the Holy Cross College, New Orleans, Louisiana*. Gretna LA: HER Publishing, 1977.

(99) O'Connor, Thomas F. "The Founding of Mount Saint Mary's College, 1808-1835." *Maryland Historical Magazine* 43 (1948): 197-209.

(100) Palmer, Steven C. "A Thwarted Try for Change." *Change* 6 (1974): 43-47.

(101) Pitt, Felix N. "Two Early Catholic Colleges in Kentucky: St. Thomas and Gethsemani." *Filson Club Historical Quarterly* 39 (1964): 133-48.

(102) Poole, Stafford. "The Founding of Missouri's First College: Saint Mary's of the Barrens, 1815-1818." *Missouri Historical Review* 64 (1970): 1-22.

(103) Ranaghan, Kevin M. "The Liturgical Renewal at Oral Roberts University." *Studia Liturgica* 9 (1973): 122-36.

(104) Rasnake, John S. "An Investigation of the Policy of the Assemblies of God on Glossolalia and Its Effects on Education in Their Colleges." M.A. thesis, East Tennessee State University, 1965.

(105) Ray, Mauldin A. "A Study of the History of Lee College, Cleveland, Tennessee." Ed.D. dissertation, University of Houston, 1964.

(106) Reddick, DeWitt C. *Wholeness and Renewal in Education: A Learning Experience at Austin College.* Sherman TX: Center for Program and Institutional Renewal, Austin College, 1979.

(107) Reid, Alfred S. *Furman University: Toward a New Identity, 1925-1975.* Durham: Duke University Press, 1976.

(108) Rittenhouse, Floyd O. "Edward A. Sutherland: Independent Reformer." *Adventist Heritage* 4 (1977): 20-34.

(109) Rogers, Tommy W. "Oakland College: An Early Presbyterian Educational Endeavor in the Old Southwest." *Journal of Presbyterian History* 43 (1965): 37-56.

(110) Royse, Nyal Dailey. "A Study of the Environment of Harding College as Perceived by Its Students and Faculty and as Anticipated by Entering Students." Ed.D. dissertation, Memphis State University, 1969.

(111) Ryan, J. J. "St. John's College, Frederick, Half a Century Ago." *Woodstock Letters* 30 (1901): 231-46.

(112) Salter, J. M. "Our College at Augusta, Georgia: Letter Dated Sacred Heart College, Augusta, Georgia, December 9, 1905." *Woodstock Letters* 34 (1905): 381-85.

(113) Springhill College. *Springhill College, Ala., 1820-1905.* Mobile: n.p., 1906.

(114) Strahan, Richard D. "A Study to Introductory Curriculum Approaches and Student Personnel Services for Evangel College." Ed.D. dissertation, University of Houston, 1955.

(115) Synan, H. Vinson. "The Background and Founding of Emmanuel College." M.A. thesis, University of Georgia, 1964.

(116) _____. *Emmanuel College: The First Fifty Years, 1919-1969.* Franklin Springs GA: Emmanuel College Library, 1968.

(117) Tyler, Lyon G. *The College of William and Mary in Virginia: Its History and Work, 1693-1907.* Richmond VA: Whittet and Shepperson, 1907.

(118) Underwood, James L. "Historical Development of Lee College." M.S. paper, University of Tennessee at Knoxville, 1954.

(119) Vollenwieder, Roy W. "Springhill College: The Early Days." *Alabama Review* 17 (1954): 127-35.

(120) Ward, Richard H. "Union University and Its Predecessors: Historical Highlights." *West Tennessee Historical Society Papers* 29 (1975): 55-63.

(121) Warford, Malcolm L. "The Making and Unmaking of a Radical Tradition: Berea College, 1855-1904." *Encounter* 38 (1977): 149-61.

(122) Williams, Eugene. "History of Trevecca Nazarene College." B.D. thesis, Nazarene Theological Seminary, 1956.

(123) Wood, George O. "The Role of the Campus Pastor at the Evangelical College, with Special Reference to Evangel College." D.Th.P. dissertation, Fuller Theological Seminary, 1970.

IV. SOUTHERN RELIGION AND EDUCATION:
STUDIES OF SEMINARIES AND THEOLOGICAL EDUCATION

(124) Abel, Paul F. "An Historical Study of the Origin and Development of Asbury Theological Seminary.'' M.A. thesis, Columbia University, 1951.

(125) ''Academic Freedom and Tenure: Concordia Seminary.'' *American Association of University Professors Bulletin* 61 (1975): 49-59.

(126) Alley, Reuben E. ''Southern Baptist Seminaries and Academic Freedom.'' *Review and Expositor* 61 (1964): 555-67.

(127) Armentrout, Donald S. ''The Beginnings of Theological Education at the University of the South: The Role of John Austin Merrick.'' *Historical Magazine of the Protestant Episcopal Church* 51 (1982): 253-67.

(128) _____. *The Quest for the Informed Priest: A History of the School of Theology*. Sewanee: School of Theology, The University of the South, 1979.

(129) Baur, John C. ''For Christ and His Kingdom.'' *Concordia Historical Institute Quarterly* 50 (1977): 99-105.

(130) Dallman, Roger H. ''Springfield Seminary.'' *Concordia Historical Institute Quarterly* 50 (1977): 106-30.

(131) Flatt, Billy W. ''An Evaluation of the Degree Programs of the Harding Graduate School of Religion as Perceived by Its Graduates, 1964-1973.'' Ed.D. dissertation, Memphis State University, 1973.

(132) Fraley, Robert O. ''A Complete History of Asbury Theological Seminary.'' Th.M. thesis, Asbury Theological Seminary, 1949.

(133) Goodwin, William A. R. *History of the Theological Seminary in Virginia and Its Historical Background: Centennial Edition*. 2 vols. New York: E. S. Gorham, 1923-24.

(134) Hahn, Stephen S. ''Lexington's Theological Library, 1832-1859.'' *South Carolina Historical Magazine* 80 (1979): 36-49.

(135) Insko, W. Robert. ''The Kentucky Seminary.'' *Register of the Kentucky Historical Society* 52 (1954): 213-32.

(136) Johnson, Inman. *Of Parsons and Professors*. Nashville: Broadman Press, 1959.

(137) Keisker, Walter. ''Then . . . Now.'' *Concordia Historical Institute Quarterly* 53 (1980): 34-38.

(138) LaMotte, Louis C. *Colored Light: The Story of the Influence of Columbia Theological Seminary, 1828-1936*. Richmond VA: Presbyterian Committee of Publication, 1937.

(139) McCall, Duke K. ''The Role of Southern Seminary in Southern Baptist Life.'' *Review and Expositor* 67 (1970): 183-93.

(140) _____. ''The Southern Baptist Theological Seminary.'' *Baptist History and Heritage* 12 (1977): 194-97, 230.

(141) McElroy, Isaac S. *The Louisville Presbyterian Theological Seminary*. Charlotte NC: Presbyterian Standard Publishing, 1929.

(142) Meigs, James T. ''The Whitsitt Controversy.'' *The Quarterly Review* 31 (1971): 41-61.

(143) Miller, H. Earl. ''The Old Seminary and the New.'' *Concordia Historical Institute Quarterly* 49 (1976): 52-63.

(144) Morro, W. C. *"Brother McGarvey": The Life of President J. W. Mc-Garvey of the College of the Bible, Lexington, Kentucky.* St. Louis: Bethany Press, 1940.

(145) Mueller, William A. "Historical Perspectives among Southern Baptists in Theological Education." *Review and Expositor* 70 (1973): 17-26.

(146) _____. *A History of Southern Baptist Theological Seminary.* Nashville: Broadman Press, 1959.

(147) _____. *The School of Providence and Prayer: A History of the New Orleans Baptist Theological Seminary.* New Orleans: Printing Department of New Orleans Baptist Theological Seminary, 1969.

(148) Parker, Harold M., Jr. "A New School Presbyterian Seminary in Woodford County." *Register of the Kentucky Historical Seminary* 74 (1976): 99-111.

(149) _____. "A School of the Prophets at Maryville." *Tennessee Historical Quarterly* 34 (1975): 72-90.

(150) Renfer, Rudolf A. "A History of Dallas Theological Seminary." Ph.D. dissertation, University of Texas at Austin, 1959.

(151) Roth, Gary G. "Wake Forest College and the Rise of Southeastern Baptist Theological Seminary." *Baptist History and Heritage* 11 (1976): 69-79.

(152) Rybolt, John E. "The Carondelet Seminary." *Missouri Historical Review* 74 (1980): 391-413.

(153) _____. "Kenrick's First Seminary." *Missouri Historical Review* 71 (1977): 139-55.

(154) Sanders, Robert L. *History of Louisville Presbyterian Theological Seminary, 1853-1953.* Louisville: Louisville Presbyterian Theological Seminary, 1953.

(155) Shipps, Howard F. *A Short History of Asbury Theological Seminary.* Wilmore KY: Asbury Theological Seminary, 1963.

(156) Soper, Marley. " 'Unser Seminar': The Story of Clinton German Seminary." *Adventist Heritage* 4 (1977): 44-55.

(157) Stevenson, Dwight E. *Lexington Theological Seminary 1865-1965.* St. Louis: Bethany Press, 1964.

(158) Thomas, Iva. *History of Holmes Theological Seminary.* Franklin Springs GA: n.p., 1959. Reprint, Greenville SC: n.p., 1969.

V. SOUTHERN RELIGION AND EDUCATION: PRIMARY, SECONDARY, AND MISCELLANEOUS ENDEAVORS

(159) Buckley, Cathryn. "The Everett Institute." *North Louisiana Historical Association Journal* 8 (1977): 119-24.

(160) DeLeon, Arnoldo. "Blowout 1910 Style: A Chicano School Boycott in West Texas." *Texana* 12 (1974): 124-40.

(161) Everman, H. E. "Early Educational Channels of Bourbon County." *Register of the Kentucky Historical Society* 73 (1975): 136-49.

(162) Ferguson, Anne Williams. "Carry Me Not, Repeat Not, Back to Ole Virginny: A Boarding School Chronicle of the 40's." *Virginia Quarterly Review* 52 (1976): 243-48.

(163) Gavelis, Vytautus. "A Descriptive Study of the Educational Attainment, Occupation, and Geographical Location of Children of Lithuanian Displaced Persons and of American Born Parents Who Attended Immaculate Conception Primary School in East St. Louis from 1948 to 1968." *Lituanus* 22 (1976): 72-75.

(164) Glauert, Ralph E. "An Uncommon Commitment: Clergymen and Their Schools in Frontier Missouri." *Missouri Historical Society Bulletin* 34 (1977): 3-16.

(165) Hitchcock, James R. "A History of Catholic Secondary Education in the Diocese of Nashville, 1837-1953." M.A. thesis, Catholic University of America, 1953.

(166) Howlett, William J. *Old St. Thomas' at Poplar Neck, Bardstown, Kentucky.* Cleveland: Dillon/Liederback, 1972. First published, 1906.

(167) Kemper, Donald J. "Catholic Integration in St. Louis, 1935-1947." *Missouri Historical Review* 73 (1978): 1-22.

(168) Kramer, William A. "Life in Perry County, Missouri, at the Turn of the Century." *Concordia Historical Institute Quarterly* 48 (1975): 10-25.

(169) Lampe, Philip E. "The Acculturation of Mexican Americans in Public and Parochial Schools." *Sociological Analysis* 36 (1975): 57-66.

(170) Lenhart, John M. "The German Catholic School in Wheeling, West Virginia, 1846-1955." *Social Justice Review* 49 (1956): 168-69.

(171) Lyon, Ralph M. "The Early Years of Livingston Female Academy." *Alabama Historical Quarterly* 37 (1975): 192-205.

(172) McCants, Sr. Dorothea Olga. "Old St. Vincent Academy." *North Louisiana Historical Association Journal* 5 (1973): 25-27.

(173) McCaul, Robert L. "Education in Georgia During the Period of Royal Government, 1752-1776: Public-School Masters and Private-Venture Teachers." *Georgia Historical Quarterly* 40 (1956): 248-59.

(174) McDermott, Jon F. "Private Schools in St. Louis, 1809-1821." *Mid-America* 11 (1940): 96-119.

(175) Malone, Michael T. "The Episcopal School of North Carolina, 1832-1842." *North Carolina Historical Review* 49 (1972): 178-94.

(176) Murphy, John J. "The Diocese of Kansas City and Its Schools." *Catholic School Journal* 52 (1952): 113-15.

(177) O'Flynn, Sr. Mary Agnes. *A Souvenir of Mount St. Joseph's Ursuline Academy: "Maple Mount," Daviess County, Kentucky.* Boston: Angel Guardian Press, 1907.

(178) O'Steen, Neal. "Pioneer Education in the Tennessee Country." *Tennessee Historical Quarterly* 35 (1976): 199-219.

(179) Poole, David R., Jr. "Educational Work at Whitefield's Orphan School in Georgia." *Methodist History* 15 (1977): 186-95.

(180) Racine, Philip N. "The Ku Klux Klan, Anti-Catholicism, and Atlanta's Board of Education, 1916-1927." *Georgia Historical Quarterly* 57 (1973): 63-75.

(181) "School for Farmers." *Jubilee* 4 (1956): 42-45.

(182) Sisters of the Visitation, St. Louis. *Centennial Souvenir: Academy of the Visitation.* St. Louis: Francis de Sales Press, 1933.

(183) Witte, Cyril M. "A History of St. Mary's Industrial School for Boys of the City of Baltimore, 1866-1950." Ph.D. dissertation, University of Notre Dame, 1955.

19 SOUTHERN CLERGY

GIVEN THE PROMINENCE of religion in Southern culture, it would seem only logical that the clergy would have an equally prominent place in Southern society. But such has not always been the case. In the colonial period, for example, when the Church of England enjoyed the status of establishment in the English colonies that became part of the United States, clergy were beset with many difficulties. The frequent conflicts with local vestries, highlighted in chapter 7, suggest that clergy did not enjoy the same status as their peers in the mother country. The situation of the colonial Anglican clergy was complicated because candidates for orders had to travel to England since there was no bishop in the colonies who could officiate at ritual ordination. Another problem was recruiting clergy, for vestry control of parishes did not provide for ''job security'' and salaries were frequently low.

Joan R. Gundersen, ''The Search for Good Men: Recruiting Ministers in Colonial Virginia'' (6), offers a reliable exposition of some of these dilemmas. On the role of the clergy and the character of colonial ministry, see Arthur P. Middleton, ''The Colonial Parson'' (12). A frequent complaint, directed particularly toward the Anglican ministry, was the quality of the individuals who served as clergy. Criticism concerned the intellectual ability, the pastoral capability, and often the moral character of parish priests. Calls for reform were common. Commissary James Blair sought to upgrade the quality of the Anglican clergy during his tenure. For that story, see Samuel C. McCulloch, ''James Blair's Plan of 1699 to Reform the Clergy of Virginia'' (11). On the popular criticism of clergy for being lazy and irresponsible, see James P. Walsh, '' 'Black Cotted Raskolls': Anti-Anglican

Criticism in Colonial Virginia'' (27). Some criticism was not unwarranted. David T. Morgan, Jr., "Scandal in Carolina: The Story of a Capricious Missionary" (14), recounts the controversy in colonial North Carolina concerning Michael Smith (d. 1698), who was accused of long absences from his duties, adultery, excessive drinking of alcoholic beverages, and improper behavior (dancing). David C. Skaggs and Gerald E. Hartdagen, "Sinners and Saints: Anglican Clerical Conduct in Colonial Maryland" (24), in looking at the period from 1700 to 1775, however, found that historians tended to emphasize only the presence of either qualified, dedicated clergy or those of questionable character. Their research found numerous examples of both.

But the colonial Anglicans were not the only ones who experienced difficulty in securing an adequate number of qualified clergy to carry on religious labors. Similar problems frequently plagued Roman Catholic efforts in Louisiana. See, for example, Alfred C. Rush, "The Supply of Clergy in Louisiana, 1763-1805" (20). Later American Catholics would face the difficulty of ministering to an ethnically diverse people, given the various patterns of immigration and in-migration that brought different groups of Catholics to parts of the South. Some illumination of this situation is provided by James Hitchcock, "Secular Clergy in Nineteenth Century America: A Diocesan Profile" (7), a case study of the Archdiocese of St. Louis between 1841 and 1899. Also see John E. Rothensteiner, "The Missouri Priest One Hundred Years Ago" (19). For a synoptic study with implications for the changing nature of the priesthood in the South, see John Tracy Ellis, ed., *The Catholic Priest in America: Historical Investigations* (4). Titles dealing with the work of many Catholic orders, male and female, are found in the listing for chapter 5.

Clergy, of course, were key elements in the evangelical ascendancy in the South both in the revivals of the Great Awakening and the frontier camp-meetings, discussed in chapter 2. Barbara A. Larson, "Samuel Davies and the Rhetoric of the New Light" (38), shows how this Presbyterian preacher of the Awakening was able to incorporate the theology of the prorevival New Light position into his sermons. Sandra Rennie argues that the clergy were central figures in providing cohesion for the Separate Baptist movement, which began to assume greater coherence in the later eighteenth century, in "The Role of the Preacher: Index to the Consolidation of the Baptist Movement in Virginia from 1760 to 1790" (18). On the frontier, the Baptist and Methodist clergy, often ill-educated in a formal sense and frequently without official ordination, effectively used an enthusiastic style of preaching in their calls for conversion and intensive personal religious experience. See Carl L. Button, "The Rhetoric of Immediacy: Baptist and Methodist Preaching on the Trans-Appalachian Frontier" (31). It was, perhaps, the simple humanity of these preachers that made their appeals plausible. On this matter, see George

W. Knight, "Treasure in Earthen Vessels: The Humanity and Humor of the Frontier Baptist Preacher" (37).

But as the frontier became more stable and church life assumed greater organization, the question of proper training and ordination assumed greater significance, especially for Baptists and Methodists. On practices regarding qualification for ordination in Southern Baptist circles, see John E. Steely, "Ministerial Certification in Southern Baptist History: Ordination" (25). Although Baptists frequently prided themselves on having a clergy drawn from the ranks of the common people, over the years they have encouraged more formal training for ministry and the educational attainment of Baptist clergy has risen. One study of the Baptist movement toward more formal education for clergy, particularly in the contemporary period, is Don F. Mabry and Paul W. Stuart, "A Study of the Educational Attainments of Southern Baptist Pastors" (10). Also see W. Morgan Patterson, "Changing Preparation for a Changing Ministry" (15). The Baptist emphasis on local congregational autonomy has endowed pastors with greater responsibility for formulating a theological stance that parishioners tend to regard as normative for the denomination. This aspect of the Baptist professional ministry is the focus of Walter B. Shurden, "The Pastor as Denominational Theologian in Southern Baptist History" (23).

Among the Southern Protestant denominations, the Presbyterians have historically been most insistent on the need for a solid educational background and formal theological training for clergy. Approaches to this preparation of clergy in the antebellum period, along with their historical roots in the Reformed tradition, form the subject of a doctoral dissertation by Robert N. Watkin, Jr., "The Forming of the Southern Presbyterian Minister: From Calvin to the American Civil War" (28). Also see Elwyn A. Smith, *The Presbyterian Ministry in America* (8:28). On views of the ministry in the Churches of Christ, see Patrick H. Casey, "The Role of the Preacher as Set Forth in the *Gospel Advocate* from 1895 through 1910" (3). Studies treating theological education per se and individual seminaries, divinity schools, and schools of theology are identified in the listing for chapter 18.

Several studies of pulpit oratory in the twentieth century suggest the multifaceted role of preaching in Southern religious life. Two articles provide a historical perspective on preaching in the Southern Baptist tradition: Thomas R. McKibbens, "The Role of Preaching in Southern Baptist History" (39), and James W. Cox, "The Southern Baptist Pulpit, 1845-1970" (32). In the early 1940s, James H. Ivey appraised what it took to be a "successful preacher" in the South and concluded that perceptions of success were linked to popularity, which was in turn tied to keeping a congregation content through sermons of spiritual uplift rather than challenging a congregation to rethink beliefs or change social mores. See his "A Study of Preaching in Southern

Churches'' (36). But at times the clergy through the pulpit have provided strong leadership for social change, or at least in helping listerners accept and adjust to changing social realities. Such was particularly true at the peak of the civil rights movement, according to the sermons and commentary found in Donald W. Shriver, Jr., ed., *The Unsilent Pulpit: Prophetic Preaching in Racial Crisis* (42). For other titles on clergy involvement in the civil rights movement, see the listing for chapter 20. A commanding oratorical style continues to reinforce perceptions of dynamic leadership according to James E. Towns in his study of prominent Southern Baptist pastor W. A. Criswell, ''The Rhetoric and Leadership of W. A. Criswell as President of the Southern Baptist Convention'' (46). For related studies concerning both Criswell and the office of president of the Southern Baptist Convention, see chapter 9. As well, preachers and their pulpits have frequently been the source for Southern religious thought. On this topic, see the listing for chapter 21.

Clergy have indeed long been near mythic figures in the Southern religious landscape. Arbiters of the divine will and catalysts of conversion, they have exercised a powerful influence in shaping Southern religious and cultural life. Yet they have also been important agents in the struggle to preserve the status quo in society. Perhaps it is the importance of the clergy to religious life that means a different current of interpretation is prevalent as well. Images of the preacher in literature suggest that the clergy have often been seen as naive idealists, hypocritical connivers, ignorant moralists, or simply Puritanical prudes unacquainted with everyday reality. The most comprehensive study of images of clergy in literature is C. Harold Woodell's doctoral dissertation, ''The Preacher in Nineteenth Century Southern Fiction'' (52), the essence of which has been published as ''The Preacher as Villain and Fool in Nineteenth-Century Southern Fiction'' (51). Also see James H. Penrod, ''Teachers and Preachers in Old Southwestern Yarns'' (50). Black clergy have had a far more expansive role, given the centrality of the Black church to community life over the years. While some titles listed in chapter 4 analyze the importance of the Black clergy, two that deal specifically with images of the Black clergy in literature are Walter C. Daniel, *Images of the Preacher in Afro-American Literature* (49), and Nancy B. Woolridge, ''The Negro Preacher in American Fiction before 1900'' (53), a University of Chicago doctoral dissertation. In addition, see Helen B. Allen, ''The Minister of the Gospel in Negro American Fiction'' (47).

Whether as agents responsible for imprinting the evangelical style on the South, as moral exemplars, as supporters or challengers of the status quo, as villains and fools, preachers and the clergy will remain vital parts of Southern religious life as long as religion continues to permeate Dixie's culture.

BIBLIOGRAPHY

Studies of individual clergy may be found in the chapters on individual denominations and movements as well as in chapters 2, 3, and 4. Clergy involvement in social issues is included in chapter 20. Also see chapter 21 on Southern religious thought. Titles concerning theological education may be found in chapter 18.

I. SOUTHERN CLERGY:
ROLE, STATUS, RECRUITMENT, AND PUBLIC PERCEPTION

(1) Bennett, Weldon B. "The Concept of the Ministry in the Thought of Representative Men of the Disciples of Christ (1804-1906)." Ph.D. dissertation, University of Southern California, 1966.

(2) Carter, James E. "The Socioeconomic Status of Baptist Ministers in Historical Perspective." *Baptist History and Heritage* 15 (1980): 37-44.

(3) Casey, Patrick H. "The Role of the Preacher as Set Forth in the *Gospel Advocate* from 1895 through 1910 with Beliefs and Consequences to 1980." D.Min. dissertation, Harding Graduate School of Religion, 1980.

(4) Ellis, John Tracy, ed. *The Catholic Priest in the United States: Historical Investigations*. Collegeville MN: St. John's University Press, 1971.

(5) Gronseth, Elbert E. "The Reaction of Presbyterian Ministers in the Knoxville Area to Specific Questions Concerning Ministerial Counseling." Thesis, University of Tennessee at Knoxville, 1961.

(6) Gundersen, Joan R. "The Search for Good Men: Recruiting Ministers in Colonial Virginia." *Historical Magazine of the Protestant Episcopal Church* 48 (1979): 453-64.

(7) Hitchcock, James. "Secular Clergy in Nineteenth Century America: A Diocesan Profile." *Records of the American Catholic Historical Society of Philadelphia* 88 (1977): 31-62.

(8) Isom, Allan Lloyd. "A Study of the Financial Condition of Church of Christ Preachers." Ed.D. dissertation, New Orleans Baptist Theological Seminary, 1972.

(9) Lemon, Robert Lyman. "Alexander Campbell's Doctrine of the Ministry." Ph.D. dissertation, Pacific School of Religion, 1968.

(10) Mabry, Don F., and Paul W. Stuart. "A Study of the Educational Attainments of Southern Baptist Pastors." *The Southern Baptist Educator* 38 (March-April 1974): 3-11.

(11) McCulloch, Samuel C. "James Blair's Plan of 1699 to Reform the Clergy of Virginia." *William and Mary Quarterly* 3d series 4 (1947): 70-86.

(12) Middleton, Arthur P. "The Colonial Parson." *William and Mary Quarterly* 3d series 26 (1969): 425-40.

(13) Miller, Rodney K. "The Influence of the Socio-Economic Status of the Anglican Clergy of Revolutionary Maryland on Their Political Organization." *Historical Magazine of the Protestant Episcopal Church* 47 (1978): 197-210.

(14) Morgan, David T., Jr. "Scandal in Carolina: The Story of a Capricious Missionary." *North Carolina Historical Review* 47 (1970): 233-43.

(15) Patterson, W. Morgan. "Changing Preparation for a Changing Ministry." *Baptist History and Heritage* 15 (1980): 14-22, 59.

(16) Posey, Walter B. "Ecclesiastical Hankerings." *Tennessee Historical Quarterly* 23 (1964): 136-44.

(17) Prestwood, W. Morgan. "Dilemmas of Deep South Clergy." *Christianity Today* 5 (16 January 1961): 8-9.

(18) Rennie, Sandra. "The Role of the Preacher: Index to the Consolidation of the Baptist Movement in Virginia from 1760 to 1790." *Virginia Magazine of History and Biography* 88 (1980): 430-41.

(19) Rothensteiner, John E. "The Missouri Priest One Hundred Years Ago." *Missouri Historical Review* 21 (1927): 562-69.

(20) Rush, Alfred C. "The Supply of Clergy in Louisiana, 1763-1805." M.A. thesis, Catholic University of America, 1938.

(21) Rymph, Raymond C., and Jeffrey K. Hadden. "The Persistence of Regionalism as a Factor in Racial Attitudes of Methodist Clergy." *Social Forces* 49 (1970): 41-50.

(22) Shurden, Walter B., ed. "Documents on the Ministry in Southern Baptist History." *Baptist History and Heritage* 15 (1980): 45-54, 64.

(23) _____. "The Pastor as Denominational Theologian in Southern Baptist History." *Baptist History and Heritage* 15 (1980): 15-22.

(22) Skaggs, David C., and Gerald E. Hartdagen. "Sinners and Saints: Anglican Clerical Conduct in Colonial Maryland." *Historical Magazine of the Protestant Episcopal Church* 47 (1978): 177-95.

(25) Steely, John E. "Ministerial Certification in Southern Baptist History: Ordination." *Baptist History and Heritage* 15 (1980): 23-29, 61.

(26) Tise, Larry E. "The Interregional Appeal of Proslavery Thought: An Ideological Profile of the Antebellum American Clergy." *Plantation Society in the Americas* 1 (1979): 58-72.

(27) Walsh, James P. " 'Black Cotted Raskolls': Anti-Anglican Criticism in Colonial Virginia." *Virginia Magazine of History and Biography* 88 (1980): 21-36.

(28) Watkin, Robert N., Jr. "The Forming of the Southern Presbyterian Minister: From Calvin to the American Civil War." Ph.D. dissertation, Vanderbilt University, 1969.

(29) Yackel, Peter G. "Benefit of Clergy in Colonial Maryland." *Maryland Historical Magazine* 69 (1974): 383-97.

(30) Zimmer, Anne Y. "The 'Paper War' in Maryland, 1772-73: The Paca-Chase Political Philosophy Tested." *Maryland Historical Magazine* 71 (1976): 177-93.

II. SOUTHERN CLERGY: PREACHING AND RHETORIC

(31) Button, Carl L. "The Rhetoric of Immediacy: Baptist and Methodist

Preaching on the Trans-Appalachian Frontier.'' Ph.D. dissertation, University of California at Los Angeles, 1972.

(32) Cox, James W. ''The Southern Baptist Pulpit, 1845-1970.'' *Review and Expositor* 67 (1970): 195-202.

(33) Eubank, W. C. ''Palmer's Century Sermon, New Orleans, January 1, 1901.'' *Southern Speech Journal* 35 (1969): 28-39.

(34) Flynt, J. Wayne, and William W. Rogers. ''Reform Oratory in Alabama, 1890-1896.'' *Southern Speech Journal* 29 (1963): 94-106.

(35) Handford, Charlene Jeanette. ''Bishop Charles Galloway's Rhetoric, 1903-1908.'' *Journal of Mississippi History* 44 (1982): 217-25.

(36) Ivey, James H. ''A Study of Preaching in Southern Churches.'' *Review and Expositor* 40 (1943): 449-57.

(37) Knight, George W. ''Treasure in Earthen Vessels: The Humanity and Humor of the Frontier Baptist Preacher.'' *Baptist History and Heritage* 7 (1972): 76-81.

(38) Larson, Barbara A. ''Samuel Davies and the Rhetoric of the New Light.'' *Speech Monographs* 38 (1971): 207-16.

(39) McKibbens, Thomas R., Jr. ''The Role of Preaching in Southern Baptist History.'' *Baptist History and Heritage* 15 (1980): 30-36, 64.

(40) Marszalek, John R., ed. ''A Civil War Sermon as Recounted in the Emma E. Holmes Diary.'' *Historical Magazine of the Protestant Episcopal Church* 46 (1977): 57-62.

(41) Pinson, William. ''The Pulpit and Race Relations.'' In *Preaching in American History*. DeWitte Holland, ed., 375-90. Nashville: Abingdon Press, 1968.

(42) Shriver, Donald W., Jr., ed. *The Unsilent Pulpit: Prophetic Preaching in Racial Crisis*. Richmond VA: John Knox Press, 1965.

(43) Stewart, Charles J. ''Civil War Preaching.'' In *Preaching in American History*. DeWitte Holland, ed., 184-205. Nashville: Abingdon Press, 1968.

(44) _____. ''The Pulpit and the Assassination of Lincoln.'' *Quarterly Journal of Speech* 50 (1964): 299-307.

(45) Taylor, Hubert V. ''Preaching on Slavery, 1831-1861.'' In *Preaching in American History*. DeWitte Holland, ed., 168-83. Nashville: Abingdon Press, 1968.

(46) Towns, James E. ''The Rhetoric and Leadership of W. A. Criswell as President of the Southern Baptist Convention.'' Ph.D. dissertation, Southern Illinois University, 1970.

III. SOUTHERN CLERGY:
IMAGES OF THE PREACHER IN LITERATURE

(47) Allen, Helen Bernice. ''The Minister of the Gospel in Negro American Fiction.'' Master's thesis, Fisk University, 1937.

(48) Colmant, Berta. "Four Preacher Tales from West Central Georgia." *Tennessee Folklore Society Bulletin* 42 (1976): 125-28.

(49) Daniel, Walter C. *Images of the Preacher in Afro-American Literature.* Washington: University Press of America, 1981.

(50) Penrod, James H. "Teachers and Preachers in Old Southwestern Yarns." *Tennessee Folklore Society Bulletin* 18 (1952): 91-96.

(51) Woodell, C. Harold. "The Preacher as Villain and Fool in Nineteenth-Century Southern Fiction." *CLA Journal* 25 (1981): 182-96.

(52) _____. "The Preacher in Nineteenth Century Southern Fiction." Ph.D. dissertation, University of North Carolina in North Carolina in Chapel Hill, 1974.

(53) Woolridge, Nancy B. "The Negro Preacher in American Fiction before 1900." Ph.D. dissertation, University of Chicago, 1942.

20 RELIGION AND SOCIETY IN THE SOUTH

WHEN SAMUEL S. HILL wrote *Southern Churches in Crisis* (2:36) in 1967, he claimed that the major "crisis" facing Southern religion concerned the ways in which the religious order was related to the social order. Hill, like many others, argued that the evangelical style that dominated the region's religious life perpetuated an individualistic ethic that had as its corollary a failure to relate creatively to the social order. Simply put, Southern religion was concerned with the salvation of souls, not the salvation or reformation of society. Much of the reluctance to develop a social ethic, of course, stemmed from the South's defensive posture toward slavery during the antebellum period, a posture that hardened as religiously motivated social reform efforts based largely in the North made abolition of slavery a major focus of their endeavor to create a "Christian America." The result was the emergence of a "culture religion" in which religion largely abandoned a prophetic role, but rather became a buttress to support prevailing cultural ways. As John Eighmy put it in his perceptive historical analysis of the social attitudes of Southern Baptists, Southern churches were *Churches in Cultural Captivity* (11).

This distance between religion and society in a formal sense and their delicate intertwining in an informal sense did not mean that social concerns had no impact on religion or that religion had no impact on the shape of society. The dominance of white evangelical Protestantism in much of the South, however, has meant that scholars have concentrated their interpretive studies primarily on the mutual influence of that strand of Southern religion and the social order. Several studies provide an overview of the diverse ways in which religion and society have indeed been closely connected in the South. Anne

C. Loveland, *Southern Evangelicals and the Social Order, 1800-1860* (22), notes the predilection of white evangelical Protestantism in the antebellum period to identify specific social activities such as dancing and card playing as "worldly" and therefore sinful, although she does not develop an argument as to why these pastimes came to be so regarded nor whether there is a necessary connection between this individualistic approach to ethical behavior and the Southern evangelical style. But she also observes that rarely did religious groups develop mechanisms to discipline members whose conduct was questionable; rather preachers and religious leaders were generally content to harangue about proper behavior. She also shows that much of the religiously based reform activity in the antebellum period was also individualistic in nature. That is, it was oriented more to alleviating the condition of certain kinds of individuals rather than altering the fabric of the social order. Hence there was concern, for example, for caring for the needs of orphans, the blind, the insane, and the like. Loveland also calls attention to the penchant for Sabbatarianism in the South, using so-called "blue laws" to regulate both private and public conduct on the sacred day of the evangelical Protestant majority.

Loveland does describe the work of national and regional societies committed to this individualistic mode of social reform, but the most comprehensive appraisal of this kind of activity is John W. Kuykendall, *"Southern Enterprize": The Work of the National Evangelical Societies in the Antebellum South* (21). Kuykendall's study suggests in part that there was more sustained activity of these "benevolent societies" than many other analysts have believed. He also notes, however, that there was a persistent suspicion of these societies in numerous religious circles, perhaps because some could see the broader implications of social reform in a culture that maintained a slave labor system. Also see James H. Moorhead, "Social Reform and the Divided Conscience of Antebellum Protestantism" (25), for a more general study of the reasons why some were wary of these reform efforts. John L. Thomas, "Romantic Reform in America, 1815-1865" (34), provides additional insight into the problem of why Southern evangelical Protestants tended to eschew social reform. Noting that emphasis on individual conversion was common to both Northern and Southern evangelical revivalism in the early nineteenth century, he argues that in the North the interaction of revivalism with Unitarianism and Transcendentalism, the need to confront problems posed by increased immigration and rapid urbanization, and the theological shifts that were underway as the "New Divinity" gradually replaced the more rigid Calvinist underpinnings of New England theology formed a matrix which made social reform a logical corollary to evangelicalism. These same forces, however, barely penetrated the South. Hence the dominance of an individualistic ethic and a consequent reluctance to link religion with social reform may have resulted from the different cultural context that nurtured Southern evangelicalism as much as it did from the presence of slavery. Also see Samuel S. Hill, ''The South's Two Cultures,'' in *Religion and the Solid South* (2:33).

Particularly in Southern Presbyterian circles, evangelical in style but divided over the matter of revivalism, an ideological perspective did emerge that gave support to the reluctance to link religion and social reform directly: the notion of the ''spirituality'' of the church. Most ardently advocated by James Henley Thornwell, this idea claims that social order, morality, and the like may be secured by means other than the religious, that the primary focus of the ministry of the church is individual holiness, and that therefore the church as a religious institution cannot link ambiguous social reform causes with the Divine will. This approach emerged contextually in part to undergird a proslavery stance, but as Jack P. Maddex has shown in ''From Theocracy to Spirituality: The Southern Presbyterian Reversal on Church and State'' (23), by Reconstruction it had become generally accepted. On Thornwell, see especially H. Shelton Smith, ''The Church and the Social Order in the Old South as Interpreted by James Henley Thornwell'' (31). Also see E. Brooks Holifield, ''Thomas Smyth: The Social Ideas of a Southern Evangelist'' (17).

The Civil War may have ended the slave labor system that many evangelical Protestants thought integral to the perpetuation of Southern culture, but it did not alter what had become a fairly entrenched view that religion and society were to be kept as two separate arenas of human life. The result was that by and large religion became a mechanism to support the status quo and, as Rufus B. Spain demonstrated in his social history of the Southern Baptists in the later nineteenth century, Southern white churches generally came to be *At Ease in Zion* (32). Nevertheless, there was still considerable interaction. David Edwin Harrell, Jr., has brilliantly probed the interplay between ''The Disciples of Christ and Social Forces in Tennessee, 1865-1900'' (15). But one consequence of the attempt to draw a line between religion and society was that religious institutions and leaders were often unprepared to confront the challenges that ensued when urbanization and industrialization began to introduce changes in the cultural fabric in the age of the ''New South.'' Although told from an elitist perspective, Frederick A. Bode, *Protestantism and the New South: North Carolina Baptists and Methodists in Political Crisis, 1894-1903* (4), is a good introduction to this dilemma. Somewhat narrower in focus, but building on similar premises, is John O. Fish's doctoral dissertation, ''Southern Methodism in the Progressive Era: A Social History'' (13). And the long-standing separation of religion and society may well be one reason why in the early twentieth century, the controversies over evolution, fundamentalism and modernism, and prohibition erupted with especial power in the South. While each of these will be treated in greater detail below, the best overview (and one that complements the studies by Loveland, Eighmy, and Spain previously noted) is James J. Thompson, Jr., *"Tried as by Fire"*: *Southern Baptists and the Religious Controversies of the 1920s* (36). Also for a general overview, see George D. Kelsey, *Social Ethics among Southern Baptists* (20), and James Sellers, *The South and Christian Ethics* (30).

In the first century and one-half of Southern religious life after the English invasion got underway, three major concerns demonstrated the links between religion and the public order: the challenge to established authority, religious and political, that accompanied the Great Awakening in many places; the War for Independence from Great Britain; and the movement for religious toleration or religious liberty and the end of religious establishment. To a great extent, all three stories are intertwined, for the challenge to authority wrought by the Awakening helped fuel both debates over independence and the call for religious liberty. The first, the role of the Awakening, has been noted in chapter 2. Literature concerning the others will be discussed here.

Religion became tinged with political fervor during the age of the American Revolution in part because advocates on both sides sought to justify their positions on religious grounds. While the New England clergy may have developed the most penetrating religious justification for independence, Southern clergy also contributed to the endeavor. See, for example, G. MacLaren Bryden, ed., "Passive Obedience Considered: In a Sermon Preached at Williamsburg, December 31st, 1775. By the Reverend David Griffith" (45). Griffith's point in the sermon was simply that when rulers failed to promote the happiness of the people, the people had a right to seek redress. But in the South, the connections between the established church and Britain frequently meant that clergy were regarded as Tory sympathizers, and indeed some of them were. Perhaps the most well-known is Maryland's Jonathan Boucher. In addition to the titles analyzing Boucher's work and Tory sympathies noted in chapter 7, also see Rodney Miller, "The Political Theology of the Anglican Clergy" (57), which focuses primarily on Boucher and the situation in Maryland; Philip Evanson, "Jonathan Boucher: The Mind of an American Loyalist" (48); and Ralph E. Fall, "The Rev. Jonathan Boucher, Turbulent Tory" (49). Boucher, of course, was not the only colonial Anglican priest to espouse a Loyalist position. The less well-known Philip Hughes, also of Maryland, who hoped to gain both wealth and prestige as a religious leader and consequently became a Tory because he thought it would grant him higher status when Britain subdued the colonies, is the subject of John R. Wennersten, "The Travail of a Tory Parson: Reverend Philip Hughes and Maryland Colonial Politics, 1767-1777" (65). Part of the religious ideology which supported the Tory position was the belief that God was a God of order by definition opposed to Revolution. On this point, see John F. Berens, " 'A God of Order and Not of Confusion': The American Loyalists and Divine Provi-

dence, 1774-1783'' (43). However, the Tories had lesser impact than their
numbers might suggest because they were never able to develop a consistent
theological position to support their politics, according to Glen T. Miller,
''Fear God and Honor the King: The Failure of the Loyalist Civil Theology
in the Revolutionary Crisis'' (55).

While the contribution of various religious groups to the Revolutionary
cause and the impact of the Revolution on them are noted in the respective
chapters treating individual denominations, several more general studies are
worthy of note here. K. Dieterich Pfisterer, ''Religion als ein Ferment der
Freiheit in der Americanischen Revolution'' (59), pays careful attention to
the role of the Baptists, especially in Virginia. Pfisterer's study should be
complemented by the work of Rhys Isaac detailed in chapter 2, most particularly Isaac's ''Dramatizing the Ideology of Revolution: Popular Mobilization in Virginia, 1774 to 1776'' (2:80) and his ''Preachers and Patriots: Popular
Culture and the Revolution in Virginia'' (2:82). James G. Leyburn, ''Presbyterian Immigrants and the American Revolution'' (52), highlights the importance of this group, arguing that because the Presbyterians were more
evenly distributed among the colonies they had more intercolonial contact and
therefore tended to see the Revolution in national terms rather than from the
perspective of an individual colony. Thomas O'Brien Hanley, *The American
Revolution and Religion: Maryland, 1770-1800* (50), is a rather pedestrian
study. Robert M. Calhoon, *Religion and the American Revolution in North
Carolina* (46), is mostly an anthology of primary sources with some interpretive comment published in connection with the national bicentennial in 1976.

While much of the discussion of moves for religious disestablishment and
religious liberty in the era of independence have concerned Virginia because
of the well-known Virginia Statutes of Religious Liberty (1786) drafted by
Thomas Jefferson, the story has a much earlier beginning in Maryland where
the desire of the proprietors to provide a place for Roman Catholic settlement
and the pragmatic need to populate the colony both decreed some provision
for religious freedom. Ironically, however, when Catholics became a political as well as religious minority, they often had to struggle for their own liberty in a hostile Protestant milieu. The most comprehensive treatment,
although somewhat uneven, is Thomas O. Hanley, *Their Rights and Liberties: The Beginnings of Religious and Political Freedom in Maryland* (78).
Hanley is at his best when discussing the 1649 Act of Toleration, which also
formed the focus of his earlier article, ''Catholic Political Thought in Colonial Maryland Government'' (75). In ''Church and State in the Maryland Ordinance of 1639'' (77), Hanley argued that this earlier law was as important
in preparing for toleration as the more famous 1649 ordinance. The pragmatism that undergirded the early commitment to religious toleration in
Maryland comes under scrutiny in John D. Krugler, ''Lord Baltimore, Ro-

man Catholics, and Toleration: Religious Policy in Maryland during the Early Catholic Years, 1634-1649'' (84). The later concern for religious freedom during the Revolutionary epoch is treated by John C. Rainbolt, ''The Struggle to Define 'Religious Liberty' in Maryland, 1776-1785'' (91).

In Virginia, the cry for religious liberty emerged not only from the Enlightenment ideology that buttressed Revolutionary politics, but also from evangelical theology, its understanding of the nature of religious experience, and its qualms about the propriety of religious establishment of any sort. Again, the work of Rhys Isaac noted in chapter 2 is basic to understanding the dynamics of the Virginia story, particularly in documenting the role of the Separate Baptists. But also, for the overall story, see Thomas E. Buckley, *Church and State in Revolutionary Virginia, 1776-1787* (69), and Gerald Bauer, ''The Quest for Religious Freedom in Virginia'' (67). Hamilton J. Eckenrode, *Separation of Church and State in Virginia* (72), remains a classic worth perusal. John S. Moore, ''The Struggle for Religious Freedom in Virginia'' (87), emphasizes the Baptist contribution, as does Jesse C. Green, Jr., ''The Early Virginia Argument for Separation of Church and State'' (73), which highlights the work of Baptist preacher John Leland. The Presbyterians and their Awakening leader Samuel Davies are also part of the story. Richard M. Gummere, ''Samuel Davies: Classical Champion of Religious Freedom'' (74), as the title suggests, shows how Davies's concern for religious liberty was linked to his own style of evangelicalism during the Awakening. Thomas E. Buckley, ''Church-State Settlement in Virginia: The Presbyterian Contribution'' (70), notes that while not all Presbyterians were in theory opposed to establishment, virtually all vocal Presbyterians in the era of Independence did argue for the equality of all religious groups before the law. Fred J. Hood's important ''The Revolution and Religious Liberty: The Conservation of the Theocratic Concept in Virginia'' (80), reminds students of the epoch that calls for religious liberty and/or toleration did not necessarily mean an abandonment of visions of a social order informed by religious principles. The parallel story for South Carolina is told by John W. Brinsfield, *Religion and Politics in Colonial South Carolina* (2:105). For a judicious study of the dynamics operating within the Anglican tradition in America that made moves toward toleration and liberty plausible, see Frederick V. Mills, *Bishops by Ballot* (2:90).

Those who concentrate on the English colonies in the South that became part of the United States frequently miss a very different story of church-state relations in the colonial period that transpired in Louisiana. There the French policy in effect for much of the colonial period brought an extensive and intimate interrelationship between ecclesiastical and civil authority and institutions. See both Charles E. O'Neill, *Church and State in French Colonial*

Louisiana: Policy and Politics to 1732 (88), and James D. Hardy, Jr., "Church and State in French Colonial Louisiana: An Essay Review" (79).

During the first half of the nineteenth century, in addition to the work of and the controversy surrounding the various voluntary societies of the benevolent empire, the major area where religion and the social order demonstrated an intimate connection was the debate over slavery. Since the literature on that topic is treated extensively in chapter 4, it will not again be covered here. The Civil War that climaxed the controversy over slavery left an impact on every religious group in the South. For its effects on individual denominations and for the story of specifically Southern denominations that emerged as a result of disputes over slavery or as a consequence of the War, see the chapters dealing with the individual denominations. C. C. Goen, *Broken Churches, Broken Nation* (118), has painstakingly demonstrated how the schisms over slavery in major American denominations precipitated the final, tragic struggle of the nation. Here concern will be to look more at the overall role of religion in the South in the time of the Confederacy and Reconstruction.

Still perhaps the best general study showing how religious forces became powerful buttresses for the Confederate case is James W. Silver, *Confederate Morale and Church Propaganda* (141). Silver argues that without the continuing religious support for the Southern war effort, the Confederacy might well have crumbled earlier. W. Harrison Daniel, "Protestantism and Patriotism in the Confederacy" (107), is a careful, detailed study of Southern religious newspapers and sermon literature during the war years demonstrating the many ways in which preachers and religious writers tied together Confederate patriotism and religious faith by claiming that support for the Confederate cause was itself a religious duty. Joseph Mitchell's more narrowly focused study, "Southern Methodist Newspapers during the Civil War" (128), reaches the same conclusion.

But not all Southern ministers endorsed the Confederate position. W. Harrison Daniel surveys the extent of loyalty to the Union in "Protestant Clergy and Union Settlement in the Confederacy" (106). Maryland Episcopal Bishop William R. Whittingham also gave much vocal support to the Union, opposing secession on the grounds that it was a Christian duty to support established government and thereby reaping much criticism among his flock, especially at the vestry level. See Richard R. Duncan, "Bishop Whittingham, the Maryland Diocese, and the Civil War" (113), and Edward N. Todd, ed., "Bishop Whittingham, Mount Calvary Church, and the Battle of Gettysburg" (148).

One vital way in which the churches lent support for the Southern war effort was in staffing a military chaplaincy that occasionally brought about religious revivals among the Confederate troops and numerous conversions among the soldiers. Three general studies summarize this ministry: Herman A. Norton, *Rebel Religion: The Story of Confederate Chaplains* (134); W. Harrison Daniel, "Southern Protestantism and Army Missions in the Confederacy" (109); and Sidney J. Romero, *Religion in the Rebel Ranks* (138). On revivals among the soldiers, see Emory Thomas, *The Confederate Nation* (147), and Charles Reagan Wilson, *Baptized in Blood* (21:60). One pastor, D. Eglinton Barr, who served a church in Baton Rouge at the outset of the war, was a Northerner by background and was imprisoned for a time by the Confederates after he engaged in chaplaincy work for the Federal forces. See Arlen L. Fowler, "Chaplain D. Eglinton Barr: A Lincoln Yankee" (117).

Every religious group in the South was drawn into the concerns of the war. Bertram W. Korn, *American Jewry and the Civil War* (126), while not restricted to Southern Jews, does discuss attitudes of the rabbis toward slavery, the controversy within Jewish circles over becoming involved in military chaplaincy work, and Union General Ulysses S. Grant's anti-Semitism. Also treating the Jewish story during the war years is Harry Simonhoff, *Jewish Participants in the Civil War* (143), a study that likewise concerns both Northern and Southern Judaism. The Roman Catholic Church, one of the few religious groups not to split into Northern and Southern divisions as a result of slavery and/or the war, has its story ably recounted by Benjamin J. Blied, *Catholics and the Civil War* (99). Chapter 4 of Blied's work specifically concerns Southern Catholicism. Some Catholics were drawn into the diplomatic work of the Confederacy. See Leo F. Stock, "Catholic Participation in the Diplomacy of the Southern Confederacy" (144). Perhaps the most controversial Southern Catholic leader in the Confederate era was Bishop Augustin Verot, Bishop of Savannah and vicar apostolic of Florida, who condemned the abuses of slavery but defended the system itself. See, in addition to titles noted in chapter 4, Willard E. Wight, "Bishop Verot and the Civil War" (153). Southern Quakers, because of their pacifism, faced an unusually awkward position. See Richard L. Zuber, "Conscientious Objectors in the Confederacy: The Quakers of North Carolina" (156).

Once the War ended, some Confederate supporters interpreted defeat in religious terms. The best general study of religious interpretations of the War is the work of William Clebsch, which draws on both Northern and Southern materials (101). There are several rather narrowly focused studies which merit mention. One concerns South Carolina Episcopalian laywoman Martha Wayles Robertson, who claimed that defeat was a sign of the sin that permeated the Confederacy. See Jonathan E. Helmreich, "A Prayer for the Spirit of Acceptance: The Journal of Martha Wayles Robertson, 1860-1866" (122). The many problems Southern churches faced in terms of rebuilding, loss of economic strength, and a low morale among adherents are recounted in a case study by Sylvia Krebs, "Funeral Meats and Second Marriages: Alabama

Churches in the Presidential Reconstruction Period'' (127). A more general study is W. Harrison Daniel, ''The Effects of the Civil War on Southern Protestantism'' (105). Of the many denominations that divided over the issues involved in the War, only the Episcopalians were able to reunite shortly after the war's close. Some Northern groups, however, stepped up involvement in Southern concerns, particularly among the freed blacks. Works detailing that work are included in the discussion in chapter 4, but also see Ralph E. Morrow, *Northern Methodism and Reconstruction* (129).Other relevant titles are noted in the chapters on individual denominations.

The end of slavery did not, of course, mean an end to racism in Southern or American life. Many religious bodies did seek to expand ministry to Southern blacks, although prejudice and discrimination were rarely far beneath the surface. The various forms such ministry took within the white denominations as well as the black denominations that emerged or increased efforts in the South are included in the discussion in chapter 4 as well as in the numerous chapters treating individual denominational groupings. Here the focus will center on the religious response to continuing racism down through the civil rights movement of the mid-twentieth century. Perhaps the most comprehensive study, which places the religious dimension in broader cultural context, is Joel Williamson, *The Crucible of Race: Black-White Relations in the American South Since Emancipation* (241). Basically an intellectual history of white attitudes on race, Williamson's thorough analysis, which emphasizes the period from 1890-1915, candidly appraises the repression and violence that accompanied the establishment of white supremacy and rigid racial separation. A valuable case study of one community that provides a prism through which to refract the entrenchment of racism following the Civil War is Harvey K. Newman, ''Piety and Segregation: White Protestant Attitudes Toward Blacks in Atlanta, 1865-1905'' (214). Also see H. Shelton Smith, *In His Image But . . .: Racism in Southern Religion, 1780-1910* (4:241), and David E. Harrell, Jr., *White Sects and Black Men in the Recent South* (12:25), both of which are discussed in other chapters.

Those whites who challenged the facile notions of white supremacy were often subject to abuse. Earl W. Porter, ''The Bassett Affair: Something to Remember'' (219), examines the difficulties encountered by John Spencer Bassett, history professor at Methodist-related Trinity College (Duke University), in 1902 when he advocated the idea of progress among black Americans. Calls for his dismissal were legion, but the school's Board of Trustees ultimately supported Bassett, although none of its members concurred with his position, on grounds of academic freedom. In many religious circles, it was the failure to take action, the acceptance of accommodation to the social status quo, that wittingly or unwittingly nurtured racism. The way this acceptance of prevalent social norms became embedded in the approach of one of the region's major denominations is the subject of John O. Fish, "Southern Methodism and Accommodation of the Negro, 1902-1915" (179). In Roman Catholicism in the South, by the late nineteenth century, the pattern of having segregated parishes in areas where black Roman Catholics were concentrated was well underway. See especially Dolores Egger Labbe, *Jim Crow Comes to Church: The Establishment of Segregated Catholic Parishes in South Louisiana* (196), and William A. Osborne, *The Segregated Covenant: Race Relations and American Catholics* (217), a more general study.

To be sure, religious attitudes were reinforced by social mores, and the racism that penetrated Southern religion was encouraged by groups such as the Ku Klux Klan, which fused some evangelical precepts with vitriolic racism as well as with strains of anti-Catholicism and anti-Semitism. While not exclusively Southern in focus, David M. Chalmers, *Hooded Americanism: The First Century of the Ku Klux Klan, 1865-1965* (168), is a well-done, popular survey of the Klan's development. Kenneth T. Jackson, *The Ku Klux Klan in the City, 1915-1930* (193), put to rest the once popular myth that the Klan was primarily a rural phenomenon in this study of Klan activities in cities including Atlanta, Memphis, Knoxville, Dallas, and others. The violence that often accompanied Klan activities made lynching part of the Southern landscape, although much of the opposition to such practices had religious roots. Jacquelyn Dowd Hall, "A Truly Subversive Affair: Women Against Lynching in the Twentieth-Century South" (185), for example, traces one strand of opposition to lynching, the Methodist Women's Missionary Council.

According to W. Edward Orser, "Racial Attitudes in Wartime: The Protestant Churches During the Second World War" (215), it was indeed that global conflict which brought home to religious leaders, Northern and Southern, the extent of white racism in the nation as a whole as well as the degree of inequality of opportunity between the races. The rethinking of positions and attitudes, and in some cases the hardening of a racist stance, which emerged in Southern Presbyterian circles following the War is appraised by Dwyn M. Mounger, "Racial Attitudes in the Presbyterian Church in the United States, 1944-1954" (211). A parallel story for Southern Baptists, more comprehensive in time span, is told by Foy D. Valentine, *A History of Southern Baptists and Race Relations, 1917-1947* (236).

Those who challenged the prevailing racism and actively sought to work from a religious base to secure social change faced an uphill battle for acceptance even after the 1954 *Brown v. Board of Education* Supreme Court decision gave special impetus to the civil rights movement in mid-century. The engaging yet penetrating autobiographical memoir of Will D. Campbell, *Brother to a Dragonfly* (163), splendidly evokes the ethos that spurred some whites to spurn racism and documents the risks to person and property that were common when one repudiated socially sanctioned ways. Among religious groups, the Jews gave the most obvious early support to civil rights activity. See P. Allen Krause, "Rabbis and Negro Rights in the South, 1954-1967" (195), and Janice Rothschild Blumberg, *One Voice* (6:97). In some of the white fundamentalist groups, opposition was the perhaps the most deep-seated, although there were occasional signs of support. That story is told in Julia Kirk Blackwelder, "Southern White Fundamentalists and the Civil Rights Movement" (160), which focuses primarily on the Assemblies of God, the Church of God (Cleveland, Tennessee), and the Southern Presbyterians. Where religious support for civil rights emerged in white Christian circles, it generally came first from the ranks of the clergy, although many were still dedicated to supporting the status quo. At times, too, intention and the realities of the social situation produced dilemmas. Ernest Q. Campbell and Thomas F. Pettigrew, *Christians in Racial Crisis: A Study of Little Rock's Ministry* (161), is a penetrating study of the virtual helplessness of the clergy in that Arkansas city when racial turmoil followed integration of the schools in 1957. Their thesis is straightforward: because the clergy had so long supported the status quo and assumed it was "of God," they were unprepared to serve as mediators in a time of social change and unable to provide effective leadership for their people as a result. For a similar, though briefer, study of the work of Baptist pastor Paul Turner when violence came to a Tennessee town in 1956 following forced desegregation of the schools, see Mary L. Cleveland, "A Baptist Pastor and Social Justice in Clinton, Tennessee" (171). In a penetrating essay, "Integration and the South: The South as a Cultural Unit" (232), Robert A. Spivey makes the case that the dilemma of segregation-desegregation, may have been a critical factor in perpetuating a sense of cultural unity and regional identity among white Southerners. The popular print media carried numerous articles criticizing the ineffectiveness of the churches in responding creatively to the racial crisis as well as pieces that noted the dilemma confronting clergy who privately advocated racial justice, but had to minister to racist congregations. A representative sampling of these articles is included in the bibliography at the close of the chapter. The limited and largely ineffective efforts to promote racial justice linked to the Social Gospel movement as it existed in the South will be noted elsewhere in this essay.

Many of the fears and emotions that fed racism also perpetuated a tradition of anti-Catholicism and anti-Semitism in the South. Much of Southern anti-Catholicism is connected with the brief ascendancy of the Know-Nothing Party in the mid-nineteenth century and the nativist sentiment it fostered. The most comprehensive studies of the fusion of political nativism and anti-Catholicism come in a series of master's theses and published doctoral dissertations written at the Catholic University of America in the 1930s and 1940s, which approached the phenomenon along state lines. These include

Mary deLourdes Gohmann, *Political Nativism in Tennessee to 1860* (248); Sr. Mary St. Patrick McConville, *Political Nativism in the State of Maryland, 1830-1860* (253); Sr. Mary Agnes Geraldine McCann, *Nativism in Kentucky to 1860* (252); Sr. Paul of the Cross McGrath, *Political Nativism in Texas, 1825-1860* (254); Sr. Mary of the Sacred Heart Ott, "The Know Nothings in Alabama, 1854-1860" (257); and Sr. M. Lucy Josephine Selig, "The Know-Nothing Party in Florida, 1852-1860" (262). Two master's theses produced at St. Louis University detail the story for Missouri: George L. McHugh, "Political Nativism in St. Louis, 1840-1857" (255), and H. Margaret Stauf, "The Anti-Catholic Movement in Missouri: Post Civil War Period" (263). The outbreak of a violent form of anti-Catholicism in Kentucky in the mid-nineteenth century is recounted by Leonard Koester, "Louisville's 'Bloody Monday'—August 6, 1855" (251). While these studies concentrate on the strain of nativism prevalent in the pre-Civil War period, Rowland T. Berthoff, "Southern Attitudes Toward Immigration, 1865-1914" (243), and J. Wayne Flynt, *Cracker Messiah: Governor Sidney J. Catts of Florida* (245), make clear that a more virulent nativism marked Southern culture in the years between 1890 and 1920.

Some political figures as well added fuel to anti-Catholic, anti-Semitic, and antiblack feelings. Perhaps the most well-known from the early twentieth century is Georgia's Tom Watson. Thomas G. Dyer, "Aaron's Rod: Theodore Roosevelt, Tom Watson, and Anti-Catholicism" (244), discusses Roosevelt's sharp criticism of Watson's anti-Catholicism in 1915. But particularly suggestive is Janet Brenner Franzoni, "Troubled Tirader: A Psychobiographical Study of Tom Watson" (247), which argues that this one-time vice-presidential candidate could at times espouse positions that were pro-Catholic, pro-Jewish, and problack. Watson died in 1922, near the start of a decade that witnessed an increase in anti-Catholic and anti-Semitic attitudes in many parts of the United States. James J. Thompson, Jr., "Southern Baptists and Anti-Catholicism in the 1920's" (264), makes a convincing case that Southern Baptists basically led Protestant anti-Catholic sentiment during the period. But not all was clear-cut. J. Wayne Flynt, "Religion in the Urban South: The Divided Religious Mind of Birmingham" (246), while documenting the ascendancy of anti-Catholicism and anti-Semitism in that city during the same decade, nevertheless notes that there were strong dissenting voices.

Studies of anti-Semitism in the United States have tended to look at such sentiment in the nation as a whole; none deals exclusively with anti-Semitism in the South. But there were in the nineteenth and early twentieth centuries numerous voices in the South that spoke of Social Christianity or a Social Gospel, which sought to apply to the social sector principles of justice and equality rooted in religious conviction. In the North, where Social Gospel advocates were more numerous, the movement was related to the rapid urbanization and industrialization of the later nineteenth century as well as to the political reform efforts associated with Progressivism. Some, but not all of the same concerns marked the less obvious Social Gospel movement in the South. While proponents of Social Christianity in the South were always a minority, their presence alone is sufficient to challenge the common assumption that Southern religion has espoused exclusively an individualistic ethic designed to keep religion and society separate and distinct spheres of human activity. John L. Eighmy provides a general overview of this important thrust in Southern religion in "Religious Liberalism in the South during the Progressive Era" (280). Institutionally, the most consistent effort to support programs and agencies concerned with meeting social needs and promoting a sense of human justice came from the Methodist Women's Home Missionary Society. The story of that group is ably told in John P. McDowell, *The Social Gospel in the South: The Woman's Home Mission Movement in the Methodist Episcopal Church, South, 1886-1939* (290). A more general study, popular rather than scholarly in form, is Noreen D. Tatum, *A Crown of Service: A Story of Women's Work in the Methodist Episcopal Church, South, from 1878-1940* (303). Often the call for a Social Gospel was linked to individuals, however, rather than to religious institutions. For example, Dale E. Soden, "The Social Gospel in Tennessee: Mark Allison Matthews" (301), details the career of this Presbyterian pastor in the town of Jackson from 1896 to 1902 while he lent advocacy to a number of programs designed to improve the condition of the working class. Occasionally, efforts to implement a Social Gospel took communitarian form. The short-lived utopian group in Georgia, the Christian Commonwealth Colony, was founded on Social Gospel principles—indeed its publication, *The Social Gospel,* gave the movement its popular label—but it proved an economic disaster. For its story, see John O. Fish, "The Christian Commonwealth Colony: A Georgia Experiment, 1896-1900" (281), and Paul D. Bolster, "Christian Socialism Comes to Georgia: The Christian Commonwealth Colony" (271).

Many proponents of a Social Gospel early recognized that racism was the most obvious area where Southern religion evidenced a gap between principles and practice. However, in the later nineteenth century, as Ralph E. Luker, "The Social Gospel and the Failure of Racial Reform, 1877-1898" (289), has observed, efforts in this area were largely unsuccessful in the South and elsewhere. The most sustained calls for racial justice came from the Fellowship of Southern Churchmen, organized in 1934 and committed to reform in other areas as well, including economics, labor, agricultural working conditions. For overviews of its work, see Robert F. Martin, "The Fellowship of Southern Churchmen" (295), and Martin's trenchant "Critique of Southern Society and Vision of a New Order: The Fellowship of Southern Churchmen, 1934-1957'' (294); David Burgess, ''The Fellowship of Southern Churchmen: Its History and Promise'' (274); and Anthony P. Dunbar, *Against the Grain: Southern Radicals and Prophets, 1929-59* (278). For many years, the organization was virtually synonymous with its longtime secretary, Howard Anderson Kester (1904-1977), who also helped organize the Southern Tenant Farmers Union. On Kester, see Robert F. Martin, ''A Prophet's Pilgrimage: The Religious Radicalism of Howard Anderson Kester, 1921-1941'' (296). In 1964, the Fellowship of Southern Churchmen was reorganized as the Committee of Southern Churchmen under the leadership of Will D. Campbell, whose work in the area of racial justice has already been noted.

In 1942, Baptist clergyman Clarence Jordan (1912-1969) and a small group of associates established Koinonia Farm near Americus, Georgia. Founded on communitarian principles and a commitment to what was perceived as the simplicity of New Testament Christianity, Koinonia also espoused racial justice, pacifism, and ecological concerns. During the civil rights movement of the 1950s, Koinonia and its residents suffered much abuse at the hands of white racists because of its commitment to racial equality and survived only with outside economic support. Although restructured, the enterprise remains in operation. A readable but uncritical study of Koinonia is Dallas Lee, *The Cotton Patch Evidence* (288). Mary S. Thomas, ''The Ordeal of Koinonia Farm'' (304), briefly discusses the reprisals that the community suffered because of its position on race. Also see Horst von Gizycki, ''Alternative Lebensformen (3): Die Christliche Kommunität der Koinonia-Partner in Georgia'' (284).

The work of Kester and Jordan and the groups with which they were identified was also concerned with rural problems—land use, the plight of the rural poor, the situation of tenant farmers, and the like. This area, too, has a longer history, going back to inroads made by the populist movement, something of a cousin in some areas to the Social Gospel, and organizations such as the Southern Farmers Alliance. On the last, see Robert C. McMath, Jr., *Populist Vanguard: A History of the Southern Farmers Alliance* (293). At times the presumed religious radicalism of the Social Gospel and the apparent socialism that marked some strands of agrarian populism had political ramifications. See, for example, Garin Burbank, *When Farmers Voted Red: The Gospel of Socialism in the Oklahoma Countryside, 1910-1924* (273). But one should not overestimate the enduring impact of such movements. Frederick A. Bode, ''Religion and Class Hegemony: A Populist Critique in North Carolina'' (270), for example, presents a strong case against the existence of an obvious Social Gospel movement in the South.

In the North, much of Social Christianity's agenda dealt with the conditions of labor as rapid industrialization changed the nature of work and the relationship of employer and employee. In the ''New South'' of the later nineteenth century, similar concerns are also apparent, though again those who supported unions or who called for better labor conditions, higher wages, and the like because of a religious commitment to justice remained a minority. Thomas A. Becnel, *Labor, Church, and the Sugar Establishment: Louisiana, 1887-1976* (269), for example, documents the support given at times to the National Agricultural Workers Union by Roman Catholic clergy and agencies. Episcopal priest Edgar Gardner Murphy (1869-1913), a progressive in matters of race and a proponent of popular education, was also an outspoken advocate of reform of child labor laws. In addition to the titles listed in chapter 7, also see Hugh C. Bailey, "Edgar Gardner Murphy and the Child Labor Movement" (267), and Ronald C. White, Jr., "Beyond the Sacred: Edgar Gardner Murphy and a Ministry of Social Reform" (305). Two studies by J. Wayne Flynt, meticulously researched, demonstrate that concern for improving the conditions of labor found strong support among some Southern Baptist leaders, although not among the rank and file: "Organized Labor, Reform, and Alabama Politics, 1920" (283), and "Alabama White Protestantism and Labor, 1900-1914" (282). Also see Daniel L. Cloyd, "Prelude to Reform: Political, Economic, and Social Thought of Alabama Baptists, 1877-1890" (7).

The complexities of the relationship between religion and concerns of labor are perhaps most vividly seen in two provocative discussions of the textile industry. Liston Pope's classic work, *Millhands and Preachers: A Study of Gastonia* (300), demonstrated both the links between social class and religious affiliation in milltown settings in North Carolina's Gaston County (now suburbs of Charlotte) and the way in which both the clergy and the churches of Gastonia became agents to support the antiunion movement in the wake of the tragic strike in Gastonia in 1929. A quarter of a century after Pope completed his work, which clearly demonstrated the support institutional religion could give to the social status quo, John R. Earle, Dean D. Knudsen, and Donald W. Shriver returned to Gastonia to see what changes, if any, had transpired in the links between religion and society. Their study, *Spindles and Spires: A Re-Study of Religion and Social Change in Gastonia* (279), revealed that the same class consciousness marked individual congregations and that for the most part clergy and churches remained resistant to the idea of labor unions, still supporting the social status quo. The occasional minister who evinced strong support for labor rarely had a long pastorate in the city. However, they did find that both clergy and churches had been instrumental in diffusing racial hostilities during the initial stages of racial desegregation and guiding Gastonia through the significant social change that ensued. Individual congregations, though, were still by and large racially separate.

Discussion of the influence as well as the limitations of the Social Gospel thrust in the South would be incomplete without taking note of the Southern

Sociological Congress. Intended to provide a forum for clergy, educators, and social workers oriented toward social reform, the Congress met annually between 1912 and 1920. For a brief time, the group brought public attention to a range of social issues running the gamut from prison reform to racial injustice. But the shifting of public concerns to World War I, the Congress's difficulty in addressing the basic problem of poverty in the South, and a religious climate that gave primary emphasis to individual conversion hastened its decline as an instrument to apply both religious principle and social research to the resolution of social problems. The most complete appraisal of the work of this organization is found in Lee M. Brooks and Alvin L. Bertrand, *History of the Southern Sociological Society* (272). Also see two articles by E. Charles Chatfield, "The Southern Sociological Congress: Organization of Uplift" (275), and "The Southern Sociological Congress: Rationale of Uplift" (276).

One area of social reform did attract considerable support: the temperance movement that culminated in Prohibition. While numerous studies trace the concern for temperance and Prohibition on a national scale, three focus particularly on the South: Charles C. Pearson and J. Edwin Hendricks, *Liquor and Anti-Liquor in Virginia* (313); James B. Sellers, *The Prohibition Movement in Alabama, 1702 to 1943* (316); and H. A. Scomp's much older study, *King Alcohol in the Realm of King Cotton* (315), which centers on Georgia between 1733 and 1887. It is perhaps ironic that opposition to the consumption of alcoholic beverages should gain wide currency in the South since two Southern states, Kentucky and Tennessee, are among the nation's leading producers of distilled whiskey. For many years, as Macel D. Ezell, "Early Attitudes Toward Alcoholic Beverages in the South" (309), demonstrated, use of alcohol was quite acceptable. But the cause of prohibition gained ground as evangelical Protestantism grew more theologically conservative, as consumption became identified with Roman Catholic immigrants and anti-Catholicism grew, and as racist attitudes saw control of alcohol as a means to impress white control on the region's black population. There were, in addition, genuine social concerns about alcohol abuse. Catholic opposition to rigid restriction on alcohol use in Oklahoma and some of the residual anti-Catholicism behind it is the focus of Thomas E. Brown, "Oklahoma's 'Bone-Dry Law' and the Roman Catholic Church" (306). Even after the national experiment in Prohibition terminated, local-option laws meant that prohibition or tight control continued to dominate much of Dixie. When local option was put on the ballot in referenda, frequently clergy led the forces opposed to a relaxation of restrictions, not always successfully. For an account of one such case, see Thomas H. Musselman, "A Crusade for Local Option: Shreveport, 1951-1952" (312). For accounts of one of the South's more colorful temperance advocates of an earlier generation, see Forrest Conklin's two essays, "Parson Brownlow Joins the Sons of Temperance" (307) and "Parson Brownlow—Temperance Advocate" (308). The Prohibition movement also benefited the same spirit that spurred attacks on other social "sins" as well as continuing Sabbatarian interest in some Southern religious circles. For example, Robert F. Sexton, "The Crusade Against Pari-Mutuel Gambling in Kentucky: A Study of Southern Progressivism in the 1920's" (366), notes how much antigambling sentiment stemmed from religious sectors as well as attacks led by religious leaders on machine politics. For a general study of the religious ideology supporting Sabbatarianism or, more popularly, "blue laws," see Louis B. Weeks, "The Scriptures and Sabbath Observance in the South" (350). Some questions about the extent to which restrictions on Sunday activity were appropriate came when organized athletics became part of the region's recreational life. David T. Javersak, "Wheeling's Sunday Sensation: The 1889 Wheeling Nailers" (348), notes the controversy in that West Virginia town over whether Sunday games violated local ordinances against work on Sunday. Similar concerns erupted on a more widespread basis as baseball enjoyed its heyday as the national pastime. See, for example, "Professional Sunday Baseball: A Study in Social Reform, 1892-1934" (349), which focuses on Atlanta, Chicago, and New York. More recent concern both to repeal and to maintain the "blue laws" that remain on the books in many communities and in some Southern states has yet to receive sustained scholarly analysis.

The decade of the 1920s not only witnessed the attempt at national prohibition and the unfortunate increase of anti-Catholic and anti-Semitic attitudes, it also saw the controversy over evolution and the confrontation between "fundamentalists" and "modernists" reach a peak. Studies of the latter that treat issues other than the links of the fundamentalist-modernist controversy to the furor over the teaching of evolutionary theory will be noted in chapter 21. An early scholarly assessment of the evangelical hostility to evolutionary theory, still worth consulting, is Virginius Dabney's chapter, "Evolution and the Evangelicals," in his *Liberalism in the South* (318). Willard B. Gatewood, Jr., has edited a helpful anthology of primary source materials that concentrates heavily on Southern materials: *Controversy in the Twenties: Fundamentalism, Modernism, and Evolution* (321). William E. Ellis, "The Fundamentalist-Modernist Schism over Evolution in the 1920's" (320), notes how internal divisions over evolution within such powerful religious groups as the Southern Baptists, Disciples of Christ, and Methodists meant that efforts to enact antievolution legislation in Kentucky were doomed. Catholics in some instances found themselves allied with their Protestant opposition in the fight against evolution. See John L. Morrison's well-documented study, "American Catholics and the Crusade against Evolution" (327). Two essays deal particularly with the impact of the evolution controversy within the

Southern Baptist Convention: James J. Thompson, Jr., "Southern Baptists and the Antievolution Controversy of the 1920's" (331), and W. Morgan Patterson, "The Southern Baptist Theologian as Controversialist: A Contrast" (328).

Willard B. Gatewood, Jr., *Preachers, Pedagogues and Politicians: The Evolution Controversy in North Carolina, 1920-1927* (324) is a careful study of the religious, educational, and political ramifications and interplay in Tarheel debates over evolution. Something of the popular outrage and the way emotions could be roused against evolution may be seen in James T. Baker's account of evangelist Mordecai Ham's attacks on evolution while conducting a revival in Elizabeth City, North Carolina, in 1924: "The Battle of Elizabeth City: Christ and Antichrist in North Carolina" (317). The story for Oklahoma is recounted in Elbert L. Watson, "Oklahoma and the Anti-Evolution Movement of the 1920's" (332). The linkage of evolution with a threat to religious orthodoxy owed some of its strength to the rhetoric of William Jennings Bryan, who made antievolution into a religious crusade. See Ferenc M. Szasz, "William Jennings Bryan, Evolution, and the Fundamentalist-Modernist Controversy" (329). Bryan, of course, made his most notorious attacks on evolutionary theory in the celebrated Scopes Trial in Dayton, Tennessee. Southerners throughout the region followed the trial avidly. See, for example, Wallace Hebert, "Louisiana Baptists and the Scopes Trial" (326), and Charles R. Wilson, " 'Mormons', Monkeys, and Morality: Reactions to the Scopes Trial in Texas" (334). As was the case in matters of race, so too with evolution: if academicians lent support to views contrary to the popular beliefs of the larger regional society, they came under severe attack. For one example, see Willard B. Gatewood, Jr., "Embattled Scholar: Howard W. Odum and the Fundamentalists, 1925-1927" (322). The more recent attempts to enact legislation either prohibiting the teaching of evolutionary theory or requiring the concomitant teaching of what has become known as "scientific creationism" await scholarly scrutiny. That such concerns may be more wide-ranging in scope, though, may be seen in the struggle over selection of public school textbooks that raged in West Virginia's Kanawha County in the early and mid-1970s. See James Humphreys, "Textbook War in West Virginia" (362).

Many of the social issues discussed here had political ramifications. Anti-Catholicism, for example, played an important role in the 1916 gubernatorial and senatorial election in Florida where some candidates attempted to appeal to religious bigotry in an effort to secure votes. J. Wayne Flynt, ed., "William V. Knott and the Gubernatorial Campaign of 1916" (337), documents Knott's loss to Sidney Catts, a well-known anti-Catholic, in the Democratic primary, while Stephen Kerber, "Park Trammell and the Florida Democratic Senatorial Primary of 1916" (340), shows how the anti-Catholic element in the gubernatorial campaign also affected the senatorial campaign. Anti-Catholic sentiment, racism, and prohibition advocacy came together in the Presidential election of 1928 that pitted wet, Catholic Democrat Alfred E. Smith against dry, Quaker Republican Herbert Hoover. But correlations in this election are not always tidy; rather, they occasionally reveal that racist ideology exceeded anti-Catholic and pro-Prohibition sentiment. Barbara C. Wingo, "The 1928 Presidential Election in Louisiana" (347), noted that while Smith did carry that state by a considerable margin, his pockets of strength varied and were concentrated in the wet, Catholic South. Republican strength centered in the dry, Protestant North and among the small number of black voters in the state. In this case, apparently, religious divisions were more important than racial divisions. A rather different story emerges from analysis of the vote in West Tennessee. G. Michael McCarthy, "The Brown Derby Campaign in West Tennessee: Smith, Hoover, and the Politics of Race" (344), emphasized the degree to which both anti-Catholic and antiblack feelings came to the fore prior to the election with many Protestant leaders openly supporting Hoover on religious grounds although it was generally known that black voters endorsed Hoover. In "Smith vs. Hoover: The Politics of Race in West Tennessee" (345), McCarthy demonstrated that in West Tennessee, where approximately one-third of the population was black, the election results revealed an overwhelming white majority for Smith because the Republicans—and consequently Hoover—were popularly identified as the "black" party. In this case, then, racism surpassed religious intolerance as a political factor.

Religious involvement in politics played a conspicuous role when Georgia's former governor, born-again Southern Baptist Jimmy Carter, ran for the White House in 1976. Carter unabashedly affirmed his belief in the spiritual foundations of politics and the ways in which his political philosophy had been shaped by religious convictions. A perceptive analysis that appears to be more of an attempt to explain to non-Americans the candid linking of religion and politics in the Carter style is F. G. Friedman, "Renaissance des Populismus in der USA: Geistig-religiöse Hintergründe der Präsidentschaftswählen" (338). Carter, of course, in his unsuccessful bid for reelection in 1980, encountered considerable religious opposition from the so-called New Religious Political Right, encompassing groups such as the Moral Majority and leaders such as Virginia's independent Baptist televangelist Jerry Falwell. While scholarly studies of the continuing impact of this injection of a blatant religious dimension into the political realm, a source of controversy in the 1984 Reagan-Mondale campaign, are yet to be written, it would appear that an intertwining of the two has gained acceptability in religious circles beyond the South at least for a time.

By the 1980s concern for women's rights, especially as related to abortion and the adoption of the proposed "equal rights amendment," had joined the national agenda of those committed to wide-ranging social reform. Although women had long been deeply involved in Southern religious life, relatively few seemed disposed to become active proponents of women's issues. The reluctance of Southern women to join in these causes has deep cultural and religious roots. Keith L. Bryant, "The Role and Status of the Female Yeomanry in the Antebellum South" (5), for example, indicated how religious activity was one arena in which it was socially acceptable for middle-class white women to participate, so long as general direction remained in the hands of men. But the ways in which some women's religious societies, specifically the Methodist Women's Home Missionary Society, could promote social involvement of a different sort have already been noted. A case study, Harvey C. Newman's "The Role of Women in Atlanta's Churches, 1865-1906" (26), points out the many dimensions of the issue and the potential conflict between socially acceptable activity and direct social involvement. A more repressive attitude towards women's religious activity came as part of the overall conservative thrust of the 1920s, according to Mollie C. Abernathy, "Southern Women, Social Reconstruction, and the Church in the 1920's" (1). Today, although many Southern religious groups have come to ordain women to the professional ministry, a regional conservatism with regard to women's issues continues. Such conservatism has led, for example, to the apparently strong support for so-called "right to life" and other anti-abortion groups among Southern Protestant women. See Priscilla Parish Williams, "Right to Life: The Southern Strategy" (369). Numerous other titles examining the vital role of women in Southern religious life may be found in the bibliographies at the close of chapters on the various denominations.

Opposition to "abortion on demand," scrutiny of proposed policies of political candidates, concern for restriction on the teaching of evolution, and advocacy of a Constitutional amendment legalizing the setting aside of specific times for voluntary prayer in the public schools are all part of the broad agenda associated with the Moral Majority and the New Religious Political Right. Estimated to have greater regional strength in the South than elsewhere, these groups are difficult to assess in terms of either regional or national influence because they are not directly linked with a particular denomination or denominations, because individuals frequently hold "membership" in more than one group linked to the general movement, and because public pronouncements reflecting the "new religious right" perspective come primarily from a handful of charismatic preachers. While there have been several popular studies of the Moral Majority and the movement it appears to represent, usually from a hostile stance, there are few scholarly studies, perhaps because the emergence of the movement in the last decade or so means it has not yet developed a history that permits solid academic analysis. The best study, which does note both Southern roots and strength, is Samuel

S. Hill and Dennis E. Owen, *The New Religious Political Right in America*
(2:31). But also see James E. Wood, Jr., "The New Religious Right and Its
Implications for Southern Baptists" (370).

Individual salvation may remain the first concern of the evangelical religious style in the South, and individual ethics may continue to be deemed
more important than a social ethic. But Southern religion has also long been
intertwined with the social sector. Much of the time the relationship has been
symbiotic, with religion and cultural mores reinforcing rather than challenging each other. At other times, on specific issues, a more prophetic stance has
emerged in religious circles, and Southern religion has at nurtured a potent,
though minority, concern for social reform.

The bibliography that follows begins with a listing of general and thematic studies and continues with separate sections identifying works on the
War for Independence; religious liberty and church-state relations; the Civil
War and the Confederacy; racism, discrimination, and the civil rights movement; nativism, anti-Catholicism, and anti-Semitism; Populism, the Social
Gospel, and labor concerns; the temperance and prohibition movements; the
controversy over evolution; politics; Sabbatarianism; charitable institutions;
other twentieth-century issues; and miscellaneous issues.

BIBLIOGRAPHY

Many of the titles listed in chapters 2, 3, 4, and 21 and in the chapters
treating individual religious groups are also relevant to the study of Religion
and Society in the South.

I. RELIGION AND THE SOCIAL ORDER IN THE SOUTH: GENERAL AND THEMATIC STUDIES

(1) Abernathy, Mollie C. "Southern Women, Social Reconstruction, and the
Church in the 1920's." *Louisiana Studies* 13 (1974): 289-312.

(2) Baker, John W. "Baptists and Politics: Revolution and Revolution." *Baptist History and Heritage* 7 (1972): 225-32.

(3) Banner, Lois W. "Religious Benevolence as Social Control: A Critique of
an Interpretation." *Journal of American History* 60 (1973): 23-41.

(4) Bode, Frederick A. *Protestantism and the New South: North Carolina Baptists and Methodists in Political Crisis, 1894-1903.* Charlottesville: University of Virginia Press, 1975.

(5) Bryant, Keith L. "The Role and Status of the Female Yeomanry in the Antebellum South." *Southern Quarterly* 18 (1980): 73-88.

(6) Campbell, Will D. "The World of the Redneck." *Christianity and Crisis*
24 (1974): 111-18.

(7) Cloyd, Daniel L. "Prelude to Reform: Political, Economic, and Social
Thought of Alabama Baptists, 1877-1890." *Alabama Review* 31 (1978): 48-
64.

(8) Crain, Joseph A. *The Development of Social Ideas among the Disciples of Christ.* St. Louis: Bethany Press, 1969.

(9) Cross, Jasper W. "The St. Louis Catholic Press and Political Issues, 1845-1861." *Records of the American Catholic Historical Society* 80 (1964): 210-23.

(10) Daniel, W. Harrison. "The Response of Virginia Baptists to Political Issues, 1865-1902." *Baptist History and Heritage* 8 (1973): 28-35.

(11) Eighmy, John L. *Churches in Cultural Captivity: A History of the Social Attitudes of Southern Baptists.* Knoxville: University of Tennessee Press, 1972.

(12) English, Carl D. "The Ethical Emphases of the Editors of Baptist Journals Published in the Southwestern Region of the United States, 1865-1915." Th.D. dissertation, Southern Baptist Theological Seminary, 1948.

(13) Fish, John O. "Southern Methodism in the Progressive Era: A Social History." Ph.D. dissertation, University of Georgia, 1969.

(14) Flynt, J. Wayne. "Baptists and Reform." *Baptist History and Heritage* 7 (1972): 211-22.

(15) Harrell, David Edwin, Jr. "The Disciples of Christ and Social Forces in Tennessee, 1865-1900." *East Tennessee Historical Society Publications* 38 (1966): 48-61.

(16) Henderson, Steven T. "Social Action in a Conservative Environment: The Christian Life Commission and Southern Baptist Churches." *Foundations* 23 (1980): 245-51.

(17) Holifield, E. Brooks. "Thomas Smyth: The Social Ideas of a Southern Evangelist." *Journal of Presbyterian History* 41 (1973): 24-39.

(18) Jones, Ronald W. "Christian Social Action and the Episcopal Church in St. Louis, Mo., 1880-1920." *Historical Magazine of the Protestant Episcopal Church* 45 (1976): 253-74.

(19) Jordan, Philip D. "The Evangelical Alliance and American Presbyterians, 1867-1873." *Journal of Presbyterian History* 51 (1973): 309-26.

(20) Kelsey, George D. *Social Ethics among Southern Baptists.* Metuchen NJ: Scarecrow Press, 1973.

(21) Kuykendall, John W. *"Southern Enterprize": The Work of the National Evangelical Societies in the Antebellum South.* Westport CT: Greenwood Press, 1982.

(22) Loveland, Anne C. *Southern Evangelicals and the Social Order, 1800-1860.* Baton Rouge: Louisiana State University Press, 1980.

(23) Maddex, Jack P. "From Theocracy to Spirituality: The Southern Presbyterian Reversal on Church and State." *Journal of Presbyterian History* 54 (1976): 438-57.

(24) Mitchell, Frank J. "The Virginia Methodist Conference and Social Issues in the Twentieth Century." Ph.D. dissertation, Duke University, 1962.

(25) Moorhead, James H. "Social Reform and the Divided Conscience of Antebellum Protestantism." *Church History* 48 (1979): 416-30.

(26) Newman, Harvey C. "The Role of Women in Atlanta's Churches, 1865-1906." *Atlanta Historical Journal* 24 (1980): 17-30.

(27) Nuesse, Celestine Joseph. *The Social Thought of American Catholics, 1634-1829.* Washington: Catholic University of America Press, 1945.

(28) Roos, David C. "The Social Thought of Barton Warren Stone and Its Significance Today for the Disciples of Christ in Western Kentucky." Ph.D. dissertation, Vanderbilt University Divinity School, 1973.

(29) Sapp, W. David. "Southern Baptist Responses to the American Economy, 1900-1980." *Baptist History and Heritage* 16 (1981): 3-12.

(30) Sellers, James. *The South and Christian Ethics.* New York: Association Press, 1962.

(31) Smith, H. Shelton. "The Church and the Social Order in the Old South as Interpreted by James Henley Thornwell." *Church History* 7 (1938): 115-24.

(32) Spain, Rufus B. *At Ease in Zion: A Social History of the Southern Baptists, 1865-1900.* Nashville: Vanderbilt University Press, 1961.

(33) Tatum, Noreen D. *A Crown of Service: A Story of Women's Work in the Methodist Episcopal Church, South, from 1878-1940.* Nashville: Parthenon Press, 1960.

(34) Thomas, John L. "Romantic Reform in America, 1815-1865." *American Quarterly* 17 (1965): 656-81.

(35) Thompson, James J., Jr. "Southern Baptists and Postwar Disillusionment, 1918-1919." *Foundations* 21 (1978): 113-22.

(36) _____. *"Tried as by Fire": Southern Baptists and the Religious Controversies of the 1920s.* Macon GA: Mercer University Press, 1982.

(37) Valentine, Foy. "Baptist Polity and Social Pronouncements." *Baptist History and Heritage* 14 (1979): 52-61.

(38) Werly, John M. "Premillennialism and the Paranoid Style." *American Studies* 18 (1977): 39-55.

(39) Weston, M. Moran. *Social Policy of the Episcopal Church in the Twentieth Century.* New York: Seabury Press, 1964.

(40) Wood, James E., Jr. "Baptist Thought and Human Rights." *Baptist History and Heritage* 13 (1978): 50-62.

II. RELIGION AND THE SOCIAL ORDER IN THE SOUTH: THE ERA OF THE AMERICAN WAR FOR INDEPENDENCE

(41) Bailey, Raymond C. "Popular Petitions and Religion in Eighteenth Century Colonial Virginia." *Historical Magazine of the Protestant Episcopal Church* 46 (1977): 419-28.

(42) Beeman, Richard R., and Rhys Isaac. "Cultural Conflict and Social Change in the Revolutionary South: Lunenberg County, Virginia." *Journal of Southern History* 46 (1980): 525-50.

(43) Berens, John F. " 'A God of Order and Not of Confusion': The American Loyalists and Divine Providence, 1774-1783." *Historical Magazine of the Protestant Episcopal Church* 47 (1978): 211-19.

(44) Bryden, G. MacLaren. "The Anti-Ecclesiastical Laws of Virginia." *Virginia Magazine of History and Biography* 64 (1956): 289-95.

(45) _____, ed. "Passive Obedience Considered: In a Sermon Preached at Williamsburg, December 31st, 1775. By the Reverend David Griffith." *Historical Magazine of the Protestant Episcopal Church* 44 (1975): 77-93.

(46) Calhoon, Robert M. *Religion and the American Revolution in North Carolina*. Raleigh: North Carolina Department of Cultural Resources, Division of Archives and History, 1976.

(47) Crow, Jeffrey J. "Tory Plots and Anglican Loyalty: The Llewelyn Conspiracy of 1777." *North Carolina Historical Review* 55 (1978): 1-17.

(48) Evanson, Philip. "Jonathan Boucher: The Mind of an American Loyalist." *Maryland Historical Magazine* 58 (1963): 123-36.

(49) Fall, Ralph E. "The Rev. Jonathan Boucher, Turbulent Tory." *Historical Magazine of the Protestant Episcopal Church* 36 (1967): 324-56.

(50) Hanley, Thomas O'Brien. *The American Revolution and Religion: Maryland, 1770-1800*. Washington: Catholic University of America Press, 1971.

(51) Holmes, David L. "The Episcopal Church and the American Revolution." *Historical Magazine of the Protestant Episcopal Church* 47 (1978): 161-91.

(52) Leyburn, James G. "Presbyterian Immigrants and the American Revolution." *Journal of Presbyterian History* 54 (1976): 9-32.

(53) McLemore, Richard A. "Tumult, Violence, Revolution and Migration." *Baptist History and Heritage* 9 (1974): 230-36.

(54) Marshall, R. W. "What Jonathan Boucher Preached." *Virginia Magazine of History and Biography* 41 (1938): 1-12.

(55) Miller, Glen T. "Fear God and Honor the King: The Failure of Loyalist Civil Theology in the Revolutionary Crisis." *Historical Magazine of the Protestant Episcopal Church* 47 (1978): 221-42.

(56) Miller, Howard. "The Grammar of Liberty: Presbyterians and the First American Constitution." *Journal of Presbyterian History* 54 (1976): 142-64.

(57) Miller, Rodney. "The Political Theology of the Anglican Clergy." *Historical Magazine of the Protestant Episcopal Church* 45 (1976): 227-36.

(58) Pauley, William E., Jr. "Religion and the American Revolution in the South." Ph.D. dissertation, Emory University, 1974.

(59) Pfisterer, K. Dieterich. "Religion als ein Ferment der Freiheit in der Amerikanischen Revolution." *Amerikastudien* 21 (1976): 217-38.

(60) "Presbyterians and the American Revolution: A Documentary Account." *Journal of Presbyterian History* 52 (1974): 299-488.

(61) Spalding, James C. "Loyalist as Royalist, Patriot as Puritan: The American Revolution as a Repetition of the English Civil Wars." *Church History* 45 (1976): 329-40.

(62) Stokes, Durward T. "Different Concepts of Government Expressed in the Sermons of Two Eighteenth Century Clergymen." *Historical Magazine of the Protestant Episcopal Church* 41 (1972): 81-94.

(63) _____. "The Presbyterian Clergy in South Carolina and the American Revolution." *South Carolina Historical Magazine* 71 (1970): 270-82.

(64) Terman, William J., Jr. "The American Revolution and the Baptist and Presbyterian Clergy in Virginia: A Study of Dissenter Opinion and Action." Ph.D. dissertation, Michigan State University, 1974.

(65) Wennersten, John R. "The Travail of a Tory Parson: Reverend Philip Hughes and Maryland Colonial Politics, 1767-1777." *Historical Magazine of the Protestant Episcopal Church* 44 (1975): 409-16.

III. RELIGION AND THE SOCIAL ORDER IN THE SOUTH: RELIGIOUS TOLERATION AND SEPARATION OF CHURCH AND STATE

(66) Andrews, Matthew P. "Separation of Church and State in Maryland." *Catholic Historical Review* 21 (1935): 164-76.

(67) Bauer, Gerald. "The Quest for Religious Freedom in Virginia." *Historical Magazine of the Protestant Episcopal Church* 41 (1972): 85-93.

(68) Brinsfield, John W. "Daniel Defoe: Writer, Statesman, and Advocate of Religious Liberty in South Carolina." *South Carolina Historical Magazine* 76 (1975): 107-11.

(69) Buckley, Thomas E., S.J. *Church and State in Revolutionary Virginia, 1776-1787.* Charlottesville: University of Virginia Press, 1977.

(70) _____. "Church-State Settlement in Virginia: The Presbyterian Contribution." *Journal of Presbyterian History* 54 (1976): 105-19.

(71) *Church and State in Eighteenth Century South Carolina.* Charleston: Dalcho Historical Society, 1965.

(72) Eckenrode, Hamilton J. *Separation of Church and State in Virginia: A Study in the Development of the Revolution.* Richmond: Virginia State Library Department of Archives and History, 1910.

(73) Green, Jesse C., Jr. "The Early Virginia Argument for Separation of Church and State." *Baptist History and Heritage* 11 (1976): 16-26.

(74) Gummere, Richard M. "Samuel Davies: Classical Champion of Religious Freedom." *Journal of Presbyterian History* 40 (1962): 67-74.

(75) Hanley, Thomas O. "Catholic Political Thought in Colonial Maryland Government." *Historical Bulletin* 32 (1953): 27-34.

(76) _____. "The Catholic Tradition of Freedom in America." *American Ecclesiastical Review* 145 (1961): 307-18.

(77) _____. "Church and State in the Maryland Ordinance of 1639." *Church History* 26 (1957): 325-41.

(78) _____. *Their Rights and Liberties: The Beginnings of Religious and Political Freedom in Maryland.* Westminster MD: Newman Press, 1969.

(79) Hardy, James D., Jr. "Church and State in French Colonial Louisiana: An Essay Review." *Louisiana History* 8 (1967): 85-95.

(80) Hood, Fred J. "Revolution and Religious Liberty: The Conservation of the Theocratic Concept in Virginia." *Church History* 40 (1971): 170-81.

(81) Johnson, Bradley T. *The Foundation of Maryland and the Origin of the Act concerning Religion of April 21, 1649.* Baltimore: Maryland Historical Society, 1883.

(82) Johnson, Thomas C. *Virginia Presbyterianism and Religious Liberty in Colonial and Revolutionary Times.* Richmond VA: Presbyterian Committee of Publication, 1907.

(83) King, William. "Lord Baltimore and His Freedom in Granting Religious Toleration." *American Catholic Historical Society of Philadelphia Records* 32 (1921): 295-313.

(84) Krugler, John D. "Lord Baltimore, Roman Catholics, and Toleration: Religious Policy in Maryland during the Early Catholic Years, 1634-1649." *Catholic Historical Review* 65 (1979): 49-75.

(85) Joiner, Edward E. "Southern Baptists and Church-State Relations, 1845-1954." Th.D. dissertation, Southern Baptist Theological Seminary, 1959.

(86) Monroe, Haskell. "Religious Toleration and Politics in Early North Carolina." *North Carolina Historical Review* 39 (1962): 267-83.

(87) Moore, John S. "The Struggle for Religious Freedom in Virginia." *Baptist History and Heritage* 11 (1976): 160-68.

(88) O'Neill, Charles E. *Church and State in French Colonial Louisiana: Policy and Politics to 1732.* New Haven: Yale University Press, 1966.

(89) Pilcher, George W. "Samuel Davies and Religious Toleration in Virginia." *Historian* 28 (1965): 48-71.

(90) Quinlivan, Mary E. "From Pragmatic Accommodation to Principled Action: The Revolution and Religious Establishment in Virginia." *West Georgia College Studies in the Social Sciences* 15 (1976): 55-64.

(91) Rainbolt, John C. "The Struggle to Define 'Religious Liberty' in Maryland, 1776-85." *Journal of Church and State* 17 (1975): 443-58.

(92) Smith, Elwyn A. "The Fundamental Church-State Tradition of the Catholic Church in the United States." *Church History* 38 (1969): 486-505.

(93) Thom, William Taylor. *The Struggle for Religious Freedom in Virginia: The Baptists.* Baltimore: Johns Hopkins University Press, 1900.

(94) Werline, Albert. *Problems of Church and State in Maryland.* South Lancaster MA: College Press, 1948.

(95) Whiting, Marvin Y. "Virginia's Experiment with Religious Uniformity: A Study of a Major Aspect of Anglican and Evangelical Theology, 1699-1789." Ph.D. dissertation, Columbia University, 1973.

(96) Wicks, Elliot K. "Thomas Jefferson—A Religious Man with a Passion for Religious Freedom." *Historical Magazine of the Protestant Episcopal Church* 46 (1967): 270-83.

IV. RELIGION AND SOCIAL ORDER IN THE SOUTH: THE CIVIL WAR AND THE CONFEDERACY

(97) Ashdown, Paul G. "Commission from a Higher Source: Church and State in the Civil War." *Historical Magazine of the Protestant Episcopal Church* 48 (1979): 321-30.

(98) Blassingame, James W. "Negro Chaplains in the Civil War." *Negro History Bulletin* 27 (1963): 24, 28.

(99) Blied, Benjamin J. *Catholics and the Civil War*. Milwaukee: By the author, 1945.

(100) Burger, Nash K. "The Diocese of Mississippi and the Confederacy." *Historical Magazine of the Protestant Episcopal Church* 14 (1940): 52+.

(101) Clebsch, William A. *Christian Interpretations of the Civil War*. Philadelphia: Fortress Press, 1969.

(102) Cushman, Joseph D., Jr. "The Episcopal Church in Florida During the Civil War." *Florida Historical Quarterly* 38 (1960): 294-301.

(103) Daniel, W. Harrison. "An Aspect of Church and State Relations in the Confederacy: Southern Protestantism and the Office of Army Chaplain." *North Carolina Historical Review* 36 (1959): 47-71.

(104) _____, ed. "Chaplains in the Army of Northern Virginia: A List Compiled in 1864 and 1865 by Robert L. Dabney." *Virginia Magazine of History and Biography* 71 (1963): 327-40.

(105) _____. "The Effects of the Civil War on Southern Protestantism." *Maryland Historical Magazine* 69 (1974): 44-63.

(106) _____. "Protestant Clergy and Union Sentiment in the Confederacy." *Tennessee Historical Quarterly* 23 (1964): 284-90.

(107) _____. "Protestantism and Patriotism in the Confederacy." *Mississippi Quarterly* 24 (1971): 117-34.

(108) _____. "Southern Presbyterians in the Confederacy." *North Carolina Historical Review* 24 (1967): 231-55.

(109) _____. "Southern Protestantism and Army Missions in the Confederacy." *Mississippi Quarterly* 17 (1964): 179-91.

(110) _____. "Southern Protestantism and Secession." *Historian* 29 (1967): 391-408.

(111) _____. "Southern Protestantism—1861 and After." *Civil War History* 5 (1960): 276-82.

(112) Davis, J. Treadwell. "The Presbyterians and the Sectional Conflict." *Southern Quarterly* 11 (1970): 117-53.

(113) Duncan, Richard R. "Bishop Whittingham, the Maryland Diocese, and the Civil War." *Maryland Historical Magazine* 61 (1966): 329-47.

(114) _____. "Maryland Methodists and the Civil War." *Maryland Historical Magazine* 59 (1964): 350-68.

(115) Dunstan, William E. III. "The Episcopal Church in the Confederacy." *Virginia Cavalcade* 19 (1970): 5-15.

(116) Fleming, Walter L. "The Churches of Alabama during the Civil War and Reconstruction." *Gulf States Historical Magazine* 1 (1902): 105-27.

(117) Fowler, Arlen L. "Chaplain D. Eglinton Barr: A Lincoln Yankee." *Historical Magazine of the Protestant Episcopal Church* 45 (1976): 435-38.

(118) Goen, C. C. *Broken Churches, Broken Nation: Denominational Schisms and the Coming of the American Civil War.* Macon GA: Mercer University Press, 1985.

(119) Griffin, J. David. "Benevolence and Malevolence in Confederate Savannah." *Georgia Historical Quarterly* 49 (1965): 347-68.

(120) Hassler, William W. "Religious Conversion of General W. Dorsey Pender, C.S.A." *Historical Magazine of the Protestant Episcopal Church* 33 (1964): 171-78.

(121) Heathcote, Charles W. "The Lutheran Church and the Civil War." Ph.D. dissertation, George Washington University, 1918.

(122) Helmreich, Jonathan E. "A Prayer for the Spirit of Acceptance: The Journal of Martha Wayles Robertson, 1860-1866." *Historical Magazine of the Protestant Episcopal Church* 46 (1977): 397-408.

(123) Kedro, Milan J. "The Civil War's Effect upon an Urban Church: the St. Louis Presbytery under Martial Law." *Missouri Historical Society Bulletin* 27 (1971): 173-93.

(124) Kibby, Leo P. "Civil War Diary of a Christian Minister: The Observations of Eri Baker Hulbert, United States Christian Commission Delegate, February-March, 1865." *Journal of the West* 3 (1964): 221-32.

(125) King, Terence. "A Confederate Chaplain at Frederick, 1862-1864." *Woodstock Letters* 58 (1929): 566-78.

(126) Korn, Bertram W. *American Jewry and the Civil War.* Cleveland: World Publishing, 1861. First published 1951.

(127) Krebs, Sylvia. "Funeral Meats and Second Marriages: Alabama Churches in the Presidential Reconstruction Period." *Alabama Historical Quarterly* 37 (1975): 206-16.

(128) Mitchell, Joseph. "Southern Methodist Newspapers during the Civil War." *Methodist History* 11 (1973): 20-39.

(129) Morrow, Ralph E. *Northern Methodism and Reconstruction.* East Lansing: Michigan State University Press, 1956.

(130) Morton, Sr. M. Rosana. "Catholic Action in the Civil War." M.A. thesis, Villanova University, 1940.

(131) Murphy, Dubose. "The Protestant Episcopal Church in Texas during the Civil War." *Historical Magazine of the Protestant Episcopal Church* 1 (1932): 90+.

(132) Nash, Michael. "Letters from a Chaplain in the War of 1861." *Woodstock Letters* 16 (1887): 144-56, 238-59; 17 (1888): 12-29, 135-49, 269-87; 18 (1889): 3-25, 153-68, 319-30; 19 (1890): 22-41, 154-63.

(133) Nicolson, John. " 'To Mock My Maker'—A Civil War Letter on Freedom of Conscience." *Historical Magazine of the Protestant Episcopal Church* 41 (1972): 67-76.

(134) Norton, Herman A. *Rebel Religion: The Story of Confederate Chaplains.* St. Louis: Bethany Press, 1961.

(135) _____. "The Role of a Religious Newspaper in Georgia during the Civil War." *Georgia Historical Quarterly* 48 (1964): 125-46.

(136) Ogilvie, Charles F. "Alabama Baptists during the Civil War and Reconstruction." Master's thesis, Southwestern Baptist Theological Seminary, 1956.

(137) O'Grady, Joseph P. "Immigrants and the Politics of Reconstruction in Richmond, Virginia." *American Catholic Historical Society of Philadelphia Records* 83 (1972): 87-101.

(138) Romero, Sidney J. *Religion in the Rebel Ranks.* Washington: University Press of America, 1983.

(139) "Sequel to a Texas Story." Province of the Most Holy Name, O.F.M. *Provincial Annals* 7 (1954): 167-71.

(140) Shankman, Arnold. "*The Christian Observer* and Civil War Censorship." *Journal of Presbyterian History* 52 (1974): 227-44.

(141) Silver, James W. *Confederate Morale and Church Propaganda.* Tuscaloosa: Confederate Publishing, 1957.

(142) _____. "The Confederate Preacher Goes to War." *North Carolina Historical Review* 33 (1956): 499-509.

(143) Simonhoff, Harry. *Jewish Participants in the Civil War.* New York: Arco Publishing, 1963.

(144) Stock, Leo F. "Catholic Participation in the Diplomacy of the Southern Confederacy." *Catholic Historical Review* 16 (1930): 1-18.

(145) Sweet, Leonard I. "The Reaction of the Protestant Episcopal Church in Virginia to the Secession Crisis: October, 1859 to May, 1861." *Historical Magazine of the Protestant Episcopal Church* 41 (1972): 137-51.

(146) Sweet, William Warren. *The Methodist Episcopal Church and the Civil War.* Cincinnati: Methodist Book Concern, 1933.

(147) Thomas, Emory. *The Confederate Nation.* New York: Harper and Row, 1979.

(148) Todd, Edward N., ed. "Bishop Whittingham, Mount Calvary Church, and the Battle of Gettysburg." *Maryland Historical Magazine* 50 (1965): 325-28.

(149) Upton, James M. "The Shakers as Pacifists in the Period between 1812 and the Civil War." *Filson Club Historical Quarterly* 47 (1973): 267-83.

(150) VanderVelde, Lewis G. *The Presbyterian Churches and the Federal Union, 1861-1869.* Cambridge MA: Harvard University Press, 1932.

(151) "View of the Bishops of Ohio and Louisiana upon the Secession of the Southern States and Its Effects upon the Ecclesiastical Allegiance of the Diocese." *Historical Magazine of the Protestant Episcopal Church* 31 (1962): 288-302.

(152) Wight, Willard E. "The Bishop of Natchez and the Confederate Chaplaincy." *Mid-America* 39 (1957): 67-72.

(153) _____. "Bishop Verot and the Civil War." *Catholic Historical Review* 47 (1961): 153-63.

(154) _____. "The Churches and the Confederate Cause." *Civil War History* 6 (1960): 362-73.

(155) _____. "Churches in the Confederacy." Ph.D. dissertation, Emory University, 1958.

(156) Zuber, Richard L. "Conscientious Objectors in the Confederacy: The Quakers of North Carolina." *Quaker History* 67 (1978): 1-19.

V. RELIGION AND THE SOCIAL ORDER IN THE SOUTH: RACISM, DISCRIMINATION, AND THE CIVIL RIGHTS MOVEMENT

(157) Anderson, John F. "Time to Heal: A Southern Church Deals with Racism." *International Review of Missions* 59 (1970): 304-310.

(158) Atkins, James. "New Voice in Birmingham." *Unitarian Register and Universalist Leader* 141 (1962): 5-7.

(159) Barnhart, Phil. *Don't Call Me Preacher: For Laymen and Other Ministers.* Grand Rapids: William B. Eerdmans, 1972.

(160) Blackwelder, Julia Kirk. "Southern White Fundamentalists and the Civil Rights Movement." *Phylon* 40 (1979): 334-41.

(161) Campbell, Ernest Q., and Thomas F. Pettigrew. *Christians in Racial Crisis: A Study of Little Rock's Ministry.* Washington: Public Affairs Press, 1959.

(162) _____, and _____. "Racial and Moral Crisis: The Role of Little Rock Ministers." *American Journal of Sociology* 64 (1959): 509-16.

(163) Campbell, Will D. *Brother to a Dragonfly.* New York: Seabury Press, 1977.

(164) _____, and James Y. Holloway, eds. *The Failure and the Hope: Essays of Southern Churchmen.* Grand Rapids: William B. Eerdmans, 1972.

(165) _____. *Race and Renewal of the Church.* Philadelphia: Westminster Press, 1962.

(166) _____. "The Role of Religion in Segregation Crises." *New South* 15 (January 1960): 3-11.

(167) Cartwright, Colbert S. "Band Together for Genuine Unity." *New South* 16 (January 1961): 6-10.

(168) Chalmers, David M. *Hooded Americanism: The First Century of the Ku Klux Klan, 1865-1965.* Garden City: Doubleday, 1965.

(169) "A Church Looks at Civil Rights in North Carolina." *New South* 18 (April 1963): 13-15.

(170) Cleveland, Len G. "Georgia Baptists and the 1954 Supreme Court Deseg- regation Decision." *Georgia Historical Quarterly* 59 (supplement 1975): 107-17.

(171) Cleveland, Mary L. "A Baptist Pastor and Social Justice in Clinton, Ten- nessee." *Baptist History and Heritage* 14 (1979): 15-19.

(172) Coleman, Charles C. *Patterns of Race Relations in the South.* New York: Exposition Press, 1949.

(173) Crooks, William H., and Ross Coggins. *Seven Who Fought.* Waco TX: Word Books, 1971.

(174) "Don't Come Unto Me: Negro Admissions Cause Clergy Sacking in Ma- con, Ga." *New Republic* 155 (12 November 1966): 9-10.

(175) Doyle, Bertram W. *The Etiquette of Race Relations in the South,* chap. 4. Chicago: University of Chicago Press, 1937.

(176) Eddy, Elizabeth M. "Student Perspectives on the Southern Church." *Phy- lon* 25 (1964): 369-81.

(177) Fair, Harold L. "Southern Methodism on Education and Race, 1900-1920." Ph.D. dissertation, Vanderbilt University, 1971.

(178) Feagin, Joe R. "Prejudice and Religious Types: A Focused Study of South- ern Fundamentalists." *Journal for the Scientific Study of Religion* 4 (1964): 3-13.

(179) Fish, John O. "Southern Methodism and Accommodation of the Negro, 1902-1915." *Journal of Negro History* 55 (1970): 200-214.

(180) Frady, Marshall. "God and Man in the South: The Church's Indifference to Civil Rights Movement." *Atlantic Monthly* 219 (1967): 37-42.

(181) Friedman, Murray. "One Episode in Southern Jewry's Response to Deseg- regation: An Historical Memoir." *American Jewish Archives* 33 (1981): 170- 83.

(182) Gaudnault, Gerard. *L'Engagement de l'Eglise dans la Revolution d'apres Martin Luther King, Jr.* Montreal: Fides, 1971.

(183) Grimke, Francis J. *Jim Crow Christianity and the Negro.* Washington: n.p., n.d.

(184) Grosse, Heinrich W. *Die Macht der Armen: Martin Luther King und der Kampf fur Sociale Gerechtigkeit.* Hamburg: Furche Verlag, 1971.

(185) Hall, Jacquelyn Dowd. "A Truly Subversive Affair: Women Against Lynching in the Twentieth-Century South." In *Women of America: A His- tory.* Carol Ruth Berkin and Mary Beth Norton, eds., 360-88. Boston: Houghton Mifflin, 1979.

(186) Hanish, Joseph J. "Catholics, Protestants and the American Negro." *Nun- tius Aulae* 43 (1961): 98-115.

(187) Hays, Brooks. *A Southern Moderate Speaks,* 195-215. Chapel Hill: Uni- versity of North Carolina Press, 1959.

(188) Hill, Davis C. "Southern Baptist Thought and Action in Race Relations." Th.D. dissertation, Southern Baptist Theological Seminary, 1952.

(189) Hill, Samuel S., Jr. "Southern Protestantism and Racial Integration." *Religion in Life* 30 (1964): 421-29.

(190) Hoge, Dean R., and Jackson W. Carroll. "Religiosity and Prejudice in Northern and Southern Churches." *Journal for the Scientific Study of Religion* 12 (1973): 181-97.

(191) Hollis, Harry N., Jr. "Reaction to Paper of Leon McBeth." *Baptist History and Heritage* 7 (1972): 169-71. See (199).

(192) Hough, Joseph C. *Black Power and White Protestants: A Christian Response to the New Negro Pluralism.* New York: Oxford University Press, 1968.

(193) Jackson, Kenneth T. *The Ku Klux Klan in the City, 1915-1930.* New York: Oxford University Press, 1967.

(194) Jordan, Clarence. "Christian Community in the South." *Journal of Religious Thought* 14 (1956-1957): 27-36.

(195) Krause, P. Allen. "Rabbis and Negro Rights in the South, 1954-1967." *American Jewish Archives* 21 (1969): 20-47.

(196) Labbe, Dolores Egger. *Jim Crow Comes to Church: The Establishment of Segregated Catholic Parishes in South Louisiana.* 2d ed. Lafayette: University of Southwestern Louisiana, 1971. Reprint, New York: Arno Press, 1978.

(197) LaFarge, John. *The Catholic Viewpoint on Race Relations.* Garden City: Hanover House, 1960.

(198) Lippy, Charles H. "Towards an Inclusive Church: Religion and Race in South Carolina Methodism, 1972-1982." In *Rethinking Methodist History.* Russell E. Richey and Kenneth E. Rowe, eds. Nashville: Abingdon Press, 1985.

(199) McBeth, Leon. "Southern Baptists and Race since 1947." *Baptist History and Heritage* 7 (1972): 155-69.

(200) McGill, Ralph. "The Agony of the Southern Minister." *New York Times Magazine* (27 September 1959). Reprinted in *No Place to Hide: The South and Human Rights.* Calvin M. Logue, ed., 289-97. Macon: Mercer University Press, 1984.

(201) McMillan, G. "Silent White Ministers of the South." *New York Times Magazine* (5 April 1964): 22 + .

(202) McNeill, Robert B. "A Georgia Minister Offers a Solution for the South." *Look* (21 May 1957): 55-58, 63-64.

(203) _____. *God Wills Us Free: The Ordeal of the Southern Minister.* New York: Hill and Wang, 1965.

(204) Malev, William S. "The Jew of the South in the Conflict on Segregation." *Conservative Judaism* 13 (1958): 35-46.

(205) Mayer, M. "The Jim Crow Christ." *Negro Digest* 13 (1964): 28-31.

(206) Miller, Francis P. "Southern Protestants and Desegregation." *New Republic* 141 (2 November 1959): 17-18.

(207) Miller, Robert M. "The Attitudes of American Protestantism toward the Negro." *Journal of Negro History* 41 (1956): 215-40.

(208) _____. "A Note on the Relation between the Protestant Churches and the Revival of the Ku Klux Klan." *Journal of Southern History* 22 (1956): 355-68.

(209) _____. "The Protestant Churches and Lynching." *Journal of Negro Education* 42 (1957): 18-31.

(210) Mosely, Clement C. "Political Influence of the Ku Klux Klan in Georgia, 1915-1925." *Georgia Historical Quarterly* 56 (1973): 235-55.

(211) Mounger, Dwyn M. "Racial Attitudes in the Presbyterian Church in the United States, 1944-1954." *Journal of Presbyterian History* 48 (1970): 38-68.

(212) "The National Council of Churches and Civil Rights." *A.M.E. Church Review* 81 (1964): 5-7.

(213) "Negro Kneel-Ins in White Churches in Savannah, Ga." *New South* 20 (July-August 1965): 22+.

(214) Newman, Harvey K. "Piety and Segregation—White Protestant Attitudes Toward Blacks in Atlanta, 1865-1905." *Georgia Historical Quarterly* 63 (1979): 238-51.

(215) Orser, W. Edward. "Racial Attitudes in Wartime: The Protestant Churches During the Second World War." *Church History* 41 (1972): 337-53.

(216) Osborne, William A. *The Race Problem in the Catholic Church in the United States between the Time of the Second Plenary Council (1866) and the Founding of the Catholic Interracial Council of New York.* Ann Arbor: University Microfilms, 1954.

(217) _____. *The Segregated Covenant: Race Relations and American Catholics.* New York: Herder and Herder, 1967.

(218) "The Other Mississippi." *New South* 18 (March 1963): 1+.

(219) Porter, Earl W. "The Bassett Affair: Something to Remember." *South Atlantic Quarterly* 72 (1973): 451-60.

(220) Prestwood, Charles M. "Dilemmas of Deep South Clergy." *Christianity Today* 5 (1961): 8-9.

(221) Rahming, Philip A. "The Church and the Civil Rights Movement in the Thought of Martin Luther King, Jr." Master's thesis, Southern Baptist Theological Seminary, 1971.

(222) Rouse, John E., Jr. "The Role of Segregation in Southern Baptist Polity." *Journal of Religious Thought* 29 (1972): 19-38.

(223) Sessions, R. P. "Are Southern Ministers Failing in the South?" *Saturday Evening Post* 234 (13 May 1961): 37+.

(224) Shockley, Donald G. "First Baptist, Birmingham: A Case Study of Wineskins Burning." *Christian Century* 87 (1970): 462-63.

(225) Shurden, Walter B. "Reaction to Paper of Henry Warnock." *Baptist History and Heritage* 7 (1972): 184-85. See (239).

(226) Simms, L. Moody, Jr. "Theodore Dubose Batton, Christian Principles, and the Race Question." *Journal of Mississippi History* 38 (1976): 47-52.

(227) Smylie, James H. "The Bible, Race, and the Changing South." *Journal of Presbyterian History* 59 (1981): 197-217.

(228) Smythe, Lewis, ed. *Southern Churches and Race Relations*. Lexington KY: College of the Bible, 1963.

(229) Southard, S. "Are Southern Churches Silent?" *Christian Century* 80 (1963): 1429-32.

(230) "Southern Catholics and Integration." *Sign* 35 (1956): 13-27.

(231) Speaks, Reuben L. "The Church and Black Liberation." *A.M.E. Zion Quarterly Review* 83 (1971): 138-48.

(232) Spivey, Robert A. "Integration and the South: The South as a Cultural Unit." *Union Seminary Quarterly Review* 11 (1956): 33-36.

(233) Storey, John W. "Southern Baptists and the Racial Controversy in the Churches and Schools During Reconstruction." *Mississippi Quarterly* 30 (1978): 211-28.

(234) _____. "Texas Baptist Leadership, the Social Gospel, and Race, 1954-1968." *Southwestern Historical Quarterly* 83 (1979): 29-46.

(235) Tomberlin, Joseph. "Florida Whites and the *Brown* Decision of 1954." *Florida Historical Quarterly* 51 (1972): 22-36.

(236) Valentine, Foy D. *A History of Southern Baptists and Race Relations, 1917-1947*. New York: Arno Press, 1980.

(237) Wamble, G. Hugh. "Negroes and Missouri Protestant Churches." *Missouri Historical Review* 61 (1967): 321-47.

(238) Warnock, Henry Y. "Modern Racial Thought and Attitudes of Southern Baptists and Methodists, 1900-1921." Ph.D. dissertation, Northwestern University, 1963.

(239) _____. "Prophets of Change: Some Southern Baptist Leaders and the Problem of Race, 1900-1921." *Baptist History and Heritage* 7 (1972): 172-83.

(240) Weeks, Louis B. "Racism, World War I, and the Christian Life: Francis J. Grimke in the Nation's Capital." *Journal of Presbyterian History* 51 (1973): 471-88.

(241) Williamson, Joel. *The Crucible of Race: Black-White Relations in the American South Since Emancipation*. New York: Oxford University Press, 1984.

(242) Wogaman, J. Philip. "A Strategy for Racial Desegregation in the Methodist Church." Ph.D. dissertation, Boston University, 1960.

VI. RELIGION AND THE SOCIAL ORDER IN THE SOUTH: NATIVISM, ANTI-SEMITISM, ANTI-CATHOLICISM

(243) Berthoff, Rowland T. "Southern Attitudes Toward Immigration, 1865-1914." *Journal of Southern History* 17 (1951): 328-60.

(244) Dyer, Thomas G. "Aaron's Rod: Theodore Roosevelt, Tom Watson, and Anti-Catholicism." *Research Studies* 44 (1976): 60-68.

(245) Flynt, J. Wayne. *Cracker Messiah: Governor Sidney J. Catts of Florida.* Baton Rouge: Louisiana State University Press, 1977.

(246) _____. "Religion in the Urban South: The Divided Religious Mind of Birmingham." *Alabama Review* 30 (1977): 108-34.

(247) Franzoni, Janet Brenner. "Troubled Tirader: A Psychobiographical Study of Tom Watson." *Georgia Historical Quarterly* 57 (1973): 493-510.

(248) Gohmann, Mary deLourdes. *Political Nativism in Tennessee to 1860.* Washington: Catholic University of America Press, 1938.

(249) Kanigel, Robert. "Did H. L. Mencken Hate the Jews?" *Menckeniana* 73 (1980): 1-7.

(250) Kennedy, Philip W. "The Know-Nothing Movement in Kentucky: The Role of M. J. Spalding, Catholic Bishop of Louisville." *Filson Club Historical Quarterly* 38 (1964): 17-35.

(251) Koester, Leonard. "Louisville's 'Bloody Monday'—August 6, 1855." *Historical Bulletin* 26 (1948): 53-54, 62-64.

(252) McCann, Sr. Mary Agnes Geraldine. *Nativism in Kentucky to 1860.* Washington: Catholic University of America Press, 1944.

(253) McConville, Sr. Mary St. Patrick. *Political Nativism in the State of Maryland, 1830-1860.* Washington: Catholic University of America Press, 1928.

(254) McGrath, Sr. Paul of the Cross. *Political Nativism in Texas, 1825-1860.* Washington: Catholic University of America Press, 1930.

(255) McHugh, George L. "Political Nativism in St. Louis, 1840-1857." M.A. thesis, St. Louis University, 1939.

(256) Moran, Denis M. "Anti-Catholicism in Early Maryland Politics: The Puritan Influence." *American Catholic Historical Society of Philadelphia Records* 61 (1950): 139-54, 213-35.

(257) Ott, Sr. Mary of the Sacred Heart. "The Know Nothings in Alabama, 1854-1860." M.A. thesis, Catholic University of America, 1945.

(258) Page, David P. "Bishop Michael J. Curley and Anti-Catholic Nativism in Florida." *Florida Historical Quarterly* 43 (1966): 101-17.

(259) Racine, Philip N. "The Ku Klux Klan, Anti-Catholicism and Atlanta's Board of Education, 1916-1927." *Georgia Historical Quarterly* 56 (1973): 63-75.

(260) Rackloff, Robert B. "Anti-Catholicism and the Florida Legislature, 1911-1919." *Florida Historical Quarterly* 48 (1972): 352-65.

(261) Schmeckebier, Lawrence F. *History of the Know-Nothing Party in Maryland.* Baltimore: Johns Hopkins University Press, 1899.

(262) Selig, Sr. M. Lucy Josephine. "The Know-Nothing Party in Florida, 1852-1860." M.A. thesis, Catholic University of America, 1944.

(263) Stauf, H. Margaret. "The Anti-Catholic Movement in Missouri: Post Civil War Period." M.A. thesis, St. Louis University, 1936.

(264) Thompson, James J., Jr. "Southern Baptists and Anti-Catholicism in the 1920's." *Mississippi Quarterly* 31 (1979): 611-25.

(265) "Those Murderous Monks of Pasco County." *Tampa Bay Historian* 1 (1979): 55-58.

(266) Tuska, Benjamin. "Know Nothingism in Baltimore, 1854-1860." *Catholic Historical Review* 11 (1925): 217-51.

VII. RELIGION AND THE SOCIAL ORDER IN THE SOUTH: POPULISM, THE SOCIAL GOSPEL, AND LABOR

(267) Bailey, Hugh C. "Edgar Gardner Murphy and the Child Labor Movement." *Alabama Review* 18 (1965): 47-59.

(268) Beasley, Jonathan P. "The Reaction of the Southern Baptist Press to the Haymarket Incident of 1886." *The Quarterly Review* 33 (1973): 37-42.

(269) Becnel, Thomas A. *Labor, Church, and the Sugar Establishment: Louisiana, 1887-1976.* Baton Rouge: Louisiana State University Press, 1980.

(270) Bode, Frederick A. "Religion and Class Hegemony: A Populist Critique in North Carolina." *Journal of Southern History* 37 (1971): 417-38.

(271) Bolster, Paul D. "Christian Socialism Comes to Georgia: The Christian Commonwealth Colony." *Georgia Review* 26 (1972): 60-70.

(272) Brooks, Lee M., and Alvin L. Bertrand. *History of the Southern Sociological Society.* University AL: University of Alabama Press, 1962.

(273) Burbank, Garin. *When Farmers Voted Red: The Gospel of Socialism in the Oklahoma Countryside, 1910-1924.* Westport CT: Greenwood Press, 1976.

(274) Burgess, David. "The Fellowship of Southern Churchmen: Its History and Promise." *Prophetic Religion* 13 (1953): 1-11.

(275) Chatfield, E. Charles. "The Southern Sociological Congress: Organization of Uplift." *Tennessee Historical Quarterly* 19 (1960): 328-47.

(276) _____. "The Southern Sociological Congress: Rationale of Uplift." *Tennessee Historical Quarterly* 20 (1961): 51-64.

(277) Cowett, Mark. "Rabbi Morris Newfield and the Social Gospel: Theology and Social Reform in the South." *American Jewish Archives* 34 (1982): 52-74.

(278) Dunbar, Anthony P. *Against the Grain: Southern Radicals and Prophets, 1929-59.* Charlottesville: University of Virginia Press, 1981.

(279) Earle, John R., et al. *Spindles and Spires: A Re-Study of Religion and Social Change in Gastonia.* Atlanta: John Knox Press, 1976.

(280) Eighmy, John L. "Religious Liberalism in the South during the Progressive Era." *Church History* 38 (1969): 359-72.

(281) Fish, John O. "The Christian Commonwealth Colony: A Georgia Experiment, 1896-1900." *Georgia Historical Quarterly* 59 (1973): 213-26.

(282) Flynt, J. Wayne. "Alabama White Protestantism and Labor, 1900-1914." *Alabama Review* 25 (1972): 192-217.

(283) _____. "Organized Labor, Reform, and Alabama Politics, 1920." *Alabama Review* 23 (1970): 163-80.

(284) Gizycki, Horst von. "Alternative Lebensformen (3): Die Christliche Kommunität der Koinonia-Partner in Georgia." *Frankfurter Hefte* 31 (1976): 35-42.

(285) Green, James R. "Propagating the Social Gospel." In *Grass-Roots Socialism: Radical Movement in the Southwest, 1895-1943*, 126-75. Baton Rouge: Louisiana State University Press, 1978.

(286) Gwaltney, Grace. "The Negro Church and the Social Gospel, 1877-1944." Master's thesis, Howard University, 1949.

(287) Johnson, Charles P. "Southern Baptists and the Social Gospel Movement." Th.D. dissertation, Southwestern Baptist Theological Seminary, 1948.

(288) Lee, Dallas. *The Cotton Patch Evidence*. New York: Harper and Row, 1971.

(289) Luker, Ralph E. "The Social Gospel and the Failure of Racial Reform, 1877-1898." *Church History* 46 (1977): 80-99.

(290) McDowell, John P. *The Social Gospel in the South: The Woman's Home Mission Movement in the Methodist Episcopal Church, South, 1886-1939*. Baton Rouge: Louisiana State University Press, 1982.

(291) McLear, Patrick E. "The Agrarian Revolt in the South: A Historiographical Essay." *Louisiana Studies* 12 (1973): 443-63.

(292) McMath, Robert C. "The Farmer's Alliance in the South." Ph.D. dissertation, University of North Carolina in Chapel Hill, 1972.

(293) _____. *Populist Vanguard: A History of the Southern Farmers Alliance*. Chapel Hill: University of North Carolina Press, 1975.

(294) Martin, Robert F. "Critique of Southern Society and Vision of a New Order: The Fellowship of Southern Churchmen, 1934-1957." *Church History* 52 (1983): 66-80.

(295) _____. "The Fellowship of Southern Churchmen." M.A. thesis, University of North Carolina in Chapel Hill, 1970.

(296) _____. "A Prophet's Pilgrimage: The Religious Radicalism of Howard Anderson Kester, 1921-1941." *Journal of Southern History* 48 (1982): 511-30.

(297) Maston, T. B. "Baptists, Social Christianity, and American Culture." *Review and Expositor* 61 (1964): 521-31.

(298) Miller, Robert Moats. "One Bible Belt State's Encounter with Populism and 'Progressive' Capitalism." *Reviews in American History* 4 (1976): 571-76.

(299) Pillar, James J. "Catholic Opposition to the Grange in Mississippi." *Journal of Mississippi History* 31 (1969): 215-28.

(300) Pope, Liston M. *Millhands and Preachers: A Study of Gastonia*. Yale Studies in Religious Education 15. New Haven: Yale University Press, 1942.

(301) Soden, Dale E. "The Social Gospel in Tennessee: Mark Allison Matthews." *Tennessee Historical Quarterly* 41 (1982): 159-70.

(302) Storey, John W. "Thomas Buford Maston and the Growth of Social Christianity among Texas Baptists." *East Texas Historical Journal* 19 (1981): 27-42.

(303) Tatum, Noreen D. *A Crown of Service: The Story of Women's Work in the Methodist Episcopal Church, South, from 1878-1940.* Nashville: Parthenon Press, 1960.

(304) Thomas, Mary S. "The Ordeal of Koinonia Farm." *Progressive* 21 (January 1957): 23-25.

(305) White, Ronald C., Jr. "Beyond the Sacred: Edgar Gardner Murphy and a Ministry of Social Reform." *Historical Magazine of the Protestant Episcopal Church* 49 (1980): 51-69.

VIII. RELIGION AND THE SOCIAL ORDER IN THE SOUTH: TEMPERANCE AND PROHIBITION

(306) Brown, Thomas E. "Oklahoma's 'Bone-Dry Law' and the Roman Catholic Church." *Chronicles of Oklahoma* 52 (1974): 316-30.

(307) Conklin, Forrest. "Parson Brownlow Joins the Sons of Temperance." *Tennessee Historical Quarterly* 39 (1980): 178-94.

(308) _____. "Parson Brownlow—Temperance Advocate." *Tennessee Historical Quarterly* 39 (1980): 293-309.

(309) Ezell, Macel D. "Early Attitudes Toward Alcoholic Beverages in the South." *Red River Valley Historical Review* 7 (1982): 64-70.

(310) Hines, Tom S., Jr. "Mississippi and the Repeal of Prohibition." *Journal of Mississippi History* 24 (1962): 1-39.

(311) Jackson, Joy. "Prohibition in New Orleans: The Unlikeliest Crusade." *Louisiana History* 19 (1978): 261-84.

(312) Musselman, Thomas H. "A Crusade for Local Option: Shreveport, 1951-1952." *North Louisiana Historical Association Journal* 6 (1975): 59-73.

(313) Pearson, Charles C., and J. Edwin Hendricks. *Liquor and Anti-Liquor in Virginia.* Durham: Duke University Press, 1967.

(314) Rorabaugh, W. J. "The Sons of Temperance in Antebellum Jasper County." *Georgia Historical Quarterly* 64 (1980): 263-79.

(315) Scomp, H. A. *King Alcohol in the Realm of King Cotton: Or, a History of the Liquor Traffic and of the Temperance Movement in Georgia from 1733 to 1887.* Chicago: Press of Blakely Printing, 1888.

(316) Sellers, James B. *The Prohibition Movement in Alabama, 1702 to 1943.* Chapel Hill: University of North Carolina Press, 1943.

IX. RELIGION AND THE SOCIAL ORDER IN THE SOUTH: FUNDAMENTALISTS, MODERNISTS, AND EVOLUTION

(317) Baker, James T. "The Battle of Elizabeth City: Christ and Anti-Christ in North Carolina." *North Carolina Historical Review* 54 (1977): 393-408.

(318) Dabney, Virginius. *Liberalism in the South.* Chapel Hill: University of North Carolina Press, 1932.

(319) Ellis, William E. "Evolution, Fundamentalism, and the Historians: An Historiographical Review." *Historian* 44 (1981): 15-35.

(320) _____. "The Fundamentalist-Modernist Schism over Evolution in the 1920's." *Register of the Kentucky Historical Society* 74 (1976): 112-23.

(321) Gatewood, Willard B., Jr., ed. *Controversy in the Twenties: Fundamentalism, Modernism, and Evolution.* Nashville: Vanderbilt University Press, 1969.

(322) _____. "Embattled Scholar: Howard W. Odum and the Fundamentalists, 1925-1927." *Journal of Southern History* 31 (1965): 375-92.

(323) _____. "The Evolution Controversy in North Carolina, 1920-1927." *Mississippi Quarterly* 16 (1964): 192-207.

(324) _____. *Preachers, Pedagogues and Politicians: The Evolution Controversy in North Carolina, 1920-1927.* Chapel Hill: University of North Carolina Press, 1966.

(325) Halliburton, R., Jr. "Adoption of Arkansas's Anti-Evolution Law." *Arkansas Historical Quarterly* 23 (1964): 27-83.

(326) Hebert, Wallace. "Louisiana Baptists and the Scopes Trial." *Louisiana Studies* 7 (1968): 329-46.

(327) Morrison, John L. "American Catholics and the Crusade Against Evolution." *American Catholic Historical Society of Philadelphia Records* 64 (1953): 59-71.

(328) Patterson, W. Morgan. "The Southern Baptist Theologian as Controversialist: A Contrast." *Baptist History and Heritage* 15 (1980): 7-14, 57.

(329) Szasz, Ferenc M. *The Divided Mind of Protestant America, 1880-1930.* University AL: University of Alabama Press, 1982.

(330) _____. "William Jennings Bryan, Evolution, and the Fundamentalist-Modernist Controversy." *Nebraska History* 58 (1975): 259-78.

(331) Thompson, James J., Jr. "Southern Baptists and the Antievolution Controversy of the 1920's." *Mississippi Quarterly* 29 (1976): 65-81.

(332) Watson, Elbert L. "Oklahoma and the Anti-Evolution Movement of the 1920's." *Chronicles of Oklahoma* 43 (1965): 396-407.

(333) Weaver, Bill L. "Kentucky Baptists' Reaction to the National Evolution Controversy." *Filson Club Historical Quarterly* 49 (1975): 266-75.

(334) Wilson, Charles R. " 'Mormons', Monkeys, and Morality: Reactions to the Scopes Trial in Texas." *East Texas Historical Journal* 12 (1925): 51-63.

X. RELIGION AND THE SOCIAL ORDER IN THE SOUTH: POLITICS

(335) Bradford, Richard H. "Religion and Politics: Alfred E. Smith and the Election of 1928 in West Virginia." *West Virginia History* 36 (1975): 213-21.

(336) East, John P. "Richard M. Weaver: The Conservatism of Affirmation." *Modern Age* 19 (1975): 338-54.

(337) Flynt, J. Wayne, ed. "William V. Knott and the Gubernatorial Campaign of 1916." *Florida Historical Quarterly* 51 (1973): 423-30.

(338) Friedman, F. G. "Renaissance des Populismus in der USA: Geistig-religiöse Hintergründe der Präsidentschaftswählen." *Stimmen der Zeit* 194 (1976): 757-65.

(339) Johnson, Benton. "Ascetic Protestantism and Political Preference in the Deep South." *American Journal of Sociology* 69 (1964): 359-66.

(340) Kerber, Stephen. "Park Trammell and the Florida Democratic Senatorial Primary of 1916." *Florida Historical Quarterly* 58 (1980): 255-72.

(341) Lichtman, Alan J. *Prejudice and the Old Politics: The Presidential Election of 1928.* Chapel Hill: University of North Carolina Press, 1979.

(342) Lisenby, William F. "Brough, Baptists, and Bombast: The Election of 1928." *Arkansas Historical Quarterly* 32 (1973): 120-31.

(343) Lucet, Charles. "Jimmy Carter: religion et politique aux USA." *Nouvelle Revue des Deux Mondes* 1 (1977): 110-17.

(344) McCarthy, G. Michael. "The Brown Derby Campaign in West Tennessee: Smith, Hoover, and the Politics of Race." *West Tennessee Historical Society Papers* 27 (1973): 81-98.

(345) _____. "Smith vs. Hoover: The Politics of Race in West Tennessee." *Phylon* 39 (1978): 154-68.

(346) Morgan, David R., and Kenneth J. Meier. "Politics and Morality: The Effect of Religion on Referenda Voting." *Social Science Quarterly* 61 (1980): 144-48.

(347) Wingo, Barbara C. "The 1928 Presidential Election in Louisiana." *Louisiana History* 18 (1977): 405-15.

XI. RELIGION AND THE SOCIAL ORDER IN THE SOUTH: SABBATARIANISM

(348) Javersak, David T. "Wheeling's Sunday Sensation: The 1889 Wheeling Nailers." *Upper Ohio Valley Historical Review* 8 (1979): 2-6.

(349) Riess, Steven. "Professional Sunday Baseball: A Study in Social Reform, 1892-1934." *Maryland Historian* 4 (1973): 95-108.

(350) Weeks, Louis B. "The Scriptures and Sabbath Observance in the South." *Journal of Presbyterian History* 59 (1981): 267-83.

XII. RELIGION AND THE SOCIAL ORDER IN THE SOUTH: CHARITABLE INSTITUTIONS

(351) Cooley, Ray N. "Religious Ministry at the Lexington, Kentucky, State Asylum, 1844-1869." *Register of the Kentucky Historical Society* 70 (1972): 94-107.

(352) Davis, Mollie C. "The Countess of Huntingdon and Whitefield's Bethesda." *Georgia Historical Quarterly* 56 (1972): 72-81.

(353) Greene, Glen Lee. *The History of Southern Baptist Hospital.* New Orleans: Southern Baptist Hospital, 1969.

(354) Lenhart, John M. "The German Catholic Orphanage in Wheeling, West Virginia, 1886-1954." *Social Justice Review* 49 (1956): 204-207.

(355) Morris, Ann N. "The History of the St. Louis Protestant Orphan Asylum." *Missouri Historical Society Bulletin* 36 (1980): 80-91.

(356) Muntsch, Albert. "Catholic Settlement Work in St. Louis." *Central Blatt and Social Justice* (now *Social Justice Review*) 4 (1911): 73-74.

(357) O'Connell, N. J. "George Whitefield and Bethesda Orphan-House." *Georgia Historical Quarterly* 54 (1970): 40-62.

(358) O'Connor, Stella. "The Charity Hospital at New Orleans: An Administrative and Financial History, 1736-1941." *Louisiana Historical Quarterly* 31 (1948): 1-109.

(359) Rothensteiner, John E. *Remembrance of the Diamond Jubilee (1925) of the German St. Vincent's Orphan Society, with a Historical Sketch.* St. Louis: St. Vincent's Orphan Society, 1925.

(360) Sayad, Elizabeth Gentry. "Alexian Brothers' Hospital: Unique Heritage." *Missouri Historical Society Bulletin* 36 (1980): 264-67.

XIII. RELIGION AND THE SOCIAL ORDER IN THE SOUTH: OTHER TWENTIETH-CENTURY ISSUES

(361) Blevins, Kent P. "Southern Baptist Attitudes Toward the Vietnam War in the Years 1965-1970." *Foundations* 23 (1980): 231-44.

(362) Humphreys, James. "Textbook War in West Virginia." *Dissent* 23 (1976): 164-70.

(363) Lefever, Harry G. "Prostitution, Politics, and Religion: The Crusade Against Vice in Atlanta in 1912." *Atlanta Historical Journal* 24 (1980): 7-29.

(364) Money, Royce L. "Church-State Relations in the Churches of Christ since 1945: A Study in Religion and Politics." Ph.D. dissertation, Baylor University, 1975.

(365) Price, Joseph L. "Attitudes of Kentucky Baptists Toward World War II." *Foundations* 21 (1978): 123-38.

(366) Sexton, Robert F. "The Crusade Against Pari-Mutuel Gambling in Kentucky: A Study of Southern Progressivism in the 1920's." *Filson Club Historical Quarterly* 50 (1976): 47-57.

(367) Sumners, Bill. "Southern Baptists and Women's Right to Vote, 1910-1920." *Baptist History and Heritage* 12 (1977): 45-51.

(368) Tedin, Kent L. "Religious Preference and Pro/Anti Activism on the Equal Rights Amendment Issue." *Pacific Sociological Review* 21 (1978): 55-66.

(369) Williams, Priscilla Parish. "Right to Life: The Southern Strategy." *Southern Exposure* 4 (1977): 82-85.

(370) Wood, James E., Jr. "The New Religious Right and Its Implications for Southern Baptists." *Foundations* 25 (1982): 153-66.

XIV. RELIGION AND THE SOCIAL ORDER IN THE SOUTH: MISCELLANEOUS TITLES

(371) Gleissner, Richard A. "Religious Causes of the Glorious Revolution in Maryland." *Maryland Historical Magazine* 64 (1969): 327-41.

(372) Gribbin, William. "The American Episcopacy and the War of 1812." *Historical Magazine of the Protestant Episcopal Church* 38 (1969): 25-36.

(373) _____. "The War of 1812 and American Presbyterianism: Religion and Politics during the Second War with Britain." *Journal of Presbyterian History* 47 (1969): 320-39.

(374) Shankman, Arnold M. "Southern Methodist Newspapers and the Coming of the Spanish-American War: A Research Note." *Journal of Southern History* 39 (1973): 93-96.

21 RELIGIOUS THOUGHT IN THE SOUTH

INTERPRETERS OF SOUTHERN RELIGION have long held that the task of doing theology in a formal sense has been of little significance to the overall story. The same claim might well be made of American religion as a whole. Perhaps the most important reason why religious thought appears inconsequential is the emphasis on affective experience in religion, a characteristic of the evangelical style that has shaped much of American religion and that continues to exercise considerable influence in the South. A religious style that elevates inner experience nearly always gives short shrift to intellectual experience, the basis for the theological enterprise. If one argues that the South has produced no great theologians, one should also argue that the United States has produced relatively few great theologians. But such a perspective, though generally correct, misses the theological sophistication of numerous individuals, usually ministers and/or seminary professors. Hence if one turns to published writings of Southern clergy and seminary academicians, including a good bit of the sermon literature, one does find clusters theologically astute and theologically provocative persons. Fortunately, scholars have been directing more attention in recent years to this neglected area.

Richard B. Davis, *Intellectual Life in the Colonial South, 1585-1763* (8), includes some discussion of religious thought in this general survey, suggesting that even in the early years of the American experience, the South had many theologically aware clergy and some laity among its people. The officially dominant Anglican Church and its clergy, though plagued by many difficulties, produced several thinkers who gave substance to the *via media* theology of the Church of England. Their contributions, as well as those of

Anglicans elsewhere in the colonies, are described and assessed by Gerald J. Goodwin in his doctoral dissertation, "The Anglican Middle Way in Early Eighteenth Century America: Anglican Religious Thought in the American Colonies, 1702-1750" (17).

One strand of religious thought popular in some circles in the late colonial period was the Deism generated by Enlightenment rationalism. Virginia's Thomas Jefferson, who wrote several short pieces on religious belief and edited a truncated version of the gospels that reflected his idiosyncratic Deism, is perhaps the most well-known of this group. Robert A. Brent, "The Jeffersonian Outlook on Religion" (5), offers a brief overview of the religious ideas of the nation's third president. While some scholars have argued that Jefferson espoused a more orthodox religious position in public than he actually held personally, William B. Huntley, "Jefferson's Public and Private Religion" (25), argues convincingly that the two are linked and consistent with each other. A. Arnold Wettstein, "Religionless Religion in the Letters and Papers from Monticello" (53), however, is convinced from his study of numerous unpublished letters and papers that Jefferson's personal perspective was more radical than many of his public pronouncements would suggest. Jefferson's attempt at editing Scripture is the focus of Charles Mabee, "Thomas Jefferson's Anti-Clerical Bible" (34). Jefferson, whatever his private religious views, was attacked as antireligious, but not to the extent that the more orthodox turned on the more revolutionary Deist and ideologue of American independence, Thomas Paine. For the response of the clergy to Paine's work, see James H. Smylie, "Clerical Perspectives on Deism: Paine's *The Age of Reason* in Virginia" (48). Smylie argues that the Virginia clergy vehemently rejected Paine's view of revelation, his exclusive claim to the use of reason, his attribution of social ills to Christianity, as well as his own constructive theological statement. Although American Unitarianism has its most obvious roots in one wing of New England Puritanism, what welcome reception it received in a few areas of the South came in part from the rationalism advocated by Jefferson and his circle. In the antebellum period, Samuel Gilman was among the more prominent Southern Unitarians. For a brief overview of Gilman's theology as well as the forces that shaped it (including the New England theological situation), see Conrad Wright's perceptive essay, "The Theological World of Samuel Gilman" (54), but also see the materials on Gilman noted in chapter 14. Some of the impetus to "liberal" theology stemmed from a fascination with the thought of John Locke. But not all persons influenced by Locke were necessarily moving in a liberal direction. See, for example, the doctoral dissertation by Billy D. Bowen discussing the ways in which Locke's ideas had an impact on the religious thought of Alexander Campbell (2).

The most significant monograph on Southern religious thought is E. Brooks Holifield's analysis of the writings of 100 antebellum clergymen located in urban areas of the South. *The Gentlemen Theologians: American Theology and Southern Culture, 1795-1860* (22) convincingly demonstrates that there was a theologically articulate and aware group of Southern clergy who were formulating a rational understanding of Christian belief, based in part on Scottish Common Sense Realism and in part on the theological movements underway in Europe. Holifield's "Mercersburg, Princeton, and the South: The Sacramental Controversy in the Nineteenth Century" (23), highlights the knowledge in the South of the historical and organic approach to Christian thought that marked the Mercersburg theology associated with the work of John Williamson Nevin and Philip Schaff and also the critical appreciation (though not always acceptance) of the more orthodox Princeton theology advanced by figures such as Archibald Alexander and Charles Hodge. Theodore Dwight Bozeman has also directed attention to the sophistication of much clerical religious thinking in the antebellum period, examining especially in the kind of logic that undergirded it and the links between that logic and then current scientific method. He presents his case in "Science, Nature, and Society: A New Approach to James Henley Thornwell" (4) and in "Inductive and Deductive Politics: Science and Society in Antebellum Presbyterian Thought" (3). Given the Presbyterian insistence on an educated ministry, it is not surprising that the more sophisticated religious thought often emerged in Presbyterian circles. Indeed a disproportionate number of the individuals noted in Holifield's *The Gentlemen Theologians* are Presbyterians. Also see Morton H. Smith, *Studies in Southern Presbyterian Theology* (8:30). Among Presbyterians and others, this antebellum theological awareness did produce an appreciation of liberal intellectual currents of the day, but Southerners were readily able to blend that liberal bent with a social conservatism focused on the status quo, a trend that continued for three-quarters of a century, according to Ralph E. Luker, "Liberal Theology and Social Conservatism: A Southern Tradition, 1840-1920" (33).

But the general retrenchment that enveloped the white South following the Civil War carried over to the realm of theology, infusing religious thought with more conservative tendencies as the nineteenth century advanced. Of course, some of the same intellectual currents that produced conservative reaction elsewhere—Darwinism and evolutionary theory, biblical criticism, philosophical shifts—also are part of the story. Sherman E. Towell's doctoral dissertation, "The Features of Southern Baptist Thought, 1845-1879" (52), discusses the impact of increasing conservatism on what is now the region's largest denomination. George Marsden, "Kingdom and Nation: New School Presbyterian Millennialism in the Civil War Era" (37), makes some reference to the way millennialist thinking penetrated Southern Presbyterian circles, helping pave the way for the fundamentalism of a later day. Indeed, today casual critics label the South as a bastion of fundamentalism without recognizing either the range of positions encompassed by that label or its broader heritage. In an earlier era, fundamentalism did not necessarily denote a narrow, rigid doctrinal perspective, but in some ways reflected an effort to restate classical evangelical Protestant orthodoxy. That viewpoint can readily be seen in the work of Edgar Young Mullins (1860-1928), professor of theology and president of the Southern Baptist Theological Seminary and one noted among his peers for his moderate position. Mullins did, however, contribute to *The Fundamentals,* a series of pamphlets that helped give the fundamentalist movement coherence in the first two decades of the twentieth century. See Bill Clark Thomas, "Edgar Young Mullins: A Baptist Exponent of Theological Restatement" (50). The broader theological milieu in which Mullins worked is the subject of James J. Thompson, Jr., "Southern Baptist Religious Thought, 1919-1931" (51). Other works about Mullins are noted in the listing for chapter 9.

The fundamentalist-modernist controversy of the 1920s struck the South as it did the rest of the nation and Canada as well, often in the context of debates over the teaching of evolutionary theory and a concern for what is popularly called biblical inerrancy. Titles that treat this controversy in the context of the debates over evolution are detailed in chapter 20. The most perceptive analyses of the fundamentalist controversy in the South have a narrow geographical or denominational focus. Willard B. Gatewood, Jr., who has also written on the connections between the fundamentalism and the furor over evolutionary theory, notes how the fundamentalist controversy had important public or political dimensions in his "Politics and Piety in North Carolina: The Fundamentalist Crusade at High Tide, 1925-1927" (14). A cognate study that also emphasizes the nonreligious aspects of the controversy is Patsy Ledbetter, "Texas Fundamentalism: Secular Phases of a Religious Conflict, 1920-1929" (28). In "Defense of the Faith: J. Frank Norris and Texas Fundamentalism, 1920-1929" (27), Ledbetter discusses the ways in which enthusiastic support for fundamentalism was to some extent most heavily concentrated in rural areas that viewed the social changes of the decade, with greater urbanization, industrialization, and in-migration, as threats to an established world view and way of life. Another essay by Willard B. Gatewood, "North Carolina Methodism and the Fundamentalist Controversy, 1920-1927" (13), probes the tension internal to that denomination and the resultant struggles for organizational dominance of various parties. Among the heirs of Alexander Campbell, fundamentalism also left its mark. See James B. North's dissertation, "The Fundamentalist Controversy among the Disciples of Christ, 1890-1930" (42), for an examination of this matter.

In some cases, strains of a more inchoate fundamentalism had been allied with dispensationalism, an attempt to divide human history into segments (dispensations) culminating in the end of time and a corresponding effort to locate current events in ths idiosyncratic chronology as signs of the nearness of the end. The connections between the two, for example, fed into the Land-mark Controversy in Southern Baptist circles in the nineteenth century. See, in addition to titles listed in chapter 9, Harold S. Smith's doctoral dissertation about a central figure in the Landmark movement, "A Critical Analysis of the Theology of J. R. Graves" (47).

In recent years, however, fundamentalism has been casually identified with the so-called "new religious right"—as discussed in chapter 20—and with a presumed resurgence of theological conservatism in Southern religion and in American religion as a whole. Leon McBeth, "Fundamentalism in the Southern Baptist Convention in Recent Years" (36), sheds some light on the impact of this newer strand of fundamentalism on the South's largest denom-ination and some reasons for its plausibility. One feature of his argument was advanced in an earlier article, "Baptist Fundamentalism: A Cultural Inter-pretation" (35), in which McBeth suggested that tacit affirmation or funda-mentalist tenets emerged as much from the tight interconnections between religion and society in the South as from clear theological conviction. E. Glenn Hinson, "Neo Fundamentalism: An Interpretation and Critique" (21), em-phasizes the importance of nontheological factors, but also cautions against seeing fundamentalism and evangelicalism as synonymous and either in its current guise as historically normative for Southern Baptists.

In popular perception at least, insistence on the inerrancy of Scripture and on a literal interpretation of the Bible are regarded as keystones of religious orthodoxy and often seen as basic to fundamentalism. Debates over the na-ture of biblical authority and scriptural interpretation came to the South as to rest of the nation as scholars began to use critical method in the analysis of biblical texts. One early controversy centered around a Disciples of Christ minister, Robert Catlett Cave (1843-1924), and a sermon he preached in St. Louis in 1889 that challenged the premises of literalism. The ensuring furor is the subject of Samuel C. Pearson, Jr., "The Cave Affair: Protestant Thought in the Gilded Age" (43). A similar controversy came to the Southern Baptist Convention in the early 1960s over the interpretation of the Book of Genesis advocated by Ralph Harrison Elliott (1925-), professor at the denomination's Midwestern Baptist Theological Seminary. See Salvador T. Martinez, "Southern Baptist Views of the Scriptures in Light of the Elliott Contro-versy" (38). One fairly common approach to understanding Southern Baptist developments, noted in chapter 9, has been to examine the impact of various controversies on the shape of the denomination. The ways in which the dis-cussions over biblical inerrancy and biblical authority are part of this broader story are presented by Walter B. Shurden in ''The Inerrancy Debate: A Comparative Study of Southern Baptist Controversies'' (46). Militant inerrantists, of course, see danger everywhere. One such advocate of inerrancy, Harold Lindsell, includes a chapter on debates within the Southern Baptist Convention in both his *The Battle for the Bible* (31) and his *The Bible in the Balance* (32).

Numerous individual titles treat more specialized topics in Southern religious thought. James Owen Renault's doctoral dissertation, ''The Development of Separate Baptist Ecclesiology in the South, 1755-1976'' (44), examines the doctrine of the church among those Baptists who first penetrated the South, a doctrine that has continued to inform Baptist consciousness. Although Separate Baptists are technically not a distinct denomination now, there are scattered individual congregations that adhere to the earlier tenets. E. Glenn Hinson has explored the relationship between Scripture and tradition in Southern Baptist thinking in ''The Authority of the Christian Heritage for Baptist Faith and Practice'' (20). The displacement of Calvinist views of predestination and free will with Arminian notions that emphasize the role of the individual in accepting the salvation offered by God in Christ comes under scrutiny in Robert T. Kendall, ''The Rise and Demise of Calvinism in the Southern Baptist Convention'' (26). Fisher H. Humphreys has written a very brief treatment of ''Current Theological Trends among Southern Baptists'' (24). The theological thrust that gave impetus to the antimission movement among some clusters of Baptists in the nineteenth century is the focus of O. Max Lee, ''Daniel Parker's Doctrine of the Two Seeds'' (29). The theological forces that helped give birth to the Cumberland Presbyterian denomination come under scrutiny in Hubert W. Morrow, ''Cumberland Presbyterian Theology: A Nineteenth Century Development in American Presbyterianism'' (41). Finally, Earl T. Sechler, *Christian Church Doctrines, Southwest Missouri, 1839-1916* (45), has examined the theological underpinnings of the distinctive stance of the Churches of Christ.

Scholars have long debated the extent to which the theological reflections of clergy and professors penetrate the popular mind. In the contemporary world, debates over the minutiae of doctrine may have little impact on the way ordinary religious folk structure their own personal belief systems or religious practice. The same may well be true for an earlier day. Two studies that have attempted to ascertain the theological perspective of the rank and file in the antebellum period have focused on attitudes toward death or the use of religious language in wills. They are Rickie Zayne Ashby, ''Philosophical and Religious Language in Early Kentucky Wills'' (1), and Dickson D. Bruce, ''Death as Testimony in the Old South'' (6). But there may be more subtle ways in which religious ideology has penetrated the popular mind, particularly if one examines nuances of the way in which religion and culture interact in the South.

The frequent claim that much of Southern religion, particularly the dominant white evangelical Protestant style, is so intertwined with the very fabric of Southern culture as to render sharp distinctions between what is "religious" and what is "cultural" difficult, if not impossible, assumes a fresh character when one asks the question of whether there might be a "civil religion" in the South. The category of civil religion derives from Rousseau's usage, but scholarly discussion for nearly two decades has revolved more around sociologist Robert Bellah's use of the term in his seminal essay, "Civil Religion in America," which appeared in 1967. Bellah contended that there existed in the United States alongside the easily identifiable religious institutions a separate clearly defined "civil religion" with its own belief structures, symbol system, rituals, and institutions. Combining strains of nationalism and patriotism with a vague theology of Divine Providence, this civil religion serves as a common reference point for American identity and for lending an interpretive framework to the events of American history. It looks to the age of the American Revolution for its basic ideology of liberty and equality and to the Civil War for a redefinition and reaffirmation of that ideology. According to Bellah, it finds sacred texts in such documents as the Declaration of Independence, the Constitution, and the Gettysburg Address. It has spawned places of pilgrimage, particularly battlefields where American blood was shed to secure the common belief system. And it has rituals, ranging from Presidential inaugurations to Fourth of July parades, which reinforce the sense of what it means to be an American. Other scholars, such as John F. Wilson (*Public Religion in American Culture,* published in 1979) have challenged this hypothesis, arguing that there are, rather, dimensions of common life in the United States why may have religious functions, but which do not constitute a separate "religion" in any formal sense of the term.

Charles Wellborn, "The Bible and Southern Politics" (58), lends some credence to Bellah's view in demonstrating how Southern political figures in the 1960s and early 1970s readily fused nationalism and religion in their speeches, thus buttressing a national civil religion. But the most provocative work in this arena in recent years is that of Charles Reagan Wilson, who has argued that there is a regional civil religion that is distinctively Southern, a "religion of the Lost Cause." Wilson makes his case in most comprehensive form in his *Baptized in Blood: The Religion of the Lost Cause, 1865-1920* (60), published in 1980, though he set forth the basic contours of his argument in two essays, "Bishop Thomas Gailor: Celebrant of Southern Tradition" (61) and "The Religion of the Lost Cause: Ritual and Organization of the Southern Civil Religion, 1865-1920" (62).

Using a dazzling array of primary sources, Wilson builds a potent case for the emergence of a Southern civil religion in the decades following the Confederate defeat to vindicate antebellum Southern mores, create a meaningful world view in which defeat in the Civil War was transformed into moral victory, and provide some transcendent source of social cohesion for a society whose foundations had been destroyed. Wilson finds evidence for the components of this regional civil religion in such varied phenomena as reunions of Confederate soldiers, eulogies at the funerals of veterans, ceremonies marking the erection of war memorials, sermons designed to provide congregations with the moral resources to rebuild a common life after defeat, and the ethos which emerged at the University of the South following the war. Other studies lend credence to Wilson's argument. For example, W. Stuart Towns, "Honoring the Confederacy in Northwest Florida: The Confederate Monument Ritual" (57), provides additional evidence of the way in which establishing war memorials became a mechanism to reaffirm commonly held values and to reassert the essential "rightness" of antebellum Southern mores. Samuel Southard, "The Southern Soldier-Saint" (56), notes the tendency in the region to elevate military personnel to the ranks of the saints wherein they become models for the proper values and proper way to order life.

The value in Wilson's argument rests in its demonstration of one of the ways in which Southerners were able to forge and maintain a workable common identity when the social structures that had ordered common life (slavery, the plantation system, and the like) were abruptly withdrawn. It also helps explain the way in which systematic racial discrimination not only magnified the separation between whites and blacks present under slavery, but became so quickly entrenched in the larger regional culture. And it illuminates why the mythic image of a "Southern way of life" has persisted not only in the South, but in the popular mind elsewhere in the nation.

But there are limitations as well. It is not clear, for example, whether the many phenomena Wilson so ably discusses actually constitute a definable, well-institutionalized religion or whether they simply represent aspects of public life that carried religious or quasi-religious meaning and function. In addition, if a civil religion is to provide a framework for meaning for a people, then the religion of the Lost Cause is quite restricted. It would seem to have functioned predominantly if not exclusively for white Southern males. The glorification of antebellum culture virtually by definition would exclude Southern blacks and native Americans from its purview; it indeed it would seem to espouse a value system that would have little relevance to their situations. The extent to which the religion of the Lost Cause would speak to the situation of white women is also questionable, though many have accepted some of its apparent premises. In the final analysis, it may be best to regard this Southern civil religion as an attempt by the white male population of the South to take selective strands of white public life and endow them with religious or quasi-religious meaning. The religion of the Lost Cause reflects in a rather different way, however, what C. C. Goen described as the "cultural captivity of the American churches" (2:27).

The bibliography that follows is divided into two sections. The first lists titles that examine various aspects of Southern religious thought and theology, including selected titles on individual figures. The second part focuses on works discussing the phenomenon of civil religion and/or the "religion of the Lost Cause" in the South.

BIBLIOGRAPHY

Numerous titles in chapters 2, 3, 4, and 20, as well as in the chapters treating individual denominations and movements (particularly synoptic and biographical studies) are also relevant to the examination of Southern religious thought and theology.

I. SOUTHERN RELIGIOUS THOUGHT AND THEOLOGY

(1) Ashby, Rickie Zayne. "Philosophical and Religious Language in Early Kentucky Wills." *Kentucky Folklore Record* 22,2 (1976): 39-44.

(2) Bowen, Billy D. "Knowledge, the Existence of God and Faith: John Locke's Influence on Alexander Campbell's Theology." Ph.D. dissertation, Michigan State University, 1978.

(3) Bozeman, Theodore Dwight. "Inductive and Deductive Politics: Science and Society in Antebellum Presbyterian Thought." *Journal of American History* 64 (1977): 704-22.

(4) _____. "Science, Nature, and Society: A New Approach to James Henley Thornwell." *Journal of Presbyterian History* 50 (1972): 306-25.

(5) Brent, Robert A. "The Jeffersonian Outlook on Religion." *Southern Quarterly* 15 (1967): 417-32.

(6) Bruce, Dickson D. "Death as Testimony in the Old South." *Southern Humanities Review* 12 (1978): 123-31.

(7) Cooke, J. W. "Albert Taylor Bledsoe: An American Philosopher and Theologian of Liberty." *Southern Humanities Review* 8 (1974): 215-27.

(8) Davis, Richard B. *Intellectual Life in the Colonial South, 1585-1763*. Knoxville: University of Tennessee Press, 1978.

(9) Farmer, James Oscar, Jr. *The Metaphysical Confederacy: James Henley Thornwell and the Synthesis of Southern Values*. Macon GA: Mercer University Press, in press.

(10) Ferguson, Richard G., Jr. "Central Themes in Shaker Thought." *Register of the Kentucky Historical Society* 74 (1976): 216-29.

(11) Garrett, James Leo, Jr. "Sources of Authority in Baptist Thought." *Baptist History and Heritage* 13 (1978): 41-49.

(12) _____. "The Theology of Walter Thomas Conner." Th.D. dissertation, Southern Baptist Theological Seminary, 1954.

(13) Gatewood, Willard B., Jr. "North Carolina Methodism and the Fundamentalist Controversy, 1920-1927." *Wesleyan Quarterly Review* 2 (1965): 67-83.

(14) _____. "Politics and Piety in North Carolina: The Fundamentalist Crusade at High Tide, 1925-1927." *North Carolina Historical Review* 42 (1965): 275-90.

(15) Gillespie, Neal C. *The Collapse of Orthodoxy: The Intellectual Ordeal of George Frederick Holmes.* Charlottesville: University Press of Virginia, 1972.

(16) _____. "The Spiritual Odyssey of George Frederick Holmes: A Study of Religious Conservatism in the Old South." *Journal of Southern History* 32 (1966): 291-307.

(17) Goodwin, Gerald J. "The Anglican Middle Way in Early Eighteenth Century America: Anglican Religious Thought in the American Colonies, 1702-1750." Ph.D. dissertation, University of Wisconsin, 1965.

(18) Hayward, Larry R. "F. E. Maddox: Chaplain of Progress, 1908." *Arkansas Historical Quarterly* 38 (1979): 146-66.

(19) Herzog, Frederick. "The Burden of Southern Theology: A Response." *Duke Divinity School Review* 38 (1973): 151-70.

(20) Hinson, E. Glenn. "The Authority of the Christian Heritage for Baptist Faith and Practice." *Search* 8 (1978): 6-24.

(21) _____. "Neo Fundamentalism: An Interpretation and Critique." *Baptist History and Heritage* 16 (1981): 33-42.

(22) Holifield, E. Brooks. *The Gentlemen Theologians: American Theology and Southern Culture, 1795-1860.* Durham: Duke University Press, 1978.

(23) _____. "Mercersburg, Princeton, and the South: The Sacramental Controversy in the Nineteenth Century." *Journal of Presbyterian History* 44 (1976): 238-57.

(24) Humphreys, Fisher H. "Current Theological Trends among Southern Baptists." *Baptist History and Heritage* 15 (1980): 43-48.

(25) Huntley, William B. "Jefferson's Public and Private Religion." *South Atlantic Quarterly* 79 (1980): 286-301.

(26) Kendall, Robert T. "The Rise and Demise of Calvinism in the Southern Baptist Convention." M.A. thesis, University of Louisville, 1973.

(27) Ledbetter, Patsy. "Defense of the Faith: J. Frank Norris and Texas Fundamentalism, 1920-1929." *Arizona and the West* 15 (1973): 45-62.

(28) _____. "Texas Fundamentalism: Secular Phases of a Religious Conflict, 1920-1929." *Red River Valley Historical Review* 8 (1981): 38-52.

(29) Lee, O. Max. "Daniel Parker's Doctrine of the Two Seeds." Th.M. thesis, Southern Baptist Theological Seminary, 1962.

(30) Lewis, Frank B. "Robert Lewis Dabney: Southern Presbyterian Apologist." Ph.D. dissertation, Duke University, 1946.

(31) Lindsell, Harold. *The Battle for the Bible*. Grand Rapids: Zondervan Publishing House, 1976.

(32) _____. *The Bible in the Balance*. Grand Rapids: Zondervan Publishing House, 1979.

(33) Luker, Ralph E. "Liberal Theology and Social Conservatism: A Southern Tradition, 1840-1920." *Church History* 50 (1981): 193-204.

(34) Mabee, Charles. "Thomas Jefferson's Anti-Clerical Bible." *Historical Magazine of the Protestant Episcopal Church* 48 (1979): 473-81. Revised in Mabee's *Reimagining America: A Theological Critique of the American Mythos and Biblical Hermeneutics*, 33-49. Macon GA: Mercer University Press, 1985.

(35) McBeth, Leon. "Baptist Fundamentalism: A Cultural Interpretation." *Baptist History and Heritage* 13 (1978): 12-19, 32.

(36) _____. "Fundamentalism in the Southern Baptist Convention in Recent Years." *Review and Expositor* 79 (1982): 85-103.

(37) Marsden, George. "Kingdom and Nation: New School Presbyterian Millennialism in the Civil War Era." *Journal of Presbyterian History* 46 (1968): 254-73.

(38) Martinez, Salvador T. "Southern Baptist Views of the Scriptures in Light of the Elliott Controversy." Th.M. thesis, Southern Baptist Theological Seminary, 1966.

(39) Miller, J. Barret. "The Theology of William Sparrow." *Historical Magazine of the Protestant Episcopal Church* 46 (1977): 443-54.

(40) Mounger, Dwyn M. "History as Interpreted by Stephen Elliott." *Historical Magazine of the Protestant Episcopal Church* 44 (1975): 285-317.

(41) Murrow, Hubert W. "Cumberland Presbyterian Theology: A Nineteenth Century Development in American Presbyterianism." *Journal of Presbyterian History* 48 (1970): 203-20.

(42) North, James B. "The Fundamentalist Controversy among the Disciples of Christ, 1890-1930." Ph.D. dissertation, University of Illinois, 1973.

(43) Pearson, Samuel C., Jr. "The Cave Affair: Protestant Thought in the Gilded Age." *Encounter* 41 (1980): 179-203.

(44) Renault, James O. "The Development of Separate Baptist Ecclesiology in the South, 1755-1976." Ph.D. dissertation, Southern Baptist Theological Seminary, 1978.

(45) Sechler, Earl T. *Christian Church Doctrines, Southwest Missouri, 1839-1916*. Springfield MO: n.p., [1961?].

(46) Shurden, Walter B. "The Inerrancy Debate: A Comparative Study of Southern Baptist Controversies." *Baptist History and Heritage* 16 (1981): 12-19.

(47) Smith, Harold S. "A Critical Analysis of the Theology of J. R. Graves." Th.D. dissertation, Southern Baptist Theological Seminary, 1966.

(48) Smylie, James H. "Clerical Perspectives on Deism: Paine's *The Age of Reason* in Virginia." *Eighteenth-Century Studies* 6 (1972-1973): 203-20.

(49) Thacker, Joseph A., Jr. "The Concept of Sin in Kentucky During the Period 1830-1860." *Register of the Kentucky Historical Society* 64 (1966): 121-28.

(50) Thomas, Bill Clark. "Edgar Young Mullins: A Baptist Exponent of Theological Restatement." Th.D. dissertation, Southern Baptist Theological Seminary, 1963.

(51) Thompson, James J., Jr. "Southern Baptist Religious Thought, 1919-1931." Ph.D. dissertation, University of Virginia, 1971.

(52) Towell, Sherman E. "The Features of Southern Baptist Thought, 1845-1879." Th.D. dissertation, Southern Baptist Theological Seminary, 1955-1956.

(53) Wettstein, A. Arnold. "Religionless Religion in the Letters and Papers from Monticello." *Religion in Life* 45 (1976): 152-60.

(54) Wright, Conrad. "The Theological World of Samuel Gilman." *Proceedings of the Unitarian Historical Society* 17,2 (1973-1975): 54-72.

II. CIVIL RELIGION IN THE SOUTH
AND THE RELIGION OF THE LOST CAUSE

(55) Berens, John F. " 'Like a Prophetic Spirit': Samuel Davies, American Eulogists, and the Deification of George Washington." *Quarterly Journal of Speech* 63 (1977): 290-97.

(56) Southard, Samuel. "The Southern Soldier-Saint." *Journal for the Scientific Study of Religion* 8 (1969): 39-46.

(57) Towns, W. Stuart. "Honoring the Confederacy in Northwest Florida: The Confederate Monument Ritual." *Florida Historical Quarterly* 55 (1978): 205-12.

(58) Wellborn, Charles. "The Bible and Southern Politics." *Religion in Life* 44 (1978): 418-27.

(59) Whitson, Mont. "Campbell's Post-Protestantism and Civil Religion." *West Virginia History* 37 (1976): 109-21.

(60) Wilson, Charles Reagan. *Baptized in Blood: The Religion of the Lost Cause, 1865-1920*. Athens: University of Georgia Press, 1980.

(61) _____. "Bishop Thomas Gailor: Celebrant of Southern Tradition." *Tennessee Historical Quarterly* 38 (1979): 322-31.

(62) _____. "The Religion of the Lost Cause: Ritual and Organization of the Southern Civil Religion, 1865-1920." *Journal of Southern History* 46 (1980): 219-38.

22 AREAS FOR FUTURE RESEARCH AND ANALYSIS

OBVIOUSLY A SUBSTANTIAL BODY of secondary literature examining many features of "religion in the South" already exists. But as has been noted frequently in the preceding chapters, several lacunae remain where considerable work needs to be done before scholarly analysis is thorough. For example, much more attention needs to be directed to the period immediately following the Civil War. There is, for example, no synoptic study of religion in the first "New South" that parallels Donald Mathews's *Religion in the Old South* (2:47) or Kenneth Bailey's *Southern White Protestantism in the Twentieth Century* (2:6), which treats the first half of the twentieth century. There are several works noted that address individual themes or changes within particular denominations during this period, but there is as yet no overall study. Yet this was a heady epoch in Southern religion, with the increasing importance of numerous independent Black denominations, the entrenchment of racism among white groups, the feeble efforts to develop a religiously grounded social consciousness to meet the challenges posed by the beginnings of urbanization and industrialization in many areas, the inroads made by the Holiness movement and Pentecostalism, and the emergence of what became known as fundamentalism.

In addition, there is a need for broader historical overviews that take much more seriously the interaction between black religion and white religion from the colonial period to the present. Separation along religious lines and the avoidance of a social ethic that would require that attention be paid to matters of race are themselves forms of interaction and cross-influence. To tell the overall story only from the perspective of the white evangelical style is a tragic flaw. As well, overviews need to deal in more sophisticated fashion with the religious life of the native American Indian peoples for whom the South is or was a home. The absence of discussion of native cultures marks much work in American studies as a whole and is not limited to those dealing with religion by any means. Yet from the onset of the European conquest of North America, native Americans have been part of the American enterprise, even if they were dismissed by whites as uncivilized, seen as potential converts to Christianity, or oppressed through inhumane governmental Indian policy. It is time that the tribal religious life of the various native American Indian groups was recognized for its own integrity and as a vital part of the overall religious mosaic.

Much more work of a critical nature needs to be done on Southern sectarianism. Here the omission may stem from the tendency of both the scholarly mind and the popular mind to relegate such groups to the religious and social fringes. Sources to study these groups are more difficult to locate since many do not keep the archival materials and institutional records to which scholars naturally turn (and to which, unfortunately, they too often restrict themselves). As David Edwin Harrell noted in his essay in *Varieties of Southern Evangelicalism* (2:28), the South has often been the nation's most fertile breeding ground for new religious sects. To neglect them is to miss part of the richness of religion in the South. Then too, there are hundreds, if not thousands, of churches in the South that are ''independent.'' That is, they are not affiliated with one of the organized denominations. To relegate these to the periphery is also to miss much of the dynamic of religious life in the region, particularly if one hopes to get any accurate sense of where ordinary folk are located religiously. And there are also several newer denominations, akin to mainline groups in belief and practice, that have established homes for themselves in Dixie. The Universal Fellowship of Metropolitan Community Churches with its special ministry to homosexuals, for example, has established flourishing congregations in numerous Southern cities from Virginia to Texas, yet its presence is not noted in the literature.

In addition, much more scholarly work needs to be directed to Southern Catholicism and Southern Judaism. Both traditions have long histories in the South, yet both are virtually ignored in general studies of Southern religion. A large body of secondary materials on facets on Southern Catholicism already exists, but the bulk lacks academic rigor and critical analysis. Much of it has been written by Catholics who are not scientific scholars for a limited Catholic audience. Fortunately there are some signs that this gap in the literature may be closing. The work of Randall Miller (5:23), for example, is bringing scholarly acumen to the study of Southern Catholicism, while the publication of a few collections of essays dealing with Southern Judaism suggests fresh interest there.

Those scholars who continue to appraise the apparent evangelical hegemony in the South need to follow the lead of Rhys Isaac (2:80-84), whose studies have been noted throughout this volume, in delving more deeply into the subtle and complex ways the evangelical world view merged with a view of social reality to tie the two together so inextricably. Work in this area should concentrate not only on the age of the Great Awakening and that of the Great Revival, but on later periods as well in order to explore how the evangelical style has maintained its seeming dominance in spite of challenges and why it remains a viable way of ordering religious life and experience.

It is also time for a fresh examination of religion in the rural South. Despite rapid industrialization and urbanization in the decades since the close of the Second World War, the South remains the most rural region of the country. Migration from rural areas to the cities, new in-migration to rural areas, industrialization of areas that were predominantly rural as recently as a decade ago, the impact of the mass media in challenging the rural world view— all need new scrutiny. The greater sensitivity to regionalism in American life has prompted several studies of religion in Appalachia, but the rural South includes much more than Appalachia. Both deserve fuller treatment.

There is need, too, for a reexamination of denominational history. Denominational history is problematic in some ways because one could argue that the major religious developments that have shaped Southern religion have rarely been restricted to a single denomination. Evangelicalism, revivalism, and the Holiness-Pentecostal movement are but three examples of phenomena vital to the understanding of Southern religion that have cut across denominational lines. Hence one could argue that denominational boundaries, just as political boundaries such as state lines, are too artificial to offer a fresh angle on Southern religion. But as long as denominations exist, there will be a need to tell their individual stories. Here the brilliant labors of David Edwin Harrell, Jr. (11:16-22), provide a model for other analysts of denominational history. What needs to be told is less the statistics of growth and development and more the reasons why and how a group gains and maintains plausibility, interacts with the broader culture, and yet distinguishes itself from parallel groups.

One area of inquiry that will grow in importance in the coming decades is the presence of clusters of people within the Southern population whose religious orientation differs considerably from most of what currently exists. The growing numbers of Mexican-Americans in parts of the South, particularly in Texas, have brought significant changes to the shape of Roman Catholicism there, as the increasing number of Cuban-Americans in South Florida has altered that area's religious landscape. Not all of these Hispanic-Americans are Roman Catholic; their impact on Southern Protestantism also warrants examination. Scholars have too long neglected the presence of large numbers of Asian immigrants in the South. The Indian population of the metropolitan Atlanta area, for example, numbers in the thousands. A Buddhist retreat center is under construction near Asheville, North Carolina. Scholars need to be sensitive to the ways in which these persons of other than European ancestry, religion, and culture are adapting their own religious traditions to the American and Southern context as well as to the appeal of some Asian groups to Americans. A mosque, the center of public Islamic worship, on the Shaw University campus in Raleigh, North Carolina, boasts a thousand devotees who use its facilities. Hence scholars should become more conscious of the penetration of Islam in the South and what impact it will have on Southern religious life. It will no longer suffice to view religion in the South through the prism of white evangelical Protestantism.

Religion in the South has probably been the subject of more studies than the religious life of any other region of the nation. But despite the vast literature to date on Southern religion, there are yet many areas which demand fresh analysis using more sophisticated interpretive constructs and others that have been hitherto been neglected. Students of Southern religion have a rich agenda for further research.

MUP *Bibliography of Religion in the South*

Designed by Margaret Jordan Brown
Composition by MUP Composition Department

Production specifications:
    text paper—60-pound Warren's Olde Style
    endpapers—Multicolor Antique Bombay
    covers (on .088 boards)—Holliston Roxite B 53525 Linen Finish
    dust jacket—Printed 3 colors, PMS 188 (burgundy), PMS 128
        (light yellow), and Black, on 100-pound enamel, and varnished

Printing (offset lithography) and binding
    by Penfield/Rowland Printing Company, Inc., Macon, Georgia

X